WORLD ATLAS

COMPACT

Previously published as *Compact Atlas of the World*

LONDON, NEW YORK, MELBOURNE, MUNICH, DELHI

LONDON, NEW YORK, MELBOURNE, MUNICH, DELHI

PUBLISHING DIRECTOR
Jonathan Metcalf

ART DIRECTOR
Philip Ormerod

ASSOCIATE PUBLISHING DIRECTOR
Liz Wheeler

ASSOCIATE PUBLISHER
Andrew Macintyre

SENIOR CARTOGRAPHIC EDITOR
Simon Mumford

PROJECT CARTOGRAPHER
Phil Rowles

PROJECT DESIGN
Nimbus Design, Langworth, UK

PRODUCTION CONTROLLER
Mandy Inness

PRODUCTION EDITOR
John Goldsmid

First American edition 2001
Published in the United States by Dorling Kindersley Publishing, Inc.,
375 Hudson Street
New York, New York 10014

A Penguin Company

12 13 14 15 16 10 9 8 7 6 5 4 3 2

002-181742-Feb/12

Published in Great Britain by Dorling Kindersley Limited

A CIP catalog record for this book is available from the Library of Congress

ISBN 978-0-7566-8984-1

DK books are available at special discounts when purchased in bulk for sales promotions, premiums, fund-raising, or educational use. For details, contact: DK Publishing Special Markets, 375 Hudson Street, New York, New York 10014 or SpecialSales@dk.com

Printed and bound in the U.S.A. by Lake Book Manufacturing, Inc.

Discover more at www.dk.com

Key to map symbols

Physical features

Elevation

6000m/19,686ft
4000m/13,124ft
3000m/9843ft
2000m/6562ft
1,000m/3281ft
500m/1640ft
250m/820ft
0
Below sea level

△   Mountain

▽   Depression

△   Volcano

)(Pass/tunnel

Sandy desert

Drainage features

Major perennial river

Minor perennial river

- - - - Seasonal river

Canal

Waterfall

Perennial lake

Seasonal lake

Wetland

Ice features

Permanent ice cap/ice shelf

Winter limit of pack ice

Summer limit of pack ice

Borders

Full international border

- - - - Disputed de facto border

· · · · · Territorial claim border

x—x—x Cease-fire line

– – – Undefined boundary

Internal administrative boundary

Communications

Major road

Minor road

Railroad

✈   International airport

Settlements

◉   Above 500,000

◉   100,000 to 500,000

○   50,000 to 100,000

○   Below 50,000

●   National capital

●   Internal administrative capital

Miscellaneous features

+   Site of interest

᠁   Ancient wall

Graticule features

Line of latitude/longitude/Equator

- - - - Tropic/Polar circle

25°   Degrees of latitude/longitude

Names

Physical features

Andes

Sahara   Landscape features

Ardennes

Land's End   Headland

Mont Blanc 4,807m   Elevation/volcano/pass

Blue Nile   River/canal/waterfall

Ross Ice Shelf   Ice feature

PACIFIC OCEAN

Sulu Sea   Sea features

Palk Strait

Chile Rise   Undersea feature

Regions

FRANCE   Country

JERSEY (to UK)   Dependent territory

KANSAS   Administrative region

Dordogne   Cultural region

Settlements

PARIS   Capital city

SAN JUAN   Dependent territory capital city

Chicago

Kettering   Other settlements

Burke

Inset map symbols

Urban area

City

Park

▪   Place of interest

▫   Suburb/district

WORLD ATLAS COMPACT

Contents

The World's Regions

North & Central America

South America

Africa

Europe

North & West Asia

South & East Asia

Australasia & Oceania

Index – Gazetteer

The Political World

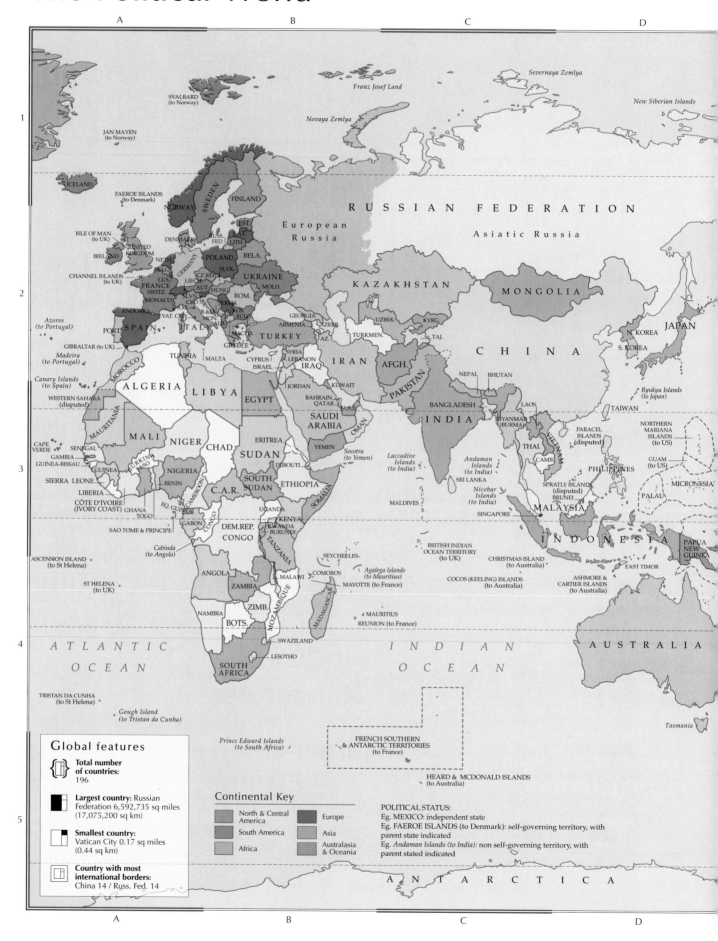

A | B | C | D

1

Severnaya Zemlya

Franz Josef Land

New Siberian Islands

SVALBARD (to Norway)

Novaya Zemlya

JAN MAYEN (to Norway)

ICELAND

FAEROE ISLANDS (to Denmark)

NORWAY

SWEDEN

FINLAND

RUSSIAN FEDERATION

Asiatic Russia

European Russia

ISLE OF MAN (to UK)

DENMARK

RUSS. FED.

EST.

LAT.

LITH.

UNITED KINGDOM

IRELAND

NETH.

BELG.

GERMANY

POLAND

BELA.

UKRAINE

KAZAKHSTAN

MONGOLIA

CHANNEL ISLANDS (to UK)

LUX.

LIECH.

CZ. REP.

SLVK.

FRANCE

SWITZ.

AUT.

HUNG.

MOLD.

2

Azores (to Portugal)

ANDORRA

MONACO

SLVN.

CRO.

S.M.

B & H.

SERBIA

ROM.

GEORGIA

ARMENIA

AZERB.

UZBEK.

KYRG.

TAJ.

N. KOREA

JAPAN

S. KOREA

PORT.

SPAIN

VAT. CITY

ITALY

MON.

ALB.

KOS.

MACED.

BULG.

GREECE

TURKEY

AZ.

TURKMEN.

CHINA

GIBRALTAR (to UK)

Madeira (to Portugal)

TUNISIA

MALTA

CYPRUS

SYRIA

LEBANON

ISRAEL

IRAQ

IRAN

AFGH.

Ryukyu Islands (to Japan)

Canary Islands (to Spain)

MOROCCO

ALGERIA

LIBYA

EGYPT

JORDAN

KUWAIT

BAHRAIN

QATAR

U.A.E.

SAUDI ARABIA

OMAN

PAKISTAN

NEPAL

BHUTAN

BANGLADESH

LAOS

TAIWAN

NORTHERN MARIANA ISLANDS (to US)

WESTERN SAHARA (disputed)

MAURITANIA

MALI

NIGER

CHAD

SUDAN

ERITREA

YEMEN

Socotra (to Yemen)

Laccadive Islands (to India)

INDIA

MYANMAR (BURMA)

PARACEL ISLANDS (disputed)

GUAM (to US)

CAPE VERDE

SENEGAL

GAMBIA

GUINEA-BISSAU

GUINEA

BURKINA FASO

NIGERIA

BENIN

CAMEROON

C.A.R.

SOUTH SUDAN

DJIBOUTI

ETHIOPIA

SOMALIA

Andaman Islands (to India)

SRI LANKA

THAI.

CAMB.

VIETNAM

PHILIPPINES

SPRATLY ISLANDS (disputed)

MICRONESIA

3

SIERRA LEONE

LIBERIA

CÔTE D'IVOIRE (IVORY COAST)

GHANA

TOGO

EQ. GUINEA

GABON

SAO TOME & PRINCIPE

CONGO

DEM. REP. CONGO

UGANDA

KENYA

RWANDA

BURUNDI

TANZANIA

SEYCHELLES

MALDIVES

Nicobar Islands (to India)

SINGAPORE

BRUNEI

MALAYSIA

INDONESIA

PAPUA NEW GUINEA

PALAU

Cabinda (to Angola)

BRITISH INDIAN OCEAN TERRITORY (to UK)

CHRISTMAS ISLAND (to Australia)

EAST TIMOR

ASHMORE & CARTIER ISLANDS (to Australia)

ASCENSION ISLAND (to St Helena)

ANGOLA

ZAMBIA

MALAWI

MOZAMBIQUE

COMOROS

MAYOTTE (to France)

Agalega Islands (to Mauritius)

COCOS (KEELING) ISLANDS (to Australia)

ST HELENA (to UK)

ZIMB.

MADAGASCAR

NAMIBIA

BOTS.

SWAZILAND

MAURITIUS

REUNION (to France)

4

ATLANTIC OCEAN

LESOTHO

SOUTH AFRICA

INDIAN OCEAN

AUSTRALIA

TRISTAN DA CUNHA (to St Helena)

Gough Island (to Tristan da Cunha)

Tasmania

Prince Edward Islands (to South Africa)

FRENCH SOUTHERN & ANTARCTIC TERRITORIES (to France)

HEARD & MCDONALD ISLANDS (to Australia)

Global features

Total number of countries: 196

Largest country: Russian Federation 6,592,735 sq miles (17,075,200 sq km)

Smallest country: Vatican City 0.17 sq miles (0.44 sq km)

Country with most international borders: China 14 / Russ. Fed. 14

Continental Key

North & Central America

South America

Africa

Europe

Asia

Australasia & Oceania

POLITICAL STATUS:
Eg. MEXICO: independent state
Eg. FAEROE ISLANDS (to Denmark): self-governing territory, with parent state indicated
Eg. *Andaman Islands (to India):* non self-governing territory, with parent stated indicated

ANTARCTICA

5

A | B | C | D

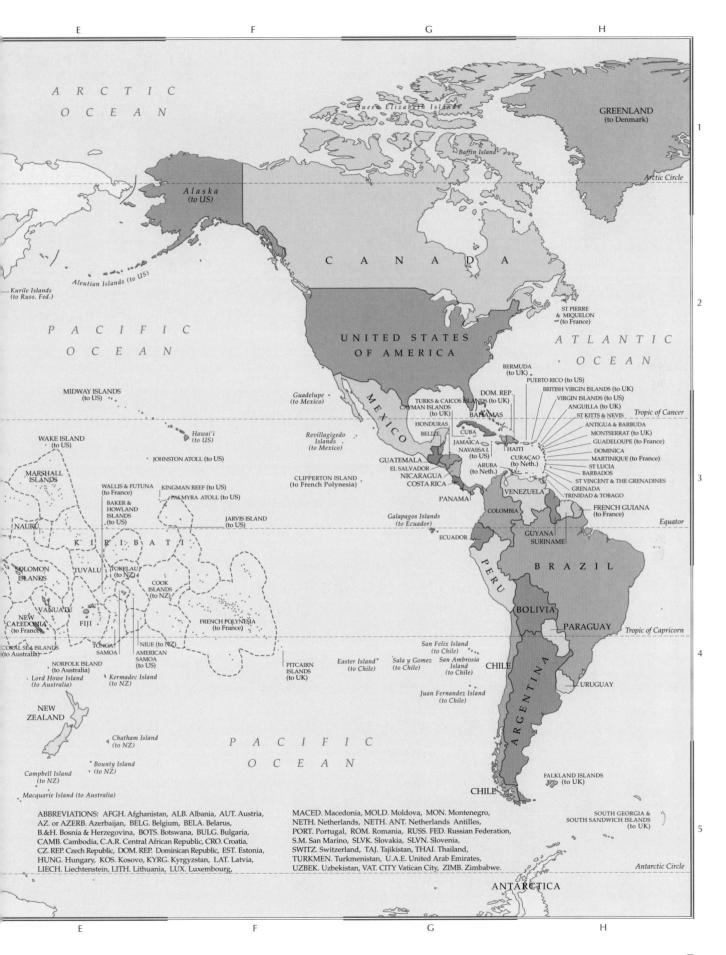

E   F   G   H

ARCTIC

OCEAN

Queen Elizabeth Islands

GREENLAND
(to Denmark)

1

Baffin Island

Arctic Circle

Alaska
(to US)

C A N A D A

Kurile Islands
(to Russ. Fed.)

Aleutian Islands (to US)

2

ST PIERRE
& MIQUELON
(to France)

PACIFIC

OCEAN

UNITED STATES
OF AMERICA

ATLANTIC

OCEAN

BERMUDA
(to UK)

PUERTO RICO (to US)

MIDWAY ISLANDS
(to US)

Guadelupe
(to Mexico)

M
E
X
I
C
O

TURKS & CAICOS ISLANDS (to UK)
CAYMAN ISLANDS (to UK)
BAHAMAS

DOM. REP.

BRITISH VIRGIN ISLANDS (to UK)
VIRGIN ISLANDS (to US)
ANGUILLA (to UK)
ST KITTS & NEVIS

Tropic of Cancer

WAKE ISLAND
(to US)

Hawai'i
(to US)

HONDURAS
BELIZE

CUBA

JAMAICA
NAVASSA I.
(to US)

HAITI

ANTIGUA & BARBUDA
MONTSERRAT (to UK)
GUADELOUPE (to France)
DOMINICA
MARTINIQUE (to France)

Revillagigedo
Islands
(to Mexico)

JOHNSTON ATOLL (to US)

GUATEMALA
EL SALVADOR
NICARAGUA
COSTA RICA

ARUBA
(to Neth.)

CURAÇAO
(to Neth.)

ST LUCIA
BARBADOS
ST VINCENT & THE GRENADINES

3

MARSHALL
ISLANDS

WALLIS & FUTUNA
(to France)

KINGMAN REEF (to US)

PALMYRA ATOLL (to US)

CLIPPERTON ISLAND
(to French Polynesia)

VENEZUELA

GRENADA
TRINIDAD & TOBAGO

FRENCH GUIANA
(to France)

NAURU

BAKER &
HOWLAND
ISLANDS
(to US)

JARVIS ISLAND
(to US)

Galapagos Islands
(to Ecuador)

COLOMBIA

Equator

K I R I B A T I

ECUADOR

GUYANA
SURINAME

SOLOMON
ISLANDS

TUVALU

TOKELAU
(to NZ)

COOK
ISLANDS
(to NZ)

P
E
R
U

B R A Z I L

VANUATU

FIJI

FRENCH POLYNESIA
(to France)

BOLIVIA

NEW
CALEDONIA
(to France)

PARAGUAY

Tropic of Capricorn

CORAL SEA ISLANDS
(to Australia)

TONGA
SAMOA

NIUE (to NZ)

AMERICAN
SAMOA
(to US)

San Felix Island
(to Chile)

Sala y Gomez
(to Chile)

San Ambrosia
Island
(to Chile)

CHILE

A
R
G
E
N
T
I
N
A

NORFOLK ISLAND
(to Australia)

PITCAIRN
ISLANDS
(to UK)

Easter Island
(to Chile)

URUGUAY

Lord Howe Island
(to Australia)

Kermadec Island
(to NZ)

Juan Fernandez Island
(to Chile)

4

NEW
ZEALAND

Chatham Island
(to NZ)

PACIFIC

OCEAN

Bounty Island
(to NZ)

Campbell Island
(to NZ)

FALKLAND ISLANDS
(to UK)

Macquarie Island (to Australia)

CHILE

SOUTH GEORGIA &
SOUTH SANDWICH ISLANDS
(to UK)

5

Antarctic Circle

ANTARCTICA

E   F   G   H

The Physical World

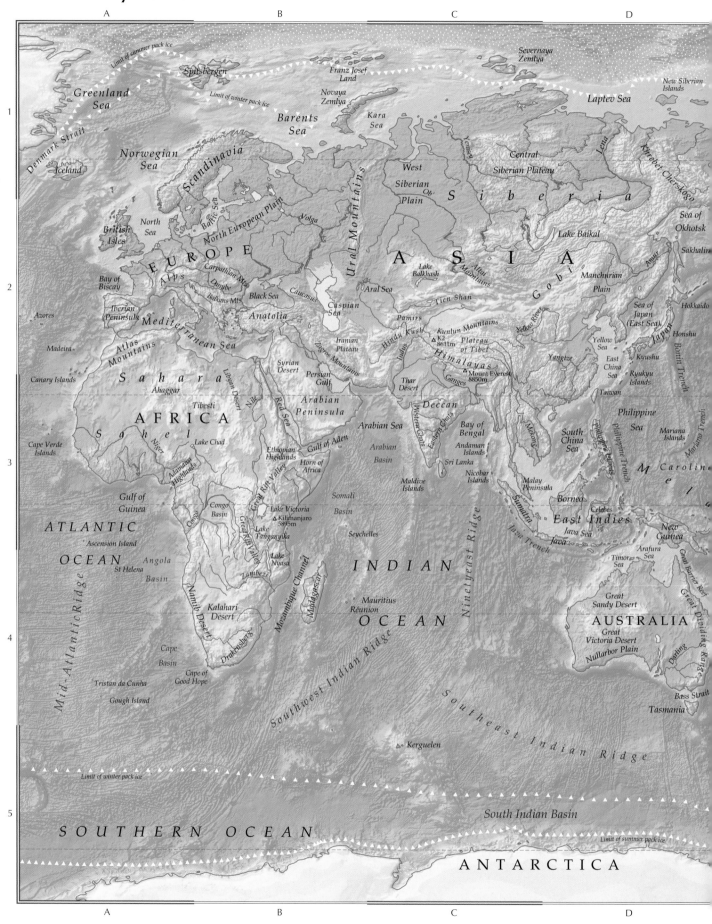

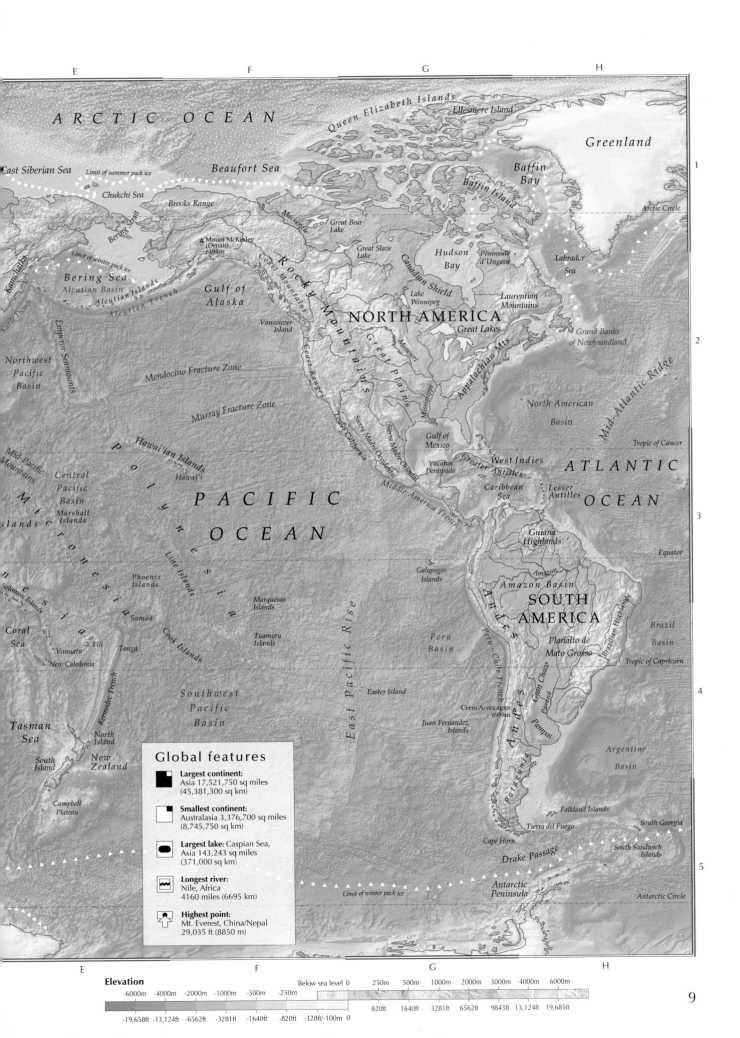

E F G H

ARCTIC OCEAN

East Siberian Sea
Limit of summer pack ice
Beaufort Sea
Queen Elizabeth Islands
Ellesmere Island
Greenland
Baffin Bay
Baffin Island
Chukchi Sea
Brooks Range
Mackenzie
Great Bear Lake
Arctic Circle
Labrador Sea
Bering Strait
Mount McKinley (Denali) 6194m
Great Slave Lake
Hudson Bay
Péninsule d'Ungava
Kamchatka
Bering Sea
Aleutian Basin
Aleutian Islands
Aleutian Trench
Gulf of Alaska
Rocky Mountains
Coast Mountains
Canadian Shield
Lake Winnipeg
NORTH AMERICA
Laurentian Mountains
Kurile Trench
Emperor Seamounts
Northwest Pacific Basin
Vancouver Island
Coast Ranges
Great Plains
Missouri
Great Lakes
Appalachian Mts
Grand Banks of Newfoundland
Mendocino Fracture Zone
Mississippi
North American Basin
Mid-Atlantic Ridge
Murray Fracture Zone
Sierra Nevada
Sierra Madre Occidental
Mid-Pacific Mountains
Hawai'ian Islands
Baja California
Sierra Madre Oriental
Gulf of Mexico
Tropic of Cancer
Central Pacific Basin
Hawai'i
Yucatán Peninsula
Greater Antilles
West Indies
ATLANTIC
Marshall Islands
PACIFIC
Middle America Trench
Caribbean Sea
Lesser Antilles
OCEAN
Micronesia
Polynesia
OCEAN
Galapagos Islands
Guiana Highlands
Equator
Solomon Islands
Phoenix Islands
Line Islands
Amazon
Amazon Basin
SOUTH AMERICA
Brazilian Highlands
Brazil Basin
Marquesas Islands
Andes
Peru Basin
Planalto de Mato Grosso
Coral Sea
Samoa
Cook Islands
Tuamotu Islands
Peru-Chile Trench
Gran Chaco
Paraná
Vanuatu
Fiji
Tonga
Tropic of Capricorn
New Caledonia
East Pacific Rise
Easter Island
Cerro Aconcagua 6959m
Pampas
Tasman Sea
Southwest Pacific Basin
Juan Fernandez Islands
Argentine Basin
South Island
North Island
New Zealand
Patagonia
Campbell Plateau
Falkland Islands
South Georgia
Tierra del Fuego
South Sandwich Islands
Cape Horn
Drake Passage
Limit of winter pack ice
Antarctic Peninsula
Antarctic Circle

Global features

■ **Largest continent:**
Asia 17,521,750 sq miles
(45,381,300 sq km)

□ **Smallest continent:**
Australasia 3,376,700 sq miles
(8,745,750 sq km)

● **Largest lake:** Caspian Sea,
Asia 143,243 sq miles
(371,000 sq km)

Longest river:
Nile, Africa
4160 miles (6695 km)

Highest point:
Mt. Everest, China/Nepal
29,035 ft (8850 m)

E F G H

Elevation

-6000m -4000m -2000m -1000m -500m -250m   Below sea level 0   250m 500m 1000m 2000m 3000m 4000m 6000m

-19,658ft -13,124ft -6562ft -3281ft -1640ft -820ft -328ft/-100m 0   820ft 1640ft 3281ft 6562ft 9843ft 13,124ft 19,685ft

Time zones

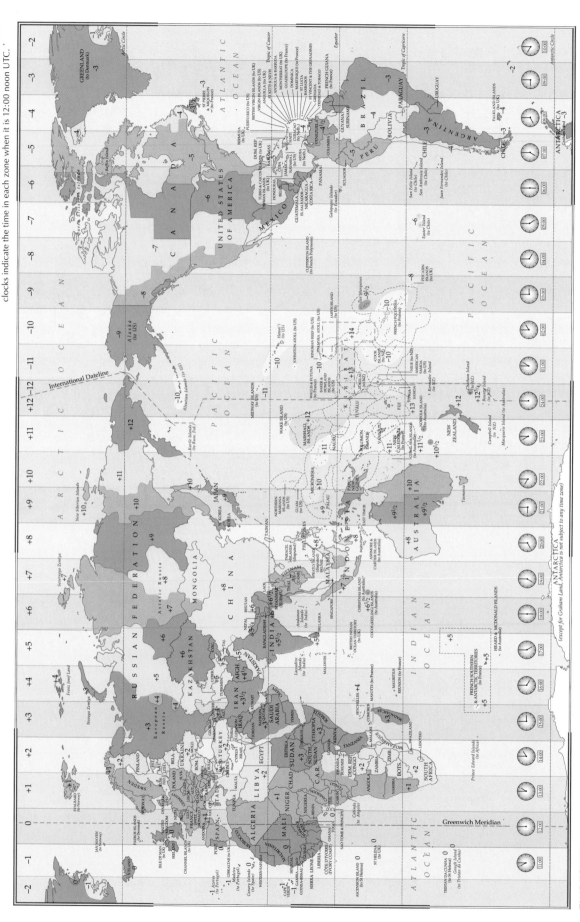

The numbers at the top of the map indicate how many hours each time zone is ahead or behind Coordinated Universal Time (UTC). The row of clocks indicate the time in each zone when it is 12:00 noon UTC.

TIME ZONES

Because Earth is a rotating sphere, the Sun shines on only half of its surface at any one time. Thus, it is simultaneously morning, evening, and night time in different parts of the world. Because of these disparities, each country or part of a country adheres to a local time. A region of the Earth's surface within which a single local time is used is called a time zone.

COORDINATED UNIVERSAL TIME (UTC)

Coordinated Universal Time (UTC) is a reference by which the local time in each time zone is set. UTC is a successor to, and closely approximates, Greenwich Mean Time (GMT). However, UTC is based on an atomic clock, whereas GMT is determined by the Sun's position in the sky relative to the 0° longitudinal meridian, which runs through Greenwich, UK.

THE INTERNATIONAL DATELINE

The International Dateline is an imaginary line from pole to pole that roughly corresponds to the 180° longitudinal meridian. It is an arbitrary marker between calendar days. The dateline is needed because of the use of local times around the world rather than a single universal time.

10

The
WORLD
ATLAS

THE MAPS IN THIS ATLAS ARE ARRANGED CONTINENT BY CONTINENT, STARTING FROM THE INTERNATIONAL DATE LINE, AND MOVING EASTWARD. THE MAPS PROVIDE A UNIQUE VIEW OF TODAY'S WORLD, COMBINING TRADITIONAL CARTOGRAPHIC TECHNIQUES WITH THE LATEST REMOTE-SENSED AND DIGITAL TECHNOLOGY.

North & Central America

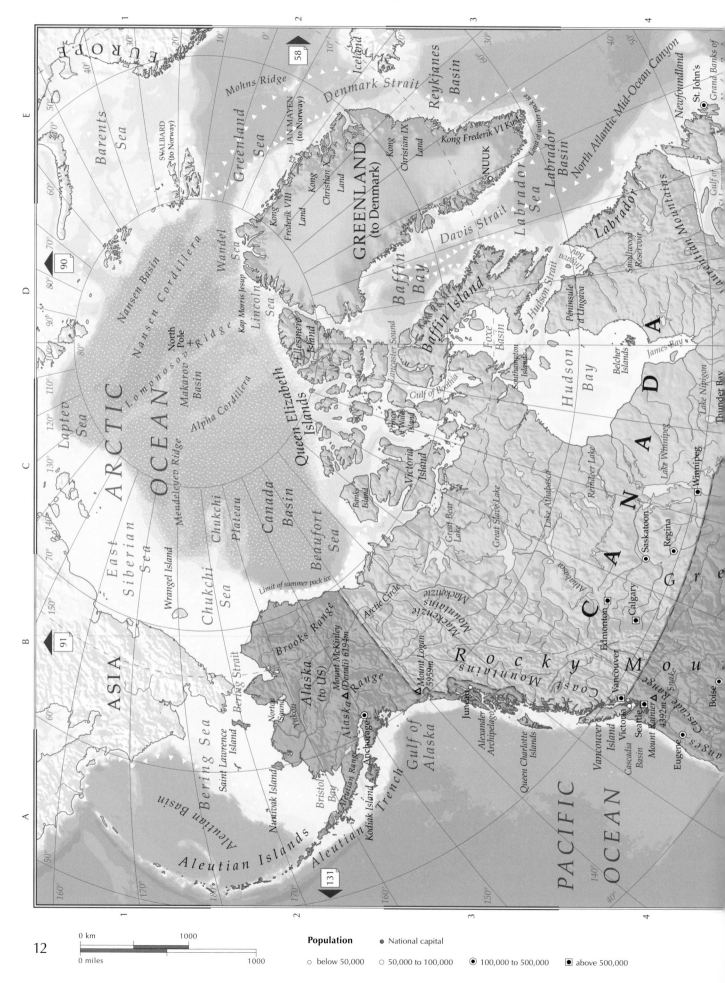

0 km 1000

0 miles 1000

Population
● National capital

○ below 50,000   ○ 50,000 to 100,000   ◉ 100,000 to 500,000   ▣ above 500,000

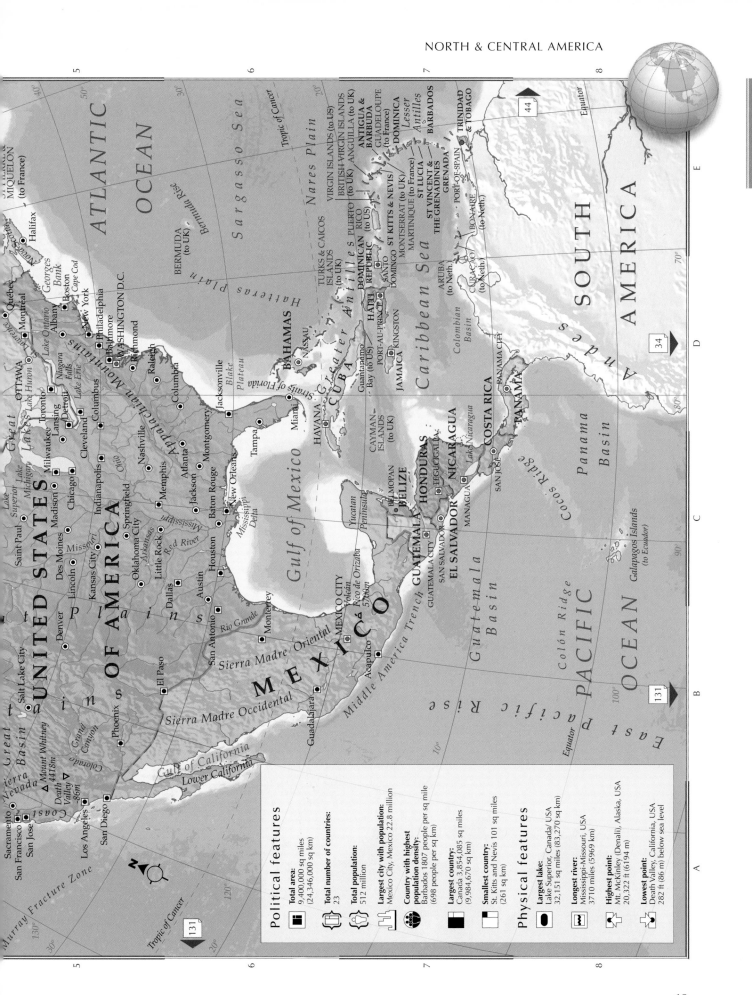

Political features

Total area:
9,400,000 sq miles
(24,346,000 sq km)

Total number of countries:
23

Total population:
512 million

Largest city with population:
Mexico City, Mexico 22.8 million

Country with highest population density:
Barbados 1807 people per sq mile
(698 people per sq km)

Largest country:
Canada 3,854,085 sq miles
(9,984,670 sq km)

Smallest country:
St. Kitts and Nevis 101 sq miles
(261 sq km)

Physical features

Largest lake:
Lake Superior, Canada/ USA
32,151 sq miles (83,270 sq km)

Longest river:
Mississippi-Missouri, USA
3710 miles (5969 km)

Highest point:
Mt. McKinley (Denali), Alaska, USA
20,322 ft (6194 m)

Lowest point:
Death Valley, California, USA
282 ft (86 m) below sea level

Western Canada & Alaska

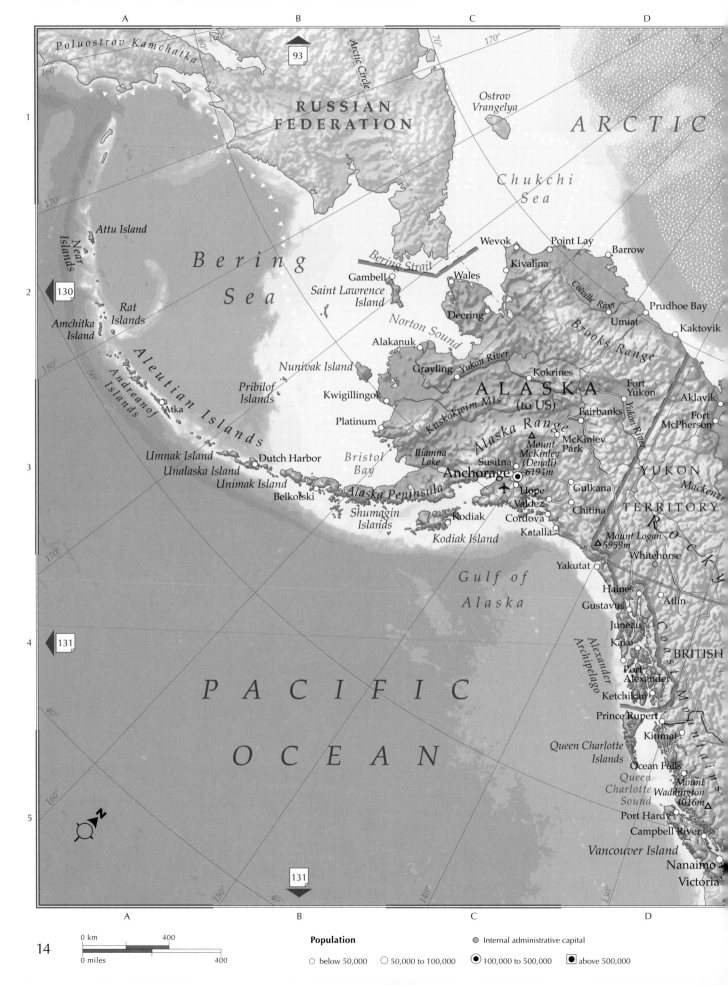

Poluostrov Kamchatka

RUSSIAN FEDERATION

Arctic Circle

Ostrov Vrangelya

ARCTIC

93

Chukchi Sea

Wevok
Point Lay
Barrow
Kivalina
Deering
Wales
Gambell
Saint Lawrence Island

Bering Strait

Colville River

Umiat
Prudhoe Bay
Kaktovik

Brooks Range

Near Islands
Attu Island

Bering Sea

130

Rat Islands
Amchitka Island

Norton Sound

Alakanuk

Grayling
Yukon River
Kokrines

Fort Yukon

ALASKA
(to US)

Aklavik
Fort McPherson

Nunivak Island

Kwigillingok
Kuskokwim Mts

Fairbanks

Aleutian Islands
Andreanof Islands
Atka

Pribilof Islands

Platinum

Alaska Range
McKinley Park

△ Mount McKinley (Denali) 6194m

YUKON

Mackenzie

Umnak Island
Unalaska Island
Unimak Island
Dutch Harbor

Bristol Bay

Iliamna Lake
Susitna

Anchorage

Hope
Valdez
Gulkana
Chitina

TERRITORY

Yukon River

Belkofski

Alaska Peninsula

Shumagin Islands

Kodiak
Cordova
Katalla

△ Mount Logan 5959m

Whitehorse

Kodiak Island

Yakutat

Rocky

Gulf of Alaska

Haines
Gustavus
Atlin

131

Juneau
Kake

Alexander Archipelago

BRITISH

PACIFIC

Port Alexander
Ketchikan

Coast Mountains

Prince Rupert

Kitimat

Queen Charlotte Islands

Ocean Falls

OCEAN

Queen Charlotte Sound

△ Mount Waddington 4016m

Port Hardy

Campbell River

Vancouver Island

131

Nanaimo
Victoria

14

0 km — 400
0 miles — 400

Population

○ below 50,000   ○ 50,000 to 100,000   ◉ 100,000 to 500,000   ▣ above 500,000

● Internal administrative capital

OCEAN

GREENLAND
(to Denmark)

Alert

133

Knud Rasmussen Land

Ellesmere Island

Axel
Heiberg
Island

Queen Elizabeth Islands

Ellef Ringnes
Island
Isachsen

Amund
Ringnes
Island

Baffin
Bay

Prince Patrick
Island

Devon Island

Mould Bay

Bathurst
Island

Cornwallis
Island

Lancaster Sound

Davis Strait

60

Melville
Island

Resolute
(Qausuittuq)

Viscount Melville
Sound

Somerset
Island

Brodeur
Peninsula

Baffin Island

Cumberland Sound

Beaufort
Sea

Banks
Island

Prince of
Wales Island

McClintock Channel

Boothia
Peninsula

Gulf of Boothia

Igloolik

Nettilling
Lake

Sachs Harbour
(Ikaahuk)

Amundsen
Gulf

Holman

Victoria
Island

King William
Island

Melville
Peninsula

Foxe
Basin

Amadjuak
Lake

Iqaluit
(Frobisher Bay)

Tuktoyaktuk

Inuvik

Paulatuk

Cambridge Bay
(Ikaluktutiak)

Gjoa Haven
(Uqsuqtuq)

Kugaaruk
(Pelly Bay)

Kugluktuk
(Coppermine)

Repulse Bay

Southampton
Island

Hudson Strait

Fort
Good Hope

Great
Bear
Lake

Echo Bay

Burnside

Back

Garry Lake

Baker Lake

NUNAVUT

Coral
Harbour

Péninsule
d'Ungava

Mackenzie

NORTHWEST
TERRITORIES

Coats
Island

Mansel
Island

QUÉBEC

Tungsten

Edzo

Yellowknife

Réliance

Rankin Inlet

Mountains

Fort Simpson

Great Slave
Lake

Lutselk'e
(Snowdrift)

Dubawnt

Whale Cove

Hudson

Fort Providence

Fort Liard

Hay River

Fort Smith

Lake Athabasca

Arviat

Bay

COLUMBIA

Fort Nelson

Reindeer Lake

Churchill

Belcher
Islands

Ware

Fort Vermilion

Wollaston Lake

Nelson

James
Bay

16

Fort St. John

Fort
McMurray

Lynn Lake

Southern
Indian Lake

CANADA

C

ALBERTA

A

N

A

D

A

Grande Prairie

Buffalo
Narrows

Thompson

ONTARIO

Prince George

SASKATCHEWAN

Flin Flon

Athabasca

Athabasca

Lake
Winnipeg

Edmonton

North Saskatchewan

The Pas

MANITOBA

Mount Robson
3954m

Leduc

Saskatchewan

Prince Albert

Red Deer

Saskatoon

Lake
Manitoba

Kamloops

Calgary

Kindersley

Yorkton

Lake Superior

Kelowna

Regina

Qu'Appelle

Winnipeg

Lake of the
Woods

Lake Huron

Medicine Hat

Brandon

Vancouver

Cranbrook

Lethbridge

Weyburn

Lake
Michigan

Milk River

Estevan

Melita

23

UNITED STATES OF AMERICA

15

Elevation

						Below sea level 0	250m	500m	1000m	2000m	3000m	4000m	6000m
-6000m	-4000m	-2000m	-1000m	-500m	-250m								
-19,658ft	-13,124ft	-6562ft	-3281ft	-1640ft	-820ft	-328ft/-100m 0	820ft	1640ft	3281ft	6562ft	9843ft	13,124ft	19,685ft

Eastern Canada

NORTHWEST TERRITORIES

NUNAVUT

SASKATCHEWAN

Hudson

Charles Island

Ivujivik

Coats Island

Mansel Island

Péninsule d' Ungava

Churchill

Southern Indian Lake

Nelson

Ottawa Islands

H u d s o n   B a y

Inukjuak (Port Harrison)

Rivière aux Feuilles

Lac Minto

M A N I T O B A

Hayes

Severn

Fort Severn

Belcher Islands

Lac Bienville

Cedar Lake

Lake Winnipeg

Peawanuk

J a m e s   B a y

Lake Winnipegosis

Sandy Lake

Winisk

Attawapiskat

Akimiski Island

Lake Manitoba

C A N

O N T A R I O

Attawapiskat

Albany

Fort Albany

Moosonee

Eastmain

Rivière de Rupert

Lac Mistassini

Chibougamau

Réservoir Gouin

Q U É

A

Lac Seul

Armstrong

Hearst

Moose

Harricana

Kenora

Dryden

Lake Nipigon

Longlac

Kapuskasing

Amos

Red River

Lake of the Woods

Nipigon

Marathon

Cochrane

Rouyn-Noranda

NORTH DAKOTA

Fort Frances

Atikokan

Tip Top Mountain △ 640m

Timmins

Rainy Lake

Thunder Bay

Foleyet

Kirkland Lake

Val-d'Or

Wawa

MINNESOTA

Lake Superior

Sault Ste. Marie

Sudbury

North Bay

Pembroke

Gatineau

Hull

Laval

OTTAWA

M I C H I G A N

SOUTH DAKOTA

Manitoulin Island

Georgian Bay

Midland

Peterborough

Kingston

U N I T E D   S T A T E S

WISCONSIN

Lake Michigan

Lake Huron

Brampton

Oshawa

Lake Ontario

O F   A M E R I C A

Kitchener

Toronto

IOWA

NEBRASKA

Sarnia

Hamilton

St. Catharines

Windsor

London

Niagara Falls

NEW YORK

Leamington

Lake Erie

Mississippi River

ILLINOIS

INDIANA

O H I O

PENNSYLVANIA

0 km 300
0 miles 300

Population ● National capital ● Internal administrative capital
○ below 50,000 ○ 50,000 to 100,000 ◉ 100,000 to 500,000 ◼ above 500,000

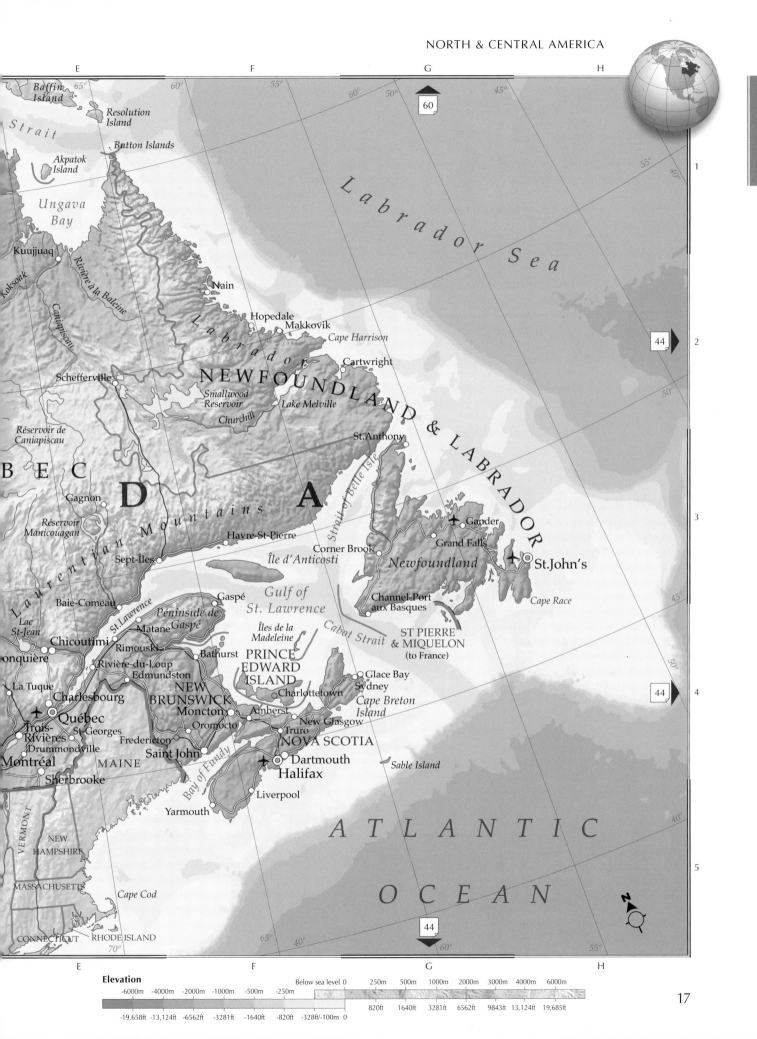

Elevation

-6000m	-4000m	-2000m	-1000m	-500m	-250m	Below sea level 0	250m 500m 1000m 2000m 3000m 4000m 6000m
-19,658ft	-13,124ft	-6562ft	-3281ft	-1640ft	-820ft	-328ft/-100m 0	820ft 1640ft 3281ft 6562ft 9843ft 13,124ft 19,685ft

USA: The Northeast

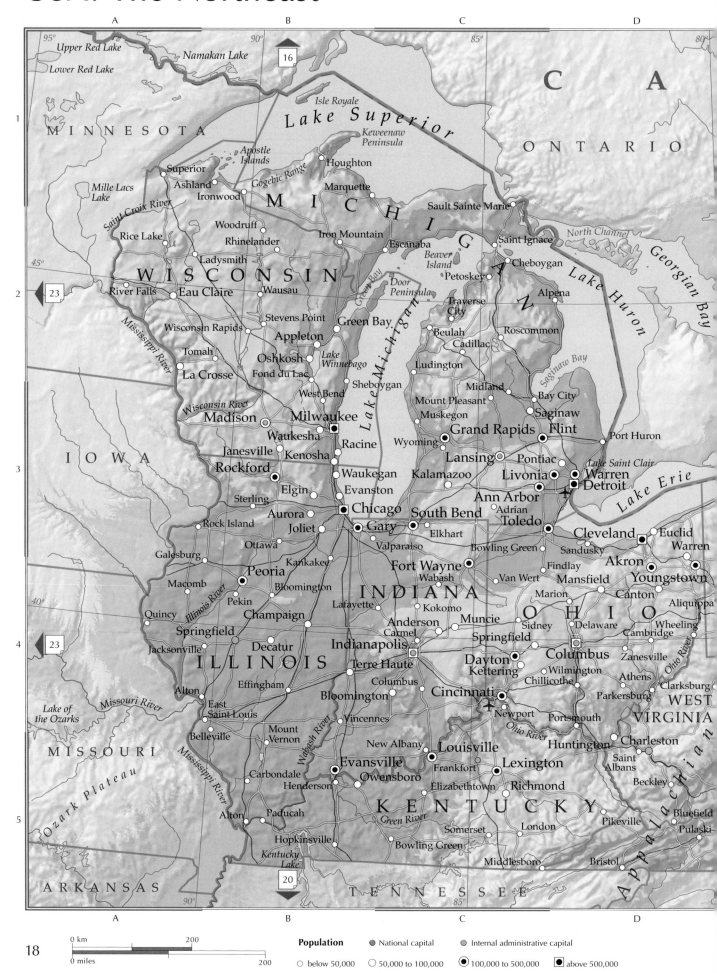

A B C D

95° 90° 85° 80°

16

Upper Red Lake
Namakan Lake
Lower Red Lake

Isle Royale

Lake Superior

Keweenaw
Peninsula

C A N A D A

O N T A R I O

1

M I N N E S O T A

Apostle
Islands

Superior
Ashland
Ironwood
Gogebic Range

Houghton

Marquette

North Channel

Georgian Bay

Mille Lacs
Lake

Saint Croix River

Woodruff
Rhinelander

Iron Mountain

Escanaba

Sault Sainte Marie

Saint Ignace

Lake Huron

M I C H I G A N

45°

Rice Lake

Ladysmith

23
River Falls Eau Claire

W I S C O N S I N

Wausau

Stevens Point

Green Bay

Beaver
Island

Cheboygan
Petoskey

Alpena

Roscommon

2

Wisconsin Rapids

Tomah

Appleton
Oshkosh

Lake
Winnebago

Traverse
City

Beulah
Cadillac

Ludington

Door
Peninsula

Green Bay

Saginaw Bay

La Crosse

Fond du Lac

Sheboygan

West Bend

Midland

Bay City

Mount Pleasant

Muskegon

Saginaw

Wisconsin River

Madison

Milwaukee

Wyoming

Grand Rapids

Flint

Port Huron

3

I O W A

Waukesha

Janesville
Rockford

Kenosha

Racine

Waukegan

Lansing

Pontiac

Kalamazoo

Livonia

Warren
Detroit

Lake Saint Clair

Lake Erie

Sterling

Elgin

Evanston

Ann Arbor

Adrian

Aurora

Chicago

South Bend

Toledo

Rock Island

Joliet

Gary

Elkhart

Cleveland

Euclid
Warren

Ottawa

Valparaiso

Bowling Green

Sandusky

Akron

Galesburg

Kankakee

Fort Wayne

Findlay

Mansfield

Youngstown

Canton

Aliquippa

4

Macomb

Peoria

Bloomington

Wabash

I N D I A N A

Van Wert

Marion

O H I O

Wheeling

Pekin

Lafayette

Kokomo

Sidney

Delaware

Zanesville

Cambridge

40°

Quincy

Champaign

Anderson
Carmel

Muncie

Springfield

Columbus

Athens

Clarksburg

23

Springfield

Decatur

Indianapolis

Dayton
Kettering

Wilmington

Chillicothe

Parkersburg

WEST

Jacksonville

I L L I N O I S

Terre Haute

Columbus

Cincinnati

Newport

Portsmouth

Huntington

Charleston

VIRGINIA

Alton

Effingham

Bloomington

Vincennes

Ohio River

Saint
Albans

Beckley

Bluefield

East
Saint Louis

Mount
Vernon

New Albany

Louisville

Lexington

Richmond

Pulaski

MISSOURI

Belleville

Evansville

Owensboro

Frankfort

Elizabethtown

5

Lake of
the Ozarks

Missouri River

Carbondale

Henderson

K E N T U C K Y

Somerset

London

Pikeville

Alton

Paducah

Green River

Bowling Green

Middlesboro

Bristol

Hopkinsville

Ozark Plateau

ARKANSAS

Kentucky
Lake

20

T E N N E S S E E

90° 85°

A B C D

0 km   200

0 miles   200

Population ● National capital ● Internal administrative capital

○ below 50,000 ○ 50,000 to 100,000 ◉ 100,000 to 500,000 ■ above 500,000

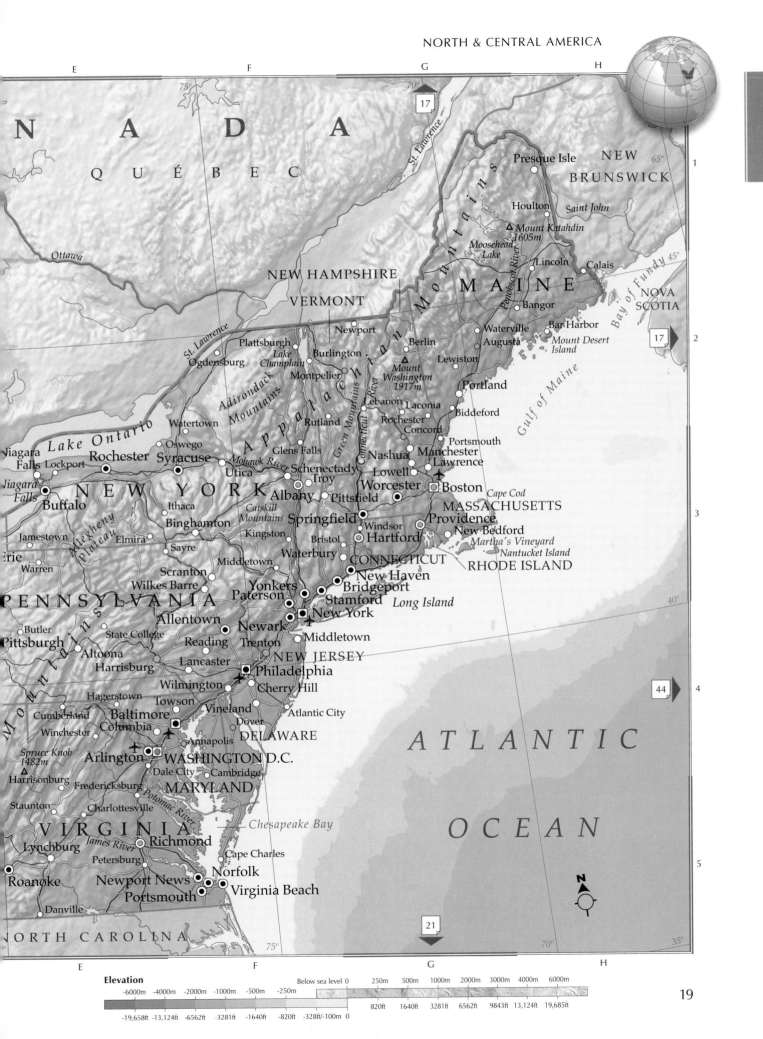

E   75°   F   70°   G   H

N A D A   1

Q U É B E C

Ottawa

St. Lawrence

Presque Isle   NEW
BRUNSWICK   65°

Houlton   Saint John

△ Mount Katahdin
1605m

Moosehead
Lake

Lincoln   Calais   45°

NEW HAMPSHIRE
VERMONT   M A I N E

Bangor   Bay of Fundy   NOVA
SCOTIA   17   2

St. Lawrence   Newport   Berlin   Waterville   Bar Harbor

Plattsburgh   Burlington   Augusta   Mount Desert
Island

Ogdensburg   Lake
Champlain   Lewiston   Gulf of Maine

Montpelier   △ Mount
Washington
1917m   Portland

Adirondack
Mountains   Lebanon   Laconia   Biddeford

Watertown   Rutland   Rochester   Portsmouth

Lake Ontario   Glens Falls   Concord

Niagara   Oswego   Mohawk River   Nashua   Manchester   Cape Cod
Falls   Lockport   Rochester   Syracuse   Schenectady   Lowell   Lawrence

Niagara   Utica   Troy   Worcester   Boston
Falls   Albany   Pittsfield   MASSACHUSETTS

Buffalo   N E W   Y O R K   Springfield   Providence

Ithaca   Catskill   Windsor   New Bedford
Mountains   Bristol   Martha's Vineyard
Erie   Binghamton   Waterbury   Hartford   Nantucket Island   3

Jamestown   Elmira   Kingston   CONNECTICUT
Warren   Sayre   RHODE ISLAND

P E N N S Y L V A N I A   Middletown   New Haven
Scranton   Yonkers   Bridgeport
Wilkes Barre   Paterson   Stamford   Long Island   40°

Butler   Allentown   Newark   New York
State College   Reading   Middletown
Pittsburgh   Altoona   Trenton
Harrisburg   Lancaster   NEW JERSEY   A T L A N T I C

Hagerstown   Philadelphia
Wilmington   Cherry Hill   4
Cumberland   Towson   Vineland   Atlantic City   44

Winchester   Baltimore   Dover
Columbia   O C E A N
Spruce Knob   Annapolis
1482m   Arlington   DELAWARE
△   WASHINGTON D.C.
Harrisonburg   Dale City   Cambridge

Fredericksburg   MARYLAND
Staunton   Potomac River

Charlottesville   Chesapeake Bay   5
V I R G I N I A
Lynchburg   James River   Richmond

Petersburg   Cape Charles
Roanoke   Norfolk
Newport News   Virginia Beach
Portsmouth   N

Danville   21

N O R T H   C A R O L I N A   75°   70°   35°

E   F   G   H

Elevation

-6000m -4000m -2000m -1000m -500m -250m

Below sea level 0   250m   500m   1000m   2000m   3000m   4000m   6000m

820ft   1640ft   3281ft   6562ft   9843ft   13,124ft   19,685ft

-19,658ft -13,124ft -6562ft -3281ft -1640ft -820ft -328ft/-100m 0

USA: The Southeast

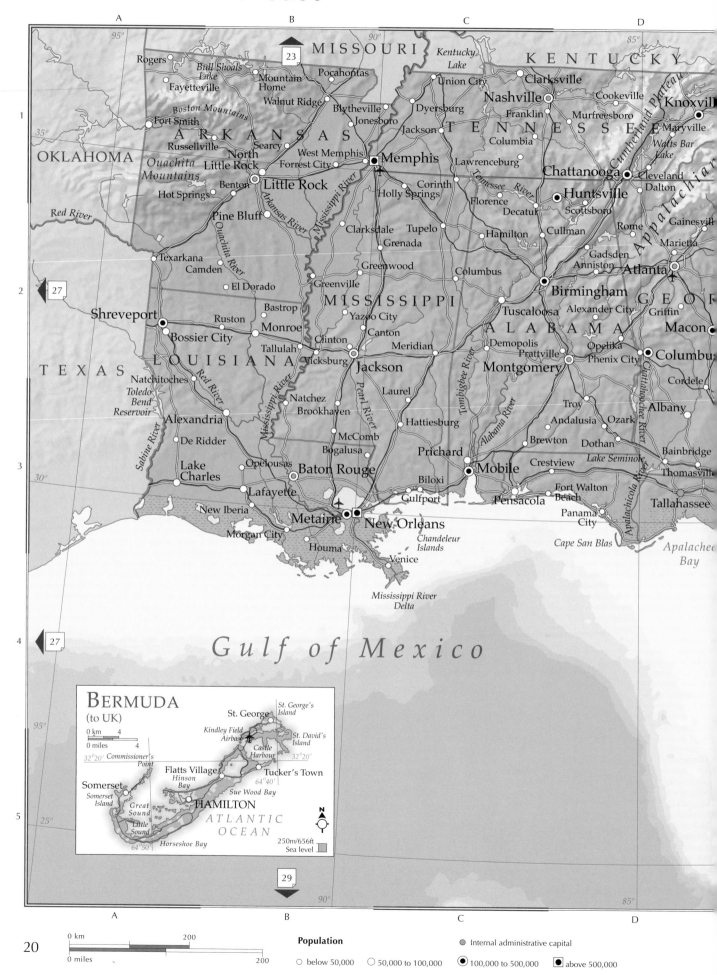

Population

○ below 50,000 ○ 50,000 to 100,000 ◉ 100,000 to 500,000 ■ above 500,000

● Internal administrative capital

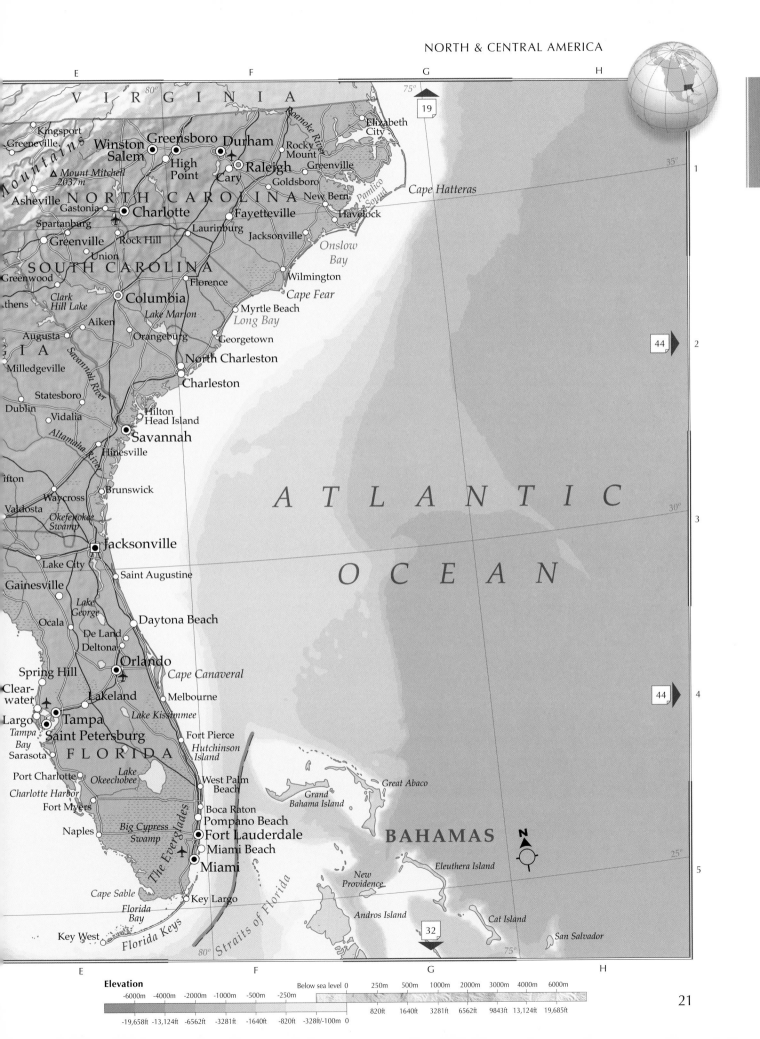

VIRGINIA

Kingsport
Greeneville
Winston Salem
Greensboro
Durham
Elizabeth City
Rocky Mount
High Point
Cary
Raleigh
Greenville
Goldsboro
△ Mount Mitchell 2037m
NORTH CAROLINA
New Bern
Havelock
Cape Hatteras
Asheville
Gastonia
Charlotte
Fayetteville
Jacksonville
Pamlico Sound
Spartanburg
Laurinburg
Onslow Bay
Greenville
Rock Hill
Union
Florence
Wilmington
SOUTH CAROLINA
Cape Fear
Greenwood
Columbia
Myrtle Beach
Long Bay
Clark Hill Lake
Lake Marion
thens
Aiken
Orangeburg
Georgetown
Augusta
North Charleston
I A
Milledgeville
Charleston
Statesboro
Dublin
Vidalia
Hilton Head Island
Altamaha River
Savannah
Hinesville
ifton
Brunswick
A T L A N T I C
Valdosta
Waycross
Okefenokee Swamp
Jacksonville
O C E A N
Lake City
Saint Augustine
Gainesville
Lake George
Ocala
Daytona Beach
De Land
Deltona
Orlando
Cape Canaveral
Spring Hill
Lakeland
Melbourne
Clear-water
Lake Kissimmee
Largo
Tampa
Saint Petersburg
Fort Pierce
Tampa Bay
Hutchinson Island
Sarasota
FLORIDA
Port Charlotte
Lake Okeechobee
West Palm Beach
Charlotte Harbor
Boca Raton
Great Abaco
Fort Myers
Pompano Beach
Grand Bahama Island
Naples
Big Cypress Swamp
Fort Lauderdale
Miami Beach
BAHAMAS
Miami
Eleuthera Island
Cape Sable
Key Largo
New Providence
Florida Bay
Andros Island
Cat Island
Key West
Florida Keys
Straits of Florida
San Salvador

19

44

44

32

Elevation

								Below sea level 0	250m	500m	1000m	2000m	3000m	4000m	6000m
-6000m	-4000m	-2000m	-1000m	-500m	-250m										
-19,658ft	-13,124ft	-6562ft	-3281ft	-1640ft	-820ft	-328ft/-100m	0		820ft	1640ft	3281ft	6562ft	9843ft	13,124ft	19,685ft

USA: Central States

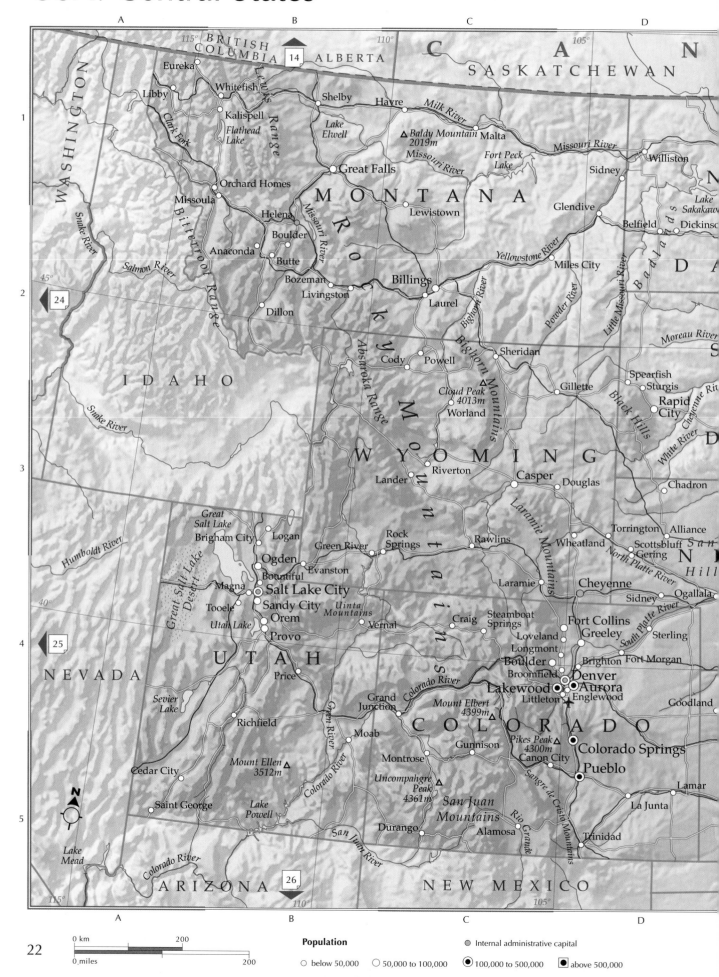

Population

○ below 50,000   ○ 50,000 to 100,000   ◉ 100,000 to 500,000   ■ above 500,000

● Internal administrative capital

0 km   200
0 miles   200

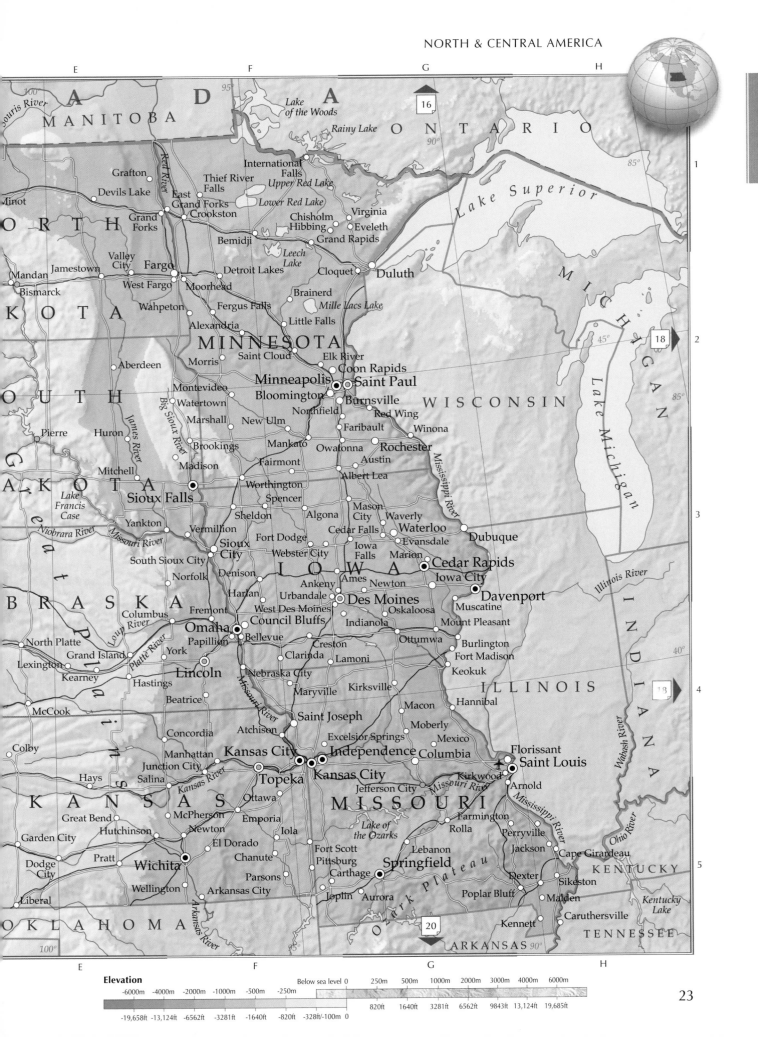

Elevation

-6000m	-4000m	-2000m	-1000m	-500m	-250m	Below sea level 0	250m	500m	1000m	2000m	3000m	4000m	6000m
-19,658ft	-13,124ft	-6562ft	-3281ft	-1640ft	-820ft	-328ft/-100m 0		820ft	1640ft	3281ft	6562ft	9843ft	13,124ft	19,685ft

USA: The West

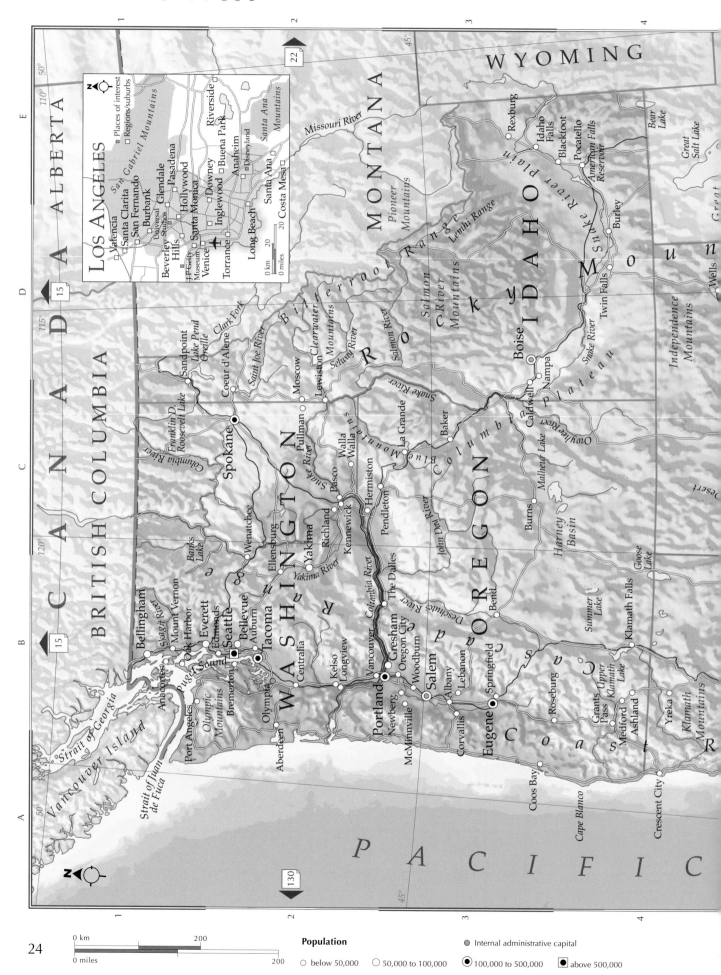

LOS ANGELES

Places of interest
Regions/suburbs

Valencia
Santa Clarita
San Fernando
Burbank
Universal Studios
Beverley Hills
Getty Museum
Venice
Santa Monica
Glendale
Pasadena
Hollywood
Inglewood
Downey
Buena Park
Anaheim
Disneyland
Santa Ana
Costa Mesa
Long Beach
Torrance
Riverside
San Gabriel Mountains
Santa Ana Mountains

WYOMING

MONTANA
Pioneer Mountains

IDAHO
Rexburg
Idaho Falls
Blackfoot
Pocatello
American Falls
Reservoir
Burley
Twin Falls
Bear Lake
Great Salt Lake
Snake River Plain
Wells
Independence Mountains

ALBERTA
CANADA

BRITISH COLUMBIA

Sandpoint
Lake Pend Oreille
Clark Fork
Bitterroot Range
Clearwater Mountains
Salmon River Mountains
Lemhi Range
Boise
Nampa
Caldwell
Owyhee River
Malheur Lake

Franklin D. Roosevelt Lake
Columbia River
Coeur d'Alene
Saint Joe River
Moscow
Lewiston
Selway River
Salmon River
Snake River
La Grande
Baker
Columbia Plateau

Spokane
Pullman
Snake River
Walla Walla
Pasco
Hermiston
Pendleton
Blue Mountains
Burns
Harney Basin
Goose Lake

Banks Lake
Wenatchee
Richland
Kennewick
John Day River

WASHINGTON

Ellensburg
Yakima
Yakima River

OREGON

Bellingham
Skagit River
Mount Vernon
Oak Harbor
Everett
Edmonds
Bellevue
Seattle
Auburn
Tacoma
Anacortes
Puget Sound
Bremerton
Olympia

Centralia
Kelso
Longview
Vancouver
Gresham
Oregon City
Woodburn
Salem
Albany
Lebanon
Springfield
Eugene

The Dalles
Deschutes River
Bend

Summer Lake
Klamath Falls
Upper Klamath Lake
Medford
Ashland
Yreka
Klamath Mountains

Port Angeles
Olympic Mountains
Aberdeen

Portland
Newberg
McMinnville
Corvallis

Coast

Roseburg
Grants Pass

Strait of Georgia
Vancouver Island
Strait of Juan de Fuca

Coos Bay
Cape Blanco
Crescent City

PACIFIC

R O C K Y   M o u n t a i n s

ROCKY MOUNTAINS

Missouri River

Great Desert

Population

○ below 50,000
○ 50,000 to 100,000
◉ 100,000 to 500,000
◼ above 500,000

● Internal administrative capital

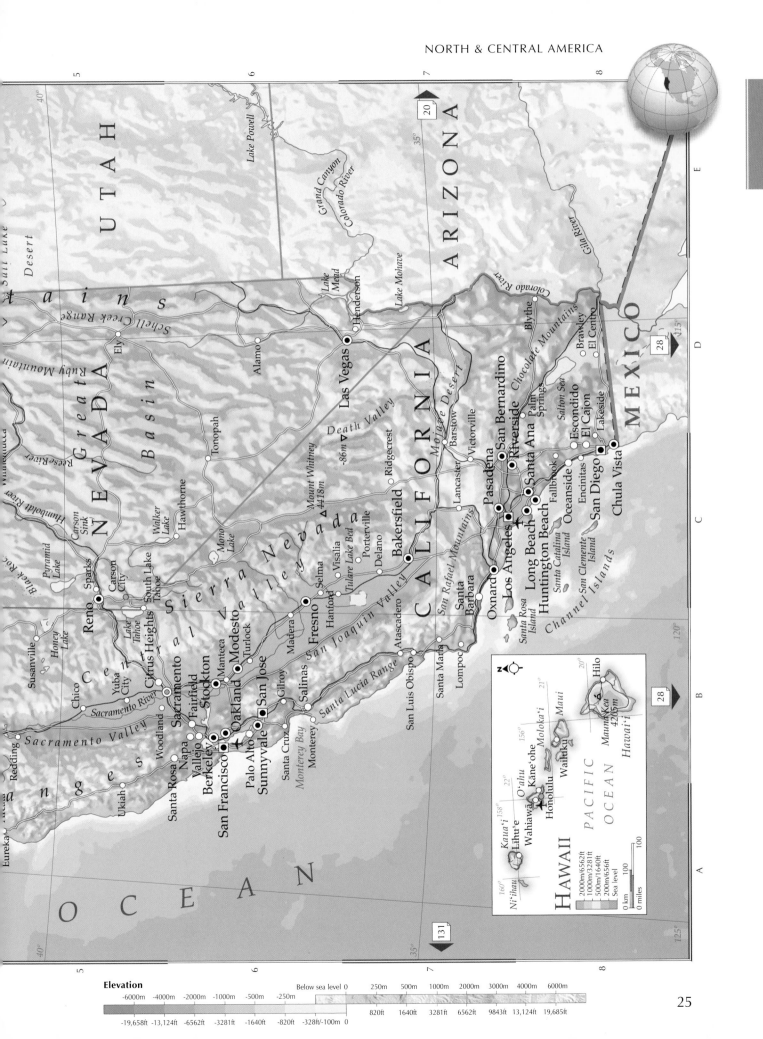

UTAH

Salt Lake Desert

Lake Powell

Grand Canyon

Colorado River

ARIZONA

20

NEVADA

Schell Creek Range

Ruby Mountains

Ely

Alamo

Great Basin

Lake Mead
Henderson
Lake Mohave

Blythe

Chocolate Mountains

Brawley
Gila River
El Centro

MEXICO

28

Reese River

Humboldt River

Tonopah

Las Vegas

Death Valley
-86m

Mojave Desert

Barstow

Victorville

San Bernardino
Riverside
Santa Ana
Palm Springs
Salton Sea

Escondido
El Cajon
Lakeside

San Diego

Chula Vista

Whitewater

Black Rock
Pyramid Lake

Sparks
Carson City

Hawthorne

Walker Lake

Mono Lake

Sierra Nevada

Mount Whitney
△4418m

Ridgecrest

Lancaster

Pasadena

Los Angeles
Long Beach
Huntington Beach

Oceanside
Encinitas
Fallbrook

San Rafael Mountains

Santa Catalina Island
San Clemente Island

Channel Islands

Susanville

Honey Lake

Reno

South Lake Tahoe
Lake Tahoe

Citrus Heights

Porterville
Delano
Visalia
Hanford
Tulare Lake Bed

Bakersfield

Madera

Fresno
Selma

San Joaquin Valley

Oxnard
Santa Barbara

Santa Rosa Island

Chico

Yuba City

Sacramento River

Woodland

Sacramento
Fairfield

Stockton
Manteca
Turlock
Modesto

Gilroy

Atascadero

Santa Lucia Range

San Luis Obispo

Santa Maria

Lompoc

Redding

Central Valley

Sacramento Valley

Ukiah

Santa Rosa
Napa
Vallejo
Berkeley
Oakland

San Francisco
Palo Alto
Sunnyvale
San Jose

Santa Cruz
Monterey Bay
Monterey

Salinas

Eureka

CALIFORNIA

OCEAN

PACIFIC OCEAN

HAWAII

Z

Kaua'i 158°
Lihu'e
Ni'ihau
160°

O'ahu
Wahiawa
Kāne'ohe
Honolulu

156°
Moloka'i
Waihuku
Maui

22°
21°
20°

Hilo
Mauna Kea
4205m
Hawai'i

PACIFIC OCEAN

2000m/6562ft
1000m/3281ft
500m/1640ft
200m/656ft
Sea level

0 km   100
0 miles   100

131

Elevation

-6000m	-4000m	-2000m	-1000m	-500m	-250m	Below sea level 0	250m	500m	1000m	2000m	3000m	4000m	6000m

| -19,658ft | -13,124ft | -6562ft | -3281ft | -1640ft | -820ft | -328ft/-100m 0 | 820ft | 1640ft | 3281ft | 6562ft | 9843ft | 13,124ft | 19,685ft |

USA: The Southwest

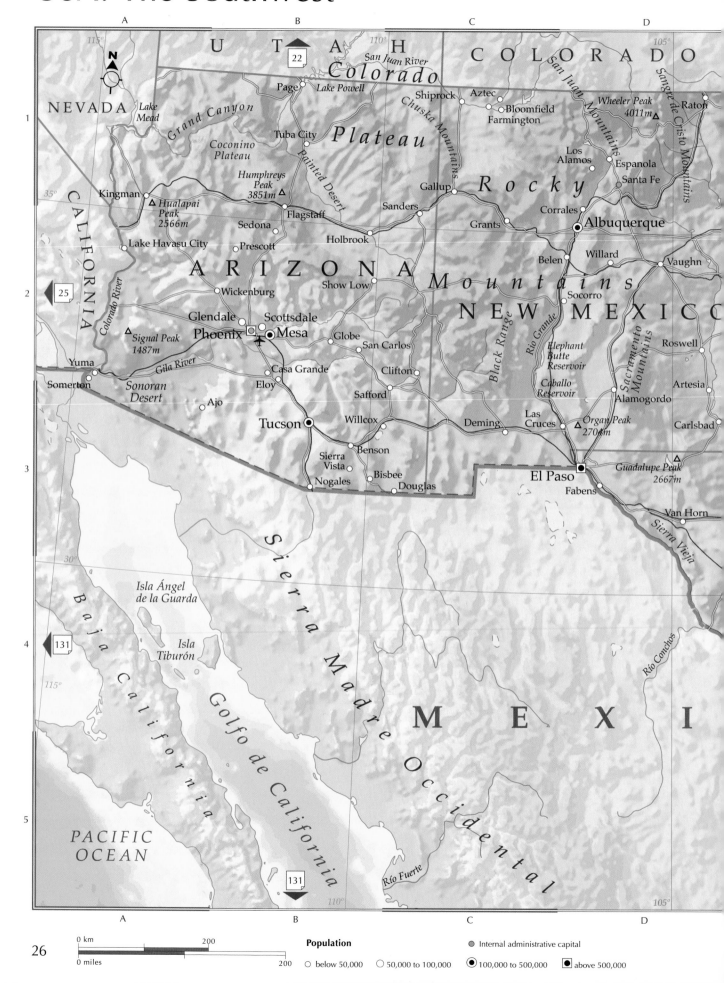

0 km   200

0 miles   200

Population

○ below 50,000   ◉ Internal administrative capital

○ 50,000 to 100,000

◉ 100,000 to 500,000   ◼ above 500,000

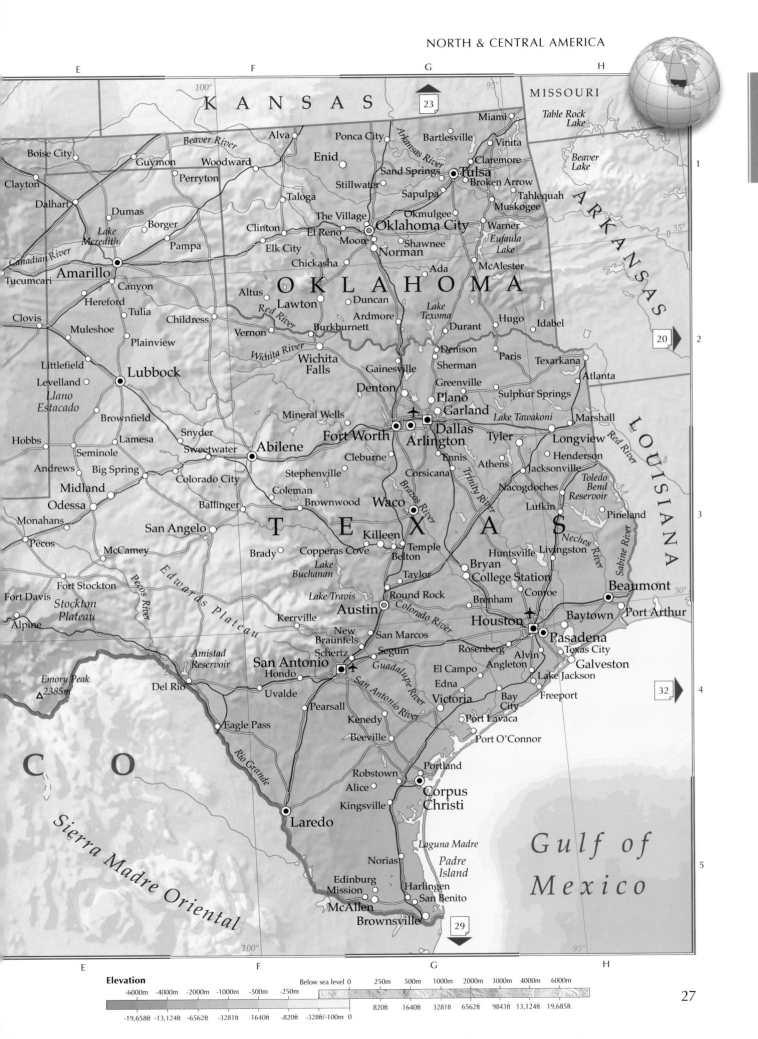

Elevation

					Below sea level 0	250m	500m	1000m	2000m	3000m	4000m	6000m

-6000m -4000m -2000m -1000m -500m -250m

820ft 1640ft 3281ft 6562ft 9843ft 13,124ft 19,685ft

-19,658ft -13,124ft -6562ft -3281ft -1640ft -820ft -328ft/-100m 0

Mexico

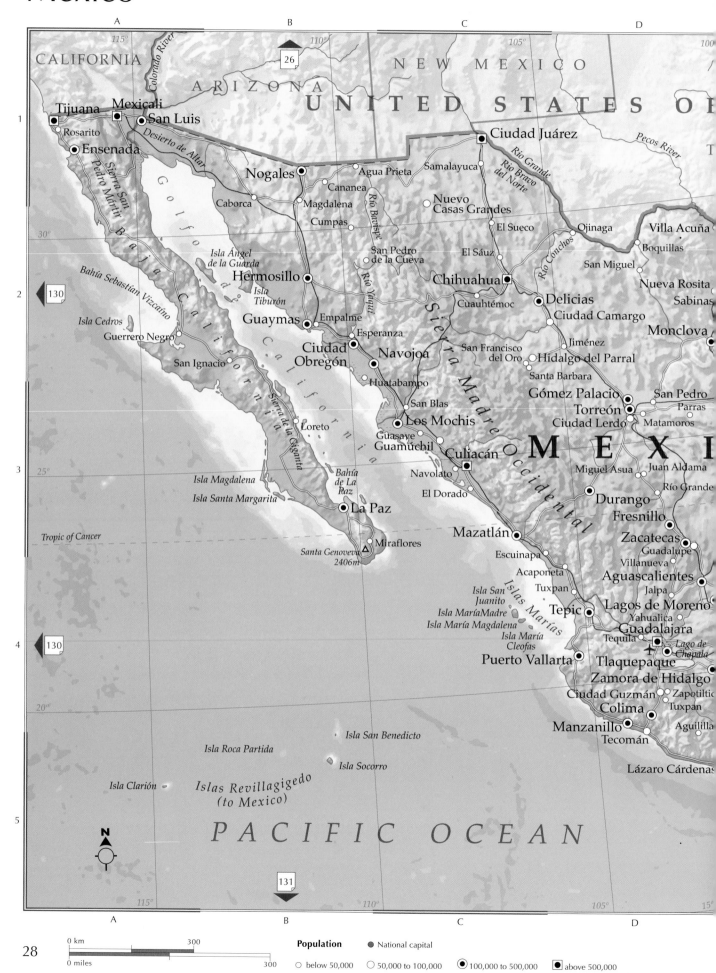

CALIFORNIA
ARIZONA
NEW MEXICO
UNITED STATES OF

Tijuana
Mexicali
San Luis
Ciudad Juárez
Pecos River
Rosarito
Ensenada
Colorado River
Desierto de Altar
Nogales
Agua Prieta
Samalayuca
Río Grande
Río Bravo
del Norte
Villa Acuña
Cananea
Caborca
Magdalena
Nuevo
Casas Grandes
El Sueco
Ojinaga
Boquillas
Cumpas
San Pedro
de la Cueva
El Sáuz
Río Conchos
San Miguel
Nueva Rosita
Isla Ángel
de la Guarda
Hermosillo
Chihuahua
Sabinas
Cuauhtémoc
Delicias
Isla
Tiburón
Ciudad Camargo
Monclova
Guaymas
Empalme
Esperanza
San Francisco
del Oro
Jiménez
Hidalgo del Parral
Ciudad
Obregón
Navojoá
Santa Barbara
Huatabampo
Gómez Palacio
San Pedro
San Blas
Torreón
Parras
Los Mochis
Ciudad Lerdo
Matamoros
Guasave
Guamúchil
Culiacán
MEXI
Miguel Asua
Juan Aldama
Navolato
Río Grande
El Dorado
Durango
Fresnillo
La Paz
Mazatlán
Zacatecas
Guadalupe
Miraflores
Escuinapa
Villanueva
Santa Genoveva
2406m
Acaponeta
Aguascalientes
Tuxpan
Jalpa
Isla San
Juanito
Tepic
Lagos de Moreno
Isla MaríaMadre
Yahualica
Isla María Magdalena
Guadalajara
Isla María
Cleofas
Tequila
Lago de
Chapala
Puerto Vallarta
Tlaquepaque
Zamora de Hidalgo
Ciudad Guzmán
Zapotiltic
Colima
Tuxpan
Manzanillo
Aguililla
Tecomán
Lázaro Cárdenas

Isla Cedros
Bahía Sebastián Vizcaíno
Guerrero Negro
San Ignacio
Isla Magdalena
Isla Santa Margarita
Loreto
Bahía
de La
Paz
Tropic of Cancer
Isla San Benedicto
Isla Roca Partida
Isla Socorro
Isla Clarión
Islas Revillagigedo
(to Mexico)

PACIFIC OCEAN

N

Golfo de California
Baja California
Sierra San Pedro Mártir
Sierra de la Giganta
Sierra Madre Occidental
Islas Marías
Río Bavispe
Río Yaqui

26
130
130
131

115°
110°
105°
100°
30°
25°
20°

28

0 km   300
0 miles   300

Population   ● National capital

○ below 50,000   ○ 50,000 to 100,000   ◉ 100,000 to 500,000   ■ above 500,000

ALABAMA
FLORIDA

20

MISSISSIPPI

LOUISIANA

Mississippi River Delta

Brazos River

Red River

Sabine River

Mississippi River

A M E R I C A

Colorado River

T E X A S

44

Gulf of Mexico

Padre Island

Piedras Negras

Río Grande

Nuevo Laredo

Sabinas Hidalgo

Ciudad Miguel Alemán

Reynosa

Río Bravo

Matamoros

Monterrey

Saltillo

Montemorelos

Laguna Madre

Linares

C O

Sierra Madre Oriental

Ciudad Victoria

Tropic of Cancer

Yucatan Channel

Ciudad Mante

Cancún

Rio Lagartos

Tizimín

Progreso

Motul

Isla Cozumel

Ciudad Madero

San Luis Potosí

Pánuco

Tampico

Mérida

Umán

Valladolid

Ticul

Peto

Río Verde

Ciudad Valles

Oxkutzcab

Tekax

Felipe Carrillo Puerto

Dolores Hidalgo

Tamazunchale

Laguna de Tamiahua

Campeche

Yucatan Peninsula

León

Tuxpán

Bahía de Campeche

Guanajuato

Poza Rica

Champotón

Chetumal

Querétaro

Papantla

Irapuato

Pachuca

Tulancingo

Laguna de Términos

Morelia

Teziutlán

Xalapa

30

MÉXICO (MEXICO CITY)

Perote

Frontera

Fransisco Escárcega

Toluca

Tlaxcala

Veracruz

Carmen

Cuernavaca

Puebla

Alvarado

Comalcalco

Uruapan

Popocatépetl 5452m

Córdoba

Coatzacoalcos

Villahermosa

BELIZE

Gulf of Honduras

Zacatepec

Tehuacán

San Andrés Tuxtla

Macuspana

Taxco

Cuautla

Tuxtepec

Minatitlán

Teapa

Presa del Infiernillo

Iguala

Ismo de Tehuantepec

San Cristóbal de Las Casas

Río Usumacinta

Río Balsas

Huajuapan

Oaxaca

Tuxtla

Sierra Madre del Sur

Chilpancingo

Ocozocuautla

Matías Romero

Chiapa de Corzo

Comitán

Ixtapa

Tecpan

Ixtepec

Presa de la Angostura

Pinotepa Nacional

Tehuantepec

Juchitán

Arriaga

Acapulco

Miahuatlán

Salina Cruz

Pijijiapán

GUATEMALA

HONDURAS

Puerto Escondido

Puerto Angel

Golfo de Tehuantepec

Escuintla

Huixtla

Tapachula

Ciudad Hidalgo

EL SALVADOR

131

Elevation

							Below sea level 0	250m	500m	1000m	2000m	3000m	4000m	6000m

-6000m -4000m -2000m -1000m -500m -250m

820ft 1640ft 3281ft 6562ft 9843ft 13,124ft 19,685ft

-19,658ft -13,124ft -6562ft -3281ft -1640ft -820ft -328ft/-100m 0

Central America

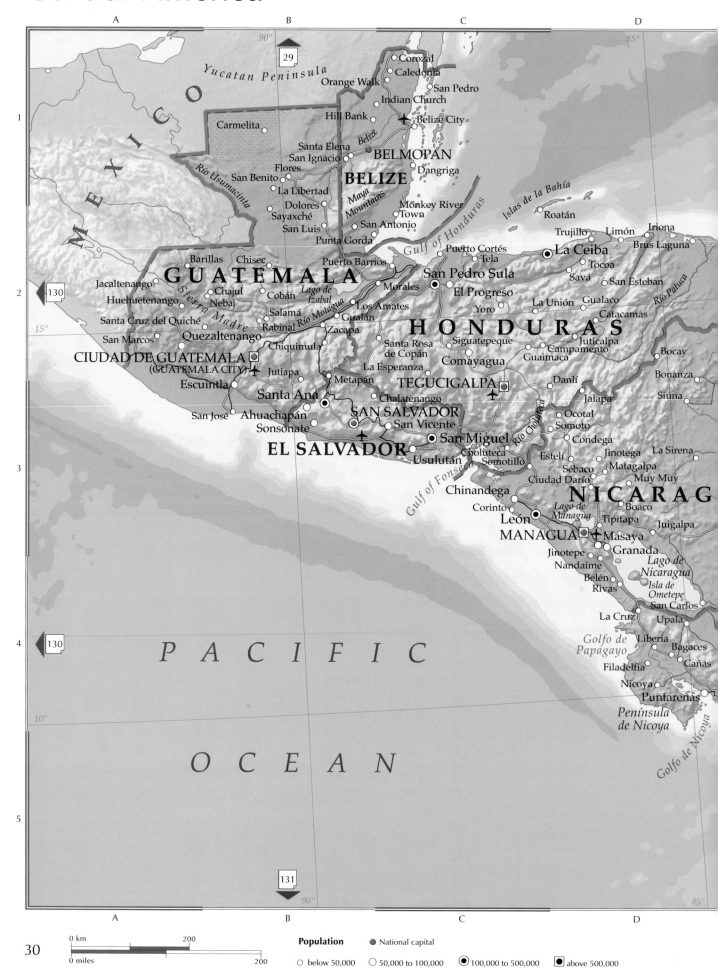

MEXICO

Yucatan Peninsula

90°   85°

29

Corozal
Caledonia
Orange Walk
San Pedro
Indian Church
Hill Bank
Belize City
Carmelita
BELMOPAN
Santa Elena
San Ignacio
Flores
Dangriga
San Benito
BELIZE
La Libertad
Dolores
Maya
Sayaxché
Mountains
Monkey River
San Luis
Town
San Antonio
Punta Gorda
Gulf of Honduras
Islas de la Bahía
Roatán
Trujillo   Limón   Iriona
Barillas   Chisec
Puerto Barrios
Puerto Cortés
Brus Laguna
Tela
La Ceiba
GUATEMALA
San Pedro Sula
Tocoa
Jacaltenango
Chajul   Cobán   Morales
El Progreso
Savá   San Esteban
Huehuetenango
Nebaj
Lago de
Izabal
Yoro   La Unión   Gualaco
Catacamas
Salamá   Los Amates
Santa Cruz del Quiché
Rabinal   Gualán
HONDURAS
Juticalpa
Bocay
San Marcos
Zacapa
Santa Rosa
Siguatepeque
Campamento
Quezaltenango
Chiquimula
de Copán
Comayagua   Guaimaca
Bonanza
CIUDAD DE GUATEMALA
La Esperanza
Danlí
Siuna
(GUATEMALA CITY)
Jutiapa
Metapán
TEGUCIGALPA
Escuintla
Chalatenango
Jalapa
Santa Ana
SAN SALVADOR
Ocotal
San José   Ahuachapán
San Vicente
Somoto
Sonsonate
San Miguel
Condega   Jinotega   La Sirena
EL SALVADOR
Usulután
Choluteca   Estelí   Matagalpa
Somotillo
Muy Muy
Ciudad Darío
Chinandega
NICARAG
Corinto
Boaco
León   Lago de
Managua   Tipitapa   Juigalpa
MANAGUA   Masaya
Jinotepe   Granada
Nandaime   Lago de
Belén   Nicaragua
Rivas   Isla de
Ometepe
San Carlos
La Cruz   Upala
Golfo de   Liberia
Papagayo   Bagaces
Filadelfia   Cañas
Nicoya
Puntarenas
Península
de Nicoya
Golfo de Nicoya

Sierra Madre

Río Usumacinta

Río Motagua

Río Choluteca

Gulf of Fonseca

Río Patuca

Belize

130

15°

130

10°

PACIFIC

OCEAN

131

90°   85°

A   B   C   D

0 km   200
0 miles   200

Population   ● National capital

○ below 50,000   ○ 50,000 to 100,000   ◉ 100,000 to 500,000   ■ above 500,000

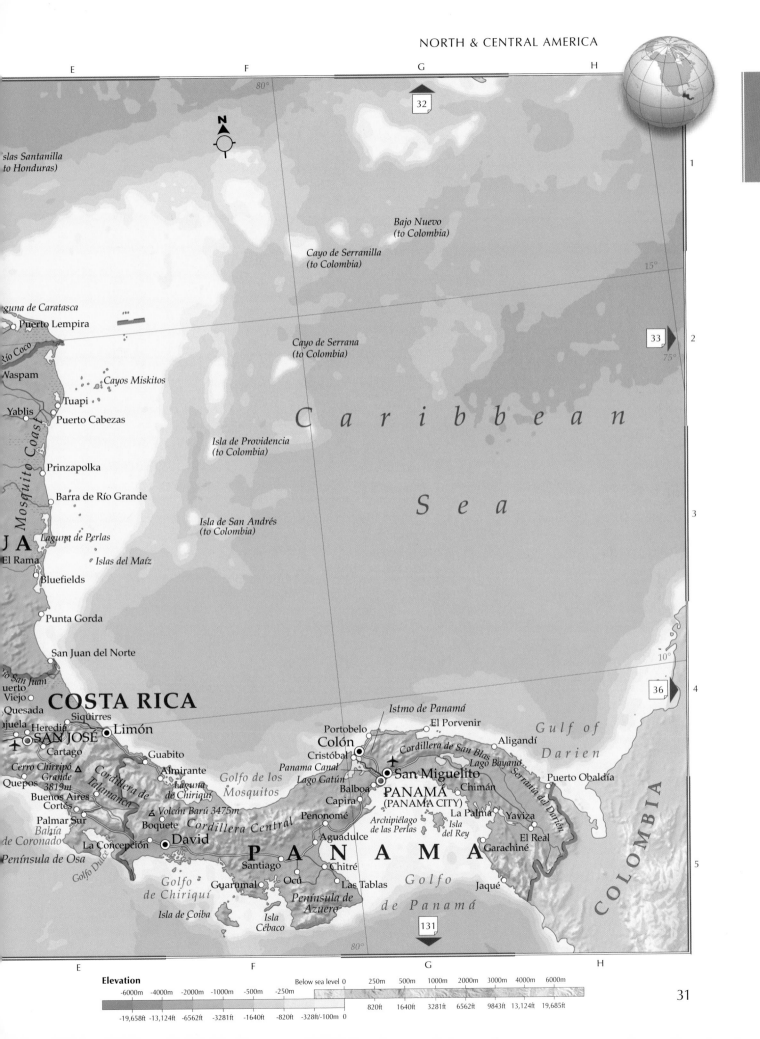

E   F   G   H

32

1

*Islas Santanilla
(to Honduras)*

*Bajo Nuevo
(to Colombia)*

*Cayo de Serranilla
(to Colombia)*

15°

guna de Caratasca

○ Puerto Lempira

*Cayo de Serrana
(to Colombia)*

33   2

75°

Río Coco

○ Naspam

Cayos Miskitos

● Tuapi

C a r i b b e a n

○ Yablis

● Puerto Cabezas

Mosquito Coast

*Isla de Providencia
(to Colombia)*

○ Prinzapolka

S e a

○ Barra de Río Grande

*Isla de San Andrés
(to Colombia)*

3

JA

○ El Rama

○ *Laguna de Perlas*

Islas del Maíz

○ Bluefields

○ Punta Gorda

○ San Juan del Norte

10°

ío San Juan

uerto
○ Viejo

36   4

○ Quesada

COSTA RICA

Istmo de Panamá

Gulf of

ajuela ○ Heredia ○ Siquirres

Portobelo ○

El Porvenir ○

Darien

⊕ ● **SAN JOSÉ** ● Limón

Colón ●

Aligandí ○

○ Cartago

Cristóbal ○

Cordillera de San Blas

○ Guabito

Panama Canal

Lago Bayano

Cerro Chirripó △

○ Almirante

Golfo de los

Lago Gatún

⊕ ● San Miguelito

Puerto Obaldía ○

Grande
3819m

Laguna
de Chiriquí

Mosquitos

Balboa ○

PANAMÁ

Chimán ○

Serranía del Darién

○ Quepos

Cordillera de

(PANAMA CITY)

○ Buenos Aires

Talamanca

○ Capira

La Palma ○

○ Cortés

Penonomé ○

Yaviza ○

○ Palmar Sur

△ *Volcán Barú 3475m*

Archipiélago
de las Perlas

Isla
del Rey

El Real ○

Bahía
de Coronado

○ Boquete

Cordillera Central

Aguadulce ○

○ Garachiné

C
O
L
O
M
B
I
A

○ La Concepción

● **David**

P A N A M A

Península de Osa

Santiago ○

Chitré ○

Golfo

5

Golfo Dulce

Golfo de Chiriquí

○ Guarumal

Ocú ○

Las Tablas ○

de Panamá

Jaqué ○

Isla de Coiba

Península de
Azuero

Isla
Cébaco

131

80°

E   F   G   H

Elevation

-6000m   -4000m   -2000m   -1000m   -500m   -250m

Below sea level 0   250m   500m   1000m   2000m   3000m   4000m   6000m

-19,658ft -13,124ft -6562ft -3281ft -1640ft -820ft -328ft/-100m 0

820ft   1640ft   3281ft   6562ft   9843ft 13,124ft 19,685ft

The Caribbean

United States of America

Gulf of Mexico

Tropic of Cancer

Straits of Florida

Florida Keys

The Everglades

Grand Bahama Island
Freeport
Marsh Harbour
Great Abaco
Bimini Islands
Berry Islands
Nicholls Town
Northeast Providence Channel
NASSAU
New Providence
Eleuthera Island
Andros Town
Rock Sound
Cat Island
Andros Island
Exuma Cays
Exuma Sound
San Salvador
BAHAMAS
Anguilla Cays
Cay Sal
George Town
Rum Cay
Great Exuma Island
Long Island
Clarence Town
Crooked Island
Crooked Island Passage
Ragged Island Range
Acklins Island
Mayaguana
Mayaguana Passage
Caicos Passage
Little Inagua
Lake Rosa
Matthew Town
Great Inagua

LA HABANA (HAVANA)
Guanabacoa
Artemisa
Cárdenas
Pinar del Río
Matanzas
Sagua la Grande
La Fé
Consolación del Sur
Santa Clara
Cienfuegos
Placetas
Archipiélago de Camagüey
Nueva Gerona
Sancti Spíritus
Morón
Ciego de Ávila
Isla de la Juventud
Cayo Largo
CUBA
Archipiélago de los Canarreos
Bahía de Cochinos
Camagüey
Nuevitas
Archipiélago de los Jardines de la Reina
Las Tunas
Holguín
Manzanillo
Bayamo
Matthew Town
Palma Soriano
Guantánamo
Cap-Haïtien
Little Cayman
Cayman Brac
Santiago de Cuba
Guantánamo Bay (to US)
Gonaïves
GEORGE TOWN
Grand Cayman
HAIT
CAYMAN ISLANDS (to UK)
Greater
NAVASSA ISLAND (to US)
Jérémie
PORT-AU-PRINCE
Montego Bay
Cayes
Spanish Town
Jamaica Channel
Jacmel
Portmore
KINGSTON
JAMAICA
Pedro Cays
Caribbean
HONDURAS
NICARAGUA
COSTA RICA
COLOMBIA

JAMAICA

Caribbean Sea

Montego Bay
Lucea
Falmouth
Discovery Bay
St Ann's Bay
Ocho Rios
The Cockpit Country
Cambridge
Annotto Bay
Buff Bay
Port Antonio
Christiana
Ewarton
Savanna-La-Mar
Mandeville
Blue Mountain Peak 2258m
Spanish Town
KINGSTON
Black River
Portmore
May Pen
Old Harbour
Morant Bay
Portland Bight

Caribbean Sea

0 km 20
0 miles 20

2000m/6562ft
1000m/3281ft
500m/1640ft
200m/656ft
Sea level

0 km 200
0 miles 200

Population

⚫ National capital

○ below 50,000　○ 50,000 to 100,000　◉ 100,000 to 500,000　◼ above 500,000

St Lucia

Gros Islet
CASTRIES
Caribbean Sea
14°00'
Anse La Raye
Dennery
Soufrière
△ Mount Gimie 950m
Micoud
Vieux Fort
61°00'

500m/1640ft
200m/656ft
Sea level

0 km 10
0 miles 10

Barbados

ATLANTIC OCEAN
Speightstown
Mt Hillaby 340m
Bathsheba
Holetown
13°10'
Welchman Hall
BRIDGETOWN
The Crane
Oistins
59°30'

200m/656ft
Sea level

0 km 10
0 miles 10

Tropic of Cancer

44

TURKS & CAICOS ISLANDS (to UK)
COCKBURN TOWN

DOMINICAN REPUBLIC
Monte Cristi
Puerto Plata
Santiago
San Francisco de Macorís
La Vega
La Romana
La Vega
Cordillera Central
SANTO DOMINGO
Isla Saona
Mona Passage
Isla Mona
Isla Beata

SAN JUAN
VIRGIN ISLANDS (to US)
Caguas
Ponce
Mayagüez
PUERTO RICO (to US)
St Croix

BRITISH VIRGIN ISLANDS (to UK)
ROAD TOWN
CHARLOTTE AMALIE

ANGUILLA (to UK)
THE VALLEY
Sint Maarten (to Netherlands)

Barbuda
ANTIGUA & BARBUDA
ST JOHN'S
BASSETERRE
Antigua
SAINT KITTS & NEVIS
PLYMOUTH
MONTSERRAT (to UK)
Grande Terre
Pointe-à-Pitre
GUADELOUPE (to France)
BASSE-TERRE
Marie-Galante
Basse-Terre

DOMINICA
ROSEAU
Martinique Passage

FORT-DE-FRANCE
MARTINIQUE (to France)
St Lucia Channel
ST LUCIA
CASTRIES
Vieux Fort
BARBADOS
BRIDGETOWN
Saint Vincent Passage
Saint Vincent
SAINT VINCENT & THE GRENADINES
KINGSTOWN
The Grenadines

GRENADA
ST GEORGE'S

ATLANTIC OCEAN
Leeward Islands
Lesser Antilles
Windward Islands
Sea
Lesser Antilles

ARUBA (to Netherlands)
ORANJESTAD
CURAÇAO (to Neth.)
BONAIRE (to Neth.)
WILLEMSTAD
Isla La Orchila
Islas Los Roques

Isla Blanquilla
Islas Los Testigos
Tobago
TRINIDAD & TOBAGO
Isla de Margarita
Isla La Tortuga
PORT-OF-SPAIN
San Fernando
Trinidad
Gulf of Paria
Golfo de Venezuela

VENEZUELA

37

Elevation

| Below sea level 0 | 250m | 500m | 1000m | 2000m | 3000m | 4000m | 6000m |

-6000m -4000m -2000m -1000m -500m -250m

-19,658ft -13,124ft -6562ft -3281ft -1640ft -820ft -328ft/-100m 0

820ft 1640ft 3281ft 6562ft 9843ft 13,124ft 19,685ft

South America

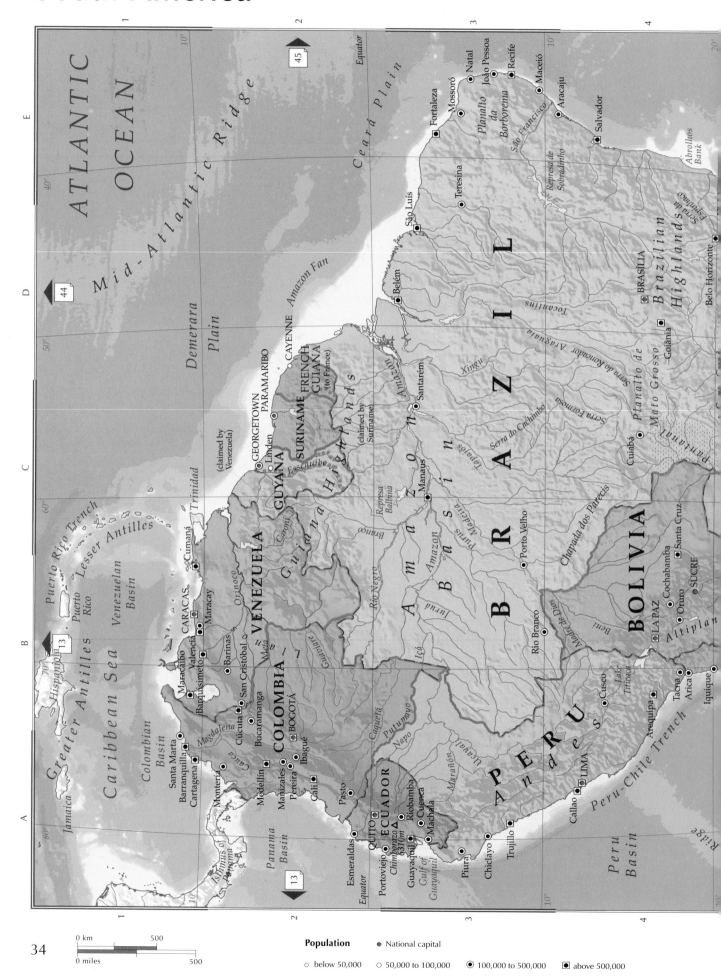

0 km   500

0 miles   500

Population   ● National capital

○ below 50,000   ◎ 50,000 to 100,000   ◉ 100,000 to 500,000   ■ above 500,000

ATLANTIC OCEAN

Mid-Atlantic Ridge

Ceará Plain

Equator

Amazon Fan

Demerara Plain

Puerto Rico Trench

Greater Antilles

Lesser Antilles

Caribbean Sea

Colombian Basin

Venezuelan Basin

Panama Basin

Isthmus of Panama

Jamaica

Hispaniola

Trinidad

Puerto Rico

Natal
João Pessoa
Recife
Maceió
Mossoró
Aracaju
Salvador
Fortaleza
Planalto da Borborema
São Francisco
Abrolhos Bank
Serra da Espinhaço

Teresina
Represa de Sobradinho

São Luís
Belém
BRASÍLIA
Belo Horizonte
Brazilian Highlands

B R A Z I L

Tocantins
Araguaia
Serra do Roncador
Planalto de Mato Grosso
Goiânia
Cuiabá
Pantanal
Paraguay

CAYENNE
PARAMARIBO
GEORGETOWN
Linden
SURINAME
FRENCH GUIANA (to France)
GUYANA
(claimed by Venezuela)
(claimed by Suriname)
Essequibo

Santarém
Amazon
Manaus
Represa Balbina
Madeira
Purus
Juruá
Amazon
A m a z o n   B a s i n
Xingu
Tapajós
Serra do Cachimbo
Serra Formosa

Guiana Highlands

VENEZUELA
CARACAS
Maracay
Valencia
Barquisimeto
Maracaibo
Barinas
San Cristóbal
Cumaná
Orinoco
Caroní
Meta
Guaviare
Branco
Rio Negro
Içá

Porto Velho
Rio Branco
Chapada dos Parecis
Chapada dos Parecis
BOLIVIA
LA PAZ
Cochabamba
Santa Cruz
Oruro
SUCRE
Altiplano
Beni
Mamoré

COLOMBIA
BOGOTÁ
Bucaramanga
Cúcuta
Medellín
Manizales
Pereira
Ibagué
Cali
Pasto
Montería
Cartagena
Barranquilla
Santa Marta
Magdalena
Cauca

ECUADOR
QUITO
Portoviejo
Chimborazo 6310m
Guayaquil
Riobamba
Cuenca
Machala
Esmeraldas
Gulf of Guayaquil
Equator

Caquetá
Putumayo
Napo
Marañón
Ucayali
Javarí
Juruá

PERU
LIMA
Callao
Trujillo
Chiclayo
Piura
Cusco
Arequipa
Tacna
Arica
Iquique
Lake Titicaca
A n d e s
Madre de Dios
Peru-Chile Trench

Peru Basin

Ridge

45
44
13
13

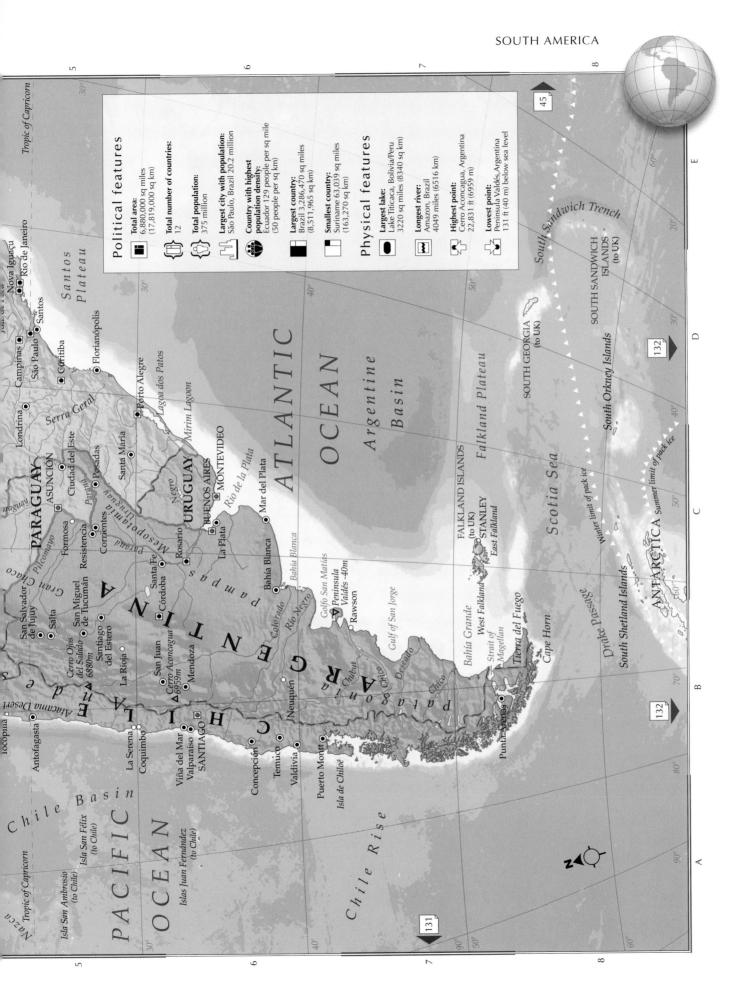

Northern South America

Caribbean Sea

Lesser Ant

ARUBA (to Netherlands)

CURAÇAO (to Neth.)

BONAIRE (to Neth.)

Península de la Guajira

Golfo de Venezuela

Islas Los Roques

Isla La Orchil

Puerto López

Punto Fijo

Ríohacha

Maicao

Coro

Puerto Cumarebo

Sabaneta

Santa Marta

Barranquilla

Ciénaga

Dabajuro

Maracaibo

Puerto Cabello

CARACAS

Cartagena

Soledad

Sabanalarga

Pico Cristóbal Colón 5775m

La Concepción

Cabimas

San Felipe

Valledupar

Machiques

Ciudad Ojeda

Carora

Valencia

Maracay

El Carmen de Bolívar

Barquisimeto

San Juan de los Morro

Sincelejo

Magangué

San Carlos del Zulia

Lago de Maracaibo

Valera

Acarigua

Valle de la Pascua

Montería

Cereté

Planeta Rica

El Vigía

Mérida

Guanare

Calabozo

San Fernando

Aguachica

Ocaña

Pico Bolívar 5007m

Barinas

Río Guanare

Caucasia

Cúcuta

San Cristóbal

Río Apure

L a V E N E

Dabeiba

Yarumal

Pamplona

Bucaramanga

Río Arauca

Barrancabermeja

Arauca

Puerto Carreño

Bello

Puerto Berrío

Río Meta

Medellín

Itagüí

Sogamoso

Río Orinoco

Puerto Ayacucho

Nuquí

Quibdó

Tunja

Yopal

A m a z o n i a

Manizales

Zipaquira

Río Guaviare

Pereira

Río Meta

Puerto Inírida

Armenia

BOGOTÁ

Villavicencio

Tuluá

Ibagué

Girardot

Buenaventura

Buga

Espinal

C O L O M B I A

Palmira

Cali

Neiva

Popayán

Garzón

San José del Guaviare

Tumaco

Pitalito

Mitú

O r i n o q u í a -

Pasto

Mocoa

Florencia

Río Vaupés

Río Apaporis

Nevado de Cumbal 4764m

Orito

Ipiales

A n d e s

Río Putumayo

Río Caquetá

Equator

E C U A D O R

Río Napo

Amazon

P E R U

Río Içá

Río Iça

Río Japurá

Río Jiruá

PANAMA

Gulf of Darien

Golfo de Panamá

PACIFIC OCEAN

Cordillera Occidental

Cordillera Central

Cordillera Oriental

Río Cauca

Río Magdalena

0 km   200

0 miles   200

Population   ● National capital

○ below 50,000   ○ 50,000 to 100,000   ◉ 100,000 to 500,000   ◼ above 500,000

ATLANTIC

OCEAN

SAINT VINCENT &
THE GRENADINES

GRENADA

TRINIDAD &
TOBAGO

Isla Blanquilla
Isla de
Margarita
Islas Los Testigos
Tobago
Tortuga
La Asunción
Porlamar
Carúpano
Cumaná
Güiria
Cariaco
Gulf of
Paria
Puerto La Cruz
Trinidad
The Serpent's Mouth
Barcelona
San Mateo
Maturín
Anaco
Araza
Cantaura
Tucupita
El Tigre
Río Orinoco
Ciudad Guayana
Upata
Ciudad
Bolívar
Embalse de Guri
Matthews
Ridge
Charity
El Callao
Spring Garden
GEORGETOWN
El Dorado
Parika
Aurora
New
Amsterdam
Río Paragua
Peters Mine
Bartica
PARAMARIBO
Nieuw Amsterdam
Salto
Angel
Rockstone
Totness
St-Laurent-du-Maroni
Kamarang
Linden
Nieuw
Nickerie
Sinnamary
Río Caura
GUYANA
Kaaimanston
Kourou
Mount Roraima
2810m
Orealla
Apoera
W. J. van
Blommesteinmeer
CAYENNE
Pakaraima Mountains
Kurupukari
SURINAME
Grand-
Santi
Ouanary
Juliana Top
1230m
Montagne
Tortue
St-Georges
(Venezuela claims all
of Guyana west of
Essequibo River)
Lethem
FRENCH
GUIANA
(to France)
Camopi
Río Orinoco
Tumuc-Humac Mountains
Acarai Mountains
(claimed by
Suriname)
(claimed by
Suriname)
Equator
Río Negro
BRAZIL
Amazon
Amazon
zon Basin
Amazon
Río Purus
Rio Tapajós

Cayuni River
Essequibo River
Courantyne River
Maroni River
Montagnes
de la Trinit
Guiana
Highlands

33

45

40

40

37

Elevation

| Below sea level 0 | | | | | | | | |

-6000m -4000m -2000m -1000m -500m -250m   250m 500m 1000m 2000m 3000m 4000m 6000m

-19,658ft -13,124ft -6562ft -3281ft -1640ft -820ft -328ft/-100m 0   820ft 1640ft 3281ft 6562ft 9843ft 13,124ft 19,685ft

Western South America

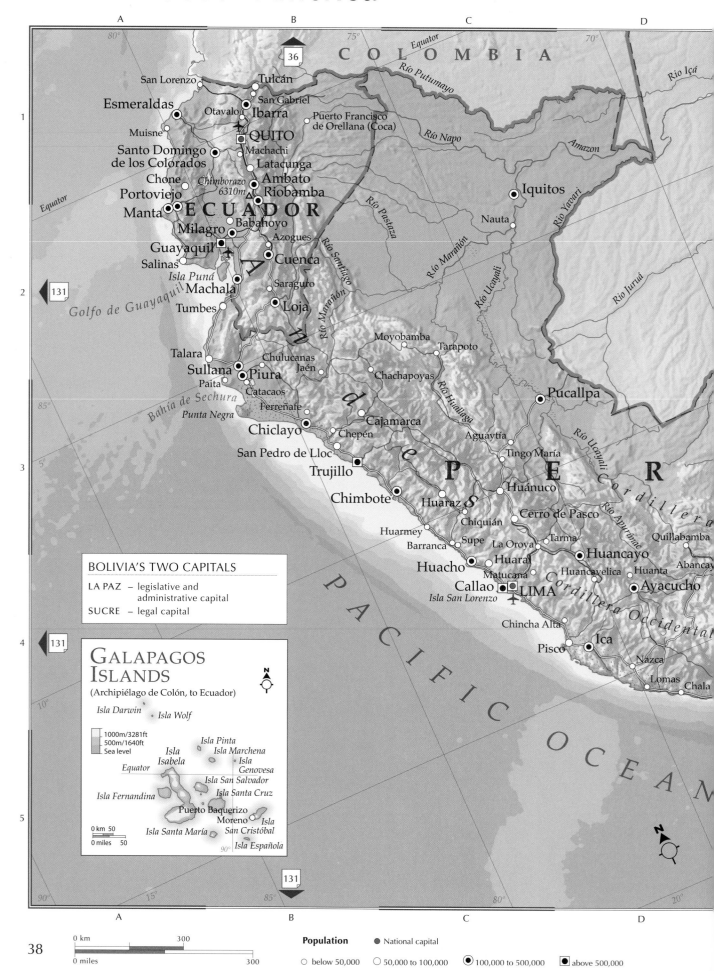

COLOMBIA

San Lorenzo
Tulcán
Esmeraldas
San Gabriel
Otavalo Ibarra
Muisne
Puerto Francisco
de Orellana (Coca)
QUITO
Machachi
Santo Domingo
de los Colorados
Latacunga
Chone
Ambato
Chimborazo Riobamba
6310m
Portoviejo
ECUADOR
Manta
Babahoyo
Milagro
Azogues
Guayaquil
Cuenca
Salinas
Isla Puná
Saraguro
Machala
Loja
Golfo de Guayaquil
Tumbes
Talara
Chulucanas
Moyobamba
Sullana
Jaén
Tarapoto
Paita
Piura
Chachapoyas
Catacaos
Ferreñafe
Bahía de Sechura
Punta Negra
Chiclayo
Cajamarca
Chepén
San Pedro de Lloc
Trujillo
Chimbote
Huaraz
Chiquián
Huarmey
Barranca
Supe
La Oroya
Tarma
Huacho
Huaral
Huancavelica
Callao
Matucana
LIMA
Isla San Lorenzo
Chincha Alta
Pisco
Ica
Nazca
Lomas
Chala

Iquitos
Nauta
Río Putumayo
Río Napo
Amazon
Río Pastaza
Río Santiago
Río Marañón
Río Ucayali
Río Yavari
Río Juruá
Río Içá
Equator

Pucallpa
Aguaytía
Tingo María
Huánuco
Cerro de Pasco
Río Apurímac
Quillabamba
Huancayo
Huanta
Abancay
Ayacucho

PERU

Cordillera Occidental
Cordillera

PACIFIC OCEAN

BOLIVIA'S TWO CAPITALS

LA PAZ – legislative and
administrative capital

SUCRE – legal capital

GALAPAGOS ISLANDS

(Archipiélago de Colón, to Ecuador)

N

Isla Darwin Isla Wolf

1000m/3281ft
500m/1640ft
Sea level

Isla Pinta
Isla Marchena
Isla Isabela
Isla Genovesa
Equator
Isla San Salvador
Isla Fernandina
Isla Santa Cruz
Puerto Baquerizo
Moreno
Isla Santa María
Isla San Cristóbal
Isla Española

0 km 50
0 miles 50

N

0 km   300
0 miles   300

Population   ● National capital

○ below 50,000   ○ 50,000 to 100,000   ◉ 100,000 to 500,000   ◼ above 500,000

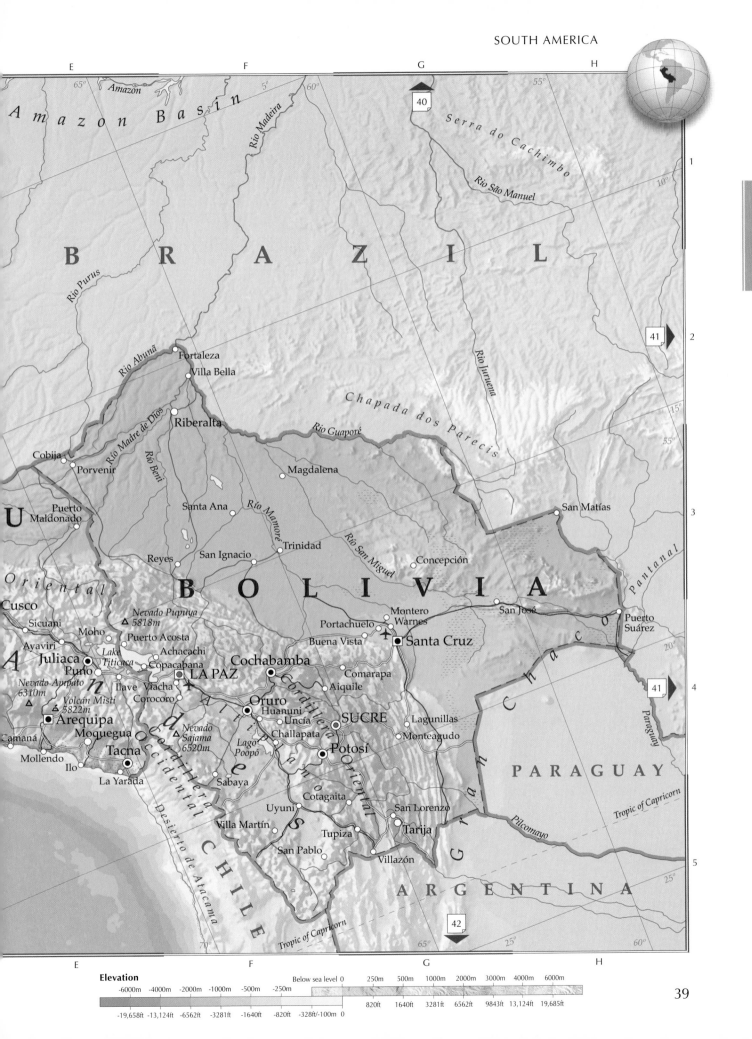

Amazon

Amazon Basin

B R A Z I L

Rio Madeira

Rio Purus

40

Serra do Cachimbo

Rio São Manuel

Rio Juruena

41

Rio Abunã

Fortaleza
Villa Bella

Chapada dos Parecis

Rio Madre de Dios

Riberalta

Rio Guaporé

Cobija
Porvenir

Rio Beni

Magdalena

San Matías

U

Puerto
Maldonado

Santa Ana

Rio Mamoré

Rio San Miguel

Pantanal

Reyes
San Ignacio
Trinidad

Concepción

Oriental

B O L I V I A

Cusco
Sicuani

Nevado Pupuya
△5818m

Montero
Warnes

San José

Puerto
Suárez

Moho
Puerto Acosta

Portachuelo

Ayaviri
A

Achacachi
Copacabana

Buena Vista

Santa Cruz

Juliaca
Puno

*Lake
Titicaca*

Cochabamba

Comarapa

Chaco

n

Nevado Ampato
6310m
△

Ilave
Viacha
Corocoro

LA PAZ

Aiquile

Lagunillas

Paraguay

Volcán Misti
△5822m

Oruro
Huanuni
Uncía

SUCRE

Arequipa

d

Nevado
△Sajama
6520m

*Lago
Poopó*

Challapata

Monteagudo

Camaná

Moquegua

e

Potosí

P A R A G U A Y

Mollendo

Tacna

Ilo

Occidental

Sabaya

Oriental

Altiplano

Cotagaita

Tropic of Capricorn

La Yarada

Desierto de Atacama

Uyuni
Villa Martín

San Lorenzo

Pilcomayo

Tarija

Tupiza

San Pablo

Villazón

A R G E N T I N A

C H I L E

42

Tropic of Capricorn

65° 5° 60° 10°

15° 55°

20°

25°

70° 65° 25° 60°

E F G H

Elevation

| -6000m | -4000m | -2000m | -1000m | -500m | -250m | Below sea level 0 | 250m | 500m | 1000m | 2000m | 3000m | 4000m | 6000m |

-19,658ft -13,124ft -6,562ft -3,281ft -1,640ft -820ft -328ft/-100m 0   820ft 1640ft 3281ft 6562ft 9843ft 13,124ft 19,685ft

Brazil

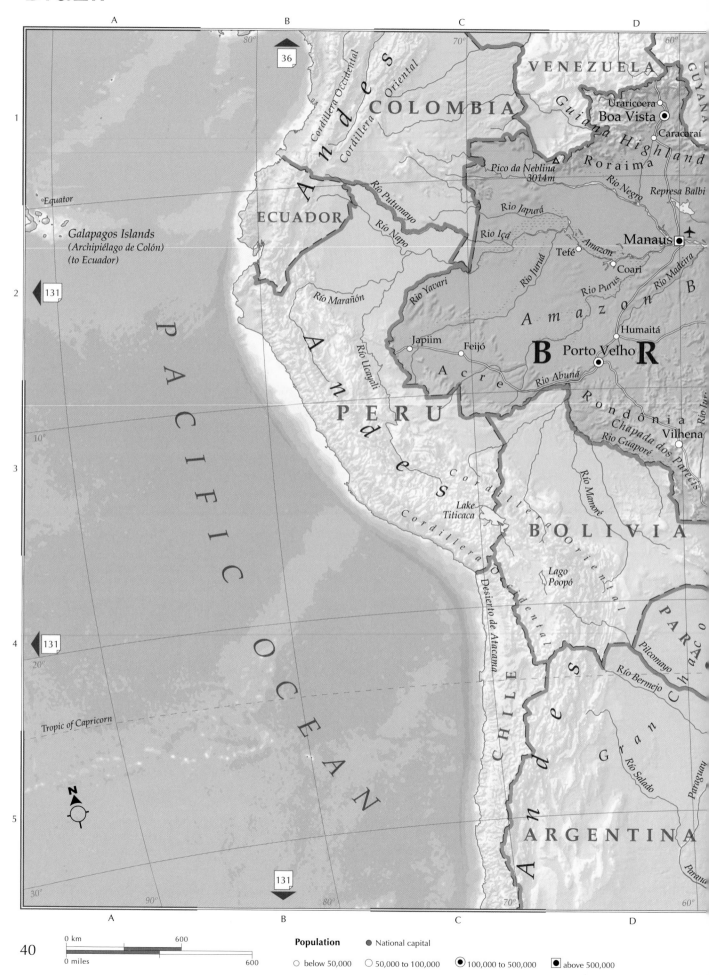

80°

VENEZUELA

GUYANA

COLOMBIA

Cordillera Occidental

Cordillera Oriental

Uraricoera

Boa Vista

Caracaraí

70°

60°

Guiana Highland

Roraima

Pico da Neblina
3014m

Río Putumayo

ECUADOR

Galapagos Islands
(Archipiélago de Colón)
(to Ecuador)

Equator

Río Napo

Río Japurá

Río Negro

Represa Balbi

Río Içá

Manaus

Tefé

Amazon

Coari

A   n   d   e   s

Río Marañón

Río Yavari

Río Juruá

Río Purus

Río Madeira

A   m   a   z   o   n

B

P A C I F I C

Japiim

Feijó

B   Porto Velho **R**

Humaitá

Río Ucayali

Acre

Río Abuná

Rondônia

Río Iu...

10°

A   n   d   e   s

Chapada dos Parecis

Vilhena

Río Guaporé

Río Mamoré

Cordillera Oriental

B O   **O L I V I A**

Lake
Titicaca

Cordillera Occidental

Lago
Poopó

O C E A N

Desierto de Atacama

PARA...

20°

CHILE

Pilcomayo

Río Bermejo

Tropic of Capricorn

30°

A   n   d   e   s

G

Río Salado

Paraguay

G   u   a   n

A R G E N T I N A

Paraná

90°

80°

70°

60°

0 km		600
0 miles		600

Population   ● National capital

○ below 50,000   ◎ 50,000 to 100,000   ◉ 100,000 to 500,000   ◼ above 500,000

ATLANTIC OCEAN

44

45

45

45

SURINAME

FRENCH GUIANA (to France)

Tumuc-Humac Mountains

Amapá

Macapá

Ilha de Marajó

Ilha Caviana de Fora

Baía de Marajó

Mouths of the Amazon

Baía de São Marcos

Alenquer

Amazon

Belém

São Luís

Parnaíba

Camocim

Santarém

Altamira

Represa de Tucuruí

Bacabal

Píripiri

Teresina

Fortaleza

Atol das Rocas

San Fernando de Noronha (to Brazil)

Itaituba

Rio Xingu

Marabá

Imperatriz

Maranhão

Ceará

Mossoró

Açu

Cabo de São Roque

Serra do Cachimbo

Carolina

Floriano

Rio Grande do Norte

Natal

Balsas

Picos

Piauí

Juazeiro do Norte

João Pessoa

Rio Tapajós

Pará

Rio Tocantins

Paraíba

Campina Grande

A Z I L

Pernambuco

Recife

Serra Formosa

Palmas do Tocantins

Represa de Sobradinho

Alagoas

Juazeiro

Maceió

Rio São Manuel

Serra dos Gradaús

Tocantins

Taguatinga

Rio São Francisco

Chapada Diamantina

Aracaju

Estância

Mato Grosso

Rio Araguaia

Goiás

Bahia

Feira de Santana

Cuiabá

Planalto

BRASÍLIA

Janaúba

Salvador

Baía de Todos os Santos

Rondonópolis

Anápolis

Central

Montes Claros

Itabuna

Goiânia

Jataí

Minas

Araçuai

Vitória da Conquista

Canavieiras

Araguari

Gerais

Pantanal

Mato Grosso do Sul

Uberlândia

Governador Valadares

Espírito Santo

Campo Grande

Uberaba

Belo Horizonte

Aquidauana

Ribeirão Preto

Divinópolis

Vitória

Presidente Prudente

Marília

Juiz de Fora

Campos

Londrina

Campinas

Nova

São Paulo

Maringá

São Paulo

Iguaçu

Rio de Janeiro

Paraná

Santos

Represa de Itaipú

Ponta Grossa

Saltos do Rio Iguaçu Iguaçu

Curitiba

Joinville

Paraná

Santa Catarina

Blumenau

Florianópolis

Passo Fundo

Rio Grande

Santa Maria

do Sul

Canoas

Bagé

Porto Alegre

Lagoa dos Patos

Río Negro

Rio Grande

URUGUAY

Mirim Lagoon

Equator

10°

20°

Tropic of Capricorn

30°

ATLANTIC OCEAN

Elevation

-6000m -4000m -2000m -1000m -500m -250m   Below sea level 0   250m 500m 1000m 2000m 3000m 4000m 6000m

-19,658ft -13,124ft -6562ft -3281ft -1640ft -820ft -328ft/-100m 0   820ft 1640ft 3281ft 6562ft 9843ft 13,124ft 19,685ft

Southern South America

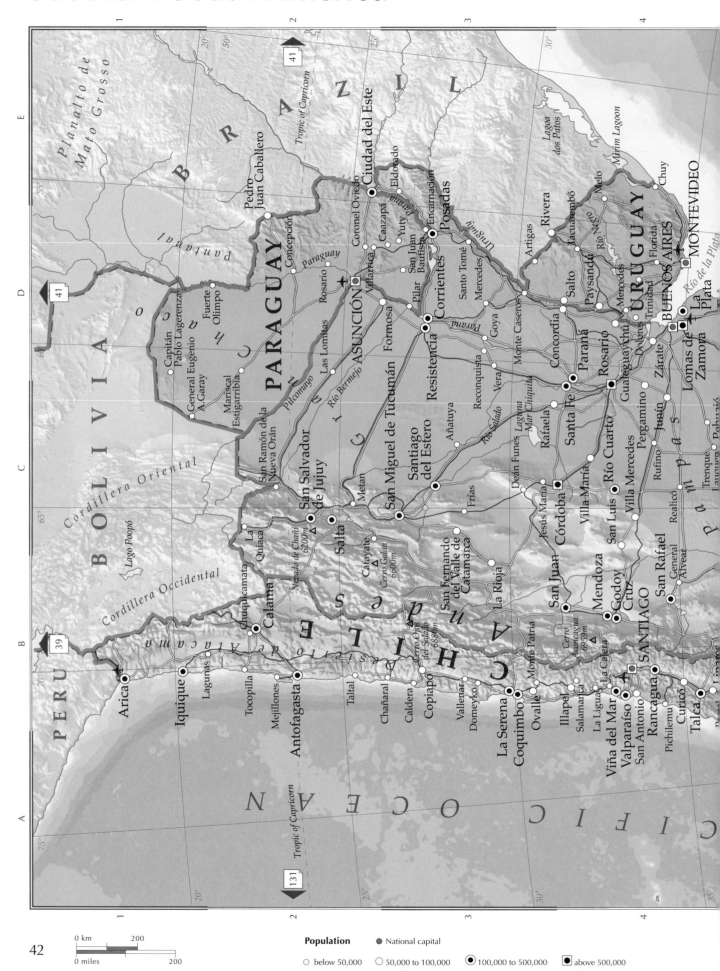

0 km   200
0 miles   200

Population   ● National capital

○ below 50,000   ○ 50,000 to 100,000   ◉ 100,000 to 500,000   ◾ above 500,000

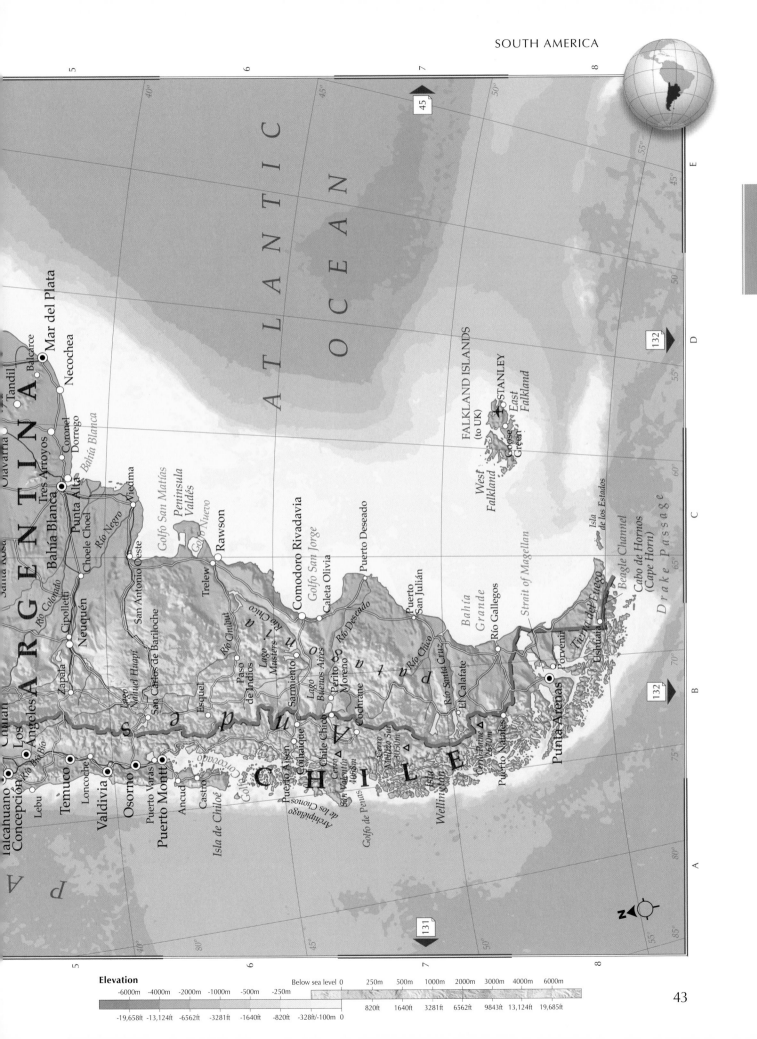

A T L A N T I C

O C E A N

P A
D

ARGENTINA

CHILE

Mar del Plata
Balcarce
Tandil
Necochea
Olavarría
Coronel
Dorrego
Bahía Blanca
Punta Alta
Tres Arroyos
Santa Rosa
Viedma
Wiedma
Golfo San Matías
Península Valdés
Golfo Nuevo
Rawson
Choele Choel
Río Negro
Río Colorado
San Antonio Oeste
Cipolletti
Neuquén
Zapala
Los Angeles
Concepción
Talcahuano
Chillán
Lebu
Río Bío Bío
Temuco
Loncoche
Valdivia
Osorno
Puerto Varas
Puerto Montt
Ancud
Castro
Isla de Chiloé
San Carlos de Bariloche
Lago Nahuel Huapi
Esquel
Paso de Indios
Río Chubut
Trelew
Sarmiento
Lago Musters
Lago Buenos Aires
Cochrane
Chile Chico
Coyhaique
Puerto Aisén
Golfo Corcovado
Archipiélago de los Chonos
Golfo de Penas
Isla Wellington
Isla San Valentín △ 4058m
Cerro Corcovado
Río Chico
Perito Moreno
Comodoro Rivadavia
Golfo San Jorge
Caleta Olivia
Puerto Deseado
Río Deseado
Puerto San Julián
Río Chico
Río Santa Cruz
El Calafate
Cerro Melizo Sur △ 3050m
Cerro Paine △ 2670m
Puerto Natales
Río Gallegos
Bahía Grande
Strait of Magellan
Punta Arenas
Porvenir
Tierra del Fuego
Ushuaia
Beagle Channel
Cabo de Hornos (Cape Horn)
Isla de los Estados
Drake Passage

FALKLAND ISLANDS (to UK)
STANLEY
East Falkland
Goose Green
West Falkland

45

132

132

131

Z ◄ ✦

Elevation

Below sea level 0	250m	500m	1000m	2000m	3000m	4000m	6000m

-6000m -4000m -2000m -1000m -500m -250m

-19,658ft -13,124ft -6562ft -3281ft -1640ft -820ft -328ft/-100m 0

820ft 1640ft 3281ft 6562ft 9843ft 13,124ft 19,685ft

The Atlantic Ocean

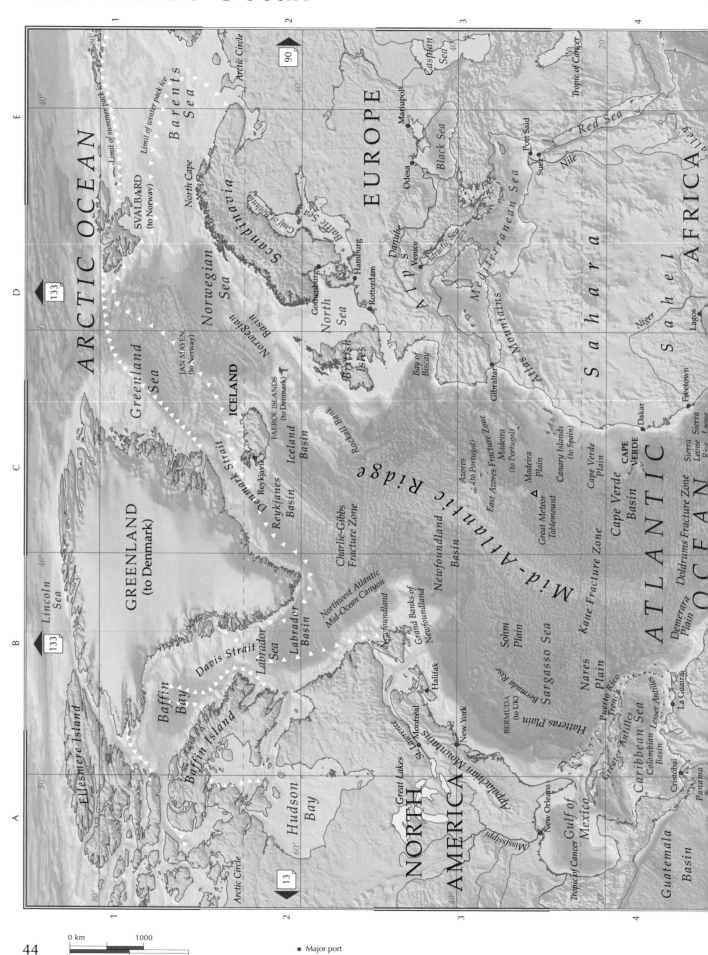

ARCTIC OCEAN

Limit of summer pack ice
Limit of winter pack ice

Arctic Circle

Lincoln Sea

Ellesmere Island

GREENLAND (to Denmark)

Baffin Bay

Baffin Island

Davis Strait

Hudson Bay

Great Lakes

NORTH AMERICA

Appalachian Mountains

St. Lawrence

Montréal

New York

New Orleans

Gulf of Mexico

Tropic of Cancer

Mississippi

Guatemala Basin

Greater Antilles

Caribbean Sea

Colombian Basin

Lesser Antilles

Cristobal

Panama

La Guaira

Demerara Plain

ATLANTIC OCEAN

Doldrums Fracture Zone

AFRICA

Sahel

Sahara

Lagos

Niger

Freetown

Sierra Leone

Sierra Leone

Dakar

Cape Verde Basin

CAPE VERDE

Cape Verde Plain

Kane Fracture Zone

Nares Plain

Puerto Rico Trench

Hatteras Plain

BERMUDA (to UK)

Bermuda Rise

Sargasso Sea

Sohm Plain

Halifax

Newfoundland

Grand Banks of Newfoundland

Newfoundland Basin

Mid-Atlantic Ridge

Madeira Plain

Great Meteor Tablemount

Madeira (to Portugal)

East Azores Fracture Zone

Azores (to Portugal)

Canary Islands (to Spain)

Atlas Mountains

Gibraltar

Bay of Biscay

Rockall Bank

British Isles

North Sea

Rotterdam

Hamburg

Gothenburg

EUROPE

Alps

Venice

Adriatic Sea

Danube

Mediterranean Sea

Black Sea

Odesa

Mariupol

Caspian Sea

Red Sea

Port Said

Suez

Nile

Tropic of Cancer

Charlie-Gibbs Fracture Zone

Northwest Atlantic Mid-Ocean Canyon

Labrador Basin

Labrador Sea

Reykjanes Basin

Denmark Strait

Reykjavik

ICELAND

Iceland Basin

FAEROE ISLANDS (to Denmark)

JAN MAYEN (to Norway)

Greenland Sea

Norwegian Basin

Norwegian Sea

Scandinavia

Gulf of Bothnia

Baltic Sea

North Cape

SVALBARD (to Norway)

Barents Sea

Arctic Circle

90

133

13

133

0 km   1000
0 miles   1000

● Major port

44

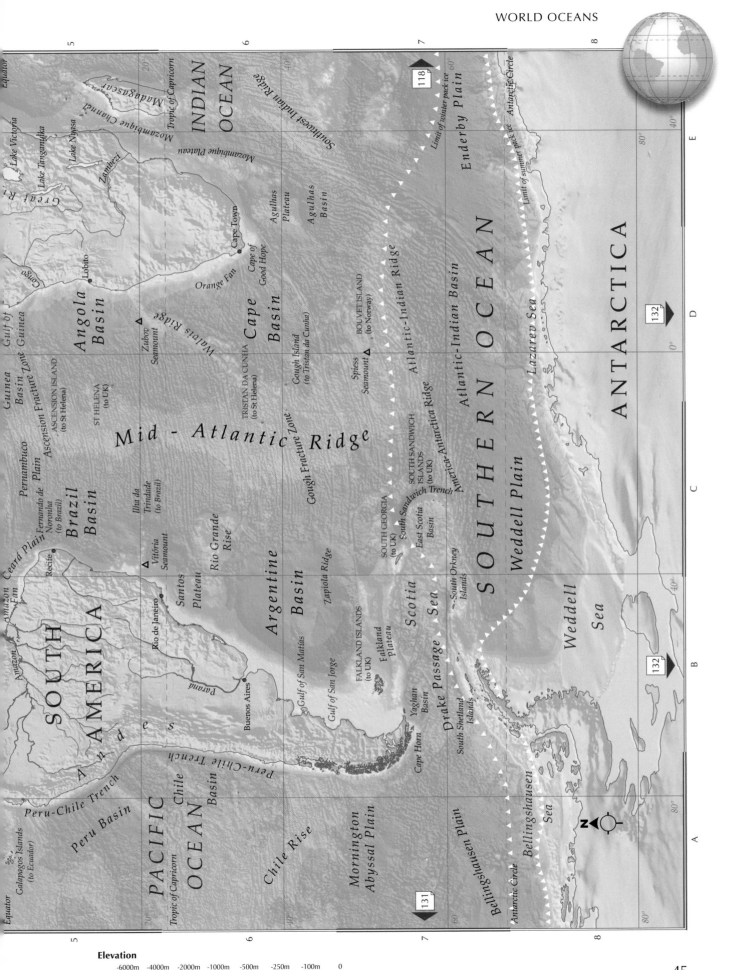

Equator

INDIAN OCEAN

Tropic of Capricorn

Southwest Indian Ridge

Madagascar

Mozambique Channel

Lake Victoria
Lake Tanganyika
Lake Nyasa
Zambezi
Great R.

Limit of winter pack ice

Enderby Plain

Antarctic Circle

Limit of summer pack ice

Cape Town

Agulhas Plateau
Agulhas Basin

Cape of Good Hope
Orange Fan

Gulf of Guinea
Congo
Lobito

Angola Basin

Mozambique Plateau

Walvis Ridge
Zubov Seamount

Cape Basin

Atlantic-Indian Ridge

ANTARCTICA

SOUTHERN OCEAN

Lazarev Sea

BOUVET ISLAND
(to Norway)

Guinea Basin
Fracture Zone

Ascension Fracture Plain
ASCENSION ISLAND
(to St Helena)

ST HELENA
(to UK)

TRISTAN DA CUNHA
(to St Helena)

Gough Island
(to Tristan da Cunha)

Spiess Seamount

Atlantic-Indian Basin

Pernambuco
Plain

Fernando de
Noronha
(to Brazil)

Mid - Atlantic Ridge

Gough Fracture Zone

America-Antarctica Ridge

Weddell Plain

Brazil Basin

Illha da
Trindade
(to Brazil)

SOUTH SANDWICH
ISLANDS
(to UK)

Ceará Plain
Amazon
Fan
Recife

Vitória
Seamount

Rio Grande
Rise

SOUTH GEORGIA
(to UK)

South Sandwich Trench

East Scotia
Basin

Amazon

SOUTH AMERICA

Santos
Plateau

Rio de Janeiro

Argentine Basin

Zapiola Ridge

Scotia Sea

South Orkney
Islands

Weddell Sea

Paraná

Buenos Aires

Gulf of San Matías

FALKLAND ISLANDS
(to UK)

Falkland
Plateau

Drake Passage

Gulf of San Jorge

Yaghan
Basin

South Shetland
Islands

A n d e s

Peru-Chile Trench

Cape Horn

Bellingshausen
Sea

PACIFIC OCEAN

Chile Basin

Chile Rise

Mornington
Abyssal Plain

Bellingshausen Plain

Peru-Chile Trench

Tropic of Capricorn

Antarctic Circle

Peru Basin

Galapagos Islands
(to Ecuador)

N

118
132
132
131

Elevation

-6000m	-4000m	-2000m	-1000m	-500m	-250m	-100m	0
-19,658ft	-13,124ft	-6562ft	-3281ft	-1640ft	-820ft	-328ft/-100m	0

Africa

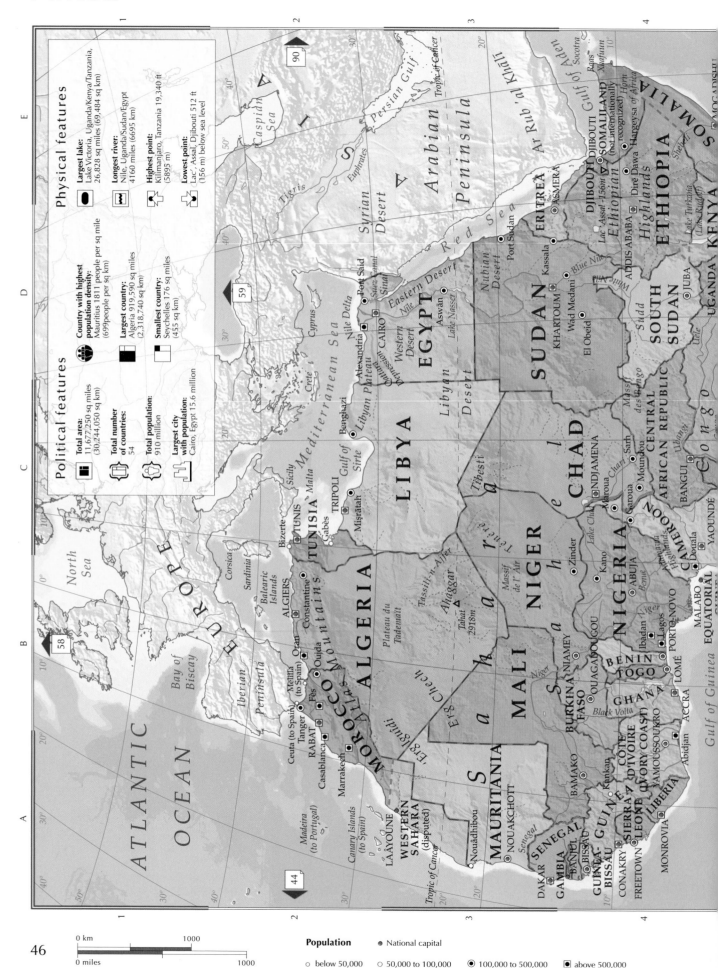

Political features

Total area:
11,677,250 sq miles
(30,244,050 sq km)

Total number of countries:
54

Total population:
910 million

Largest city with population:
Cairo, Egypt 15.6 million

Physical features

Largest lake:
Lake Victoria, Uganda/Kenya/Tanzania, 26,828 sq miles (69,484 sq km)

Longest river:
Nile, Uganda/Sudan/Egypt 4160 miles (6695 km)

Highest point:
Kilimanjaro, Tanzania 19,340 ft (5895 m)

Lowest point:
Lac' Assal, Djibouti 512 ft (156 m) below sea level

Country with highest population density:
Mauritius 1811 people per sq mile (699 people per sq km)

Largest country:
Algeria 919,590 sq miles (2,318,740 sq km)

Smallest country:
Seychelles 176 sq miles (455 sq km)

Population

● National capital

○ below 50,000   ◎ 50,000 to 100,000   ◉ 100,000 to 500,000   ■ above 500,000

0 km   1000

0 miles   1000

Equator

Somali
Basin

Kismaayo

Aldabra
Group

COMOROS
MORONI
MAYOTTE
(to France)

ANTANANARIVO
Mahajanga
Fianarantsoa
Nacala
Nampula

Toliara

Tropic of Capricorn

Madagascar
Basin

MADAGASCAR

Madagascar
Plateau

INDIAN

OCEAN

Southwest Indian Ridge

Prince Edward Islands
(to South Africa)

Crozet
Plateau

Kirinyaga
5200m
NAIROBI
Kilimanjaro
5895m
Mombasa
Tanga
Pemba
Zanzibar
Dar es Salaam

Kisumu
Lake Victoria
KIGALI
RWANDA
BUJUMBURA
BURUNDI
Masai
Steppe
DODOMA
TANZANIA
Lake
Tanganyika
Lake Rukwa
Lake Nyasa
Ruvuma

Beira

Mozambique Channel

Bukavu

Great Rift Valley

MALAWI
LILONGWE
Blantyre
Zambezi

Mozambique Plateau

Kalemie
Lake Mweru
Ndola
Kitwe

Lubumbashi

ZAMBIA
LUSAKA
Lake
Kariba
HARARE
ZIMBABWE
Bulawayo

MOZAMBIQUE

MAPUTO
TSHWANE/PRETORIA
MBABANE
SWAZILAND
Durban

Ilebo
Kananga

DEM. REP.
CONGO
KINSHASA

Basin

Kasai

Kwango

Lualaba
Luoua

Luena

Chando

Victoria Falls
Zambezi

Francistown
GABORONE
BOTSWANA
Kalahari
Desert
Okavango
Delta
Johannesburg
BLOEMFONTEIN
MASERU
LESOTHO

SOUTH AFRICA

Drakensberg

East London
Port Elizabeth

Agulhas
Plateau

Agulhas
Basin

MATADI
BRAZZAVILLE
CONGO
GABON
Port-Gentil
LIBREVILLE

SAO TOME
& PRINCIPE
SAO
TOMÉ

Cabinda
(to Angola)
LUANDA
Cuango
Cuanza
Huambo
Môco 2619m
Lubango
Namibe

ANGOLA
Bié
Plateau
Cubango
Cunene

WINDHOEK
NAMIBIA
Etosha
Pan
Namib Desert
Nossob

Kalahari
Desert
Vaal
Orange River
Great Karoo
CAPE TOWN
Cape of
Good Hope

Orange Fan

Ascension Fracture Zone
ASCENSION ISLAND
(to Saint Helena)

SAINT HELENA
(to UK)

Guinea
Basin

Angola
Basin

ATLANTIC

OCEAN

Walvis Ridge

Cape
Basin

Mid-Atlantic
Ridge

Tropic of Capricorn

TRISTAN DA CUNHA
(to Saint Helena)

Gough Island
(to Tristan da Cunha)

Atlantic-Indian Ridge

Winter limit of pack ice

119

132

132

45

47

Northwest Africa

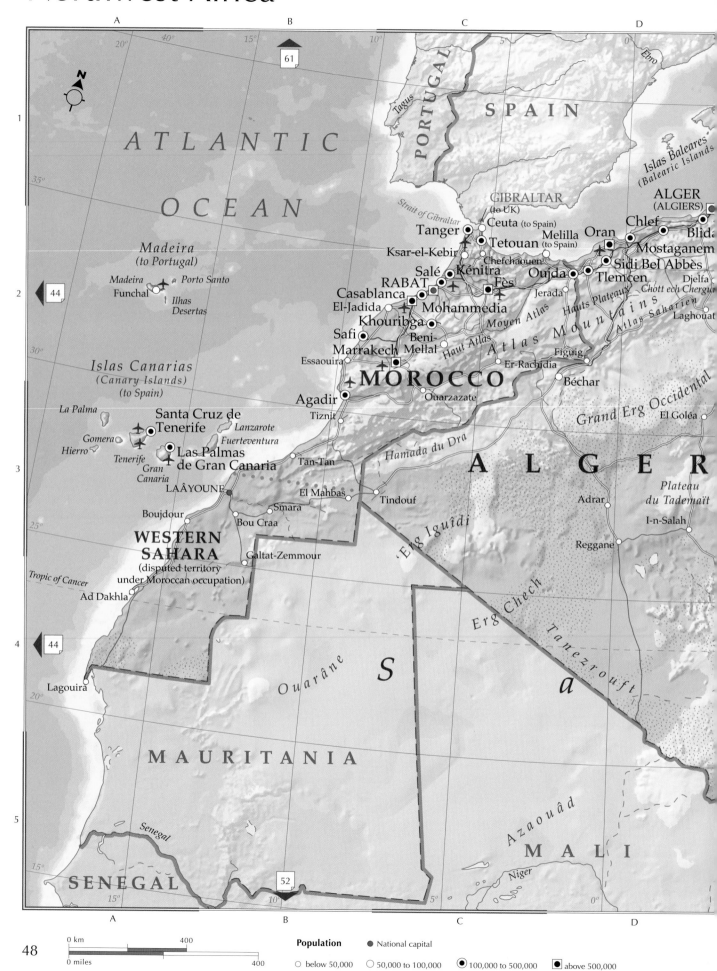

ATLANTIC

OCEAN

Madeira
(to Portugal)

44

Madeira • *Porto Santo*
Funchal *Ilhas*
Desertas

PORTUGAL

SPAIN

Tagus

Ebro

Islas Baleares
(Balearic Islands)

GIBRALTAR
(to UK)

Strait of Gibraltar

Ceuta (to Spain)

ALGER
(ALGIERS)

Tanger
Tetouan
Melilla
(to Spain)
Oran

Chlef

Blida

Ksar-el-Kebir
Chefchaouen
Mostaganem

Salé Kénitra
RABAT
Casablanca
El-Jadida Mohammedia
Khouribga
Safi Beni-
Marrakech Mellal
Essaouira

Fès

Oujda
Sidi Bel Abbès
Tlemcen

Djelfa
Jerada
Chott ech Chergui

Hauts Plateaux

Moyen Atlas

Haut Atlas

Laghouat

Er-Rachidia

Atlas

Mountains

Atlas Saharien

Figuig

Islas Canarias
(Canary Islands)
(to Spain)

La Palma

Gomera

Hierro

Santa Cruz de
Tenerife

Lanzarote

Fuerteventura

Tenerife

Las Palmas
de Gran Canaria

Gran
Canaria

MOROCCO

Agadir

Tiznit

Ouarzazate

Béchar

Grand Erg Occidental

El Goléa

LAÂYOUNE

Tan-Tan

Hamada du Dra

A L G E R

Plateau
du Tademaït

Boujdour

El Mahbas

Tindouf

Adrar

I-n-Salah

Smara
Bou Craa

WESTERN
SAHARA
(disputed territory
under Moroccan occupation)

Galtat-Zemmour

'Erg Iguîdi

Erg Chech

Reggane

Tropic of Cancer

Ad Dakhla

44

S

Ouarâne

Erg Chech

Tanezrouft

a

Lagouira

MAURITANIA

Azaouâd

M A L I

Senegal

Niger

SENEGAL

52

48

Population ● National capital

0 km   400

0 miles   400

○ below 50,000 ◎ 50,000 to 100,000 ◉ 100,000 to 500,000 ■ above 500,000

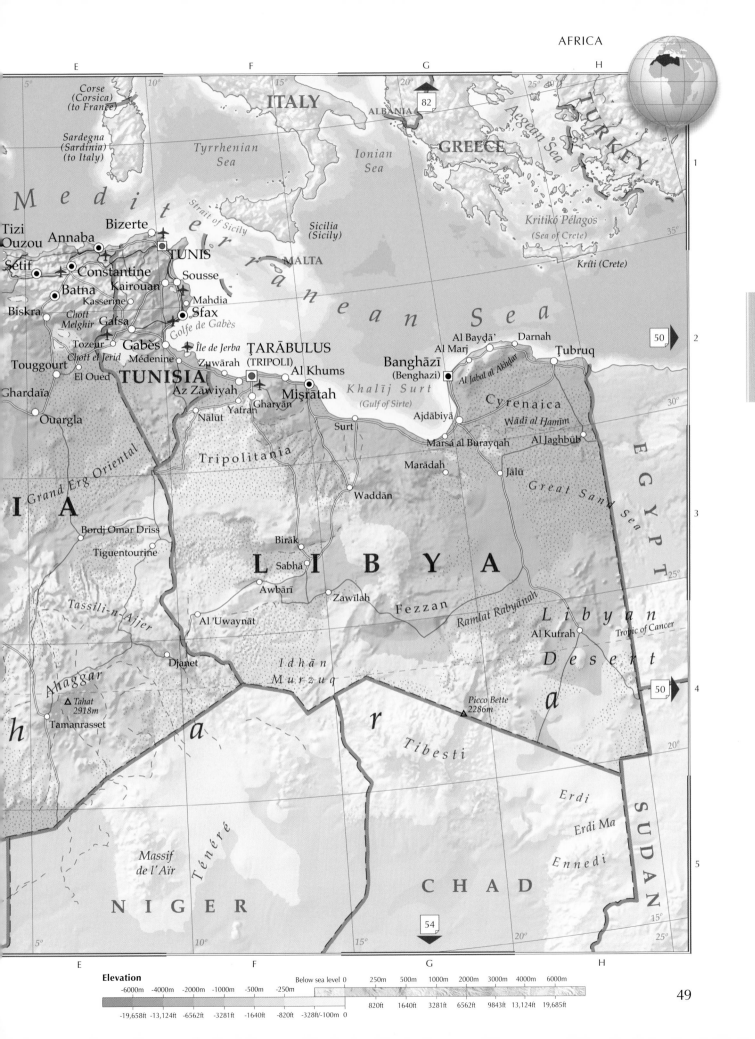

Elevation

						Below sea level 0	250m	500m	1000m	2000m	3000m	4000m	6000m
-6000m	-4000m	-2000m	-1000m	-500m	-250m								
-19,658ft	-13,124ft	-6562ft	-3281ft	-1640ft	-820ft	-328ft/-100m 0	820ft	1640ft	3281ft	6562ft	9843ft	13,124ft	19,685ft

Northeast Africa

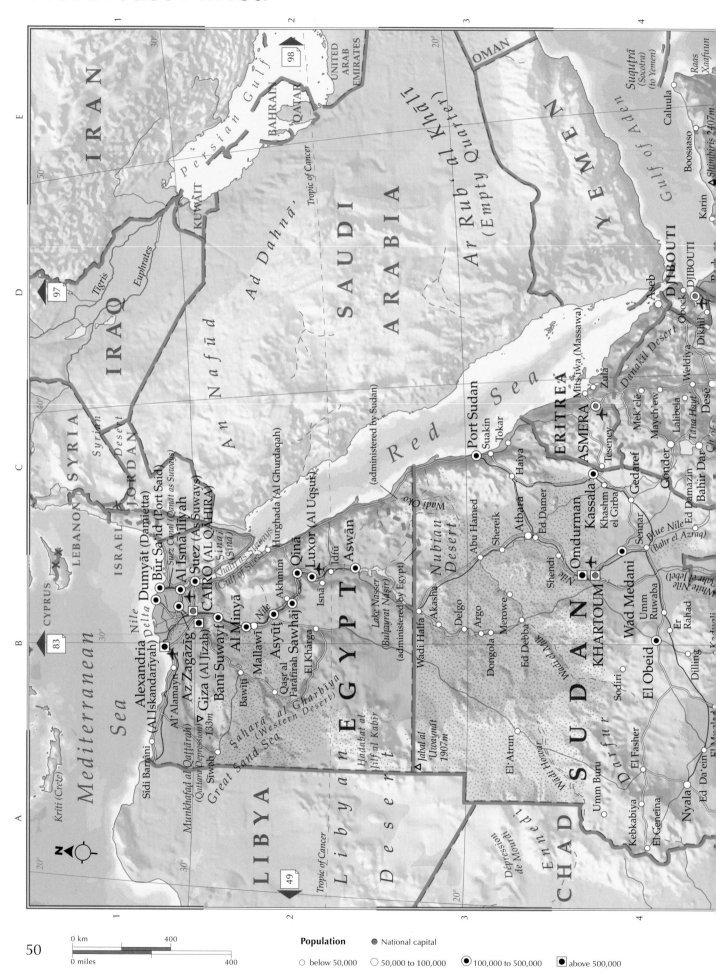

IRAN

Persian Gulf

OMAN

UNITED ARAB EMIRATES

BAHRAIN

QATAR

KUWAIT

SYRIA

IRAQ

Tigris

Euphrates

Syrian Desert

LEBANON

JORDAN

ISRAEL

CYPRUS

Kríti (Crete)

Mediterranean Sea

Sidi Barrâni

Al 'Alamayn

Alexandria (Al Iskandarïyah)

Dumyât (Damietta)

Bûr Sa'îd (Port Said)

Al Ismâ'ilïyah

Suez (As Suways)

Suez Canal (Qanât as Suways)

Az Zagâzïg

CAIRO (AL QÂHIRA)

Giza (Al Jïzah)

Banî Suwayf

Al Minyâ

Mallawi

Asyût

Sawhâj

Akhmîm

Qasr al Farâfirah

Bawîti

Qinâ

Hurghada (Al Ghurdaqah)

Luxor (Al Uqsur)

Isnâ

Idfû

Aswân

El Khârga

Siwah

Munkhafad al Qattârah (Qattara Depression) -133m

Saharâ' al Gharbïya (Western Desert)

Great Sand Sea

Libyan Desert

Hadabat al Jilf al Kabîr

Jabal al 'Uwaynât 1907m

LIBYA

EGYPT

Nile

Nile Delta

Sinai

Gulf of Suez (Khalîj as Suways)

Tropic of Cancer

SAUDI ARABIA

An Nafûd

Ad Dahnâ'

Ar Rub' al Khâlî (Empty Quarter)

Red Sea

Port Sudan

Suakin

Tokar

(administered by Sudan)

Wadi Oko

Lake Nasser (Buhayrat Nâsir) (administered by Egypt)

Wadi Halfa

Akasha

Delgo

Argo

Dongola

Ed Debba

Merowe

Abu Hamed

Shereik

Atbara

Ed Damer

Haiya

Nubian Desert

Shendi

Nile

KHARTOUM

Omdurman

Khashm el Girba

Kassala

Gedaref

Teseney

ASMERA

ERITREA

Mits'iwa (Massawa)

Zula

Danakil Desert

Aseb

Obock

DJIBOUTI

DJIBOUTI

Dikhil

Gulf of Aden

YEMEN

Suqutrâ (Socotra) (to Yemen)

Raas Xaafuun

Shimbiris 2407m

Boosaaso

Caluula

Karin

Mek'elê

Maych'ew

Weldiya

Lalibela

Gonder

Bahir Dar

Ed Damazin

Sennar

Blue Nile (Bahr el Azraq)

Wad Medani

Umm Ruwaba

Er Rahad

El Obeid

Sodiri

Dilling

Kebkabiya

El Fasher

Umm Buru

El'Atrun

Darfur

CHAD

SUDAN

White Nile (Bahr el Jebel)

Nile (Wadi el Milk)

Ed Da'ein

Nyala

El Geneina

Dépression de Mourdi

Ennedi

Wâdi Howar

Bahr el Azraq

50

Population

● National capital

○ below 50,000   ◔ 50,000 to 100,000   ◉ 100,000 to 500,000   ◼ above 500,000

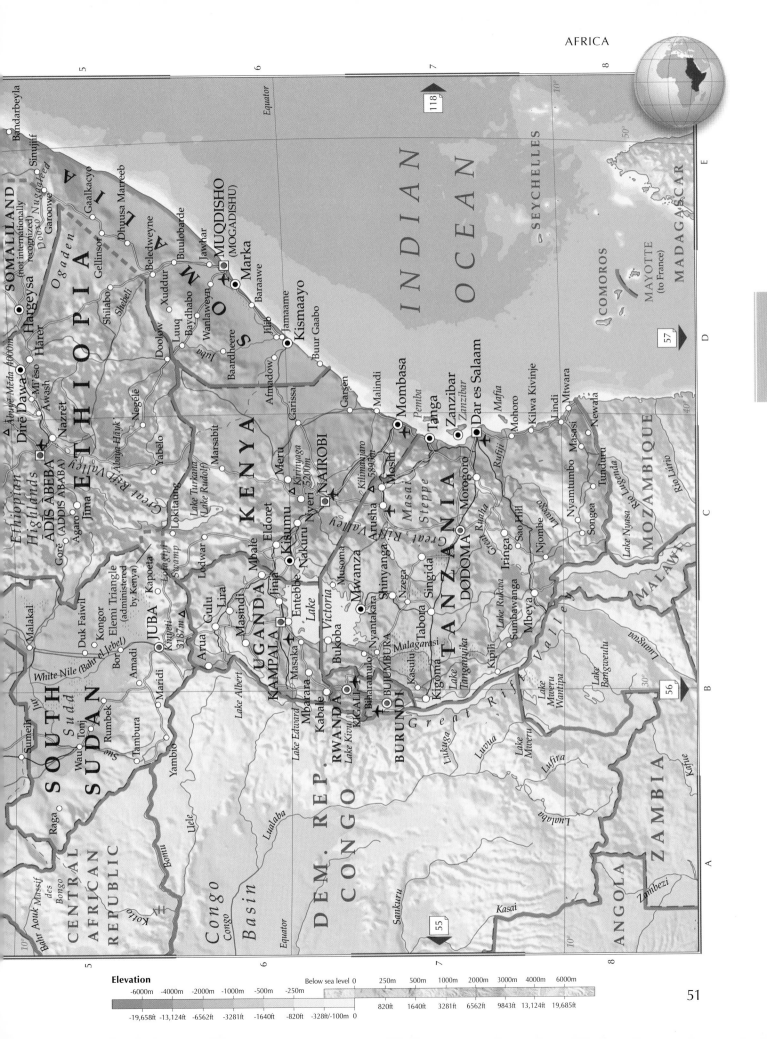

Map labels

5 · 6 · 7 · 8

Equator

118

INDIAN OCEAN

SEYCHELLES

E

50°

Bandarbeyla

SOMALILAND
(not internationally
recognized)

Sinujiif
Dooxo Nugaaleed
Garoowe

Ogaden

Gaalkacyo

Dhuusa Marreeb

ETHIOPIA

SOMALIA

Hargeysa
Härer
Mr'ēso Härer
Awash
Nazrēt
Abuyē Mēda 4000m

Gellinsor
Xuddur
Beledweyne
Jawhar
Buulobarde

MUQDISHO
(MOGADISHU)
Marka
Baraawe

Shilabo
Doolow
Luuq
Baydhabo
Wanlaweyn
Jilib
Jamaame
Kismaayo
Buur Gaabo

Negēlē
Yabēlo
Baardheere

Afmadow

Malindi

Mombasa
Pemba
Tanga
Zanzibar
Dar es Salaam
Mafia
Mohoro
Kilwa Kivinje
Lindi
Mtwara

COMOROS
MAYOTTE
(to France)

MADAGASCAR

D
40°

57

Ethiopian
Highlands
ĀDĪS ĀBEBA
(ADDIS ABABA)
Gorē
Agaro
Jima

Lake Abaya–Hāyk'

Marsabit
Garissa
Garsen

KENYA
Meru
Kirinyaga
NAIROBI
Nyeri
Kilimanjaro 5895m
Moshi
Arusha
Masai Steppe

Great Rift Valley

TANZANIA
Moregoro
DODOMA
Iringa
Njombe
Songea
Masasi
Tunduru
Newala

MOZAMBIQUE
Rio Lúrio

C
30°

Great Rift Valley

Lake Turkana
(Lake Rudolf)
Lokitaung
Lodwar
Eldoret
Mbale
Kisumu
Nakuru
Musoma
Mwanza
Nzega
Singida
Tabora
Shinyanga
Nyantakara
Nyamtumbo
Sao Hill
Mbeya
Sumbawanga
Lake Rukwa

MALAWI
Lake Nyasa
(Lake Malawi)

SOUTH SUDAN
Sudd
Malakal
Duk Faiwil
Kongor
Bor
Amadi
White Nile (Bahr el Jebel)
Rumbek
Tambura
Yambio

UGANDA
Gulu
Lira
Masindi
Arua
Kapoeta 3187m
JUBA
Kampala
Entebbe
Lake Victoria
Masaka
Bukoba
Mbarara
Kabale

Kakyeli

RWANDA
KIGALI
Lake Kivu
Bujumbura
BURUNDI
Biharamulo
Kasulu
Kigoma
Lake Tanganyika
Malagarasi
Kasai
Luvua
Lukuga
Lake Mweru

DEM. REP. CONGO
Congo Basin
Congo
Lualaba
Sankuru
Equator

CENTRAL AFRICAN REPUBLIC
Bahr Aouk
Massif des Bongo
Kotto

ANGOLA
ZAMBIA
Zambezi
Kafue
Lake Bangweulu
Lufira
Luapula

55

56

A B C D E

10° · 40° · 30°

Elevation legend

Elevation

Below sea level 0 · 250m · 500m · 1000m · 2000m · 3000m · 4000m · 6000m

-6000m · -4000m · -2000m · -1000m · -500m · -250m

820ft · 1640ft · 3281ft · 6562ft · 9843ft · 13,124ft · 19,685ft

-19,658ft · -13,124ft · -6562ft · -3281ft · -1640ft · -820ft · -328ft/-100m · 0

West Africa

WESTERN SAHARA
(disputed territory under Moroccan occupation)

'Aïn Ben Tili
Bîr Mogreïn

Erg Iguîdi

Kâghet
El Hank
Ouarâne
Erg

Fdérik   Zouérat
Touâjîl

Nouâdhibou

Choûm
Akchâr   Atâr   Chinguetti
Akjoujt   Oujeft
El Mreyyé

MAURITANIA

Idîni   Tîchît
NOUAKCHOTT   Tidjikja
Boutilimit   Magta
Lahjar   Boûmdeïd   Aoukâr
Rkîz   Aleg   Oualâta
Rosso   Kaédi   Tâmchekket   Ayoûn el 'Atroûs
Richard Toll   Dagana   Kiffa   Néma
Saint Louis   Senegal   Matam   Kobenni   Amourj
Louga   Sélibabi   Timbedgha   Bassikounou
Mékhé   SENEGAL   Nioro
DAKAR   Thiès   Mbaké   Nioro
Mbour   Diourbel   Kayes   Ténenkou
Sokone   Kaolack   Kokolani   Ségou
BANJUL   GAMBIA   Tambacounda   Toukoto   Koulikoro   Bani
Bignona   Kolda   Gambia   Kita   San
Ziguinchor   Sédhiou   Bafing   BAMAKO
Bafatá   Koutiala
BISSAU   Gaoual   Dinguiraye   Bagoé   Sikasso
GUINEA-   Boké   Labé   Pita   Tikinsso   Siguiri   Bougouni
BISSAU   Kindia   Mamou   Faranah   Kankan   Tengréla
CONAKRY   Tokounou   Odienné   Ferkessédougou
SIERRA   Makeni   Kissidougou   Boundiali   Korhogo
FREETOWN   LEONE   Beyla   CÔTE
Bo   Kenema   D'IVOIRE
Nzérékoré   Katiola
Gbanga   (IVORY COAST)
Tubmanburg   Đanané   Lac de Kossou
MONROVIA   Harbel   YAMOUSSOUKRO
Zwedru   Gagnoa
Buchanan   LIBERIA   Divo
Harper   Sassandra
San-Pédro

ATLANTIC OCEAN

CAPE VERDE
Ilhas de Barlavento
Santo Antão   Mindelo
São Vicente   Pedra Lume
São Nicolau   Sal
Boa Vista
Santiago   Maio
Fogo   PRAIA
Ilhas de Sotavento

Tropic of Cancer

52

Population   ● National capital

○ below 50,000   ◎ 50,000 to 100,000   ◉ 100,000 to 500,000   ▣ above 500,000

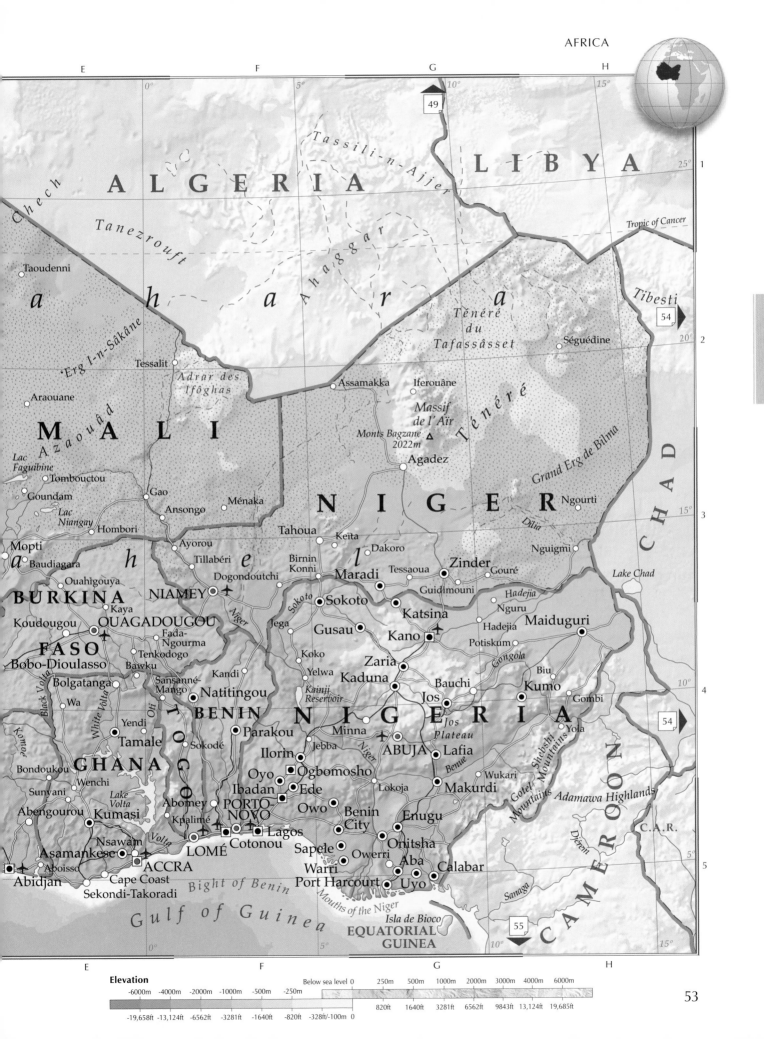

E   F   G   H

0°   5°   10°   15°   1

ALGERIA   *Tassili-n-Ajjer*   **LIBYA**   25°

49

Chech   *Tropic of Cancer*

Tanezrouft   *Ahaggar*   *Tibesti*   54   20°   2

Taoudenni

a   *h*   *a   r   a*   *Ténéré du Tafassâsset*   Séguédine

'Erg I-n-Sâkâne   Tessalit   Assamakka   Iferouâne

Araouane   *Adrar des Ifôghas*   *Massif de l'Air*   *Grand Erg de Bilma*   **C**

MALI   Monts Bagzane 2022m   *Ténéré*   **H**

Lac Faguibine   Agadez   **A**

Tombouctou   Gao   **N   I   G   E   R**   Ngourti   **D**   15°   3

Goundam   Ansongo   Ménaka   *Dilia*   Nguigmi

Lac Niangay   Hombori   Tahoua   Keïta   Dakoro   Lake Chad

Mopti   Ayorou   Birnin   Tessaoua   Zinder   Gouré

a   Baudiagara   *h*   Tillabéri   *e*   Dogondoutchi   Konni   *l*   Maradi   Guidimouni   *Hadejia*

BURKINA   **NIAMEY**   *Sokoto*   Sokoto   Katsina   Nguru

Koudougou   Kaya   Jega   Gusau   Kano   Hadejia   **Maiduguri**

OUAGADOUGOU   Fada-   *Niger*   Koko   Zaria   Potiskum

FASO   Ngourma   Yelwa   Kaduna   Bauchi   Biu   Kumo

Bobo-Dioulasso   Tenkodogo   Kandi   *Kainji Reservoir*   Jos   *Congola*   Gombi   10°   4

Bolgatanga   Bawku   Sansanné-   Natitingou   **N   I   G   E   R   I   A**   Yola   54

Wa   Mango   **BENIN**   Minna   *Jos Plateau*   *Shebshi Mountains*

Yendi   Parakou   *Niger*   **ABUJA**   Lafia   Wukari   *Gotel Mountains*   **C**

GHANA   Tamale   Sokodé   Ilorin   Jebba   *Benue*   Makurdi   *Adamawa Highlands*   **A**

Bondoukou   *Oti*   Oyo   Ogbomosho   Lokoja   **M**

Sunyani   Wenchi   **T**   Ibadan   Ede   Owo   Enugu   *Dierem*   **E**   C.A.R.

Abengourou   Kumasi   *Lake Volta*   Abomey   **PORTO-**   Benin   Onitsha   **R**   5°   5

Asamankese   Nsawam   Kpalimé   **NOVO**   Owo   City   Aba   Calabar   **O**

Abidjan   Aboisso   ACCRA   **LOMÉ**   Cotonou   Sapele   Owerri   Uyo   *Sanaga*   **O**

Cape Coast   *Bight of Benin*   Warri   Port Harcourt   **N**

Sekondi-Takoradi   *Mouths of the Niger*

Gulf of Guinea   *Isla de Bioco*   55   **CAMEROON**

0°   5°   **EQUATORIAL**   10°   15°
GUINEA

E   F   G   H

Elevation

Below sea level 0   250m   500m   1000m   2000m   3000m   4000m   6000m

-6000m   -4000m   -2000m   -1000m   -500m   -250m

820ft   1640ft   3281ft   6562ft   9843ft   13,124ft   19,685ft

-19,658ft   -13,124ft   -6562ft   -3281ft   -1640ft   -820ft   -328ft/-100m   0

Central Africa

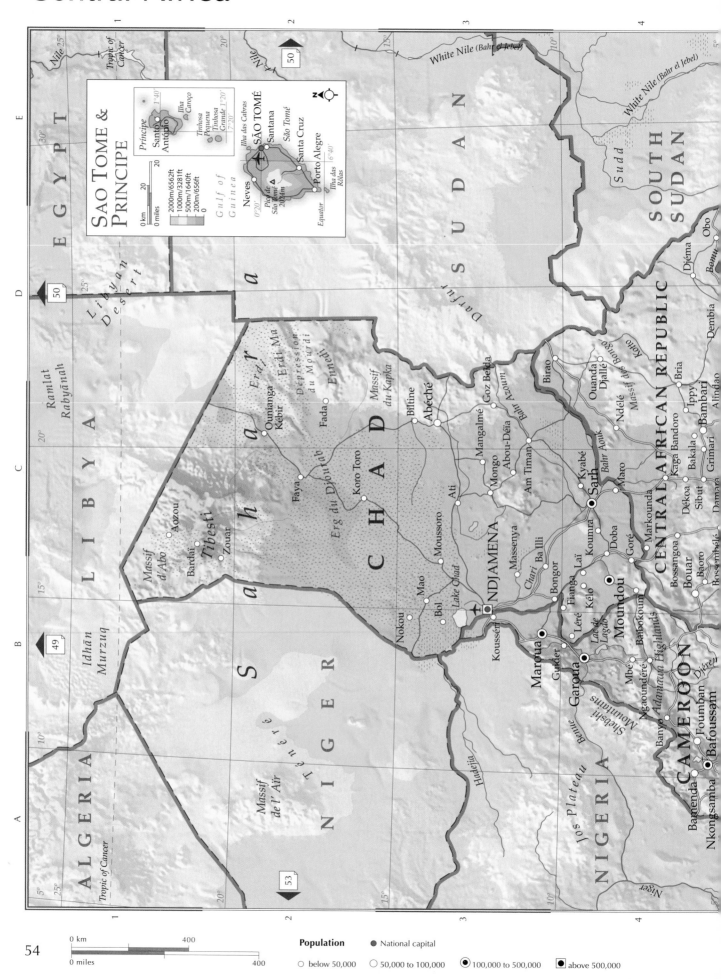

SÃO TOMÉ & PRINCIPE

Príncipe
Santo
António
Ilha Cabras
Ilha das Cabras
SÃO TOMÉ
Santana
Santa Cruz
São Tomé
Porto Alegre
Ilha das
Rôlas
Neves
Pico de
São Tomé
2024m
Equator
Gulf of
Guinea

2000m/6562ft
1000m/3281ft
500m/1640ft
200m/656ft

0 km 20
0 miles 20

EGYPT
Nile
Tropic of Cancer
*Libyan
Desert*
*Ramlat
Rabyānah*

LIBYA
*Idhān
Murzuq*

ALGERIA
Tropic of Cancer

*Massif
d'Abo*
Aozou
Bardaï
Zouar
Tibesti

*Massif
de l'Aïr*

NIGER
Ténéré

Sahara

CHAD
Erdi
Erdi Ma
Ouninga
Kébir
Fada
*Dépression
du Mourdi*
Ennedi
*Massif
du Kapka*
Biltine
Abéché
Koro Toro
Faya
Erg du Djourab
Ati
Mongo
Am Timan
Moussoro
Mao
Bol
Lake Chad
Nokou
NDJAMENA
Massenya
Masseny
Chari Ba Illi
Bongor
Kousséri
Goz Beïda
Mangalmé
Abou-Déïa
Bahr Azoum
Bahr Aouk
Birao
Kyabé
Sarh
Maro
Markounda
Doba
Goré
Koumra
Laï
Kélo
Fianga
Léré
*Lac de
Léré*
Lagdo
Moundou
Bafoussam
Baïbokoum
Bossangoa

SUDAN
Darfur

**SOUTH
SUDAN**
White Nile (Bahr el Jebel)
White Nile (Bahr el Jebel)
Sudd

CENTRAL AFRICAN REPUBLIC
Ouanda
Djallé
Ndélé
Kaga Bandoro
Bozoum
Bouar
Bouca
Massif des Bongo
Koho
Djéma
Dembia
Obo
Bémal
Bria
Ippy
Bambari
Alindao
Bakala
Grimari
Dékoa
Sibut
Damara
Bossembélé
Baoro

CAMEROON
Maroua
Guider
Garoua
Mbé
Ngaoundéré
Adamaua Highlands
Banyo
Tignère
*Shebshi
Mountains*
Bénoué
Foumban
Djérem
Bafoussam
Bamenda
Nkongsamba

NIGERIA
Jos Plateau
Hadejia
Niger
Benue

53

49
50
50

Population
● National capital
○ below 50,000
◎ 50,000 to 100,000
◉ 100,000 to 500,000
■ above 500,000

0 km   400
0 miles   400

54

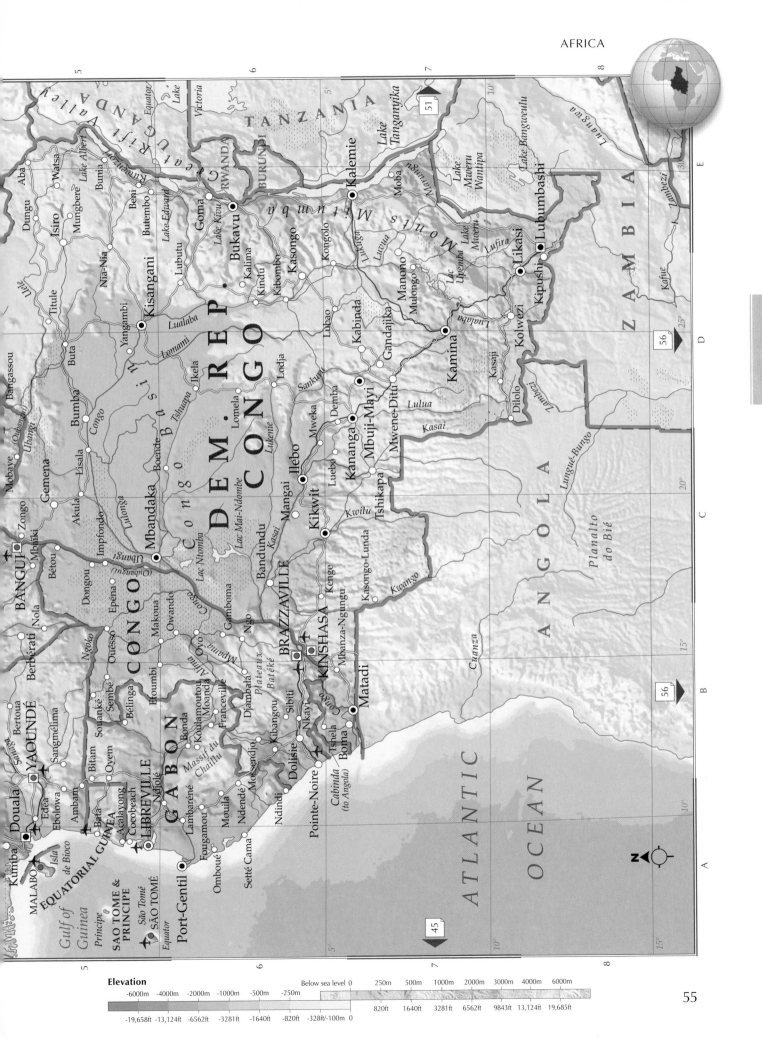

Elevation

| Below sea level 0 | 250m | 500m | 1000m | 2000m | 3000m | 4000m | 6000m |

| -6000m | -4000m | -2000m | -1000m | -500m | -250m |

| -19,658ft | -13,124ft | -6562ft | -3281ft | -1640ft | -820ft | -328ft/-100m | 0 |

| 820ft | 1640ft | 3281ft | 6562ft | 9843ft | 13,124ft | 19,685ft |

Southern Africa

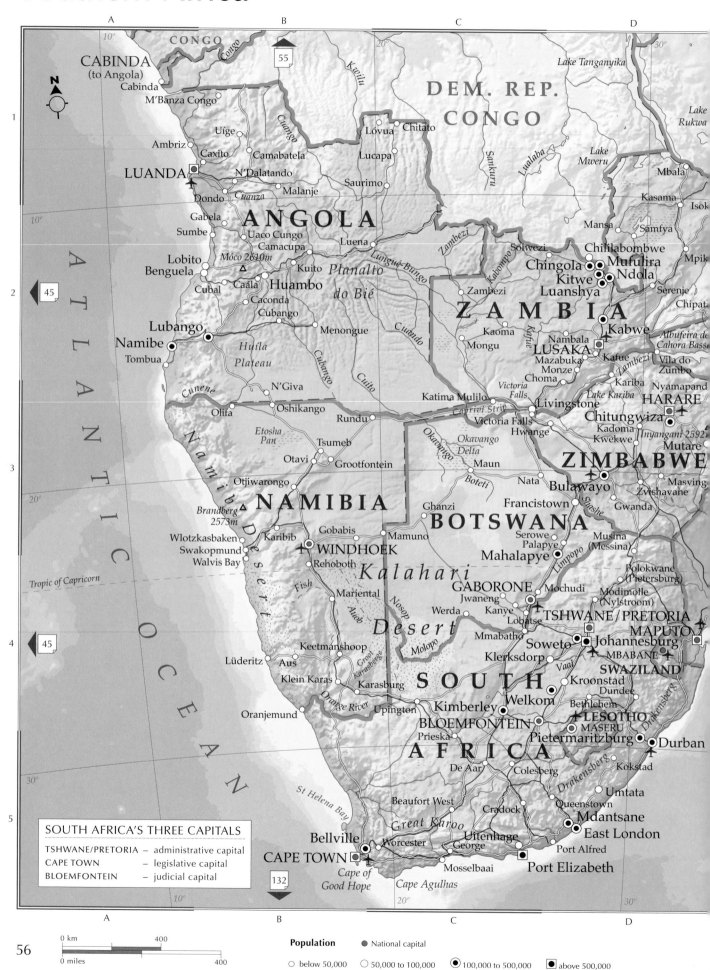

CABINDA
(to Angola)
Cabinda
M'Banza Congo

CONGO
Congo

55

DEM. REP.
CONGO

Lake Tanganyika

Lake Rukwa

Uíge
Ambriz
Caxito
LUANDA
Dondo
Gabela
Sumbe

Lóvua
Chitato
Camabatela
N'Dalatando
Malanje
Cuanza
Lucapa
Saurimo

Mbala
Kasama
Isok

ANGOLA

Luena

Zambezi

Mansa
Samfya
Mpik

Lobito
Benguela
Uaco Cungo
Camacupa
Môco 2610m
Cubal
Caála
Huambo
Caconda
Cubango

Planalto
do Bié

Lungué-Bungo

Solwezi
Chililabombwe
Chingola
Mufulira
Kitwe
Ndola
Luanshya

Serenje
Chipat

Lubango
Namibe
Tombua

Menongue

Cuando

ZAMBIA
Kaoma
Mongu

Nambala
LUSAKA
Mazabuka
Monze
Choma

Kabwe
Albufeira de
Cahora Bass
Kafue
Zambezi
Vila do
Zumbo

Huíla
Plateau

Cunene
N'Giva
Olifa
Oshikango

Cubango
Cuito

Katima Mulilo
Caprivi Strip
Victoria
Falls

Livingstone
Victoria Falls

Lake Kariba
Kariba
Nyamapand
HARARE
Chitungwiza

Rundu

Okavango

Hwange

Kadoma
Kwekwe

Inyangani 2592
Mutare

Etosha
Pan
Tsumeb
Otavi
Grootfontein

Okavango
Delta

Maun

Boteti

Nata

ZIMBABWE

Masving
Zvishavane

Otjiwarongo

NAMIBIA

Brandberg
2573m

Karibib
Gobabis
Mamuno

Ghanzi

Bulawayo
Gwanda

Francistown

BOTSWANA

Serowe
Palapye

Musina
(Messina)

Wlotzkasbaken
Swakopmund
Walvis Bay

WINDHOEK
Rehoboth

Kalahari

Mahalapye

Limpopo

Polokwane
(Pietersburg)

Tropic of Capricorn

Fish

Mariental

Auob

Desert

Nosop

GABORONE
Jwaneng
Kanye

Mochudi

Modimolle
(Nylstroom)

TSHWANE / PRETORIA
MAPUTO

Lüderitz
Aus
Klein Karas

Keetmanshoop

Karasburg

Groot Karasberge

Molopo

Werda

Mmabatho

Lobatse

Mmabatho

Soweto
Johannesburg
Klerksdorp

MBABANE
SWAZILAND

Kroonstad
Dundee

Oranjemund

Orange River

Upington

Kimberley
Welkom
BLOEMFONTEIN
Prieska

Bethlehem

LESOTHO
MASERU

Pietermaritzburg
Durban

SOUTH

Vaal

Drakensberg

De Aar
Colesberg
Kokstad

AFRICA

Umtata
Queenstown

St Helena Bay

Beaufort West
Cradock

Great Karoo

Mdantsane
East London
Port Alfred

Bellville
CAPE TOWN

132

Worcester
George

Uitenhage
Mosselbaai

Port Elizabeth

Cape of
Good Hope
Cape Agulhas

ATLANTIC OCEAN

SOUTH AFRICA'S THREE CAPITALS
TSHWANE/PRETORIA – administrative capital
CAPE TOWN – legislative capital
BLOEMFONTEIN – judicial capital

0 km   400

0 miles   400

Population   ● National capital

○ below 50,000   ○ 50,000 to 100,000   ◉ 100,000 to 500,000   ◼ above 500,000

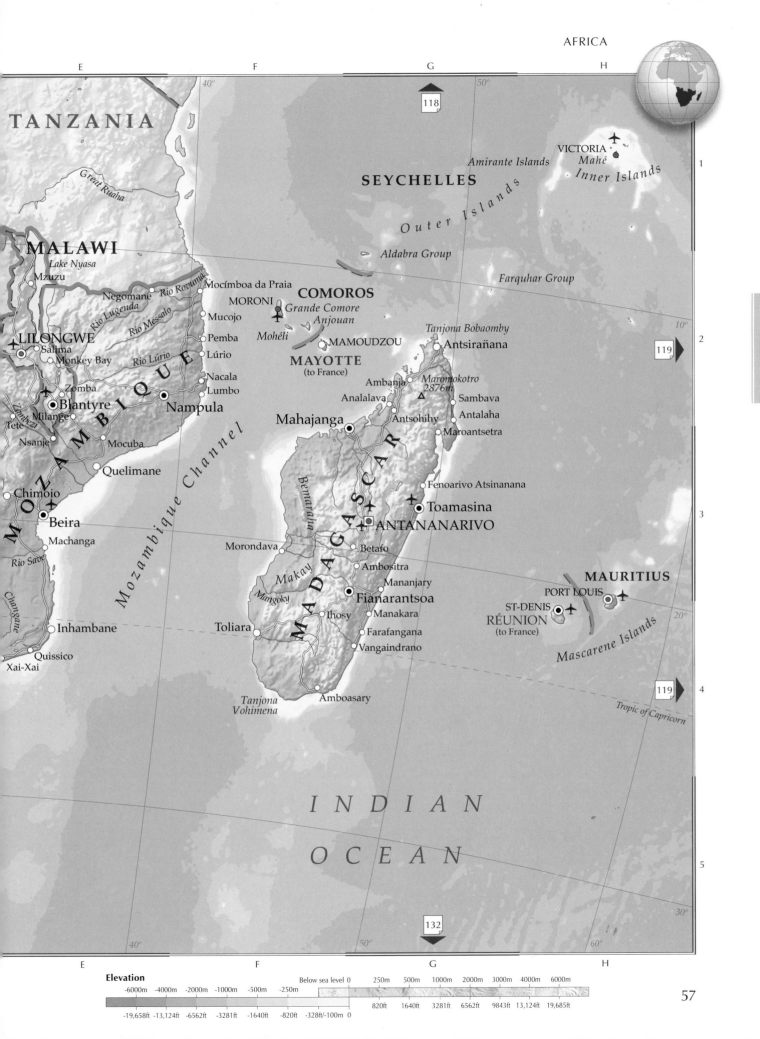

TANZANIA

SEYCHELLES

Amirante Islands

VICTORIA
Mahé
Inner Islands

Outer Islands

Aldabra Group

Farquhar Group

MALAWI

Lake Nyasa
Mzuzu

Negomane • Rio Rovuma • Mocímboa da Praia

Rio Lugenda

COMOROS

MORONI
Grande Comore
Anjouan

Tanjona Bobaomby

Rio Messalo

Mucojo

Mohéli

Antsirañana

LILONGWE
Salima

Pemba

MAMOUDZOU

Monkey Bay

Rio Lúrio

Lúrio

MAYOTTE
(to France)

Maromokotro
2876m

Ambanja

Zomba

Nacala

Analalava

Sambava

Blantyre
Milange

Lumbo

Nampula

Antsohihy

Antalaha

Tete

Mahajanga

Maroantsetra

Nsanje

Mocuba

M O Z A M B I Q U E

Quelimane

Bemaraha

Fenoarivo Atsinanana

Chimoio

Beira

Mozambique Channel

Toamasina

ANTANANARIVO

Machanga

M A D A G A S C A R

Betafo

Rio Save

Morondava

Ambositra

MAURITIUS

Makay

Mananjary

PORT LOUIS

Changane

Mangoky

Fianarantsoa

ST-DENIS

Inhambane

Manakara

RÉUNION
(to France)

Quissico

Toliara

Ihosy

Xai-Xai

Farafangana

Mascarene Islands

Vangaindrano

Amboasary

*Tanjona
Vohimena*

Tropic of Capricorn

I N D I A N

O C E A N

Elevation

-6000m	-4000m	-2000m	-1000m	-500m	-250m		Below sea level 0	250m	500m	1000m	2000m	3000m	4000m	6000m
-19,658ft	-13,124ft	-6562ft	-3281ft	-1640ft	-820ft	-328ft/-100m	0		820ft	1640ft	3281ft	6562ft	9843ft	13,124ft 19,685ft

Europe

Political features

Total area:
4,809,200 sq miles
(12,456,000 sq km)

Total number of countries:
44

Total population:
697 million

Largest city with population:
Moscow, European Russia 13.75 million

Country with highest population density:
Monaco 40,719 people per sq mile
(15,661 people per sq km)

Largest country:
European Russia 1,527,341 sq miles
(3,955,818 sq km)

Smallest country:
Vatican City, Italy 0.17 sq miles
(0.44 sq km)

Physical features

Largest lake:
Lake Lagoda, European Russia
7,100 sq miles (18,390 sq km)

Longest river:
Volga, European Russia
2,290 miles (3,688 km)

Highest point:
El'brus, Caucasus, European Russia
18,510ft (5,642 m)

Lowest point:
Volga Delta, Caspian Sea, European
Russia 92 ft (28m) below sea level

Population   ● National capital

○ below 50,000   ◎ 50,000 to 100,000   ◉ 100,000 to 500,000   ■ above 500,000

0 km 500
0 miles 500

Barents Sea

North Cape

Ostrov Kolguyev

Arctic Circle

Murmansk

Kola Peninsula

White Sea

Archangel

Northern Dvina

Ural Mountains

Ob'

Irtysh

R U S S I A N

Lake Onega

Perm'

Tampere

Lake Ladoga

Turku HELSINKI

Saint Petersburg

Vologda

Ufa

Åland

Uppsala TALLINN

Kazan'

STOCKHOLM

Yaroslavl'

Ul'yanovsk

Gotland

ESTONIA

Nizhniy Novgorod

Samara

Orenburg

Baltic Sea

RĪGA

MOSCOW

Ural

LATVIA

LITHUANIA

Kaliningrad Kaunas

Vitsyebsk

Central Russian Upland

Volga Uplands

Gdańsk

VILNIUS

Aral Sea

KALININGRAD (to Russ. Fed.)

MINSK

Syr Darya

Bydgoszcz

Babruysk

Homyel'

Voronezh

Łódź Brest

Pripet Marshes

Ural

WARSAW

Dnieper Lowlands

Amu Darya

POLAND

Bug

Don

Kraków

L'viv

KIEV

Kharkiv

Volgograd

Dnieper

UKRAINE

Dnipropetrovs'k

Astrakhan'

Volga Delta -28m

SLOVAKIA

Dniester

Donets'k

Rostov-na-Donu

Chernivtsi

BUDAPEST

MOLDOVA

CHIŞINĂU

Stavropol'

Caspian Sea

HUNGARY

Cluj-Napoca

Odesa

Sea of Azov

ROMANIA

Crimea

C a u c a s u s

Braşov

Simferopol'

El'brus 5642m

BELGRADE

BUCHAREST

Constanţa

Black Sea

SERBIA

Danube

KOSOVO BULGARIA

Varna

(disputed) Balkan Mountains

MONT. PRISTINA

Burgas

PODGORICA SOFIA

SKOPJE

MACED. TURKEY

TIRANA

Aegean Sea

Anatolia

ALBANIA

Pindus Mountains

Zagros Mountains

GREECE

ATHENS

Piraeus

Peloponnese

Tigris

Euphrates

Sea

Cyprus

Irákleio

Crete

FINLAND

Gulf of Bothnia

Kölen

DEN

E u r o p e a n   P l a i n

F E D E R A T I O N

BELARUS

n

The North Atlantic

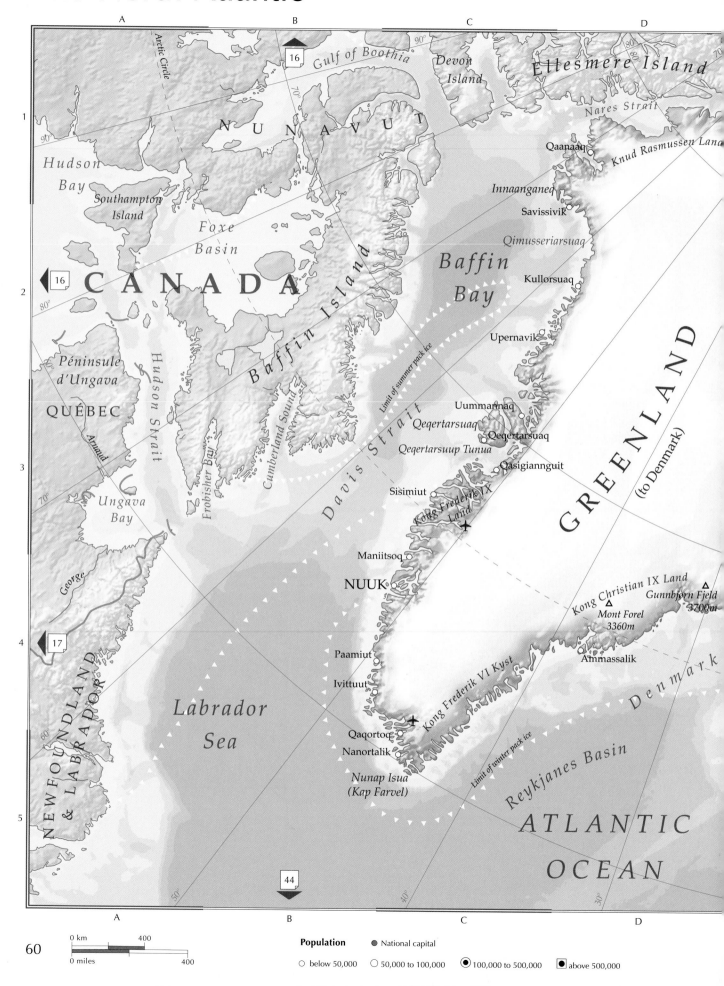

Gulf of Boothia

Devon Island

Ellesmere Island

Nares Strait

NUNAVUT

Hudson Bay

Southampton Island

Foxe Basin

CANADA

Baffin Island

Qaanaaq

Knud Rasmussen Land

Innaanganeq

Savissivik

Qimusseriarsuaq

Baffin Bay

Kullorsuaq

Upernavik

Péninsule d'Ungava

QUÉBEC

Hudson Strait

Cumberland Sound

Limit of summer pack ice

Uummannaq

Qeqertarsuaq

Qeqertarsuaq

Qeqertarsuup Tunua

Qasigiannguit

GREENLAND
(to Denmark)

Arnaud

Frobisher Bay

Davis Strait

Sisimiut

Kong Frederik IX Land

Ungava Bay

Maniitsoq

Kong Christian IX Land

Gunnbjørn Fjeld 3700m

Mont Forel 3360m

George

NUUK

NEWFOUNDLAND & LABRADOR

Paamiut

Ivittuut

Kong Frederik VI Kyst

Ammassalik

Denmark

Labrador Sea

Qaqortoq

Nanortalik

Reykjanes Basin

Limit of winter pack ice

Nunap Isua (Kap Farvel)

ATLANTIC OCEAN

Arctic Circle

16

16

17

44

0 km   400
0 miles   400

Population   ● National capital

○ below 50,000   ○ 50,000 to 100,000   ◉ 100,000 to 500,000   ◼ above 500,000

ARCTIC

OCEAN

*Lincoln
Sea*

Kap Morris Jesup

*Wandel
Sea*

Zemlya
Frantsa-Iosifa

133

Kvitøya

Independence Fjord

Nord

SVALBARD
(to Norway)

Nordaustlandet

*Novaya
Zemlya*

Kong Karls Land

Kong Frederik VIII Land

Spitsbergen

Barentsøya

*Barents
Sea*

LONGYEARBYEN
Barentsburg

Edgeøya

88

*Greenland
Sea*

Storfjorden

Limit of winter pack ice

Bjørnøya
(to Norway)

*Kong Christian X
Land*

Δ *Petermann Bjerg
2940m*

Daneborg

*Nordkapp
(North Cape)*

Limit of summer pack ice

Mohns Ridge

FINLAND

Kong Oscar Fjord

Ittoqqortoormiit

Kangertittivaq

JAN MAYEN
(to Norway)

Arctic Circle

Kangikajik

*Norwegian
Sea*

Vestfjorden

S t r a i t

Norwegian Basin

62

ICELAND

Bolungarvík
Siglufjördhur   Raufarhöfn
Ísafjördhur
Húsavík
Akureyri
Seydhisfjördhur
Stykkishólmur   Neskaupstadhur
Faxaflói **REYKJAVÍK**
Selfoss *Vatnajökull*   Djúpivogur
Thorlákshöfn   Δ *Hvannadalshnúkur
2119m*
Surtsey
Vestmannaeyjar

S
W
E
D
E
N

*Gulf
of
Bothnia*

N O R W A Y

N

FAEROE ISLANDS
(to Denmark)

TÓRSHAVN

63

*Shetland
Islands*

Elevation

| -6000m | -4000m | -2000m | -1000m | -500m | -250m | Below sea level 0 | 250m | 500m | 1000m | 2000m | 3000m | 4000m | 6000m |

-19,658ft | -13,124ft | -6562ft | -3281ft | -1640ft | -820ft | -328ft/-100m 0

820ft | 1640ft | 3281ft | 6562ft | 9843ft | 13,124ft | 19,685ft

Scandinavia & Finland

RUSSIAN FEDERATION

FINLAND

SWEDEN

Barents Sea

ARCTIC OCEAN

Norwegian Sea

Nordkapp (North Cape)

Arctic Circle

88
133
133
61

0 km	200		
0 miles	200		

Population
● National capital
○ below 50,000 ○ 50,000 to 100,000 ◉ 100,000 to 500,000 ▣ above 500,000

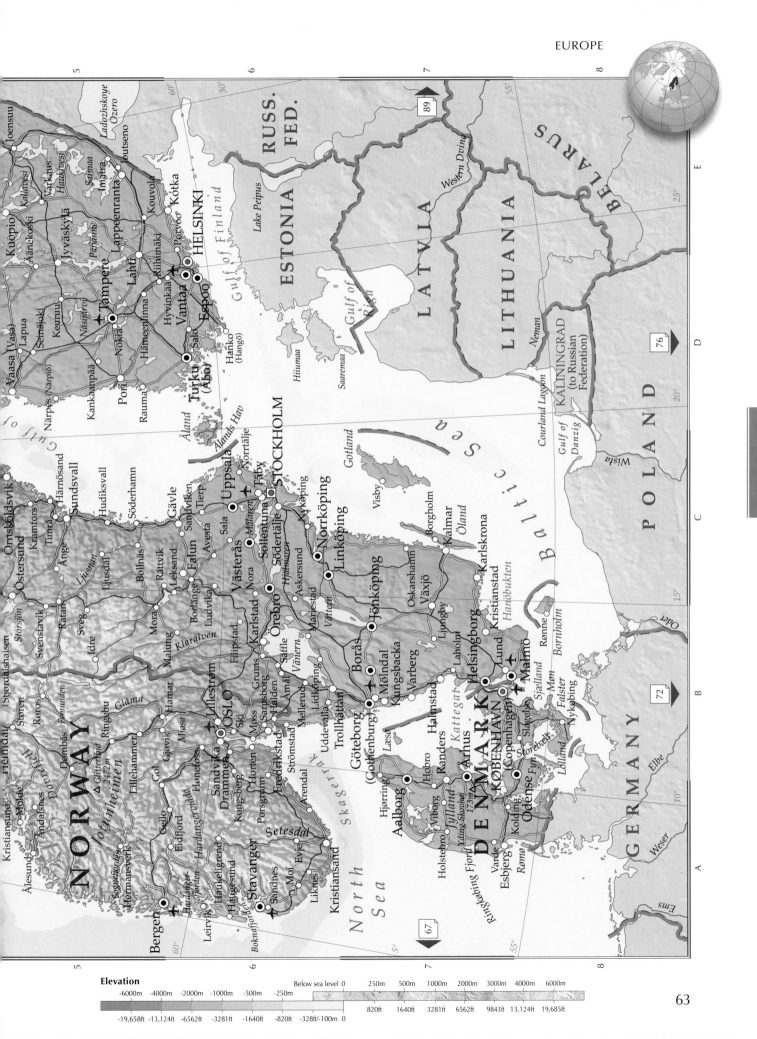

Elevation

| -6000m | -4000m | -2000m | -1000m | -500m | -250m | Below sea level 0 | 250m | 500m | 1000m | 2000m | 3000m | 4000m | 6000m |

| -19,658ft | -13,124ft | -6562ft | -3281ft | -1640ft | -820ft | -328ft/-100m | 0 | 820ft | 1640ft | 3281ft | 6562ft | 9843ft | 13,124ft | 19,685ft |

The Low Countries

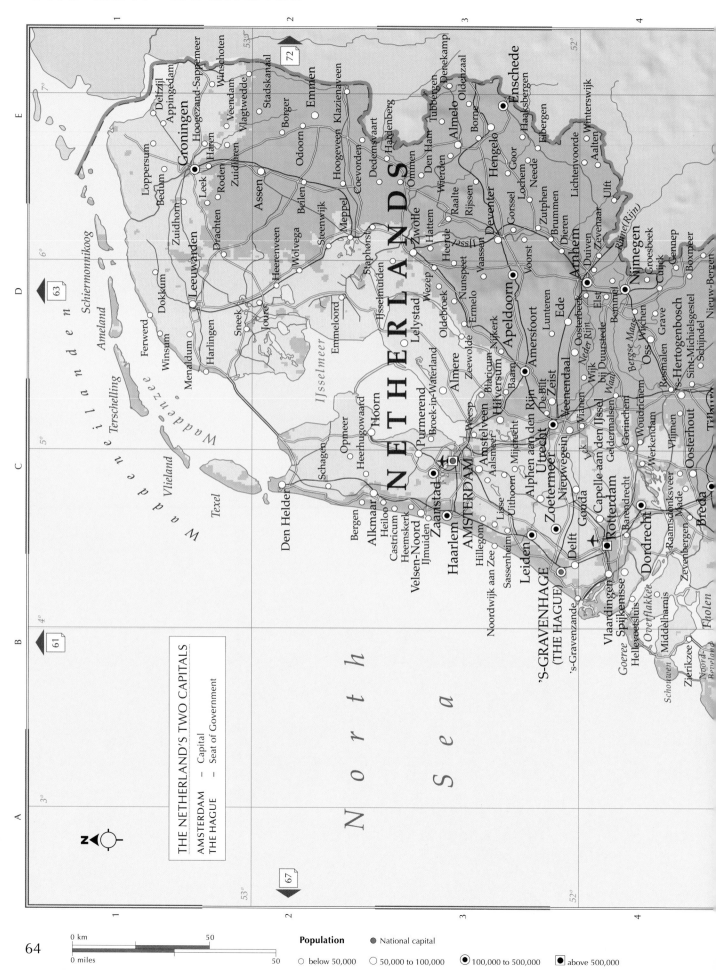

Population

- ● National capital
- ○ below 50,000
- ○ 50,000 to 100,000
- ◉ 100,000 to 500,000
- ■ above 500,000

0 km   50
0 miles   50

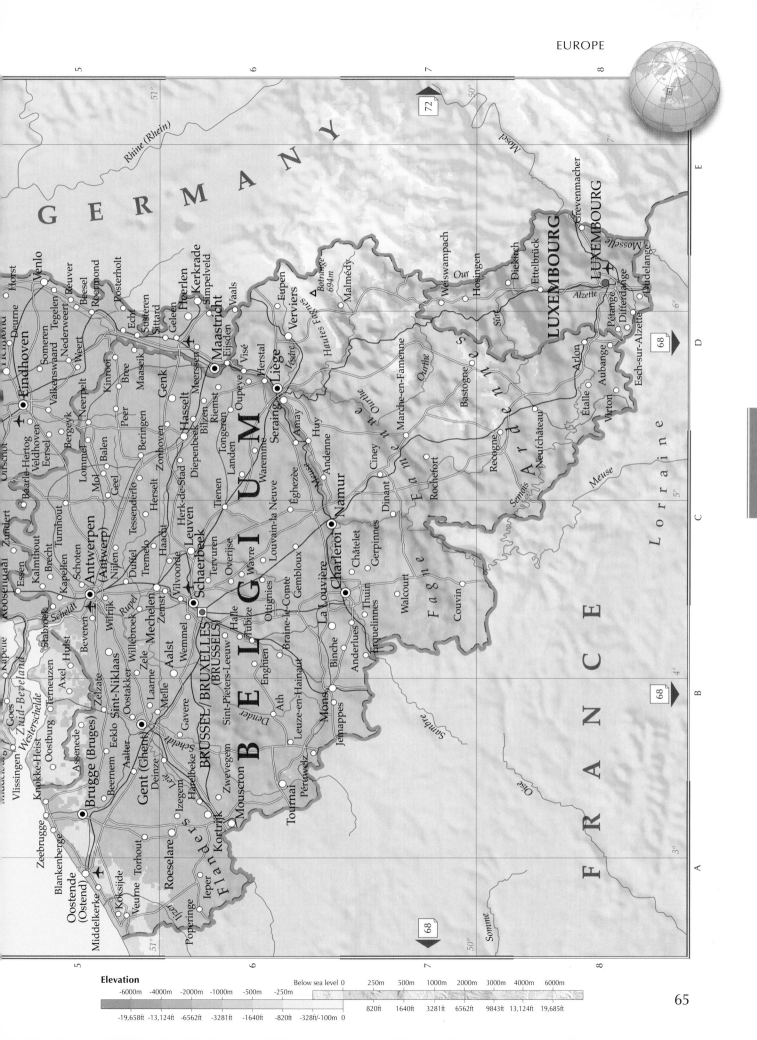

G E R M A N Y

B E L G I U M

LUXEMBOURG

F R A N C E

L o r r a i n e

Elevation

| | | | | | | | Below sea level 0 | 250m | 500m | 1000m | 2000m | 3000m | 4000m | 6000m |

| -6000m | -4000m | -2000m | -1000m | -500m | -250m |

| -19,658ft | -13,124ft | -6562ft | -3281ft | -1640ft | -820ft | -328ft/-100m | 0 |

820ft 1640ft 3281ft 6562ft 9843ft 13,124ft 19,685ft

The British Isles

North Sea

ATLANTIC OCEAN

SCOTLAND

Shetland Islands
- Unst
- Yell
- Fetlar
- Mainland
- Lerwick

Fair Isle

Orkney Islands
- Sanday
- Kirkwall
- Mainland
- Hoy
- John o'Groats

Thurso
Ben Hope 927m
Ullapool
North West Highlands
Moray Firth
Elgin
Inverness
Loch Ness
Aviemore
Spey
Dee
Grampian Mountains
Fraserburgh
Peterhead
Aberdeen
Montrose
Arbroath
Dundee
Forfar
Tay
St Andrews
Firth of Forth
Perth
Dunfermline
Forth
Stirling
Edinburgh
Glasgow
Hamilton
Galashiels
Hawick
Berwick-upon-Tweed
Cheviot Hills
Tyne
Newcastle upon Tyne
South Shields
Sunderland

The Minch
Ben Nevis 1343 m
Fort William
Loch Lomond
Clyde
Greenock
Paisley
East Kilbride
Kilmarnock
Prestwick
Isle of Arran
Ayr
Southern Uplands
Dumfries

Isle of Lewis
Stornoway
Harris
North Uist
South Uist
Barra
St Kilda
Outer Hebrides
The Little Minch
Isle of Skye
Stromeferry
Mallaig
Rhum
Eigg
Coll
Tiree
Isle of Mull
Firth of Lorn
Oban
Jura
Islay
Inner Hebrides
Kintyre

NORTHERN IRELAND
Coleraine
Londonderry

0 km   100
0 miles   100

Population
- National capital
- Internal administrative capital
- ○ below 50,000
- ○ 50,000 to 100,000
- ◉ 100,000 to 500,000
- ▣ above 500,000

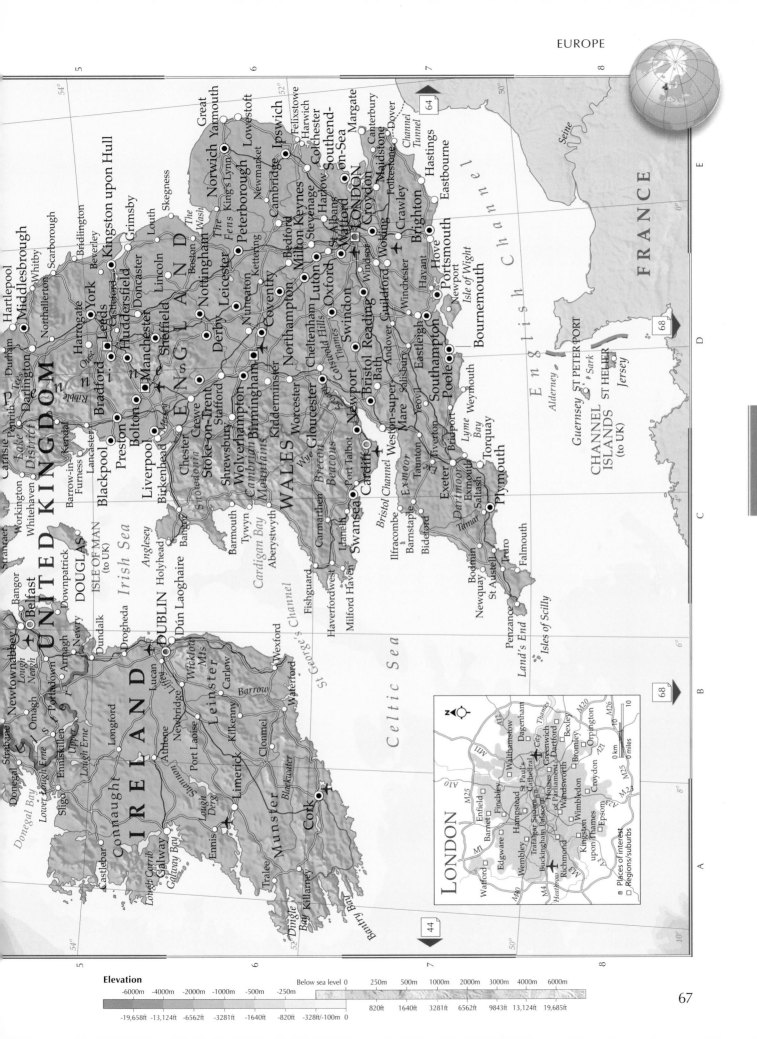

Elevation

Below sea level 0	250m	500m	1000m	2000m	3000m	4000m	6000m
	820ft	1640ft	3281ft	6562ft	9843ft	13,124ft	19,685ft

-6000m	-4000m	-2000m	-1000m	-500m	-250m
-19,658ft	-13,124ft	-6562ft	-3281ft	-1640ft	-820ft	-328ft/-100m	0

France, Andorra & Monaco

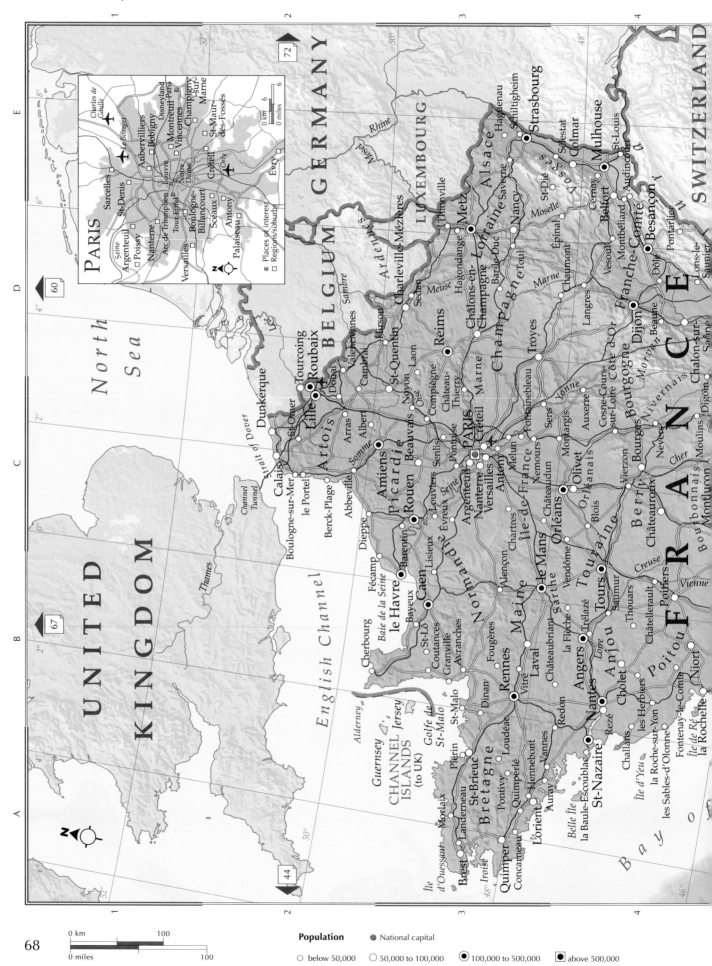

PARIS (inset map)

Charles de Gaulle · le Bourget · St-Denis · Sarcelles · Argenteuil · Poissy · Nanterre · Aubervilliers · Bobigny · Disneyland · Montreuil-Paris · Villiers · Champigny-sur-Marne · St-Maur-des-Fossés · Vincennes · Louvre · Notre Dame · Arc de Triomphe · Tour Eiffel · Versailles · Boulogne-Billancourt · Sceaux · Créteil · Antony · Orly · Palaiseau · Evry · Seine

- ■ Places of interest
- □ Regions/suburbs

North Sea

GERMANY

LUXEMBOURG

BELGIUM

SWITZERLAND

UNITED KINGDOM

English Channel

Strait of Dover

Channel Tunnel

CHANNEL ISLANDS (to UK)

FRANCE

Strasbourg · Mulhouse · Colmar · Sélestat · St-Louis · Schiltigheim · Haguenau · St-Dié · Vosges · Cernay · Belfort · Montbéliard · Audincourt · Besançon · Pontarlier · Dole · Lons-le-Saunier · Chalon-sur-Saône · Digoin · Moulins

Rhine · Mosel · Ardennes · Sambre · Meuse · Marne · Yonne

Thionville · Metz · Hagondange · Nancy · Bar-le-Duc · Toul · Épinal · Chaumont · Langres · Dijon · Beaune · Morvan · Nivernais · Bourgogne · Nevers · Château-Thierry · Reims · Châlons-en-Champagne · Charleville-Mézières · Sedan · Hirson · Laon · Compiègne · St-Quentin · Valenciennes · Cambrai · Troyes · Auxerre · Sens · Montargis · Fontainebleau · Cosne-Cours-sur-Loire · Côte-d'Or

Tourcoing · Roubaix · Lille · Denain · Douai · Arras · Albert · Somme · Amiens · Beauvais · Senlis · Pontoise · Melun · Nemours · Montargis · Châteaudun · Orléans · Olivet · Orléanais · Blois · Vierzon · Bourges · Châteauroux · Berry · Vienne

Dunkerque · St-Omer · Calais · le Portel · Boulogne-sur-Mer · Berck-Plage · Abbeville · Artois · Picardie · Rouen · Barentin · Évreux · Louviers · Chartres · Alençon · Île-de-France · Paris · Créteil · Argenteuil · Nanterre · Versailles · Antony · Seine · Maine · le Mans · Sarthe · la Flèche · Vendôme · Tours · Touraine · Creuse · Poitiers

Fécamp · Dieppe · Baie de la Seine · le Havre · Caen · Bayeux · Lisieux · Normandie · Saumur · Thouars · Châtellerault · Poitou

Cherbourg · St-Lô · Coutances · Granville · Avranches · Fougères · Vitré · Laval · Châteaubriant · Angers · Anjou · Cholet · les Herbiers · Fontenay-le-Comte · Niort · la Rochelle · île de Ré

St-Brieuc · Dinan · St-Malo · Golfe de St-Malo · Jersey · Guernsey · Alderney · Rennes · Redon · Nantes · Rezé · St-Nazaire · la Baule-Escoublac · Challans · île d'Yeu · la Roche-sur-Yon · les Sables-d'Olonne

Morlaix · Landerneau · Brest · Quimper · Concarneau · île d'Ouessant · Iroise · Pontivy · Loudéac · Quimperlé · Hennebont · Lorient · Auray · Vannes · Belle Île · Bretagne · Loire

Thames

Bay of

Population scales and map key as shown

Population
- ○ below 50,000
- ○ 50,000 to 100,000
- ◉ 100,000 to 500,000
- ■ above 500,000
- ● National capital

0 km — 100
0 miles — 100

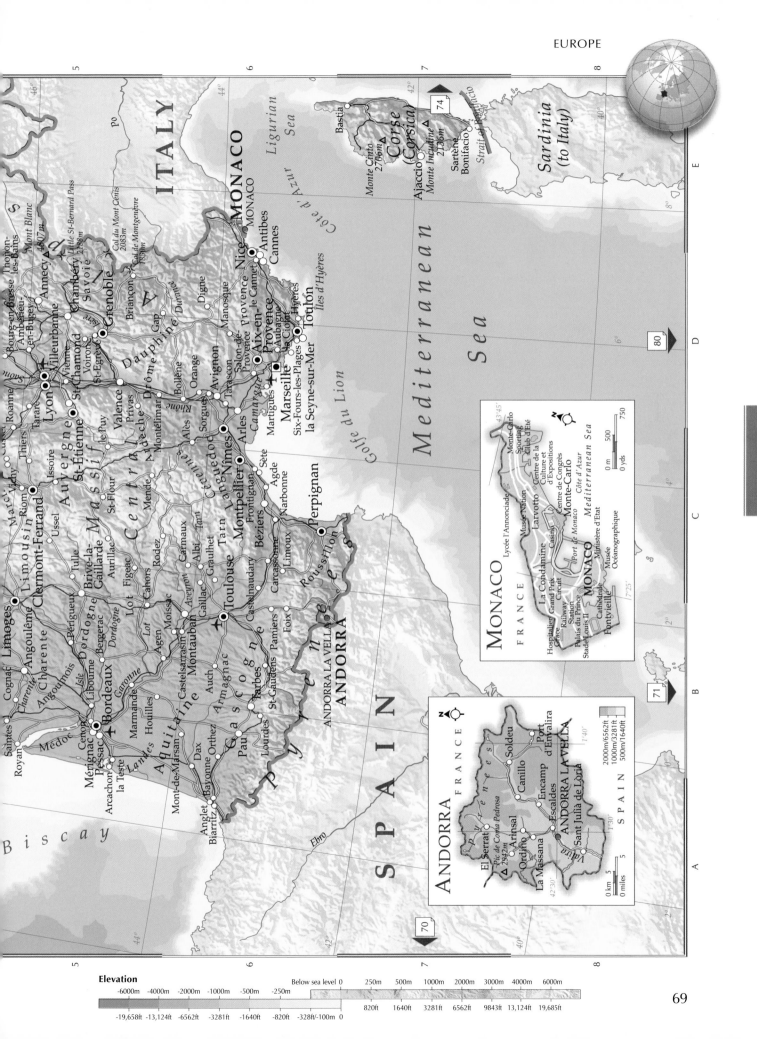

ITALY

SPAIN

Mediterranean Sea

Ligurian Sea

Corse (Corsica)

Sardinia (to Italy)

Biscay

Elevation

-6000m	-4000m	-2000m	-1000m	-500m	-250m	

Below sea level 0   250m   500m   1000m   2000m   3000m   4000m   6000m

-19,658ft -13,124ft -6562ft -3281ft -1640ft -820ft -328ft/-100m 0

820ft   1640ft   3281ft   6562ft   9843ft   13,124ft   19,685ft

MONACO

FRANCE

Monte-Carlo

Mediterranean Sea

0 m   500   750
0 yds

ANDORRA

FRANCE

ANDORRA LA VELLA

SPAIN

2000m/6562ft
1000m/3281ft
500m/1640ft

0 km   5
0 miles   5

Spain & Portugal

Bay of Biscay

ATLANTIC

OCEAN

PORTUGAL

S P

Sistema Central

MADRID

Galicia

Asturias

Cordillera Cantábrica

Castilla-León

Extremadura

Sierra Morena

Andalucía

Algarve

Costa Verde

Costa del Sol

Cities and towns

A Coruña (La Coruña), Ferrol, Luarca, Gijón (Xixón), Costa Verde, Santander, Betanzos, Larache, Avilés, Villaviciosa, Llanes, Pravia, Tineo, Oviedo, Villalba, Mieres del Camino, Torrelavega, Santa Comba, Pola de Lena, Cabañaquinta, Reinosa, Cabo Fisterra, Lugo, Chantada, Monforte de Lemos, Ponferrada, León, Outes, Santiago, Muros, Lalín, O Carballiño, Astorga, Ribeira, Pontevedra, Ourense (Orense), Benavente, Palencia, Lerma, Marín, Porteareas, Xinzo de Limia, Zamora, Valladolid, Aranda de Duero, Vigo, Muíño/Minho, Ponte da Barca, Bragança, Embalse de Ricobayo, Toro, Duero, Viana do Castelo, Braga, Guimarães, Chaves, Medina del Campo, Burgos, Póvoa de Varzim, Vila do Conde, Vila Real, Embalse de Almendra, Salamanca, Segovia, Sierra de Guadarrón, Matosinhos, Porto (Oporto), Lamego, Douro, Vila Nova de Gaia, São João da Madeira, Ovar, Albergaria-a-Velha, Viseu, Ávila, Aveiro, Ílhavo, Alto da Torre 1993m, Guarda, Ciudad-Rodrigo, Béjar, Sierra de Gredos, Coimbra, Covilhã, Plasencia, Talavera de la Reina, Aranjuez, Figueira da Foz, Serra da Estrela, Coria, Embalse de Valdecañas, Getafe, Leiria, Castelo Branco, Tagus, Toledo, Ocaña, Tomar, Embalse de Alcántara, Cáceres, Entroncamento, Abrantes, Trujillo, Peniche, Caldas da Rainha, Portalegre, Herrera del Duque, Daimiel, Torres Vedras, Santarém, Mérida, Villanueva de la Serena, Sintra, Coruche, Estremoz, Elvas, Don Benito, Ciudad Real, Cascais, LISBOA (LISBON), Badajoz, Castuera, Puertollano, Almada, Barreiro, Évora, Almendralejo, Setúbal, Serra d'Ossa, Zafra, Villafranca de los Barros, Pozoblanco, La Carolina, Alcácer do Sal, Barragem do Alqueva, Jerez de los Caballeros, Azuaga, Baía de Setúbal, Sines, Beja, Montoro, Bailén, Guadiana, Cortegana, Sierra Morena, Córdoba, Linares, Ourique, Nerva, Bujalance, Jaén, Valverde del Camino, La Algaba, Carmona, Palma del Río, Martos, Alcaudete, Portimão, Ayamonte, Lepe, Sevilla (Seville), Ecija, Lucena, Osuna, Lagos, Faro, Isla Cristina, Huelva, Dos Hermanas, Antequera, Archidona, Granada, Cabo de São Vicente, Tavira, Olhão, Las Cabezas de San Juan, Lebrija, Olvera, Álora, Ronda, Motril, Sanlúcar de Barrameda, Ubrique, Estepona, El Puerto de Santa María, Jerez de la Frontera, Coín, Málaga, Cádiz, San Fernando, Vejer de la Frontera, Marbella, Fuengirola, Barbate de Franco, Algeciras, GIBRALTAR (to UK), Ceuta (to Spain), Strait of Gibraltar, MOROCCO, Golfo de Cádiz, Costa de la Luz

AZORES (to Portugal)

Corvo

Flores

São Jorge

Faial

Pico

Graciosa

Terceira

São Miguel

Ponta Delgada

Santa Maria

0 km 100

0 miles 100

200m/656ft

Sea level

Population   ● National capital

○ below 50,000   ○ 50,000 to 100,000   ◉ 100,000 to 500,000   ■ above 500,000

0 km   100

0 miles   100

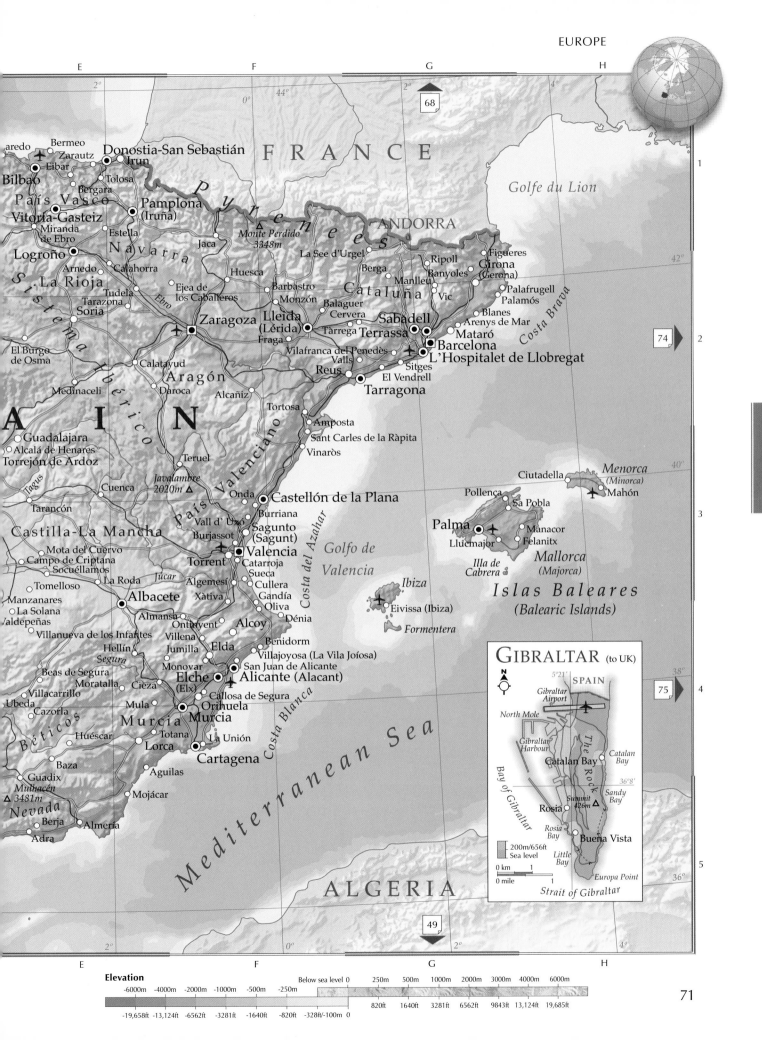

FRANCE

ANDORRA

Pyrenees

Golfe du Lion

aredo
Bermeo
Zarautz
Eibar
Donostia-San Sebastián
Irun
Bilbao
Tolosa
País Vasco
Bergara
Pamplona
Vitoria-Gasteiz
(Iruña)
Miranda
de Ebro
Estella
Logroño
Navarra
Jaca
Monte Perdido
3348m
La See d'Urgel
Arnedo
Calahorra
Huesca
Berga
Ripoll
Figueres
La Rioja
Tarazona
Ejea de
los Caballeros
Barbastro
Cataluña
Manlleu
Girona
(Gerona)
Soria
Monzón
Banyoles
Palafrugell
El Burgo
de Osma
Zaragoza
Lleida
(Lérida)
Balaguer
Cervera
Vic
Palamós
Blanes
Calatayud
Fraga
Tárrega
Terrassa
Sabadell
Arenys de Mar
Mataró
Aragón
Daroca
Vilafranca del Penedès
Barcelona
Medinaceli
Alcañiz
Valls
Sitges
L'Hospitalet de Llobregat
Reus
El Vendrell
A I N
Tortosa
Tarragona
Guadalajara
Amposta
Alcalá de Henares
Torrejón de Ardoz
Sant Carles de la Ràpita
Vinaròs
Teruel
Javalambre
2020m
Cuenca
Onda
Castellón de la Plana
Ciutadella
Menorca
(Minorca)
Tarancón
Burriana
Vall d' Uxó
Sagunto
(Sagunt)
Pollença
Sa Pobla
Mahón
Castilla-La Mancha
Burjassot
Valencia
Golfo de
Valencia
Palma
Manacor
Mota del Cuervo
Catarroja
Sueca
Torrent
Felanitx
Campo de Criptana
Socuéllamos
Algemesí
Llucmajor
Tomelloso
La Roda
Cullera
Xàtiva
Gandía
Illa de
Cabrera
Mallorca
(Majorca)
Manzanares
Albacete
Oliva
La Solana
Almansa
Dénia
Ibiza
Islas Baleares
aldepeñas
Ontinyent
Alcoy
(Balearic Islands)
Villanueva de los Infantes
Villena
Hellín
Jumilla
Elda
Benidorm
Eivissa (Ibiza)
Segura
Monovar
Villajoyosa (La Vila Joíosa)
Beas de Segura
San Juan de Alicante
Formentera
Moratalla
Cieza
Elche
Alicante (Alacant)
Villacarrillo
Mula
(Elx)
Ubeda
Callosa de Segura
Cazorla
Murcia
Orihuela
Béticos
Murcia
Huéscar
Totana
La Unión
Baza
Lorca
Cartagena
Guadix
Aguilas
Mulhacén
3481m
Mojácar
Nevada
Mediterranean Sea
Berja
Almería
Adra

ALGERIA

68
74
75
49

GIBRALTAR (to UK)
N
SPAIN
5°21'
Gibraltar
Airport
North Mole
Gibraltar
Harbour
Catalan Bay
Catalan Bay
Bay of Gibraltar
The Rock
36°8'
Sandy
Bay
Rosia
Summit
426m
Rosia
Bay
Buena Vista
Little
Bay
200m/656ft
Sea level
Europa Point
0 km   1
0 mile   1
Strait of Gibraltar

Elevation

						Below sea level 0	250m	500m	1000m	2000m	3000m	4000m	6000m
-6000m	-4000m	-2000m	-1000m	-500m	-250m								
-19,658ft	-13,124ft	-6562ft	-3281ft	-1640ft	-820ft	-328ft/-100m 0	820ft	1640ft	3281ft	6562ft	9843ft	13,124ft	19,685ft

Germany & The Alpine States

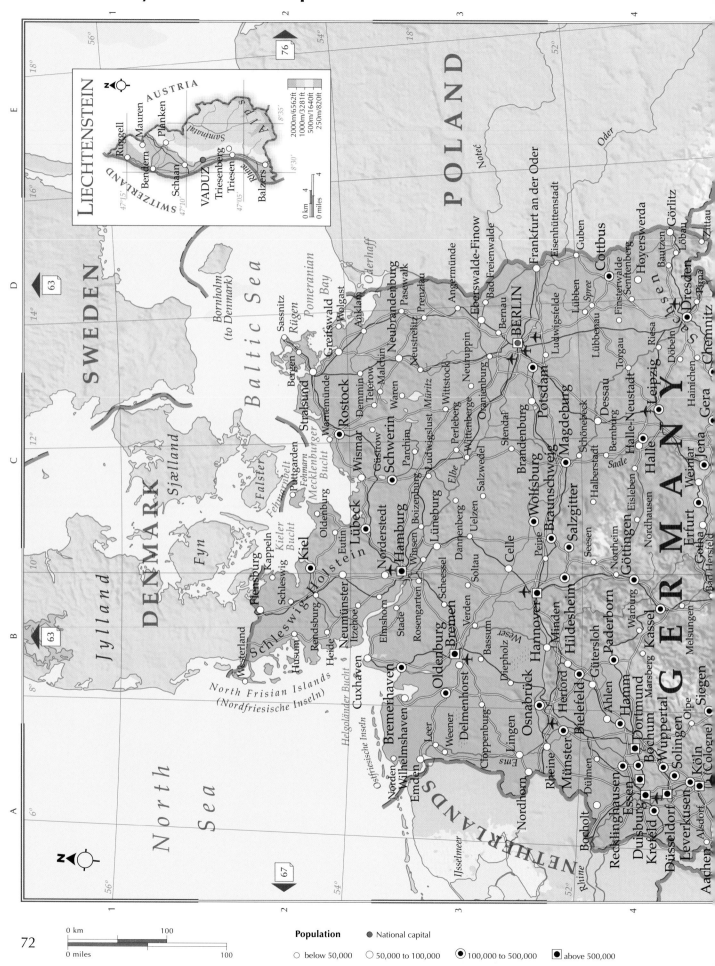

LIECHTENSTEIN

AUSTRIA
SWITZERLAND

Ruggell
Mauren
Planken
Bendern
Schaan
VADUZ
Triesenberg
Triesen
Balzers

Rhine
Saminatal
Alps

2000m/6562ft
1000m/3281ft
500m/1640ft
250m/820ft

0 km 4
0 miles 4

SWEDEN

POLAND

Bornholm
(to Denmark)

Baltic Sea

Oder
Noteć

Pomeranian Bay

Greifswald Bay
Wolgast
Ahlbeck
Oderhaff

Sassnitz
Rügen
Bergen
Stralsund
Wismar
Rostock
Warnemünde

Frankfurt an der Oder
Eisenhüttenstadt
Guben
Cottbus
Finsterwalde
Senftenberg
Hoyerswerda
Görlitz
Löbau
Bautzen
Dresden
Pirna
Chemnitz
Zittau

Neubrandenburg
Pasewalk
Prenzlau
Angermünde
Bad Freienwalde
Eberswalde-Finow

Demmin
Malchin
Teterow
Güstrow
Waren
Schwerin
Parchim
Ludwigslust
Wittstock
Neuruppin
Oranienburg
Bernau
BERLIN
Potsdam
Ludwigsfelde
Lübben
Lübbenau
Spree
Torgau
Riesa
Döbeln
Hainichen
Gera
Jena
Weimar
Erfurt
Gotha

Müritz
Neustrelitz
Wittenberge
Perleberg
Brandenburg
Magdeburg
Schönebeck
Stendal
Salzwedel
Halberstadt
Bernburg
Dessau
Wittenberg
Halle-Neustadt
Halle
Leipzig
Bad Hersfeld

Lübeck
Eutin
Oldenburg
Mecklenburger Bucht
Fehmarn
Puttgarden
Fehmarnbelt
Kieler Bucht

DENMARK
Sjælland
Fyn
Falster
Kappeln
Schleswig
Flensburg
Kiel
Neumünster
Rendsburg
Itzehoe
Heide
Husum
Westerland
North Frisian Islands
(Nordfriesische Inseln)

Jylland

North Sea

Norderstedt
Hamburg
Witzen Boizenburg
Lüneburg
Dannenberg
Uelzen
Salzwedel
Celle
Seesen
Northeim
Göttingen
Eisleben
Nordhausen
Melsungen
Kassel
Marsberg

Elmshorn
Stade
Rosengarten
Scheessel
Verden
Soltau
Bremen
Verden
Bassum
Diepholz
Minden
Hildesheim
Peine
Braunschweig
Wolfsburg
Salzgitter
Hannover
Herford
Bielefeld
Gütersloh
Paderborn
Warburg

Cuxhaven
Bremerhaven
Wilhelmshaven
Delmenhorst
Oldenburg
Leer
Weener
Cloppenburg
Lingen
Osnabrück
Rheine
Münster
Ahlen
Hamm
Dortmund
Bochum
Wuppertal
Solingen
Olpe
Siegen

Helgoländer Bucht
Ostfriesische Inseln
Norden
Emden
Nordhorn
Dülmen
Bocholt
Recklinghausen
Essen
Duisburg
Krefeld
Düsseldorf
Leverkusen
Köln
(Cologne)
Alsdorf
Aachen

Ems
Weser
Elbe
Saale
Rhine
IJsselmeer

NETHERLANDS

GERMANY

Population

- ○ below 50,000
- ◎ 50,000 to 100,000
- ◉ 100,000 to 500,000
- ■ above 500,000

● National capital

0 km 100
0 miles 100

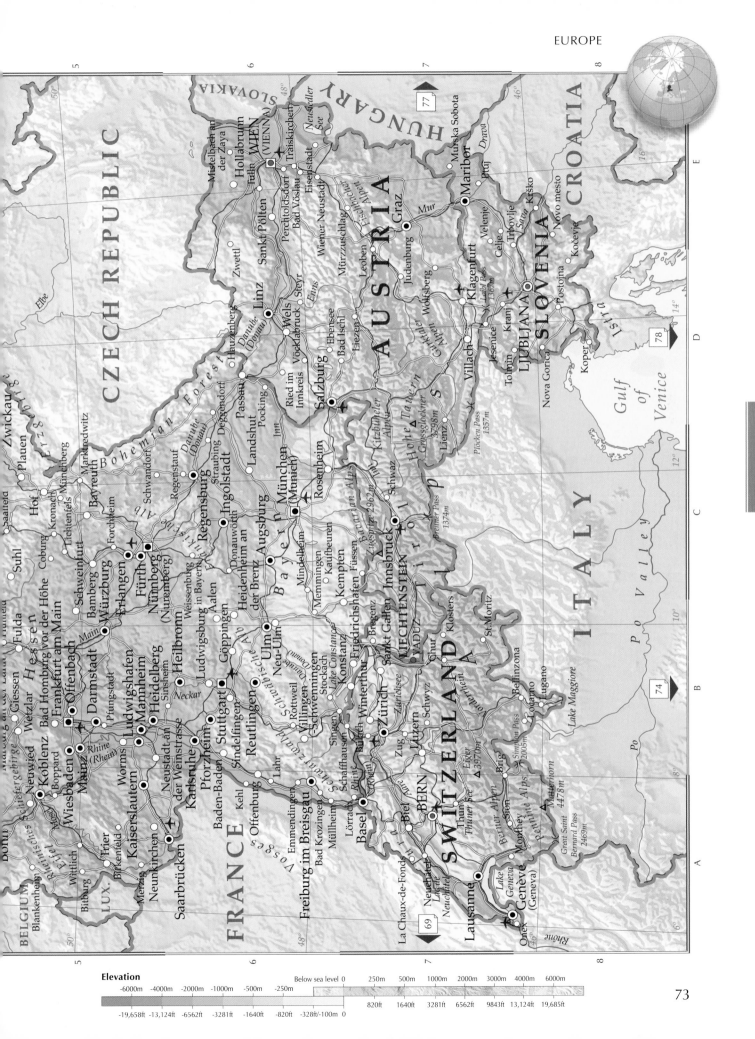

Elevation

						Below sea level 0	250m	500m	1000m	2000m	3000m	4000m	6000m

-6000m -4000m -2000m -1000m -500m -250m

-19,658ft -13,124ft -6562ft -3281ft -1640ft -820ft -328ft/-100m 0   820ft 1640ft 3281ft 6562ft 9843ft 13,124ft 19,685ft

Italy

SLOVAKIA

HUNGARY

BOSNIA & HERZEGOVINA

CROATIA

Dalmatia

Adriatic Sea

SLOVENIA

SAN MARINO

Dogana
Serravalle
Fiorina
Cailungo
Faetano
Monte Titano
739m
Montegiardino
Murata
Gualdicciolo
Borgo Maggiore
SAN MARINO
ITALY
Chiesanuova

500m/1640ft
200m/656ft
100m/328ft

0 km   2
0 miles   2

Trieste
Udine
Tarvisio
Monfalcone
Portogruaro
Gemona del Friuli
Pordenone
Bressanone
Cortina d'Ampezzo
Alpi
Dolomitiche
Merano
Bolzano
Trento
Bassano del Grappa
Arco
Lago di Garda
Treviso
Venezia (Venice)
Mestre
Gulf of Venice
Chioggia
Rovigo
Foci del Po
Edolo
Como
Lago di Como
Bergamo
Brescia
Vicenza
Padova
Monselice
Ostiglia
Adige
Po
Comacchio
Ravenna
Forlì
Rimini
SAN MARINO
SAN MARINO
Fano
Pesaro
Falconara Marittima
Ancona
Civitanova Marche
Fermo
Ascoli Piceno
Giulianova
Teramo
Pescara
Ortona
Chieti
Termoli

Istra

Drava
Sava

GERMANY

AUSTRIA

SWITZERLAND
LIECHTENSTEIN
Brenner Pass
1374m
Inn
Rhine
Lake Constance
Lake Maggiore
Lago Maggiore
Varese
Monza
Sesto San Giovanni
Rho
Milano (Milan)
Pavia
Novara
Vercelli
Casteggio
Piacenza
Cremona
Mantova
Verona
Parma
Reggio nell'Emilia
Modena
Carpi
Ferrara
Bologna
Imola
Faenza
Cesena
Appennino
Pistoia
Prato
Firenze (Florence)
Lucca
Arno
Pisa
Viareggio
Massa
Carrara
La Spezia
Savona
Genova (Genoa)
Appennino Ligure
Golfo di Genova
Finale Ligure
Imperia
San Remo
Ventimiglia
MONACO
Rhône
Great Saint Bernard Pass 2469m
Aosta
Gran Paradiso 4061m
Mont Blanc 4807m
Little St-Bernard Pass 2188m
Susa
Rivoli
Moncalieri
Torino (Turin)
Asti
Alessandria
Mondovì
Cuneo
Savigliano
Po
Piemonte
FRANCE

Lombardia

Lago Trasimeno
Perugia
Foligno
Todi
Sansepolcro
Arezzo
Siena
Chianti
Toscana
Grosseto
Orbetello
Portoferraio
Isola d'Elba
Piombino
Cecina
Livorno
Archipelago Toscano
Civitavecchia
Viterbo
Terni
L'Aquila
Avezzano
Tivoli
ROMA (ROME)
VATICAN CITY
Appennino Abruzzese
Umbro-Marchigiano
Marche
Appennino Umbro-Marchigiano

Corse (Corsica) (to France)
Strait of Bonifacio
Isola Asinara
La Maddalena

Ligurian Sea

Creese

Population

● National capital

○ below 50,000
○ 50,000 to 100,000
◉ 100,000 to 500,000
■ above 500,000

0 km   100
0 miles   100

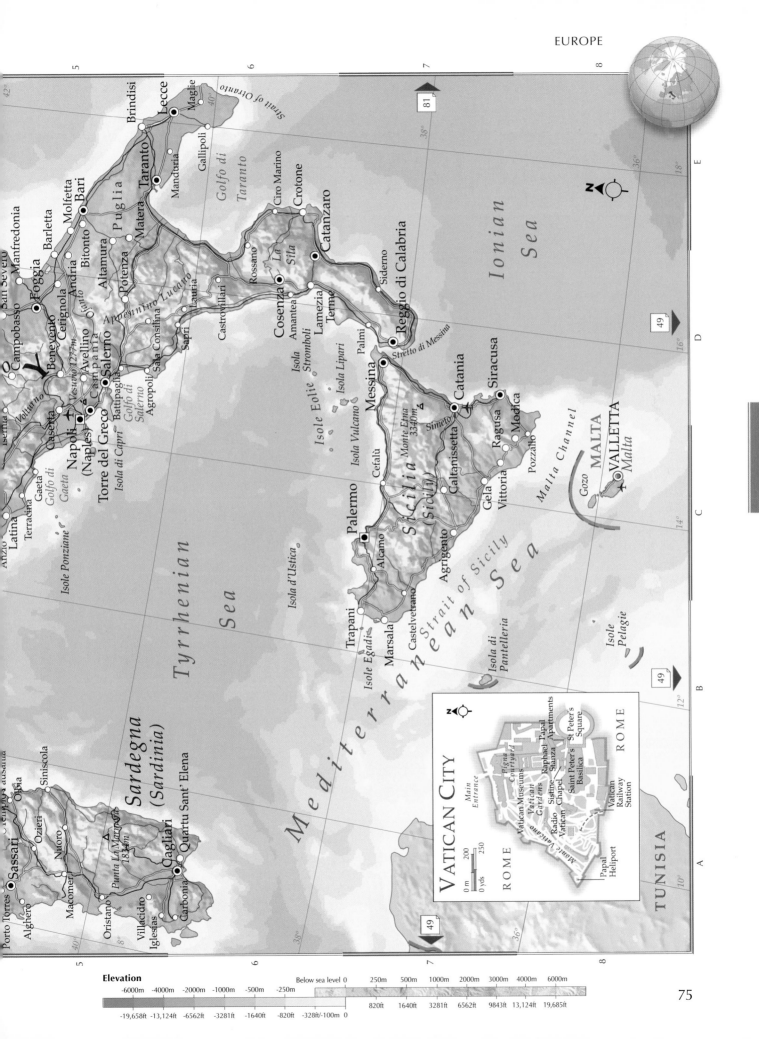

Map labels

Seas and water features:
Strait of Otranto
Golfo di Taranto
Ionian Sea
Strait of Messina
Stretto di Messina
Tyrrhenian Sea
Mediterranean Sea
Strait of Sicily
Malta Channel
Golfo di Gaeta
Golfo di Salerno

Cities and places (northeast/Puglia):
Lecce
Maglie
Brindisi
Gallipoli
Manduria
Taranto
Bari
Molfetta
Barletta
Manfredonia
San Severo
Bitonto
Andria
Altamura
Puglia
Matera
Foggia
Cerignola
Campobasso
Benevento
Avellino
Salerno
Potenza
Appennino Lucano
Campania
Sala Consilina
Sapri
Lauria
Castrovillari
Rossano
Ciro Marino
Crotone
La Sila
Catanzaro
Cosenza
Amantea
Isola Stromboli
Lamezia Terme
Siderno
Reggio di Calabria
Palmi

Naples area:
Isernia
Volturno
Vesuvio 1277m
Caserta
Napoli (Naples)
Torre del Greco
Isola di Capri
Battipaglia
Agropoli
Gaeta
Terracina
Latina
Anzio
Isole Ponziane

Islands:
Isole Eolie
Isola Lipari
Isola Vulcano
Isola d'Ustica
Cefalù

Sicily:
Messina
Monte Etna 3340m
Simeto
Catania
Siracusa
Medica
Ragusa
Caltanissetta
Gela
Vittoria
Pozzallo
Palermo
Alcamo
Agrigento
Castelvetrano
Marsala
Trapani
Isole Egadi
Sicilia (Sicily)

Malta:
Gozo
MALTA
VALLETTA
Malta

Other:
Isola di Pantelleria
Isole Pelagie
TUNISIA

Sardinia:
Sardegna (Sardinia)
Sassari
Porto Torres
Alghero
Olbia
Siniscola
Ozieri
Nuoro
Macomer
Oristano
Punta La Marmora 1834m
Villacidro
Iglesias
Carbonia
Cagliari
Quartu Sant'Elena

Vatican City inset

VATICAN CITY

ROME

Main Entrance
Pigna Courtyard
Vatican Museums
Vatican Gardens
Radio Vatican
Musei Vaticano
Papal Apartments
Raphael Stanza
Sistine Chapel
Saint Peter's Basilica
St Peter's Square
Vatican Railway Station
Papal Heliport

0 m   200
0 yds   250

ROME

Elevation

Below sea level 0	250m	500m	1000m	2000m	3000m	4000m	6000m

-6000m -4000m -2000m -1000m -500m -250m

-19,658ft -13,124ft -6562ft -3281ft -1640ft -820ft -328ft/-100m 0

820ft 1640ft 3281ft 6562ft 9843ft 13,124ft 19,685ft

Central Europe

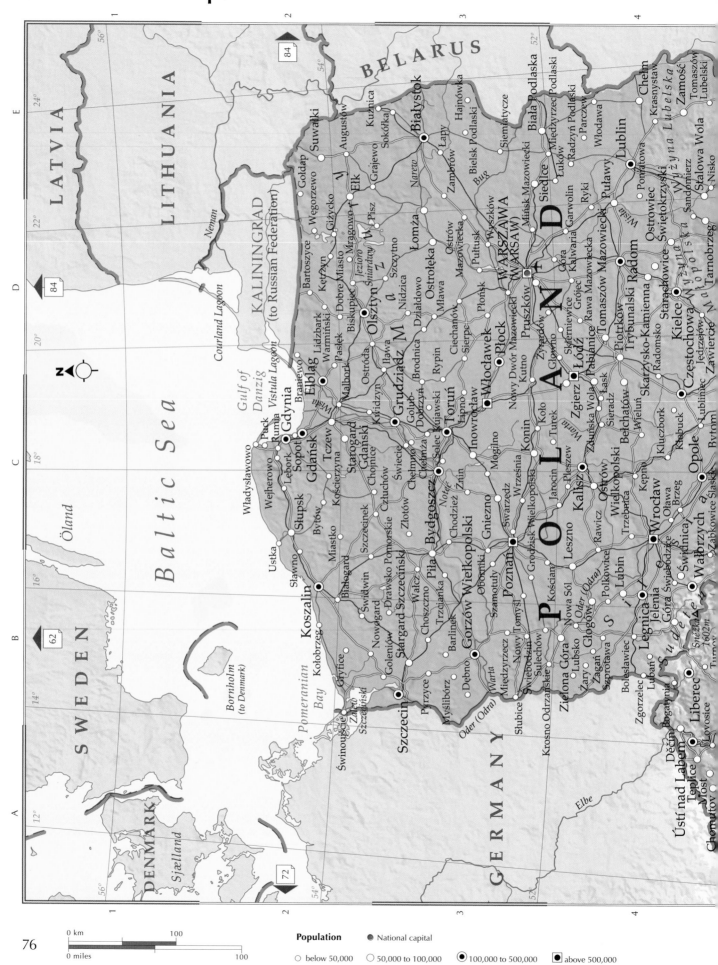

SWEDEN

LATVIA

LITHUANIA

KALININGRAD
(to Russian Federation)

BELARUS

DENMARK

GERMANY

P O L A N D

Baltic Sea

Öland

Bornholm
(to Denmark)

Sjælland

Pomeranian Bay

Gulf of Danzig

Courland Lagoon

Vistula Lagoon

Neman

Elbe

Oder (Odra)

Warta

Noteć

Wisła

Narew

Bug

Świnoujście · Złoto Szczecińskie · Ustka · Sławno · Koszalin · Kołobrzeg · Gryfice · Białogard · Świdwin · Nowogard · Goleniów · Stargard Szczeciński · Pyrzyce · Myślibórz · Dębno · Barlinek · Międzyrzecz · Nowy Tomyśl · Świebodzin · Sulechów · Zielona Góra · Żary · Żagań · Szprotawa · Lubsko · Krosno Odrzańskie · Słubice · Gubin · Zgorzelec · Żnin

Władysławowo · Puck · Rumia · Wejherowo · Gdynia · Sopot · Gdańsk · Tczew · Lębork · Słupsk · Bytów · Kościerzyna · Kartuzy · Starogard Gdański · Chojnice · Człuchów · Miastko · Szczecinek · Drawsko Pomorskie · Złotów · Wałcz · Piła · Trzcianka · Chodzież · Czarnków · Oborniki · Szamotuły · Poznań · Gorzów Wielkopolski · Leszno · Kościan · Nowa Sól · Głogów · Polkowice · Lubin · Bolesławiec · Lubań · Jelenia Góra · Świeradów

Braniewo · Elbląg · Lidzbark Warmiński · Pasłęk · Malbork · Kwidzyn · Grudziądz · Golub-Dobrzyń · Świecie · Chełmno · Chełmża · Toruń · Bydgoszcz · Inowrocław · Mogilno · Gniezno · Września · Konin · Koło · Turek · Kalisz · Jarocin · Pleszew · Ostrów Wielkopolski · Krotoszyn · Rawicz · Trzebnica · Wołów · Wrocław · Oława · Brzeg · Oleśnica · Wieluń · Kępno · Kluczbork · Namysłów · Kłobuck · Opole · Strzelin · Ząbkowice Śląskie · Świdnica · Wałbrzych · Legnica · Świebodzice

Suwałki · Gołdap · Węgorzewo · Giżycko · Mrągowo · Kętrzyn · Bartoszyce · Biskupiec · Dobre Miasto · Olsztyn · Nidzica · Działdowo · Ostróda · Iława · Brodnica · Rypin · Lipno · Sierpc · Ciechanów · Mława · Płońsk · Nowy Dwór Mazowiecki · Kutno · Płock · Włocławek · Pułtusk · Wyszków · Ostrołęka · Ostrów Mazowiecka · Mińsk Mazowiecki · WARSZAWA (WARSAW) · Pruszków · Żyrardów · Skierniewice · Góra Kalwaria · Grójec · Rawa Mazowiecka · Łowicz · Zgierz · Łódź · Pabianice · Łask · Sieradz · Zduńska Wola · Bełchatów · Piotrków Trybunalski · Tomaszów Mazowiecki

Augustów · Grajewo · Ełk · Pisz · Szczytno · Łomża · Zambrów · Kolno · Ostrów · Białystok · Sokółka · Kuźnica · Hajnówka · Bielsk Podlaski · Siemiatycze · Łapy · Siedlce · Łuków · Garwolin · Ryki · Dęblin · Puławy · Radzyń Podlaski · Międzyrzec Podlaski · Parczew · Biała Podlaska · Włodawa · Lublin · Radom · Starachowice · Skarżysko-Kamienna · Szydłowiec · Ostrowiec Świętokrzyski · Kielce · Końskie · Radomsko · Częstochowa · Zawiercie · Jędrzejów · Sandomierz · Stalowa Wola · Nisko · Tarnobrzeg · Krasnystaw · Chełm · Zamość · Tomaszów Lubelski · Pońiatowa

Wyżyna Lubelska · *Wyżyna Małopolska* · *Mazury* · *Pojezierze Mazurskie* · *Sudety* · *Pojezierze Pomorskie*

Śnieżka 1602m

Ústí nad Labem · Děčín · Teplice · Most · Chomutov · Liberec · Lovosice · Bogatynia · Turnov

Jezioro Śniardwy

0 km 100
0 miles 100

Population ● National capital

○ below 50,000 ○ 50,000 to 100,000 ◉ 100,000 to 500,000 ■ above 500,000

84 · 84 · 62 · 72

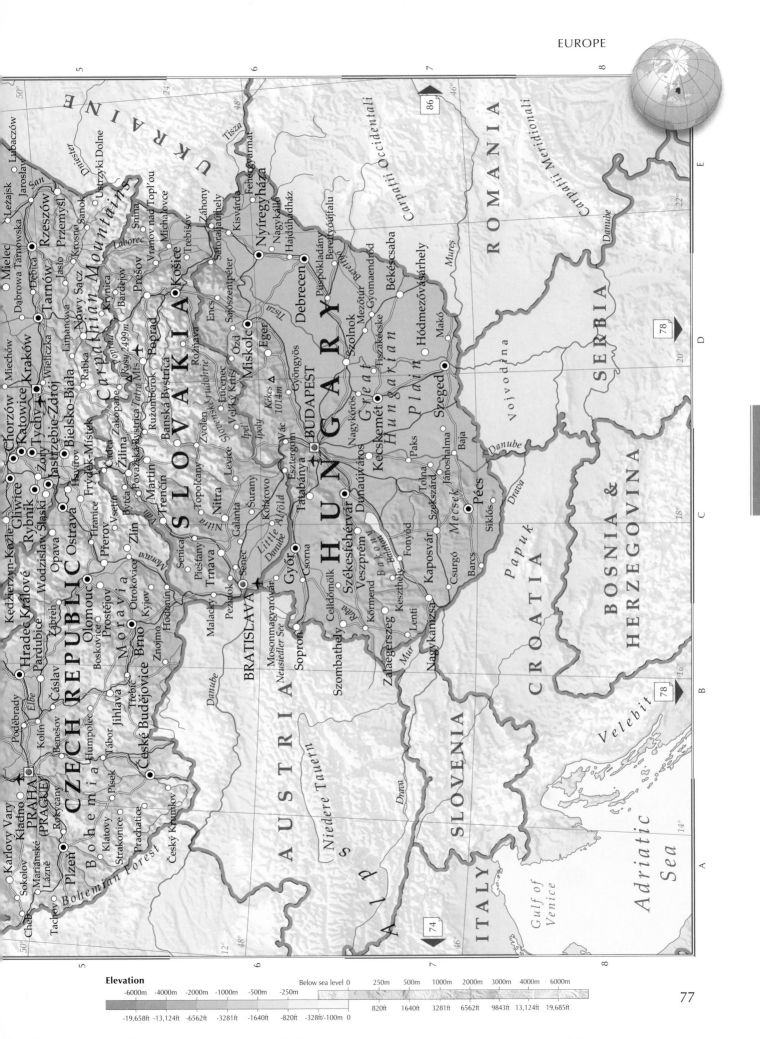

Elevation

| -6000m | -4000m | -2000m | -1000m | -500m | -250m | Below sea level 0 | 250m | 500m | 1000m | 2000m | 3000m | 4000m | 6000m |

| -19,658ft | -13,124ft | -6562ft | -3281ft | -1640ft | -820ft | -328ft/-100m 0 | | | 820ft | 1640ft | 3281ft | 6562ft | 9843ft | 13,124ft | 19,685ft |

Southeast Europe

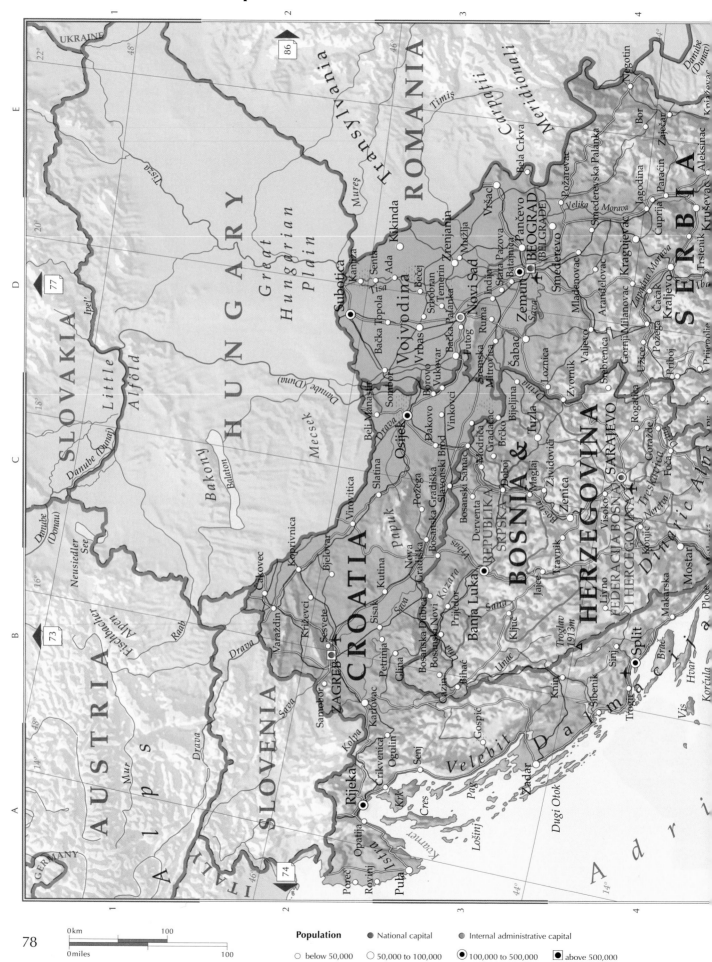

Population   ● National capital   ● Internal administrative capital

○ below 50,000   ○ 50,000 to 100,000   ◉ 100,000 to 500,000   ■ above 500,000

0 km   100

0 miles   100

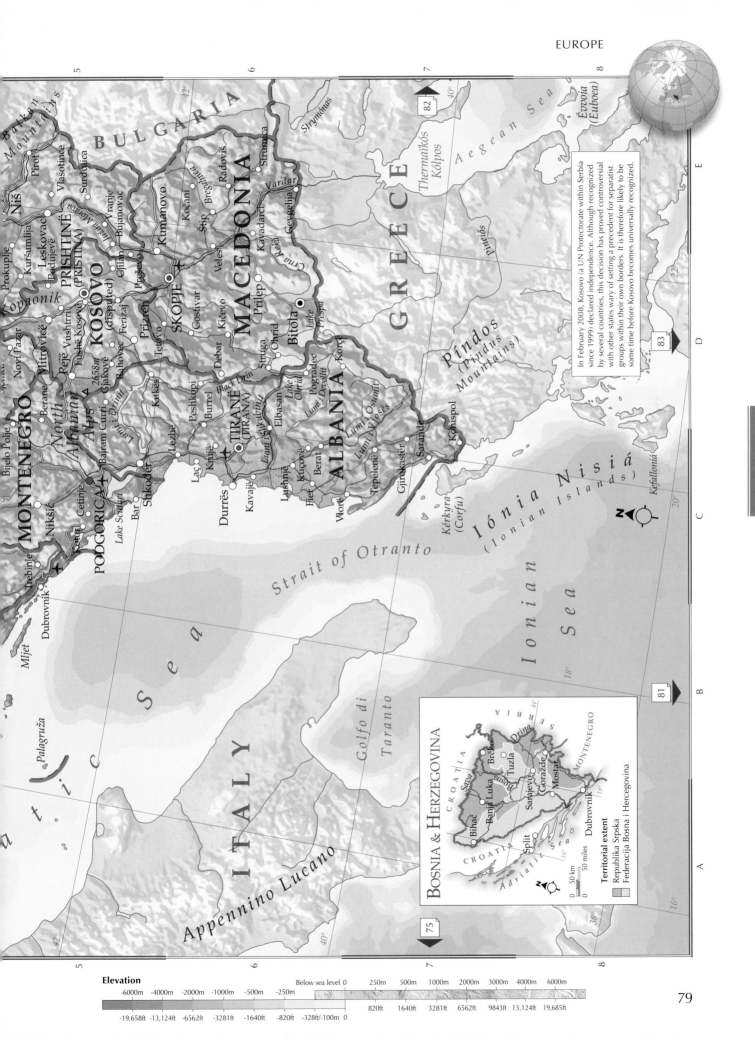

In February 2008, Kosovo (a UN Protectorate within Serbia since 1999) declared independence. Although recognized by several countries, this decision has proved controversial with other states wary of setting a precedent for separatist groups within their own borders. It is therefore likely to be some time before Kosovo becomes universally recognized.

BOSNIA & HERZEGOVINA

Territorial extent
Republika Srpska
Federacija Bosna i Hercegovina

Elevation

							Below sea level 0	250m	500m	1000m	2000m	3000m	4000m	6000m
-6000m	-4000m	-2000m	-1000m	-500m	-250m			820ft	1640ft	3281ft	6562ft	9843ft	13,124ft	19,685ft
-19,658ft	-13,124ft	-6562ft	-3281ft	-1640ft	-820ft	-328ft/-100m 0								

The Mediterranean

ATLANTIC

OCEAN

*Bay of
Biscay*

Quimper

St-Nazaire
Île d'Yeu
Nantes

Tours
Loire

Île de Ré
Île d'Oléron

Limoges

F R A N C E

Dijon

Seine

Zürich
BERN
SWITZ.

Lyon
*Mont Blanc
4807m*

LIECH.
VADUZ

GERMANY

München
(Munich)

Innsbruck

Milano
(Milan)

Venezia
(Venice)

Clermont-Ferrand

Bordeaux

Dordogne

Garonne

*Massif
Central*

Nîmes
Montpellier

Toulouse

Marseille

MONACO

Nice
Côte d'Azur

Torino
(Turin)

Rhône

Po

Bologna

Genova
(Genoa)

*Golfo di
Genova*

Pisa

*Ligurian
Sea*

ROMA
(ROME)

**SAN
MARINO**

*Gulf
of
Venice*

*Alpi
Dolomitiche*

Santander

A Coruña

Vigo

Porto

PORTUGAL

Bilbao

Cordillera Cantábrica

Duero

Valladolid

Sistema Ibérico

Ebro

Pyrenees

ANDORRA

Perpignan

Zaragoza

Barcelona

Tarragona

Costa Brava

Golfe du Lion

*Corse
(Corsica)*

Ajaccio

*Isola
d'Elba*

**VATICAN
CITY**

Isola Asinara

Sassari

*Sardegna
(Sardinia)*

*Tyrrhenian
Sea*

LISBOA
(LISBON)

Tagus

MADRID

Sistema Central

S P A I N

Castellón
de la Plana

Valencia

*Menorca
(Minorca)*

*Mallorca
(Majorca)*

Palma

*Golfo de
Valencia*

Ibiza

Formentera

*Islas Baleares
(Balearic Islands)*

Cagliari

M e d i t

Sevilla
(Seville)

Sierra Morena

Guadalquivir

Sistemas Béticos

Murcia

Alicante

Costa Blanca

Cartagena

*Cap
Bougaroun*

**ALGER
(ALGIERS)**

Tizi Ouzou

Annaba

*Golfe de
Tunis*

TUNIS

*Sicilia
(Sicily)*

Palermo

Cap Bon

*Isola di
Pantelle*

Golfo de
Cádiz

Cádiz

Málaga

Almería

Costa del Sol

**GIBRALTAR
(to UK)**

Strait of Gibraltar

Ceuta (to Spain)

Tanger

Tétouan

Melilla
(to Spain)

Oran

Mostaganem

Atlas Tellien

Constantine

Sétif

Massif de l'Aurès

*Chott el
Hodna*

Sousse

Sfax

*Golfe
de
Hammamet*

*Isole
Pelag.*

*Îles de
Kerkenah*

Fès

Tlemcen

Oujda

*Chott ech
Chergui*

MOROCCO

RABAT

Casablanca

Moyen Atlas

Haut Atlas

Hauts Plateaux

Atlas Mountains

Chott Melghir

A L G E R I A

*Chott
el Jerid*

Gabès

*Golfe de
Gabès*

Île de Jerba

TUNISIA

Safi

**TARABULUS
(TRIPOLI)**

Gharyān

MALTA

Mediterranean Sea

14°30'

36°

Victoria

Nadur

*Comino
(Kemmuna)*

Gozo

Mġarr

Mellieħa

Mosta

Malta

Ħamrun

Rabat

St Julian's

Sliema

VALLETTA

Paola

Birżebbuġa

250m/820ft
100m/328ft
Sea Level

0 km   10
0 miles   10

CYPRUS

**TURKISH REPUBLIC OF
NORTHERN CYPRUS**
(recognized only
by Turkey)

Mediterranean Sea

Lapta
(Lápithos)

Girne
(Kerýneia)

Yenierenköy
(Agialoúsa)

Güzelyurt Körfezi
(Kólpos Mórfou)

Değirmenlik
(Kythréa)

*Gazimağusa Körfezi
(Kólpos Ammóchostos)*

Pólis

35°

NICOSIA

Gazimağusa
(Ammóchostos,
Famagusta)

Páfos

Tróodos

Dhekélia

Lárnaka

*Sovereign
Base Area
(to UK)*

Akrotíri

*Sovereign
Base Area
(to UK)*

Lemesós
(Limassol)

34°

33°

1000m/3281ft
500m/1640ft
250m/820ft
Sea Level

0 km   25
0 miles   25

S a h a r a

0 km   400
0 miles   400

Population   ● National capital

○ below 50,000   ○ 50,000 to 100,000   ◉ 100,000 to 500,000   ■ above 500,000

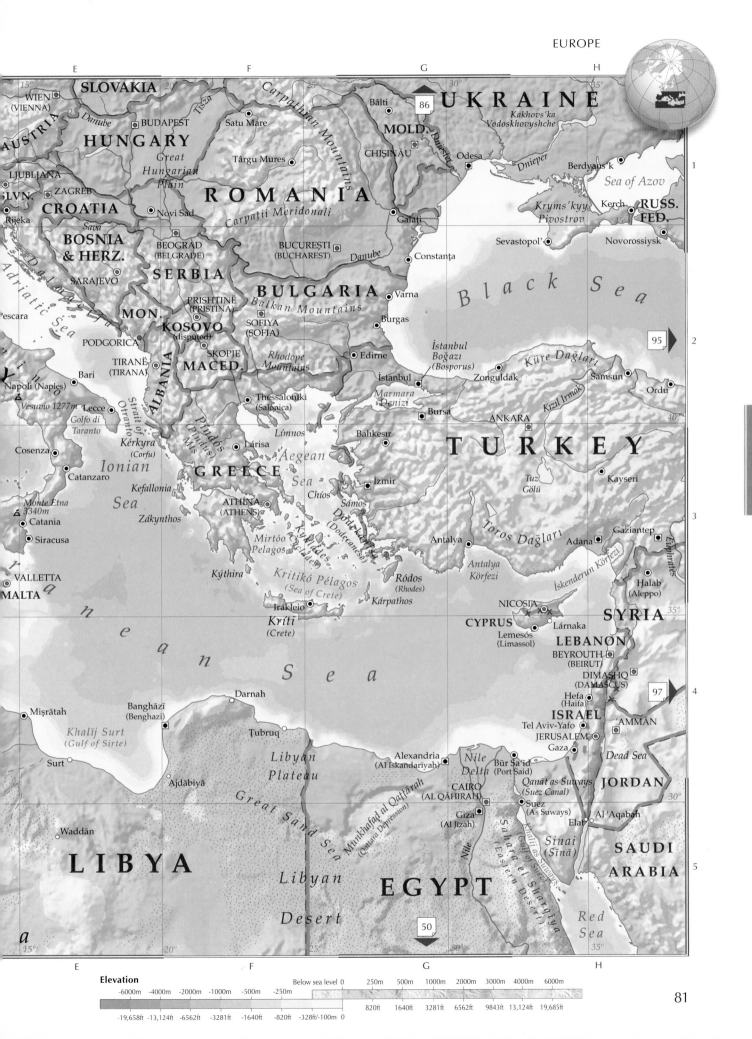

SLOVAKIA

WIEN
(VIENNA)

AUSTRIA

Danube

BUDAPEST

HUNGARY

Great
Hungarian
Plain

Tisza

Carpathian Mountains

Satu Mare

Bâlti

86

UKRAINE

MOLD.

CHIŞINĂU

Dniester

Kakhovs'ka
Vodoskhovyshche

Odesa

Dnieper

Berdyans'k

1

Sea of Azov

LJUBLJANA

SLVN.

ZAGREB

CROATIA

Rijeka

Sava

Novi Sad

ROMANIA

Târgu Mures

Carpaţii Meridonali

Galaţi

Kryms'kyy
Pivostrov

Kerch

RUSS.
FED.

Sevastopol'

Novorossiysk

Adriatic Sea

Dalmatia

escara

BOSNIA
& HERZ.

SARAJEVO

SERBIA

BEOGRAD
(BELGRADE)

PRISHTINË
(PRISTINA)

Danube

BUCUREŞTI
(BUCHAREST)

Constanţa

Black Sea

Varna

2

95

MON.

PODGORICA

KOSOVO
(disputed)

SOFIYA
(SOFIA)

BULGARIA

Balkan Mountains

Burgas

İstanbul
Boğazı
(Bosporus)

TIRANË
(TIRANA)

SKOPJE

MACED.

Rhodope
Mountains

Edirne

İstanbul

Zonguldak

Küre Dağları

Samsun

Ordu

Bari

ALBANIA

Napoli (Naples)

Vesuvio 1277m

Lecce

Strait of Otranto

Kérkyra
(Corfu)

Pindus
(Pindos)
Mts

Thessaloníki
(Salonica)

Límnos

Lárisa

Marmara
Denizi

Bursa

ANKARA

Balıkesır

Kızıl Irmak

40°

TURKEY

Golfo di
Taranto

Cosenza

Ionian

Catanzaro

Kefallonia

Aegean
Sea

İzmir

Chíos

Sámos

Tuz
Gölü

Kayseri

3

Monte Etna
3340m

Catania

Siracusa

Sea

Zákynthos

ATHINA
(ATHENS)

Kýklades
(Cyclades)

Dodekánisa
(Dodecanese)

Antalya

Toros Dağları

Antalya
Körfezi

Adana

Gaziantep

Euphrates

VALLETTA

MALTA

Kýthira

Mirtóo
Pélagos

Kritikó Pélagos
(Sea of Crete)

Ródos
(Rhodes)

Kárpathos

İskenderun Körfezi

Halab
(Aleppo)

NICOSIA

CYPRUS

Lemesós
(Limassol)

Lárnaka

SYRIA

35°

Mediterranean

Irákleio

Kríti
(Crete)

LEBANON

BEYROUTH
(BEIRUT)

DIMASHQ
(DAMASCUS)

Hefa
(Haifa)

97

4

Sea

Darnah

Banghāzī
(Benghazi)

Mişrātah

Khalīj Surt
(Gulf of Sirte)

Ţubruq

ISRAEL

Tel Aviv-Yafo

JERUSALEM

Gaza

AMMAN

Dead Sea

Surt

Ajdābiyā

Alexandria
(Al Iskandarīyah)

Nile
Delta

Būr Sa'īd
(Port Said)

Qanāt as Suways
(Suez Canal)

JORDAN

30°

Waddān

Libyan
Plateau

Great Sand Sea

Munkhafad al Qattārah
(Qatara Depression)

CAIRO
(AL QĀHIRAH)

Giza
(Al Jīzah)

Suez
(As Suways)

Elat

Al 'Aqabah

Khalīj as Suways
(Gulf of Suez)

Aş Şahrā' al Sharqīyah
(Eastern Desert)

Sinai
(Sīnā)

SAUDI

LIBYA

Libyan

EGYPT

50

Desert

Nile

Red
Sea

ARABIA

5

a

15°

20°

25°

30°

35°

E

F

G

H

Elevation

-6000m -4000m -2000m -1000m -500m -250m

Below sea level 0 250m 500m 1000m 2000m 3000m 4000m 6000m

-19,658ft -13,124ft -6562ft -3281ft -1640ft -820ft -328ft/-100m 0

820ft 1640ft 3281ft 6562ft 9843ft 13,124ft 19,685ft

Bulgaria & Greece

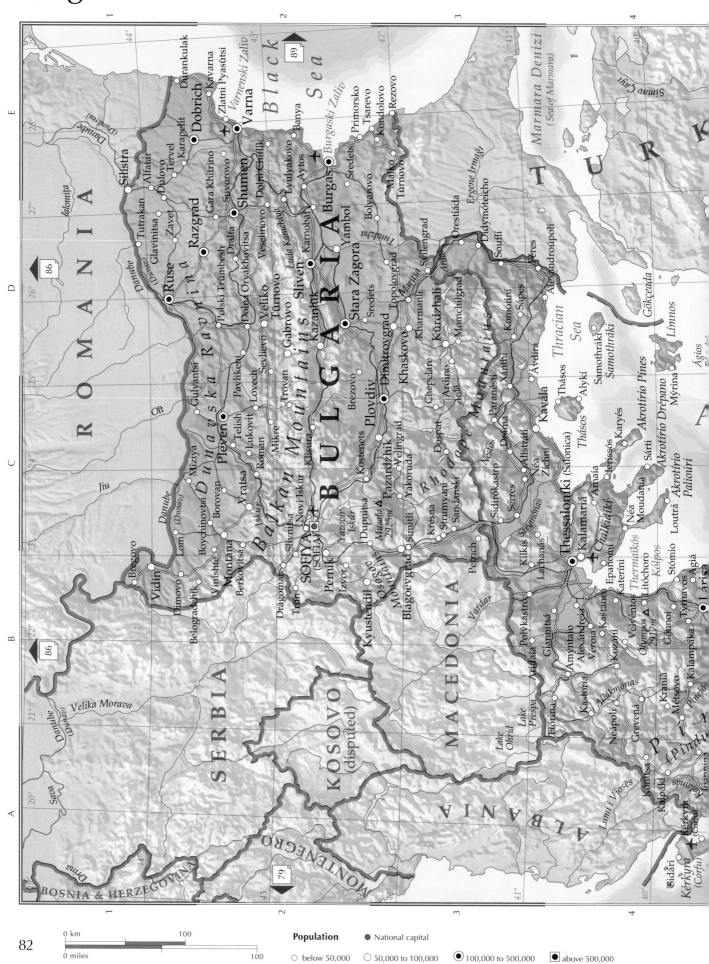

Population   ● National capital

○ below 50,000   ○ 50,000 to 100,000   ◉ 100,000 to 500,000   ◼ above 500,000

0 km   100

0 miles   100

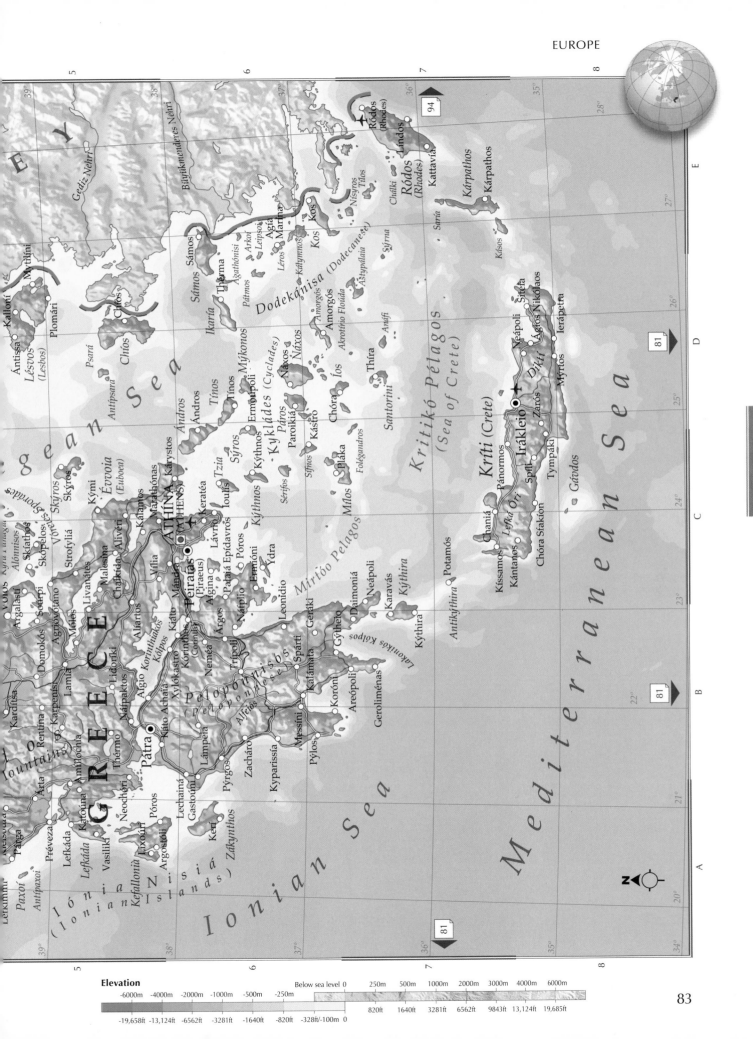

Elevation

-6000m	-4000m	-2000m	-1000m	-500m	-250m	Below sea level 0	250m	500m	1000m	2000m	3000m	4000m	6000m
-19,658ft	-13,124ft	-6562ft	-3281ft	-1640ft	-820ft	-328ft/-100m 0	820ft	1640ft	3281ft	6562ft	9843ft	13,124ft	19,685ft

The Baltic States & Belarus

Population ● National capital

○ below 50,000 ○ 50,000 to 100,000 ◉ 100,000 to 500,000 ■ above 500,000

0 km   100

0 miles   100

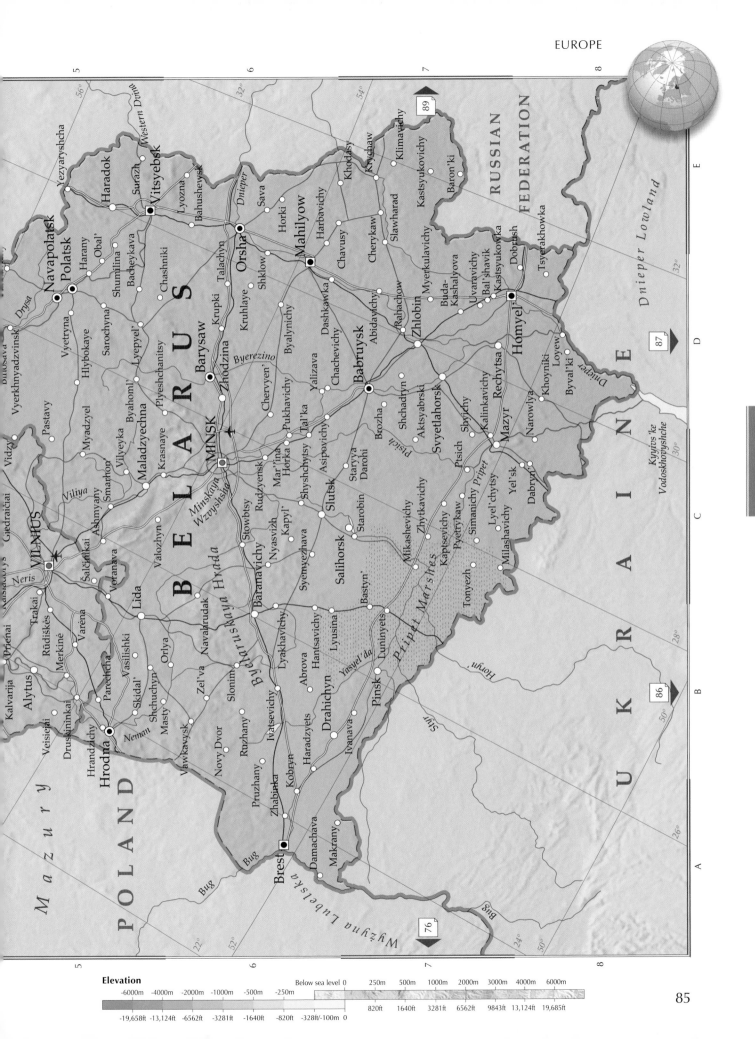

Elevation

| -6000m | -4000m | -2000m | -1000m | -500m | -250m | Below sea level 0 | 250m | 500m | 1000m | 2000m | 3000m | 4000m | 6000m |

| -19,658ft | -13,124ft | -6562ft | -3281ft | -1640ft | -820ft | -328ft/-100m 0 | 820ft | 1640ft | 3281ft | 6562ft | 9843ft | 13,124ft | 19,685ft |

85

Ukraine, Moldova & Romania

POLAND

BELARUS

Małopolska

Wyżyna Lubelska

Carpathian Mountains

Tatra Mountains

SLOVAKIA

Slovenské Rudohorie

HUNGARY

Great Hungarian Plain

UKR

MOLDOVA

Podil's'ka Vysochina

Carpathian Mountains

Transnistria

Transylvania

Muntii Apuseni

ROMANIA

Carpatii Meridionali

SERBIA

Velika Morava

Danube

Wallachia

Danube (Dunărea)

Dunavska Ravnina

BULGARIA

Lacul Razim
Lacul Sinoie

Pripet
Pripet Marshes
Kovel'
Sarny
Olevs'k
Ovruch
Volodymyr-Volyns'kyy
Novovolyns'k
Kivertsi
Korosten
Sokal'
Luts'k
Rivne
Malyn
Dubno
Novohrad-Volyns'kyy
Radomyshl'
Chervonohrad
Slavuta
Shepetivka
Zhytomyr
Zhovkva
Kremenets'
Polonne
Berdychiv
Yavoriv
Izyaslav
L'viv
Zolochiv
Zbarazh
Starokostyantyniv
Horodok
Khmel'nyts'kyy
Sambir
Khodoriv
Berezhany
Ternopil'
Drohobych
Zhydachiv
Vinnytsya
Boryslav
Kozyatyn
Stryy
Kalush
Chortkiv
Lypovets'
Dolyna
Zhmerynka
Haysyn
Ivano-Frankivs'k
Uzhhorod
Nadvirna
Kam"yanets'-Podil's'kyy
Tul'chyn
Mukacheve
Kolomyya
Mohyliv-Podil's'kyy
Berehove
Chernivtsi
Dniester
Vynohradiv
Khust
Hora Hoverla 2061m
Darabani
Soroca
Balta
Negreşti-Oaş
Rădăuţi
Dorohoi
Satu Mare
Solca
Botoşani
Bălţi
Rîbniţa
Kotovs'k
Baia Mare
Borşa
Suceava
Carei
Baia Sprie
Fălticeni
Paşcani
Marghita
Năsăud
Târgu-Neamţ
Iaşi
Călăraşi
Orhei
Dubăsari
Şimleu Silvaniei
Zalău
Bistriţa
Topliţa
Bicaz
Roman
CHIŞINĂU (KISHINEV)
Străşeni
Oradea
Dej
Reghin
Piatra-Neamţ
Tighina (Bendery)
Aleşd
Beiuş
Cluj-Napoca
Gheorgheni
Bacău
Hînceşti
Tiraspol
Salonta
Turda
Ludus
Târgu Mureş
Miercurea-Ciuc
Vaslui
Curtici
Ineu
Abrud
Aiud
Medias
Cristuru Secuiesc
Târgu Ocna
Bârlad
Comrat
Arad
Alba Iulia
Rupea
Basarabeasca
Sânnicolau Mare
Mures
Deva
Sibiu
Făgăraş
Târgu Secuiesc
Adjud
Ciadîr-Lunga
Lipova
Hunedoara
Codlea
Sfântu Gheorghe
Taraclia
Jimbolia
Timişoara
Hateg
Cisnădie
Vârful Moldoveanu 2544m
Câmpulung
Braşov
Focşani
Cahul
Artsyz
Lugoj
Oţelu Roşu
Petroşani
Râşnov
Sinaia
Râmnicu Sărat
Galaţi
Bolhrad
Bocşa
Reşiţa
Câmpina
Reni
Ozero Yalpuh
Braila
Kiliya
Reşiţa
Anina
Târgu Jiu
Călimăneşti
Curtea de Argeş
Moreni
Buzău
Macin
Izmayil
Oraviţa
Moldova Nouă
Râmnicu Vâlcea
Mizil
Isaccea
Tulcea
Orşova
Motru
Pitesti
Târgovişte
Ploieşti
Babadag
Drobeta-Turnu Severin
Strehaia
Drăgăşani
Titu
Urziceni
Ţăndărei
Hârşova
Filiaşi
Bâlea
Buftea
Ialomiţa
Slobozia
Feteşti
Craiova
Slatina
BUCUREŞTI (BUCHAREST)
Bâlea
Caracal
Călăraşi
Medgidia
Calafat
Bâileşti
Roşiori de Vede
Alexandria
Olteniţa
Constanţa
Corabia
Oll
Turnu Măgurele
Giurgiu
Techirghiol
Eforie Sud
Zimnicea
Mangalia

0 km 100
0 miles 100

Population   ● National capital

○ below 50,000   ○ 50,000 to 100,000   ◉ 100,000 to 500,000   ◼ above 500,000

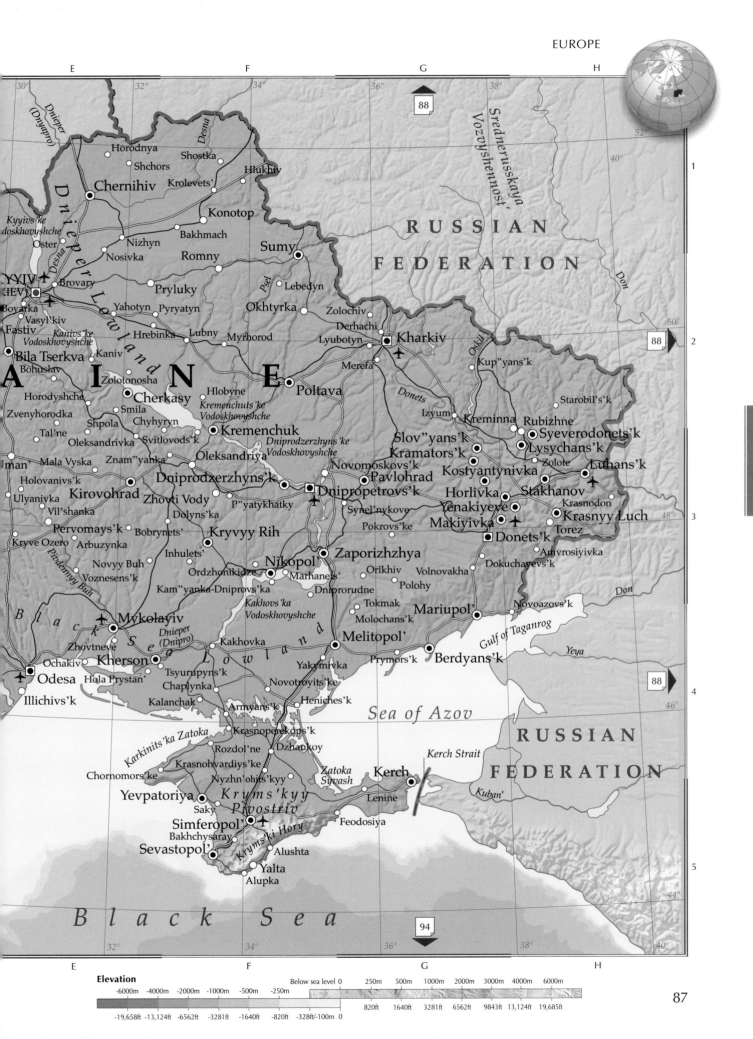

RUSSIAN

FEDERATION

UKRAINE

Black Sea

Dnieper Lowland

RUSSIAN

FEDERATION

Sea of Azov

Black Sea

Kryms'kyy Pivostriv

Cities and Features (reading the map):

Dnieper (Dnypro), Horodnya, Shchors, Shostka, Chernihiv, Krolevets', Hlukhiv, Desna, Konotop, Bakhmach, Nizhyn, Romny, Sumy, Nosivka, Pryluky, Lebedyn, Okhtyrka, Zolochiv, Derhachi, Srednerusskaya Vozvyshennost', Don

KYYIV, KIEV, Brovary, Yahotyn, Pyryatyn, Hrebinka, Lubny, Myrhorod, Lyubotyn, Kharkiv, Merefa, Kup"yans'k, Oskil, Boyarka, Vasyl'kiv, Fastiv, Kaniv, Bila Tserkva, Bohuslav, Zolotonosha, Cherkasy, Poltava, Donets, Izyum, Starobil's'k, Kremminna, Rubizhne, Syeverodonets'k

Horodyshche, Zvenyhorodka, Smila, Chyhyryn, Hlobyne, Kremenchuts'ke Vodoskhovyshche, Slov"yans'k, Lysychans'k, Tal'ne, Shpola, Svitlovods'k, Oleksandrivka, Kremenchuk, Dniprodzerzhyns'ke Vodoskhovyshche, Kramators'k, Zolote, Luhans'k, Kostyantynivka, Uman', Mala Vyska, Znam"yanka, Oleksandriya, Novomoskovs'k, Dniprodzerzhyns'k, Dnipropetrovs'k, Pavlohrad, Horlivka, Stakhanov, Krasnodon

Holovanivs'k, Kirovohrad, Zhovti Vody, Vil'shanka, Dolyns'ka, P"yatykhatky, Synel'nykove, Yenakiyeve, Krasnyy Luch, Pervomays'k, Bobrynets', Kryvyy Rih, Pokrovs'ke, Makiyivka, Torez, Kryve Ozero, Arbuzynka, Inhulets', Zaporizhzhya, Donets'k, Amvrosiyivka, Novyy Buh, Voznesens'k, Ordzhonikidze, Nikopol, Marhanets', Orikhiv, Volnovakha, Dokuchayevs'k, Don, Pivdennyy Buh, Kam"yanka-Dniprovs'ka, Dniprorudne, Polohy, Novoazovs'k, Mykolayiv, Kakhovs'ka Vodoskhovyshche, Tokmak, Mariupol', Zhovtneve, Molochans'k, Gulf of Taganrog, Yeya, Kherson, Kakhovka, Melitopol', Berdyans'k, Ochakiv, Dnieper (Dnipro), Yakymivka, Prymors'k, Odesa, Hola Prystan', Tsyurupyns'k, Chaplynka, Novotroyits'ke, Illichivs'k, Kalanchak, Heniches'k, Armyans'k, Sea of Azov

Karkinits'ka Zatoka, Krasnoperekops'k, Rozdol'ne, Dzhankoy, Kerch Strait, Kuban', Chornomors'ke, Krasnohvardiys'ke, Nyzhn'ohirs'kyy, Zatoka Syvash, Kerch, Yevpatoriya, Saky, Simferopol', Lenine, Bakhchysaray, Feodosiya, Sevastopol', Alushta, Yalta, Alupka, Kryms'ki Hory

Black Sea

Elevation

-6000m -4000m -2000m -1000m -500m -250m   Below sea level 0 250m 500m 1000m 2000m 3000m 4000m 6000m

-19,658ft -13,124ft -6562ft -3281ft -1640ft -820ft -328ft/-100m 0   820ft 1640ft 3281ft 6562ft 9843ft 13,124ft 19,685ft

European Russia

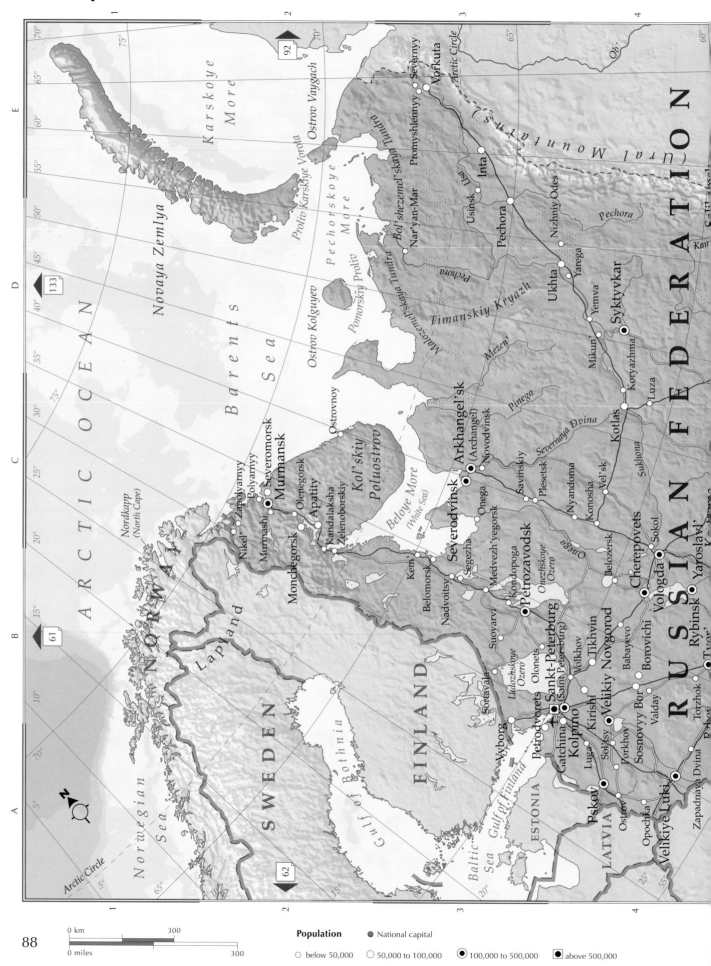

0 km   300

0 miles   300

Population   ● National capital

○ below 50,000   ○ 50,000 to 100,000   ◉ 100,000 to 500,000   ◼ above 500,000

Elevation

-6000m	-4000m	-2000m	-1000m	-500m	-250m	Below sea level 0	250m	500m	1000m	2000m	3000m	4000m	6000m

| -19,658ft | -13,124ft | -6562ft | -3281ft | -1640ft | -820ft | -328ft/-100m | 0 | 820ft | 1640ft | 3281ft | 6562ft | 9843ft | 13,124ft | 19,685ft |

North & West Asia

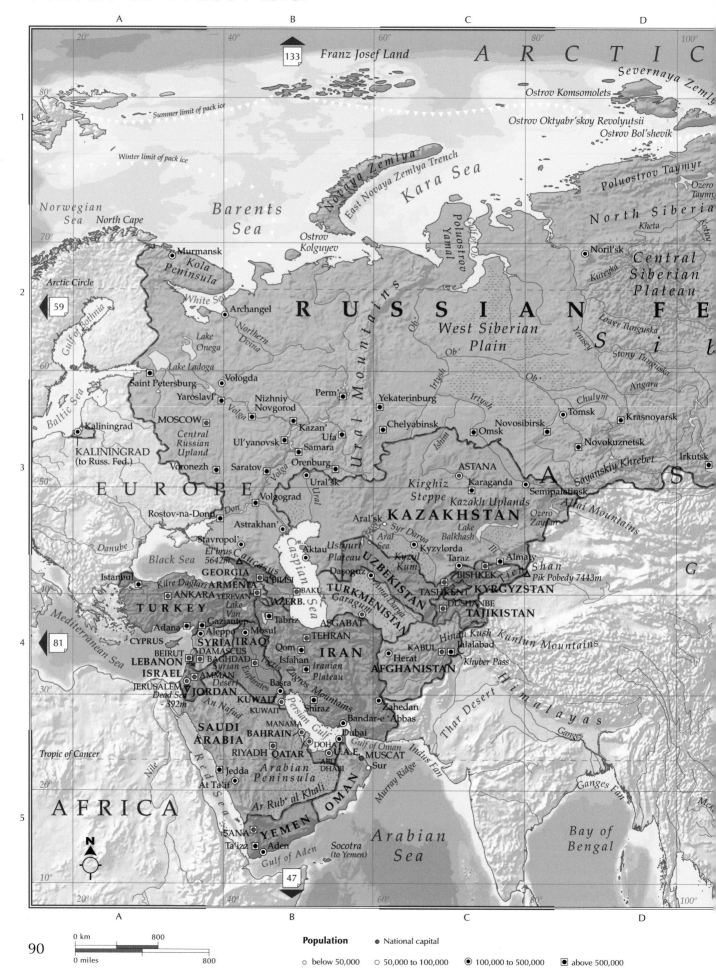

ARCTIC

Franz Josef Land

Severnaya Zemlya

Ostrov Komsomolets

Ostrov Oktyabr'skoy Revolyutsii
Ostrov Bol'shevik

Poluostrov Taymyr

Ozero Taymy

Summer limit of pack ice

Winter limit of pack ice

Novaya Zemlya

East Novaya Zemlya Trench

Kara Sea

North Siberia

Kheta

Kotuy

Norwegian Sea

North Cape

Barents Sea

Ostrov Kolguyev

Gulf of Ob

Poluostrov Yamal

Noril'sk

Central Siberian Plateau

Kureyka

Arctic Circle

Murmansk

Kola Peninsula

White Sea

RUSSIAN FE

Lower Tunguska

Archangel

Northern Devina

Ural Mountains

Ob'

West Siberian Plain

Irtysh

Si

Stony Tunguska

Lake Onega

Lake Ladoga

Vologda

Perm'

Yekaterinburg

Ob'

Irtysh

Tomsk

Chulym

Angara

Saint Petersburg

Yaroslavl'

Nizhniy Novgorod

Chelyabinsk

Novosibirsk

Krasnoyarsk

Gulf of Bothnia

Baltic Sea

Kaliningrad

MOSCOW

Volga

Kazan'

Ufa

Omsk

Novokuznetsk

Central Russian Upland

Ul'yanovsk

Samara

ASTANA

Sayanskiy Khrebet

Irkutsk

KALININGRAD
(to Russ. Fed.)

Voronezh

Saratov

Orenburg

Ishim

Karaganda

A

S

Volga

EUROPE

Ural'sk

Kirghiz Steppe

Semipalatinsk

Altai Mountains

Volgograd

Ural

Kazakh Uplands

Ozero Zaysan

G

Rostov-na-Donu

Don

Astrakhan'

Aral'sk

KAZAKHSTAN

Lake Zaysan

Stavropol'

Ustyurt Plateau

Syr Darya

Aral Sea

Lake Balkhash

Ili

Almaty

El'brus 5642m

Caucasus

Caspian Sea

Aktau

Kyzyl Kum

Kyzylorda

Taraz

BISHKEK

Shan

Pik Pobedy 7443m

Black Sea

GEORGIA

TBILISI

Dasoguz

UZBEKISTAN

KYRGYZSTAN

Istanbul

Küre Daglari

ARMENIA

BAKU

Amu Darya

TASHKENT

DUSHANBE

Kirklareli

ANKARA

YEREVAN

AZERB.

TURKMENISTAN

Garagum

TAJIKISTAN

TURKEY

Lake Van

Tabriz

ASGABAT

Hindu Kush

Kunlun Mountains

Gaziantep

Mosul

TEHRAN

KABUL

Jalalabad

Adana

Aleppo

Qom

IRAN

Herat

Khyber Pass

CYPRUS

SYRIA

IRAQ

Isfahan

AFGHANISTAN

BEIRUT

DAMASCUS

BAGHDAD

Iranian Plateau

LEBANON

Syrian Desert

Tigris

Euphrates

Zagros Mountains

ISRAEL

AMMAN

Basra

Shiraz

Zahedan

JERUSALEM

JORDAN

KUWAIT

Persian Gulf

Bandar-e 'Abbas

Dead Sea -392m

An Nafud

KUWAIT

MANAMA

OMAN

Thar Desert

Himalayas

Dubai

Ganges

SAUDI ARABIA

BAHRAIN

DOHA

U.A.E.

MUSCAT

Indus Fan

Tropic of Cancer

RIYADH

QATAR

ABU DHABI

Sur

Ganges Fan

Jedda

Arabian Peninsula

At Ta'if

Red Sea

Ar Rub' al Khali

OMAN

Murray Ridge

Gulf of Oman

Bay of Bengal

AFRICA

SANA

YEMEN

Ta'izz

Aden

Socotra (to Yemen)

Arabian Sea

Gulf of Aden

Nile

Mediterranean Sea

N

90

0 km   800
0 miles   800

Population   ● National capital

○ below 50,000   ○ 50,000 to 100,000   ◉ 100,000 to 500,000   ▣ above 500,000

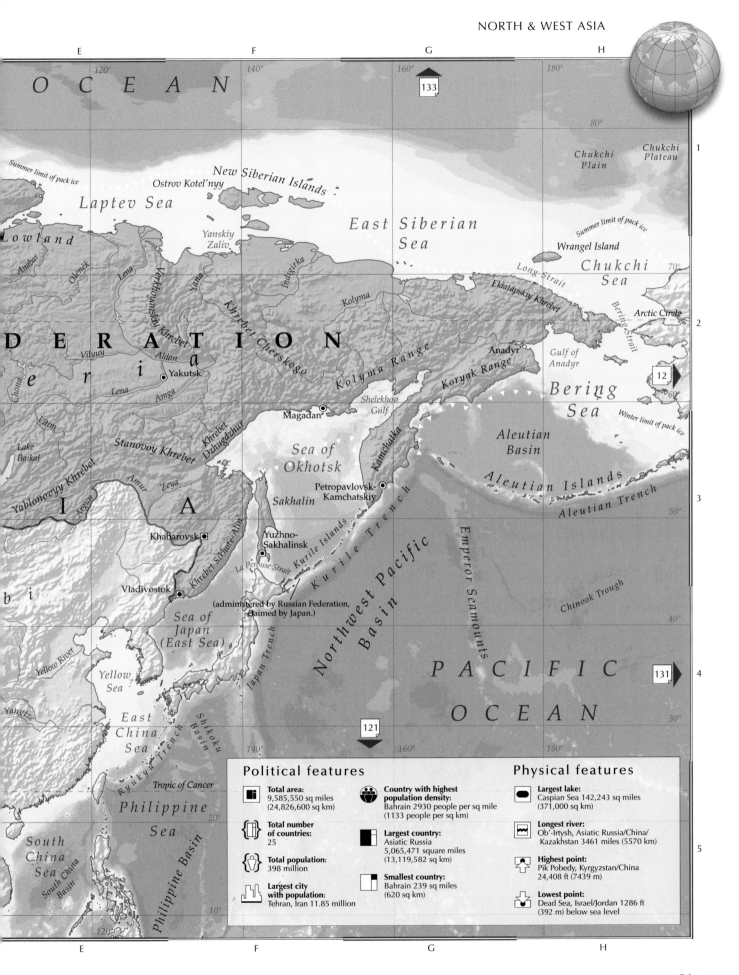

O C E A N

133

Chukchi
Plain

Chukchi
Plateau

Summer limit of pack ice

Laptev Sea

New Siberian Islands

Ostrov Kotel'nyy

East Siberian
Sea

Summer limit of pack ice

Lowland

Yanskiy
Zaliv

Wrangel Island

Chukchi
Sea

Anabar

Olenek

Lena

Yana

Indigirka

Long Strait

Ekiatapskiy Khrebet

Bering Strait

Arctic Circle

Vilyuy

Khrebet Cherskogo

Kolyma

Kolyma Range

Koryak Range

Anadyr

Gulf of
Anadyr

12

D E R A T I O N

e r i a

Chona

Yakutsk

Aldan

Bering
Sea

Lena

Amga

Shelekhov
Gulf

Vitim

Magadan

Kamchatka

Aleutian
Basin

Lake
Baikal

Stanovoy Khrebet

Khrebet
Dzhugdzhur

Sea of
Okhotsk

Aleutian Islands

Yablonovyy Khrebet

Amur

Zeya

Sakhalin

Petropavlovsk-
Kamchatskiy

Aleutian Trench

Argun

Winter limit of pack ice

I   A

Khabarovsk

Yuzhno-
Sakhalinsk

Kurile Islands

Kurile Trench

Emperor Seamounts

Chinook Trough

Khrebet Sikhote-Alin

La Perouse Strait

Vladivostok

(administered by Russian Federation,
claimed by Japan.)

Northwest Pacific
Basin

b   i

Sea of
Japan
(East Sea)

Japan Trench

P A C I F I C

131

Yellow River

Yellow
Sea

Shikoku
Basin

O C E A N

121

Yangtze

East
China
Sea

Ryukyu Trench

Tropic of Cancer

Philippine

Sea

South
China
Sea

South China
Basin

Philippine Basin

Political features

Total area:
9,585,550 sq miles
(24,826,600 sq km)

**Country with highest
population density:**
Bahrain 2930 people per sq mile
(1133 people per sq km)

**Total number
of countries:**
25

Largest country:
Asiatic Russia
5,065,471 square miles
(13,119,582 sq km)

Total population:
398 million

**Largest city
with population:**
Tehran, Iran 11.85 million

Smallest country:
Bahrain 239 sq miles
(620 sq km)

Physical features

Largest lake:
Caspian Sea 142,243 sq miles
(371,000 sq km)

Longest river:
Ob'-Irtysh, Asiatic Russia/China/
Kazakhstan 3461 miles (5570 km)

Highest point:
Pik Pobedy, Kyrgyzstan/China
24,408 ft (7439 m)

Lowest point:
Dead Sea, Israel/Jordan 1286 ft
(392 m) below sea level

Russia & Kazakhstan

0 km   600
0 miles   600

Population   ● National capital

○ below 50,000   ○ 50,000 to 100,000   ◉ 100,000 to 500,000   ■ above 500,000

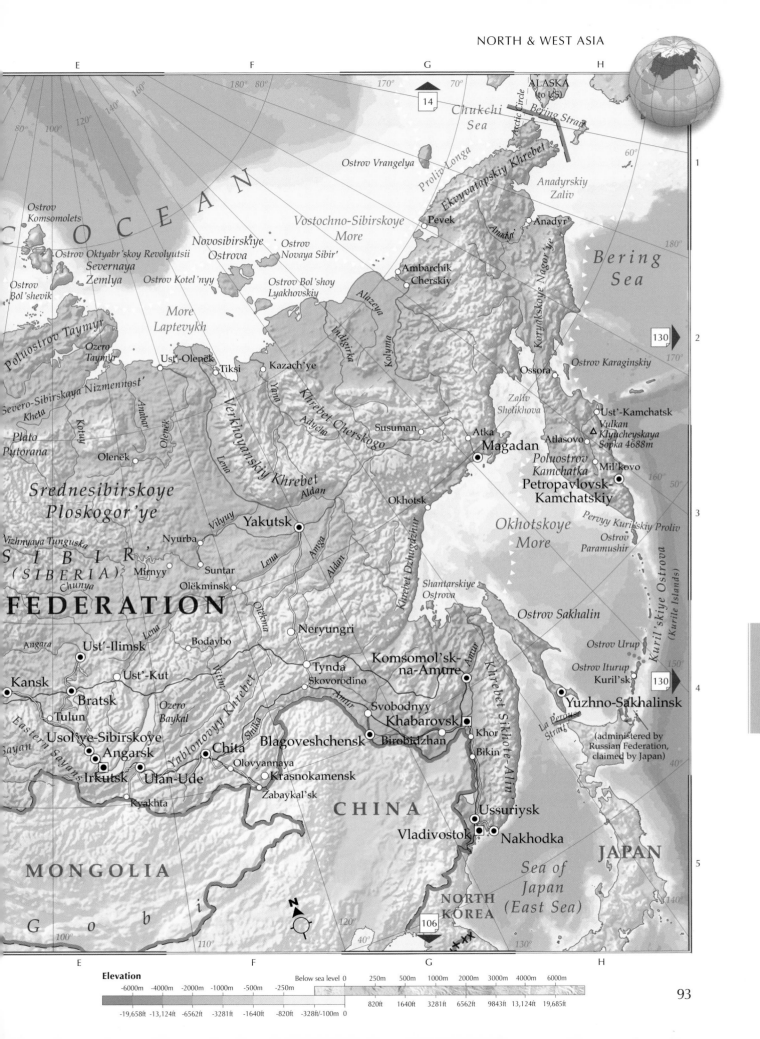

ALASKA
(to US)

*Chukchi
Sea*

Arctic Circle

Bering Strait

C O C E A N

*Ostrov
Komsomolets*

Ostrov Vrangelya

Prolip Longa

Ekvyvatapskiy Khrebet

*Anadyrskiy
Zaliv*

*Bering
Sea*

Ostrov Oktyabr'skoy Revolyutsii

*Severnaya
Zemlya*

*Novosibirskiye
Ostrova*

*Vostochno-Sibirskoye
More*

*Ostrov
Novaya Sibir'*

Pevek

Anadyr'

Anadyr'

130

*Ostrov
Bol'shevik*

Ostrov Kotel'nyy

*Ostrov Bol'shoy
Lyakhovskiy*

Ambarchik
Cherskiy

Koryakskoye Nagor'ye

Ostrov Karaginskiy

Poluostrov Taymyr

*More
Laptevykh*

Alazeya

Ossora

*Zaliv
Shelikhova*

Ostrov Karaginskiy

*Ozero
Taymyr*

Ust'-Olenëk Tiksi

Kazach'ye

Indigirka

Kolyma

Ust'-Kamchatsk

Severo-Sibirskaya Nizmennost'

Kheta

Yana

Khrebet Cherskogo

Susuman

Atka

Atlasovo

Vulkan
Klyucheyskaya
Sopka 4688m

Kotuy

Anabar

Olenëk

Adycha

Magadan

*Poluostrov
Kamchatka*

Mil'kovo

*Plato
Putorana*

Olenëk

Lena

Aldan

Okhotsk

Petropavlovsk-
Kamchatskiy

*Srednesibirskoye
Ploskogor'ye*

Vilyuy

Yakutsk

*Okhotskoye
More*

Pervyy Kurilskiy Proliv

*Ostrov
Paramushir*

Vizhnyaya Tunguska

Nyurba

Lena

Anga

Aldan

Khrebet Dzhugdzhur

S I B I R '
(SIBERIA)

Mirnyy

Suntar

*Shantarskiye
Ostrova*

Chunya

Olëkminsk

Ostrov Sakhalin

Ostrov Urup

F E D E R A T I O N

Olëkma

Neryungri

Ostrov Iturup

130

Angara

Ust'-Ilimsk

Bodaybo

Vitim

Tynda

Amur

Khrebet Sikhote-Alin'

Kuril'sk

Yuzhno-Sakhalinsk

Kansk

Ust'-Kut

Skovorodino

Kuril'skiye Ostrova (Kurile Islands)

Bratsk

*Ozero
Baykal*

Svobodnyy

Khabarovsk

*La Perouse
Strait*

Tulun

Komsomol'sk-
na-Amure

Khor

(administered by
Russian Federation,
claimed by Japan)

Eastern Sayans

Usol'ye-Sibirskoye

Yablonovyy Khrebet

Amur

Blagoveshchensk

Birobidzhan

Bikin

Angarsk

Chita

Shilka

Olovyannaya

Sayan

Irkutsk

Ulan-Ude

Krasnokamensk

C H I N A

Ussuriysk

Kyakhta

Zabaykal'sk

Vladivostok

Nakhodka

J A P A N

M O N G O L I A

*Sea of
Japan
(East Sea)*

G o b i

N

NORTH
KOREA

106

Elevation

						Below sea level 0	250m	500m	1000m	2000m	3000m	4000m	6000m
-6000m	-4000m	-2000m	-1000m	-500m	-250m								
-19,658ft	-13,124ft	-6562ft	-3281ft	-1640ft	-820ft	-328ft/-100m	0	820ft	1640ft	3281ft	6562ft	9843ft	13,124ft	19,685ft

Turkey & The Caucasus

ROMANIA

Danube

Iacul Sinoie

BULGARIA

Varnenski Zaliv

Burgaski Zaliv

Maritsa

UKRAINE

Kryms'kyy Pivostriv

Black Sea

82

Kırklareli

Edirne

Ergene Çayi

Çorlu

Tekirdag

İstanbul *İstanbul Boğazı (Bosporus)*

İzmit

Adapazarı

Zonguldak

Bartın

Cide

İnebolu

Sinop

Gerze

Küre Dağları

Karabük

Kastamonu

Kargı

Çerkeş

Bafra

Samsun

Ünye

Ordu

Canik Dağları

Marmara Denizi (Sea of Marmara)

İznik Gölü

Bursa

Bilecik

Bolu

Gerede

Çankırı

Kızıl Irmak

Merzifon

Çorum

Tokat

Zara

Çanakkale Boğazı (Dardanelles)

Bandırma

Yalova

Çanakkale

Balıkesir

Simav Çayı

Bozüyük

Eskişehir

ANKARA

Kalecik

Alaca

Sorgun

Yıldızeli

Sivas

Edremit

Ayvalık

Kütahya

Simav

Polatlı

Kırıkkale

Hirfanli Baraji

Şarkışla

Boğazlıyan

T U R K

Lésvos

Akhisar

Gediz

Kulu

Tuz Gölü

Bünyan

Manisa

Gediz Nehri

Uşak

Afyon

Cihanbeyli

Akşehir

Nevşehir

İncesu

Gürün

Menemen

İzmir

Chios

Ödemiş

Alaşehir

Dinar

Anatolia

Aksaray

Kayseri

Sámos

Aydın

Nazilli

Denizli

Beyşehir Gölü

Konya

Niğde

Göksun

Güne

Söke

Büyükmenderes Nehri

Burdur

Burdur Gölü

İsparta

Kahramanmaraş

Milas

Tavas

Suğla Gölü

Ereğli

Muğla

Karaman

Ceyhan

Gaziantep

Bodrum

Marmaris

Dalaman

Antalya

Manavgat

Alanya

Toros Dağları

Mut

Tarsus

Mersin (İçel)

Adana

Osmaniye

İskenderun

Kilis

Fethiye

Kaş

Finike

Antalya Körfezi

Anamur

Silifke

Antakya

Kırıkhan

Dodekánisa (Dodécanèse)

Ródos (Rhodes)

Kárpathos

G R E E C E

CYPRUS

TURKISH REPUBLIC OF NORTHERN CYPRUS
(recognized only by Turkey)

Orantes

M e d i t e r r a n e a n

S e a

LEBANON

50

86

N

S

0 km   200

0 miles   200

Population   ⬤ National capital

○ below 50,000   ◎ 50,000 to 100,000   ◉ 100,000 to 500,000   ■ above 500,000

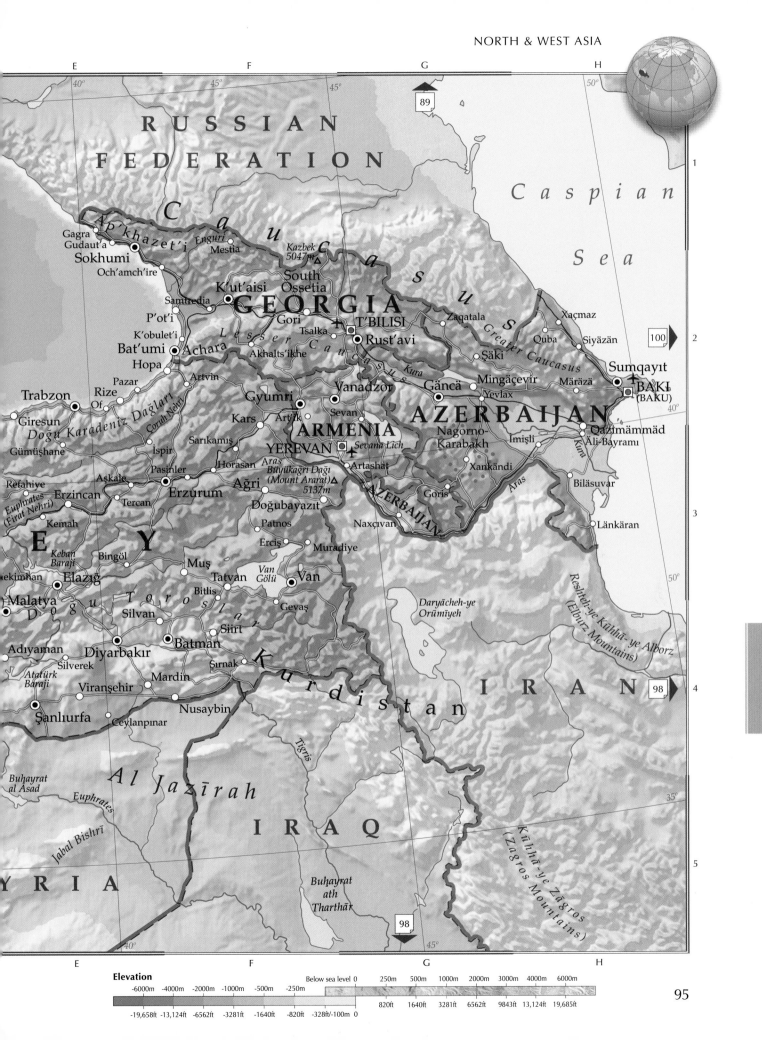

RUSSIAN

FEDERATION

Caspian

Sea

Gagra
Gudaut'a
Sokhumi
Och'amch'ire

Ap'khazet'i
Enguri
Mestia

C   a   u   c   a   s   u   s

Kazbek
5047m △

C   a   u   c   a   s   u   s

Xaçmaz

K'ut'aisi
South
Ossetia

Samtredia
P'ot'i
K'obulet'i
Bat'umi ● Achara
Hopa

GEORGIA

Gori
Tsalka
Akhalts'ikhe

T'BILISI
Rust'avi

Zaqatala

Quba
Siyäzän

Greater Caucasus

Märäzä

Sumqayıt

BAKI
(BAKU)

Lesser   Caucasus

Kura

Şäki

Mingäçevir
Yevlax

Pazar
Rize
Of

Artvin

Trabzon
Giresun
Gümüşhane

Doğu Karadeniz Dağları
Çoruh Nehri

İspir

Gyumri
Kars
Sarıkamış

Artik
Sevan

Vanadzor

Gäncä

AZERBAIJAN

Qazımämmäd
Äli-Bayramı

ARMENIA
YEREVAN

Sevana Lich

Nagorno-
Karabakh

İmişli

Biläsuvar

Refahiye
Erzincan
Kemah

Aşkale
Tercan
Erzurum

Horasan
Pasinler

Aras
Büyükağrı Dağı
(Mount Ararat) △
5137m

Artashat

Xankändi

Goris

Aras

E   Y

Bingöl

Muş

Tatvan
Bitlis

Ağrı

Doğubayazıt

Patnos
Erciş

AZERBAIJAN

Länkäran

Elazığ
Malatya

Doğu
Toroslar

Keban
Barajı

Silvan

Muradiye

Van
Gölü

Van

Gevaş

Naxçıvan

Daryācheh-ye
Orūmīyeh

Reshteh-ye Kūhhā-ye Alborz
(Elburz Mountains)

Adıyaman
Silverek

Diyarbakır

Batman

Siirt

Şırnak

Kurdistan

IRAN

Şanlıurfa
Viranşehir
Ceylanpınar

Mardin

Nusaybin

Atatürk
Barajı

Tigris

Buhayrat
al Asad
Jabal Bishrī

Euphrates

Al Jazīrah

IRAQ

Buhayrat
ath
Tharthār

Kūhhā-ye Zāgros
(Zagros Mountains)

Y R I A

Refahiye
Erzincan

Kemah

Euphrates
(Firat Nehri)

Elevation

| -6000m | -4000m | -2000m | -1000m | -500m | -250m | Below sea level 0 | 250m | 500m | 1000m | 2000m | 3000m | 4000m | 6000m |

-19,658ft -13,124ft -6562ft -3281ft -1640ft -820ft -328ft/-100m 0   820ft 1640ft 3281ft 6562ft 9843ft 13,124ft 19,685ft

The Near East

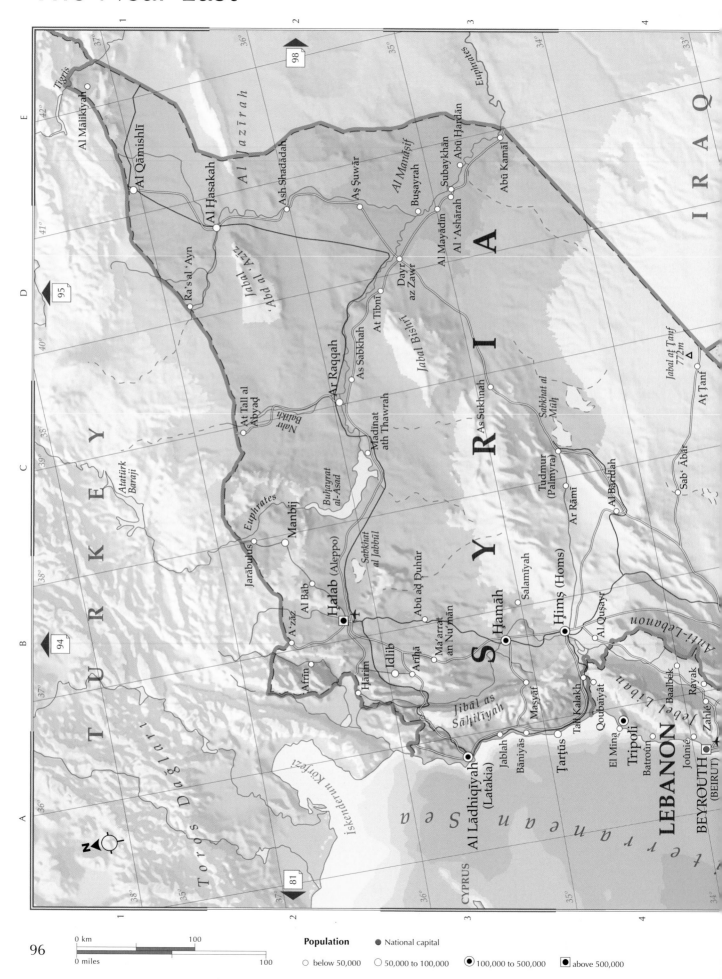

TURKEY

Tigris
Al Mālikīyah
Al Qāmishlī
Al Ḥasakah
Ash Shadādah
Ra's al 'Ayn
At Tall al Abyaḍ
Jarābulus
Manbij
A'zāz
Al Bāb
Afrīn
Ḥārim
Idlib
Arīḥā
Ḥalab (Aleppo)
Ma'arrat an Nu'mān
Abū aḍ Ḍuhūr
Sabkhat al Jabbūl
Buḥayrat al-Asad
Nahr Balīkh
Madīnat ath Thawrah
Ar Raqqah
As Sabkhah
At Tibnī
Aṣ Ṣuwār
Al Manāṣif
Buṣayrah
Subaykhān
Abū Ḥardān
Abū Kamāl
Al Mayādīn
Al 'Ashārah
Dayr az Zawr
Jabal Bishrī
Jabal 'Abd al 'Azīz
Al Jazīrah
Atatürk Barajı
Euphrates

SYRIA

As Sukhnah
Tudmur (Palmyra)
Ar Rāmī
Sabkhat al-Mūḥ
Salamīyah
Ḥamāh
Ḥimṣ (Homs)
Al Quṣayr
Al Bāridah
Sab' Ābār
Jabal aṭ Ṭanf 772m
At Ṭanf

IRAQ

Jibāl as Sāḥilīyah
Maṣyāf
Tall Kalakh
Qoubaiyāt
Baalbek
Rayak
Jounié
Zaḥlé
Anti-Lebanon
Jebel Liban

Al Lādhiqīyah (Latakia)
Jablah
Bāniyās
Ṭarṭūs
El Mina
Tripoli
Batroûn

LEBANON
BEYROUTH (BEIRUT)

CYPRUS

İskenderun Körfezi

Mediterranean Sea

Toros Dağları

Population   National capital

○ below 50,000   ○ 50,000 to 100,000   ◉ 100,000 to 500,000   ◼ above 500,000

0 km   100
0 miles   100

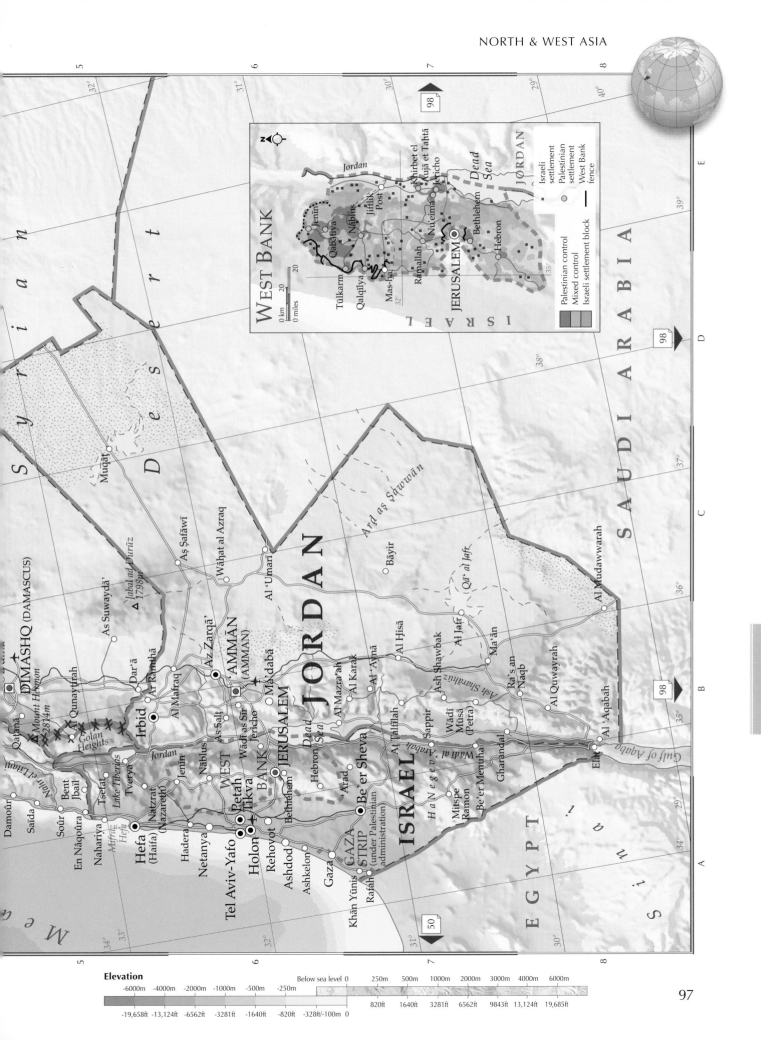

WEST BANK

Israeli settlement	⊙
Palestinian settlement	■
West Bank fence	—

Palestinian control
Mixed control
Israeli settlement block

0 km 20
0 miles 20

Jordan
Khirbet el Aujā et Tahtā
Jenin
Jiftlik Post
Qabātiya
Nāblus
Nu'eima
Jericho
Dead Sea
JORDAN
Tulkarm
Qalqīlya
Mas-ha
Ramallah
Bethlehem
Hebron
JERUSALEM
ISRAEL

S y r i a n   D e s e r t

SAUDI ARABIA

JORDAN

Muqāt
As Safāwī
Wāhat al Azraq
Al 'Umari
Ard as Sawwān
Bāyir
Qa' al Jafr
Al Mudawwarah
Al Quwayrah

DIMASHQ (DAMASCUS)
As Suwaydā'
Jabal ad Durūz 1798m △
Al 'Aqabah

Qatanā
△ Mount Hermon 2814m
Al Qunaytirah
Golan Heights
Irbid
Ar Ramthā
Az Zarqā'
AMMAN ('AMMAN)
Mādabā
Al Mazra'ah
Al Karak
At 'Aynā
Al Hisā
Ash Shawbak
Al Jafr
Ma'ān
Ra's an Naqb

Damoûr
Saïda
Soûr
Bent Jbaïl
En Nâqoûra
Nahariya
Hefa (Haifa)
Nahr el Lītāni
Tseŕat
Lake Tiberius
Tverya
Jordan
Jenin
Nāblus
WEST BANK
Ramallah
Dar'ā
Al Mafraq
As Salt
Wādi as Sir
Jericho
Hadera
Natanya
Natzrat (Nazareth)
Petah Tikva
Holon
Rehovot
Ashdod
Ashkelon
Gaza
GAZA STRIP (under Palestinian administration)
Khān Yūnis
Rafah
Tel Aviv-Yafo
JERUSALEM
Bethlehem
Hebron
Arad
Be'er Sheva
Dead Sea
At Tafīlah
Sappir
Wādi Mūsā (Petra)
Ash Sharāh
Gharandal
Be'er Menuha
Mitspe Ramon
Ha Negev
Wādi al 'Arabah
Elat
Al 'Aqabah
Gulf of Aqaba

J O R D A N

I S R A E L

E G Y P T

S i n a i

M e d ...

Elevation

| -6000m | -4000m | -2000m | -1000m | -500m | -250m | Below sea level 0 | 250m | 500m | 1000m | 2000m | 3000m | 4000m | 6000m |

-19,658ft -13,124ft -6562ft -3281ft -1640ft -820ft -328ft/-100m 0   820ft   1640ft   3281ft   6562ft   9843ft   13,124ft   19,685ft

The Middle East

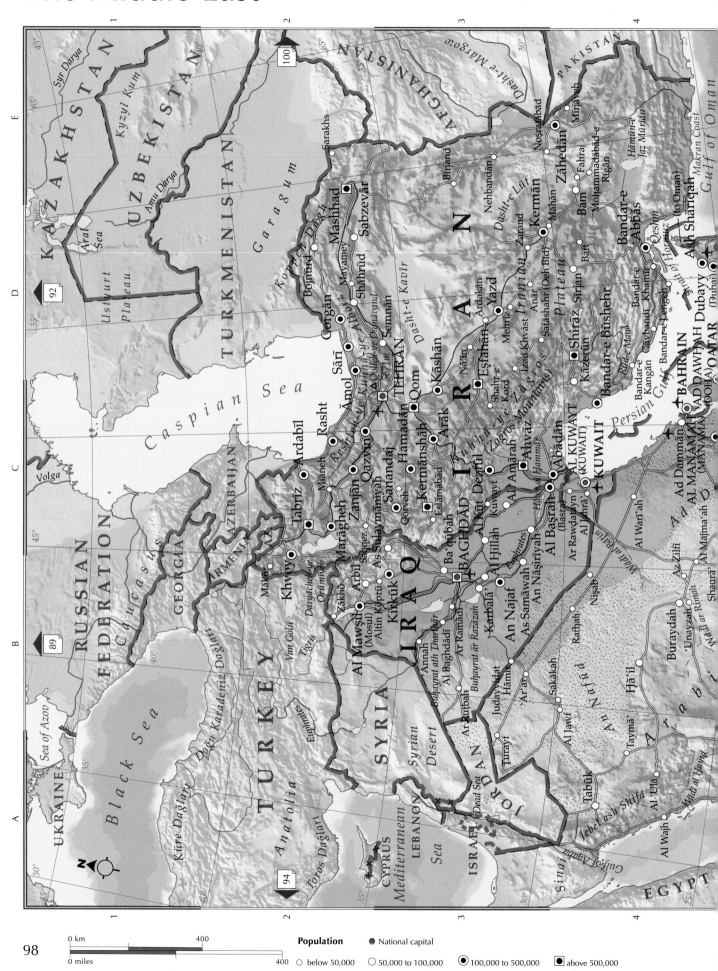

0 km   400

0 miles   400

Population   ● National capital

○ below 50,000   ○ 50,000 to 100,000   ◉ 100,000 to 500,000   ■ above 500,000

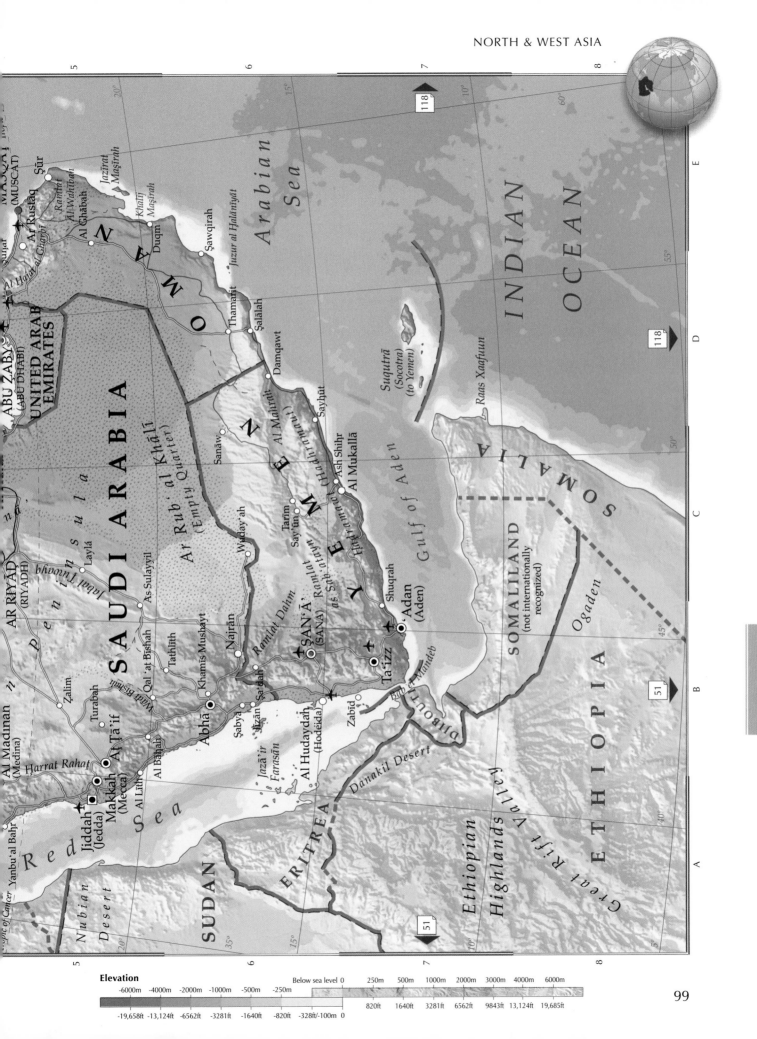

Elevation

| Below sea level 0 | 250m | 500m | 1000m | 2000m | 3000m | 4000m | 6000m |

-6000m -4000m -2000m -1000m -500m -250m

-19,658ft -13,124ft -6562ft -3281ft -1640ft -820ft -328ft/-100m 0

820ft 1640ft 3281ft 6562ft 9843ft 13,124ft 19,685ft

Central Asia

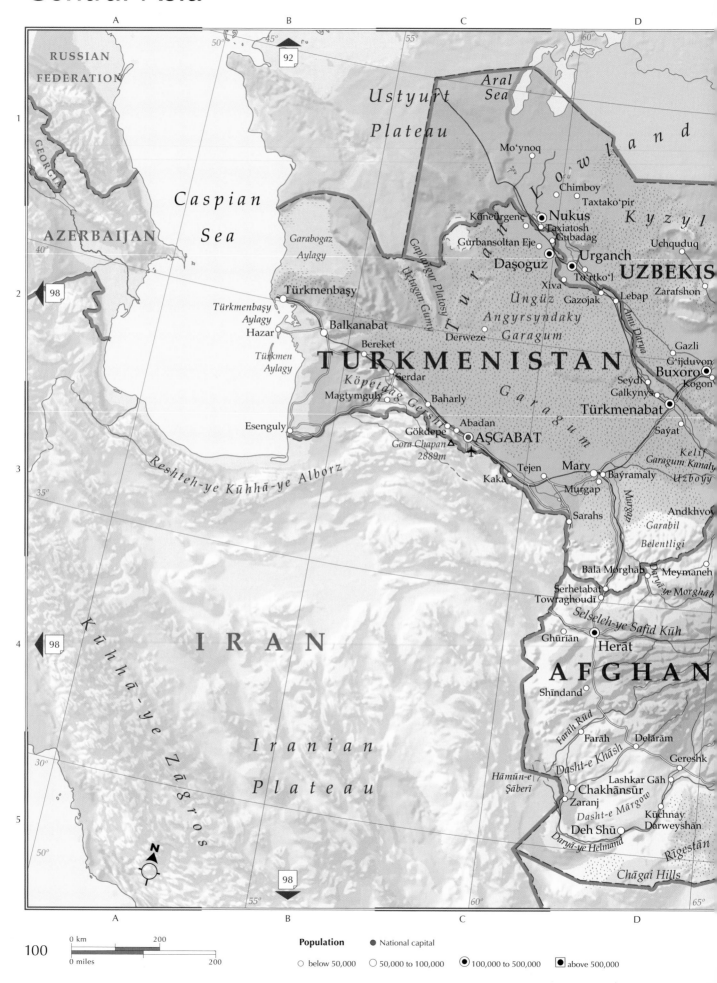

RUSSIAN
FEDERATION

GEORGIA

AZERBAIJAN

Caspian

Sea

Ustyurt

Plateau

Aral

Sea

Mo'ynoq

T u r a n   L o w l a n d

Chimboy

Taxtako'pir

K y z y l

Köneürgenç

Nukus

Taxiatosh

Gubadag

Uchquduq

Gurbansoltan Eje

Garabogaz

Aylagy

Daşoguz

Urganch

UZBEKIS

Gaplaŋgyr Platosy

Uçtagan Gumy

To'rtko'l

Xiva

Üngüz

Gazojak

Lebap

Zarafshon

Türkmenbaşy

Türkmenbaşy

Aylagy

Hazar

Balkanabat

Bereket

Derweze

Angyrsyndaky

Garagum

Gazli

G'ijduvon

Buxoro

Türkmen

Aylagy

Köpetdag Gershi

Serdar

TURKMENISTAN

Garagum

Seýdi

Galkynyş

Kogon

Magtymguly

Baharly

Türkmenabat

Esenguly

Gökdepe

Abadan

AŞGABAT

Gora Chapan

2889m

Reshteh-ye Kūhhā-ye Alborz

Tejen

Mary

Bayramaly

Saýat

Kelif

Garagum Kanaly

Uzboýy

Kaka

Murgap

Andkhvo

Sarahs

Garabil

Belentligi

Murgab

Balā Morghāb

Meymaneh

Serhetabat

Towraghoudī

Daryā-ye Morghāb

Selseleh-ye Safid Kūh

Ghūriān

Herāt

AFGHAN

IRAN

Shīndand

Kūhhā-ye Zāgros

Iranian

Plateau

Farāh Rūd

Farāh

Delārām

Gereshk

Dasht-e Khāsh

Hāmūn-e

Şāberī

Lashkar Gāh

Chakhānsūr

Zaranj

Dasht-e Mārgow

Kŭchnay

Darweyshān

Deh Shū

Daryā-ye Helmand

Rīgestān

Chāgai Hills

0 km   200

0 miles   200

Population   ● National capital

○ below 50,000   ◎ 50,000 to 100,000   ◉ 100,000 to 500,000   ◼ above 500,000

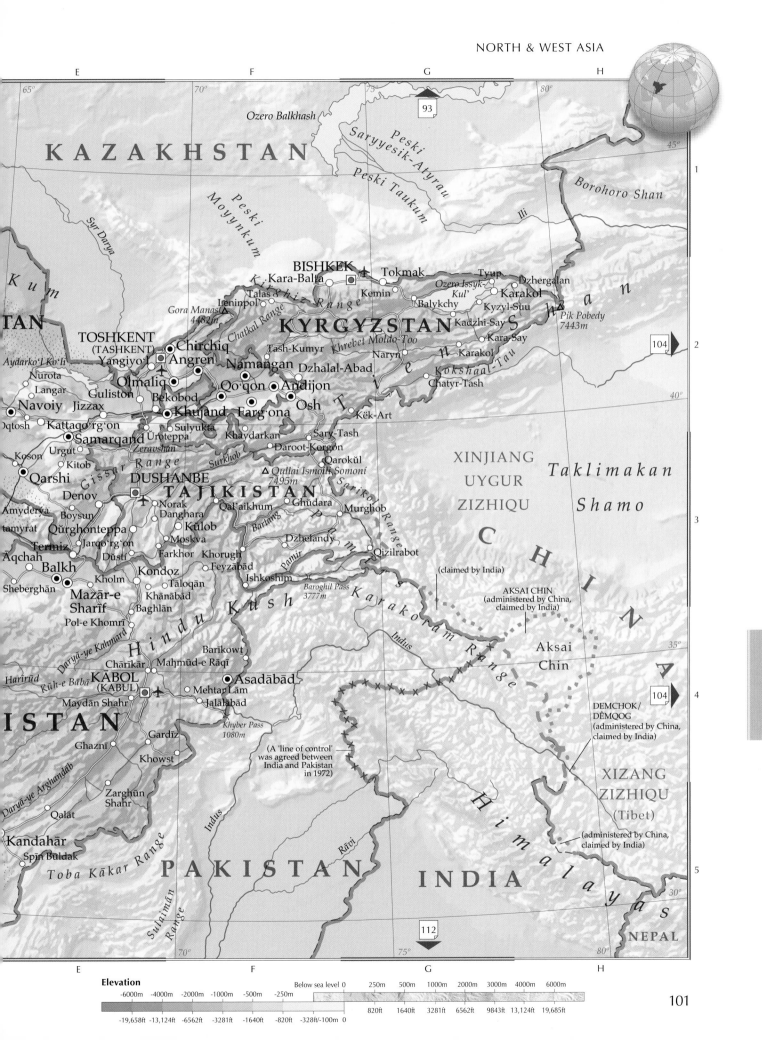

E   F   G   H

65°   70°   75°   80°

93

KAZAKHSTAN

Ozero Balkhash

Peski Saryyesik-Atyrau

Peski Taukum

Peski Moyynkum

Borohoro Shan

1

45°

Ili

Syr Darya

K u m

TAN

104

2

Aydarko'l Ko'li

BISHKEK
Kara-Balta • Tokmak
Kirghiz Range • Kemin
Talas • Leninpol • Balykchy
Gora Manas △ *4482m*
Chatkal Range

Ozero Issyk-Kul' • Tyup
• Dzhergalan
Karakol
Kyzyl-Suu
Kadzhi-Say
Kara-Say
△ *Pik Pobedy 7443m*

KYRGYZSTAN

TOSHKENT
(TASHKENT) • Chirchiq
Yangiyo'l • Angren
Olmaliq • Namangan • Dzhalal-Abad
Nurota • Guliston • Bekobod • Qo'qon • Andijon
Langar • Jizzax • Khujand • Farg'ona • Osh
Navoiy

Tash-Kumyr
Khrebet Moldo-Too
Naryn
Karakol
Chatyr-Tash

Kokshaal-Tau

△
n

Kёk-Art

40°

Oqtosh • Kattaqo'rg'on
Samarqand • Üroteppa • Sulyukta
Koson • Urgut
Kitob

Zeravshan Range
Surkhob

Khaydarkan
Sary-Tash
Daroot-Korgon
Qarokül

**XINJIANG
UYGUR
ZIZHIQU**

*Taklimakan
Shamo*

Qarshi

Gissar Range
DUSHANBE
TAJIKISTAN
Norak
Denov • Danghara
Boysun • Kŭlob
Amyderya • Moskva
tamyrat • Qürghonteppa • Jarqo'rg'on • Farkhor
Termiz • Düsti • Khorugh • Feyzābād
Aqchah • Kondoz
Balkh • Kholm • Tāloqān
Sheberghān • Khānābād
Mazār-e Sharīf • Baghlān
Pol-e Khomrī

△ *Qullai Ismoili Somoni 7495m*
Qal'aikhum
Ghŭdara
Bartang
Murghob
Dzhelandy
Qizilrabot
Ishkoshim
Baroghil Pass 3777m

Pamir
Sarikol Range
Rushan Range

C H I N A

3

(claimed by India)

AKSAI CHIN
(administered by China,
claimed by India)

Karakoram Range
Indus

Aksai
Chin

35°

104

4

Hindu Kush
Darya-ye Kahmard
Harirūd • *Kŭh-e Bābā*
Barīkowt
Charīkar • Maḥmūd-e Rāqī
KĀBOL
(KABUL)
Maydān Shahr
●Asadābād
Mehtar Lām
Jalālābād

DEMCHOK/
DÊMQOG
(administered by China,
claimed by India)

ISTAN

Ghaznī • Gardīz
Khowst
Khyber Pass 1080m
(A 'line of control'
was agreed between
India and Pakistan
in 1972)

**XIZANG
ZIZHIQU**
(Tibet)

(administered by China,
claimed by India)

Daryā-ye Arghandāb
Zarghūn Shahr
Qalāt
Kandahār
Spīn Būldak

Toba Kākar Range
Sulaimān Range
Indus
Rāvi

P A K I S T A N

I N D I A

30°

Himalayas

NEPAL

5

112

E   F   G   H

Elevation

-6000m -4000m -2000m -1000m -500m -250m   Below sea level 0 250m 500m 1000m 2000m 3000m 4000m 6000m

-19,658ft -13,124ft -6562ft -3281ft -1640ft -820ft -328ft/-100m 0

820ft 1640ft 3281ft 6562ft 9843ft 13,124ft 19,685ft

South & East Asia

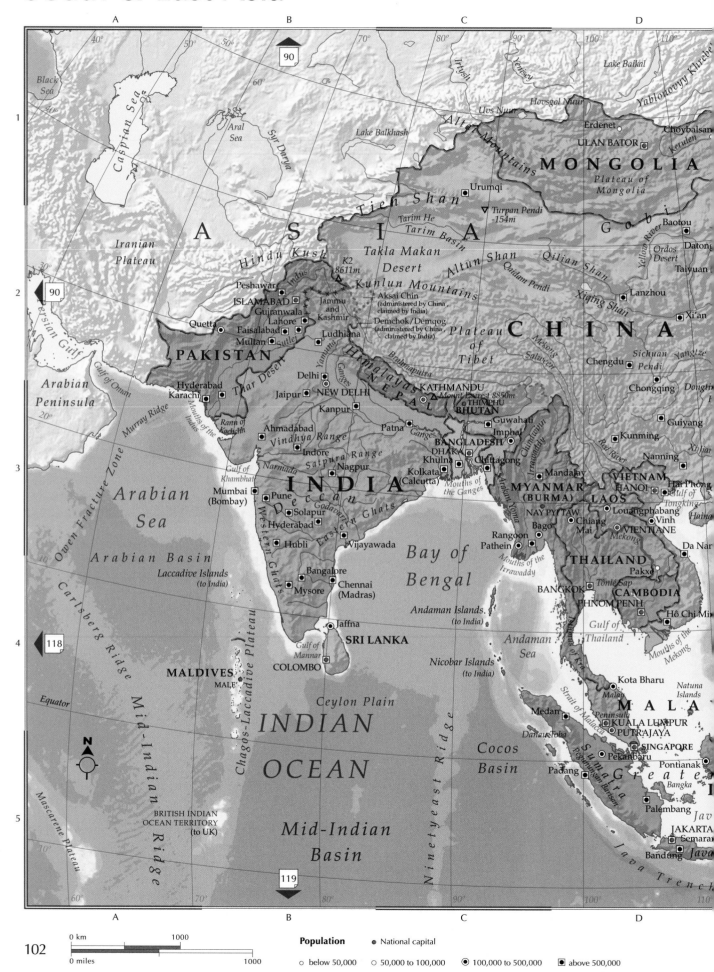

Black Sea

Caspian Sea

Aral Sea

Syr Darya

Iranian Plateau

Hindu Kush

Peshawar

ISLAMABAD

Gujranwala

Lahore

Quetta

Faisalabad

Multan

Sutlej

Indus

PAKISTAN

Thar Desert

Hyderabad

Karachi

Mouths of the Indus

Rann of Kachchh

Gulf of Khambhat

Persian Gulf

Arabian Peninsula

Gulf of Oman

Arabian Sea

Murray Ridge

Owen Fracture Zone

Arabian Basin

Laccadive Islands (to India)

Carlsberg Ridge

Mascarene Plateau

Chagos-Laccadive Plateau

Equator

MALDIVES

MALE

BRITISH INDIAN OCEAN TERRITORY (to UK)

Mid-Indian Ridge

N

INDIAN

OCEAN

Ceylon Plain

Mid-Indian Basin

K2 8611m

Tien Shan

Tarim He

Tarim Basin

Takla Makan Desert

Kunlun Mountains

Aksai Chin (administered by China claimed by India)

Demchok / Demqog (administered by China claimed by India)

Jammu and Kashmir

A S I A

Altun Shan

Plateau of Tibet

Mekong

Salween

Delhi

Jaipur

NEW DELHI

Kanpur

Yamuna

Ganges

Himalayas

NEPAL

KATHMANDU

THIMPHU

BHUTAN

Mount Everest 8850m

Brahmaputra

Ahmadabad

Indore

Narmada

Vindhya Range

Satpura Range

Nagpur

Godavari

INDIA

Deccan

Mumbai (Bombay)

Pune

Solapur

Hyderabad

Hubli

Western Ghats

Eastern Ghats

Bangalore

Mysore

Chennai (Madras)

Vijayawada

Kolkata (Calcutta)

Patna

Ganges

Mouths of the Ganges

DHAKA

Khulna

BANGLADESH

Chittagong

Guwahati

Imphal

Chindwin

Irrawaddy

Arakan Yoma

Mandalay

MYANMAR (BURMA)

NAY PYI TAW

Bago

Rangoon

Pathein

Mouths of the Irrawaddy

Bay of Bengal

Andaman Islands (to India)

Andaman Sea

Nicobar Islands (to India)

Jaffna

SRI LANKA

COLOMBO

Gulf of Mannar

Cocos Basin

Ninetyeast Ridge

Urumqi

Turpan Pendi -154m

Altun Shan

Qaidam Pendi

Qilian Shan

Xiqing Shan

Lanzhou

Xi'an

C H I N A

Chengdu

Sichuan Pendi

Yangtze

Chongqing

Dongting

Guiyang

Kunming

Nanning

Xijiang

VIETNAM

HANOI

Hai Phong

Gulf of Tongking

Hainan

Da Nang

LAOS

Louangphabang

Vinh

VIENTIANE

Chiang Mai

Mekong

THAILAND

Pakxe

BANGKOK

Tônlé Sap

CAMBODIA

PHNOM PENH

Hô Chi Minh

Gulf of Thailand

Isthmus of Kra

Mouths of the Mekong

Mongolia

Lake Baikal

Yablonovyy Khrebet

Hovsgol Nuur

Uvs Nuur

Altai Mountains

Kerulen

Erdenet

ULAN BATOR

Choybalsan

M O N G O L I A

Plateau of Mongolia

Gobi

Baotou

Ordos Desert

Datong

Taiyuan

Yellow River

Irtysh

Yenisey

Lake Balkhash

Kota Bharu

Natuna Islands

Malay Peninsula

MALA

Strait of Malacca

Medan

Danau Toba

KUALA LUMPUR

PUTRAJAYA

SINGAPORE

Pekanbaru

Pontianak

Padang

Sumatra

Pegunungan Barisan

Greater

Palembang

Bangka

JAKARTA

Semarang

Bandung

Java

Java Trench

0 km 1000
0 miles 1000

Population   ● National capital

○ below 50,000   ○ 50,000 to 100,000   ◉ 100,000 to 500,000   ■ above 500,000

Political features

Total area:
7,936,200 sq miles
(20,554,700 sq km)

Total number of countries:
24

Total population:
3979 million

Largest city with population:
Tokyo, Japan 34.2 million

Country with highest population density:
Singapore 20,339 people per sq mile
(7869 people per sq km)

Largest country:
China 3,705,386 sq miles
(9,596,960 sq km)

Smallest country:
Maldives 116 sq miles
(300 sq km)

Physical features

Largest lake:
Tônlé Sap, Cambodia
1000 sq miles (2850 sq km)

Longest river:
Chang Jiang (Yangtze), China
3965 miles (6380 km)

Highest point:
Mount Everest, China/Nepal
29,035 ft (8850 m)

Lowest point:
Turpan Pendi (Turfan Basin), China
505 ft (154 m) below sea level

Western China & Mongolia

RUSSIAN FED

KAZAKHSTAN

Kazakhskiy

Melkosopochnik

Ozero Balkhash

Kulunda Steppe

Yenisey

Zapadnyy Sayan

Hövsgöl Nuur

Uvs Nuur

Ulaangom

Mörön

Ozero Zaysan

Ölgiy

Altay

Hyargas Nuur

Tsetserleg

Hangayn Nuruu

Har Us Nuur

Har Nuur

MONG

Hovd

KYRGYZSTAN

Ozero Issyk-Kul'

Yining

Karamay

Gurbanfünggüt Shamo

Kuytun

Shihezi

Fukang

Jimsar

Ürümqi

Qitai

Turpan

Altay

Bayanhongor

△ *Aj Bogd Uul 3802m*

Ulungur Hu

G

Atas Bogd 2695m △

Hami

Dalian Hob

Borohoro Shan

Tien Shan

△ *Tomür Feng 7443m*

Korla

Bosten Hu

Turpan Pendi

Kuruktag

Xingxingxia

GANSU

Tarim He

Tarim Basin

Kashi

Yengisar

Shache

XINJIANG UYGUR

ZIZHIQU

Lop Nur

Qilian Shan

TAJIKISTAN

AFGH.

Yecheng

(claimed by India)

Pishan

Moyu

Taklimakan Shamo

Ruoqiang

Altun Shan

Danghe Nanshan

Qinghai Hu

Hotan

Qira

Qaidam Pendi

Dulan

Qinghai Hu

PAKISTAN

Karakoram Range

K2 △ *8611m*

Kashmir

Hotan

Kunlun Shan

Golmud

Burhan Budai Shan

A'nyêmaqên Shan

AKSAI CHIN

JAMMU AND KASHMIR

Indus

AKSAI CHIN (administered by China, claimed by India)

CHI

QINGHAI

DÊMCHOK / DÊMQOG (administered by China, claimed by India)

Qingzang Gaoyuan (Plateau of Tibet)

Tongtian He

Bayan Har Shan

Gar Xincun

Zanda

Rutog

XIZANG

Gozhê

Tanggula Shan

Amdo

Yushu

Mekong

H

Himalayas

ZIZHIQU

(Tibet)

Tangra Yumco

Siling Co

Nagqu

Qamdo

Gyaring Co

Ngangzê Co

Nam Co

Damxung

Saltween

Hengduan Shan

Jinsha Jiang

Brahmaputra

Nyainqêntanglha Shan

NEPAL

Yamuna

Ganges

Lhazê

Xigazê

Maizhokunggar

Lhasa

Gonggar

Gyangzê

ARUNACHAL PRADESH (claimed by China)

△ *Mount Everest 8850m*

INDIA

BHUTAN

INDIA

MYANMAR (BURMA)

104

0 km — 400

0 miles — 400

Population   ● National capital   ● Internal administrative capital

○ below 50,000   ○ 50,000 to 100,000   ◎ 100,000 to 500,000   ■ above 500,000

ERATION

RUSS. FED.

Ozero Baykal

Ergun Jagdaqi

HEILONGJIANG

Hulun Buir (Hailar)

Sühbaatar

Manzhouli

Hulun Nur

Lake Khanka

Darhan Choybalsan

JILIN

Erdenet

Bulgan

ULAANBAATAR (ULAN BATOR)

Dzuunmod Öndörhaan

Menengiyn Tal

Hulingol

OLIA Baruun-Urt

Tongliao

Sea of Japan (East Sea)

Xilinhot

Saynshand

Liao He

Erenhot

Chifeng (Ulanhad)

LIAONING

NORTH KOREA

Dalandzadgad

Altayn Nuruu

Ulan Qab (Jining)

Liaodong Wan

Korea Bay

SOUTH KOREA

bi

Lang Shan

Hohhot

BEIJING

Korea Bay

Baotou

TIANJIN

Bo Hai

Wuhai (Haibowan)

Huang He (Yellow River)

Yellow Sea

Yabrai Shan

Tengger Shamo

Mu Us Shadi

HEBEI

SHANDONG

JAPAN

Xining

NINGXIA

Great Wall of China

SHANXI

N

Huang He (Yellow River)

GANSU

HENAN

JIANGSU

East

SHAANXI

SHANGHAI SHI

Han Shui

ANHUI

China

HUBEI

ZHEJIANG

Sea

Chang Jiang (Yangtze)

SICHUAN

CHONGQING

JIANGXI

Nansei-shotō (to Japan)

HUNAN

FUJIAN

Tropic of Cancer

YUNNAN

GUIZHOU

TAIWAN

NEI MONGOL ZIZHIQU (Inner Mongolia)

Du Hinggan Ling

Argun (Ergun He)

Shilka

Amur (Heilong Jiang)

Onon

Onon Gol

Selenga

Kerulen

93

106

108

107

Elevation

-6000m -4000m -2000m -1000m -500m -250m

Below sea level 0 250m 500m 1000m 2000m 3000m 4000m 6000m

-19,658ft -13,124ft -6562ft -3281ft -1640ft -820ft -328ft/-100m 0

820ft 1640ft 3281ft 6562ft 9843ft 13,124ft 19,685ft

Eastern China & Korea

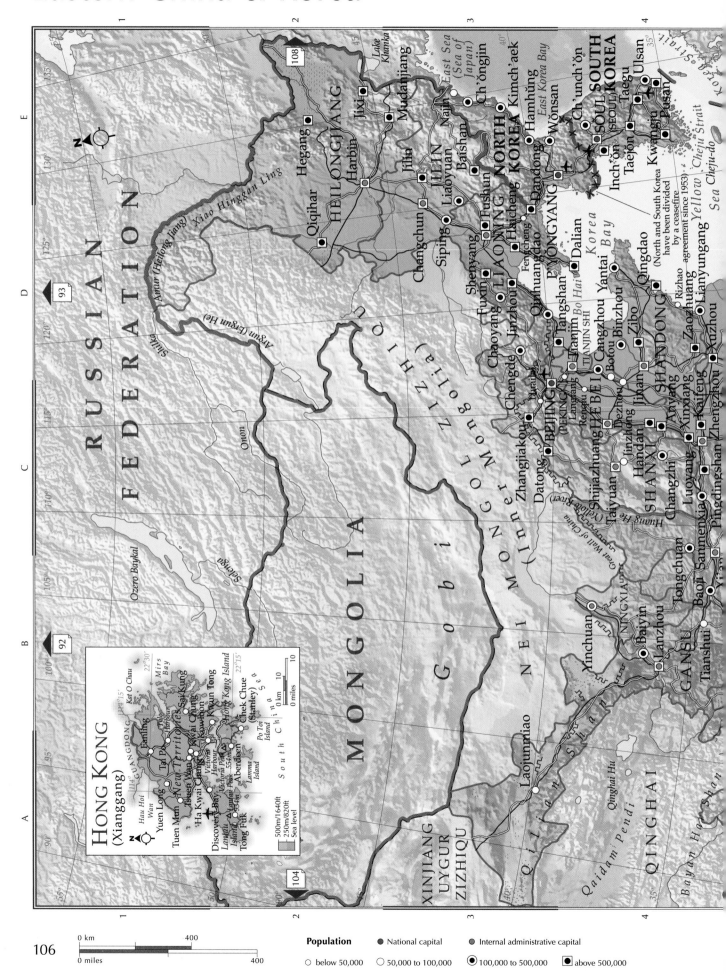

RUSSIAN FEDERATION

MONGOLIA

NEI MONGGOL (Inner Mongolia)

Nei Monggol Zizhiqu

HEILONGJIANG

JILIN

LIAONING

NORTH KOREA

SOUTH KOREA

HEBEI

SHANDONG

SHANXI

NINGXIA

GANSU

QINGHAI

XINJIANG UYGUR ZIZHIQU

GUANGDONG

Lake Khanka

East Sea (Sea of Japan)

East Korea Bay

Korea Bay

Bo Hai

Yellow Sea

Cheju Strait

Cheju-do

Korea Strait

Great Wall of China

Huang He (Yellow River)

Ozero Baykal

Selenga

Onon

Shilka

Amur (Heilong Jiang)

Argun (Ergun He)

Xiao Hinggan Ling

Gobi

Qilian Shan

Bayan Har Shan

Qinghai Hu

Qaidam Pendi

South China Sea

Cities and towns

Hegang · Jixi · Mudanjiang · Harbin · Qiqihar · Jilin · Changchun · Siping · Baishan · Liaoyuan · Fushun · Shenyang · Fuxin · Chaoyang · Jinzhou · Qinhuangdao · Fengcheng · Haicheng · Jinxi · Chengde · Zhangjiakou · Datong · Beijing (PEKING) · Langfang · Tangshan · Tianjin (TIANJIN SHI) · Renqiu · Cangzhou · Binzhou · Bofou · Yantai · Qingdao · Weihai · Rizhao · Zibo · Jinan · Dezhou · Shijiazhuang · Handan · Jinzhong · Taiyuan · Changzhi · Anyang · Xinxiang · Kaifeng · Luoyang · Zhengzhou · Sanmenxia · Pingdingshan · Yichuan · Yinchuan · Baiyin · Lanzhou · Tianshui · Tongchuan · Baoji · Laojunmiao

North Korea: Ch'ŏngjin · Najin · Kimch'aek · Hamhŭng · Wŏnsan · PYONGYANG · Dandong · Dalian

South Korea: Ch'unch'ŏn · SEOUL (SŎUL) · Inch'ŏn · Taejŏn · Taegu · Ulsan · Pusan · Kwangju

(North and South Korea have been divided by a ceasefire agreement since 1953)

HONG KONG (Xianggang)

GUANGDONG

Hau Hoi Wan · Yuen Long · Tuen Mun · Penling · Sha Tau Kok · Tai Po · Kat O Chau · Mirs Bay · Tolo Harbour · Sai Kung · New Territories · Tseun Wan · Kwai Chung · Kwun Tong · Kowloon · Ha Kwai Chung · Lantau Island · Discovery Bay · Victoria Harbour · Victoria Peak 554m · Aberdeen · Hong Kong Island · Kwun Tong · Chek Chue (Stanley) · Po Toi Island · Lamma Island · Tong Fuk

500m/1640ft · 250m/820ft · Sea level

Population · ● National capital · ● Internal administrative capital
○ below 50,000 · ○ 50,000 to 100,000 · ◉ 100,000 to 500,000 · ■ above 500,000

0 km 400 · 0 miles 400

Elevation

| Below sea level 0 | 250m | 500m | 1000m | 2000m | 3000m | 4000m | 6000m |

-6000m -4000m -2000m -1000m -500m -250m

-19,658ft -13,124ft -6562ft -3281ft -1640ft -820ft -328ft/-100m 0

820ft 1640ft 3281ft 6562ft 9843ft 13,124ft 19,685ft

Japan

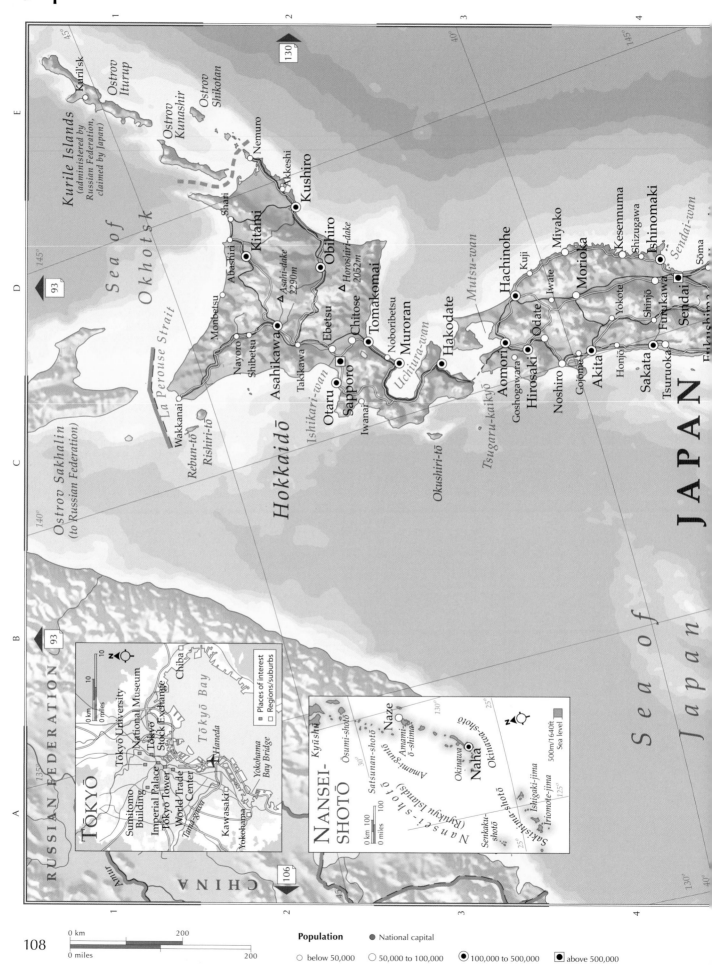

RUSSIAN FEDERATION

Kuril'sk

Ostrov Iturup

Kurile Islands
(administered by
Russian Federation,
claimed by Japan)

Ostrov Shikotan

Ostrov Kunashir

Ostrov Shikotan

Nemuro

Shari

Akkeshi

Kushiro

Sea of Okhotsk

Abashiri

Kitami

Obihiro

△ *Asahi-dake 2290m*

△ *Horoshiri-dake 2052m*

Monbetsu

Nayoro

Shibetsu

Ebetsu

Chitose

Tomakomai

Tomakomai

Noboribetsu

Muroran

Mutsu-wan

Miyako

Hachinohe

Kuji

Iwate

Morioka

Kesennuma

Shizugawa

Ishinomaki

Sendai-wan

Sōma

La Perouse Strait

Wakkanai

Rebun-tō

Rishiri-tō

Takikawa

Asahikawa

Otaru

Sapporo

Iwanai

Hokkaidō

Ishikari-wan

Uchiura-wan

Hakodate

Okushiri-tō

Tsugaru-kaikyō

Aomori

Goshogawara

Hirosaki

Odate

Noshiro

Gojōme

Akita

Yokote

Honjō

Shinjō

Funakawa

Sendai

Fukushima

Sakata

Tsuruoka

Ostrov Sakhalin
(to Russian Federation)

Sea of Japan

JAPAN

TŌKYŌ

RUSSIAN FEDERATION

Chiba

Tokyo University
National Museum
Tokyo Stock Exchange

Sumitomo Building
Imperial Palace
Tokyo Tower
World Trade Center

Tōkyō Bay

Haneda

Kawasaki

Yokohama

Yokohama Bay Bridge

Tama-gawa

Amur

CHINA

■ Places of interest
□ Regions/suburbs

NANSEI-SHOTŌ

Kyūshū

Ōsumi-shotō

Satsunan-shotō

Naze

Amami-gunto

Amami-ō-shima

Okinawa

Naha

Okinawa

Nansei-shotō
(Ryukyu Islands)

Senkaku-shotō

Sakishima-shotō

Ishigaki-jima

Iriomote-jima

500m/1640ft
Sea level

Population   ● National capital

○ below 50,000   ○ 50,000 to 100,000   ◉ 100,000 to 500,000   ◼ above 500,000

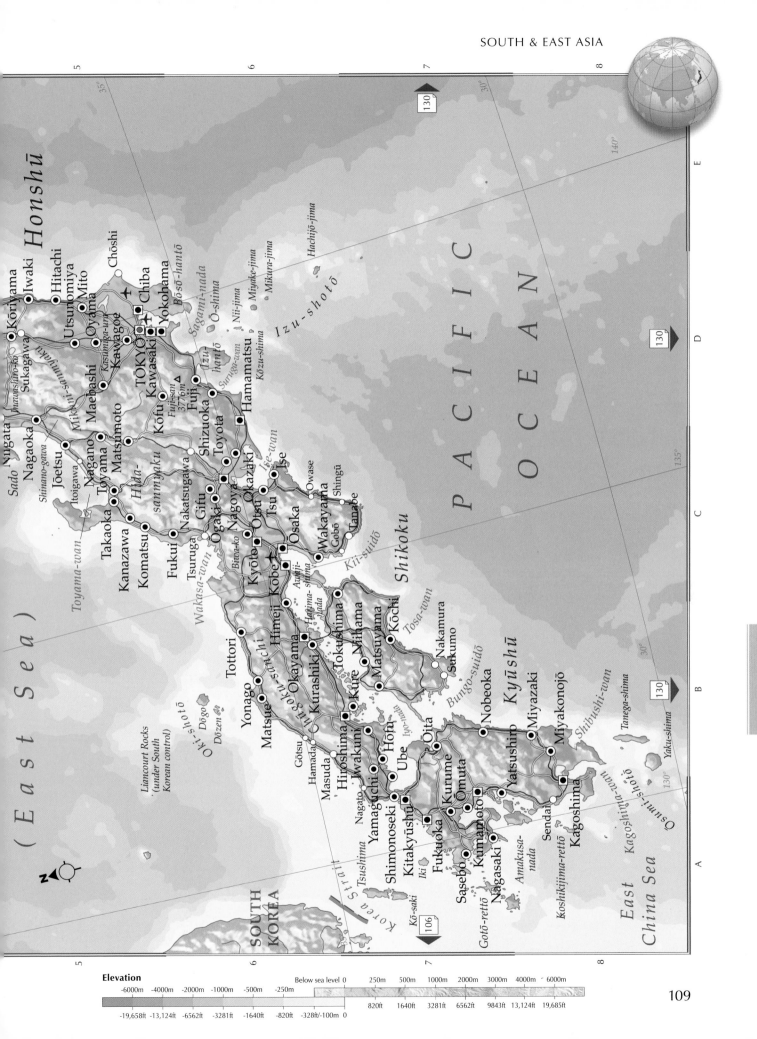

PACIFIC OCEAN

(E a s t   S e a)

Honshū

Shikoku

Kyūshū

SOUTH KOREA

East China Sea

Elevation

				Below sea level 0	250m	500m	1000m	2000m	3000m	4000m	6000m

-6000m -4000m -2000m -1000m -500m -250m

820ft 1640ft 3281ft 6562ft 9843ft 13,124ft 19,685ft

-19,658ft -13,124ft -6562ft -3281ft -1640ft -820ft -328ft/-100m 0

South India & Sri Lanka

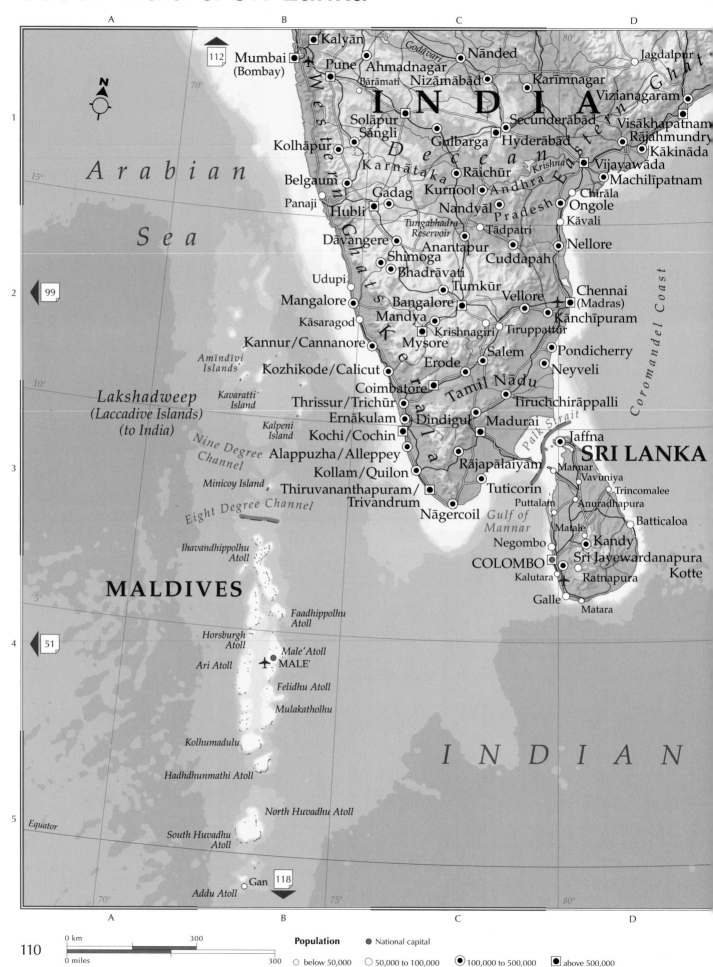

Arabian Sea

Kalyān
112 Mumbai (Bombay)
Pune
Ahmadnagar
Nānded
Jagdalpur

Bārāmati
Nizāmābād
Karīmnagar
Vizianagaram

Solāpur
Secunderābād
Visākhapatnam

Sāngli
Gulbarga
Hyderābād
Rājahmundry

Kolhāpur
Kākināda

Belgaum
Raichūr
Krishna
Vijayawāda

Panaji
Gadag
Kurnool
Andhra
Machilīpatnam

Hubli
Nandyāl
Pradesh
Chirāla
Ongole

Tungabhadra Reservoir
Tādpatri
Kāvali

Dāvangere
Anantapur
Nellore

Shimoga
Cuddapah

Udupi
Bhadrāvati
Tumkūr

Mangalore
Bangalore
Vellore
Chennai (Madras)

Mandya
Kānchīpuram

Kāsaragod
Krishnagiri
Tiruppattūr

Kannur/Cannanore
Mysore
Salem
Pondicherry

Kozhikode/Calicut
Erode
Neyveli

Amīndivi Islands
Coimbatore
Tamil Nādu

Lakshadweep (Laccadive Islands) (to India)
Kavaratti Island
Thrissur/Trichūr
Tiruchchirāppalli

Ernākulam
Dindigul
Madurai

Kalpeni Island
Kochi/Cochin
Jaffna

Nine Degree Channel
Alappuzha/Alleppey
SRI LANKA

Kollam/Quilon
Rājapālaiyam
Mannar

Minicoy Island
Tuticorin
Vavuniya

Thiruvananthapuram/Trivandrum
Trincomalee

Eight Degree Channel
Nāgercoil
Gulf of Mannar
Puttalam
Anuradhapura

MALDIVES
Matale
Batticaloa

Ihavandhippolhu Atoll
Negombo
Kandy

COLOMBO
Sri Jayewardanapura
Kotte

Faadhippolhu Atoll
Kalutara
Ratnapura

Horsburgh Atoll
Galle

Ari Atoll
Male' Atoll
MALE'
Matara

Felidhu Atoll

Mulakatholhu

INDIAN

Kolhumadulu

Hadhdhunmathi Atoll

North Huvadhu Atoll

South Huvadhu Atoll

Gan 118
Addu Atoll

Equator

110

0 km   300
0 miles   300

Population   ● National capital

○ below 50,000   ○ 50,000 to 100,000   ◉ 100,000 to 500,000   ◼ above 500,000

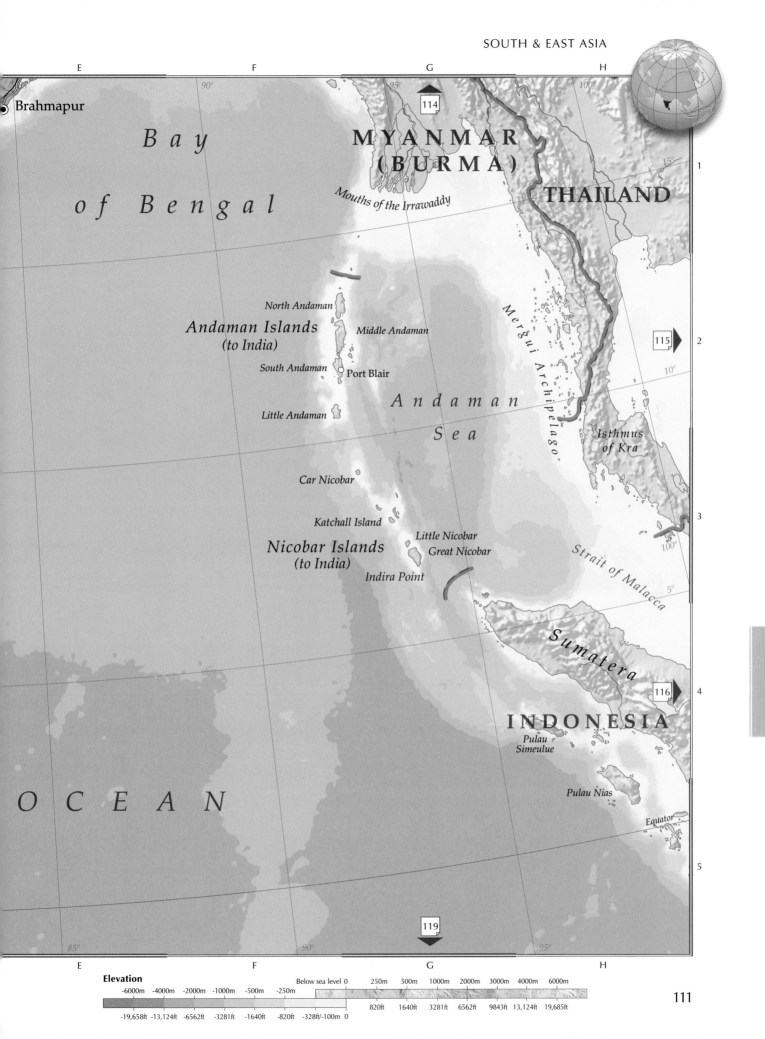

Brahmapur

Bay

of Bengal

MYANMAR
(BURMA)

THAILAND

Mouths of the Irrawaddy

114

115

North Andaman

Andaman Islands
(to India)

Middle Andaman

South Andaman — Port Blair

A n d a m a n

S e a

Little Andaman

Mergui Archipelago

*Isthmus
of Kra*

Car Nicobar

Katchall Island

Nicobar Islands
(to India)

Little Nicobar
Great Nicobar

Indira Point

Strait of Malacca

116

INDONESIA

Sumatera

*Pulau
Simeulue*

O C E A N

Pulau Nias

Equator

119

Elevation

| Below sea level 0 | 250m | 500m | 1000m | 2000m | 3000m | 4000m | 6000m |

-6000m -4000m -2000m -1000m -500m -250m

820ft 1640ft 3281ft 6562ft 9843ft 13,124ft 19,685ft

-19,658ft -13,124ft -6562ft -3281ft -1640ft -820ft -328ft/-100m 0

Northern India, Pakistan & Bangladesh

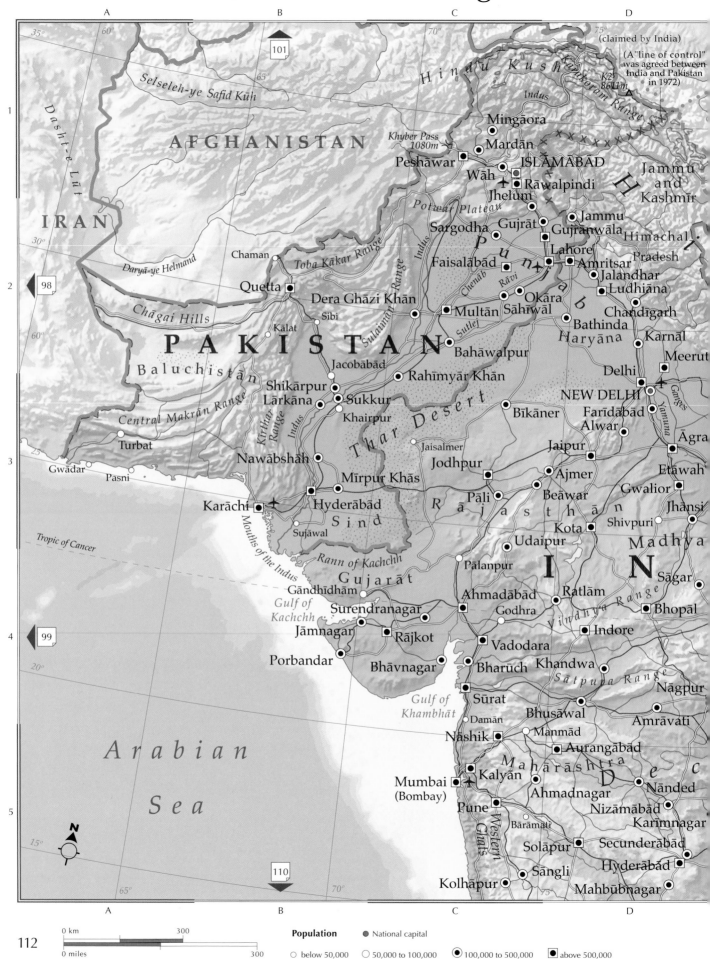

AFGHANISTAN

Selseleh-ye Safid Kūh

Hindu Kush

Karakoram Range

(claimed by India)

(A "line of control" was agreed between India and Pakistan in 1972)

K2 8611m

Indus

Dasht-e Lūt

IRAN

Daryā-ye Helmand

Chaman

Quetta

Chāgai Hills

Kālat

PAKISTAN

Baluchistān

Central Makrān Range

Turbat

Gwādar   Pasni

Toba Kākar Range

Sibi

Dera Ghāzi Khān

Sulaimān Range

Indus

Kirthar Range

Shikārpur
Lārkāna
Jacobābād
Sukkur
Khairpur

Nawābshāh

Mīrpur Khās

Karachi

Mouths of the Indus

Hyderābād

Sind

Sujāwal

Mingaora

Khyber Pass 1080m

Peshāwar   Mardān

Wāh   ISLĀMĀBAD
Rāwalpindi
Jhelum

Potwar Plateau

Sargodha   Gujrāt   Gujrānwāla

Jammu and Kashmīr

Jammu

Himachal Pradesh

Lahore
Amritsar
Jalandhar
Ludhiāna

Faisalābād

Chenāb

Rāvi

Okāra
Sāhīwāl

Multān

Sutlej

Bahāwalpur

Chandīgarh

Bathinda

Haryāna

Karnāl

Meerut

Delhi

NEW DELHI

Rahīmyār Khān

Thar Desert

Bīkāner

Farīdābād
Alwar

Āgra

Etāwah

Jaisalmer

Jodhpur

Jaipur

Ajmer

Pāli   Beāwar

Kota

Gwalior

Jhānsi

Shivpuri

Sāgar

Rājasthān

Udaipur

Madhya

INDIA

Tropic of Cancer

Rann of Kachchh

Gujarāt

Gāndhīdhām

Gulf of Kachchh

Surendranagar

Jāmnagar

Porbandar

Bhāvnagar

Pālanpur

Ahmadābād

Ratlām

Godhra

Rājkot

Vadodara

Bharūch

Gulf of Khambhāt

Sūrat

Daman

Bhopal

Indore

Khandwa

Satpura Range

Vindhya Range

Nāgpur

Amrāvati

Bhusāwal

Manmād

Nāshik

Arabian Sea

Mumbai (Bombay)

Kalyān

Pune

Bārāmati

Solāpur

Kolhāpur

Sāngli

Maharāshtra

Aurangābād

Ahmadnagar

Nizāmābād

Karīmnagar

Secunderābād

Hyderābād

Nānded

Mahbūbnagar

Western Ghats

Deccan

N

0 km   300
0 miles   300

Population   ● National capital

○ below 50,000   ◎ 50,000 to 100,000   ◉ 100,000 to 500,000   ■ above 500,000

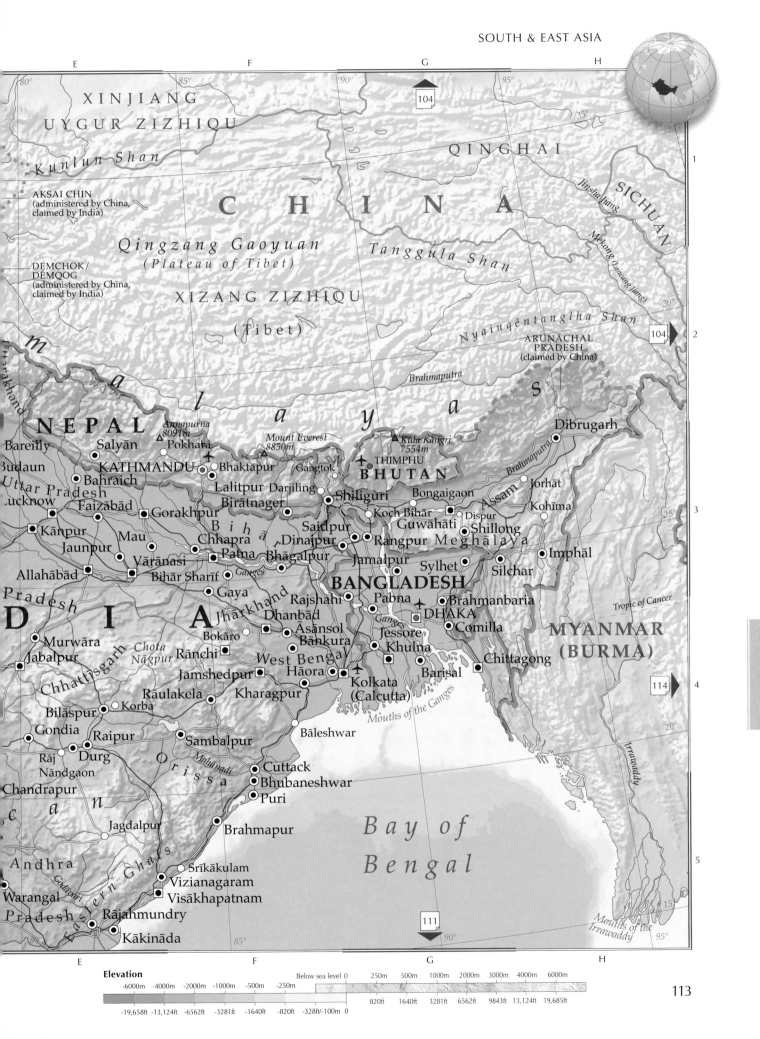

XINJIANG
UYGUR ZIZHIQU
Kunlun Shan
QINGHAI
SICHUAN
CHINA
AKSAI CHIN
(administered by China,
claimed by India)
Qingzang Gaoyuan
(Plateau of Tibet)
Tanggula Shan
DEMCHOK /
DÊMQOG
(administered by China,
claimed by India)
XIZANG ZIZHIQU
(Tibet)
Nyainqêntanglha Shan
ARUNACHAL
PRADESH
(claimed by China)
Brahmaputra
Jinsha Jiang
Mekong (Lancang Jiang)

H i m a l a y a s

Dibrugarh
NEPAL
Annapurna
8091m
Pokhara
Mount Everest
8850m
Kula Kangri
7554m
THIMPHU
Brahmaputra
Bareilly
Salyan
Budaun
KATHMANDU
Bahraich
Bhaktapur
Gangtok
BHUTAN
Assam
Jorhat
Uttar Pradesh
Lucknow
Lalitpur
Darjiling
Shiliguri
Bongaigaon
Kohima
Faizabad
Gorakhpur
Biratnager
Koch Bihar
Dispur
Guwahati
Shillong
Meghalaya
Imphal
Kanpur
Jaunpur
Mau
B i h a r
Chhapra
Saidpur
Dinajpur
Rangpur
Varanasi
Patna
Bhagalpur
Jamalpur
Sylhet
Silchar
Allahabad
Bihar Sharif
Ganges
Gaya
BANGLADESH
Pradesh
Jharkhand
Rajshahi
Pabna
Brahmanbaria
Tropic of Cancer
D I A
Dhanbad
Ganges
DHAKA
MYANMAR
(BURMA)
Murwara
Bokaro
Asansol
Bankura
Jessore
Comilla
Jabalpur
Chota
Nagpur
Ranchi
West Bengal
Khulna
Chittagong
Chhattisgarh
Jamshedpur
Haora
Barisal
Bilaspur
Korba
Raulakela
Kharagpur
Kolkata
(Calcutta)
Mouths of the Ganges
Gondia
Raipur
Sambalpur
Baleshwar
Raj
Nandgaon
Durg
Mahanadi
Orissa
Cuttack
Bhubaneshwar
Chandrapur
Puri
D e c c a n
Jagdalpur
Brahmapur
Bay of
Bengal
Andhra
Eastern Ghats
Srikakulam
Vizianagaram
Warangal
Godavari
Visakhapatnam
Pradesh
Rajahmundry
Mouths of the
Irrawaddy
Kakinada
Irrawaddy

Elevation

| Below sea level 0 | 250m | 500m | 1000m | 2000m | 3000m | 4000m | 6000m |

-6000m -4000m -2000m -1000m -500m -250m

-19,658ft -13,124ft -6562ft -3281ft -1640ft -820ft -328ft/-100m 0

820ft 1640ft 3281ft 6562ft 9843ft 13,124ft 19,685ft

104
104
114
111

Mainland Southeast Asia

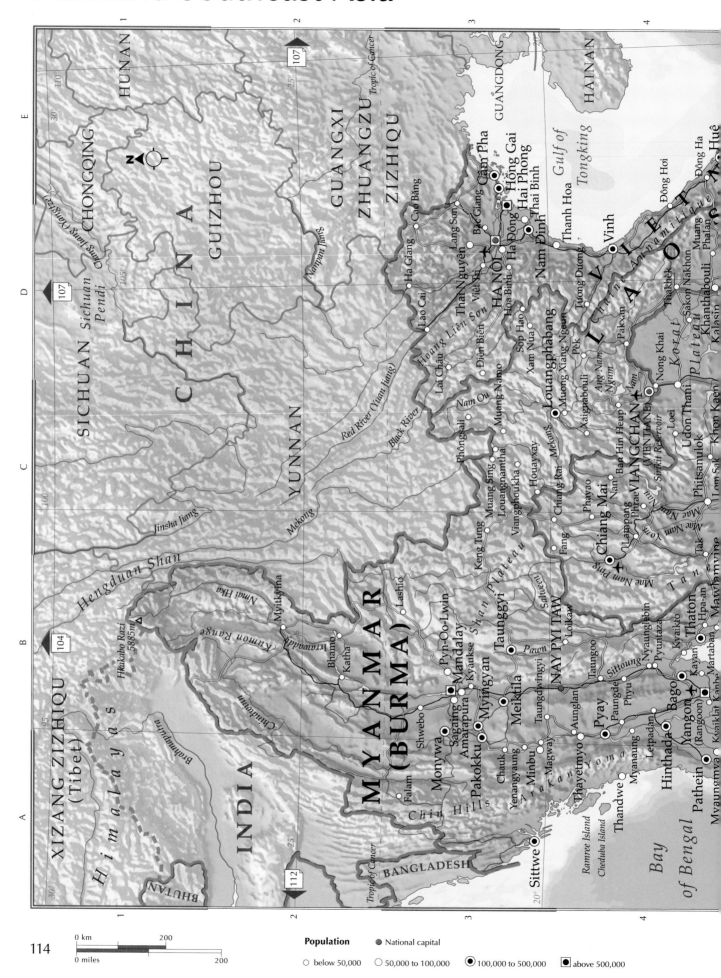

0 km   200

0 miles   200

Population   ● National capital

○ below 50,000   ◎ 50,000 to 100,000   ◉ 100,000 to 500,000   ◼ above 500,000

117

116

116

111

THAILAND

CAMBODIA

KRUNG THEP (BANGKOK)

PHNUM PENH

MALAYSIA

INDONESIA

South China
Sea

Gulf of
Thailand

Andaman
Sea

INDIAN
OCEAN

Strait of Malacca

Malay
Peninsula

Mergui Archipelago

Bilauktaung Range

Mouths of the Irrawaddy

Mouths of the Mekong

Hồi An
Tam Ky
Quảng Ngãi
Đà Nẵng
Salavan
Muang Khôngxêdôn
Pakxé
Champasak
Surin
Roi Et
Ubon Ratchathani
Buriram
Nakhon Ratchasima
Sara Buri
Lop Buri
Nakhon Sawan
Ayutthaya
Nakhon Pathom
Phetchaburi
Ratchaburi
Chon Buri
Samut Prakan
Pattaya
Rayong
Chanthaburi
Reang Kesei
Bătdâmbâng
Phumi Sâmraông
Chuŏr Phnum
Krălănh
Siěmréab
Kâmpóng Thum
Moŭng Roessei
Pouthĭsăt
Chuŏr Phnum Krâvanh
Kâmpóng Spœ
Kâmpóng Chhnăng
Kâmpóng Saôm
Kâmpôt
Suŏng
Kâmpóng Cham
Trâpeăng Vêng
Svay Riěng
Krâchéh
Stœ̆ng Trêng
Virôchey
Samakhixai
Khong
Tônlé Kong
Tônlé Srepôk
Play Cu
Tuy Hoa
Quy Nhon
Cam Ranh
Nha Trang
Da Lat
Di Linh
Biên Hoa
Hồ Chí Minh
Vung Tau
My Tho
Tra Vinh
Cần Thơ
Soc Trăng
Bac Liêu
Ca Mau
Rach Gia
Châu Đốc
Long Xuyên
Vinh Rach Gia
Kâmpông Saôm
Ko Kut
Ko Chang
Ao Krung Thep
Ban Hua Hin
Chumphon
Lang Suan
Ko Phangan
Ko Samui
Surat Thani
Sichon
Nakhon Si Thammarat
Pak Phanang
Thung Song
Thale Luang
Phatthalung
Songkhla
Pattani
Narathiwat
Yala
Hat Yai
Trang
Ko Lanta
Ko Ta Ru Tao
Pulau Langkawi
Pulau Pinang
Phuket
Ko Phuket
Phang-Nga
Ko Phra Thong
Zadetkyi Kyun
Ranong
Tenasserim
Lanbi Kyun
Letsôk-aw Kyun
Daung Kyun
Kadan Kyun
Mali Kyun
Myeik
Daewi
Ye
Kyaikkami
Bogale
Labutta
Mudon

Rang-
Thăp Cham
Phan Thiết
Phan Rang-
Côn Đảo

Kepulauan Natuna
(to Indonesia)

Sumatera
(Sumatra)

Pulau Simeulue

Andaman Islands
(to India)
North Andaman
Middle Andaman
South Andaman
Little Andaman

Nicobar Islands
(to India)
Car Nicobar
Katchall Island
Little Nicobar
Great Nicobar

Isthmus of Kra

Srinagarind Reservoir

Mekong

Tônlé Sap

Stœ̆ng Sên

Phnum Dângrêk

Tônlé Kong

15°
10°
5°
10°
5°
15°

Elevation

-6000m	-4000m	-2000m	-1000m	-500m	-250m	Below sea level 0	250m	500m	1000m	2000m	3000m	4000m	6000m
-19,658ft	-13,124ft	-6562ft	-3281ft	-1640ft	-820ft	-328ft/-100m 0	820ft	1640ft	3281ft	6562ft	9843ft	13,124ft	19,685ft

Maritime Southeast Asia

SINGAPORE

MALAYSIA

Johore Strait

Causeway

Lim Chu Kang
Choa Chu Kang
Jurong Industrial Estate
Hougang New Town
Bukit Panjang
Bukit Timah 176m
Queenstown
City
Telok Blangah
Bedok New Town
Changi
Pulau Tekong
Pulau Ubin

Selat Pandan
Pulau Sudong
Sentosa
Pulau Pawai

Strait of Singapore

0 km 10
0 miles 10

1°20'
104°
103°50'
103°40'
10°

Urban areas
Open areas
Nature reserves

MYANMAR (BURMA)

115

LAOS

THAILAND

Mekong

VIETNAM

CAMBODIA

Gulf of Tongking

Hainan Dao (to China)

110°

PARACEL ISLANDS
(disputed by China, Taiwan and Vietnam)

South China

Sea

SPRATLY ISLANDS
(disputed by China, Malaysia, Philippines, Taiwan and Vietnam)

Mouths of the Mekong

111

Andaman Sea

Nicobar Islands (to India)

Gulf of Thailand

Isthmus of Kra

Palawan

Balabac Strait

Gunung Kinabalu 4101m

Kota Kinabalu
Sabah

BANDAR SERI BEGAWAN
BRUNEI
Miri

Banda Aceh
Sigli
Langsa
Meulaboh
Medan
Tebingtinggi
Pematangsiantar
Pulau Simeulue
Kepulauan Banyak
Danau Toba
Sibolga
Pulau Nias

George Town
Butterworth
Taiping
Ipoh
Pulau Pinang

Strait of Malacca

Klang
PUTRAJAYA
Melaka
Muar
Batu Pahat

Kota Bharu
Kuala Terengganu
Dungun
Cukai
Kuantan
KUALA LUMPUR
Keluang
Johor Bahru
SINGAPORE

Kepulauan Natuna

Selat Serasan

MALAYSIA

Bintulu
Sibu
Sarawak
Sri Aman
Kuching
Singkawang
Sidas
Pontianak
Sungai Kapuas

Banjaran Tiramabo

Batang Rajang

Pegunungan Müller

Sungai Kayan

Borneo

Equator

Pekanbaru
Solok
Rengat
Padang
Pulau Siberut
Kepulauan Mentawai
Sungaipenuh
Bengkulu
Lahat

Kepulauan Lingga

Kualatungkal

Batang Hari
Jambi
Pangkalpinang
Palembang

Bangka

Selat Karimata

Pulau Belitung

Sungai Mahakam

Samarinda
Balikpapan

Kalimantan

Sampit

Amuntai
Kandangan

Sungai Barito

Banjarmasin

111

INDIAN
OCEAN

Sumatera (Sumatra)

Kotabumi
Bandar Lampung
Serang
Sukabumi

Pegunungan Barisan

Selat Sunda

JAKARTA
Bogor
Bandung
Tasikmalaya
Cilacap
Magelang
Yogyakarta
Surakarta

Cirebon
Tegal
Pekalongan

INDONESIA

Pulau Laut
Makassar

Java Sea

Pulau Madura
Semarang
Kudus
Kediri
Madiun
Malang

Surabaya
Probolinggo
Jember
Mataram

Denpasar
Pulau Lombok

Jawa (Java)
Bali

MALAYSIA'S TWO CAPITALS

KUALA LUMPUR – Capital
PUTRAJAYA – Administrative capital

119

0 km 200
0 miles 200

Population ● National capital

○ below 50,000 ◎ 50,000 to 100,000 ◉ 100,000 to 500,000 ◼ above 500,000

Luzon Strait
Babuyan Island
Babuyan Channel

109

NORTHERN
MARIANA
ISLANDS
(to US)

GUAM
(to US)

Tuguegarao
Ilagan
Baguio
Luzon
Angeles
Dagupan
Cabanatuan
MANILA
Lucena
Batangas
Naga
Mindoro
Legazpi City

Philippine
Sea

PHILIPPINES

Calbayog
Sibuyan
Sea
Samar
Roxas City
Cadiz
Panay
Island
Tacloban
Leyte
Iloilo
Bacolod
City
Cebu
Palawan

Butuan
Cagayan de Oro
Iligan
Bislig
Negros
Bohol Sea
Mindanao

Puerto
Princesa

Sulu Sea

122

MICRONESIA

Yap

P A C I F I C

Zamboanga
Basilan
Moro
Gulf
Lebak
Davao
Davao Gulf
General
Santos
andakan
Sulu Archipelago

Babeldaob

P A L A U

Kepulauan
Talaud

O C E A N

Celebes Sea

Kepulauan Sangir

Pulau Morotai

Manado
Bitung
Gorontalo
Pulau
Halmahera

Pulau Waigeo

Pulau
Biak
Kepulauan Banggai

Palu
Gulf of
Tomini

Molucca Sea

Halmahera
Sea
Sorong
Jazirah
Doberai

Manokwari
Pulau
Yapen

Jayapura

Equator

122

Sulawesi
(Celebes)
Kepulauan
Sula
Maluku (Moluccas)
Teluk Berau
Pulau
Misool

Teluk
Canderawasih

Pegunungan Maoke

PAPUA

Palu
Pegunungan
Quarles
Danau
Towuti
Waflia
Wahai
Ceram Sea

Puncak Jaya
5030m

Sungai Mamberamo

NEW

Parepare
N
Tifu
Kendari
Pulau
Buru
Ambon
S
I
A
Papua
(Irian Jaya)

GUINEA

Singkang
Teluk Bone
Kolaka
Pulau
Buton
Pulau
Seram
Kepulauan
Kai

New Guinea

Watampone
Makassar
Bulukumba
Banda Sea

Kepulauan
Aru

Sungai Digul

Flores
Sea

Tenggara
Flores
Pulau
Wetar
Kepulauan Alor
Kepulauan
Tanimbar
Pulau Yamdena

Arafura

Selat Sumba
Savu Sea
DILI
Timor
Kepulauan Leti

EAST TIMOR

Sea

Torres Strait

Pulau
Sumba
Nikiniki
Kupang
Timor Sea

126

A U S T R A L I A

Elevation

| -6000m | -4000m | -2000m | -1000m | -500m | -250m | Below sea level 0 | 250m | 500m | 1000m | 2000m | 3000m | 4000m | 6000m |

-19,658ft -13,124ft -6562ft -3281ft -1640ft -820ft -328ft/-100m 0   820ft 1640ft 3281ft 6562ft 9843ft 13,124ft 19,685ft

The Indian Ocean

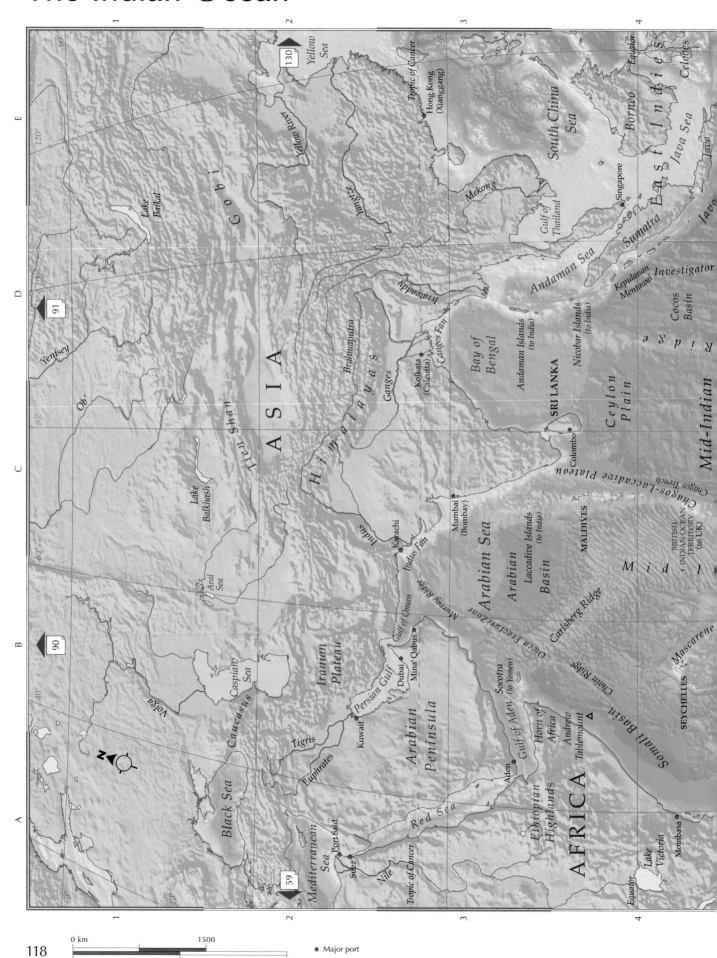

0 km   1500

0 miles   1500

● Major port

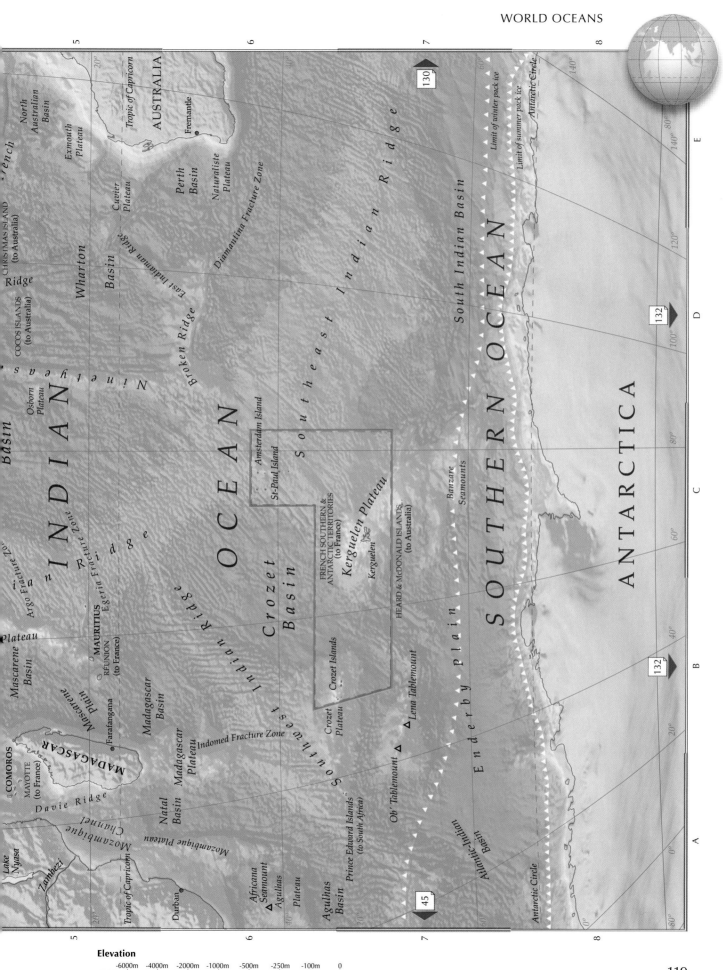

AUSTRALIA

Fremantle

Tropic of Capricorn

20°

North Australian Basin

Exmouth Plateau

CHRISTMAS ISLAND (to Australia)

French

Cuvier Plateau

Perth Basin

Naturaliste Plateau

Wharton Basin

COCOS ISLANDS (to Australia)

Ridge

Diamantina Fracture Zone

East Indiaman Ridge

Broken Ridge

S o u t h e a s t   I n d i a n   R i d g e

South Indian Basin

Ninetyeast Ridge

Osborn Plateau

basin

I N D I A N

O C E A N

Amsterdam Island

St-Paul Island

FRENCH SOUTHERN & ANTARCTIC TERRITORIES (to France)

Kerguelen Plateau

Kerguelen

SOUTHERN OCEAN

Limit of winter pack ice

Limit of summer pack ice

Antarctic Circle

Fan

Egeria Fracture Zone

Argo Fracture Zone

MAURITIUS

RÉUNION (to France)

Southwest Indian Ridge

Crozet Basin

Crozet Plateau

Crozet Islands

HEARD & McDONALD ISLANDS (to Australia)

Banzare Seamounts

ANTARCTICA

Plateau

Mascarene Basin

Mascarene Plateau

Farafangana

Madagascar Basin

Madagascar Plateau

Indomed Fracture Zone

Lena Tablemount

Ob' Tablemount

E n d e r b y   P l a i n

COMOROS

MAYOTTE (to France)

MADAGASCAR

Davie Ridge

Natal Basin

Mozambique Plateau (to South Africa)

Mozambique Channel

Prince Edward Islands (to South Africa)

Atlantic-Indian Basin

Lake Nyasa

Zambezi

Tropic of Capricorn

20°

Durban

Africana Seamount

Agulhas Plateau

Agulhas Basin

Antarctic Circle

40°

20°

0°

20°

40°

60°

80°

100°

120°

140°

E

D

C

B

A

132

132

45

130

Elevation

-6000m -4000m -2000m -1000m -500m -250m -100m 0

-19,658ft -13,124ft -6562ft -3281ft -1640ft -820ft -328ft/-100m 0

Australasia & Oceania

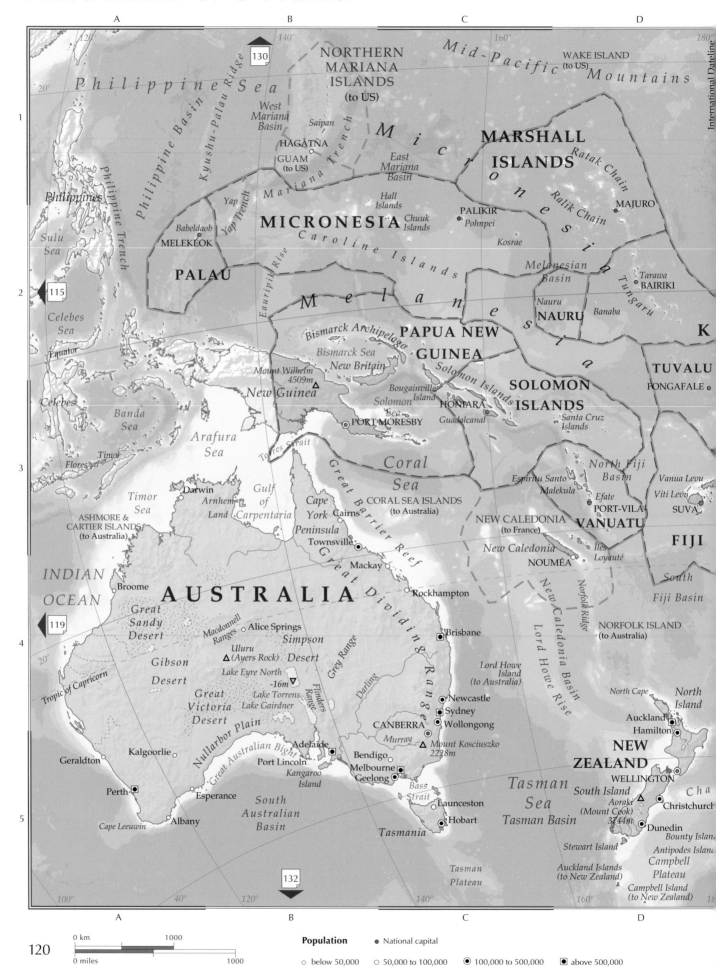

A · B · C · D

NORTHERN MARIANA ISLANDS
(to US)

Mid-Pacific Mountains

WAKE ISLAND
(to US)

Philippine Sea

Philippine Basin

Kyushu-Palau Ridge

West Mariana Basin

Saipan

MARSHALL ISLANDS

Ratak Chain

HAGÁTÑA
GUAM (to US)

East Mariana Basin

MAJURO

Philippines

Philippine Trench

Yap

Yap Trench

Hall Islands

PALIKIR
Pohnpei

Ralik Chain

Sulu Sea

Babeldaob

MICRONESIA

Chuuk Islands

Kosrae

Caroline Islands

Melanesian Basin

Tarawa
BAIRIKI

MELEKEOK

Eauripik Rise

PALAU

Melanesia

Nauru
NAURU

Banaba

Tungaru

Celebes Sea

Equator

K

Celebes

Banda Sea

Bismarck Archipelago

Bismarck Sea

New Britain

PAPUA NEW GUINEA

TUVALU

FONGAFALE

Mount Wilhelm 4509m

New Guinea

Bougainville Island

Solomon Islands

SOLOMON ISLANDS

North Fiji Basin

Vanua Levu

Timor

Flores

Solomon Sea

HONIARA

Santa Cruz Islands

Espiritu Santo
Malekula

Efate
PORT-VILA

Viti Levu
SUVA

Arafura Sea

PORT MORESBY

Guadalcanal

Torres Strait

Coral Sea

CORAL SEA ISLANDS
(to Australia)

NEW CALEDONIA
(to France)

New Caledonia

VANUATU

Îles Loyauté

FIJI

Timor Sea

Darwin

Arnhem Land

Gulf of Carpentaria

Cape York

Cairns

NOUMÉA

South Fiji Basin

ASHMORE & CARTIER ISLANDS
(to Australia)

Peninsula

Townsville

Great Barrier Reef

New Caledonia Ridge

Norfolk Ridge

INDIA OCEAN

Broome

AUSTRALIA

Rockhampton

Lord Howe Island
(to Australia)

NORFOLK ISLAND
(to Australia)

Great Sandy Desert

Alice Springs

Macdonnell Ranges

Simpson Desert

Brisbane

Lord Howe Rise

Gibson Desert

Uluru (Ayers Rock)

Grey Range

North Cape

North Island

Tropic of Capricorn

Lake Eyre North -16m

Great Victoria Desert

Lake Torrens
Lake Gairdner

Flinders Range

Darling

Newcastle
Sydney
Wollongong

Auckland
Hamilton

CANBERRA

Murray

Mount Kosciuszko 2228m

NEW ZEALAND

Geraldton

Kalgoorlie

Nullarbor Plain

Adelaide
Port Lincoln

Bendigo

Melbourne
Geelong

WELLINGTON

Tasman Sea

South Island

Aoraki (Mount Cook) 3744m

Christchurch

Perth

Esperance

Great Australian Bight

Kangaroo Island

South Australian Basin

Bass Strait

Launceston

Tasman Basin

Dunedin

Bounty Islan

Antipodes Island

Campbell Plateau

Albany

Cape Leeuwin

Hobart

Tasmania

Stewart Island

Auckland Islands
(to New Zealand)

Tasman Plateau

Campbell Island
(to New Zealand)

A · B · C · D

0 km — 1000
0 miles — 1000

Population   ● National capital

○ below 50,000   ○ 50,000 to 100,000   ◉ 100,000 to 500,000   ▣ above 500,000

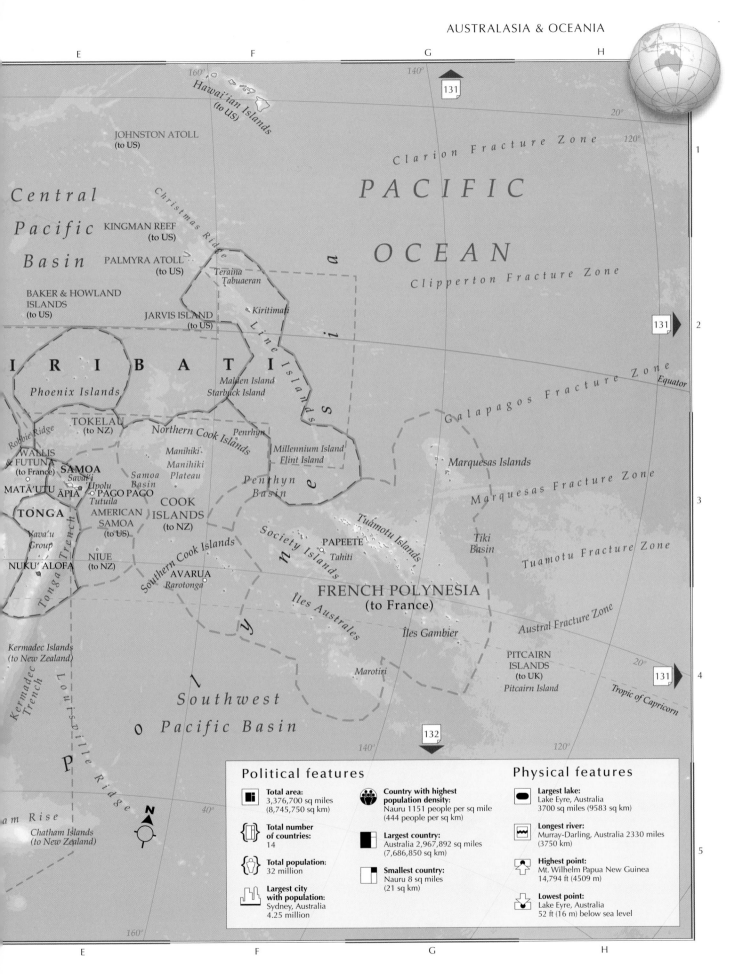

E — 160° — F — G — 140° — H — 120° — 20° — 1

131

Hawai'ian Islands
(to US)

JOHNSTON ATOLL
(to US)

Central

Pacific

Basin

KINGMAN REEF
(to US)

PALMYRA ATOLL
(to US)

BAKER & HOWLAND
ISLANDS
(to US)

JARVIS ISLAND
(to US)

Teraina
Tabuaeran

Kiritimati

P A C I F I C

O C E A N

Clarion Fracture Zone

Clipperton Fracture Zone

131

Equator

Galapagos Fracture Zone

Christmas Ridge

Line Islands

K I R I B A T I

Phoenix Islands

Malden Island
Starbuck Island

TOKELAU
(to NZ)

Northern Cook Islands

Penrhyn

Millennium Island
Flint Island

Marquesas Islands

Marquesas Fracture Zone

Robbie Ridge

WALLIS
& FUTUNA
(to France)

Manihiki
Manihiki
Plateau

SAMOA

MATA'UTU

Savai'i
Upolu

ĀPIA

PAGO PAGO
Tutuila

*Samoa
Basin*

*Penrhyn
Basin*

COOK
ISLANDS
(to NZ)

Society Islands

PAPEETE
Tahiti

Tuamotu Islands

*Tiki
Basin*

Tuamotu Fracture Zone

TONGA

Vava'u
Group

AMERICAN
SAMOA
(to US)

Southern Cook Islands

AVARUA
Rarotonga

FRENCH POLYNESIA
(to France)

Îles Australes

Îles Gambier

Austral Fracture Zone

NUKU'ALOFA

NIUE
(to NZ)

Tonga Trench

PITCAIRN
ISLANDS
(to UK)

Pitcairn Island

20°

131

Kermadec Islands
(to New Zealand)

Marotiri

Southwest

Pacific Basin

Tropic of Capricorn

Kermadec Trench

Louisville Ridge

140°

132

120°

...am Rise

Chatham Islands
(to New Zealand)

160°

N

40°

E — F — G — H

Political features

Total area:
3,376,700 sq miles
(8,745,750 sq km)

**Total number
of countries:**
14

Total population:
32 million

**Largest city
with population:**
Sydney, Australia
4.25 million

**Country with highest
population density:**
Nauru 1151 people per sq mile
(444 people per sq km)

Largest country:
Australia 2,967,892 sq miles
(7,686,850 sq km)

Smallest country:
Nauru 8 sq miles
(21 sq km)

Physical features

Largest lake:
Lake Eyre, Australia
3700 sq miles (9583 sq km)

Longest river:
Murray-Darling, Australia 2330 miles
(3750 km)

Highest point:
Mt. Wilhelm Papua New Guinea
14,794 ft (4509 m)

Lowest point:
Lake Eyre, Australia
52 ft (16 m) below sea level

The Southwest Pacific

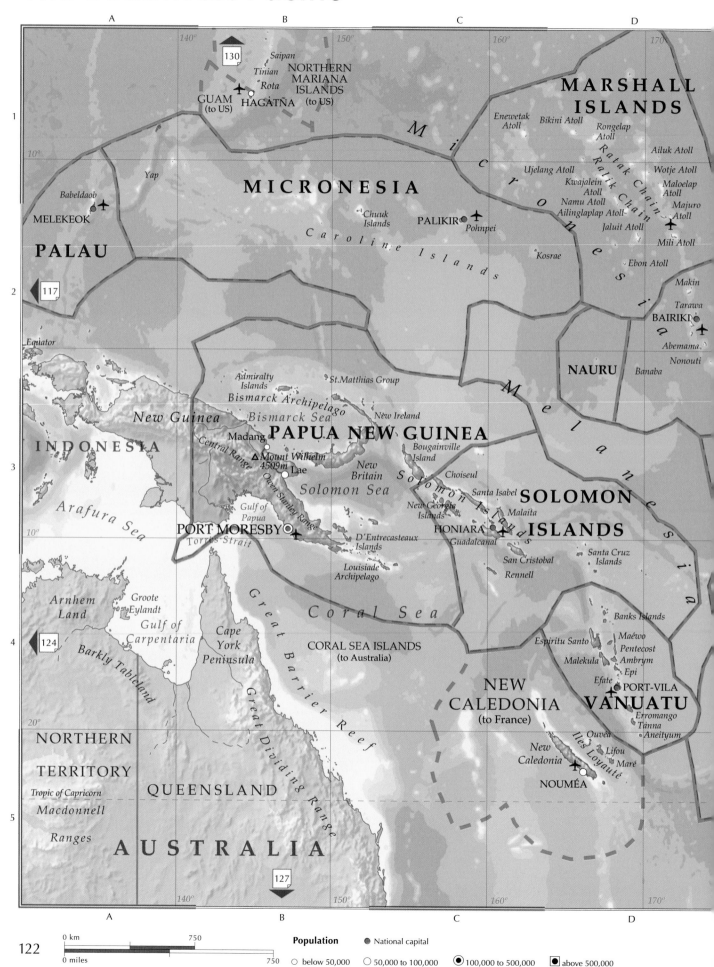

MARSHALL ISLANDS

Saipan
Tinian
Rota
NORTHERN MARIANA ISLANDS (to US)
GUAM (to US)
HAGÁTÑA
130

Eneuetak Atoll
Bikini Atoll
Rongelap Atoll
Ailuk Atoll
Ujelang Atoll
Wotje Atoll
Kwajalein Atoll
Maloelap Atoll
Namu Atoll
Majuro Atoll
Ailinglaplap Atoll
Jaluit Atoll
Mili Atoll

Yap

MICRONESIA

Babeldaob
MELEKEOK
Chuuk Islands
PALIKIR
Pohnpei
Caroline Islands
Kosrae
Ebon Atoll

PALAU

117

Makin
Tarawa
BAIRIKI
Abemama
Nonouti

Equator

NAURU
Banaba

Admiralty Islands
St.Matthias Group
Bismarck Archipelago
New Ireland
New Guinea
Bismarck Sea
PAPUA NEW GUINEA

INDONESIA
Madang
Central Range
△ Mount Wilhelm 4509m
Lae
New Britain
Solomon Sea
Bougainville Island
Choiseul
Santa Isabel
New Georgia Islands
Malaita
SOLOMON ISLANDS

Melanesia

Owen Stanley Range
Gulf of Papua
PORT MORESBY
Torres Strait
D'Entrecasteaux Islands
HONIARA
Guadalcanal
San Cristobal
Rennell
Louisiade Archipelago
Santa Cruz Islands

Arafura Sea

Arnhem Land
Groote Eylandt
Gulf of Carpentaria
Cape York Peninsula
Great Barrier Reef
Coral Sea
CORAL SEA ISLANDS (to Australia)

Banks Islands
Espiritu Santo
Maéwo
Pentecost
Malekula
Ambrym
Epi
Efate
PORT-VILA
VANUATU
Erromango
Tanna
Aneityum

Barkly Tableland
124

NORTHERN TERRITORY
Great Dividing Range
QUEENSLAND

NEW CALEDONIA (to France)

Ouvéa
Îles Loyauté
Lifou
Maré
New Caledonia
NOUMÉA

Tropic of Capricorn
Macdonnell Ranges

AUSTRALIA
127

0 km   750
0 miles   750

Population   ● National capital

○ below 50,000   ○ 50,000 to 100,000   ◉ 100,000 to 500,000   ■ above 500,000

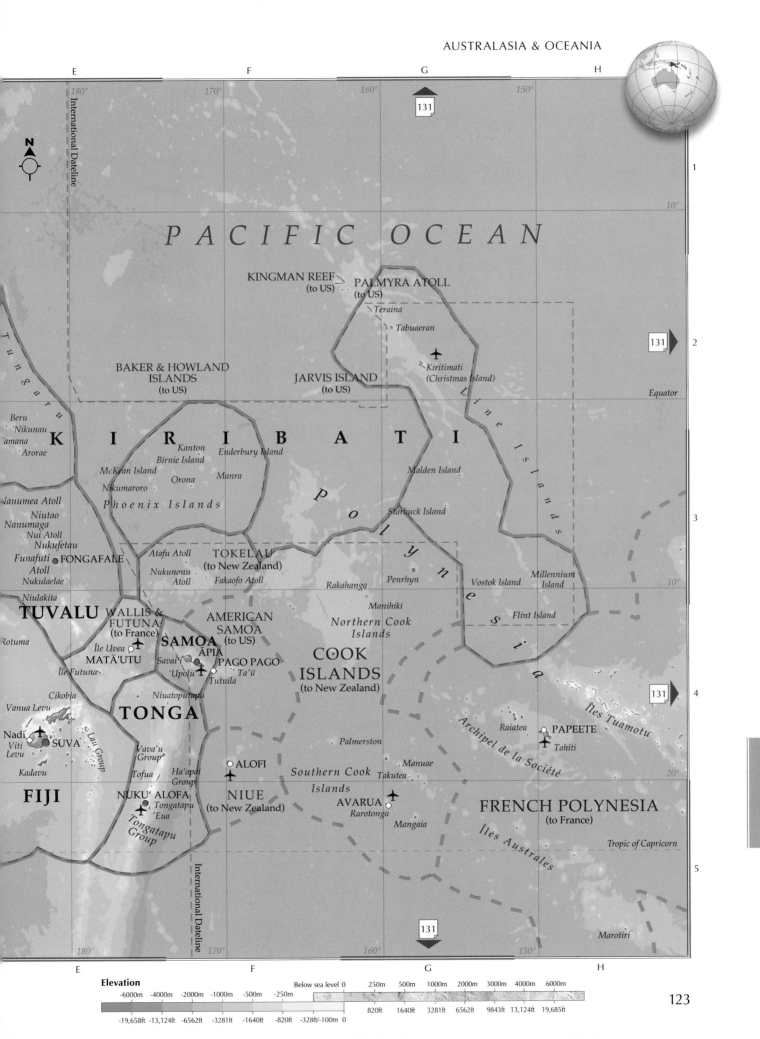

E   F   G   H

180°   *170°*   *160°*   *150°*

131

International Dateline

N

1

10°

PACIFIC OCEAN

131   2

KINGMAN REEF
(to US)

PALMYRA ATOLL
(to US)

Teraina

Tabuaeran

BAKER & HOWLAND
ISLANDS
(to US)

JARVIS ISLAND
(to US)

*Kiritimati
(Christmas Island)*

Line Islands

Equator

Beru
Nikunau
amana
Arorae

K I R I B A T I

Kanton

Birnie Island

McKean Island

Enderbury Island

Malden Island

Nikumaroro

Orona

Manra

P o l

Phoenix Islands

Starbuck Island

3

Nanumea Atoll
Niutao
Nanumaga
Nui Atoll
Nukufetau
Funafuti ● FONGAFALE
Atoll
Nukulaelae

Atafu Atoll

*Nukunonu
Atoll*

TOKELAU
(to New Zealand)

Fakaofo Atoll

Rakahanga

Penrhyn

Vostok Island

*Millennium
Island*

y

n

10°

Niulakita

TUVALU

WALLIS &
FUTUNA
(to France)

AMERICAN
SAMOA
(to US)

Manihiki

*Northern Cook
Islands*

Flint Island

e

s

Rotuma

Île Uvea ○
MATĀ'UTU

SAMOA
ĀPIA ●

Savai'i ○

Upolu

PAGO PAGO

Ta'ū

Tutuila

i

a

COOK
ISLANDS
(to New Zealand)

Raiatea
● PAPEETE

Cikobia

Niuatoputapu

Archipel de la Société

Îles Tuamotu

131   4

Vanua Levu

TONGA

Palmerston

Tahiti

Nadi
*Viti
Levu* ● SUVA

*Vava'u
Group*

Manuae

*Southern Cook
Islands*

Takutea

20°

Kadavu

Tofua

● ALOFI

*Ha'apai
Group*

Avarua ○
AVARUA

FRENCH POLYNESIA
(to France)

FIJI

NUKU'ALOFA

NIUE
(to New Zealand)

Rarotonga

Mangaia

Tongatapu
'Eua

*Tongatapu
Group*

Îles Australes

Tropic of Capricorn

International Dateline

131

5

180°   *170°*   *160°*   *150°*

Marotiri

E   F   G   H

Elevation

-6000m	-4000m	-2000m	-1000m	-500m	-250m	Below sea level 0	250m	500m	1000m	2000m	3000m	4000m	6000m
-19,658ft	-13,124ft	-6562ft	-3281ft	-1640ft	-820ft	-328ft/-100m 0	820ft	1640ft	3281ft	6562ft	9843ft	13,124ft	19,685ft

Western Australia

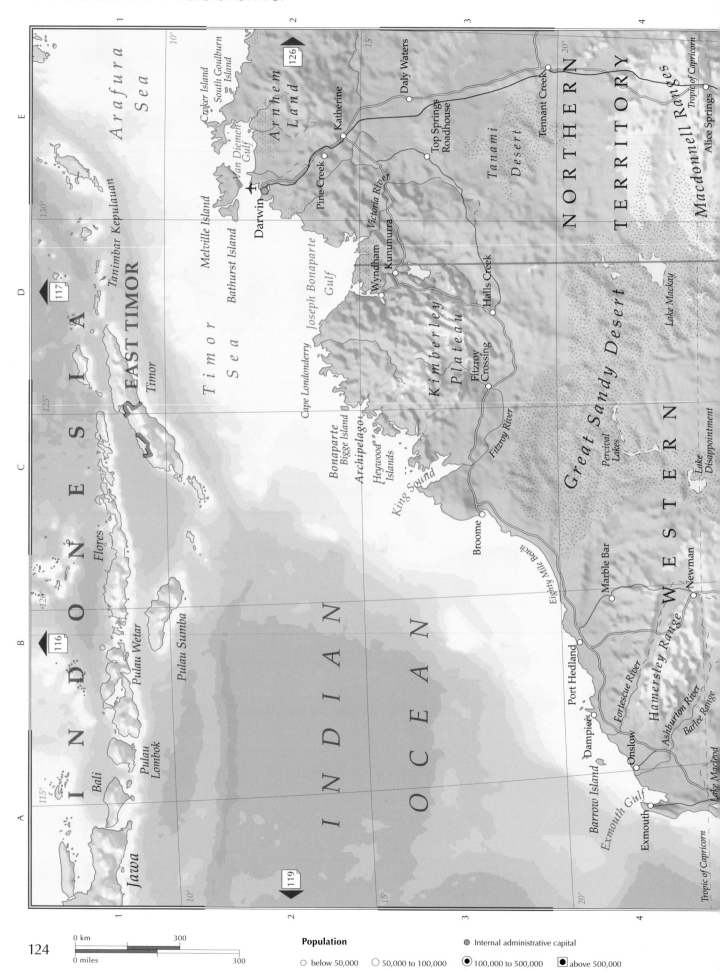

Arafura Sea

Croker Island
South Goulburn Island
Van Diemen Gulf
Arnhem Land

Daly Waters
Katherine

Pine Creek
Top Springs Roadhouse
Tanami Desert
Tennant Creek

Darwin
Melville Island
Bathurst Island

NORTHERN TERRITORY

Joseph Bonaparte Gulf

Wyndham
Kununurra
Victoria River

Halls Creek

Macdonnell Ranges
Alice Springs
Tropic of Capricorn

Cape Londonderry

Kimberley Plateau

Fitzroy Crossing

Great Sandy Desert

Lake Mackay

Timor Sea

Bonaparte Archipelago
Bigge Island
Heywood Islands
King Sound

Fitzroy River

Percival Lakes
Lake Disappointment

Tanimbar Kepulauan

EAST TIMOR

Timor

INDONESIA

Flores

Pulau Wetar

Pulau Sumba

Broome

Eighty Mile Beach

Marble Bar
Newman

WESTERN

Port Hedland

Dampier
Onslow

Hamersley Range
Fortescue River
Ashburton River
Barlee Range

Bali

Pulau Lombok

Jawa

INDIAN OCEAN

Barrow Island
Exmouth Gulf
Exmouth
Lake Macleod

Tropic of Capricorn

0 km   300
0 miles   300

Population

○ below 50,000
○ 50,000 to 100,000
◉ 100,000 to 500,000
◼ above 500,000

● Internal administrative capital

AUSTRALIA

SOUTH AUSTRALIA

AUSTRALIA

WESTERN AUSTRALIA

Gibson Desert

Great Victoria Desert

Musgrave Ranges

△ Uluru (Ayers Rock) 867m

Lake Amadeus

Nullarbor Plain

Great Australian Bight

INDIAN OCEAN

Coober Pedy
Tarcoola
Lake Everard
Lake Gairdner
Penong
Ceduna
Lake Gairdner
Elliston
Port Lincoln

Eucla

Reid

Zanthus
Balladonia
Norseman
Coolgardie
Lake Cowan
Kalgoorlie
Southern Cross
Merredin
Esperance

Lake Rebecca
Lake Carey
Lake Wells
Lake Carnegie

Robinson Range

Meekatharra
Mount Magnet
Lake Moore
Lake Barlee

Albany
Katanning
Wagin
Narrogin
Manjimup
Collie
Brookton
Northam
Bunbury
Busselton
Augusta
Mandurah
Rockingham
Fremantle
Perth
Gingin
Moora

Geraldton
Kalbarri

Murchison River
Gascoyne River

Carnarvon
Denham
Shark Bay
Bernier Island
Dorre Island
Dirk Hartog Island

Elevation

| -6000m | -4000m | -2000m | -1000m | -500m | -250m | Below sea level 0 | 250m | 500m | 1000m | 2000m | 3000m | 4000m | 6000m |

-19,658ft -13,124ft -6562ft -3281ft -1640ft -820ft -328ft/-100m 0   820ft 1640ft 3281ft 6562ft 9843ft 13,124ft 19,685ft

Eastern Australia

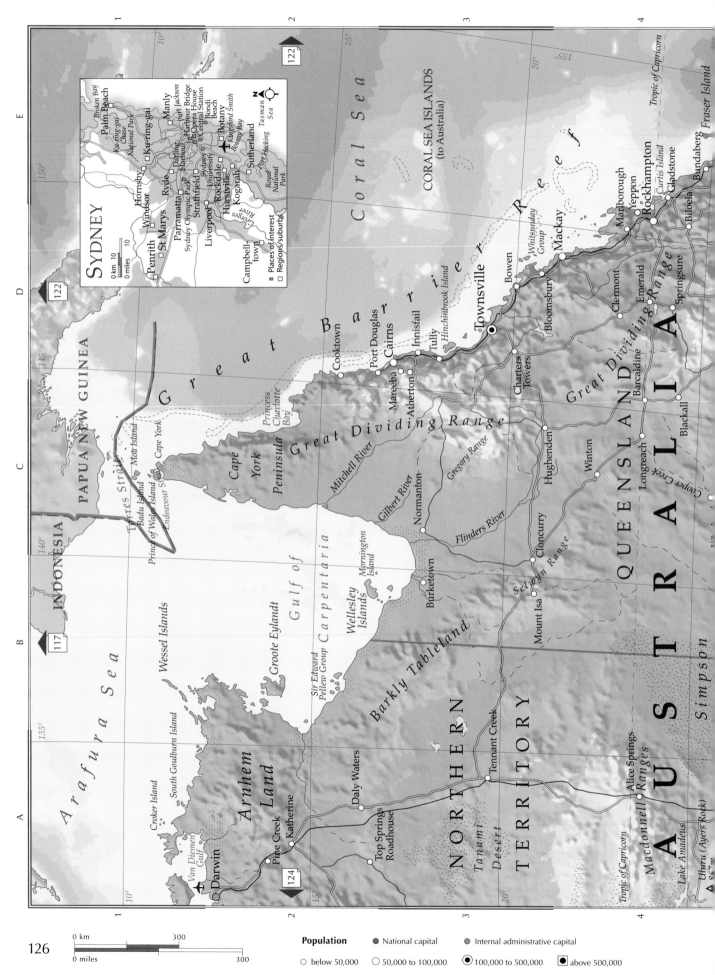

SYDNEY

Broken Bay
Palm Beach
Ku-ring-gai Chase National Park
Ku-ring-gai
Manly
Port Jackson
Harbour Bridge
Central Station
Opera House
Botany
Bondi
Kingsford Smith
Botany Bay
Sutherland
Port Hacking
Royal National Park

Hornsby
Windsor
Ryde
St Marys
Parramatta
Sydney Olympic Park
Strathfield
Penrith
Liverpool
Lewisham
Rockdale
Hurstville
Kogarah

Georges River

Campbell-town

0 km 10
0 miles 10

■ Places of interest
□ Regions/suburbs

Coral Sea

CORAL SEA ISLANDS
(to Australia)

Tropic of Capricorn

Fraser Island
Bundaberg
Biloela
Gladstone
Curtis Island
Rockhampton
Yeppon
Marlborough
Springsure
Emerald
Clermont
Barcaldine
Blackall
Mackay
Whitsunday Group
Bloomsbury
Bowen
Townsville
Charters Towers
Hughenden
Winton
Longreach

Great Barrier Reef

Cooktown
Port Douglas
Cairns
Mareeba
Atherton
Innisfail
Tully
Hinchinbrook Island

Great Dividing Range

QUEENSLAND

Cooper Creek

Hinchinbrook Island

PAPUA NEW GUINEA

INDONESIA

Torres Strait
Badu Island
Moa Island
Cape York
Prince of Wales Island
Endeavour Strait

Cape York Peninsula

Princess Charlotte Bay

Mitchell River

Gilbert River

Gregory Range

Normanton

Flinders River

Selwyn Range

Cloncurry
Mount Isa

Burketown

Barkly Tableland

Gulf of Carpentaria

Mornington Island

Wellesley Islands

Sir Edward Pellew Group

Groote Eylandt

Wessel Islands

South Goulburn Island

Croker Island

Van Diemen Gulf

Arafura Sea

Darwin
Pine Creek
Katherine

Arnhem Land

Daly Waters
Top Springs Roadhouse

Tennant Creek

NORTHERN TERRITORY

Tanami Desert

Simpson

Alice Springs
Macdonnell Ranges
Lake Amadeus
Uluru (Ayers Rock)

Tropic of Capricorn

AUSTRALIA

Tasman Sea

126

0 km 300
0 miles 300

Population
● National capital
● Internal administrative capital
○ below 50,000
○ 50,000 to 100,000
◉ 100,000 to 500,000
■ above 500,000

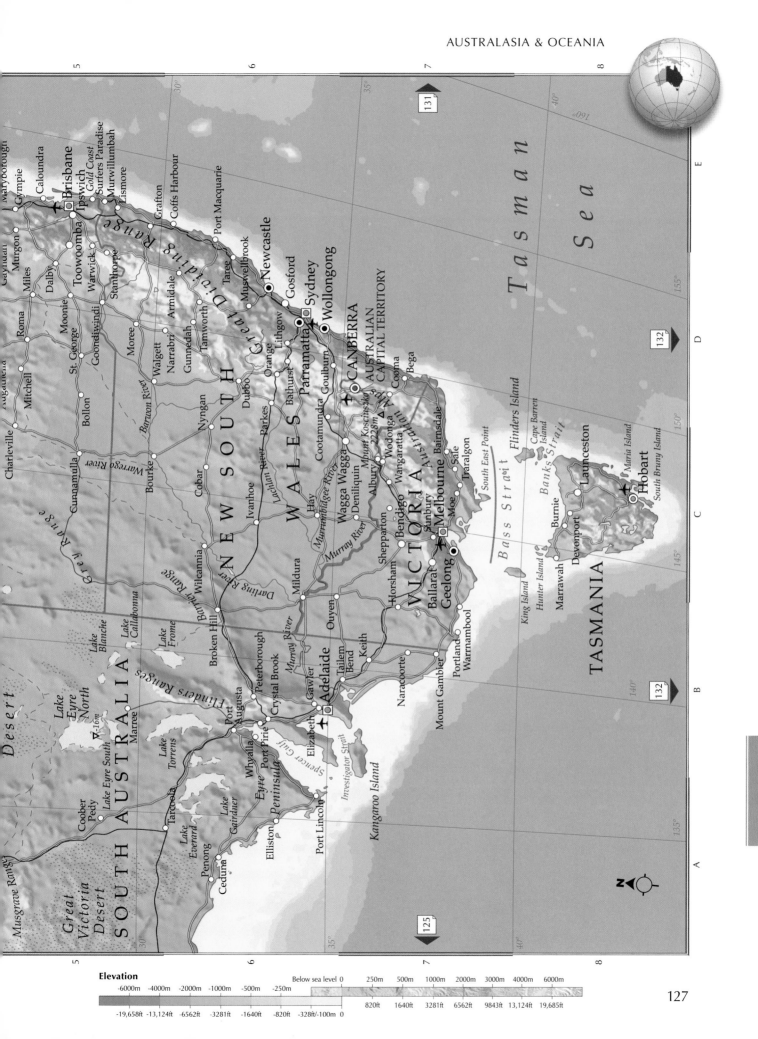

Elevation

-6000m	-4000m	-2000m	-1000m	-500m	-250m	Below sea level 0	250m	500m	1000m	2000m	3000m	4000m	6000m

| -19,658ft | -13,124ft | -6562ft | -3281ft | -1640ft | -820ft | -328ft/-100m 0 | 820ft | 1640ft | 3281ft | 6562ft | 9843ft | 13,124ft | 19,685ft |

New Zealand

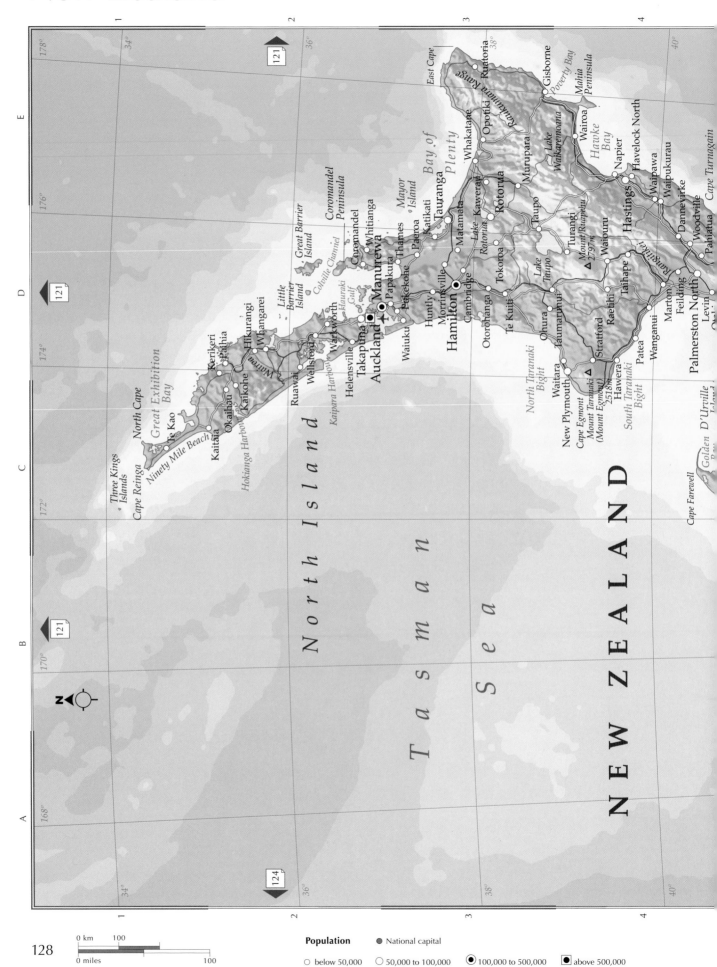

Population
● National capital
○ below 50,000 ○ 50,000 to 100,000 ◉ 100,000 to 500,000 ◼ above 500,000

0 km 100
0 miles 100

Elevation

129

The Pacific Ocean

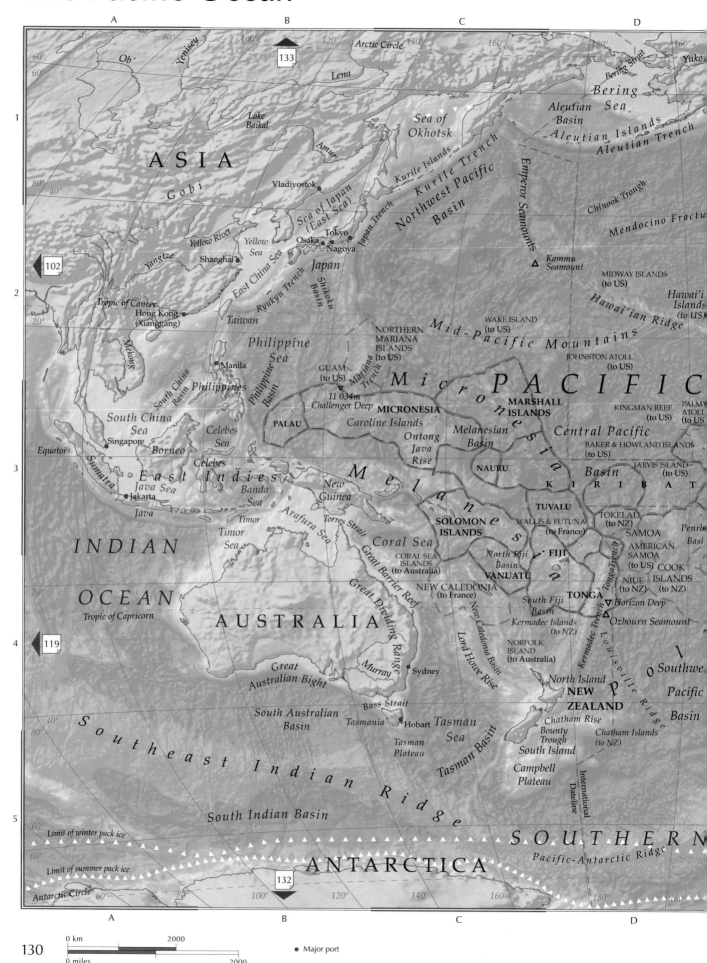

ASIA

Ob'
Yenisey
Lena
Arctic Circle
Lake Baikal
Amur
Gobi
Sea of Okhotsk
Kurile Islands
Kurile Trench
Northwest Pacific Basin
Emperor Seamounts
Bering Sea
Aleutian Basin
Aleutian Islands
Aleutian Trench
Bering Strait
Yuko
Chinook Trough
Mendocino Fractu

Vladivostok
Sea of Japan (East Sea)
Japan Trench
Kammu Seamount
MIDWAY ISLANDS (to US)
Yellow River
Yellow Sea
Tokyo
Osaka
Nagoya
Shanghai
East China Sea
Japan
Shikoku Basin
Hawai'ian Ridge
Hawai'i Islands (to US)
Yangtze

Tropic of Cancer
Hong Kong (Xianggang)
Taiwan
Ryukyu Trench
WAKE ISLAND (to US)
Mid-Pacific Mountains

Philippine Sea
NORTHERN MARIANA ISLANDS (to US)
JOHNSTON ATOLL (to US)
Mekong
Manila
Philippine Basin
GUAM (to US)
Mariana Trench
11 034m Challenger Deep
MICRONESIA
Micronesia
MARSHALL ISLANDS
PACIFIC
KINGMAN REEF (to US)
PALMY ATOLL (to US)

South China Basin
Philippines
PALAU
Caroline Islands
Melanesian Basin
Central Pacific
BAKER & HOWLAND ISLANDS (to US)
South China Sea
Singapore
Celebes Sea
Ontong Java Rise
NAURU
Basin
JARVIS ISLAND (to US)
Equator
Borneo
Celebes
East Indies
Melanesia
KIRIBAT
Sumatra
Java Sea
Banda Sea
New Guinea
TUVALU
TOKELAU (to NZ)
Jakarta
Timor
Arafura Sea
Torres Strait
SOLOMON ISLANDS
WALLIS & FUTUNA (to France)
SAMOA
Penrh Basi
Java
Timor Sea
Great Barrier Reef
Coral Sea
CORAL SEA ISLANDS (to Australia)
North Fiji Basin
FIJI
AMERICAN SAMOA (to US)
COOK ISLANDS (to NZ)

INDIAN
VANUATU
NIUE (to NZ)
NEW CALEDONIA (to France)
South Fiji Basin
TONGA
Horizon Deep
Ozbourn Seamount
OCEAN
Tropic of Capricorn
AUSTRALIA
Great Dividing Range
New Caledonia Basin
Kermadec Islands (to NZ)
Kermadec Trench
Tonga Trench
Louisville Ridge
Southwe
NORFOLK ISLAND (to Australia)
Pacific Basin

Great Australian Bight
Murray
Sydney
Lord Howe Rise
North Island
NEW ZEALAND
Bass Strait
Tasman Sea
Chatham Rise
South Australian Basin
Tasmania
Hobart
Tasman Plateau
Bounty Trough
Chatham Islands (to NZ)
Southeast Indian Ridge
Tasman Basin
South Island
Campbell Plateau
International Dateline

South Indian Basin
SOUTHERN
Limit of winter pack ice
Pacific-Antarctic Ridge
Limit of summer pack ice
ANTARCTICA
Antarctic Circle

0 km   2000
0 miles   2000

● Major port

130

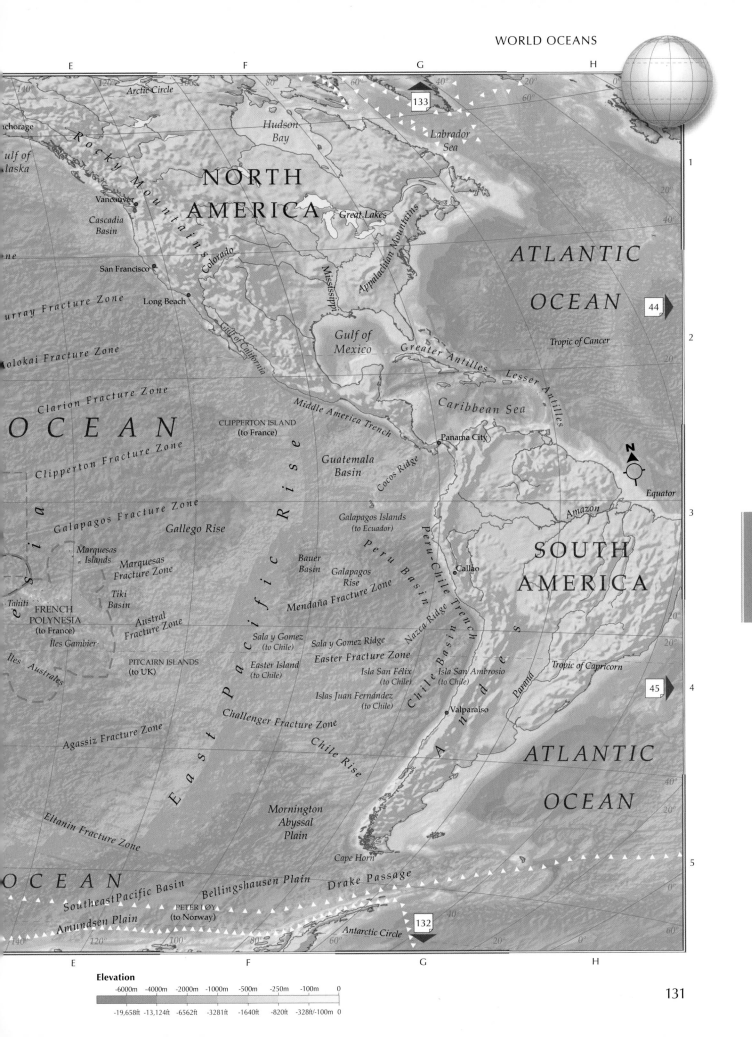

Elevation

-6000m	-4000m	-2000m	-1000m	-500m	-250m	-100m	0
-19,658ft	-13,124ft	-6562ft	-3281ft	-1640ft	-820ft	-328ft/-100m	0

Labels on map:

Arctic Circle
Hudson Bay
Labrador Sea
NORTH AMERICA
Great Lakes
ATLANTIC OCEAN
nchorage
Gulf of Alaska
Rocky Mountains
Vancouver
Cascadia Basin
San Francisco
Colorado
Appalachian Mountains
Long Beach
Mississippi
Tropic of Cancer
Gulf of California
Gulf of Mexico
Greater Antilles
Lesser Antilles
urray Fracture Zone
olokai Fracture Zone
Caribbean Sea
Clarion Fracture Zone
OCEAN
Middle America Trench
CLIPPERTON ISLAND (to France)
Clipperton Fracture Zone
Guatemala Basin
Cocos Ridge
Panama City
N
Galapagos Fracture Zone
Gallego Rise
Galapagos Islands (to Ecuador)
Equator
sia
Marquesas Islands
Marquesas Fracture Zone
Bauer Basin
Galapagos Rise
Peru Basin
SOUTH AMERICA
Amazon
Tahiti
Tiki Basin
Mendaña Fracture Zone
Callao
Peru-Chile Trench
FRENCH POLYNESIA (to France)
Austral Fracture Zone
East Pacific Rise
Îles Gambier
Sala y Gomez (to Chile)
Sala y Gomez Ridge
Nazca Ridge
Tropic of Capricorn
Îles Australes
PITCAIRN ISLANDS (to UK)
Easter Island (to Chile)
Easter Fracture Zone
Isla San Félix (to Chile)
Isla San Ambrosio (to Chile)
Chile Basin
Andes
Paraná
Islas Juan Fernández (to Chile)
Valparaíso
Challenger Fracture Zone
Agassiz Fracture Zone
Chile Rise
ATLANTIC OCEAN
Mornington Abyssal Plain
Eltanin Fracture Zone
OCEAN
Southeast Pacific Basin
Bellingshausen Plain
Cape Horn
Drake Passage
Amundsen Plain
PETER I ØY (to Norway)
Antarctic Circle

Antarctica

45

ATLANTIC

OCEAN

SOUTH GEORGIA
(to UK)

SOUTH SANDWICH
ISLANDS
(to UK)

South Sandwich Trench

America-Antarctica Ridge

Limit of winter pack ice

Atlantic-Indian Basin

SOUTHERN

OCEAN

Enderby Plain

Scotia
Sea

Antarctic Circle

Lazarev Sea

Weddell Plain

Orcadas
(Argentina)

South Orkney
Islands

Signy
(UK)

South Shetland
Islands

Sanae
(South Africa)

Georg von Neumayer
(Germany)

Novolazarevskaya
(Russian Federation)

Dronning Maud
Land

Lützow
Holmbukta

Molodezhnaya
(Russian Federation)

Syowa
(Japan)

119

Drake Passage

43

Esperanza
(Argentina)

Capitán Arturo Prat
(Chile)

Palmer
(US)

Antarctic Peninsula

Limit of summer pack ice

Halley
(UK)

Weddell
Sea

Coats
Land

Enderby
Land

Mawson
(Australia)

Belgrano II
(Argentina)

Berkner
Island

Cape
Darnley

Rothera
(UK)

San Martin
(Argentina)

Palmer Land

Ronne
Ice Shelf

Mackenzie
Bay

Prydz Bay

Alexander
Island

Princess
Elizabeth
Land

Davis
(Australia)

ANTARCTICA

Bellingshausen
Sea

Vinson Massif
4897m

PETER I ØY
(to Norway)

Ellsworth
Land

West
Antarctica

Transantarctic Mountains

Amundsen-Scott
(US)
South
Pole

East

Antarctica

Davis
Sea

Mirny
(Russian Federation)

South
Geomagnetic
Pole

Vostok
(Russian Federation)

Shackleton
Ice Shelf

Limit of winter pack ice

Limit of summer pack ice

Amundsen
Sea

Marie Byrd Land

Mount Sidley
4181m

Mount Siple
3100m

Mount Kirkpatrick
4528m

Mount Markham
4351m

Ross Ice
Shelf

Roosevelt
Island

Scott Base
(N.Z)

McMurdo Base
(US)

Mount Erebus
3794m

Victoria Land

Wilkes
Land

Casey
(Australia)

Cape
Poinsett

131

Amundsen
Plain

Ross
Sea

Terre
Adélie

130

SOUTHERN

OCEAN

Cape Adare

Leningradskaya
(Russian Federation)

George V
Land

Dumont d'Urville
(France)

South

Indian

Basin

Pacific-Antarctic Ridge

Scott Island

Balleny Islands

Macquarie Ridge

Udintsev Fracture Zone

Eltanin Fracture Zone

● Antarctic research station

130

0 km 500
0 miles 500

Elevation

Below sea level 0 250m 500m 1000m 2000m 3000m 4000m 6000m

-6000m -4000m -2000m -1000m -500m -250m

-19,658ft -13,124ft -6562ft -3281ft -1640ft -820ft -328ft/-100m 0

820ft 1640ft 3281ft 6562ft 9843ft 13,124ft 19,685ft

Arctic Ocean

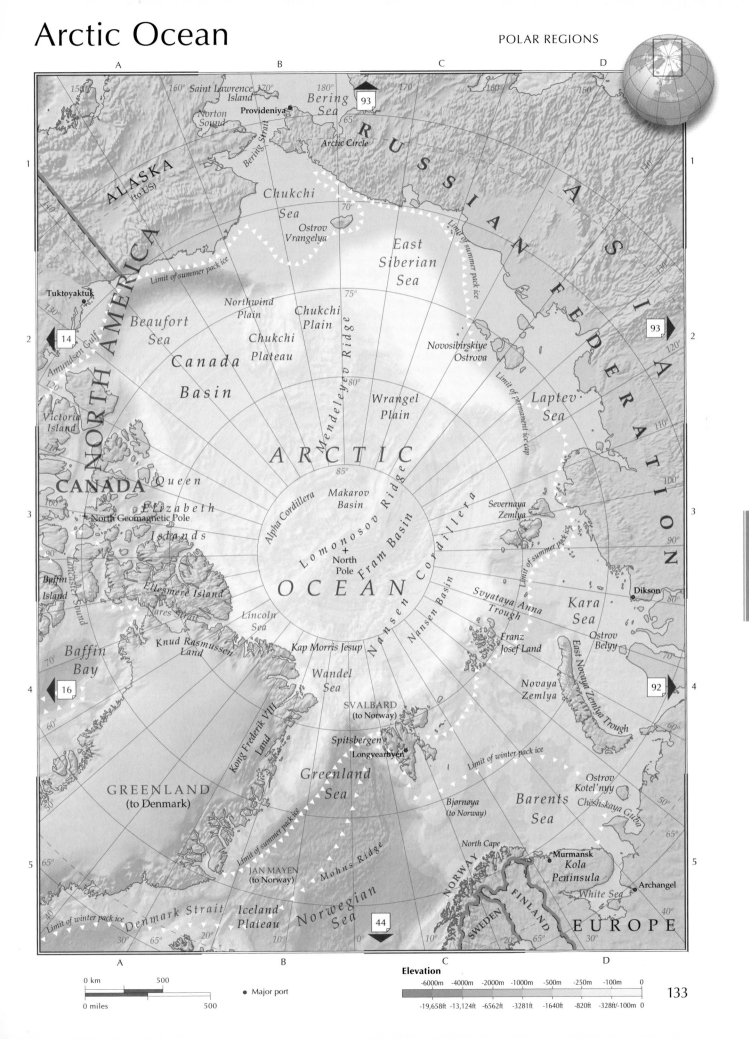

RUSSIAN FEDERATION

ASIA

NORTH AMERICA

CANADA

ALASKA (to US)

EUROPE

NORWAY

SWEDEN

FINLAND

GREENLAND (to Denmark)

SVALBARD (to Norway)

JAN MAYEN (to Norway)

ARCTIC OCEAN

Seas and Water Features
- Bering Sea
- Chukchi Sea
- East Siberian Sea
- Laptev Sea
- Kara Sea
- Barents Sea
- White Sea
- Beaufort Sea
- Baffin Bay
- Lincoln Sea
- Wandel Sea
- Greenland Sea
- Norwegian Sea
- Chëshskaya Guba
- Norton Sound
- Amundsen Gulf
- Bering Strait
- Lancaster Sound
- Nares Strait
- Denmark Strait

Physical Features
- Chukchi Plain
- Chukchi Plateau
- Northwind Plain
- Canada Basin
- Wrangel Plain
- Mendeleyev Ridge
- Makarov Basin
- Alpha Cordillera
- Lomonosov Ridge
- Fram Basin
- Nansen Basin
- Nansen Cordillera
- Svyataya Anna Trough
- East Novaya Zemlya Trough
- Mohns Ridge
- Iceland Plateau
- Knud Rasmussen Land
- Kong Frederik VIII Land

Places and Labels
- Saint Lawrence Island
- Providerniya
- Arctic Circle
- Ostrov Vrangelya
- Novosibirskiye Ostrova
- Severnaya Zemlya
- Franz Josef Land
- Novaya Zemlya
- Ostrov Belyy
- Ostrov Kotel'nyy
- Dikson
- North Cape
- Murmansk
- Kola Peninsula
- Archangel
- Bjørnøya (to Norway)
- Spitsbergen
- Longyearbyen
- Tuktoyaktuk
- Victoria Island
- Queen Elizabeth Islands
- North Geomagnetic Pole
- Buffin Island
- Ellesmere Island
- Kap Morris Jesup
- North Pole

Limit of summer pack ice
Limit of winter pack ice
Limit of permanent ice cap

Elevation

-6000m	-4000m	-2000m	-1000m	-500m	-250m	-100m	0
-19,658ft	-13,124ft	-6562ft	-3281ft	-1640ft	-820ft	-328ft/-100m	0

0 km — 500
0 miles — 500

● Major port

Country Profiles

This Factfile is intended as a guide to a world that is continually changing as political fashions and personalities come and go. Nevertheless, all the material in these factfiles has been researched from the most up-to-date and authoritative sources to give an incisive portrait of the geographical, political, and social characteristics that make each country so unique.

There are currently 196 independent countries in the world - more than at any previous time - and over 60 dependencies. Antarctica is the only land area on Earth that is not officially part of, and does not belong to, any single country.

Country profile key

Formation Date of independence / date current borders were established

Population Total population / population density – based on total *land* area

Languages An asterisk (*) denotes the official language(s)

Calorie consumption Average number of calories consumed daily per person

---

AFGHANISTAN
Central Asia

Page 100 D4

In 2001, following a US-led offensive, the hard-line Muslim taliban militia was replaced by a new interim government under Hamid Karazi

Official name Islamic Republic of Afghanistan
Formation 1919 / 1919
Capital Kabul
Population 29.1 million / 116 people per sq mile (45 people per sq km)
Total area 250,000 sq. miles (647,500 sq. km)
Languages Pashtu*, Tajik, Dari*, Farsi, Uzbek, Turkmen
Religions Sunni Muslim 80%, Shi'a Muslim 19%, Other 1%
Ethnic mix Pashtun 38%, Tajik 25%, Hazara 19%, Uzbek and Turkmen 15%, Other 3%
Government Presidential system
Currency Afghani = 100 puls
Literacy rate 28%
Calorie consumption 1539 kilocalories

ALBANIA
Southeast Europe

Page 79 C6

Lying at the southeastern end of the Adriatic Sea, Albania held its first multiparty elections in 1991, after nearly five decades of communism.

Official name Republic of Albania
Formation 1912 / 1921
Capital Tirana
Population 3.2 million / 302 people per sq mile (117 people per sq km)
Total area 11,100 sq. miles (28,748 sq. km)
Languages Albanian*, Greek
Religions Sunni Muslim 70%, Albanian Orthodox 20%, Roman Catholic 10%
Ethnic mix Albanian 98%, Greek 1%, Other 1%
Government Parliamentary system
Currency Lek = 100 qindarka (qintars)
Literacy rate 96%
Calorie consumption 2904 kilocalories

ALGERIA
North Africa

Page 48 C3

Algeria achieved independence from France in 1962. Today, its military-dominated government faces a severe challenge from Islamic extremists.

Official name People's Democratic Republic of Algeria
Formation 1962 / 1962
Capital Algiers
Population 35.4 million / 38 people per sq mile (15 people per sq km)
Total area 919,590 sq. miles (2,381,740 sq. km)
Languages Arabic*, Tamazight (Kabyle, Shawia, Tamashek), French
Religions Sunni Muslim 99%, Christian & Jewish 1%
Ethnic mix Arab 75%, Berber 24%, European & Jewish 1%
Government Presidential system
Currency Algerian dinar = 100 centimes
Literacy rate 75%
Calorie consumption 3104 kilocalories

ANDORRA
Southwest Europe

Page 69 B6

A tiny landlocked principality, Andorra lies high in the eastern Pyrenees between France and Spain. It held its first full elections in 1993.

Official name Principality of Andorra
Formation 1278 / 1278
Capital Andorra la Vella
Population 84,825 / 471 people per sq mile (182 people per sq km)
Total area 181 sq. miles (468 sq. km)
Languages Spanish, Catalan*, French, Portuguese
Religions Roman Catholic 94%, Other 6%
Ethnic mix Spanish 46%, Andorran 28%, Other 18%, French 8%
Government Parliamentary system
Currency Euro = 100 cents
Literacy rate 99%
Calorie consumption Not available

ANGOLA
Southern Africa

Page 56 B2

Located in southwest Africa, Angola was in an almost constant state of civil war for nearly 30 years, until a peace deal was agreed in 2002.

Official name Republic of Angola
Formation 1975 / 1975
Capital Luanda
Population 19 million / 39 people per sq mile (15 people per sq km)
Total area 481,351 sq. miles (1,246,700 sq. km)
Languages Portuguese*, Umbundu, Kimbundu, Kikongo
Religions Roman Catholic 68%, Protestant 20%, Indigenous beliefs 12%
Ethnic mix Ovimbundu 37%, Kimbundu 25%, Other 25%, Bakongo 13%
Government Presidential system
Currency Readjusted kwanza = 100 lwei
Literacy rate 70%
Calorie consumption 1949 kilocalories

ANTIGUA & BARBUDA
West Indies

Page 33 H3

Lying on the Atlantic edge of the Leeward Islands, Antigua and Barbuda's area includes the uninhabited islet of Redonda.

Official name Antigua and Barbuda
Formation 1981 / 1981
Capital St. John's
Population 87,884 / 517 people per sq mile (200 people per sq km)
Total area 170 sq. miles (442 sq. km)
Languages English*, English patois
Religions Anglican 45%, Other Protestant 42%, Roman Catholic 10%, Other 3%
Ethnic mix Black African 95%, Other 5%
Government Parliamentary system
Currency East Caribbean dollar = 100 cents
Literacy rate 99%
Calorie consumption 2319 kilocalories

ARGENTINA
South America

Page 43 B5

Most of the southern half of South America is occupied by Argentina. The country returned to civilian rule in 1983 after a series of military coups.

Official name Republic of Argentina
Formation 1816 / 1816
Capital Buenos Aires
Population 40.7 million / 39 people per sq mile (15 people per sq km)
Total area 1,068,296 sq. miles (2,766,890 sq. km)
Languages Spanish*, Italian, Amerindian languages
Religions Roman Catholic 70%, Other 18%, Protestant 9%, Muslim 2%, Jewish 1%
Ethnic mix Indo-European 97%, Mestizo 2%, Amerindian 1%
Government Presidential system
Currency Argentine peso = 100 centavos
Literacy rate 98%
Calorie consumption 3001 kilocalories

ARMENIA
Southwest Asia

Page 95 F3

Smallest of the former USSR's republics, Armenia lies in the Lesser Caucasus mountains. Territorial war with Azerbaijan ended in a 1994 ceasefire.

Official name Republic of Armenia
Formation 1991 / 1991
Capital Yerevan
Population 3.1 million / 269 people per sq mile (104 people per sq km)
Total area 11,506 sq. miles (29,800 sq. km)
Languages Armenian*, Azeri, Russian
Religions Armenian Apostolic Church (Orthodox) 88%, Other 6%, Armenian Catholic Church 6%
Ethnic mix Armenian 98%, Other 1%, Yezidi 1%
Government Parliamentary system
Currency Dram = 100 luma
Literacy rate 99%
Calorie consumption 2250 kilocalories

AUSTRALIA
Australasia & Oceania

Page 120 A4

An island continent located between the Indian and Pacific oceans, Australia was settled by Europeans 200 years ago, but now has many Asian immigrants.

Official name Commonwealth of Australia
Formation 1901 / 1901
Capital Canberra
Population 21.5 million / 7 people per sq mile (3 people per sq km)
Total area 2,967,893 sq. miles (7,686,850 sq. km)
Languages English*, Italian, Cantonese, Greek, Arabic, Vietnamese, Aboriginal languages
Religions Roman Catholic 26%, Nonreligious 19%, Anglican 19%, Other 17%, Other Christian 13%, United Church 6%
Ethnic mix
Government Parliamentary system
Currency Australian dollar = 100 cents
Literacy rate 99%
Calorie consumption 3186 kilocalories

AUSTRIA
Central Europe

Page 73 D7

Bordering eight countries in the heart of Europe, Austria was created in 1920 after the collapse of the Austro-Hungarian Empire the previous year.

Official name Republic of Austria
Formation 1918 / 1919
Capital Vienna
Population 8.4 million / 263 people per sq mile (102 people per sq km)
Total area 32,378 sq. miles (83,858 sq. km)
Languages German*, Croatian, Slovenian, Hungarian (Magyar)
Religions Roman Catholic 78%, Nonreligious 9%, Other 8%, Protestant 5%
Ethnic mix Austrian 93%, Croat, Slovene, and Hungarian 6%, Other 1%
Government Parliamentary system
Currency Euro = 100 cents
Literacy rate 99%
Calorie consumption 3760 kilocalories

AZERBAIJAN
Southwest Asia

Page 95 G2

Situated on the western coast of the Caspian Sea, Azerbaijan was the first Soviet republic to declare independence from Moscow in 1991.

Official name Republic of Azerbaijan
Formation 1991 / 1991
Capital Baku
Population 8.9 million / 266 people per sq mile (103 people per sq km)
Total area 33,436 sq. miles (86,600 sq. km)
Languages Azeri*, Russian
Religions Shi'a Muslim 68%, Sunni Muslim 26%, Russian Orthodox 3%, Armenian Apostolic Church (Orthodox) 2%, Other 1%
Ethnic mix Azeri 91%, Other 3%, Armenian 2%, Russian 2%, Lazs 2%
Government Presidential system
Currency New manat = 100 gopik
Literacy rate 99%
Calorie consumption 2996 kilocalories

BAHAMAS
West Indies

Page 32 C1

Located in the western Atlantic, off the Florida coast, the Bahamas comprise some 700 islands and 2,400 cays, only 30 of which are inhabited.

Official name Commonwealth of the Bahamas
Formation 1973 / 1973
Capital Nassau
Population 300,000 / 78 people per sq mile (30 people per sq km)
Total area 5382 sq. miles (13,940 sq. km)
Languages English*, English Creole, French Creole
Religions Baptist 32%, Anglican 20%, Roman Catholic 19%, Other 17%, Methodist 6%, Church of God 6%
Ethnic mix Black African 85%, European 12%, Asian and Hispanic 3%
Government Parliamentary system
Currency Bahamian dollar = 100 cents
Literacy rate 96%
Calorie consumption 2701 kilocalories

BAHRAIN
Southwest Asia

Page 98 C4

Bahrain is an archipelago of 33 islands between the Qatar peninsula and the Saudi Arabian mainland. Only three of these islands are inhabited.

Official name Kingdom of Bahrain
Formation 1971 / 1971
Capital Manama
Population 800,000 / 2930 people per sq mile (1133 people per sq km)
Total area 239 sq. miles (620 sq. km)
Languages Arabic
Religions Muslim (mainly Shi'a) 99%, Other 1%
Ethnic mix Bahraini 63%, Asian 19%, Other Arab 10%, Iranian 8%
Government Mixed monarchical–parliamentary system
Currency Bahraini dinar = 1000 fils
Literacy rate 91%
Calorie consumption Not available

BANGLADESH
South Asia

Page 113 G3

Bangladesh lies at the north of the Bay of Bengal. It seceded from Pakistan in 1971 and, after much political instability, returned to democracy in 1991.

Official name People's Republic of Bangladesh
Formation 1971 / 1971
Capital Dhaka
Population 164 million / 3180 people per sq mile (1228 people per sq km)
Total area 55,598 sq. miles (144,000 sq. km)
Languages Bengali*, Urdu, Chakma, Marma (Magh), Garo, Khasi, Santhali, Tripuri, Mro
Religions Muslim (mainly Sunni) 88%, Hindu 11%, Other 1%
Ethnic mix Bengali 98%, Other 2%
Government Parliamentary system
Currency Taka = 100 poisha
Literacy rate 56%
Calorie consumption 2250 kilocalories

BARBADOS
West Indies

Page 33 H4

Barbados is the most easterly of the Caribbean Windward Islands. Under British rule for 339 years, it became fully independent in 1966.

Official name Barbados
Formation 1966 / 1966
Capital Bridgetown
Population 300,000 / 1807 people per sq mile (698 people per sq km)
Total area 166 sq. miles (430 sq. km)
Languages Bajan (Barbadian English), English*
Religions Anglican 40%, Other 24%, Nonreligious 17%, Pentecostal 8%, Methodist 7%, Roman Catholic 4%
Ethnic mix Black African 92%, Other 3%, White 3%, Mixed race 2%
Government Parliamentary system
Currency Barbados dollar = 100 cents
Literacy rate 99%
Calorie consumption 3055 kilocalories

BELARUS
Eastern Europe

Page 85 B6

Formerly known as White Russia, Belarus lies landlocked in eastern Europe. The country reluctantly became independent of the USSR in 1991.

Official name Republic of Belarus
Formation 1991 / 1991
Capital Minsk
Population 9.6 million / 120 people per sq mile (46 people per sq km)
Total area 80,154 sq. miles (207,600 sq. km)
Languages Belarussian*, Russian*
Religions Orthodox Christian 80%, Roman Catholic 14%, Other 4%, Protestant 2%
Ethnic mix Belarussian 81%, Russian 11%, Polish 4%, Ukrainian 2%, Other 2%
Government Presidential system
Currency Belarussian rouble = 100 kopeks
Literacy rate 99%
Calorie consumption 3086 kilocalories

BELGIUM
Northwest Europe

Page 65 B6

Located in northwestern Europe, Belgium's history has been marked by the division between its Flemish- and French-speaking communities.

Official name Kingdom of Belgium
Formation 1830 / 1919
Capital Brussels
Population 10.7 million / 844 people per sq mile (326 people per sq km)
Total area 11,780 sq. miles (30,510 sq. km)
Languages Dutch*, French*, German*
Religions Roman Catholic 88%, Other 10%, Muslim 2%
Ethnic mix Fleming 58%, Walloon 33%, Other 6%, Italian 2%, Moroccan 1%
Government Parliamentary system
Currency Euro = 100 cents
Literacy rate 99%
Calorie consumption 3690 kilocalories

BARBADOS / BELIZE
Central America

Page 30 B1

The last Central American country to gain independence, this former British colony lies on the eastern shore of the Yucatan Peninsula.

Official name Belize
Formation 1981 / 1981
Capital Belmopan
Population 300,000 / 34 people per sq mile (13 people per sq km)
Total area 8867 sq. miles (22,966 sq. km)
Languages English Creole, Spanish, English*, Mayan, Garifuna (Carib)
Religions Roman Catholic 62%, Other 16%, Anglican 12%, Methodist 6%, Mennonite 4%
Ethnic mix Mestizo 49%, Creole 25%, Maya 11%, Garifuna 6%, Other 6%, Asian Indian 3%
Government Parliamentary system
Currency Belizean dollar = 100 cents
Literacy rate 75%
Calorie consumption 2719 kilocalories

BENIN
West Africa

Page 53 F4

Stretching north from the West African coast, Benin became one of the pioneers of African democratization in 1990, ending years of military rule.

Official name Republic of Benin
Formation 1960 / 1960
Capital Porto-Novo
Population 9.2 million / 215 people per sq mile (83 people per sq km)
Total area 43,483 sq. miles (112,620 sq. km)
Languages Fon, Bariba, Yoruba, Adja, Houeda, Somba, French*
Religions Indigenous beliefs and Voodoo 50%, Christian 30%, Muslim 20%
Ethnic mix Fon 41%, Other 21%, Adja 16%, Yoruba 12%, Bariba 10%
Government Presidential system
Currency CFA franc = 100 centimes
Literacy rate 42%
Calorie consumption 2512 kilocalories

BHUTAN
South Asia

Page 113 G3

The landlocked Buddhist kingdom of Bhutan is perched in the eastern Himalayas between India and China. Gradual reforms protect its cultural identity.

Official name Kingdom of Bhutan
Formation 1656 / 1865
Capital Thimphu
Population 700,000 / 39 people per sq mile (15 people per sq km)
Total area 18,147 sq. miles (47,000 sq. km)
Languages Dzongkha*, Nepali, Assamese
Religions Mahayana Buddhist 75%, Hindu 25%
Ethnic mix Drukpa 50%, Nepalese 35%, Other 15%
Government Mixed monarchical–parliamentary system
Currency Ngultrum = 100 chetrum
Literacy rate 56%
Calorie consumption Not available

BOLIVIA
South America

Page 39 F3

Bolivia lies landlocked high in central South America. Mineral riches once made it the region's wealthiest state. Today, it is the poorest.

Official name Plurinational State of Bolivia
Formation 1825 / 1938
Capital La Paz (administrative); Sucre (judicial)
Population 10 million / 24 people per sq mile (9 people per sq km)
Total area 424,162 sq. miles (1,098,580 sq. km)
Languages Aymara*, Quechua*, Spanish*
Religions Roman Catholic 93%, Other 7%
Ethnic mix Quechua 37%, Aymara 32%, Mixed race 13%, European 10%, Other 8%
Government Presidential system
Currency Boliviano = 100 centavos
Literacy rate 91%
Calorie consumption 2093 kilocalories

BRAZIL
South America

Page 40 C2

Brazil covers more than half of South America and is the site of the world's largest rain forest. The country has immense natural resources.

Official name Federative Republic of Brazil
Formation 1822 / 1828
Capital Brasília
Population 195 million / 60 people per sq mile (23 people per sq km)
Total area 3,286,470 sq. miles (8,511,965 sq. km)
Languages Portuguese*, German, Italian, Spanish, Polish, Japanese, Amerindian languages
Religions Roman Catholic 74%, Protestant 15%, Atheist 7%, Other 3%, Afro-American Spiritist 1%
Ethnic mix White 54%, Mixed race 38%, Black 6%, Other 2%
Government Presidential system
Currency Real = 100 centavos
Literacy rate 90%
Calorie consumption 3099 kilocalories

BURKINA FASO
West Africa

Page 53 E4

Known as Upper Volta until 1984, the West African state of Burkina Faso has been under military rule for most of its post-independence history.

Official name Burkina Faso
Formation 1960 / 1960
Capital Ouagadougou
Population 16.3 million / 154 people per sq mile (60 people per sq km)
Total area 105,869 sq. miles (274,200 sq. km)
Languages Mossi, Fulani, French*, Tuareg, Dyula, Songhai
Religions Muslim 55%, Christian 25%, Traditional beliefs 20%
Ethnic mix Mossi 48%, Other 21%, Peul 10%, Lobi 7%, Bobo 7%, Mandé 7%
Government Presidential system
Currency CFA franc = 100 centimes
Literacy rate 29%
Calorie consumption 2669 kilocalories

CAMEROON
Central Africa

Page 54 A4

Situated on the central West African coast, Cameroon was effectively a one-party state for 30 years. Multiparty elections were held in 1992.

Official name Republic of Cameroon
Formation 1960 / 1961
Capital Yaoundé
Population 20 million / 111 people per sq mile (43 people per sq km)
Total area 183,567 sq. miles (475,400 sq. km)
Languages Bamileke, Fang, Fulani, French*, English*
Religions Roman Catholic 35%, Traditional beliefs 25%, Muslim 22%, Protestant 18%
Ethnic mix Cameroon highlanders 31%, Other 21%, Equatorial Bantu 19%, Kirdi 11%, Fulani 10%, Northwestern Bantu 8%
Government Presidential system
Currency CFA franc = 100 centimes
Literacy rate 71%
Calorie consumption 2259 kilocalories

BOSNIA & HERZEGOVINA
Southeast Europe

Page 78 B3

At the heart of the western Balkans, Bosnia and Herzegovina was the focus of the bitter conflict surrounding the breakup of the former Yugoslavia.

Official name Bosnia and Herzegovina
Formation 1992 / 1992
Capital Sarajevo
Population 3.8 million / 192 people per sq mile (74 people per sq km)
Total area 19,741 sq. miles (51,129 sq. km)
Languages Bosnian*, Serbian*, Croatian*
Religions Muslim (mainly Sunni) 40%, Orthodox Christian 31%, Roman Catholic 15%, Other 14%
Ethnic mix Bosniak 48%, Serb 34%, Croat 16%, Other 2%
Government Parliamentary system
Currency Marka = 100 pfeninga
Literacy rate 98%
Calorie consumption 3084 kilocalories

BRUNEI
Southeast Asia

Page 116 D3

Lying on the northwestern coast of the island of Borneo, Brunei is surrounded and divided in two by the Malaysian state of Sarawak.

Official name Sultanate of Brunei
Formation 1984 / 1984
Capital Bandar Seri Begawan
Population 400,000 / 197 people per sq mile (76 people per sq km)
Total area 2228 sq. miles (5770 sq. km)
Languages Malay*, English, Chinese
Religions Muslim (mainly Sunni) 66%, Buddhist 14%, Christian 10%, Other 10%
Ethnic mix Malay 67%, Chinese 16%, Other 11%, Indigenous 6%
Government Monarchy
Currency Brunei dollar = 100 cents
Literacy rate 95%
Calorie consumption 2987 kilocalories

BURUNDI
Central Africa

Page 51 B7

Small, landlocked Burundi lies just south of the Equator, on the Nile-Congo watershed in Central Africa. Since 1993 it has been marked by violent ethnic conflict.

Official name Republic of Burundi
Formation 1962 / 1962
Capital Bujumbura
Population 8.5 million / 858 people per sq mile (331 people per sq km)
Total area 10,745 sq. miles (27,830 sq. km)
Languages Kirundi*, French*, Kiswahili
Religions Roman Catholic 62%, Traditional beliefs 23%, Muslim 10%, Protestant 5%
Ethnic mix Hutu 85%, Tutsi 14%, Twa 1%
Government Presidential system
Currency Burundian franc = 100 centimes
Literacy rate 67%
Calorie consumption 1680 kilocalories

CANADA
North America

Page 15 E4

Canada extends from its US border north to the Arctic Ocean. In recent years, French-speaking Quebec has sought independence from the rest of the country.

Official name Canada
Formation 1867 / 1949
Capital Ottawa
Population 33.9 million / 10 people per sq mile (4 people per sq km)
Total area 3,855,171 sq. miles (9,984,670 sq. km)
Languages English*, French*, Chinese, Italian, German, Ukrainian, Portuguese, Inuktitut, Cree
Religions Roman Catholic 44%, Protestant 29%, Other and nonreligious 27%
Ethnic mix
Government Parliamentary system
Currency Canadian dollar = 100 cents
Literacy rate 99%
Calorie consumption 3530 kilocalories

BOTSWANA
Southern Africa

Page 56 C3

Once the British protectorate of Bechuanaland, Botswana lies landlocked in southern Africa. Diamonds provide it with a prosperous economy.

Official name Republic of Botswana
Formation 1966 / 1966
Capital Gaborone
Population 2 million / 9 people per sq mile (4 people per sq km)
Total area 231,803 sq. miles (600,370 sq. km)
Languages Setswana, English*, Shona, San, Khoikhoi, isiNdebele
Religions Christian (mainly Protestant) 70%, Nonreligious 20%, Traditional beliefs 6%, Other (including Muslim) 4%
Ethnic mix Tswana 79%, Kalanga 11%, Other 10%
Government Presidential system
Currency Pula = 100 thebe
Literacy rate 84%
Calorie consumption 2235 kilocalories

BULGARIA
Southeast Europe

Page 82 C2

Located in southeastern Europe, Bulgaria has made slow progress toward democracy since the fall of its communist regime in 1990.

Official name Republic of Bulgaria
Formation 1908 / 1947
Capital Sofia
Population 7.5 million / 176 people per sq mile (68 people per sq km)
Total area 42,822 sq. miles (110,910 sq. km)
Languages Bulgarian*, Turkish, Romani
Religions Bulgarian Orthodox 83%, Muslim 12%, Other 4%, Roman Catholic 1%
Ethnic mix Bulgarian 84%, Turkish 9%, Roma 5%, Other 2%
Government Parliamentary system
Currency Lev = 100 stotinki
Literacy rate 98%
Calorie consumption 2761 kilocalories

CAMBODIA
Southeast Asia

Page 115 D5

Located in mainland Southeast Asia, Cambodia has emerged from two decades of civil war and invasion from Vietnam.

Official name Kingdom of Cambodia
Formation 1953 / 1953
Capital Phnom Penh
Population 15.1 million / 222 people per sq mile (86 people per sq km)
Total area 69,900 sq. miles (181,040 sq. km)
Languages Khmer*, French, Chinese, Vietnamese, Cham
Religions Buddhist 93%, Muslim 6%, Christian 1%
Ethnic mix Khmer 90%, Vietnamese 5%, Other 4%, Chinese 1%
Government Parliamentary system
Currency Riel = 100 sen
Literacy rate 78%
Calorie consumption 2245 kilocalories

CAPE VERDE
Atlantic Ocean

Page 52 A2

Off the west coast of Africa, in the Atlantic Ocean, lies the group of islands that make up Cape Verde, a Portuguese colony until 1975.

Official name Republic of Cape Verde
Formation 1975 / 1975
Capital Praia
Population 500,000 / 321 people per sq mile (124 people per sq km)
Total area 1557 sq. miles (4033 sq. km)
Languages Portuguese Creole, Portuguese*
Religions Roman Catholic 97%, Other 2%, Protestant (Church of the Nazarene) 1%
Ethnic mix Mestiço 71%, African 28%, European 1%
Government Mixed presidential–parliamentary system
Currency Escudo = 100 centavos
Literacy rate 85%
Calorie consumption 2549 kilocalories

CENTRAL AFRICAN REPUBLIC
Central Africa

Page 54 C4

This landlocked country lies between the basins of the Chad and Congo rivers. Its arid north sustains less than 2% of the population.

Official name Central African Republic
Formation 1960 / 1960
Capital Bangui
Population 4.5 million / 19 people per sq mile (7 people per sq km)
Total area 240,534 sq. miles (622,984 sq. km)
Languages Sango, Banda, Gbaya, French*
Religions Traditional beliefs 35%, Roman Catholic 25%, Protestant 25%, Muslim 15%
Ethnic mix Baya 33%, Banda 27%, Other 17%, Mandjia 13%, Sara 10%
Government Presidential system
Currency CFA franc = 100 centimes
Literacy rate 55%
Calorie consumption 1956 kilocalories

CHAD
Central Africa

Page 54 C3

Landlocked in north central Africa, Chad has been torn by intermittent periods of civil war since it gained independence from France in 1960.

Official name Republic of Chad
Formation 1960 / 1960
Capital N'Djamena
Population 11.5 million / 24 people per sq mile (9 people per sq km)
Total area 495,752 sq. miles (1,284,000 sq. km)
Languages French*, Sara, Arabic*, Maba
Religions Muslim 51%, Christian 35%, Animist 7%, Traditional beliefs 7%
Ethnic mix Other 30%, Sara 28%, Mayo-Kebbi 12%, Arab 12%, Ouaddai 9%, Kanem-Bornou 9%
Government Presidential system
Currency CFA franc = 100 centimes
Literacy rate 34%
Calorie consumption 2040 kilocalories

CHILE
South America

Page 42 B3

Chile extends in a ribbon down the west coast of South America. It returned to democracy in 1989 after a referendum rejected its military dictator.

Official name Republic of Chile
Formation 1818 / 1883
Capital Santiago
Population 17.1 million / 59 people per sq mile (23 people per sq km)
Total area 292,258 sq. miles (756,950 sq. km)
Languages Spanish*, Amerindian languages
Religions Roman Catholic 89%, Other and nonreligious 11%
Ethnic mix Mestizo and European 90%, Other Amerindian 9%, Mapuche 1%
Government Presidential system
Currency Chilean peso = 100 centavos
Literacy rate 99%
Calorie consumption 2957 kilocalories

CHINA
East Asia

Page 104 C4

This vast East Asian country was dominated by Mao Zedong for almost 30 years, but since the 1980's it has emerged as one of the world's major political and economic powers.

Official name People's Republic of China
Formation 960 / 1999
Capital Beijing
Population 1.35 billion / 376 people per sq mile (145 people per sq km)
Total area 3,705,386 sq. miles (9,596,960 sq. km)
Languages Mandarin*, Wu, Cantonese, Hsiang, Min, Hakka, Kan
Religions Nonreligious 59%, Traditional beliefs 20%, Other 13%, Buddhist 6%, Muslim 2%
Ethnic mix Han 92%, Other 4%, Zhuang 1%, Hui 1%, Manchu 1%, Miao 1%
Government One-party state
Currency Renminbi (known as yuan) = 10 jiao = 100 fen
Literacy rate 94%
Calorie consumption 2974 kilocalories

COLOMBIA
South America

Page 36 B3

Lying in northwest South America, Colombia is one of the world's most violent countries, with powerful drugs cartels and guerrilla activity.

Official name Republic of Colombia
Formation 1819 / 1903
Capital Bogotá
Population 46.3 million / 115 people per sq mile (45 people per sq km)
Total area 439,733 sq. miles (1,138,910 sq. km)
Languages Spanish*, Wayuu, Páez, and other Amerindian languages
Religions Roman Catholic 95%, Other 5%
Ethnic mix Mestizo 58%, White 20%, European–African 14%, African 4%, frican–Amerindian 3%, Amerindian 1%
Government Presidential system
Currency Colombian peso = 100 centavos
Literacy rate 93%
Calorie consumption 2662 kilocalories

COMOROS
Indian Ocean

Page 57 F2

In the Indian Ocean, between Mozambique and Madagascar, lie the Comoros, comprising three main islands, and a number of smaller islets.

Official name Union of the Comoros
Formation 1975 / 1975
Capital Moroni
Population 700,000 / 813 people per sq mile (314 people per sq km)
Total area 838 sq. miles (2170 sq. km)
Languages Arabic*, Comoran*, French*
Religions Muslim (mainly Sunni) 98%, Other 1%, Roman Catholic 1%
Ethnic mix Comoran 97%, Other 3%
Government Presidential system
Currency Comoros franc = 100 centimes
Literacy rate 74%
Calorie consumption 1857 kilocalories

CONGO
Central Africa

Page 55 B5

Astride the Equator in west central Africa, this former French colony emerged from 26 years of Marxist-Leninist rule in 1990.

Official name Republic of the Congo
Formation 1960 / 1960
Capital Brazzaville
Population 3.8 million / 29 people per sq mile (11 people per sq km)
Total area 132,046 sq. miles (342,000 sq. km)
Languages Kongo, Teke, Lingala, French*
Religions Traditional beliefs 50%, Roman Catholic 35%, Protestant 13%, Muslim 2%
Ethnic mix Bakongo 51%, Teke 17%, Other 16%, Mbochi 11%, Mbédé 5%
Government Presidential system
Currency CFA franc = 100 centimes
Literacy rate 87%
Calorie consumption 2513 kilocalories

COLOMBIA / CONGO, DEM. REP.
Central Africa

Page 55 C6

Straddling the Equator in east central Africa, Dem. Rep. Congo is one of Africa's largest countries. It achieved independence from Belgium in 1960.

Official name Democratic Republic of the Congo
Formation 1960 / 1960
Capital Kinshasa
Population 67.8 million / 77 people per sq mile (30 people per sq km)
Total area 905,563 sq. miles (2,345,410 sq. km)
Languages Kiswahili, Tshiluba, Kikongo, Lingala, French*
Religions Roman Catholic 50%, Protestant 20%, Traditional beliefs and other 20%, Muslim 10%
Ethnic mix Other 55%, Mongo, Luba, Kongo, and Mangbetu-Azande 45%
Government Presidential system
Currency Congolese franc = 100 centimes
Literacy rate 67%
Calorie consumption 1585 kilocalories

COSTA RICA
Central America

Page 31 E4

Costa Rica is the most stable country in Central America. Its neutrality in foreign affairs is long-standing, but it has very strong ties with the US.

Official name Republic of Costa Rica
Formation 1838 / 1838
Capital San José
Population 4.6 million / 233 people per sq mile (90 people per sq km)
Total area 19,730 sq. miles (51,100 sq. km)
Languages Spanish*, English Creole, Bribri, Cabecar
Religions Roman Catholic 71%, Evangelical 14%, Nonreligious 11%, Other 4%
Ethnic mix Mestizo and European 94%, Black 3%, Chinese 1%, Other 1%, Amerindian 1%
Government Presidential system
Currency Costa Rican colón = 100 céntimos
Literacy rate 96%
Calorie consumption 2813 kilocalories

CÔTE D'IVOIRE
West Africa

Page 52 D4

One of the larger nations along the coast of West Africa, Côte d'Ivoire remains under the influence of its former colonial ruler, France.

Official name Republic of Côte d'Ivoire
Formation 1960 / 1960
Capital Yamoussoukro
Population 21.6 million / 176 people per sq mile (68 people per sq km)
Total area 124,502 sq. miles (322,460 sq. km)
Languages Akan, French*, Krou, Voltaique
Religions Muslim 38%, Roman Catholic 25%, Traditional beliefs 25%, Protestant 6%, Other 6%
Ethnic mix Akan 42%, Voltaique 18%, Mandé du Nord 17%, Krou 11%, Mandé du Sud 10%, Other 2%
Government Presidential system
Currency CFA franc = 100 centimes
Literacy rate 55%
Calorie consumption 2515 kilocalories

CROATIA
Southeast Europe

Page 78 B2

Post-independence fighting in this former Yugoslav republic initially thwarted plans to capitalize on its location along the eastern Adriatic coast. A return to stability has resolved this situation.

Official name Republic of Croatia
Formation 1991 / 1991
Capital Zagreb
Population 4.4 million / 202 people per sq mile (78 people per sq km)
Total area 21,831 sq. miles (56,542 sq. km)
Languages Croatian*
Religions Roman Catholic 88%, Other 7%, Orthodox Christian 4%, Muslim 1%
Ethnic mix Croat 90%, Serb 5%, Other 5%
Government Parliamentary system
Currency Kuna = 100 lipa
Literacy rate 99%
Calorie consumption 2987 kilocalories

CUBA
West Indies

Page 32 C2

Cuba is the largest island in the Caribbean and the only communist country in the Americas. It was led by Fidel Castro for almost 40 years until he stepped down in 2008.

Official name Republic of Cuba
Formation 1902 / 1902
Capital Havana
Population 11.2 million / 262 people per sq mile (101 people per sq km)
Total area 42,803 sq. miles (110,860 sq. km)
Languages Spanish
Religions Nonreligious 49%, Roman Catholic 40%, Atheist 6%, Other 4%, Protestant 1%
Ethnic mix Mulatto (mixed race) 51%, White 37%, Black 11%, Chinese 1%
Government One-party state
Currency Cuban peso = 100 centavos
Literacy rate 99%
Calorie consumption 3295 kilocalories

CYPRUS
Southeast Europe

Page 80 C5

Cyprus lies in the eastern Mediterranean. Since 1974, it has been partitioned between the Turkish-occupied north and the Greek south (which joined the EU in 2004).

Official name Republic of Cyprus
Formation 1960 / 1960
Capital Nicosia
Population 900,000 / 252 people per sq mile (97 people per sq km)
Total area 3571 sq. miles (9250 sq. km)
Languages Greek*, Turkish*
Religions Orthodox Christian 78%, Muslim 18%, Other 4%
Ethnic mix Greek 81%, Turkish 11%, Other 8%
Government Presidential system
Currency Euro (new Turkish lira in TRNC) = 100 cents (euro); 100 kurus (Turkish lira)
Literacy rate 98%
Calorie consumption 3199 kilocalories

CZECH REPUBLIC
Central Europe

Page 77 A5

Once part of Czechoslovakia in eastern Europe, it became independent in 1993, after peacefully dissolving its federal union with Slovakia.

Official name Czech Republic
Formation 1993 / 1993
Capital Prague
Population 10.4 million / 342 people per sq mile (132 people per sq km)
Total area 30,450 sq. miles (78,866 sq. km)
Languages Czech*, Slovak, Hungarian (Magyar)
Religions Roman Catholic 39%, Atheist 38%, Other 18%, Protestant 3%, Hussite 2%
Ethnic mix Czech 90%, Moravian 4%, Other 4%, Slovak 2%
Government Parliamentary system
Currency Czech koruna = 100 haleru
Literacy rate 99%
Calorie consumption 3317 kilocalories

DENMARK
Northern Europe

Page 63 A7

The country occupies the Jutland peninsula and over 400 islands in Scandinavia. Greenland and the Faeroe Islands are self-governing associated territories.

Official name Kingdom of Denmark
Formation 950 / 1944
Capital Copenhagen
Population 5.5 million / 336 people per sq mile (130 people per sq km)
Total area 16,639 sq. miles (43,094 sq. km)
Languages Danish
Religions Evangelical Lutheran 95%, Roman Catholic 3%, Muslim 2%
Ethnic mix Danish 96%, Other (including Scandinavian and Turkish) 3%, Faeroese and Inuit 1%
Government Parliamentary system
Currency Danish krone = 100 øre
Literacy rate 99%
Calorie consumption 3397 kilocalories

DJIBOUTI
East Africa

Page 50 D4

A city state with a desert hinterland, Djibouti lies in northeast Africa. Once known as French Somaliland, its economy relies on its port.

Official name Republic of Djibouti
Formation 1977 / 1977
Capital Djibouti
Population 900,000 / 101 people per sq mile (39 people per sq km)
Total area 8494 sq. miles (22,000 sq. km)
Languages Somali, Afar, French*, Arabic*
Religions Muslim (mainly Sunni) 94%, Christian 6%
Ethnic mix Issa 60%, Afar 35%, Other 5%
Government Presidential system
Currency Djibouti franc = 100 centimes
Literacy rate 70%
Calorie consumption 2210 kilocalories

DOMINICA
West Indies

Page 33 H4

The Caribbean island Dominica resisted European colonization until the 18th century, when it first came under the French, and then, the British

Official name Commonwealth of Dominica
Formation 1978 / 1978
Capital Roseau
Population 72,969 / 252 people per sq mile (97 people per sq km)
Total area 291 sq. miles (754 sq. km)
Languages French Creole, English*
Religions Roman Catholic 77%, Protestant 15%, Other 8%
Ethnic mix Black 87%, Mixed race 9%, Carib 3%, Other 1%
Government Parliamentary system
Currency East Caribbean dollar = 100 cents
Literacy rate 88%
Calorie consumption 3115 kilocalories

DOMINICAN REPUBLIC
West Indies

Page 33 E2

The republic occupies the eastern two-thirds of the island of Hispaniola in the Caribbean. Frequent coups and a strong US influence mark its recent past.

Official name Dominican Republic
Formation 1865 / 1865
Capital Santo Domingo
Population 10.2 million / 546 people per sq mile (211 people per sq km)
Total area 18,679 sq. miles (48,380 sq. km)
Languages Spanish*, French Creole
Religions Roman Catholic 95%, Other and nonreligious 5%
Ethnic mix Mixed race 73%, European 16%, Black African 11%
Government Presidential system
Currency Dominican Republic peso = 100 centavos
Literacy rate 88%
Calorie consumption 2263 kilocalories

EAST TIMOR
Southeast Asia

Page 116 F5

This new nation occupies the eastern half of the island of Timor. Invaded by Indonesiain 1975, it declared independence in 1999.

Official name Democratic Republic of Timor-Leste
Formation 2002 / 2002
Capital Dili
Population 1.2 million / 213 people per sq mile (82 people per sq km)
Total area 5756 sq. miles (14,874 sq. km)
Languages Tetum (Portuguese/Austronesian)*, Bahasa Indonesia, Portuguese
Religions Roman Catholic 95%, Other (including Muslim and Protestant) 5%
Ethnic mix Not available
Government Parliamentary system
Currency US dollar = 100 cents
Literacy rate 51%
Calorie consumption 2016 kilocalories

ECUADOR
South America

Page 38 A2

Ecuador sits high on South America's western coast. Once part of the Inca heartland, its territory includes the Galapagos Islands, to the west.

Official name Republic of Ecuador
Formation 1830 / 1942
Capital Quito
Population 13.8 million / 129 people per sq mile (50 people per sq km)
Total area 109,483 sq. miles (283,560 sq. km)
Languages Spanish*, Quechua, other Amerindian languages
Religions Roman Catholic 95%, Protestant, Jewish, and other 5%
Ethnic mix Mestizo 77%, White 11%, Amerindian 7%, Black African 5%
Government Presidential system
Currency US dollar = 100 cents
Literacy rate 84%
Calorie consumption 2304 kilocalories

EGYPT
North Africa

Page 50 B2

Egypt occupies the northeast corner of Africa. The 30 year regime of Hosni Mubarak was brought to an end by a popular uprising in the "Arab Spring" of 2011.

Official name Arab Republic of Egypt
Formation 1936 / 1982
Capital Cairo
Population 84.5 million / 220 people per sq mile (85 people per sq km)
Total area 386,660 sq. miles (1,001,450 sq. km)
Languages Arabic*, French, English, Berber
Religions Muslim (mainly Sunni) 90%, Coptic Christian and other 9%, Other Christian 1%
Ethnic mix Egyptian 99%, Nubian, Armenian, Greek, and Berber 1%
Government Transitional regime
Currency Egyptian pound = 100 piastres
Literacy rate 72%
Calorie consumption 3163 kilocalories

EL SALVADOR
Central America

Page 30 B3

El Salvador is Central America's smallest state. A 12-year war between US-backed government troops and left-wing guerrillas ended in 1992.

Official name Republic of El Salvador
Formation 1841 / 1841
Capital San Salvador
Population 6.2 million / 775 people per sq mile (299 people per sq km)
Total area 8124 sq. miles (21,040 sq. km)
Languages Spanish
Religions Roman Catholic 80%, Evangelical 18%, Other 2%
Ethnic mix Mestizo 90%, White 9%, Amerindian 1%
Government Presidential system
Currency Salvadorean colón & US dollar = 100 centavos (colón); 100 cents (US dollar)
Literacy rate 84%
Calorie consumption 2585 kilocalories

EQUATORIAL GUINEA
Central Africa

Page 55 A5

The country comprises the Rio Muni mainland and five islands on the west coast of central Africa. Free elections were first held in 1988.

Official name Republic of Equatorial Guinea
Formation 1968 / 1968
Capital Malabo
Population 700,000 / 65 people per sq mile (25 people per sq km)
Total area 10,830 sq. miles (28,051 sq. km)
Languages Spanish*, Fang, Bubi, French*
Religions Roman Catholic 90%, Other 10%
Ethnic mix Fang 85%, Other 11%, Bubi 4%
Government Presidential system
Currency CFA franc = 100 centimes
Literacy rate 93%
Calorie consumption Not available

ERITREA
East Africa

Page 50 C3

Lying on the shores of the Red Sea, Eritrea effectively seceded from Ethopia in 1993, following a 30-year war for independence.

Official name State of Eritrea
Formation 1993 / 2002
Capital Asmara
Population 5.2 million / 115 people per sq mile (44 people per sq km)
Total area 46,842 sq. miles (121,320 sq. km)
Languages Tigrinya*, English*, Tigre, Afar, Arabic*, Saho, Bilen, Kunama, Nara, Hadareb
Religions Christian 50%, Muslim 48%, Other 2%
Ethnic mix Tigray 50%, Tigre 31%, Other 9%, Saho 5%, Afar 5%
Government Transitional regime
Currency Nakfa = 100 cents
Literacy rate 67%
Calorie consumption 1587 kilocalories

ESTONIA
Northeast Europe

Page 84 D2

Estonia is the smallest and most developed of the three Baltic states. It has the highest standard of living of any of the former Soviet republics.

Official name Republic of Estonia
Formation 1991 / 1991
Capital Tallinn
Population 1.3 million / 75 people per sq mile (29 people per sq km)
Total area 17,462 sq. miles (45,226 sq. km)
Languages Estonian*, Russian
Religions Evangelical Lutheran 56%, Orthodox Christian 25%, Other 19%
Ethnic mix Estonian 69%, Russian 25%, Other 4%, Ukrainian 2%
Government Parliamentary system
Currency Euro = 100 cents
Literacy rate 99%
Calorie consumption 3129 kilocalories

ETHIOPIA
East Africa

Page 51 C5

Located in northeast Africa, Ethiopia was a Marxist regime from 1974–91. It has suffered a series of economic, civil, and natural crises.

Official name Federal Democratic Republic of Ethiopia
Formation 1896 / 2002
Capital Addis Ababa
Population 85 million / 198 people per sq mile (77 people per sq km)
Total area 435,184 sq. miles (1,127,127 sq. km)
Languages Amharic*, Tigrinya, Galla, Sidamo, Somali, English, Arabic
Religions Orthodox Christian 40%, Muslim 40%, Traditional beliefs 15%, Other 5%
Ethnic mix Oromo 40%, Amhara 25%, Other 35%
Government Parliamentary system
Currency Birr = 100 cents
Literacy rate 36%
Calorie consumption 1952 kilocalories

FIJI
Australasia & Oceania

Page 123 E5

A volcanic archipelago, Fiji comprises 882 islands in the southern Pacific Ocean. Ethnic Fijians and Indo-Fijians have been in conflict since 1987.

Official name Republic of the Fiji Islands
Formation 1970 / 1970
Capital Suva
Population 900,000 / 128 people per sq mile (49 people per sq km)
Total area 7054 sq. miles (18,270 sq. km)
Languages Fijian, English*, Hindi, Urdu, Tamil, Telugu
Religions Hindu 38%, Methodist 37%, Roman Catholic 9%, Muslim 8%, Other 8%
Ethnic mix Melanesian 51%, Indian 44%, Other 5%
Government Transitional regime
Currency Fiji dollar = 100 cents
Literacy rate 94%
Calorie consumption 3033 kilocalories

FINLAND
Northern Europe

Page 62 D4

Finland's distinctive language and national identity have been influenced by both its Scandinavian and its Russian neighbors.

Official name Republic of Finland
Formation 1917 / 1947
Capital Helsinki
Population 5.3 million / 45 people per sq mile (17 people per sq km)
Total area 130,127 sq. miles (337,030 sq. km)
Languages Finnish*, Swedish*, Sámi
Religions Evangelical Lutheran 83%, Other 15%, Roman Catholic 1%, Orthodox Christian 1%
Ethnic mix Finnish 93%, Other (including Sámi) 7%
Government Parliamentary system
Currency Euro = 100 cents
Literacy rate 99%
Calorie consumption 3215 kilocalories

FRANCE
Western Europe

Page 68 B4

Straddling Western Europe from the English Channel to the Mediterranean Sea, France, is one of the world's leading industrial powers.

Official name French Republic
Formation 987 / 1919
Capital Paris
Population 62.6 million / 295 people per sq mile (114 people per sq km)
Total area 211,208 sq. miles (547,030 sq. km)
Languages French*, Provençal, German, Breton, Catalan, Basque
Religions Roman Catholic 88%, Muslim 8%, Protestant 2%, Jewish 1%, Buddhist 1%
Ethnic mix French 90%, North African (mainly Algerian) 6%, German (Alsace) 2%, Other 2%
Government Mixed presidential–parliamentary system
Currency Euro = 100 cents
Literacy rate 99%
Calorie consumption 3553 kilocalories

GABON
Central Africa

Page 55 A5

A former French colony straddling the Equator on Africa's west coast, it returned to multiparty politics in 1990, after 22 years of one-party rule.

Official name Gabonese Republic
Formation 1960 / 1960
Capital Libreville
Population 1.5 million / 15 people per sq mile (6 people per sq km)
Total area 103,346 sq. miles (267,667 sq. km)
Languages Fang, French*, Punu, Sira, Nzebi, Mpongwe
Religions Christian (mainly Roman Catholic) 55%, Traditional beliefs 40%, Other 4%, Muslim 1%
Ethnic mix Fang 26%, Shira-punu 24%, Other 16%, Foreign residents 15%, Nzabi-duma 11%, Mbédé-Teke 8%
Government Presidential system
Currency CFA franc = 100 centimes
Literacy rate 88%
Calorie consumption 2730 kilocalories

GAMBIA
West Africa

Page 52 B3

A narrow state on the west coast of Africa, Gambia was renowned for its stability until its government was overthrown in a coup in 1994.

Official name Republic of the Gambia
Formation 1965 / 1965
Capital Banjul
Population 1.8 million / 466 people per sq mile (180 people per sq km)
Total area 4363 sq. miles (11,300 sq. km)
Languages Mandinka, Fulani, Wolof, Jola, Soninke, English*
Religions Sunni Muslim 90%, Christian 8%, Traditional beliefs 2%
Ethnic mix Mandinka 42%, Fulani 18%, Wolof 16%, Jola 10%, Serahuli 9%, Other 5%
Government Presidential system
Currency Dalasi = 100 butut
Literacy rate 46%
Calorie consumption 2345 kilocalories

GEORGIA
Southwest Asia

Page 95 F2

Located on the eastern shore of the Black Sea, Georgia's northern provinces have been torn by civil war since independence from the USSR in 1991.

Official name Georgia
Formation 1991 / 1991
Capital Tbilisi
Population 4.2 million / 156 people per sq mile (60 people per sq km)
Total area 26,911 sq. miles (69,700 sq. km)
Languages Georgian*, Russian, Azeri, Armenian, Mingrelian, Ossetian, Abkhazian
Religions Georgian Orthodox 74%, Russian Orthodox 10%, Muslim 10%, Other 6%
Ethnic mix Georgian 84%, Armenian 6%, Azeri 6%, Russian 2%, Other 1%, Ossetian 1%
Government Presidential system
Currency Lari = 100 tetri
Literacy rate 99%
Calorie consumption 2813 kilocalories

GERMANY
Northern Europe

Page 72 B4

Europe's strongest economic power, Germany's democratic west and Communist east were re-unified in 1990, after the fall of the east's regime.

Official name Federal Republic of Germany
Formation 1871 / 1990
Capital Berlin
Population 82.1 million / 608 people per sq mile (235 people per sq km)
Total area 137,846 sq. miles (357,021 sq. km)
Languages German*, Turkish
Religions Protestant 34%, Roman Catholic 33%, Other 30%, Muslim 3%
Ethnic mix German 92%, Other 3%, Other European 3%, Turkish 2%
Government Parliamentary system
Currency Euro = 100 cents
Literacy rate 99%
Calorie consumption 3530 kilocalories

GHANA
West Africa

Page 53 E5

Once known as the Gold Coast, Ghana in West Africa has experienced intermittent periods of military rule since independence in 1957.

Official name Republic of Ghana
Formation 1957 / 1957
Capital Accra
Population 24.3 million / 274 people per sq mile (106 people per sq km)
Total area 92,100 sq. miles (238,540 sq. km)
Languages Twi, Fanti, Ewe, Ga, Adangbe, Gurma, Dagomba (Dagbani), English*
Religions Christian 69%, Muslim 16%, Traditional beliefs 9%, Other 6%
Ethnic mix Akan 49%, Mole-Dagbani 17%, Ewe 13%, Other 9%, Ga and Ga-Adangbe 8%, Guan 4%
Government Presidential system
Currency Cedi = 100 pesewas
Literacy rate 67%
Calorie consumption 2849 kilocalories

GREECE
Southeast Europe

Page 83 A5

Greece is the southernmost Balkan nation. High government debt lead to the introduction of austerity measures in 2011, resulting in widespread social unrest.

Official name Hellenic Republic
Formation 1829 / 1947
Capital Athens
Population 11.2 million / 222 people per sq mile (86 people per sq km)
Total area 50,942 sq. miles (131,940 sq. km)
Languages Greek*, Turkish, Macedonian, Albanian
Religions Orthodox Christian 98%, Other 1%, Muslim 1%
Ethnic mix Greek 98%, Other 2%
Government Parliamentary system
Currency Euro = 100 cents
Literacy rate 97%
Calorie consumption 3700 kilocalories

GRENADA
West Indies

Page 33 G5

The Windward island of Grenada became a focus of attention in 1983, when the US mounted an invasion to sever its growing links with Cuba.

Official name Grenada
Formation 1974 / 1974
Capital St. George's
Population 108,419 / 828 people per sq mile (319 people per sq km)
Total area 131 sq. miles (340 sq. km)
Languages English*, English Creole
Religions Roman Catholic 68%, Anglican 17%, Other 15%
Ethnic mix Black African 82%, Mulatto (mixed race) 13%, East Indian 3%, Other 2%
Government Parliamentary system
Currency East Caribbean dollar = 100 cents
Literacy rate 96%
Calorie consumption 2320 kilocalories

GUATEMALA
Central America

Page 30 A2

The largest state on the Central American isthmus, Guatemala returned to civilian rule in 1986, after 32 years of repressive military rule.

Official name Republic of Guatemala
Formation 1838 / 1838
Capital Guatemala City
Population 14.4 million / 344 people per sq mile (133 people per sq km)
Total area 42,042 sq. miles (108,890 sq. km)
Languages Quiché, Mam, Cakchiquel, Kekchí, Spanish*
Religions Roman Catholic 65%, Protestant 33%, Other and nonreligious 2%
Ethnic mix Amerindian 60%, Mestizo 30%, Other 10%
Government Presidential system
Currency Quetzal = 100 centavos
Literacy rate 74%
Calorie consumption 2171 kilocalories

GUINEA
West Africa

Page 52 C4

Facing the Atlantic Ocean, on the west coast of Africa, Guinea became the first French colony in Africa to gain independence, in 1958.

Official name Republic of Guinea
Formation 1958 / 1958
Capital Conakry
Population 10.3 million / 109 people per sq mile (42 people per sq km)
Total area 94,925 sq. miles (245,857 sq. km)
Languages Pulaar, Malinké, Soussou, French*
Religions Muslim 85%, Christian 8%, Traditional beliefs 7%
Ethnic mix Peul 40%, Malinké 30%, Soussou 20%, Other 10%
Government Presidential system
Currency Guinea franc = 100 centimes
Literacy rate 40%
Calorie consumption 2529 kilocalories

GUINEA-BISSAU
West Africa

Page 52 B4

Known as Portuguese Guinea during its days as a colony, Guinea-Bissau is situated on Africa's west coast, bordered by Senegal and Guinea.

Official name Republic of Guinea-Bissau
Formation 1974 / 1974
Capital Bissau
Population 1.6 million / 147 people per sq mile (57 people per sq km)
Total area 13,946 sq. miles (36,120 sq. km)
Languages Portuguese Creole, Balante, Fulani, Malinké, Portuguese*
Religions Traditional beliefs 50%, Muslim 40%, Christian 10%
Ethnic mix Balante 30%, Fulani 20%, Other 16%, Mandyako 14%, Mandinka 13%, Papel 7%
Government Presidential system
Currency CFA franc = 100 centimes
Literacy rate 52%
Calorie consumption 2288 kilocalories

GUYANA
South America

Page 37 F3

The only English-speaking country in South America, Guyana gained independence from Britain in 1966, and became a republic in 1970.

Official name Cooperative Republic of Guyana
Formation 1966 / 1966
Capital Georgetown
Population 800,000 / 11 people per sq mile (4 people per sq km)
Total area 83,000 sq. miles (214,970 sq. km)
Languages English Creole, Hindi, Tamil, Amerindian languages, English*
Religions Christian 57%, Hindu 28%, Muslim 10%, Other 5%
Ethnic mix East Indian 43%, Black African 30%, Mixed race 17%, Amerindian 9%, Other 1%
Government Presidential system
Currency Guyanese dollar = 100 cents
Literacy rate 99%
Calorie consumption 2753 kilocalories

HAITI
West Indies

Page 32 D3

Haiti shares the Caribbean island of Hispaniola with the Dominican Republic. At independence, in 1804, it became the world's first Black republic.

Official name Republic of Haiti
Formation 1804 / 1884
Capital Port-au-Prince
Population 10.2 million / 959 people per sq mile (370 people per sq km)
Total area 10,714 sq. miles (27,750 sq. km)
Languages French Creole*, French*
Religions Roman Catholic 55%, Protestant 28%, Other (including Voodoo) 16%, Nonreligious 1%
Ethnic mix Black African 95%, Mulatto (mixed race) and European 5%
Government Presidential system
Currency Gourde = 100 centimes
Literacy rate 62%
Calorie consumption 1848 kilocalories

HONDURAS
Central America

Page 30 C2

Honduras straddles the Central American isthmus. The country returned to full democratic civilian rule in 1984, after a succession of military regimes.

Official name Republic of Honduras
Formation 1838 / 1838
Capital Tegucigalpa
Population 7.6 million / 176 people per sq mile (68 people per sq km)
Total area 43,278 sq. miles (112,090 sq. km)
Languages Spanish*, Garífuna (Carib), English Creole
Religions Roman Catholic 97%, Protestant 3%
Ethnic mix Mestizo 90%, Black African 5%, Amerindian 4%, White 1%
Government Presidential system
Currency Lempira = 100 centavos
Literacy rate 84%
Calorie consumption 2601 kilocalories

HUNGARY
Central Europe

Page 77 C6

Hungary is bordered by seven states in Central Europe. It has changed its economic and political policies to develop closer ties with the EU.

Official name Republic of Hungary
Formation 1918 / 1947
Capital Budapest
Population 10 million / 280 people per sq mile (108 people per sq km)
Total area 35,919 sq. miles (93,030 sq. km)
Languages Hungarian (Magyar)*
Religions Roman Catholic 52%, Calvinist 16%, Other 15%, Nonreligious 14%, Lutheran 3%
Ethnic mix Magyar 90%, Roma 4%, German 3%, Serb 2%, Other 1%
Government Parliamentary system
Currency Forint = 100 fillér
Literacy rate 99%
Calorie consumption 3438 kilocalories

ICELAND
Northwest Europe

Page 61 E4

Europe's westernmost country, Iceland lies in the North Atlantic, straddling the mid-Atlantic ridge. Its spectacular, volcanic landscape is largely uninhabited.

Official name Republic of Iceland
Formation 1944 / 1944
Capital Reykjavík
Population 300,000 / 8 people per sq mile (3 people per sq km)
Total area 39,768 sq. miles (103,000 sq. km)
Languages Icelandic*
Religions Evangelical Lutheran 84%, Other (mostly Christian) 10%, Nonreligious 3%, Roman Catholic 3%
Ethnic mix Icelandic 94%, Other 5%, Danish 1%
Government Parliamentary system
Currency Icelandic króna = 100 aurar
Literacy rate 99%
Calorie consumption 3330 kilocalories

INDIA
South Asia

Page 112 D4

Separated from the rest of Asia by the Himalayan mountain ranges, India forms a subcontinent. It is the world's second most populous country.

Official name Republic of India
Formation 1947 / 1947
Capital New Delhi
Population 1.21 billion / 1058 people per sq mile (408 people per sq km)
Total area 1,269,338 sq. miles (3,287,590 sq. km)
Languages Hindi*, English*, Urdu, Bengali, Marathi, Telugu, Tamil, Bihari, Gujarati, Kanarese
Religions Hindu 81%, Muslim 13%, Sikh 2%, Christian 2%, Buddhist 1%, Other 1%
Ethnic mix Indo-Aryan 72%, Dravidian 25%, Mongoloid and other 3%
Government Parliamentary system
Currency Indian rupee = 100 paise
Literacy rate 66%
Calorie consumption 2301 kilocalories

INDONESIA
Southeast Asia

Page 116 C4

Formerly the Dutch East Indies, Indonesia, the world's largest archipelago, stretches over 5,000 km (3,100 miles), from the Indian Ocean to the Pacific Ocean.

Official name Republic of Indonesia
Formation 1949 / 1999
Capital Jakarta
Population 232 million / 335 people per sq mile (129 people per sq km)
Total area 741,096 sq. miles (1,919,440 sq. km)
Languages Javanese, Sundanese, Madurese, Bahasa Indonesia*, Dutch
Religions Sunni Muslim 86%, Protestant 6%, Roman Catholic 3%, Hindu 2%, Other 2%, Buddhist 1%
Ethnic mix Javanese 41%, Other 29%, Sundanese 15%, Coastal Malays 12%, Madurese 3%
Government Presidential system
Currency Rupiah = 100 sen
Literacy rate 92%
Calorie consumption 2535 kilocalories

IRAN
Southwest Asia

Page 98 B3

Since the 1979 revolution led by Ayatollah Khomeini, which sent Iran's Shah into exile, this Middle Eastern country has become the world's largest theocracy.

Official name Islamic Republic of Iran
Formation 1502 / 1990
Capital Tehran
Population 75.1 million / 119 people per sq mile (46 people per sq km)
Total area 636,293 sq. miles (1,648,000 sq. km)
Languages Farsi*, Azeri, Luri, Gilaki, Mazanderani, Kurdish, Turkmen, Arabic, Baluchi
Religions Shi'a Muslim 89%, Sunni Muslim 9%, Other 2%
Ethnic mix Persian 51%, Azari 24%, Other 10%, Lur and Bakhtiari 8%, Kurdish 7%
Government Islamic theocracy
Currency Iranian rial = 100 dinars
Literacy rate 85%
Calorie consumption 3042 kilocalories

IRAQ
Southwest Asia

Page 98 B3

Oil-rich Iraq is situated in the central Middle East. A US-led invasion in 2003 toppled the regime of Saddam Hussein, prompting an insurgency that led to huge political and social turmoil.

Official name Republic of Iraq
Formation 1932 / 1990
Capital Baghdad
Population 31.5 million / 187 people per sq mile (72 people per sq km)
Total area 168,753 sq. miles (437,072 sq. km)
Languages Arabic*, Kurdish*, Turkic languages, Armenian, Assyrian
Religions Shi'a Muslim 60%, Sunni Muslim 35%, Other (including Christian) 5%
Ethnic mix Arab 80%, Kurdish 15%, Turkmen 3%, Other 2%
Government Parliamentary system
Currency New Iraqi dinar = 1000 fils
Literacy rate 78%
Calorie consumption 2197 kilocalories

IRELAND
Northwest Europe

Page 67 A6

The Republic of Ireland occupies about 85% of the island of Ireland. Large government debt caused a major financial crisis leading to intervention by the EU and IMF in 2010.

Official name Ireland
Formation 1922 / 1922
Capital Dublin
Population 4.6 million / 173 people per sq mile (67 people per sq km)
Total area 27,135 sq. miles (70,280 sq. km)
Languages English*, Irish Gaelic*
Religions Roman Catholic 87%, Other and nonreligious 10%, Anglican 3%
Ethnic mix Irish 99%, Other 1%
Government Parliamentary system
Currency Euro = 100 cents
Literacy rate 99%
Calorie consumption 3532 kilocalories

ISRAEL
Southwest Asia

Page 97 A7

Israel was created as a new state in 1948 on the east coast of the Mediterranean. Following wars with its Arab neighbors, it has extended its boundaries.

Official name State of Israel
Formation 1948 / 1994
Capital Jerusalem (not internationally recognized)
Population 7.3 million / 930 people per sq mile (359 people per sq km)
Total area 8019 sq. miles (20,770 sq. km)
Languages Hebrew*, Arabic*, Yiddish, German, Russian, Polish, Romanian, Persian
Religions Jewish 76%, Muslim (mainly Sunni) 16%, Other 4%, Druze 2%, Christian 2%
Ethnic mix Jewish 76%, Arab 20%, Other 4%
Government Parliamentary system
Currency Shekel = 100 agorot
Literacy rate 99%
Calorie consumption 3540 kilocalories

ITALY
Southern Europe

Page 74 B3

Projecting into the Mediterranean Sea in Southern Europe, Italy is an ancient land, but also one of the continent's newest unified states.

Official name Italian Republic
Formation 1861 / 1947
Capital Rome
Population 60.1 million / 529 people per sq mile (204 people per sq km)
Total area 116,305 sq. miles (301,230 sq. km)
Languages Italian*, German, French, Rhaeto-Romanic, Sardinian
Religions Roman Catholic 85%, Other and nonreligious 13%, Muslim 2%
Ethnic mix Italian 94%, Other 4%, Sardinian 2%
Government Parliamentary system
Currency Euro = 100 cents
Literacy rate 99%
Calorie consumption 3657 kilocalories

JAMAICA
West Indies

Page 32 C3

First colonized by the Spanish and then, from 1655, by the English, Jamaica was the first of the Caribbean island nations to achieve independence, in 1962.

Official name Jamaica
Formation 1962 / 1962
Capital Kingston
Population 2.7 million / 646 people per sq mile (249 people per sq km)
Total area 4243 sq. miles (10,990 sq. km)
Languages English Creole, English*
Religions Other and nonreligious 45%, Other Protestant 20%, Church of God 18%, Baptist 10%, Anglican 7%
Ethnic mix Black African 91%, Mulatto (mixed race) 7%, European and Chinese 1%, East Indian 1%
Government Parliamentary system
Currency Jamaican dollar = 100 cents
Literacy rate 86%
Calorie consumption 2848 kilocalories

JAPAN
East Asia

Page 108 C4

Japan comprises four principal islands and over 3,000 smaller ones. With the emperor as constitutional head, it is now one of the world's most powerful economies.

Official name Japan
Formation 1590 / 1972
Capital Tokyo
Population 127 million / 874 people per sq mile (337 people per sq km)
Total area 145,882 sq. miles (377,835 sq. km)
Languages Japanese*, Korean, Chinese
Religions Shinto and Buddhist 76%, Buddhist 16%, Other (including Christian) 8%
Ethnic mix Japanese 99%, Other (mainly Korean) 1%
Government Parliamentary system
Currency Yen = 100 sen
Literacy rate 99%
Calorie consumption 2806 kilocalories

JORDAN
Southwest Asia

Page 97 B6

The kingdom of Jordan lies east of Israel. In 1993, King Hussein responded to calls for greater democracy by agreeing to multiparty elections.

Official name Hashemite Kingdom of Jordan
Formation 1946 / 1967
Capital Amman
Population 6.5 million / 189 people per sq mile (73 people per sq km)
Total area 35,637 sq. miles (92,300 sq. km)
Languages Arabic*
Religions Sunni Muslim 92%, Christian 6%, Other 2%
Ethnic mix Arab 98%, Circassian 1%, Armenian 1%
Government Monarchy
Currency Jordanian dinar = 1000 fils
Literacy rate 92%
Calorie consumption 2977 kilocalories

KAZAKHSTAN
Central Asia

Page 92 B4

Second largest of the former Soviet republics, mineral-rich Kazakhstan has the potential to become the major Central Asian economic power.

Official name Republic of Kazakhstan
Formation 1991 / 1991
Capital Astana
Population 15.8 million / 15 people per sq mile (6 people per sq km)
Total area 1,049,150 sq. miles (2,717,300 sq. km)
Languages Kazakh*, Russian, Ukrainian, German, Uzbek, Tatar, Uighur
Religions Muslim (mainly Sunni) 47%, Orthodox Christian 44%, Other 7%, Protestant 2%
Ethnic mix Kazakh 57%, Russian 27%, Other 8%, Ukrainian 3%, Uzbek 3%, German 2%
Government Presidential system
Currency Tenge = 100 tiyn
Literacy rate 99%
Calorie consumption 3359 kilocalories

KENYA
East Africa

Page 51 C6

Kenya became a multiparty democracy in 1992 and was led by President Daniel Moi from 1978 until 2002 when he was barred from re-election and Mwai Kibaki subsequently became president.

Official name Republic of Kenya
Formation 1963 / 1963
Capital Nairobi
Population 40.9 million / 187 people per sq mile (72 people per sq km)
Total area 224,961 sq. miles (582,650 sq. km)
Languages Kiswahili*, English*, Kikuyu, Luo, Kalenjin, Kamba
Religions Christian 80%, Muslim 10%, Traditional beliefs 9%, Other 1%
Ethnic mix Other 28%, Kikuyu 22%, Luo 14%, Luhya 14%, Kamba 11%, Kalenjin 11%
Government Mixed Presidential–Parliamentary system
Currency Kenya shilling = 100 cents
Literacy rate 87%
Calorie consumption 2060 kilocalories

KIRIBATI
Australasia & Oceania

Page 123 F3

Part of the British colony of the Gilbert and Ellice Islands until independence in 1979, Kiribati comprises 33 islands in the mid-Pacific Ocean.

Official name Republic of Kiribati
Formation 1979 / 1979
Capital Bairiki (Tarawa Atoll)
Population 100,743 / 368 people per sq mile (142 people per sq km)
Total area 277 sq. miles (717 sq. km)
Languages English*, Kiribati
Religions Roman Catholic 55%, Kiribati Protestant Church 36%, Other 9%
Ethnic mix Micronesian 99%, Other 1%
Government Elections involving informal groupings
Currency Australian dollar = 100 cents
Literacy rate 99%
Calorie consumption 2854 kilocalories

KOSOVO (not yet fully recognized)
Southeast Europe

Page 79 D5

In February 2008, Kosovo controversially declared independence from Serbia. It faces numerous economic and political challenges as it seeks to gain full international recognition.

Official name Republic of Kosovo
Formation 2008 / 2008
Capital Priština
Population 1.83 million / 433 people per sq mile (167 people per sq km)
Total area 4212 sq. miles (10,908 sq. km)
Languages Albanian*, Serbian*, Bosniak, Gorani, Roma, Turkish
Religions Muslim 92%, Orthodox Christian 4%, Roman Catholic 4%
Ethnic mix Albanian 92%, Serb 4%, Bosniak and Gorani 2%, Roma 1%, Turkish 1%
Government Parliamentary system
Currency Euro = 100 cents
Literacy rate 92%
Calorie consumption Not available

KUWAIT
Southwest Asia

Page 98 C4

Kuwait lies on the northwest extreme of the Persian Gulf. The state was a British protectorate from 1914 until 1961, when full independence was granted.

Official name State of Kuwait
Formation 1961 / 1961
Capital Kuwait City
Population 3.1 million / 451 people per sq mile (174 people per sq km)
Total area 6880 sq. miles (17,820 sq. km)
Languages Arabic*, English
Religions Sunni Muslim 45%, Shi'a Muslim 40%, Christian, Hindu, and other 15%
Ethnic mix Kuwaiti 45%, Other Arab 35%, South Asian 9%, Other 7%, Iranian 4%
Government Monarchy
Currency Kuwaiti dinar = 1000 fils
Literacy rate 94%
Calorie consumption 3038 kilocalories

KYRGYZSTAN
Central Asia

Page 101 F2

A mountainous, landlocked state in Central Asia. The most rural of the ex-Soviet republics, it only gradually developed its own cultural nationalism.

Official name Kyrgyz Republic
Formation 1991 / 1991
Capital Bishkek
Population 5.6 million / 73 people per sq mile (28 people per sq km)
Total area 76,641 sq. miles (198,500 sq. km)
Languages Kyrgyz*, Russian*, Uzbek, Tatar, Ukrainian
Religions Muslim (mainly Sunni) 70%, Orthodox Christian 30%
Ethnic mix Kyrgyz 69%, Uzbek 14%, Russian 9%, Other 6%, Uighur 1%, Dungan 1%
Government Transitional regime
Currency Som = 100 tyiyn
Literacy rate 99%
Calorie consumption 2672 kilocalories

LAOS
Southeast Asia

Page 114 D4

A former French colony, independent in 1953, Laos lies landlocked in Southeast Asia. It has been under communist rule since 1975.

Official name Lao People's Democratic Republic
Formation 1953 / 1953
Capital Vientiane
Population 6.4 million / 72 people per sq mile (28 people per sq km)
Total area 91,428 sq. miles (236,800 sq. km)
Languages Lao*, Mon-Khmer, Yao, Vietnamese, Chinese, French
Religions Buddhist 65%, Other (including animist) 34%, Christian 1%
Ethnic mix Lao Loum 66%, Lao Theung 30%, Other 2%, Lao Soung 2%
Government One-party state
Currency New kip = 100 at
Literacy rate 73%
Calorie consumption 2227 kilocalories

LESOTHO
Southern Africa

Page 56 D4

The landlocked kingdom of Lesotho is entirely surrounded by South Africa, which provides all its land transportation links with the outside world.

Official name Kingdom of Lesotho
Formation 1966 / 1966
Capital Maseru
Population 2.1 million / 179 people per sq mile (69 people per sq km)
Total area 11,720 sq. miles (30,355 sq. km)
Languages English*, Sesotho*, isiZulu
Religions Christian 90%, Traditional beliefs 10%
Ethnic mix Sotho 99%, European and Asian 1%
Government Parliamentary system
Currency Loti & South African rand = 100 lisente
Literacy rate 90%
Calorie consumption 2468 kilocalories

LIECHTENSTEIN
Central Europe

Page 73 B7

Tucked in the Alps between Switzerland and Austria, Liechtenstein became an independent principality of the Holy Roman Empire in 1719.

Official name Principality of Liechtenstein
Formation 1719 / 1719
Capital Vaduz
Population 35,236 / 568 people per sq mile (220 people per sq km)
Total area 62 sq. miles (160 sq. km)
Languages German*, Alemannish dialect, Italian
Religions Roman Catholic 79%, Other 13%, Protestant 8%
Ethnic mix Liechtensteiner 66%, Other 12%, Swiss 10%, Austrian 6%, German 3%, Italian 3%
Government Parliamentary system
Currency Swiss franc = 100 rappen/centimes
Literacy rate 99%
Calorie consumption Not available

MACEDONIA
Southeast Europe

Page 79 D6

Landlocked in the southern Balkans, Macedonia has been affected by sanctions imposed on its northern trading partners and by Greek antagonism.

Official name Republic of Macedonia
Formation 1991 / 1991
Capital Skopje
Population 2 million / 201 people per sq mile (78 people per sq km)
Total area 9781 sq. miles (25,333 sq. km)
Languages Macedonian*, Albanian*, Turkish, Romani, Serbian
Religions Orthodox Christian 65%, Muslim 29%, Roman Catholic 4%, Other 2%
Ethnic mix Macedonian 64%, Albanian 25%, Turkish 4%, Roma 3%, Other 2%, Serb 2%
Government Mixed presidential–parliamentary system
Currency Macedonian denar = 100 deni
Literacy rate 97%
Calorie consumption 2983 kilocalories

LATVIA
Northeast Europe

Page 84 C3

Situated on the east coast of the Baltic Sea, Lativa, like its Baltic neighbors, became independent in 1991. It retains a large Russian population.

Official name Republic of Latvia
Formation 1991 / 1991
Capital Riga
Population 2.2 million / 88 people per sq mile (34 people per sq km)
Total area 24,938 sq. miles (64,589 sq. km)
Languages Latvian*, Russian
Religions Other 43%, Lutheran 24%, Roman Catholic 18%, Orthodox Christian 15%
Ethnic mix Latvian 59%, Russian 28%, Belarussian 4%, Other 4%, Ukrainian 3%, Polish 2%
Government Parliamentary system
Currency Lats = 100 santimi
Literacy rate 99%
Calorie consumption 3019 kilocalories

LIBERIA
West Africa

Page 52 C5

Liberia faces the Atlantic Ocean in equatorial West Africa. Africa's oldest republic, it was established in 1847. Today, it is torn by civil war.

Official name Republic of Liberia
Formation 1847 / 1847
Capital Monrovia
Population 4.1 million / 110 people per sq mile (43 people per sq km)
Total area 43,000 sq. miles (111,370 sq. km)
Languages Kpelle, Vai, Bassa, Kru, Grebo, Kissi, Gola, Loma, English*
Religions Traditional beliefs 40%, Christian 40%, Muslim 20%
Ethnic mix Indigenous tribes (12 groups) 49%, Kpellé 20%, Bassa 16%, Gio 8%, Krou 7%
Government Presidential system
Currency Liberian dollar = 100 cents
Literacy rate 59%
Calorie consumption 2163 kilocalories

LITHUANIA
Northeast Europe

Page 84 B4

The largest, most powerful and stable of the Baltic states, Lithuania was the first Baltic country to declare independence from Moscow, in 1991.

Official name Republic of Lithuania
Formation 1991 / 1991
Capital Vilnius
Population 3.3 million / 131 people per sq mile (51 people per sq km)
Total area 25,174 sq. miles (65,200 sq. km)
Languages Lithuanian*, Russian
Religions Roman Catholic 79%, Other 15%, Russian Orthodox 4%, Protestant 2%
Ethnic mix Lithuanian 85%, Polish 6%, Russian 5%, Other 3%, Belarussian 1%
Government Parliamentary system
Currency Litas = 100 centu
Literacy rate 99%
Calorie consumption 3419 kilocalories

MADAGASCAR
Indian Ocean

Page 57 F4

Lying in the Indian Ocean, Madagascar is the world's fourth largest island. Free elections in 1993 ended 18 years of radical socialist government.

Official name Republic of Madagascar
Formation 1960 / 1960
Capital Antananarivo
Population 20.1 million / 90 people per sq mile (35 people per sq km)
Total area 226,656 sq. miles (587,040 sq. km)
Languages Malagasy*, French*, English*
Religions Traditional beliefs 52%, Christian (mainly Roman Catholic) 41%, Muslim 7%
Ethnic mix Other Malay 46%, Merina 26%, Betsimisaraka 15%, Betsileo 12%, Other 1%
Government Transitional regime
Currency Ariary = 5 iraimbilanja
Literacy rate 64%
Calorie consumption 2133 kilocalories

LEBANON
Southwest Asia

Page 96 A4

Lebanon is dwarfed by its two powerful neighbors, Syria and Israel. The state started rebuilding in 1989, after 14 years of intense civil war.

Official name Republic of Lebanon
Formation 1941 / 1941
Capital Beirut
Population 4.3 million / 1089 people per sq mile (420 people per sq km)
Total area 4015 sq. miles (10,400 sq. km)
Languages Arabic*, French, Armenian, Assyrian
Religions Muslim 60%, Christian 39%, Other 1%
Ethnic mix Arab 95%, Armenian 4%, Other 1%
Government Parliamentary system
Currency Lebanese pound = 100 piastres
Literacy rate 90%
Calorie consumption 3107 kilocalories

LIBYA
North Africa

Page 49 F3

Situated on north Africa's Mediterranean coast, Libya has been under the leadership of Colonel Gaddafi since 1969. Civil war to oust his regime began during the 2011 "Arab Spring."

Official name Libyan Republic (post Gaddafi regime)
Formation 1951 / 1951
Capital Tripoli
Population 6.5 million / 10 people per sq mile (4 people per sq km)
Total area 679,358 sq. miles (1,759,540 sq. km)
Languages Arabic*, Tuareg
Religions Muslim (mainly Sunni) 97%, Other 3%
Ethnic mix Arab and Berber 97%, Other 3%
Government Transitional regime
Currency Libyan dinar = 1000 dirhams
Literacy rate 89%
Calorie consumption 3144 kilocalories

LUXEMBOURG
Northwest Europe

Page 65 D8

Making up part of the plateau of the Ardennes in Western Europe, Luxembourg is Europe's last independent duchy and one of its richest states.

Official name Grand Duchy of Luxembourg
Formation 1867 / 1867
Capital Luxembourg-Ville
Population 500,000 / 501 people per sq mile (193 people per sq km)
Total area 998 sq. miles (2586 sq. km)
Languages Luxembourgish*, German*, French*
Religions Roman Catholic 97%, Protestant, Orthodox Christian, and Jewish 3%
Ethnic mix Luxembourger 62%, Foreign residents 38%
Government Parliamentary system
Currency Euro = 100 cents
Literacy rate 99%
Calorie consumption 3685 kilocalories

MALAWI
Southern Africa

Page 57 E1

A former British colony, Malawi lies landlocked in southeast Africa. Its name means "the land where the sun is reflected in the water like fire."

Official name Republic of Malawi
Formation 1964 / 1964
Capital Lilongwe
Population 15.7 million / 432 people per sq mile (167 people per sq km)
Total area 45,745 sq. miles (118,480 sq. km)
Languages Chewa, Lomwe, Yao, Ngoni, English*
Religions Protestant 55%, Roman Catholic 20%, Muslim 20%, Traditional beliefs 5%
Ethnic mix Bantu 99%, Other 1%
Government Presidential system
Currency Malawi kwacha = 100 tambala
Literacy rate 74%
Calorie consumption 2127 kilocalories

MALAYSIA
Southeast Asia

Page 116 B3

Malaysia's three separate territories include Malaya, Sarawak, and Sabah. A financial crisis in 1997 ended a decade of spectacular financial growth.

Official name Federation of Malaysia
Formation 1963 / 1965
Capital Kuala Lumpur; Putrajaya (administrative)
Population 27.9 million / 220 people per sq mile (85 people per sq km)
Total area 127,316 sq. miles (329,750 sq. km)
Languages Bahasa Malaysia*, Malay, Chinese, Tamil, English
Religions Muslim (mainly Sunni) 61%, Buddhist 19%, Christian 9%, Hindu 6%, Other 5%
Ethnic mix Malay 53%, Chinese 26%, Indigenous tribes 12%, Indian 8%, Other 1%
Government Parliamentary system
Currency Ringgit = 100 sen
Literacy rate 92%
Calorie consumption 2908 kilocalories

MALDIVES
Indian Ocean

Page 110 A4

Only 200 of the more than 1,000 Maldivian small coral islands in the Indian Ocean, are inhabited. Government rests in the hands of a few influential families.

Official name Republic of Maldives
Formation 1965 / 1965
Capital Male'
Population 300,000 / 2586 people per sq mile (1000 people per sq km)
Total area 116 sq. miles (300 sq. km)
Languages Dhivehi (Maldivian)*, Sinhala, Tamil, Arabic
Religions Sunni Muslim 100%
Ethnic mix Arab–Sinhalese–Malay 100%
Government Presidential system
Currency Rufiyaa = 100 laari
Literacy rate 97%
Calorie consumption Not available

MALI
West Africa

Page 53 E2

Landlocked in the heart of West Africa, Mali held its first free elections in 1992, more than 30 years after it gained independence from France.

Official name Republic of Mali
Formation 1960 / 1960
Capital Bamako
Population 13.3 million / 28 people per sq mile (11 people per sq km)
Total area 478,764 sq. miles (1,240,000 sq. km)
Languages Bambara, Fulani, Senufo, Soninke, French*
Religions Muslim (mainly Sunni) 90%, Traditional beliefs 6%, Christian 4%
Ethnic mix Bambara 52%, Other 14%, Fulani 11%, Saracolé 7%, Soninka 7%, Tuareg 5%, Mianka 4%
Government Presidential system
Currency CFA franc = 100 centimes
Literacy rate 23%
Calorie consumption 2579 kilocalories

MALTA
Southern Europe

Page 80 A5

The Maltese archipelago lies off southern Sicily, midway between Europe and North Africa. The only inhabited islands are Malta, Gozo, and Kemmuna.

Official name Republic of Malta
Formation 1964 / 1964
Capital Valletta
Population 400,000 / 3226 people per sq mile (1250 people per sq km)
Total area 122 sq. miles (316 sq. km)
Languages Maltese*, English*
Religions Roman Catholic 98%, Other and nonreligious 2%
Ethnic mix Maltese 96%, Other 4%
Government Parliamentary system
Currency Euro = 100 cents
Literacy rate 92%
Calorie consumption 3592 kilocalories

MARSHALL ISLANDS
Australasia & Oceania

Page 122 D1

A group of 34 atolls, the Marshall Islands were under US rule as part of the UN Trust Territory of the Pacific Islands until 1986. The economy depends on US aid.

Official name Republic of the Marshall Islands
Formation 1986 / 1986
Capital Majuro
Population 67,182 / 960 people per sq mile (371 people per sq km)
Total area 70 sq. miles (181 sq. km)
Languages Marshallese*, English*, Japanese, German
Religions Protestant 90%, Roman Catholic 8%, Other 2%
Ethnic mix Micronesian 90%, Other 10%
Government Presidential system
Currency US dollar = 100 cents
Literacy rate 91%
Calorie consumption Not available

MAURITANIA
West Africa

Page 52 C2

Situated in northwest Africa, two-thirds of Mauritania's territory is desert. A former French colony, it achieved independence in 1960.

Official name Islamic Republic of Mauritania
Formation 1960 / 1960
Capital Nouakchott
Population 3.4 million / 9 people per sq mile (3 people per sq km)
Total area 397,953 sq. miles (1,030,700 sq. km)
Languages Hassaniyah Arabic*, Wolof, French
Religions Sunni Muslim 100%
Ethnic mix Maure 81%, Wolof 7%, Tukolor 5%, Other 4%, Soninka 3%
Government Presidential system
Currency Ouguiya = 5 khoums
Literacy rate 58%
Calorie consumption 2823 kilocalories

MAURITIUS
Indian Ocean

Page 57 H3

Located to the east of Madagascar in the Indian Ocean, Mauritius became a republic 25 years after it gained independence. Tourism is a mainstay of its economy.

Official name Republic of Mauritius
Formation 1968 / 1968
Capital Port Louis
Population 1.3 million / 1811 people per sq mile (699 people per sq km)
Total area 718 sq. miles (1860 sq. km)
Languages French Creole, Hindi, Urdu, Tamil, Chinese, English*, French
Religions Hindu 48%, Roman Catholic 24%, Muslim 17%, Protestant 9%, Other 2%
Ethnic mix Indo-Mauritian 68%, Creole 27%, Sino-Mauritian 3%, Franco-Mauritian 2%
Government Parliamentary system
Currency Mauritian rupee = 100 cents
Literacy rate 88%
Calorie consumption 2936 kilocalories

MEXICO
North America

Page 28 D3

Located between the United States of America and the Central American states, Mexico was a Spanish colony for 300 years until 1836.

Official name United Mexican States
Formation 1836 / 1848
Capital Mexico City
Population 111 million / 150 people per sq mile (58 people per sq km)
Total area 761,602 sq. miles (1,972,550 sq. km)
Languages Spanish*, Nahuatl, Mayan, Zapotec, Mixtec, Otomi, Totonac, Tzotzil, Tzeltal
Religions Roman Catholic 77%, Other 14%, Protestant 6%, Nonreligious 3%
Ethnic mix Mestizo 60%, Amerindian 30%, European 9%, Other 1%
Government Presidential system
Currency Mexican peso = 100 centavos
Literacy rate 93%
Calorie consumption 3245 kilocalories

MICRONESIA
Australasia & Oceania

Page 122 B1

The Federated States of Micronesia, situated in the western Pacific, comprise 607 islands and atolls grouped into four main island states.

Official name Federated States of Micronesia
Formation 1986 / 1986
Capital Palikir (Pohnpei Island)
Population 106,836 / 394 people per sq mile (152 people per sq km)
Total area 271 sq. miles (702 sq. km)
Languages Trukese, Pohnpeian, Kosraean, Yapese, English*
Religions Roman Catholic 50%, Protestant 47%, Other 3%
Ethnic mix Chuukese 49%, Pohnpeian 24%, Other 14%, Kosraean 6%, Yapese 5%, Asian 2%
Government Nonparty system
Currency US dollar = 100 cents
Literacy rate 81%
Calorie consumption Not available

MOLDOVA
Southeast Europe

Page 86 D3

The smallest and most densely populated of the ex-Soviet republics, Moldova has strong linguistic and cultural links with Romania to the west.

Official name Republic of Moldova
Formation 1991 / 1991
Capital Chisinau
Population 3.6 million / 277 people per sq mile (107 people per sq km)
Total area 13,067 sq. miles (33,843 sq. km)
Languages Moldovan*, Ukrainian, Russian
Religions Orthodox Christian 93%, Other 6%, Baptist 1%
Ethnic mix Moldovan 84%, Ukrainian 7%, Gagauz 5%, Russian 2%, Bulgarian 1%, Other 1%
Government Parliamentary system
Currency Moldovan leu = 100 bani
Literacy rate 99%
Calorie consumption 2907 kilocalories

MONACO
Southern Europe

Page 69 E6

The smallest and most densely populated of the ex-Soviet republics, Moldova has strong linguistic and cultural links with Romania to the west.

Official name Principality of Monaco
Formation 1861 / 1861
Capital Monaco-Ville
Population 30,539 / 40,719 people per sq mile (15,661 people per sq km)
Total area 0.75 sq. miles (1.95 sq. km)
Languages French*, Italian, Monégasque, English
Religions Roman Catholic 89%, Protestant 6%, Other 5%
Ethnic mix French 47%, Other 21%, Italian 16%, Monégasque 16%
Government Mixed monarchical–parliamentary system
Currency Euro = 100 cents
Literacy rate 99%
Calorie consumption Not available

MONGOLIA
East Asia

Page 104 D2

Lying between Russia and China, Mongolia is a vast and isolated country with a small population. Over two-thirds of the country is desert.

Official name Mongolia
Formation 1924 / 1924
Capital Ulan Bator
Population 2.7 million / 4 people per sq mile (2 people per sq km)
Total area 604,247 sq. miles (1,565,000 sq. km)
Languages Khalkha Mongolian*, Kazakh, Chinese, Russian
Religions Tibetan Buddhist 50%, Nonreligious 40%, Shamanist and Christian 6%, Muslim 4%
Ethnic mix Khalkh 95%, Kazakh 4%, Other 1%
Government Mixed presidential–parliamentary system
Currency Tugrik (tögrög) = 100 möngö
Literacy rate 98%
Calorie consumption 2254 kilocalories

MONTENEGRO
Southeast Europe

Page 79 C5

Montenegro voted to split from Serbia in 2006. Since then the country has developed politically and economically with a view towards eventual membership of the EU.

Official name Montenegro
Formation 2006 / 2006
Capital Podgorica
Population 600,000 / 113 people per sq mile (43 people per sq km)
Total area 5332 sq. miles (13,812 sq. km)
Languages Montenegrin*, Serbian, Albanian, Bosniak, Croatian
Religions Orthodox Christian 74%, Muslim 18%, Other 4%, Roman Catholic 4%
Ethnic mix Montenegrin 43%, Serb 32%, Other 12%, Bosniak 8%, Albanian 5%
Government Parliamentary system
Currency Euro = 100 cents
Literacy rate 98%
Calorie consumption 2445 kilocalories

MOROCCO
North Africa

Page 48 C2

A former French colony in northwest Africa, independent in 1956, Morocco has occupied the disputed territory of Western Sahara since 1975.

Official name Kingdom of Morocco
Formation 1956 / 1969
Capital Rabat
Population 32.4 million / 188 people per sq mile (73 people per sq km)
Total area 172,316 sq. miles (446,300 sq. km)
Languages Arabic*, Tamazight (Berber), French, Spanish
Religions Muslim (mainly Sunni) 99%, Other (mostly Christian) 1%
Ethnic mix Arab 70%, Berber 29%, European 1%
Government Mixed monarchical–parliamentary system
Currency Moroccan dirham = 100 centimes
Literacy rate 56%
Calorie consumption 3230 kilocalories

MOZAMBIQUE
Southern Africa

Page 57 E3

Mozambique lies on the southeast African coast. It was torn by a civil war between the Marxist government and a rebel group from 1977–1992.

Official name Republic of Mozambique
Formation 1975 / 1975
Capital Maputo
Population 23.4 million / 77 people per sq mile (30 people per sq km)
Total area 309,494 sq. miles (801,590 sq. km)
Languages Makua, Xitsonga, Sena, Lomwe, Portuguese*
Religions Traditional beliefs 56%, Christian 30%, Muslim 14%
Ethnic mix Makua Lomwe 47%, Tsonga 23%, Malawi 12%, Shona 11%, Yao 4%, Other 3%
Government Presidential system
Currency New metical = 100 centavos
Literacy rate 55%
Calorie consumption 2071 kilocalories

MYANMAR (BURMA)
Southeast Asia

Page 114 A3

Myanmar forms the eastern shores of the Bay of Bengal and the Andaman Sea in Southeast Asia. Since 1988 it has been ruled by a repressive military regime.

Official name Union of Myanmar
Formation 1948 / 1948
Capital Nay Pyi Taw
Population 50.5 million / 199 people per sq mile (77 people per sq km)
Total area 261,969 sq. miles (678,500 sq. km)
Languages Burmese*, Shan, Karen, Rakhine, Chin, Yangbye, Kachin, Mon
Religions Buddhist 89%, Christian 4%, Muslim 4%, Other 2%, Animist 1%
Ethnic mix Burman (Bamah) 68%, Other 12%, Shan 9%, Karen 7%, Rakhine 4%
Government Presidential system
Currency Kyat = 100 pyas
Literacy rate 92%
Calorie consumption 2438 kilocalories

NAMIBIA
Southern Africa

Page 56 B3

Located in southwestern Africa, Namibia became free of South African control in 1990, after years of uncertainty and guerrilla activity.

Official name Republic of Namibia
Formation 1990 / 1994
Capital Windhoek
Population 2.2 million / 7 people per sq mile (3 people per sq km)
Total area 318,694 sq. miles (825,418 sq. km)
Languages Ovambo, Kavango, English*, Bergdama, German, Afrikaans
Religions Christian 90%, Traditional beliefs 10%
Ethnic mix Ovambo 50%, Other tribes 22%, Kavango 9%, Herero 7%, Damara 7%, Other 5%
Government Presidential system
Currency Namibian dollar & South African rand = 100 cents
Literacy rate 88%
Calorie consumption 2349 kilocalories

NAURU
Australasia & Oceania

Page 122 D3

Nauru lies in the Pacific, 2,480 miles (4,000 km) northeast of Australia. For many years phosphate deposits provided great wealth but these are now virtually exhausted.

Official name Republic of Nauru
Formation 1968 / 1968
Capital None
Population 9322 / 1151 people per sq mile (444 people per sq km)
Total area 8.1 sq. miles (21 sq. km)
Languages Nauruan*, Kiribati, Chinese, Tuvaluan, English
Religions Nauruan Congregational Church 60%, Roman Catholic 35%, Other 5%
Ethnic mix Nauruan 93%, Chinese 5%, Other Pacific islanders 1%, European 1%
Government Nonparty system
Currency Australian dollar = 100 cents
Literacy rate 95%
Calorie consumption Not available

NEPAL
South Asia

Page 113 E3

Nepal lies between India and China, on the shoulder of the southern Himalayas. In 2008, after many years of unrest, Nepal was declared a republic and the monarchy was dissolved .

Official name Federal Democratic Republic of Nepal
Formation 1769 / 1769
Capital Kathmandu
Population 29.9 million / 566 people per sq mile (219 people per sq km)
Total area 54,363 sq. miles (140,800 sq. km)
Languages Nepali*, Maithili, Bhojpuri
Religions Hindu 81%, Buddhist 11%, Muslim 4%, Other (including Christian) 4%
Ethnic mix Other 52%, Chhetri 16%, Hill Brahman 13%, Magar 7%, Tharu 7%, Tamang 5%
Government Transitional regime
Currency Nepalese rupee = 100 paisa
Literacy rate 59%
Calorie consumption 2349 kilocalories

NETHERLANDS
Northwest Europe

Page 64 C3

Astride the delta of five major rivers in northwest Europe, the Netherlands has a long trading tradition. Rotterdam is the world's largest port.

Official name Kingdom of the Netherlands
Formation 1648 / 1839
Capital Amsterdam; The Hague (administrative)
Population 16.7 million / 1275 people per sq mile (492 people per sq km)
Total area 16,033 sq. miles (41,526 sq. km)
Languages Dutch*, Frisian
Religions Roman Catholic 36%, Other 34%, Protestant 27%, Muslim 3%
Ethnic mix Dutch 82%, Other 12%, Surinamese 2%, Turkish 2%, Moroccan 2%
Government Parliamentary system
Currency Euro = 100 cents
Literacy rate 99%
Calorie consumption 3243 kilocalories

NEW ZEALAND
Australasia & Oceania

Page 128 A4

One of the Pacific Rim countries, New Zealand lies southeast of Australia, and comprises the North and South Islands, separated by the Cook Strait.

Official name New Zealand
Formation 1947 / 1947
Capital Wellington
Population 4.3 million / 41 people per sq mile (16 people per sq km)
Total area 103,737 sq. miles (268,680 sq. km)
Languages English*, Maori*
Religions Anglican 24%, Other 22%, Presbyterian 18%, Nonreligious 16%, Roman Catholic 15%, Methodist 5%
Ethnic mix European 75%, Maori 15%, Other 7%, Samoan 3%
Government Parliamentary system
Currency New Zealand dollar = 100 cents
Literacy rate 99%
Calorie consumption 3150 kilocalories

NICARAGUA
Central America

Page 30 D3

Nicaragua lies at the heart of Central America. An 11-year war between left-wing Sandinistas and right-wing US-backed Contras ended in 1989.

Official name Republic of Nicaragua
Formation 1838 / 1838
Capital Managua
Population 5.8 million / 127 people per sq mile (49 people per sq km)
Total area 49,998 sq. miles (129,494 sq. km)
Languages Spanish*, English Creole, Miskito
Religions Roman Catholic 80%, Protestant Evangelical 17%, Other 3%
Ethnic mix Mestizo 69%, White 17%, Black 9%, Amerindian 5%
Government Presidential system
Currency Córdoba oro = 100 centavos
Literacy rate 80%
Calorie consumption 2400 kilocalories

NIGER
West Africa

Page 53 F3

Niger lies landlocked in West Africa, but it is linked to the sea by the River Niger. Since 1973 it has suffered civil unrest and two major droughts.

Official name Republic of Niger
Formation 1960 / 1960
Capital Niamey
Population 15.9 million / 33 people per sq mile (13 people per sq km)
Total area 489,188 sq. miles (1,267,000 sq. km)
Languages Hausa, Djerma, Fulani, Tuareg, Teda, French*
Religions Muslim 99%, Other (including Christian) 1%
Ethnic mix Hausa 53%, Djerma and Songhai 21%, Tuareg 11%, Fulani 7%, Kanuri 6%, Other 2%
Government Presidential system
Currency CFA franc = 100 centimes
Literacy rate 30%
Calorie consumption 2306 kilocalories

NIGERIA
West Africa

Page 53 F4

Africa's most populous state Nigeria, in West Africa, is a federation of 30 states. It adopted civilian rule in 1999 after 33 years of military government.

Official name Federal Republic of Nigeria
Formation 1960 / 1961
Capital Abuja
Population 158 million / 450 people per sq mile (174 people per sq km)
Total area 356,667 sq. miles (923,768 sq. km)
Languages Hausa, English*, Yoruba, Ibo
Religions Muslim 50%, Christian 40%, Traditional beliefs 10%
Ethnic mix Other 29%, Hausa 21%, Yoruba 21%, Ibo 18%, Fulani 11%
Government Presidential system
Currency Naira = 100 kobo
Literacy rate 61%
Calorie consumption 2708 kilocalories

NORTH KOREA
East Asia

Page 106 E3

North Korea comprises the northern half of the Korean peninsula. A communist state since 1948, it is largely isolated from the outside world.

Official name Democratic People's Republic of Korea
Formation 1948 / 1953
Capital Pyongyang
Population 24 million / 516 people per sq mile (199 people per sq km)
Total area 46,540 sq. miles (120,540 sq. km)
Languages Korean*
Religions Atheist 100%
Ethnic mix Korean 100%
Government One-party state
Currency North Korean won = 100 chon
Literacy rate 99%
Calorie consumption 2146 kilocalories

NORWAY
Northern Europe

Page 63 A5

The Kingdom of Norway traces the rugged western coast of Scandinavia. Settlements are largely restricted to southern and coastal areas.

Official name Kingdom of Norway
Formation 1905 / 1905
Capital Oslo
Population 4.9 million / 41 people per sq mile (16 people per sq km)
Total area 125,181 sq. miles (324,220 sq. km)
Languages Norwegian* (Bokmål "book language" and Nynorsk "new Norsk"), Sámi
Religions Evangelical Lutheran 88%, Other and nonreligious 8%, Muslim 2%, Roman Catholic 1%, Pentecostal 1%
Ethnic mix Norwegian 93%, Other 6%, Sámi 1%
Government Parliamentary system
Currency Norwegian krone = 100 øre
Literacy rate 99%
Calorie consumption 3455 kilocalories

OMAN
Southwest Asia

Page 99 D6

Situated on the eastern coast of the Arabian Peninsula, Oman is the least developed of the Gulf states, despite modest oil exports.

Official name Sultanate of Oman
Formation 1951 / 1951
Capital Muscat
Population 2.9 million / 35 people per sq mile (14 people per sq km)
Total area 82,031 sq. miles (212,460 sq. km)
Languages Arabic*, Baluchi, Farsi, Hindi, Punjabi
Religions Ibadi Muslim 75%, Other Muslim and Hindu 25%
Ethnic mix Arab 88%, Baluchi 4%, Indian and Pakistani 3%, Persian 3%, African 2%
Government Monarchy
Currency Omani rial = 1000 baisa
Literacy rate 87%
Calorie consumption Not available

PAKISTAN
South Asia

Page 112 B2

Pakistan was created in 1947 as an independent Muslim state. Today, this nuclear armed country is struggling to deal with complex domestic and international tensions.

Official name Islamic Republic of Pakistan
Formation 1947 / 1971
Capital Islamabad
Population 185 million / 621 people per sq mile (240 people per sq km)
Total area 310,401 sq. miles (803,940 sq. km)
Languages Punjabi, Sindhi, Pashtu, Urdu*, Baluchi, Brahui
Religions Sunni Muslim 77%, Shi'a Muslim 20%, Hindu 2%, Christian 1%
Ethnic mix Punjabi 56%, Pathan (Pashtun) 15%, Sindhi 14%, Mohajir 7%, Other 4%, Baluchi 4%
Government Presidential system
Currency Pakistani rupee = 100 paisa
Literacy rate 56%
Calorie consumption 2251 kilocalories

PALAU
Australasia & Oceania

Page 122 A2

The Palau archipelago, a group of over 200 islands, lies in the western Pacific Ocean. Since independence in 1994 it has prospered on a thriving tourist industry.

Official name Republic of Palau
Formation 1994 / 1994
Capital Melekeok
Population 20,956 / 107 people per sq mile (41 people per sq km)
Total area 177 sq. miles (458 sq. km)
Languages Palauan*, English, Japanese, Angaur, Tobi, Sonsorolese
Religions Christian 66%, Modekngei 34%
Ethnic mix Palauan 74%, Filipino 16%, Other 6%, Chinese and other Asian 4%
Government Nonparty system
Currency US dollar = 100 cents
Literacy rate 98%
Calorie consumption Not available

PANAMA
Central America

Page 31 F5

Southernmost of the Central American countries. The Panama Canal (returned to Panama from US control in 2000) links the Pacific and Atlantic oceans.

Official name Republic of Panama
Formation 1903 / 1903
Capital Panama City
Population 3.5 million / 119 people per sq mile (46 people per sq km)
Total area 30,193 sq. miles (78,200 sq. km)
Languages English Creole, Spanish*, Amerindian languages, Chibchan languages
Religions Roman Catholic 84%, Protestant 15%, Other 1%
Ethnic mix Mestizo 70%, Black 14%, White 10%, Amerindian 6%
Government Presidential system
Currency Balboa & US dollar = 100 centésimos
Literacy rate 94%
Calorie consumption 2451 kilocalories

PAPUA NEW GUINEA
Australasia & Oceania

Page 122 B3

Achieving independence from Australia in 1975, PNG occupies the eastern section of the island of New Guinea and several other island groups.

Official name Independent State of Papua New Guinea
Formation 1975 / 1975
Capital Port Moresby
Population 6.9 million / 39 people per sq mile (15 people per sq km)
Total area 178,703 sq. miles (462,840 sq. km)
Languages Pidgin English, Papuan, English*, Motu, 800 (est.) native languages
Religions Protestant 60%, Roman Catholic 37%, Other 3%
Ethnic mix Melanesian and mixed race 100%
Government Parliamentary system
Currency Kina = 100 toea
Literacy rate 60%
Calorie consumption 2193 kilocalories

PARAGUAY
South America

Page 42 D2

Landlocked in central South America. Its post-independence history has included periods of military rule. Free elections were held in 1993.

Official name Republic of Paraguay
Formation 1811 / 1938
Capital Asunción
Population 6.5 million / 42 people per sq mile (16 people per sq km)
Total area 157,046 sq. miles (406,750 sq. km)
Languages Guaraní, Spanish*, German
Religions Roman Catholic 90%, Protestant (including Mennonite) 10%
Ethnic mix Mestizo 91%, Other 7%, Amerindian 2%
Government Presidential system
Currency Guaraní = 100 céntimos
Literacy rate 95%
Calorie consumption 2622 kilocalories

PERU
South America

Page 38 C3

Once the heart of the Inca empire, before the Spanish conquest in the 16th century, Peru lies on the Pacific coast of South America.

Official name Republic of Peru
Formation 1824 / 1941
Capital Lima
Population 29.5 million / 60 people per sq mile (23 people per sq km)
Total area 496,223 sq. miles (1,285,200 sq. km)
Languages Spanish*, Quechua, Aymara
Religions Roman Catholic 81%, Other 19%
Ethnic mix Amerindian 45%, Mestizo 37%, White 15%, Other 3%
Government Presidential system
Currency New sol = 100 céntimos
Literacy rate 90%
Calorie consumption 2426 kilocalories

PHILIPPINES
Southeast Asia

Page 117 E1

An archipelago of 7,107 islands between the South China Sea and the Pacific. After 21 years of dictatorship, democracy was restored in 1986.

Official name Republic of the Philippines
Formation 1946 / 1946
Capital Manila
Population 93.6 million / 813 people per sq mile (314 people per sq km)
Total area 115,830 sq. miles (300,000 sq. km)
Languages Filipino, English*, Tagalog*, Cebuano, Ilocano, Hiligaynon, many other local languages
Religions Roman Catholic 81%, Protestant 9%, Muslim 5%, Other (including Buddhist) 5%
Ethnic mix Other 34%, Tagalog 28%, Cebuano 13%, Ilocano 9%, Hiligaynon 8%, Bisaya 8%
Government Presidential system
Currency Philippine peso = 100 centavos
Literacy rate 95%
Calorie consumption 2518 kilocalories

POLAND
Northern Europe

Page 76 B3

With its seven international borders and strategic location in the heart of Europe, Poland has always played an important role in European affairs.

Official name Republic of Poland
Formation 1918 / 1945
Capital Warsaw
Population 38 million / 323 people per sq mile (125 people per sq km)
Total area 120,728 sq. miles (312,685 sq. km)
Languages Polish*
Religions Roman Catholic 93%, Other and nonreligious 5%, Orthodox Christian 2%
Ethnic mix Polish 98%, Other 2%
Government Parliamentary system
Currency Zloty = 100 groszy
Literacy rate 99%
Calorie consumption 3397 kilocalories

PORTUGAL
Southwest Europe

Page 70 B3

Facing the Atlantic on the western side of the Iberian Peninsula, Portugal is the most westerly country on the European mainland.

Official name Republic of Portugal
Formation 1139 / 1640
Capital Lisbon
Population 10.7 million / 301 people per sq mile (116 people per sq km)
Total area 35,672 sq. miles (92,391 sq. km)
Languages Portuguese*
Religions Roman Catholic 92%, Protestant 4%, Nonreligious 3%, Other 1%
Ethnic mix Portuguese 98%, African and other 2%
Government Parliamentary system
Currency Euro = 100 cents
Literacy rate 95%
Calorie consumption 3583 kilocalories

QATAR
Southwest Asia

Page 98 C4

Projecting north from the Arabian Peninsula into the Persian Gulf, Qatar's reserves of oil and gas make it one of the region's wealthiest states.

Official name State of Qatar
Formation 1971 / 1971
Capital Doha
Population 1.5 million / 353 people per sq mile (136 people per sq km)
Total area 4416 sq. miles (11,437 sq. km)
Languages Arabic*
Religions Muslim (mainly Sunni) 95%, Other 5%
Ethnic mix Qatari 20%, Other Arab 20%, Indian 20%, Nepalese 13%, Filipino 10%, Other 10%, Pakistani 7%
Government Monarchy
Currency Qatar riyal = 100 dirhams
Literacy rate 95%
Calorie consumption Not available

ROMANIA
Southeast Europe

Page 86 B4

Romania lies on the Black Sea coast. Since the overthrow of its communist regime in 1989, it has been slowly converting to a free-market economy.

Official name Romania
Formation 1878 / 1947
Capital Bucharest
Population 21.2 million / 238 people per sq mile (92 people per sq km)
Total area 91,699 sq. miles (237,500 sq. km)
Languages Romanian*, Hungarian (Magyar), Romani, German
Religions Romanian Orthodox 87%, Protestant 5%, Roman Catholic 5%, Other 3%
Ethnic mix Romanian 89%, Magyar 7%, Roma 3%, Other 1%
Government Presidential system
Currency New Romanian leu = 100 bani
Literacy rate 98%
Calorie consumption 3510 kilocalories

RUSSIAN FEDERATION
Europe / Asia

Page 92 D4

Still the world's largest state, despite the breakup of the USSR in 1991, the Russian Federation is a major power on the world stage, controlling vast mineral and energy reserves.

Official name Russian Federation
Formation 1480 / 1991
Capital Moscow
Population 140 million / 21 people per sq mile (8 people per sq km)
Total area 6,592,735 sq. miles (17,075,200 sq. km)
Languages Russian*, Tatar, Ukrainian, Chavash, various other national languages
Religions Orthodox Christian 75%, Muslim 14%, Other 11%
Ethnic mix Russian 80%, Other 12%, Tatar 4%, Ukrainian 2%, Chavash 1%, Bashkir 1%
Government Mixed Presidential–Parliamentary system
Currency Russian rouble = 100 kopeks
Literacy rate 99%
Calorie consumption 3272 kilocalories

RWANDA
Central Africa

Page 51 B6

Rwanda lies just south of the Equator in east central Africa. Since independence from France in 1962, ethnic tensions have dominated politics.

Official name Republic of Rwanda
Formation 1962 / 1962
Capital Kigali
Population 10.3 million / 1069 people per sq mile (413 people per sq km)
Total area 10,169 sq. miles (26,338 sq. km)
Languages Kinyarwanda*, French, Kiswahili, English
Religions Christian 94%, Muslim 5%, Traditional beliefs 1%
Ethnic mix Hutu 85%, Tutsi 14%, Other (including Twa) 1%
Government Presidential system
Currency Rwanda franc = 100 centimes
Literacy rate 71%
Calorie consumption 2054 kilocalories

ST KITTS AND NEVIS
West Indies

Page 33 G3

Separated by a channel, the two islands of Saint Kitts and Nevis are part of the Leeward Islands chain in the Caribbean. Nevis is the less developed of the two.

Official name Federation of Saint Christopher and Nevis
Formation 1983 / 1983
Capital Basseterre
Population 50,314 / 362 people per sq mile (140 people per sq km)
Total area 101 sq. miles (261 sq. km)
Languages English*, English Creole
Religions Anglican 33%, Methodist 29%, Other 22%, Moravian 9%, Roman Catholic 7%
Ethnic mix Black 95%, Mixed race 3%, White 1%, Other and Amerindian 1%
Government Parliamentary system
Currency East Caribbean dollar = 100 cents
Literacy rate 98%
Calorie consumption 2452 kilocalories

ST LUCIA
West Indies

Page 33 G4

Among the most beautiful of the Caribbean Windward Islands, Saint Lucia retains both French and British influences from its colonial history.

Official name Saint Lucia
Formation 1979 / 1979
Capital Castries
Population 161,557 / 685 people per sq mile (265 people per sq km)
Total area 239 sq. miles (620 sq. km)
Languages English*, French Creole
Religions Roman Catholic 90%, Other 10%
Ethnic mix Black 83%, Mulatto (mixed race) 13%, Asian 3%, Other 1%
Government Parliamentary system
Currency East Caribbean dollar = 100 cents
Literacy rate 95%
Calorie consumption 2744 kilocalories

ST VINCENT & THE GRENADINES
West Indies

Page 33 G4

Formerly ruled by Britain, these volcanic islands form part of the Caribbean Windward Islands. Agriculture, notably banana production, dominates the economy.

Official name Saint Vincent and the Grenadines
Formation 1979 / 1979
Capital Kingstown
Population 103,869 / 793 people per sq mile (305 people per sq km)
Total area 150 sq. miles (389 sq. km)
Languages English*, English Creole
Religions Anglican 46%, Methodist 28%, Roman Catholic 13%, Other 12%
Ethnic mix Black 66%, Mulatto (mixed race) 19%, Other 12%, Carib 2%
Government Parliamentary system
Currency East Caribbean dollar = 100 cents
Literacy rate 88%
Calorie consumption 2806 kilocalories

SAMOA
Australasia & Oceania

Page 123 F4

The southern Pacific islands of Samoa gained independence from New Zealand in 1962. Four of the nine islands are inhabited.

Official name Independent State of Samoa
Formation 1962 / 1962
Capital Apia
Population 200.000 / 183 people per sq mile (71 people per sq km)
Total area 1104 sq. miles (2860 sq. km)
Languages Samoan*, English*
Religions Christian 99%, Other 1%
Ethnic mix Polynesian 91%, Euronesian 7%, Other 2%
Government Parliamentary system
Currency Tala = 100 sene
Literacy rate 99%
Calorie consumption 2878 kilocalories

SAN MARINO
Southern Europe

Page 74 C3

Perched on the slopes of Monte Titano in the Italian Appennino, San Marino has maintained its independence since the 4th century AD.

Official name Republic of San Marino
Formation 1631 / 1631
Capital San Marino
Population 31,817 / 1326 people per sq mile (522 people per sq km)
Total area 23.6 sq. miles (61 sq. km)
Languages Italian*
Religions Roman Catholic 93%, Other and nonreligious 7%
Ethnic mix Sammarinese 88%, Italian 10%, Other 2%
Government Parliamentary system
Currency Euro = 100 cents
Literacy rate 99%
Calorie consumption Not available

SÃO TOMÉ & PRÍNCIPE
West Africa

Page 55 A5

A former Portuguese colony off Africa's west coast, comprising two main islands and smaller islets. The 1991 elections ended 15 years of Marxism.

Official name Democratic Republic of São Tomé and Príncipe
Formation 1975 / 1975
Capital São Tomé
Population 179,506 / 484 people per sq mile (187 people per sq km)
Total area 386 sq. miles (1001 sq. km)
Languages Portuguese Creole, Portuguese*
Religions Roman Catholic 84%, Other 16%
Ethnic mix Black 90%, Portuguese and Creole 10%
Government Presidential system
Currency Dobra = 100 céntimos
Literacy rate 89%
Calorie consumption 2662 kilocalories

SAUDI ARABIA
Southwest Asia

Page 99 B5

Occupying most of the Arabian Peninsula, the desert kingdom of Saudi Arabia, rich in oil and gas, covers an area the size of Western Europe.

Official name Kingdom of Saudi Arabia
Formation 1932 / 1932
Capital Riyadh
Population 26.2 million / 32 people per sq mile (12 people per sq km)
Total area 756,981 sq. miles (1,960,582 sq. km)
Languages Arabic*
Religions Sunni Muslim 85%, Shi'a Muslim 15%
Ethnic mix Arab 72%, Foreign residents (mostly south and southeast Asian) 20%, Afro-Asian 8%
Government Monarchy
Currency Saudi riyal = 100 halalat
Literacy rate 86%
Calorie consumption 3133 kilocalories

SENEGAL
West Africa

Page 52 B3

A former French colony, Senegal achieved independence in 1960. Its capital, Dakar, stands on the westernmost cape of Africa.

Official name Republic of Senegal
Formation 1960 / 1960
Capital Dakar
Population 12.9 million / 174 people per sq mile (67 people per sq km)
Total area 75,749 sq. miles (196,190 sq. km)
Languages Wolof, Pulaar, Serer, Diola, Mandinka, Malinké, Soninké, French*
Religions Sunni Muslim 95%, Christian (mainly Roman Catholic) 4%, Traditional beliefs 1%
Ethnic mix Wolof 43%, Serer 15%, Peul 14%, Other 14%, Toucouleur 9%, Diola 5%
Government Presidential system
Currency CFA franc = 100 centimes
Literacy rate 50%
Calorie consumption 2318 kilocalories

SERBIA
Southeast Europe

Page 78 D4

One of seven states to emerge from the former Yugoslavia, Serbia has struggled to find stability amid ongoing ethnic and nationalist tensions.

Official name Republic of Serbia
Formation 2006 / 2008
Capital Belgrade
Population 9.9 million / 331 people per sq mile (128 people per sq km)
Total area 29,905 sq. miles (77,453 sq. km)
Languages Serbian*, Hungarian (Magyar)
Religions Orthodox Christian 85%, Roman Catholic 6%, Other 6%, Muslim 3%
Ethnic mix Serb 83%, Other 10%, Magyar 4%, Bosniak 2%, Roma 1%
Government Parliamentary system
Currency Serbian dinar = 100 para
Literacy rate 98%
Calorie consumption 2729 kilocalories

SEYCHELLES
Indian Ocean

Page 57 G1

A former British colony comprising 115 islands in the Indian Ocean. Under one-party rule for 16 years, it became a multiparty democracy in 1993.

Official name Republic of Seychelles
Formation 1976 / 1976
Capital Victoria
Population 89,188 / 858 people per sq mile (330 people per sq km)
Total area 176 sq. miles (455 sq. km)
Languages French Creole*, English*, French*
Religions Roman Catholic 82%, Anglican 6%, Other (including Muslim) 6%, Other Christian 3%, Hindu 2%, Seventh-day Adventist 1%
Ethnic mix Creole 89%, Indian 5%, Other 4%, Chinese 2%
Government Presidential system
Currency Seychelles rupee = 100 cents
Literacy rate 92%
Calorie consumption 2426 kilocalories

SIERRA LEONE
West Africa

Page 52 C4

The West African state of Sierra Leone achieved independence from the British in 1961. Today, it is one of the world's poorest nations.

Official name Republic of Sierra Leone
Formation 1961 / 1961
Capital Freetown
Population 5.8 million / 210 people per sq mile (81 people per sq km)
Total area 27,698 sq. miles (71,740 sq. km)
Languages Mende*, Temne, Krio, English
Religions Muslim 60%, Christian 30%, Traditional beliefs 10%
Ethnic mix Mende 35%, Temne 32%, Other 21%, Limba 8%, Kuranko 4%
Government Presidential system
Currency Leone = 100 cents
Literacy rate 41%
Calorie consumption 2128 kilocalories

SINGAPORE
Southeast Asia

Page 116 A1

A city state linked to the southernmost tip of the Malay Peninsula by a causeway, Singapore is one of Asia's most important commercial centers.

Official name Republic of Singapore
Formation 1965 / 1965
Capital Singapore
Population 4.8 million / 20,339 people per sq mile (7869 people per sq km)
Total area 250 sq. miles (648 sq. km)
Languages Mandarin*, Malay*, Tami*l, English*
Religions Buddhist 55%, Taoist 22%, Muslim 16%, Hindu, Christian, and Sikh 7%
Ethnic mix Chinese 74%, Malay 14%, Indian 9%, Other 3%
Government Parliamentary system
Currency Singapore dollar = 100 cents
Literacy rate 95%
Calorie consumption Not available

SLOVAKIA
Central Europe

Page 77 C6

Landlocked in Central Europe, Slovakia has been independent since 1993. It is the less developed half of the former Czechoslovakia.

Official name Slovak Republic
Formation 1993 / 1993
Capital Bratislava
Population 5.4 million / 285 people per sq mile (110 people per sq km)
Total area 18,859 sq. miles (48,845 sq. km)
Languages Slovak*, Hungarian (Magyar), Czech
Religions Roman Catholic 69%, Other 13%, Nonreligious 13%, Greek Catholic (Uniate) 4%, Orthodox Christian 1%
Ethnic mix Slovak 86%, Magyar 10%, Roma 2%, Other 1%, Czech 1%
Government Parliamentary system
Currency Euro = 100 cents
Literacy rate 99%
Calorie consumption 2885 kilocalories

SLOVENIA
Central Europe

Page 73 D8

Northernmost of the former Yugoslav republics, Slovenia has the closest links with Western Europe. In 1991, it gained independence with little violence.

Official name Republic of Slovenia
Formation 1991 / 1991
Capital Ljubljana
Population 2 million / 256 people per sq mile (99 people per sq km)
Total area 7820 sq. miles (20,253 sq. km)
Languages Slovenian*
Religions Roman Catholic 58%, Other 28%, Atheist 10%, Muslim 2%, Orthodox Christian 2%
Ethnic mix Slovene 83%, Other 12%, Serb 2%, Croat 2%, Bosniak 1%
Government Parliamentary system
Currency Euro = 100 cents
Literacy rate 99%
Calorie consumption 3220 kilocalories

SOLOMON ISLANDS
Australasia & Oceania

Page 122 C3

The Solomon archipelago comprises several hundred islands scattered in the southwestern Pacific. Independence from Britain came in 1978.

Official name Solomon Islands
Formation 1978 / 1978
Capital Honiara
Population 500,000 / 46 people per sq mile (18 people per sq km)
Total area 10,985 sq. miles (28,450 sq. km)
Languages English*, Pidgin English, Melanesian Pidgin, around 120 others
Religions Church of Melanesia (Anglican) 34%, Roman Catholic 19%, South Seas Evangelical Church 17%, Methodist 11%, Other 19%
Ethnic mix Melanesian 93%, Polynesian 4%, Other 3%
Government Parliamentary system
Currency Solomon Islands dollar = 100 cents
Literacy rate 77%
Calorie consumption 2434 kilocalories

SOMALIA
East Africa

Page 51 E5

Italian and British Somaliland were united in 1960 to create this semiarid state occupying the horn of Africa. It has suffered years of civil war.

Official name Somalia
Formation 1960 / 1960
Capital Mogadishu
Population 9.4 million / 39 people per sq mile (15 people per sq km)
Total area 246,199 sq. miles (637,657 sq. km)
Languages Somali*, Arabic*, English, Italian
Religions Sunni Muslim 99%, Christian 1%
Ethnic mix Somali 85%, Other 15%
Government Transitional regime
Currency Somali shilin = 100 senti
Literacy rate 24%
Calorie consumption 1762 kilocalories

SOUTH AFRICA
Southern Africa

Page 56 C4

South Africa is the most southerly nation on the African continent. The multiracial elections of 1994 overturned 80 years of white minority rule.

Official name Republic of South Africa
Formation 1934 / 1994
Capital Pretoria (Tshwane); Cape Town; Bloemfontein
Population 50.5 million / 107 people per sq mile (41 people per sq km)
Total area 471,008 sq. miles (1,219,912 sq. km)
Languages English, isiZulu, isiXhosa, Afrikaans, Sepedi, Setswana, Sesotho, Xitsonga, siSwati, Tshivenda, isiNdebele
Religions Christian 68%, Traditional beliefs and animist 29%, Muslim 2%, Hindu 1%
Ethnic mix Black 80%, White 9%, Colored 9%, Asian 2%
Government Presidential system
Currency Rand = 100 cents
Literacy rate 89%
Calorie consumption 2986 kilocalories

SOUTH KOREA
East Asia

Page 106 E4

South Korea occupies the southern half of the Korean peninsula. It was separated from the communist North in 1948.

Official name Republic of Korea
Formation 1948 / 1953
Capital Seoul
Population 48.5 million / 1272 people per sq mile (491 people per sq km)
Total area 38,023 sq. miles (98,480 sq. km)
Languages Korean*
Religions Mahayana Buddhist 47%, Protestant 38%, Roman Catholic 11%, Confucianist 3%, Other 1%
Ethnic mix Korean 100%
Government Presidential system
Currency South Korean won = 100 chon
Literacy rate 99%
Calorie consumption 3074 kilocalories

SOUTH SUDAN
East Africa

Page 51 B5

Predominantly Christian, the South Sudanese fought a long-running civil war against the mainly Muslim northerners until the region finally gained independence from Sudan in 2011.

Official name Republic of South Sudan
Formation 2011 / 2011
Capital Juba
Population 8.3 million / 33 people per sq mile (13 people per sq km)
Total area 248,777 sq. miles (644,329 sq. km)
Languages Arabic, Dinka, Nuer, Zande, Bari, Shilluk, Lotuko
Religions Not available
Ethnic mix Dinka 40%, Nuer 15%, Shilluk/Anwak 10%, Azande 10%, Arab 10%, Bari 10%, Other 5%
Government Presidential system
Currency South Sudan Pound = 100 piastres
Literacy rate 37%
Calorie consumption Not available

SPAIN
Southwest Europe

Page 70 D2

Lodged between mainland Europe and Africa, the Atlantic and the Mediterranean, Spain has occupied a pivotal position since it was united in 1492.

Official name Kingdom of Spain
Formation 1492 / 1713
Capital Madrid
Population 45.3 million / 235 people per sq mile (91 people per sq km)
Total area 194,896 sq. miles (504,782 sq. km)
Languages Spanish*, Catalan*, Galician*, Basque*
Religions Roman Catholic 96%, Other 4%
Ethnic mix Castilian Spanish 72%, Catalan 17%, Galician 6%, Basque 2%, Other 2%, Roma 1%
Government Parliamentary system
Currency Euro = 100 cents
Literacy rate 98%
Calorie consumption 3271 kilocalories

SRI LANKA
South Asia

Page 110 D3

The island republic of Sri Lanka is separated from India by the narrow Palk Strait. The 26 year civil war between the Sinhalese and Tamil ended in 2009.

Official name Democratic Socialist Republic of Sri Lanka
Formation 1948 / 1948
Capital Colombo
Population 20.4 million / 816 people per sq mile (315 people per sq km)
Total area 25,332 sq. miles (65,610 sq. km)
Languages Sinhala*, Tamil*, Sinhala-Tamil, English
Religions Buddhist 69%, Hindu 15%, Muslim 8%, Christian 8%
Ethnic mix Sinhalese 74%, Tamil 18%, Moor 7%, Other 1%
Government Mixed presidential–parliamentary system
Currency Sri Lanka rupee = 100 cents
Literacy rate 91%
Calorie consumption 2392 kilocalories

SUDAN
East Africa

Page 50 B4

In 1989, an army coup installed a military Islamic fundamentalist regime. Split from South Sudan in 2011 following years of civil war.

Official name Republic of the Sudan
Formation 1956 / 2011
Capital Khartoum
Population 34 million / 47 people per sq mile (18 people per sq km)
Total area 718,722 sq. miles (1,861,481 sq. km)
Languages Arabic, Nubian, Beja, Fur
Religions Almost 100% Muslim (mainly Sunni)
Ethnic mix Arab 60%, Other 18%, Nubian 10%, Beja 8%, Fur 3%, Zaghawa 1%
Government Presidential system
Currency New Sudanese pound = 100 piastres
Literacy rate 70%
Calorie consumption 2266 kilocalories

SURINAME
South America

Page 37 G3

Suriname is a former Dutch colony on the north coast of South America. Democracy was restored in 1991, after almost 11 years of military rule.

Official name Republic of Suriname
Formation 1975 / 1975
Capital Paramaribo
Population 500,000 / 8 people per sq mile (3 people per sq km)
Total area 63,039 sq. miles (163,270 sq. km)
Languages Sranan (creole), Dutch*, Javanese, Sarnami Hindi, Saramaccan, Chinese, Carib
Religions Hindu 27%, Protestant 25%, Roman Catholic 23%, Muslim 20%, Traditional beliefs 5%
Ethnic mix East Indian 27%, Creole 18%, Black 15%, Javanese 15%, Mixed race 13%, Other 12%
Government Parliamentary system
Currency Surinamese dollar = 100 cents
Literacy rate 95%
Calorie consumption 2468 kilocalories

SWAZILAND
Southern Africa

Page 56 D4

The tiny southern African kingdom of Swaziland gained independence from Britain in 1968. It is economically dependent on South Africa.

Official name Kingdom of Swaziland
Formation 1968 / 1968
Capital Mbabane
Population 1.2 million / 181 people per sq mile (70 people per sq km)
Total area 6704 sq. miles (17,363 sq. km)
Languages English*, siSwati*, isiZulu, Xitsonga
Religions Traditional beliefs 40%, Other 30%, Roman Catholic 20%, Muslim 10%
Ethnic mix Swazi 97%, Other 3%
Government Monarchy
Currency Lilangeni = 100 cents
Literacy rate 87%
Calorie consumption 2307 kilocalories

SWEDEN
Northern Europe

Page 62 B4

The largest Scandinavian country in both population and area, Sweden's strong industrial base helps to fund its extensive welfare system.

Official name Kingdom of Sweden
Formation 1523 / 1921
Capital Stockholm
Population 9.3 million / 59 people per sq mile (23 people per sq km)
Total area 173,731 sq. miles (449,964 sq. km)
Languages Swedish*, Finnish, Sámi
Religions Evangelical Lutheran 75%, Other 13%, Muslim 5%, Other Protestant 5%, Roman Catholic 2%
Ethnic mix Swedish 86%, Foreign-born or first-generation immigrant 12%, Finnish & Sámi 2%
Government Parliamentary system
Currency Swedish krona = 100 öre
Literacy rate 99%
Calorie consumption 3116 kilocalories

SWITZERLAND
Central Europe

Page 73 A7

One of the world's most prosperous countries, with a long tradition of neutrality in foreign affairs, it lies at the center of Western Europe.

Official name Swiss Confederation
Formation 1291 / 1857
Capital Bern
Population 7.6 million / 495 people per sq mile (191 people per sq km)
Total area 15,942 sq. miles (41,290 sq. km)
Languages German*, Swiss-German, French*, Italian*, Romansch
Religions Roman Catholic 42%, Protestant 35%, Other and nonreligious 19%, Muslim 4%
Ethnic mix German 64%, French 20%, Other 9.5%, Italian 6%, Romansch 0.5%
Government Parliamentary system
Currency Swiss franc = 100 rappen/centimes
Literacy rate 99%
Calorie consumption 3421 kilocalories

SYRIA
Southwest Asia

Page 96 B3

Stretching from the eastern Mediterranean to the River Tigris, Syria's borders were created on its independence from France in 1946.

Official name Syrian Arab Republic
Formation 1941 / 1967
Capital Damascus
Population 22.5 million / 317 people per sq mile (122 people per sq km)
Total area 71,498 sq. miles (184,180 sq. km)
Languages Arabic*, French, Kurdish, Armenian, Circassian, Turkic languages, Assyrian, Aramaic
Religions Sunni Muslim 74%, Alawi 12%, Christian 10%, Druze 3%, Other 1%
Ethnic mix Arab 90%, Kurdish 9%, Armenian, Turkmen, and Circassian 1%
Government One-party state
Currency Syrian pound = 100 piastres
Literacy rate 84%
Calorie consumption 3049 kilocalories

TAIWAN
East Asia

Page 107 D6

The island republic of Taiwan lies 80 miles (130 km) off the southeast coast of mainland China. China considers it to be one of its provinces.

Official name Republic of China (ROC)
Formation 1949 / 1949
Capital Taipei
Population 23.1 million / 1852 people per sq mile (715 people per sq km)
Total area 13,892 sq. miles (35,980 sq. km)
Languages Amoy Chinese, Mandarin Chinese*, Hakka Chinese
Religions Buddhist, Confucianist, and Taoist 93%, Christian 5%, Other 2%
Ethnic mix Han (pre-20th-century migration) 84%, Han (20th-century migration) 14%, Aboriginal 2%
Government Presidential system
Currency Taiwan dollar = 100 cents
Literacy rate 98%
Calorie consumption Not available

TAJIKISTAN
Central Asia

Page 101 F3

Tajikistan lies landlocked on the western slopes of the Pamirs in Central Asia. The Tajiks' language and traditions are similar to those of Iran.

Official name Republic of Tajikistan
Formation 1991 / 1991
Capital Dushanbe
Population 7.1 million / 129 people per sq mile (50 people per sq km)
Total area 55,251 sq. miles (143,100 sq. km)
Languages Tajik*, Uzbek, Russian
Religions Sunni Muslim 95%, Shi'a Muslim 3%, Other 2%
Ethnic mix Tajik 80%, Uzbek 15%, Other 3%, Russian 1%, Kyrgyz 1%
Government Presidential system
Currency Somoni = 100 diram
Literacy rate 99%
Calorie consumption 2127 kilocalories

TANZANIA
East Africa

Page 51 B7

The East African state of Tanzania was formed in 1964 by the union of Tanganyika and Zanzibar. A third of its area is game reserve or national park.

Official name United Republic of Tanzania
Formation 1964 / 1964
Capital Dodoma
Population 45 million / 132 people per sq mile (51 people per sq km)
Total area 364,898 sq. miles (945,087 sq. km)
Languages Kiswahili*, Sukuma, Chagga, Nyamwezi, Hehe, Makonde, Yao, Sandawe, English*
Religions Christian 63%, Muslim 35%, Other 2%
Ethnic mix Native African (over 120 tribes) 99%, European, Asian, and Arab 1%
Government Presidential system
Currency Tanzanian shilling = 100 cents
Literacy rate 73%
Calorie consumption 2017 kilocalories

THAILAND
Southeast Asia

Page 115 C5

Thailand lies at the heart of mainland Southeast Asia. Continuing rapid industrialization has resulted in massive congestion in the capital.

Official name Kingdom of Thailand
Formation 1238 / 1907
Capital Bangkok
Population 68.1 million / 345 people per sq mile (133 people per sq km)
Total area 198,455 sq. miles (514,000 sq. km)
Languages Thai*, Chinese, Malay, Khmer, Mon, Karen, Miao
Religions Buddhist 95%, Muslim 4%, Other (including Christian) 1%
Ethnic mix Thai 83%, Chinese 12%, Malay 3%, Khmer and Other 2%
Government Parliamentary system
Currency Baht = 100 satang
Literacy rate 94%
Calorie consumption 2529 kilocalories

TOGO
West Africa

Page 53 F4

Togo lies sandwiched between Ghana and Benin in West Africa. The 1993–94 presidential elections were the first since its independence in 1960.

Official name Republic of Togo
Formation 1960
Capital Lomé
Population 6.8 million / 324 people per sq mile (125 people per sq km)
Total area 21,924 sq. miles (56,785 sq. km)
Languages Ewe, Kabye, Gurma, French*
Religions Christian 47%, Traditional beliefs 33%, Muslim 14%, Other 6%
Ethnic mix Ewe 46%, Other African 41%, Kabye 12%, European 1%
Government Presidential system
Currency CFA franc = 100 centimes
Literacy rate 57%
Calorie consumption 2146 kilocalories

TONGA
Australasia & Oceania

Page 123 E4

Northeast of New Zealand, in the South Pacific, Tonga is an archipelago of 170 islands, 45 of which are inhabited. Politics is effectively controlled by the king.

Official name Kingdom of Tonga
Formation 1970 / 1970
Capital Nuku'alofa
Population 105,916 / 381 people per sq mile (147 people per sq km)
Total area 289 sq. miles (748 sq. km)
Languages English*, Tongan*
Religions Free Wesleyan 41%, Other 17%, Roman Catholic 16%, Church of Jesus Christ of Latter-day Saints 14%, Free Church of Tonga 12%
Ethnic mix Tongan 98%, Other 2%
Government Monarchy
Currency Pa'anga (Tongan dollar) = 100 seniti
Literacy rate 99%
Calorie consumption Not available

TRINIDAD AND TOBAGO
West Indies

Page 33 H5

The former British colony of Trinidad and Tobago is the most southerly of the West Indies, lying just 9 miles (15 km) off the coast of Venezuela.

Official name Republic of Trinidad and Tobago
Formation 1962 / 1962
Capital Port-of-Spain
Population 1.3 million / 656 people per sq mile (253 people per sq km)
Total area 1980 sq. miles (5128 sq. km)
Languages English Creole, English*, Hindi, French, Spanish
Religions Other 30%, Roman Catholic 26%, Hindu 23%, Anglican 8%, Baptist 7%, Muslim 6%
Ethnic mix East Indian 40%, Black 38%, Mixed race 20%, White & Chinese 1%, Other 1%
Government Parliamentary system
Currency Trinidad and Tobago dollar = 100 cents
Literacy rate 99%
Calorie consumption 2713 kilocalories

TUNISIA
North Africa

Page 49 E2

Tunisia, in North Africa, has traditionally been one of the more liberal Arab states. The 24 year regime of Zine El Abidine Ben Ali was ended during the "Arab Spring" revolutions of 2011.

Official name Republic of Tunisia
Formation 1956 / 1956
Capital Tunis
Population 10.4 million / 173 people per sq mile (67 people per sq km)
Total area 63,169 sq. miles (163,610 sq. km)
Languages Arabic*, French
Religions Muslim (mainly Sunni) 98%, Christian 1%, Jewish 1%
Ethnic mix Arab and Berber 98%, European 1%, Jewish 1%
Government Transitional regime
Currency Tunisian dinar = 1000 millimes
Literacy rate 78%
Calorie consumption 3312 kilocalories

TURKEY
Asia / Europe

Page 94 B3

Lying partly in Europe, but mostly in Asia, Turkey's position gives it significant influence in the Mediterranean, Black Sea, and Middle East.

Official name Republic of Turkey
Formation 1923 / 1939
Capital Ankara
Population 75.7 million / 255 people per sq mile (98 people per sq km)
Total area 301,382 sq. miles (780,580 sq. km)
Languages Turkish*, Kurdish, Arabic, Circassian, Armenian, Greek, Georgian, Ladino
Religions Muslim (mainly Sunni) 99%, Other 1%
Ethnic mix Turkish 70%, Kurdish 20%, Other 8%, Arab 2%
Government Parliamentary system
Currency Turkish lira = 100 kurus
Literacy rate 91%
Calorie consumption 3482 kilocalories

TURKMENISTAN
Central Asia

Page 100 B2

Stretching from the Caspian Sea into the deserts of Central Asia, the ex-Soviet state of Turkmenistan has adjusted better than most to independence.

Official name Turkmenistan
Formation 1991 / 1991
Capital Ashgabat
Population 5.2 million / 28 people per sq mile (11 people per sq km)
Total area 188,455 sq. miles (488,100 sq. km)
Languages Turkmen*, Uzbek, Russian, Kazakh, Tatar
Religions Sunni Muslim 89%, Orthodox Christian 9%, Other 2%
Ethnic mix Turkmen 85%, Other 6%, Uzbek 5%, Russian 4%
Government One-party state
Currency New manat = 100 tenge
Literacy rate 99%
Calorie consumption 2754 kilocalories

TUVALU
Australasia & Oceania

Page 123 E3

The former Ellice Islands, linked to the Gilbert Islands as a British colony until 1978, Tuvalu is an isolated chain of nine atolls in the Central Pacific.

Official name Tuvalu
Formation 1978 / 1978
Capital Fongafale (Funafuti Atoll)
Population 10,544 / 1054 people per sq mile (406 people per sq km)
Total area 10 sq. miles (26 sq. km)
Languages Tuvaluan, Kiribati, English*
Religions Church of Tuvalu 97%, Other 1%, Baha'i 1%, Seventh-day Adventist 1%
Ethnic mix Polynesian 96%, Micronesian 4%
Government Nonparty system
Currency Australian dollar and Tuvaluan dollar = 100 cents
Literacy rate 98%
Calorie consumption Not available

UGANDA
East Africa

Page 51 B6

Uganda lies landlocked in East Africa. It was ruled by one of Africa's more eccentric leaders, the dictator Idi Amin Dada, from 1971–1980.

Official name Republic of Uganda
Formation 1962 / 1962
Capital Kampala
Population 33.8 million / 439 people per sq mile (169 people per sq km)
Total area 91,135 sq. miles (236,040 sq. km)
Languages Luganda, Nkole, Chiga, Lango, Acholi, Teso, Lugbara, English*
Religions Christian 85%, Muslim (mainly Sunni) 12%, Other 3%
Ethnic mix Other 50%, Baganda 17%, Banyakole 10%, Basoga 9%, Bakiga 7%, Iteso 7%
Government Presidential system
Currency New Uganda shilling = 100 cents
Literacy rate 74%
Calorie consumption 2247 kilocalories

UKRAINE
Eastern Europe

Page 86 C2

Bordered by seven states, the former "breadbasket of the Soviet Union" balances assertive nationalism with concerns over its relations with Russia.

Official name Ukraine
Formation 1991 / 1991
Capital Kiev
Population 45.4 million / 195 people per sq mile (75 people per sq km)
Total area 223,089 sq. miles (603,700 sq. km)
Languages Ukrainian*, Russian, Tatar
Religions Christian (mainly Orthodox) 95%, Other 5%
Ethnic mix Ukrainian 78%, Russian 17%, Other 5%
Government Presidential system
Currency Hryvna = 100 kopiykas
Literacy rate 99%
Calorie consumption 3230 kilocalories

UNITED ARAB EMIRATES
Southwest Asia

Page 99 D5

Bordering the Persian Gulf on the northern coast of the Arabian Peninsula, is the United Arab Emirates, a working federation of seven states.

Official name United Arab Emirates
Formation 1971 / 1972
Capital Abu Dhabi
Population 4.7 million / 146 people per sq mile (56 people per sq km)
Total area 32,000 sq. miles (82,880 sq. km)
Languages Arabic*, Farsi, Indian and Pakistani languages, English
Religions Muslim (mainly Sunni) 96%, Christian, Hindu, and other 4%
Ethnic mix Asian 60%, Emirian 25%, Other Arab 12%, European 3%
Government Monarchy
Currency UAE dirham = 100 fils
Literacy rate 90%
Calorie consumption 3138 kilocalories

UNITED KINGDOM
Northwest Europe

Page 67 B5

Separated from continental Europe by the North Sea and the English Channel, the UK comprises England, Wales, Scotland, and Northern Ireland.

Official name United Kingdom of Great Britain and Northern Ireland
Formation 1707 / 1922
Capital London
Population 61.9 million / 664 people per sq mile (256 people per sq km)
Total area 94,525 sq. miles (244,820 sq. km)
Languages English*, Welsh* (in Wales), Gaelic
Religions Anglican 45%, Other & nonreligious 39%, Roman Catholic 9%, Presbyterian 4%, Muslim 3%
Ethnic mix English 80%, Scottish 9%, West Indian, Asian, & other 5%, Welsh 3%, Northern Irish 3%
Government Parliamentary system
Currency Pound sterling = 100 pence
Literacy rate 99%
Calorie consumption 3442 kilocalories

UNITED STATES
North America

Page 13 B5

Stretching across the most temperate part of North America, and with many natural resources, the USA is the sole truly global superpower.

Official name United States of America
Formation 1776 / 1959
Capital Washington D.C.
Population 318 million / 90 people per sq mile (35 people per sq km)
Total area 3,717,792 sq. miles (9,626,091 sq. km)
Languages English*, Spanish, Chinese, French, German, Tagalog, Vietnamese, Italian, Korean, Russian, Polish
Religions Protestant 52%, Roman Catholic 25%, Other & nonreligious 20%, Jewish 2%, Muslim 1%
Ethnic mix White 62%, Hispanic 13%, Black American/African 13%, Other 8%, Asian 4%
Government Presidential system
Currency US dollar = 100 cents
Literacy rate 99%
Calorie consumption 3770 kilocalories

URUGUAY
South America

Page 42 D4

Uruguay is situated in southeastern South America. It returned to civilian government in 1985, after 12 years of military dictatorship.

Official name Eastern Republic of Uruguay
Formation 1828 / 1828
Capital Montevideo
Population 3.4 million / 50 people per sq mile (19 people per sq km)
Total area 68,039 sq. miles (176,220 sq. km)
Languages Spanish*
Religions Roman Catholic 66%, Other and nonreligious 30%, Jewish 2%, Protestant 2%
Ethnic mix White 90%, Mestizo 6%, Black 4%
Government Presidential system
Currency Uruguayan peso = 100 centésimos
Literacy rate 98%
Calorie consumption 2818 kilocalories

UZBEKISTAN
Central Asia

Page 100 D2

Sharing the Aral Sea coastline with its northern neighbor, Kazakhstan, Uzbekistan lies on the ancient Silk Road between Asia and Europe.

Official name Republic of Uzbekistan
Formation 1991 / 1991
Capital Tashkent
Population 27.8 million / 161 people per sq mile (62 people per sq km)
Total area 172,741 sq. miles (447,400 sq. km)
Languages Uzbek*, Russian, Tajik, Kazakh
Religions Sunni Muslim 88%, Orthodox Christian 9%, Other 3%
Ethnic mix Uzbek 80%, Other 6%, Russian 6%, Tajik 5%, Kazakh 3%
Government Presidential system
Currency Som = 100 tiyin
Literacy rate 99%
Calorie consumption 2525 kilocalories

VANUATU
Australasia & Oceania

Page 122 D4

An archipelago of 82 islands and islets in the Pacific Ocean, it was ruled jointly by Britain and France from 1906 until independence in 1980.

Official name Republic of Vanuatu
Formation 1980 / 1980
Capital Port Vila
Population 200,000 / 42 people per sq mile (16 people per sq km)
Total area 4710 sq. miles (12,200 sq. km)
Languages Bislama* (Melanesian pidgin), English*, French*, other indigenous languages
Religions Presbyterian 37%, Other 19%, Roman Catholic 15%, Anglican 15%, Traditional beliefs 8%, Seventh-day Adventist 6%
Ethnic mix ni-Vanuatu 94%, European 4%, Other 2%
Government Parliamentary system
Currency Vatu = 100 centimes
Literacy rate 82%
Calorie consumption 2722 kilocalories

VATICAN CITY
Southern Europe

Page 75 A8

The Vatican City, seat of the Roman Catholic Church, is a walled enclave in the city of Rome. It is the world's smallest fully independent state.

Official name State of the Vatican City
Formation 1929 / 1929
Capital Vatican City
Population 832 / 4894 people per sq mile (1891 people per sq km)
Total area 0.17 sq. miles (0.44 sq. km)
Languages Italian*, Latin*
Religions Roman Catholic 100%
Ethnic mix Not avaailable
Government Papal state
Currency Euro = 100 cents
Literacy rate 99%
Calorie consumption Not available

VENEZUELA
South America

Page 36 D2

Located on the north coast of South America, Venezuela has the continent's most urbanized society. Most people live in the northern cities.

Official name Bolivarian Republic of Venezuela
Formation 1830 / 1830
Capital Caracas
Population 29 million / 85 people per sq mile (33 people per sq km)
Total area 352,143 sq. miles (912,050 sq. km)
Languages Spanish*, Amerindian languages
Religions Roman Catholic 96%, Protestant 2%, Other 2%
Ethnic mix Mestizo 69%, White 20%, Black 9%, Amerindian 2%
Government Presidential system
Currency Bolívar fuerte = 100 céntimos
Literacy rate 95%
Calorie consumption 2582 kilocalories

VIETNAM
Southeast Asia

Page 114 D4

Situated in the far east of mainland Southeast Asia, the country has made great progress towards recovery after the devastating 1962–75 Vietnam War.

Official name Socialist Republic of Vietnam
Formation 1976 / 1976
Capital Hanoi
Population 89 million / 708 people per sq mile (274 people per sq km)
Total area 127,243 sq. miles (329,560 sq. km)
Languages Vietnamese*, Chinese, Thai, Khmer, Muong, Nung, Miao, Yao, Jarai
Religions Other 74%, Buddhist 14%, Roman Catholic 7%, Cao Dai 3%, Protestant 2%
Ethnic mix Vietnamese 86%, Other 8%, Thai 2%, Muong 2%, Tay 2%
Government One-party state
Currency Đông = 10 hao = 100 xu
Literacy rate 93%
Calorie consumption 2769 kilocalories

YEMEN
Southwest Asia

Page 99 C7

Located in southern Arabia, Yemen was formerly two countries – a socialist regime in the south, and a republic in the north. Both united in 1990.

Official name Republic of Yemen
Formation 1990 / 1990
Capital Sana
Population 24.3 million / 112 people per sq mile (43 people per sq km)
Total area 203,849 sq. miles (527,970 sq. km)
Languages Arabic*
Religions Sunni Muslim 55%, Shi'a Muslim 42%, Christian, Hindu, and Jewish 3%
Ethnic mix Arab 99%, Afro-Arab, Indian, Somali, and European 1%
Government Presidential system
Currency Yemeni rial = 100 fils
Literacy rate 62%
Calorie consumption 2032 kilocalories

ZAMBIA
Southern Africa

Page 56 C2

Zambia lies landlocked at the heart of southern Africa. In 1991, it made a peaceful transition from single-party rule to multiparty democracy.

Official name Republic of Zambia
Formation 1964 / 1964
Capital Lusaka
Population 13.3 million / 47 people per sq mile (18 people per sq km)
Total area 290,584 sq. miles (752,614 sq. km)
Languages Bemba, Tonga, Nyanja, Lozi, Lala-Bisa, Nsenga, English*
Religions Christian 63%, Traditional beliefs 36%, Muslim and Hindu 1%
Ethnic mix Bemba 34%, Other African 26%, Tonga 16%, Nyanja 14%, Lozi 9%, European 1%
Government Presidential system
Currency Zambian kwacha = 100 ngwee
Literacy rate 71%
Calorie consumption 1885 kilocalories

ZIMBABWE
Southern Africa

Page 56 D3

The former British colony of Southern Rhodesia became fully independent as Zimbabwe in 1980, after 15 years of troubled white minority rule.

Official name Republic of Zimbabwe
Formation 1980 / 1980
Capital Harare
Population 12.6 million / 84 people per sq mile (33 people per sq km)
Total area 150,803 sq. miles (390,580 sq. km)
Languages Shona, isiNdebele, English*
Religions Syncretic (Christian/traditional beliefs) 50%, Christian 25%, Traditional beliefs 24%, Other (including Muslim) 1%
Ethnic mix Shona 71%, Ndebele 16%, Other African 11%, White 1%, Asian 1%
Government Presidential system
Currency Zimbabwe dollar suspended in 2009
Literacy rate 92%
Calorie consumption 2207 kilocalories

Overseas Territories and Dependencies

Despite the rapid process of decolonization since the end of the Second World War, around 10 million people in more than 50 territories around the world continue to live under the protection of a parent state.

AUSTRALIA

ASHMORE & CARTIER ISLANDS
Indian Ocean
Claimed 1931
Capital not applicable
Area 2 sq miles (5 sq km)
Population None

CHRISTMAS ISLAND
Indian Ocean
Claimed 1958
Capital The Settlement
Area 52 sq miles (135 sq km)
Population 1402

COCOS ISLANDS
Indian Ocean
Claimed 1955
Capital West Island
Area 5.5 sq miles (14 sq km)
Population 596

CORAL SEA ISLANDS
Southwest Pacific
Claimed 1969
Capital None
Area Less than 1.2 sq miles (3 sq km)
Population below 10 (scientists)

HEARD & McDONALD ISLANDS
Indian Ocean
Claimed 1947
Capital not applicable
Area 161 sq miles (417 sq km)
Population None

NORFOLK ISLAND
Southwest Pacific
Claimed 1774
Capital Kingston
Area 13.3 sq miles (34 sq km)
Population 2169

DENMARK

FAEROE ISLANDS
North Atlantic
Claimed 1380
Capital Tórshavn
Area 540 sq miles (1399 sq km)
Population 49,267

GREENLAND
North Atlantic
Claimed 1380
Capital Nuuk
Area 840,000 sq miles (2,175,516 sq km)
Population 57,670

FRANCE

CLIPPERTON ISLAND
East Pacific
Claimed 1935
Capital not applicable
Area 2.7 sq miles (7 sq km)
Population None

FRENCH GUIANA
South America
Claimed 1817
Capital Cayenne
Area 35,135 sq miles (90,996 sq km)
Population 225,651

FRENCH POLYNESIA
South Pacific
Claimed 1843
Capital Papeete
Area 1,608 sq miles (4165 sq km)
Population 300,000

GUADELOUPE
West Indies
Claimed 1635
Capital Basse-Terre
Area 629 sq miles (1628 sq km)
Population 452,000

MARTINIQUE
West Indies
Claimed 1635
Capital Fort-de-France
Area 425 sq miles (1100 sq km)
Population 400,000

MAYOTTE
Indian Ocean
Claimed 1843
Capital Mamoudzou
Area 144 sq miles (374 sq km)
Population 194,159

NEW CALEDONIA
Southwest Pacific
Claimed 1853
Capital Nouméa
Area 7,374 sq miles (19,103 sq km)
Population 300,000

RÉUNION
Indian Ocean
Claimed 1638
Capital Saint-Denis
Area 970 sq miles (2512 sq km)
Population 800,000

ST. PIERRE & MIQUELON
North America
Claimed 1604
Capital Saint-Pierre
Area 93 sq miles (242 sq km)
Population 5888

WALLIS & FUTUNA
South Pacific
Claimed 1842
Capital Matá'Utu
Area 106 sq miles (274 sq km)
Population 15,398

NETHERLANDS

ARUBA
West Indies
Claimed 1643
Capital Oranjestad
Area 75 sq miles (194 sq km)
Population 106,113

BONAIRE
West Indies
Claimed 1816
Capital Kralendijk
Area 113 sq miles (294 sq km)
Population 15,800

CURAÇAO
West Indies
Claimed 1815
Capital Willemstad
Area 171 sq miles (444 sq km)
Population 142,180

SABA
West Indies
Claimed 1816
Capital The Bottom
Area 5 sq miles (13 sq km)
Population 2000

SINT-EUSTATIUS
West Indies
Claimed 1784
Capital Oranjestad
Area 8 sq miles (21 sq km)
Population 3100

SINT-MAARTEN
West Indies
Claimed 1648
Capital Phillipsburg
Area 13 sq miles (34 sq km)
Population 37,429

NEW ZEALAND

COOK ISLANDS
South Pacific
Claimed 1901
Capital Avarua
Area 91 sq miles (235 sq km)
Population 11,124

NIUE
South Pacific
Claimed 1901
Capital Alofi
Area 102 sq miles (264 sq km)
Population 1311

TOKELAU
South Pacific
Claimed 1926
Capital not applicable
Area 4 sq miles (10 sq km)
Population 1384

NORWAY

BOUVET ISLAND
South Atlantic
Claimed 1928
Capital not applicable
Area 22 sq miles (58 sq km)
Population None

JAN MAYEN
North Atlantic
Claimed 1929
Capital not applicable
Area 147 sq miles (381 sq km)
Population 18 (scientists)

PETER I ISLAND
Antarctica
Claimed 1931
Capital not applicable
Area 69 sq miles (180 sq km)
Population None

SVALBARD
Arctic Ocean
Claimed 1920
Capital Longyearbyen
Area 24,289 sq miles (62,906 sq km)
Population 2019

UNITED KINGDOM

ANGUILLA
West Indies
Claimed 1650
Capital The Valley
Area 37 sq miles (96 sq km)
Population 15,094

ASCENSION ISLAND
South Atlantic
Claimed 1673
Capital Georgetown
Area 34 sq miles (88 sq km)
Population 880

BERMUDA
North Atlantic
Claimed 1612
Capital Hamilton
Area 20 sq miles (53 sq km)
Population 68,679

BRITISH INDIAN OCEAN TERRITORY
Indian Ocean
Claimed 1814
Capital Diego Garcia
Area 23 sq miles (60 sq km)
Population 4000

BRITISH VIRGIN ISLANDS
West Indies
Claimed 1672
Capital Road Town
Area 59 sq miles (153 sq km)
Population 25,383

CAYMAN ISLANDS
West Indies
Claimed 1670
Capital George Town
Area 100 sq miles (259 sq km)
Population 51,384

FALKLAND ISLANDS
South Atlantic
Claimed 1832
Capital Stanley
Area 4699 sq miles (12,173 sq km)
Population 3140

GIBRALTAR
Southwest Europe
Claimed 1713
Capital Gibraltar
Area 2.5 sq miles (6.5 sq km)
Population 28,956

GUERNSEY
Northwest Europe
Claimed 1066
Capital St Peter Port
Area 25 sq miles (65 sq km)
Population 65,068

ISLE OF MAN
Northwest Europe
Claimed 1765
Capital Douglas
Area 221 sq miles (572 sq km)
Population 84,655

JERSEY
Northwest Europe
Claimed 1066
Capital St. Helier
Area 45 sq miles (116 sq km)
Population 94,161

MONTSERRAT
West Indies
Claimed 1632
Capital Plymouth (currently uninhabitable)
Area 40 sq miles (102 sq km)
Population 5140

PITCAIRN ISLANDS
South Pacific
Claimed 1887
Capital Adamstown
Area 18 sq miles (47 sq km)
Population 48

ST. HELENA
South Atlantic
Claimed 1673
Capital Jamestown
Area 47 sq miles (122 sq km)
Population 7700

SOUTH GEORGIA &
   THE SOUTH SANDWICH ISLANDS
South Atlantic
Capital not applicable
Claimed 1775
Area 1387 sq miles (3592 sq km)
Population None

TRISTAN DA CUNHA
South Atlantic
Claimed 1612
Capital Edinburgh
Area 38 sq miles (98 sq km)
Population 264

TURKS & CAICOS ISLANDS
West Indies
Claimed 1766
Capital Cockburn Town
Area 166 sq miles (430 sq km)
Population 44,819

UNITED STATES OF AMERICA

AMERICAN SAMOA
South Pacific
Claimed 1900
Capital Pago Pago
Area 75 sq miles (195 sq km)
Population 67,242

BAKER & HOWLAND ISLANDS
Central Pacific
Claimed 1856
Capital not applicable
Area 0.54 sq miles (1.4 sq km)
Population None

GUAM
West Pacific
Claimed 1898
Capital Hagåtña
Area 212 sq miles (549 sq km)
Population 183,286

JARVIS ISLAND
Central Pacific
Claimed 1856
Capital not applicable
Area 1.7 sq miles (4.5 sq km)
Population None

NORTHERN MARIANA ISLANDS
West Pacific
Claimed 1947
Capital Saipan
Area 177 sq miles (457 sq km)
Population 46,050

PALMYRA ATOLL
Central Pacific
Claimed 1898
Capital not applicable
Area 5 sq miles (12 sq km)
Population None

PUERTO RICO
West Indies
Claimed 1898
Capital San Juan
Area 3515 sq miles (9104 sq km)
Population 4.0 million

VIRGIN ISLANDS
West Indies
Claimed 1917
Capital Charlotte Amalie
Area 137 sq miles (355 sq km)
Population 109,666

WAKE ISLAND
Central Pacific
Claimed 1898
Capital not applicable
Area 2.5 sq miles (6.5 sq km)
Population 150 (US air base)

Geographical comparisons

Largest countries

Russ. Fed.	6,592,735 sq miles	(17,075,200 sq km)
Canada	3,854,085 sq miles	(9,984,670 sq km)
USA	3,717,792 sq miles	(9,629,091 sq km)
China	3,705,386 sq miles	(9,596,960 sq km)
Brazil	3,286,470 sq miles	(8,511,965 sq km)
Australia	2,967,893 sq miles	(7,686,850 sq km)
India	1,269,339 sq miles	(3,287,590 sq km)
Argentina	1,068,296 sq miles	(2,766,890 sq km)
Kazakhstan	1,049,150 sq miles	(2,717,300 sq km)
Algeria	919,590 sq miles	(2,318,740 sq km)

Smallest countries

Vatican City	0.17 sq miles	(0.44 sq km)
Monaco	0.75 sq miles	(1.95 sq km)
Nauru	8 sq miles	(21 sq km)
Tuvalu	10 sq miles	(26 sq km)
San Marino	24 sq miles	(61 sq km)
Liechtenstein	62 sq miles	(160 sq km)
Marshall Islands	70 sq miles	(181 sq km)
St. Kitts & Nevis	101 sq miles	(261 sq km)
Maldives	116 sq miles	(300 sq km)
Malta	124 sq miles	(320 sq km)

Largest islands

Greenland	849,400 sq miles (2,200,000 sq km)
New Guinea	312,000 sq miles (808,000 sq km)
Borneo	292,222 sq miles (757,050 sq km)
Madagascar	229,300 sq miles (594,000 sq km)
Sumatra	202,300 sq miles (524,000 sq km)
Baffin Island	183,800 sq miles (476,000 sq km)
Honshu	88,800 sq miles (230,000 sq km)
Britain	88,700 sq miles (229,800 sq km)
Victoria Island	81,900 sq miles (212,000 sq km)
Ellesmere Island	75,700 sq miles (196,000 sq km)

Richest countries

(GNI per capita, in US$)

Luxembourg	65,630
Norway	59,590
Switzerland	54,930
Liechtenstein	50,000
Denmark	47,390
Iceland	46,320
USA	43,740
Sweden	41,060
Ireland	40,150
Japan	38,980

Poorest countries

(GNI per capita, in US$)

Burundi	100
Somalia	120
Congo, Dem. Rep.	120
Liberia	130
Malawi	160
Ethiopia	160
Guinea-Bissau	180
Sierra Leone	220
Eritrea	220
Afghanistan	222

Most populous countries

China	1,350,000,000
India	1,210,000,000
USA	318,000,000
Indonesia	232,000,000
Brazil	195,000,000
Pakistan	185,000,000

Most populous countries *continued*

Bangladesh	164,000,000
Nigeria	158,000,000
Russian Federation	140,000,000
Japan	127,000,000

Least populous countries

Vatican City	832
Nauru	9,322
Tuvalu	10,544
Palau	20,956
Monaco	30,539
San Marino	31,817
Liechtenstein	32,236
St. Kitts & Nevis	50,314
Marshall Islands	67,182
Dominica	72,969

Most densely populated countries

Monaco	40,719 people per sq mile (15,661 per sq km)
Singapore	20,339 people per sq mile (7869 per sq km)
Vatican City	4894 people per sq mile (1891 per sq km)
Malta	3226 people per sq mile (1250 per sq km)
Bangladesh	3180 people per sq mile (1228 per sq km)
Bahrain	2930 people per sq mile (1133 per sq km)
Maldives	2586 people per sq mile (1000 per sq km)
Taiwan	1852 people per sq mile (715 per sq km)
Mauritius	1811 people per sq mile (699 per sq km)
Barbados	1807 people per sq mile (698 per sq km)

Most sparsely populated countries

Mongolia	4 people per sq mile	(2 per sq km)
Namibia	7 people per sq mile	(3 per sq km)
Australia	7 people per sq mile	(3 per sq km)
Iceland	8 people per sq mile	(3 per sq km)
Suriname	8 people per sq mile	(3 per sq km)
Botswana	8 people per sq mile	(3 per sq km)
Mauritania	8 people per sq mile	(3 per sq km)
Libya	9 people per sq mile	(4 per sq km)
Canada	9 people per sq mile	(4 per sq km)
Guyana	10 people per sq mile	(4 per sq km)

Most widely spoken languages

1. Chinese (Mandarin)	6. Arabic
2. English	7. Bengali
3. Hindi	8. Portuguese
4. Spanish	9. Malay-Indonesian
5. Russian	10. French

Largest conurbations

Tokyo	34,200,000
Mexico City	22,800,000
Seoul	22,300,000
New York	21,900,000
São Paulo	20,200,000
Mumbai	19,850,000
Delhi	19,700,000
Shanghai	18,150,000
Los Angeles	18,000,000
Osaka	16,800,000
Jakarta	16,550,000
Kolkata	15,650,000
Cairo	15,600,000
Manila	14,950,000
Karachi	14,300,000
Moscow	13,750,000
Buenos Aires	13,450,000
Dacca	13,250,000

Largest conurbations *continued*

Rio de Janeiro	12,150,000
Beijing	12,100,000
London	12,000,000
Tehran	11,850,000
Istanbul	11,500,000
Lagos	11,100,000
Shenzhen	10,700,000

Longest rivers

Nile (NE Africa)	4160 miles	(6695 km)
Amazon (South America)	4049 miles	(6516 km)
Yangtze (China)	3915 miles	(6299 km)
Mississippi/Missouri (US)	3710 miles	(5969 km)
Ob'-Irtysh (Russ. Fed.)	3461 miles	(5570 km)
Yellow River (China)	3395 miles	(5464 km)
Congo (Central Africa)	2900 miles	(4667 km)
Mekong (Southeast Asia)	2749 miles	(4425 km)
Lena (Russian Federation)	2734 miles	(4400 km)
Mackenzie (Canada)	2640 miles	(4250 km)
Yenisey (Russ. Federation)	2541 miles	(4090 km)

Highest mountains

(Height above sea level)

Everest	29,035 ft	(8850 m)
K2	28,253 ft	(8611 m)
Kanchenjunga I	28,210 ft	(8598 m)
Makalu I	27,767 ft	(8463 m)
Cho Oyu	26,907 ft	(8201 m)
Dhaulagiri I	26,796 ft	(8167 m)
Manaslu I	26,783 ft	(8163 m)
Nanga Parbat I	26,661 ft	(8126 m)
Annapurna I	26,547 ft	(8091 m)
Gasherbrum I	26,471 ft	(8068 m)

Largest bodies of inland water

(Area & depth)

Caspian Sea	143,243 sq miles (371,000 sq km)	3215 ft (980 m)
Lake Superior	32,151 sq miles (83,270 sq km)	1289 ft (393 m)
Lake Victoria	26,560 sq miles (68,880 sq km)	328 ft (100 m)
Lake Huron	23,436 sq miles (60,700 sq km)	751 ft (229 m)
Lake Michigan	22,402 sq miles (58,020 sq km)	922 ft (281 m)
Lake Tanganyika	12,703 sq miles (32,900 sq km)	4700 ft (1435 m)
Great Bear Lake	12,274 sq miles (31,790 sq km)	1047 ft (319 m)
Lake Baikal	11,776 sq miles (30,500 sq km)	5712 ft (1741 m)
Great Slave Lake	10,981 sq miles (28,440 sq km)	459 ft (140 m)
Lake Erie	9915 sq miles (25,680 sq km)	197 ft (60 m)

Deepest ocean features

Challenger Deep, Mariana Trench (Pacific)	36,201 ft (11,034 m)
Vityaz III Depth, Tonga Trench (Pacific)	35,704 ft (10,882 m)
Vityaz Depth, Kurile-Kamchatka Trench (Pacific)	34,588 ft (10,542 m)
Cape Johnson Deep, Philippine Trench (Pacific)	34,441 ft (10,497 m)
Kermadec Trench (Pacific)	32,964 ft (10,047 m)
Ramapo Deep, Japan Trench (Pacific)	32,758 ft (9984 m)
Milwaukee Deep, Puerto Rico Trench (Atlantic)	30,185 ft (9200 m)
Argo Deep, Torres Trench (Pacific)	30,070 ft (9165 m)
Meteor Depth, South Sandwich Trench (Atlantic)	30,000 ft (9144 m)
Planet Deep, New Britain Trench (Pacific)	29,988 ft (9140 m)

Greatest waterfalls

(Mean flow of water)

Boyoma (Congo, Dem. Rep.)	600,400 cu. ft/sec (17,000 cu.m/sec)
Khône (Laos/Cambodia)	410,000 cu. ft/sec (11,600 cu.m/sec)
Niagara (USA/Canada)	195,000 cu. ft/sec (5500 cu.m/sec)
Grande (Uruguay)	160,000 cu. ft/sec (4500 cu.m/sec)
Paulo Afonso (Brazil)	100,000 cu. ft/sec (2800 cu.m/sec)
Urubupunga (Brazil)	97,000 cu. ft/sec (2750 cu.m/sec)
Iguaçu (Argentina/Brazil)	62,000 cu. ft/sec (1700 cu.m/sec)
Maribondo (Brazil)	53,000 cu. ft/sec (1500 cu.m/sec)
Victoria (Zimbabwe)	39,000 cu. ft/sec (1100 cu.m/sec)

Greatest waterfalls *continued*

Kabalega (Uganda)	42,000 cu. ft/sec (1200 cu.m/sec)
Churchill (Canada)	35,000 cu. ft/sec (1000 cu.m/sec)
Cauvery (India)	33,000 cu. ft/sec (900 cu.m/sec)

Highest waterfalls

Angel (Venezuela)	3212 ft	(979 m)
Tugela (South Africa)	3110 ft	(948 m)
Utigard (Norway)	2625 ft	(800 m)
Mongefossen (Norway)	2539 ft	(774 m)
Mtarazi (Zimbabwe)	2500 ft	(762 m)
Yosemite (USA)	2425 ft	(739 m)
Ostre Mardola Foss (Norway)	2156 ft	(657 m)
Tyssestrengane (Norway)	2119 ft	(646 m)
*Cuquenan (Venezuela)	2001 ft	(610 m)
Sutherland (New Zealand)	1903 ft	(580 m)
*Kjellfossen (Norway)	1841 ft	(561 m)

* indicates that the total height is a single leap

Largest deserts

Sahara	3,450,000 sq miles (9,065,000 sq km)
Gobi	500,000 sq miles (1,295,000 sq km)
Ar Rub al Khali	289,600 sq miles (750,000 sq km)
Great Victorian	249,800 sq miles (647,000 sq km)
Sonoran	120,000 sq miles (311,000 sq km)
Kalahari	120,000 sq miles (310,800 sq km)
Garagum	115,800 sq miles (300,000 sq km)
Takla Makan	100,400 sq miles (260,000 sq km)
Namib	52,100 sq miles (135,000 sq km)
Thar	33,670 sq miles (130,000 sq km)

NB – Most of Antarctica is a polar desert, with only 2 inches (50 mm) of precipitation annually

Hottest inhabited places

Djibouti (Djibouti)	86.0°F	(30.0°C)
Timbouctou (Mali)	84.7°F	(29.3°C)
Tirunelveli (India)	84.7°F	(29.3°C)
Tuticorin (India)	84.7°F	(29.3°C)
Nellore (India)	84.5°F	(29.2°C)
Santa Marta (Colombia)	84.5°F	(29.2°C)
Aden (Yemen)	84.0°F	(29.0°C)
Madurai (India)	84.0°F	(29.0°C)
Niamey (Niger)	84.0°F	(29.0°C)

Driest inhabited places

Aswân (Egypt)	0.02 in	(0.5 mm)
Luxor (Egypt)	0.03 in	(0.7 mm)
Arica (Chile)	0.04 in	(1.1 mm)
Ica (Peru)	0.10 in	(2.3 mm)
Antofagasta (Chile)	0.20 in	(4.9 mm)
El Minya (Egypt)	0.20 in	(5.1 mm)
Asyût (Egypt)	0.20 in	(5.2 mm)
Callao (Peru)	0.50 in	(12.0 mm)
Trujillo (Peru)	0.55 in	(14.0 mm)
El Faiyûm (Egypt)	0.80 in	(19.0 mm)

Wettest inhabited places

Buenaventura (Colombia)	265 in	(6743 mm)
Monrovia (Liberia)	202 in	(5131 mm)
Pago Pago (American Samoa)	196 in	(4990 mm)
Moulmein (Myanmar)	191 in	(4852 mm)
Lae (Papua New Guinea)	183 in	(4645 mm)
Baguio (Luzon I., Philippines)	180 in	(4573 mm)
Sylhet (Bangladesh)	176 in	(4457 mm)
Padang (Sumatra, Indonesia)	166 in	(4225 mm)
Bogor (Java, Indonesia)	166 in	(4225 mm)
Conakry (Guinea)	171 in	(4341 mm)

Aa – Almería

A

Aa see Gauja
Aachen 72 A4 Dut. Aken, Fr. Aix-la-Chapelle; anc. Aquae Grani, Aquisgranum. Nordrhein-Westfalen, W Germany
Aaiún see Laâyoune
Aalborg 63 B7 var. Ålborg, Ålborg-Nørresundby; anc. Alburgum. Nordjylland, N Denmark
Aalen 73 B6 Baden-Württemberg, S Germany
Aalsmeer 64 C3 Noord-Holland, C Netherlands
Aalst 65 B6 Oost-Vlaanderen, C Belgium
Aalten 64 E4 Gelderland, E Netherlands
Aalter 65 B5 Oost-Vlaanderen, NW Belgium
Aanaarjävri see Inarijärvi
Äänekoski 63 D5 Länsi-Suomi, W Finland
Aar see Aare
Aare 73 A7 var. Aar. river W Switzerland
Aarhus see Århus
Aarlen see Arlon
Aat see Ath
Aba 55 E5 Orientale, NE Dem. Rep. Congo
Aba 53 G5 Abia, S Nigeria
Abā as Su'ūd see Najrān
Abaco Island see Great Abaco, N Bahamas
Ābādān 98 C4 Khūzestān, SW Iran
Abadan 100 C3 prev. Bezmein, Büzmeýin, Rus. Byuzmeyin. Ahal Welaýaty, C Turkmenistan
Abai see Blue Nile
Abakan 92 D4 Respublika Khakasiya, S Russian Federation
Abancay 38 D4 Apurímac, SE Peru
Abariringa see Kanton
Abashiri 108 D2 var. Abasiri. Hokkaidō, NE Japan
Abasiri see Abashiri
Ābay Wenz see Blue Nile
Abbaia see Ābaya Hāyk'
Abbatis Villa see Abbeville
Abbazia see Opatija
Abbeville 68 C2 anc. Abbatis Villa. Somme, N France
'Abd al 'Azīz, Jabal 96 D2 mountain range NE Syria
Abéché 54 C3 var. Abécher, Abeshr. Ouaddaï, SE Chad
Abécher see Abéché
Abela see Ávila
Abellinum see Avellino
Abemama 122 D2 var. Apamama; prev. Roger Simpson Island. atoll Tungaru, W Kiribati
Abengourou 53 E5 E Côte d'Ivoire
Aberbrothock see Arbroath
Abercorn see Mbala
Aberdeen 66 D3 anc. Devana. NE Scotland, United Kingdom
Aberdeen 23 E2 South Dakota, N USA
Aberdeen 24 B2 Washington, NW USA
Abergwaun see Fishguard
Abertawe see Swansea
Aberystwyth 67 C6 W Wales, United Kingdom
Abeshr see Abéché
Abhā 99 B6 'Asīr, SW Saudi Arabia
Abidavichy 85 D7 Rus. Obidovichi. Mahilyowskaya Voblasts', E Belarus
Abidjan 53 E5 S Côte d'Ivoire
Abilene 27 F3 Texas, SW USA
Abingdon see Pinta, Isla
Abkhazia see Ap'khazet'i
Åbo see Turku
Aboisso 53 E5 SE Côte d'Ivoire
Abo, Massif d' 54 B1 mountain range NW Chad
Abomey 53 F5 S Benin
Abou-Déïa 54 C3 Salamat, SE Chad
Aboudouhour see Abū aḑ Ḑuhūr
Abou Kémal see Abū Kamāl
Abrantes 70 B3 var. Abrántes. Santarém, C Portugal
Abrashlare see Brezovo
Abrolhos Bank 34 E4 undersea bank W Atlantic Ocean
Abrova 85 B6 Rus. Obrovo. Brestskaya Voblasts', SW Belarus
Abrud 86 B4 Ger. Gross-Schlatten, Hung. Abrudbánya. Alba, SW Romania
Abrudbánya see Abrud
Abruzzese, Appennino 74 C4 mountain range C Italy
Absaroka Range 22 B2 mountain range Montana/Wyoming, NW USA
Abū aḑ Ḑuhūr 96 B3 Fr. Aboudouhour. Idlib, NW Syria
Abu Dhabi see Abū Ẓabī
Abu Hamed 50 C3 River Nile, N Sudan
Abū Ḩardān 96 E3 var. Hajîne. Dayr az Zawr, E Syria
Abuja 53 G4 country capital (Nigeria) Federal Capital District, C Nigeria
Abū Kamāl 96 E3 Fr. Abou Kémal. Dayr az Zawr, E Syria
Abula see Ávila
Abunã, Rio 40 C2 var. Río Abuná. river Bolivia/Brazil
Abut Head 129 B6 headland South Island, New Zealand
Abuye Meda 50 D4 mountain C Ethiopia
Abū Ẓabī 99 C5 var. Abū Ẓabī, Eng. Abu Dhabi. country capital (United Arab Emirates) Abū Ẓaby, C United Arab Emirates
Abū Ẓabī see Abū Ẓabī
Abyaḑ, Al Baḩr al see White Nile
Abyla see Ávila
Abyssinia see Ethiopia
Acalayong 55 A5 SW Equatorial Guinea
Acaponeta 28 D4 Nayarit, C Mexico
Acapulco 29 E5 var. Acapulco de Juárez. Guerrero, S Mexico
Acapulco de Juárez see Acapulco
Acarai Mountains 37 F4 Sp. Serra Acaraí. mountain range Brazil/Guyana
Acaraí, Serra see Acarai Mountains
Acarigua 36 D2 Portuguesa, N Venezuela
Accra 53 E5 country capital (Ghana) SE Ghana
Achacachi 39 E4 La Paz, W Bolivia
Achara 95 F2 var. Ajaria. autonomous republic SW Georgia
Acklins Island 32 C2 island SE Bahamas
Aconcagua, Cerro 42 B4 mountain W Argentina
Açores/Açores, Arquipélago dos/Açores, Ilhas dos see Azores
A Coruña 70 B1 Cast. La Coruña, Eng. Corunna; anc. Caronium. Galicia, NW Spain
Acre 40 C2 off. Estado do Acre. state W Brazil
Acre 40 C2 off. Estado do Acre. region W Brazil
Açu 41 G2 var. Assu. Rio Grande do Norte, E Brazil
Acunum Acusio see Montélimar
Ada 78 D3 Vojvodina, N Serbia
Ada 27 G2 Oklahoma, C USA
Ada Bazar see Adapazarı
Adalia see Antalya
Adalia, Gulf of see Antalya Körfezi
Adama see Nazrēt
'Adan 99 B7 Eng. Aden. SW Yemen
Adana 94 D4 var. Seyhan. Adana, S Turkey
Adâncata see Horlivka
Adapazarı 94 B2 prev. Ada Bazar. Sakarya, NW Turkey
Adare, Cape 132 B4 cape Antarctica
Ad Dahna 98 C4 desert E Saudi Arabia
Ad Dakhla 48 A4 var. Dakhla. SW Western Sahara
Ad Dalanj see Dilling
Ad Damar see Ed Damer
Ad Damazīn see Ed Damazin
Ad Dāmir see Ed Damer
Ad Dammān 98 C4 var. Dammām. Ash Sharqīyah, NE Saudi Arabia
Ad Dāmūr see Damoûr
Ad Dawḩah 98 C4 Eng. Doha. country capital (Qatar) C Qatar
Aḑ Ḑiffah see Libyan Plateau
Addis Ababa see Ādīs Ābeba
Addoo Atoll see Addu Atoll
Addu Atoll 110 A5 var. Addoo Atoll, Seenu Atoll. atoll S Maldives
Adelaide 127 B6 state capital South Australia
Adelsberg see Postojna
Aden see 'Adan
Aden, Gulf of 99 C7 gulf SW Arabian Sea
Adige 74 C2 Ger. Etsch. river N Italy
Adirondack Mountains 19 F2 mountain range New York, NE USA
Ādīs Ābeba 51 C5 Eng. Addis Ababa. country capital (Ethiopia) Ādīs Ābeba, C Ethiopia
Adıyaman 95 E4 Adıyaman, SE Turkey
Adjud 86 C4 Vrancea, E Romania
Admiralty Islands 122 B3 island group N Papua New Guinea
Adra 71 E5 Andalucía, S Spain
Adrar 48 D3 C Algeria
Adrian 18 C3 Michigan, N USA
Adrianople/Adrianopolis see Edirne
Adriatico, Mare see Adriatic Sea
Adriatic Sea 81 E2 Alb. Deti Adriatik, It. Mare Adriatico, SCr. Jadransko More, Slvn. Jadransko Morje. sea N Mediterranean Sea
Adriatik, Deti see Adriatic Sea
Adycha 93 F2 river NE Russian Federation
Aegean Sea 83 C5 Gk. Aigaíon Pelagos, Aigaío Pélagos, Turk. Ege Denizi. sea NE Mediterranean Sea
Aegviidu 84 D2 Ger. Charlottenhof. Harjumaa, NW Estonia
Aegyptus see Egypt
Aelana see Al 'Aqabah
Aelok see Ailuk Atoll
Aelōninlaplap see Ailinglaplap Atoll
Aemona see Ljubljana
Aeolian Islands 75 C6 var. Isole Lipari, Eng. Aeolian Islands, Lipari Islands. island group S Italy
Aeolian Islands see Eolie, Isole
Æsernia see Isernia
Afar Depression see Danakil Desert
Afars et des Issas, Territoire Français des see Djibouti
Afghānestān, Dowlat-e Eslāmī-ye see Afghanistan
Afghanistan 100 C4 off. Islamic Republic of Afghanistan, Per. Dowlat-e Eslāmī-ye Afghānestān; prev. Republic of Afghanistan. country C Asia
Afmadow 51 D6 Jubbada Hoose, S Somalia
Africa 46 continent
Africa, Horn of 46 E4 physical region Ethiopia/Somalia
Africana Seamount 119 A6 seamount SW Indian Ocean
'Afrīn 96 B2 Ḩalab, N Syria
Afyon 94 B3 prev. Afyonkarahisar. Afyon, W Turkey
Agadès see Agadez
Agadez 53 G3 prev. Agadès. Agadez, C Niger
Agadir 48 B3 SW Morocco
Agana/Agaña see Hagåtña
Āgaro 51 C5 Oromīya, C Ethiopia
Agassiz Fracture Zone 121 G5 fracture zone S Pacific Ocean
Agatha see Agde
Agathónisi 83 D6 island Dodekánisa, Greece, Aegean Sea
Agde 69 C6 anc. Agatha. Hérault, S France
Agedabia see Ajdābiyā
Agen 69 B5 anc. Aginnum. Lot-et-Garonne, SW France
Agendicum see Sens
Aghri Dagh see Büyükağrı Dağı
Agiá 82 B4 var. Ayiá. Thessalía, C Greece
Agialoúsa see Yenierenköy
Agía Marína 83 E6 Léros, Dodekánisa, Greece, Aegean Sea
Aginnum see Agen
Ágios Efstrátios 82 D4 var. Áyios Evstrátios, Hagios Evstrátios. island E Greece
Ágios Nikólaos 83 D8 var. Áyios Nikólaos. Kríti, Greece, E Mediterranean Sea
Āgra 112 D3 Uttar Pradesh, N India
Agra and Oudh, United Provinces of see Uttar Pradesh
Agram see Zagreb
Ağrı 95 F3 var. Karaköse; prev. Karakılısse. Ağrı, NE Turkey
Agri Dagi see Büyükağrı Dağı
Agrigento 75 C7 Gk. Akragas; prev. Girgenti. Sicilia, Italy, C Mediterranean Sea
Agriovótano 83 C5 Évvoia, C Greece
Agropoli 75 D5 Campania, S Italy
Aguachica 36 B2 Cesar, N Colombia
Aguadulce 31 F5 Coclé, S Panama
Agua Prieta 28 B1 Sonora, NW Mexico
Aguascalientes 28 D4 Aguascalientes, C Mexico
Aguaytía 38 C3 Ucayali, C Peru
Águilas 71 E4 Murcia, SE Spain
Aguililla 28 D4 Michoacán, SW Mexico
Agulhas Basin 47 D8 undersea basin SW Indian Ocean
Agulhas Plateau 45 D6 undersea plateau SW Indian Ocean
Ahaggar 53 F2 high plateau region SE Algeria
Ahlen 72 B4 Nordrhein-Westfalen, W Germany
Ahmadābād 112 C4 var. Ahmedabad. Gujarāt, W India
Ahmadnagar 112 C5 var. Ahmednagar. Mahārāshtra, W India
Ahmedabad see Ahmadābād
Ahmednagar see Ahmadnagar
Ahuachapán 30 B3 Ahuachapán, W El Salvador
Ahvāz 98 C3 var. Ahwāz; prev. Nāsiri. Khūzestān, SW Iran
Ahvenanmaa see Åland
Ahwāz see Ahvāz
Aigaíon Pelagos/Aigaío Pélagos see Aegean Sea
Aígina 83 C6 var. Aíyina, Egina. Aígina, C Greece
Aígio 83 B5 var. Egio; prev. Aíyion. Dytikí Ellás, S Greece
Aiken 21 E2 South Carolina, SE USA
Ailinglaplap Atoll 122 D2 var. Aelōnlaplap. atoll Ralik Chain, S Marshall Islands
Ailuk Atoll 122 D1 var. Aelok. atoll Ratak Chain, NE Marshall Islands
Ainaži 84 D3 Est. Heinaste, Ger. Hainasch. Limbaži, N Latvia
'Aïn Ben Tili 52 D1 Tiris Zemmour, N Mauritania
Aintab see Gaziantep
Aïoun el Atrous/Aïoun el Atroûss see 'Ayoûn el 'Atroûs
Aiquile 39 F4 Cochabamba, C Bolivia
Aïr see Aïr, Massif de l'
Air du Azbine see Aïr, Massif de l'
Aïr, Massif de l' 53 G2 var. Aïr, Air du Azbine, Asben. mountain range NC Niger
Aiud 86 B4 Ger. Strassburg, Hung. Nagyenyed; prev. Engeten. Alba, SW Romania
Aix see Aix-en-Provence
Aix-en-Provence 69 D6 var. Aix; anc. Aquae Sextiae. Bouches-du-Rhône, SE France
Aix-la-Chapelle see Aachen
Aíyina see Aígina
Aíyion see Aígio
Aizkraukle 84 C4 Aizkraukle, S Latvia
Ajaccio 69 E7 Corse, France, C Mediterranean Sea
Ajaria see Achara
Ajastan see Armenia
Aj Bogd Uul 104 D2 mountain SW Mongolia
Ajdābiyā 49 G2 var. Agedabia, Ajdābiyah. NE Libya
Ajdābiyah see Ajdābiyā
Ajjinena see El Geneina
Ajmer 112 D3 var. Ajmere. Rājasthān, N India
Ajo 26 A3 Arizona, SW USA
Akaba see Al 'Aqabah
Akamagaseki see Shimonoseki
Akasha 50 B3 Northern, N Sudan
Akchâr 52 C2 desert W Mauritania
Aken see Aachen
Akermanceaster see Bath
Akhalts'ikhe 95 F2 SW Georgia
Akhisar 94 A3 Manisa, W Turkey
Akhmīm 50 B2 var. Akhmîm; anc. Panopolis. C Egypt
Akhtubinsk 89 C7 Astrakhanskaya Oblast', SW Russian Federation
Akhtyrka see Okhtyrka
Akimiski Island 16 C3 island Nunavut, C Canada
Akinovka 87 F4 Zaporiz'ka Oblast', S Ukraine
Akita 108 D4 Akita, Honshū, C Japan
Akjoujt 52 C2 prev. Fort-Repoux. Inchiri, W Mauritania
Akkeshi 108 E2 Hokkaidō, NE Japan
Aklavik 14 D3 Northwest Territories, NW Canada
Akmola see Astana
Akmolinsk see Astana
Aknavásár see Târgu Ocna
Akpatok Island 17 E1 island Nunavut, E Canada
Akragas see Agrigento
Akron 18 D4 Ohio, N USA
Akrotiri see Akrotírion
Akrotírion 80 C5 var. Akrotiri. UK air base S Cyprus
Aksai Chin 102 B2 Chin. Aksayqin. disputed region China/India
Aksaray 94 C4 Aksaray, C Turkey
Aksayqin see Aksai Chin
Akşehir 94 B4 Konya, W Turkey
Aktash see Oqtosh
Aktau 92 A4 Kaz. Aqtaū; prev. Shevchenko. Mangistau, W Kazakhstan
Aktjubinsk/Aktyubinsk see Aktobe
Aktobe 92 B4 Kaz. Aqtöbe; prev. Aktjubinsk, Aktyubinsk. Aktyubinsk, NW Kazakhstan
Aktsyabrski 85 C7 Rus. Oktyabr'skiy; prev. Karpilovka. Homyel'skaya Voblasts', SE Belarus
Aktyubinsk see Aktobe
Akula 55 C5 Equateur, NW Dem. Rep. Congo
Akureyri 61 E4 Nordhurland Eystra, N Iceland
Akyab see Sittwe
Alabama 20 C2 off. State of Alabama, also known as Camellia State, Heart of Dixie, The Cotton State, Yellowhammer State. state S USA
Alabama River 20 C3 river Alabama, S USA
Alaca 94 C3 Çorum, N Turkey
Alacant see Alicante
Alagoas 41 G2 off. Estado de Alagoas. region E Brazil
Alagoas 41 G2 off. Estado de Alagoas. state E Brazil
Alais see Alès
Alajuela 31 E4 Alajuela, C Costa Rica
Alakanuk 14 C2 Alaska, USA
Al 'Alamayn 50 B1 var. El 'Alamein. N Egypt
Al 'Amārah 98 C3 var. Amara. Maysān, E Iraq
Alamo 25 D6 Nevada, W USA
Alamogordo 26 D3 New Mexico, SW USA
Alamosa 22 C5 Colorado, C USA
Åland 63 C6 var. Aland Islands, Fin. Ahvenanmaa. island group SW Finland
Aland Islands see Åland
Aland Sea see Ålands Hav
Ålands Hav 63 C6 var. Aland Sea. strait Baltic Sea/Gulf of Bothnia
Alanya 94 C4 Antalya, S Turkey
Al 'Aqabah 97 B8 var. Akaba, Aqaba, 'Aqaba; anc. Aelana, Elath. Al 'Aqabah, SW Jordan
Al 'Arabīyah as Su'ūdīyah see Saudi Arabia
Alasca, Golfo de see Alaska, Gulf of
Alaşehir 94 A4 Manisa, W Turkey
Al 'Asharah 96 E3 var. Ashara. Dayr az Zawr, E Syria
Alaska 14 C3 off. State of Alaska, also known as Land of the Midnight Sun, The Last Frontier, Seward's Folly; prev. Russian America. state NW USA
Alaska, Gulf of 14 C4 var. Golfo de Alasca. gulf Canada/USA
Alaska Peninsula 14 C3 peninsula Alaska, USA
Alaska Range 12 B2 mountain range Alaska, USA
Al-Asnam see Chlef
Alattio see Alta
Al Awaynāt see Al 'Uwaynāt
Alaykel'/Alay-Kuu see Kök-Art
Al 'Aynā 97 B7 Al Karak, W Jordan
Alazeya 93 G2 river NE Russian Federation
Al Bāb 96 B2 Ḩalab, N Syria
Albacete 71 E3 Castilla-La Mancha, C Spain
Al Baghdādī 98 B3 var. Khān al Baghdādī. Al Anbār, SW Iraq
Al Bāha see Al Bāḩah
Al Bāḩah 99 B5 var. Al Bāha. Al BāḨah, SW Saudi Arabia
Al Baḩrayn see Bahrain
Alba Iulia 86 B4 Ger. Weissenburg, Hung. Gyulafehérvár; prev. Bălgrad, Karlsburg, Károly-Fehérvár. Alba, W Romania
Albania 79 C7 off. Republic of Albania, Alb. Republika e Shqipqërisë, Shqipëria; prev. People's Socialist Republic of Albania. country SE Europe
Albania see Aubagne
Albany 125 B7 Western Australia
Albany 20 D3 Georgia, SE USA
Albany 19 F3 state capital New York, NE USA
Albany 24 B3 Oregon, NW USA
Albany 16 C3 river Ontario, S Canada
Alba Regia see Székesfehérvár
Al Bāridah 96 C4 var. Bāridah. Ḩimş, C Syria
Al Başrah 98 C3 Eng. Basra, hist. Busra, Bussora. Al Başrah, SE Iraq
Al Batrūn see Batroûn
Al Bayḑā' 49 G2 var. Beida. NE Libya
Albemarle Island see Isabela, Isla
Albemarle Sound 21 G1 inlet W Atlantic Ocean
Albergaria-a-Velha 70 B2 Aveiro, N Portugal
Albert 68 C3 Somme, N France
Alberta 15 E4 province SW Canada
Albert Edward Nyanza see Edward, Lake
Albert, Lake 51 B6 var. Albert Nyanza, Lac Mobutu Sese Seko. lake Uganda/Dem. Rep. Congo
Albert Lea 23 F3 Minnesota, N USA
Albert Nyanza see Albert, Lake
Albertville see Kalemie
Albi 69 C6 anc. Albiga. Tarn, S France
Albiga see Albi
Ålborg see Aalborg
Ålborg-Nørresundby see Aalborg
Alborz, Reshteh-ye Kūhhā-ye 98 C2 Eng. Elburz Mountains. mountain range N Iran
Albuquerque 26 D2 New Mexico, SW USA
Al Burayqah see Marsá al Burayqah
Alburgum see Aalborg
Albury 127 C7 New South Wales, SE Australia
Alcácer do Sal 70 B4 Setúbal, W Portugal
Alcalá de Henares 71 E3 Ar. Alkal'a; anc. Complutum. Madrid, C Spain
Alcamo 75 C7 Sicilia, Italy, C Mediterranean Sea
Alcañiz 71 F2 Aragón, NE Spain
Alcántara, Embalse de 70 C3 reservoir W Spain
Alcaudete 70 D4 Andalucía, S Spain
Alcázar see Ksar-el-Kebir
Alcazarquivir see Ksar-el-Kebir
Alcoi see Alcoy
Alcoy 71 F4 Cat. Alcoi. País Valenciano, E Spain
Aldabra Group 57 G2 island group SW Seychelles
Aldan 93 F3 river NE Russian Federation
al Dar al Baida see Rabat
Alderney 68 A2 island Channel Islands
Aleg 52 C3 Brakna, SW Mauritania
Aleksandriya see Oleksandriya
Aleksandropol' see Gyumri
Aleksandrovka see Oleksandrivka
Aleksandrovsk see Zaporizhzhya
Aleksin 89 B5 Tul'skaya Oblast', W Russian Federation
Aleksinac 78 E4 Serbia, SE Serbia
Alençon 68 B3 Orne, N France
Alenquer 41 E2 Pará, NE Brazil
Alep/Aleppo see Ḩalab
Alert 15 F1 Ellesmere Island, Nunavut, N Canada
Alès 69 C6 prev. Alais. Gard, S France
Aleşd 86 B3 Hung. Élesd. Bihor, SW Romania
Alessandria 74 B2 Fr. Alexandrie. Piemonte, N Italy
Ålesund 63 A5 Møre og Romsdal, S Norway
Aleutian Basin 91 G3 undersea basin Bering Sea
Aleutian Islands 14 A3 island group Alaska, USA
Aleutian Range 12 A2 mountain range Alaska, USA
Aleutian Trench 91 H3 trench S Bering Sea
Alexander Archipelago 14 D4 island group Alaska, USA
Alexander City 20 D2 Alabama, S USA
Alexander Island 132 A3 island Antarctica
Alexander Range see Kirghiz Range
Alexandra 129 B7 Otago, South Island, New Zealand
Alexándreia 82 B4 var. Alexándria. Kentrikí Makedonía, N Greece
Alexandretta see İskenderun
Alexandretta, Gulf of see İskenderun Körfezi
Alexandria 50 B1 Ar. Al Iskandarīyah. N Egypt
Alexandria 86 C5 Teleorman, S Romania
Alexandria 20 B3 Louisiana, S USA
Alexandria 23 F2 Minnesota, N USA
Alexándria see Alexándreia
Alexandrie see Alessandria
Alexandroúpoli 82 D3 var. Alexandroúpolis, Turk. Dedeagaç, Dedeagach. Anatolikí Makedonía kai Thráki, NE Greece
Alexandroúpolis see Alexandroúpoli
Al Fāshir see El Fasher
Alfatar 82 E1 Silistra, NE Bulgaria
Alfeiós 83 B6 prev. Alfiós; anc. Alpheius, Alpheus. river S Greece
Alfiós see Alfeiós
Alföld see Great Hungarian Plain
Al-Furāt see Euphrates
Alga 92 B4 Kaz. Algha. Aktyubinsk, NW Kazakhstan
Algarve 70 B4 cultural region S Portugal
Algeciras 70 C5 Andalucía, SW Spain
Algemesí 71 F3 País Valenciano, E Spain
Al-Genain see El Geneina
Alger 49 E1 var. Algiers, El Djazaïr, Al Jazair. country capital (Algeria) N Algeria
Algeria 48 C3 off. Democratic and Popular Republic of Algeria. country N Africa
Algeria, Democratic and Popular Republic of see Algeria
Algerian Basin 58 C5 var. Balearic Plain. undersea basin W Mediterranean Sea
Algha see Alga
Al Ghābah 99 E5 var. Ghaba. C Oman
Alghero 75 A5 Sardegna, Italy, C Mediterranean Sea
Al Ghurdaqah see Hurghada
Algiers see Alger
Al Golea see El Goléa
Algona 23 F3 Iowa, C USA
Al Hajar al Gharbi 99 D5 mountain range N Oman
Al Hamad see Syrian Desert
Al Ḩasakah 96 D2 var. Al Hasijah, El Haseke, Fr. Hassetché. Al Ḩasakah, NE Syria
Al Hasijah see Al Ḩasakah
Al Ḩillah 98 B3 var. Hilla. Bābil, C Iraq
Al Ḩisā 97 B7 Aţ Ţafilah, W Jordan
Al Ḩudaydah 99 B6 Eng. Hodeida. W Yemen
Al Hufūf 98 C4 var. Hofuf. Ash Sharqīyah, NE Saudi Arabia
Aliákmonas
Aliákmonas 82 B4 prev. Aliákmon; anc. Haliacmon. river N Greece
Alíartos 83 C5 Stereá Ellás, C Greece
Alicante 71 F4 Cat. Alacant, Lat. Lucentum. País Valenciano, SE Spain
Alice 27 G5 Texas, SW USA
Alice Springs 126 A4 Northern Territory, C Australia
Alifu Atoll see Ari Atoll
Aligandí 31 G4 Kuna Yala, NE Panama
Aliki see Alykí
Alima 55 B6 river C Congo
Al Imārāt al 'Arabīyah al Muttaḩidah see United Arab Emirates
Alindao 54 C4 Basse-Kotto, S Central African Republic
Aliquippa 18 D4 Pennsylvania, NE USA
Al Iskandarīyah see Alexandria
Al Ismā'īlīya 50 B1 var. Ismailia, Ismâ'ilîya. N Egypt
Alistráti 82 C3 Kentrikí Makedonía, NE Greece
Alivéri 83 C5 var. Alivérion. Évvoia, C Greece
Alivérion see Alivéri
Al Jabal al Akhḑar 49 G2 mountain range NE Libya
Al Jafr 97 B7 Ma'ān, S Jordan
Al Jaghbūb 49 H3 NE Libya
Al Jahrā' 98 C4 var. Al Jahrah, Jahra. C Kuwait
Al Jahrah see Al Jahrā'
Al Jamāhīrīyah al 'Arabīyah al Lībīyah ash Sha'bīyah al Ishtirākīy see Libya
Al Jawf 98 B4 off. Jauf. Al Jawf, NW Saudi Arabia
Al Jawlān see Golan Heights
Al Jazair see Alger
Al Jazīrah 96 E2 physical region Iraq/Syria
Al Jīzah see Gîza
Al Junaynah see El Geneina
Alkal'a see Alcalá de Henares
Al Karak 97 B7 var. El Kerak, Karak, Kerak; anc. Kir Moab, Kir of Moab. Al Karak, W Jordan
Al-Kasr al-Kebir see Ksar-el-Kebir
Al Khalīl see Hebron
Al Khārijah 50 B2 var. El Khârga. C Egypt
Al Khums 49 F2 var. Homs, Khoms, Khums. NW Libya
Alkmaar 64 C2 Noord-Holland, NW Netherlands
Al Kufrah 49 H4 SE Libya
Al Kūt 98 C3 var. Kūt al 'Amārah, Kut al Imara. Wāsiţ, E Iraq
Al-Kuwait see Al Kuwayt
Al Kuwayt 98 C4 var. Al-Kuwait, Eng. Kuwait, Kuwait City; prev. Qurein. country capital (Kuwait) E Kuwait
Al Lādhiqīyah 96 A3 Eng. Latakia, Fr. Lattaquié; anc. Laodicea, Laodicea ad Mare. Al Lādhiqīyah, W Syria
Allahābād 113 E3 Uttar Pradesh, N India
Allanmyo see Aunglan
Allegheny Plateau 19 E3 mountain range New York/Pennsylvania, NE USA
Allenstein see Olsztyn
Allentown 19 F4 Pennsylvania, NE USA
Alleppey 110 C3 var. Alappuzha. Kerala, SW India
Alliance 22 D3 Nebraska, C USA
Al Līth 99 B5 Makkah, SW Saudi Arabia
Al Lubnān see Lebanon
Alma-Ata see Almaty
Almada 70 B4 Setúbal, W Portugal
Al Madīnah 99 A5 Eng. Medina. Al Madīnah, W Saudi Arabia
Al Mafraq 97 B6 var. Mafraq. Al Mafraq, N Jordan
Al Mahdīyah see Mahdia
Al Mahrah 99 C6 mountain range E Yemen
Al Majma'ah 98 B4 Ar Riyāḑ, C Saudi Arabia
Al Mālikīyah 96 E1 var. Malkiye. Al Ḩasakah, N Syria
Almalyk see Olmaliq
Al Mamlakah see Morocco
Al Mamlaka al Urdunīya al Hashemīyah see Jordan
Al Manāmah 98 C4 Eng. Manama. country capital (Bahrain) N Bahrain
Al Manāşif 96 E3 mountain range E Syria
Almansa 71 F4 Castilla-La Mancha, C Spain
Al-Mariyya see Almería
Al Marj 49 G2 var. Barka, It. Barce. NE Libya
Almaty 92 C5 var. Alma-Ata. Almaty, SE Kazakhstan
Al Mawşil 98 B2 Eng. Mosul. Nīnawá, N Iraq
Al Mayādīn 96 D3 var. Mayadin, Fr. Meyadine. Dayr az Zawr, E Syria
Al Mazra' see Al Mazra'ah
Al Mazra'ah 97 B6 var. Al Mazra', Mazra'a. Al Karak, W Jordan
Almelo 64 E3 Overijssel, E Netherlands
Almendra, Embalse de 70 C2 reservoir Castilla-León, NW Spain
Almendralejo 70 C4 Extremadura, W Spain
Almere 64 C3 var. Almere-stad. Flevoland, C Netherlands
Almere-stad see Almere
Almería 71 E5 Ar. Al-Mariyya; anc. Unci, Lat. Portus Magnus. Andalucía, S Spain

Al'met'yevsk – Arinsal

Al'met'yevsk 89 D5 Respublika Tatarstan, W Russian Federation
Al Mīnā' see El Mina
Al Minyā 50 B2 var. El Minya, Minya. C Egypt
Almirante 31 E4 Bocas del Toro, NW Panama
Al Mudawwarah 97 B8 Ma'ān, SW Jordan
Al Mukallā 99 C6 var. Mukalla. SE Yemen
Al Obayyid see El Obeid
Alofi 123 F4 dependent territory capital (Niue) W Niue
Aloha State see Hawai'i
Aloja 84 D3 Limbaži, N Latvia
Alónnisos 83 C5 island Vóreies Sporádes, Greece, Aegean Sea
Álora 70 D5 Andalucía, S Spain
Alor, Kepulauan 117 E5 island group E Indonesia
Al Oued see El Oued
Alpen see Alps
Alpena 18 D2 Michigan, N USA
Alpes see Alps
Alpha Cordillera 133 B3 var. Alpha Ridge. seamount range Arctic Ocean
Alpha Ridge see Alpha Cordillera
Alpheius see Alfeiós
Alphen see Alphen aan den Rijn
Alphen aan den Rijn 64 C3 var. Alphen. Zuid-Holland, C Netherlands
Alpheus see Alfeiós
Alpi see Alps
Alpine 27 E4 Texas, SW USA
Alps 80 C1 Fr. Alpes, Ger. Alpen, It. Alpi. mountain range C Europe
Al Qaḍārif see Gedaref
Al Qāhirah see Cairo
Al Qāmishlī 96 E1 var. Kamishli, Qamishly. Al Ḥasakah, NE Syria
Al Qaṣrayn see Kasserine
Al Qayrawān see Kairouan
Al-Qsar al-Kbir see Ksar-el-Kebir
Al Qubayyāt see Qoubaïyât
Al Quds/Al Quds ash Sharīf see Jerusalem
Alqueva, Barragem do 70 C4 reservoir Portugal/Spain
Al Qunayṭirah 97 B5 var. El Kuneitra, El Quneitra, Kuneitra, Qunaytra. Al Qunayṭirah, SW Syria
Al Quṣayr 96 B4 var. El Quseir, Quṣayr, Fr. Kousseir. Ḥimṣ, W Syria
Al Quwayrah 97 B8 var. El Quweira. Al 'Aqabah, SW Jordan
Alsace 68 E3 Ger. Elsass; anc. Alsatia. cultural region NE France
Alsatia see Alsace
Alsdorf 72 A4 Nordrhein-Westfalen, W Germany
Alt see Olt
Alta 62 D2 Fin. Alattio. Finnmark, N Norway
Altai see Altai Mountains
Altai Mountains 104 C2 var. Altai, Chin. Altay Shan, Rus. Altay. mountain range Asia/Europe
Altamaha River 21 E3 river Georgia, SE USA
Altamira 41 E2 Pará, NE Brazil
Altamura 75 E5 anc. Lupatia. Puglia, SE Italy
Altar, Desierto de 28 A1 var. Sonoran Desert. desert Mexico/USA
Altar, Desierto de see Sonoran Desert
Altay 104 C2 Xinjiang Uygur Zizhiqu, NW China
Altay 104 D2 prev. Yösönbulag. Govĭ-Altay, W Mongolia
Altay Altai Mountains, Asia/Europe
Altay Shan see Altai Mountains
Altbetsche see Bečej
Altenburg see București, Romania
Altin Köprü 98 B3 var. Altun Kupri. At Ta'mīn, N Iraq
Altiplano 39 F4 physical region W South America
Altkanischa see Kanjiža
Alton 18 B5 Illinois, N USA
Alton 18 B4 Missouri, C USA
Altoona 19 E4 Pennsylvania, NE USA
Alto Paraná see Paraná
Altpasua see Stara Pazova
Alt-Schwanenburg see Gulbene
Altsohl see Zvolen
Altun Kupri see Altin Köprü
Altun Shan 104 C3 var. Altyn Tagh. mountain range NW China
Altus 27 F2 Oklahoma, C USA
Altyn Tagh see Altun Shan
Al Ubayyiḍ see El Obeid
Alūksne 84 D3 Ger. Marienburg. Alūksne, NE Latvia
Al 'Ulā 98 A4 Al Madīnah, NW Saudi Arabia
Al 'Umarī 97 C6 'Ammān, E Jordan
Alupka 87 F5 Respublika Krym, S Ukraine
Al Uqṣur see Luxor
Al Urdunn see Jordan
Alushta 87 F5 Respublika Krym, S Ukraine
Al 'Uwaynāt 49 F4 var. Al Awaynāt. SW Libya
Alva 27 F1 Oklahoma, C USA
Alvarado 29 F4 Veracruz-Llave, E Mexico
Alvin 27 H4 Texas, SW USA
Al Wajh 98 A4 Tabūk, NW Saudi Arabia
Alwar 112 D3 Rājasthān, N India
Al Warī'ah 98 C4 Ash Sharqīyah, N Saudi Arabia
Al Yaman see Yemen
Alykí 82 C4 var. Aliki. Thásos, N Greece
Alytus 85 B5 Pol. Olita. Alytus, S Lithuania
Alzette 65 D8 river S Luxembourg
Amadeus, Lake 125 D5 seasonal lake Northern Territory, C Australia
Amadi 51 B5 W Equatoria, S South Sudan
Amadjuak Lake 15 G3 lake Baffin Island, Nunavut, N Canada
Amakusa-nada 109 A7 gulf SW Japan
Åmål 63 B6 Västra Götaland, S Sweden
Amami-gunto 108 A3 island group SW Japan
Amami-o-shim 108 A3 island S Japan
Amantea 75 D6 Calabria, SW Italy
Amapá 41 E1 off. Estado de Amapá; prev. Território de Amapá. region NE Brazil
Amapá 41 E1 off. Estado de Amapá; prev. Território de Amapá. state NE Brazil
Amapá, Estado de see Amapá
Amapá, Território de see Amapá
Amara see Al 'Amārah
Amarapura 114 B3 Mandalay, C Myanmar (Burma)
Amarillo 27 E2 Texas, SW USA
Amay 65 C6 Liège, E Belgium
Amazon 41 E1 Sp. Amazonas. river Brazil/Peru
Amazonas see Amazon
Amazon Basin 40 D2 basin N South America
Amazon, Mouths of the 41 F1 delta NE Brazil
Ambam 55 B5 Sud, S Cameroon
Ambanja 57 G2 Antsirañana, N Madagascar
Ambarchik 93 G2 Respublika Sakha (Yakutiya), NE Russian Federation
Ambato 38 B1 Tungurahua, C Ecuador
Ambérieu-en-Bugey 69 D5 Ain, E France
Ambianum see Amiens
Amboasary 57 F4 Toliara, S Madagascar
Amboina see Ambon
Ambon 117 F4 prev. Amboina, Amboyna. Pulau Ambon, E Indonesia
Ambositra 57 G3 Fianarantsoa, SE Madagascar
Amboyna see Ambon
Ambracia see Árta
Ambre, Cap d' see Bobaomby, Tanjona
Ambrim see Ambrym
Ambriz 56 A1 Bengo, NW Angola
Ambrym 122 D4 var. Ambrim. island C Vanuatu
Amchitka Island 14 A2 island Aleutian Islands, Alaska, USA
Amdo 104 C5 Xizang Zizhiqu, W China
Ameland 64 D1 Fris. It Amelân. island Waddeneilanden, N Netherlands
Amelân, It see Ameland
America see United States of America
America-Antarctica Ridge 45 C7 undersea ridge S Atlantic Ocean
America in Miniature see Maryland
American Falls Reservoir 24 E4 reservoir Idaho, NW USA
American Samoa 123 E4 US unincorporated territory W Polynesia
Amersfoort 64 D3 Utrecht, C Netherlands
Ames 23 F3 Iowa, C USA
Amfilochía 83 A5 var. Amfilokhía. Dytikí Ellás, C Greece
Amfilokhía see Amfilochía
Amga 93 F3 river NE Russian Federation
Amherst 17 F4 Nova Scotia, SE Canada
Amherst see Kyaikkami
Amida see Diyarbakır
Amiens 68 C3 anc. Ambianum, Samarobriva. Somme, N France
Amíndaion/Amindeo see Amýntaio
Amindivi Islands 110 A2 island group Lakshadweep, India, N Indian Ocean
Amirante Islands 57 G1 var. Amirantes Group. island group C Seychelles
Amirantes Group see Amirante Islands
Amistad, Presa de la see Amistad Reservoir
Amistad Reservoir 27 F4 var. Presa de la Amistad. reservoir Mexico/USA
Amisus see Samsun
Ammaia see Portalegre
'Ammān 97 B6 var. Amman; anc. Philadelphia, Bibl. Rabbah Ammon, Rabbath Ammon. country capital (Jordan) 'Ammān, NW Jordan
Ammassalik 60 D4 var. Angmagssalik. Tunu, S Greenland
Ammóchostos see Gazimağusa
Ammóchostos, Kólpos see Gazimağusa Körfezi
Amnok-kang see Yalu
Amoea see Portalegre
Amoentai see Amuntai
Āmol 98 D2 var. Amul. Māzandarān, N Iran
Amorgós 83 D6 Amorgós, Kykládes, Greece, Aegean Sea
Amorgós 83 D6 island Kykládes, Greece, Aegean Sea
Amos 16 D4 Québec, SE Canada
Amourj 52 D3 Hodh ech Chargui, SE Mauritania
Amoy see Xiamen
Ampato, Nevado 39 E4 mountain S Peru
Amposta 71 F2 Cataluña, NE Spain
Amraoti see Amrāvati
Amrāvati 112 D4 prev. Amraoti. Mahārāshtra, C India
Amritsar 112 D2 Punjab, N India
Amstelveen 64 C3 Noord-Holland, C Netherlands
Amsterdam 64 C3 country capital (Netherlands) Noord-Holland, C Netherlands
Amsterdam Island 119 C6 island NE French Southern and Antarctic Territories
Am Timan 54 C3 Salamat, SE Chad
Amu Darya 100 D2 Rus. Amudar'ya, Taj. Dar"yoi Amu, Turkm. Amyderya, Uzb. Amudaryo; anc. Oxus. river C Asia
Amu-Dar'ya see Amyderya
Amudar'ya/Amudaryo/Amu, Dar"yoi see Amu Darya
Amul see Āmol
Amund Ringnes Island 15 F2 Island Nunavut, N Canada
Amundsen Basin see Fram Basin
Amundsen Plain 132 A4 abyssal plain S Pacific Ocean
Amundsen-Scott 132 B3 US research station Antarctica
Amundsen Sea 132 A4 sea S Pacific Ocean
Amuntai 116 D4 prev. Amoentai. Borneo, C Indonesia
Amur 93 G4 Chin. Heilong Jiang. river China/Russian Federation
Amvrosiyevka see Amvrosiyivka
Amvrosiyivka 87 H3 Rus. Amvrosiyevka. Donets'ka Oblast', SE Ukraine
Amyderya 101 E3 Rus. Amu-Dar'ya. Lebap Welaýaty, NE Turkmenistan
Amyderya see Amu Darya
Amýntaio 82 B4 var. Amindeo; prev. Amíndaion. Dytikí Makedonía, N Greece
Anabar 93 E2 river NE Russian Federation
An Abhainn Mhór see Blackwater
Anaco 37 E2 Anzoátegui, NE Venezuela
Anaconda 22 B2 Montana, NW USA
Anacortes 24 B1 Washington, NW USA
Anadolu Dağları see Doğu Karadeniz Dağları
Anadyr' 93 H1 Chukotskiy Avtonomnyy Okrug, NE Russian Federation
Anadyr' 93 G1 river NE Russian Federation
Anadyr, Gulf of see Anadyrskiy Zaliv
Anadyrskiy Zaliv 93 H1 Eng. Gulf of Anadyr. gulf NE Russian Federation
Anáfi 83 D7 anc. Anaphe. island Kykládes, Greece, Aegean Sea
'Ānah see 'Annah
Anaheim 24 E2 California, W USA
Anaiza see 'Unayzah
Analalava 57 G2 Mahajanga, NW Madagascar
Anamur 94 C5 İçel, S Turkey
Anantapur 110 C2 Andhra Pradesh, S India
Anaphe see Anáfi
Anápolis 41 F3 Goiás, C Brazil
Anār 98 D3 Kermān, C Iran
Anatolia 94 C4 plateau C Turkey
Anatom see Aneityum
Añatuya 42 C3 Santiago del Estero, N Argentina
An Bhearú see Barrow
Anchorage 14 C3 Alaska, USA
Ancona 74 C3 Marche, C Italy
Ancud 43 B6 prev. San Carlos de Ancud. Los Lagos, S Chile
Ancyra see Ankara
Åndalsnes 63 A5 Møre og Romsdal, S Norway
Andalucía 70 D4 cultural region S Spain
Andalusia 20 C3 Alabama, S USA
Andaman Islands 102 B4 island group India, NE Indian Ocean
Andaman Sea 102 C4 sea NE Indian Ocean
Andenne 65 C6 Namur, SE Belgium
Anderlues 65 B7 Hainaut, S Belgium
Anderson 18 C4 Indiana, N USA
Andes 42 B3 mountain range W South America
Andhra Pradesh 113 E5 cultural region E India
Andijon 101 F2 Rus. Andizhan. Andijon Viloyati, E Uzbekistan
Andikíthira see Antikýthira
Andipaxi see Antípaxoi
Andípsara see Antípsara
Ándissa see Ántissa
Andizhan see Andijon
Andkhvoy 100 D3 Fāryāb, N Afghanistan
Andorra 69 A7 off. Principality of Andorra, Cat. Valls d'Andorra, Fr. Vallée d'Andorre. country SW Europe
Andorra see Andorra la Vella
Andorra la Vella 69 A8 var. Andorra, Fr. Andorre la Vielle, Sp. Andorra la Vieja. country capital (Andorra) C Andorra
Andorra la Vieja see Andorra la Vella
Andorra, Principality of see Andorra
Andorra, Valls d'/Andorra, Vallée d' see Andorra
Andorre la Vielle see Andorra la Vella
Andover 67 D7 S England, United Kingdom
Andøya 62 C2 island C Norway
Andreanof Islands 14 A3 island group Aleutian Islands, Alaska, USA
Andrews 27 E3 Texas, SW USA
Andrew Tablemount 118 A4 var. Gora Andryu. seamount W Indian Ocean
Andria 75 D5 Puglia, SE Italy
An Droichead Nua see Newbridge
Andropov see Rybinsk
Ándros 83 D6 Ándros, Kykládes, Greece, Aegean Sea
Ándros 83 C6 island Kykládes, Greece, Aegean Sea
Andros Island 32 B2 island NW Bahamas
Andros Town 32 C1 Andros Island, NW Bahamas
Andryu, Gora see Andrew Tablemount
Aneityum 122 D5 var. Anatom; prev. Kéamu. island S Vanuatu
Ānewetak see Enewetak Atoll
Angara 93 E4 river C Russian Federation
Angarsk 93 E4 Irkutskaya Oblast', S Russian Federation
Ånge 63 C5 Västernorrland, C Sweden
Ángel de la Guarda, Isla 28 B2 island NW Mexico
Angeles 117 E1 off. Angeles City. Luzon, N Philippines
Angeles City see Angeles
Angel Falls 37 E3 Eng. Angel Falls. waterfall E Venezuela
Angel Falls see Ángel, Salto
Angerburg see Węgorzewo
Ångermanälven 62 C4 river N Sweden
Angermünde 72 D3 Brandenburg, NE Germany
Angers 68 B4 anc. Juliomagus. Maine-et-Loire, NW France
Anglesey 67 C5 island NW Wales, United Kingdom
Anglet 69 A6 Pyrénées-Atlantiques, SW France
Angleton 27 H4 Texas, SW USA
Anglia see England
Anglo-Egyptian Sudan see Sudan
Angmagssalik see Ammassalik
Ang Nam Ngum 114 C4 lake C Laos
Angola 56 B2 off. Republic of Angola; prev. People's Republic of Angola, Portuguese West Africa. country SW Africa
Angola Basin 47 B5 undersea basin E Atlantic Ocean
Angola, People's Republic of see Angola
Angola, Republic of see Angola
Angora see Ankara
Angostura see Ciudad Bolívar
Angostura, Presa de la 29 G5 reservoir SE Mexico
Angoulême 69 B5 anc. Iculisma. Charente, W France
Angoumois 69 B5 cultural region W France
Angra Pequena see Lüderitz
Angren 101 F2 Toshkent Viloyati, E Uzbekistan
Anguilla 33 G3 UK dependent territory E West Indies
Anguilla Cays 32 B2 islets SW Bahamas
Anhui 106 C5 var. Anhui Sheng, Anhwei, Wan. province E China
AnhuiSheng/Anhwei Wan see Anhui
Anicium see le Puy
Anina 86 A4 Ger. Steierdorf, Hung. Stájerlakanina; prev. Ştaierdorf-Anina, Steierdorf-Anina, Steyerlak-Anina. Caraş-Severin, SW Romania
Anjou 68 B4 cultural region NW France
Anjouan 57 F2 var. Ndzouani, Nzwani. island SE Comoros
Ankara 94 C3 prev. Angora; anc. Ancyra. country capital (Turkey) Ankara, C Turkey
Ankeny 23 F3 Iowa, C USA
Anklam 72 D2 Mecklenburg-Vorpommern, NE Germany
An Mhuir Cheilteach see Celtic Sea
Annaba 49 E1 prev. Bône. NE Algeria
An Nafud 98 B4 desert NW Saudi Arabia
'Annah 98 B3 var. 'Ānah. Al Anbār, NW Iraq
An Najaf 98 B3 var. Najaf. An Najaf, S Iraq
Annamitique, Chaîne 114 D4 mountain range C Laos
Annapolis 19 F4 state capital Maryland, NE USA
Annapurna 113 E3 mountain C Nepal
An Nāqūrah see En Nâqoûra
Ann Arbor 18 C3 Michigan, N USA
An Nāṣirīyah 98 C3 var. Nasiriya. Dhī Qār, SE Iraq
Anneciacum see Annecy
Annecy 69 D5 anc. Anneciacum. Haute-Savoie, E France
An Nīl al Abyaḍ see White Nile
An Nīl al Azraq see Blue Nile
Anniston 20 D2 Alabama, S USA
Annotto Bay 32 B4 C Jamaica
An Ómaigh see Omagh
Anqing 106 D5 Anhui, E China
Anse La Raye 33 F1 NW Saint Lucia
Anshun 106 B6 Guizhou, S China
Ansongo 53 E3 Gao, E Mali
An Srath Bán see Strabane
Antakya 94 D4 anc. Antioch, Antiochia. Hatay, S Turkey
Antalaha 57 G2 Antsirañana, NE Madagascar
Antalya 94 B4 prev. Adalia; anc. Attaleia, Bibl. Attalia. Antalya, SW Turkey
Antalya, Gulf of 94 B4 var. Gulf of Adalia, Eng. Gulf of Antalya. gulf SW Turkey
Antalya, Gulf of see Antalya Körfezi
Antananarivo 57 G3 prev. Tananarive. country capital (Madagascar) Antananarivo, C Madagascar
Antarctica 132 B3 continent
Antarctic Peninsula 132 A2 peninsula Antarctica
Antep see Gaziantep
Antequera 70 D5 anc. Anticaria, Antiquaria. Andalucía, S Spain
Antequera see Oaxaca
Antibes 69 D6 anc. Antipolis. Alpes-Maritimes, SE France
Anticaria see Antequera
Anticosti, Île d' 17 F3 Eng. Anticosti Island. island Québec, E Canada
Anticosti Island see Anticosti, Île d'
Antigua 33 G3 island S Antigua and Barbuda, Leeward Islands
Antigua and Barbuda 33 G3 country E West Indies
Antikýthira 83 B7 var. Andikíthira. island S Greece
Anti-Lebanon 96 B4 var. Jebel esh Sharqi, Ar. Al Jabal ash Sharqī, Fr. Anti-Liban. mountain range Lebanon/Syria
Anti-Liban see Anti-Lebanon
Antioch see Antakya
Antiochia see Antakya
Antípaxoi 83 A5 var. Andipaxi. island Iónia Nisiá, Greece, C Mediterranean Sea
Antipodes Islands 120 D5 island group S New Zealand
Antipolis see Antibes
Antípsara 83 D5 var. Andípsara. island E Greece
Antiquaria see Antequera
Ántissa 83 D5 var. Ándissa. Lésvos, E Greece
An tIúr see Newry
Antivari see Bar
Antofagasta 42 B2 Antofagasta, N Chile
Antony 68 E2 Hauts-de-Seine, N France
An tSionainn see Shannon
Antsirañana 57 G2 province N Madagascar
Antsohihy 57 G2 Mahajanga, NW Madagascar
An-tung see Dandong
Antwerpen 65 C5 Eng. Antwerp, Fr. Anvers. Antwerpen, N Belgium
Anuradhapura 110 D3 North Central Province, C Sri Lanka
Anvers see Antwerpen
Anyang 106 C4 Henan, C China
A'nyêmaqên Shan 104 D4 mountain range C China
Anykščiai 84 C4 Utena, E Lithuania
Anzio 75 C5 Lazio, C Italy
Ao Krung Thep 115 C5 var. Krung Thep Mahanakhon, Eng. Bangkok. country capital (Thailand) Bangkok, C Thailand
Aomen see Macao
Aomori 108 D3 Aomori, Honshū, C Japan
Aóos see Vjosës, Lumi i
Aoraki 129 B6 prev. Aorangi, Mount Cook. mountain South Island, New Zealand
Aorangi see Aoraki
Aosta 74 A1 anc. Augusta Praetoria. Valle d'Aosta, NW Italy
Aoukâr 52 D3 var. Aouker. plateau C Mauritania
Aouk, Bahr 54 C4 river Central African Republic/Chad
Aouker see Aoukâr
Aozou 54 C1 Borkou-Ennedi-Tibesti, N Chad
Apalachee Bay 20 D3 bay Florida, SE USA
Apalachicola River 20 D3 river Florida, SE USA
Apamama see Abemama
Apaporis, Río 36 C4 river Brazil/Colombia
Apatity 88 C2 Murmanskaya Oblast', NW Russian Federation
Ape 84 D3 Alūksne, NE Latvia
Apeldoorn 64 D3 Gelderland, E Netherlands
Apennines 74 E2 Eng. Apennines. mountain range Italy/San Marino
Apennines see Appennino
Āpia 123 F4 country capital (Samoa) Upolu, SE Samoa
Ap'khazet'i 95 E1 var. Abkhazia. autonomous republic NW Georgia
Apoera 37 G3 Sipaliwini, NW Suriname
Apostle Islands 18 B1 island group Wisconsin, N USA
Appalachian Mountains 13 D5 mountain range E USA
Appingedam 64 E1 Groningen, NE Netherlands
Appleton 18 B2 Wisconsin, N USA
Apulia see Puglia
Apure, Río 36 C2 river W Venezuela
Apurímac, Río 38 D3 river S Peru
Apuseni, Munţii 86 A4 mountain range W Romania
Aqaba/'Aqaba see Al 'Aqabah
Aqaba, Gulf of 98 A4 var. Gulf of Elat, Ar. Khalīj al 'Aqabah; anc. Sinus Aelaniticus. gulf NE Red Sea
'Aqabah, Khalīj al see Aqaba, Gulf of
Āqchah 101 E3 var. Āqcheh. Jowzjān, N Afghanistan
Āqcheh see Āqchah
Aqmola see Astana
Aqtöbe see Aktobe
Aquae Augustae see Dax
Aquae Calidae see Bath
Aquae Flaviae see Chaves
Aquae Grani see Aachen
Aquae Sextiae see Aix-en-Provence
Aquae Solis see Bath
Aquae Tarbelicae see Dax
Aquidauana 41 E4 Mato Grosso do Sul, S Brazil
Aquila/Aquila degli Abruzzi see L'Aquila
Aquisgranum see Aachen
Aquitaine 69 B6 cultural region SW France
'Arabah, Wadi al 97 B7 Heb. Ha'Arava. dry watercourse Israel/Jordan
Arabian Basin 102 A4 undersea basin N Arabian Sea
Arabian Desert see Sahara el Sharqîya
Arabian Peninsula 99 B5 peninsula SW Asia
Arabian Sea 102 A3 sea NW Indian Ocean
Arabicus, Sinus see Red Sea
'Arabī, Khalīj al see Gulf, The
'Arabīyah as Su'ūdīyah, Al Mamlakah al see Saudi Arabia
'Arabīyah Jumhūrīyah, Miṣr al see Egypt
Arab Republic of Egypt see Egypt
Aracaju 41 G3 state capital Sergipe, E Brazil
Araçuai 41 F3 Minas Gerais, SE Brazil
Arad 97 B7 Southern, S Israel
Arad 86 A4 Arad, W Romania
Arafura Sea 120 A3 Ind. Laut Arafuru. sea W Pacific Ocean
Arafuru, Laut see Arafura Sea
Aragón 71 E2 autonomous community E Spain
Araguaia, Río 41 E3 var. Araguaya. river C Brazil
Araguari 41 F3 Minas Gerais, SE Brazil
Araguaya see Araguaia, Río
Ara Jovis see Aranjuez
Arāk 98 C3 prev. Sultānābād. Markazī, W Iran
Arakan Yoma 114 A3 mountain range W Myanmar (Burma)
Araks/Arak's see Aras
Aral see Aralsk, Kazakhstan
Aral Sea 100 C1 Kaz. Aral Tengizi, Rus. Aral'skoye More, Uzb. Orol Dengizi. inland sea Kazakhstan/Uzbekistan
Aral'sk 92 B4 Kaz. Aral. Kzylorda, SW Kazakhstan
Aral'skoye More/Aral Tengizi see Aral Sea
Aranda de Duero 70 D2 Castilla-León, N Spain
Aranđelovac 78 D4 prev. Arandjelovac. Serbia, C Serbia
Arandjelovac see Aranđelovac
Aranjuez 70 D3 anc. Ara Jovis. Madrid, C Spain
Araouane 53 E2 Tombouctou, N Mali
'Ar'ar 98 B3 Al Ḥudūd ash Shamālīyah, NW Saudi Arabia
Ararat, Mount see Büyükağrı Dağı
Aras 95 G3 Arm. Arak's, Az. Araz Nehri, Per. Rūd-e Aras, Rus. Araks; prev. Araxes. river SW Asia
Aras, Rūd-e see Aras
Arauca 36 C2 Arauca, NE Colombia
Arauca, Río 36 C2 river Colombia/Venezuela
Arausio see Orange
Araxes see Aras
Araz Nehri see Aras
Arbela see Arbīl
Arbīl 98 B2 var. Erbil, Irbīl, Kurd. Hawlêr; anc. Arbela. Arbīl, N Iraq
Arbroath 66 D3 anc. Aberbrothock. E Scotland, United Kingdom
Arbuzinka see Arbuzynka
Arbuzynka 87 E3 Rus. Arbuzinka. Mykolayivs'ka Oblast', S Ukraine
Arcachon 69 B5 Gironde, SW France
Arcae Remorum see Châlons-en-Champagne
Arcata 24 A4 California, W USA
Archangel see Arkhangel'sk
Archangel Bay see Chëshskaya Guba
Archidona 70 D5 Andalucía, S Spain
Arco 74 C2 Trentino-Alto Adige, N Italy
Arctic Mid Oceanic Ridge see Nansen Cordillera
Arctic Ocean 133 B3 ocean
Arda 82 C3 var. Ardhas, Gk. Ardas. river Bulgaria/Greece
Ardabīl 98 C2 var. Ardebil. Ardabīl, NW Iran
Ardakān 98 D3 Yazd, C Iran
Ardas 82 D3 var. Ardhas, Bul. Arda. river Bulgaria/Greece
Arḍ aş Şawwān 97 C7 var. Ardh es Suwwān. plain S Jordan
Ardeal see Transylvania
Ardebil see Ardabīl
Ardèche 69 C5 cultural region E France
Ardennes 65 C8 physical region Belgium/France
Ardhas see Arda/Ardas
Ardh es Suwwān see Arḍ aş Şawwān
Ardino 82 D3 Kŭrdzhali, S Bulgaria
Ard Mhacha see Armagh
Ardmore 27 G2 Oklahoma, C USA
Arel see Arlon
Arelas/Arelate see Arles
Arendal 63 A6 Aust-Agder, S Norway
Arensburg see Kuressaare
Arenys de Mar 71 G2 Cataluña, NE Spain
Areópoli 83 B7 prev. Areópolis. Pelopónnisos, S Greece
Areópolis see Areópoli
Arequipa 39 E4 Arequipa, SE Peru
Arezzo 74 C3 anc. Arretium. Toscana, C Italy
Argalastí 83 C5 Thessalía, C Greece
Argenteuil 68 D1 Val-d'Oise, N France
Argentina 43 B5 off. Argentine Republic. country S South America
Argentina Basin see Argentine Basin
Argentine Basin 35 C7 var. Argentina Basin. undersea basin SW Atlantic Ocean
Argentine Republic see Argentina
Argentine Rise see Falkland Plateau
Argentoratum see Strasbourg
Arghandab, Darya-ye 101 E5 river SE Afghanistan
Argirocastro see Gjirokastër
Argo 50 B3 Northern, N Sudan
Argo Fracture Zone 119 C5 tectonic Feature C Indian Ocean
Árgos 83 B6 Pelopónnisos, S Greece
Argostóli 83 A5 var. Argostólion. Kefallonía, Iónia Nisiá, Greece, C Mediterranean Sea
Argostólion see Argostóli
Argun 103 E1 Chin. Ergun He, Rus. Argun'. river China/Russian Federation
Argyrokastron see Gjirokastër
Århus 63 B7 var. Aarhus. Århus, C Denmark
Aria see Herāt
Ari Atoll 110 A4 var. Alifu Atoll. atoll C Maldives
Arica 42 B1 hist. San Marcos de Arica. Tarapacá, N Chile
Aridaía 82 B3 var. Aridea, Aridhaía. Dytikí Makedonía, N Greece
Aridea see Aridaía
Aridhaía see Aridaía
Arīhā 96 B3 Eng. Jericho. Al Karak, W Jordan
Ariminum see Rimini
Arinsal 69 A7 NW Andorra Europe

Arizona – Baldy Mountain

Arizona *26 A2* *off.* State of Arizona, *also known as* Copper State, Grand Canyon State. *state* SW USA
Arkansas *20 A1* *off.* State of Arkansas, *also known as* The Land of Opportunity. *state* S USA
Arkansas City *23 F5* Kansas, C USA
Arkansas River *27 G1* *river* C USA
Arkhangel'sk *92 B2* *Eng.* Archangel. Arkhangel'skaya Oblast', NW Russian Federation
Arkoí *83 E6* *island* Dodekánisa, Greece, Aegean Sea
Arles *69 D6* *var.* Arles-sur-Rhône; *anc.* Arelas, Arelate. Bouches-du-Rhône, SE France
Arles-sur-Rhône *see* Arles
Arlington *27 G2* Texas, SW USA
Arlington *19 E4* Virginia, NE USA
Arlon *65 D8* *Dut.* Aarlen, *Ger.* Arel, *Lat.* Orolaunum. Luxembourg, SE Belgium
Armagh *67 B5* *Ir.* Ard Mhacha. S Northern Ireland, United Kingdom
Armagnac *69 B6* *cultural region* S France
Armenia *36 B3* Quindío, W Colombia
Armenia *95 F3* *off.* Republic of Armenia, *var.* Ajastan, *Arm.* Hayastani Hanrapetut'yun; *prev.* Armenian Soviet Socialist Republic. *country* SW Asia
Armenian Soviet Socialist Republic *see* Armenia
Armenia, Republic of *see* Armenia
Armidale *127 D6* New South Wales, SE Australia
Armstrong *16 B3* Ontario, S Canada
Armyans'k *87 F4* *Rus.* Armyansk. Respublika Krym, S Ukraine
Arnaía *82 C4* *Cont.* Arnea. Kentrikí Makedonía, N Greece
Arnaud *60 A3* *river* Québec, E Canada
Arnea *see* Arnaía
Arnedo *71 E2* La Rioja, N Spain
Arnhem *64 D4* Gelderland, SE Netherlands
Arnhem Land *126 A2* *physical region* Northern Territory, N Australia
Arno *74 B3* *river* C Italy
Arnold *23 G4* Missouri, C USA
Arnswalde *see* Choszczno
Aroe Islands *see* Aru, Kepulauan
Arorae *123 E3* *atoll* Tungaru, W Kiribati
Arrabona *see* Győr
Ar Rahad *see* Er Rahad
Ar Ramādī *98 B3* *var.* Ramadi, Rumadiya. Al Anbār, SW Iraq
Ar Rāmī *96 C4* Ḩimş, C Syria
Ar Ramthā *97 B5* *var.* Ramtha. Irbid, N Jordan
Arran, Isle of *66 C4* *island* SW Scotland, United Kingdom
Ar Raqqah *96 C2* *var.* Rakka; *anc.* Nicephorium. Ar Raqqah, N Syria
Arras *68 C2* *anc.* Nemetocenna. Pas-de-Calais, N France
Ar Rawḑatayn *98 C4* *var.* Raudhatain. N Kuwait
Arretium *see* Arezzo
Arriaca *see* Guadalajara
Arriaga *29 G5* Chiapas, SE Mexico
Ar Riyāḑ *99 C5* *Eng.* Riyadh. *country capital* (Saudi Arabia) Ar Riyāḑ, C Saudi Arabia
Ar Rub 'al Khali *99 C6* *Eng.* Empty Quarter, Great Sandy Desert. *desert* SW Asia
Ar Rustāq *99 E5* *var.* Rostak, Rustaq. N Oman
Ar Ruţbah *98 B3* *var.* Rutba. Al Anbār, SW Iraq
Árta *83 A5* *anc.* Ambracia. Ípeiros, W Greece
Artashat *95 F3* S Armenia
Artemisa *32 B2* La Habana, W Cuba
Artesia *26 D3* New Mexico, SW USA
Arthur's Pass *129 C6* *pass* South Island, New Zealand
Artigas *42 D3* *prev.* San Eugenio, San Eugenio del Cuareim. Artigas, N Uruguay
Art'ik *95 F2* W Armenia
Artois *68 C2* *cultural region* N France
Artsiz *see* Artsyz
Artsyz *86 D4* *Rus.* Artsiz. Odes'ka Oblast', SW Ukraine
Artvin *95 F2* Artvin, NE Turkey
Arua *51 B6* NW Uganda
Aruba *36 C1* *var.* Oruba. *Dutch autonomous region* S West Indies
Aru Islands *see* Aru, Kepulauan
Aru, Kepulauan *117 G4* *Eng.* Aru Islands; *prev.* Aroe Islands. *island group* E Indonesia
Arunāchal Pradesh *113 G3* *prev.* North East Frontier Agency, North East Frontier Agency of Assam. *cultural region* NE India
Arusha *51 C7* Arusha, N Tanzania
Arviat *15 G4* *prev.* Eskimo Point. Nunavut, C Canada
Arvidsjaur *62 C4* Norrbotten, N Sweden
Arys' *92 B5* *Kaz.* Arys. Yuzhnyy Kazakhstan, S Kazakhstan
Arys *see* Arys'
Asadābād *101 F4* *var.* Asaḏābād; *prev.* Chaghasarāy. Konar, E Afghanistan
Asaḏābād *see* Asadābād
Asad, Buḩayrat al *96 C2* *Eng.* Lake Assad. *lake* N Syria
Asahi-dake *108 D2* *mountain* Hokkaidō, N Japan
Asahikawa *108 D2* Hokkaidō, N Japan
Asamankese *53 E5* SE Ghana
Āsānsol *113 F4* West Bengal, NE India
Asben *see* Aïr, Massif de l'
Ascension Fracture Zone *47 A5* *tectonic Feature* C Atlantic Ocean
Ascension Island *45 C5* *dependency of St.Helena* C Atlantic Ocean
Ascoli Piceno *74 C4* *anc.* Asculum Picenum. Marche, C Italy
Asculum Picenum *see* Ascoli Piceno
'Aseb *50 D4* *var.* Assab, *Amh.* Āseb. SE Eritrea
Assen *64 E2* Drenthe, NE Netherlands
Aşgabat *100 C3* *prev.* Ashgabat, Ashkhabad, Poltoratsk. *country capital* (Turkmenistan) Ahal Welaýaty, C Turkmenistan
Ashara *see* Al 'Ashārah
Ashburton *129 C6* Canterbury, South Island, New Zealand
Ashburton River *124 A4* *river* Western Australia
Ashdod *97 A6* *anc.* Azotos, *Lat.* Azotus. Central, W Israel
Asheville *21 E1* North Carolina, SE USA
Ashgabat *see* Aşgabat
Ashkelon *97 A6* *prev.* Ashqelon. Southern, C Israel
Ashkhabad *see* Aşgabat
Ashland *24 B4* Oregon, NW USA
Ashland *18 B1* Wisconsin, N USA
Ashmore and Cartier Islands *120 A3* *Australian external territory* E Indian Ocean
Ashmyany *85 C5* *Rus.* Oshmyany. Hrodzyenskaya Voblasts', W Belarus
Ashqelon *see* Ashkelon
Ash Shadādah *96 D2* *var.* Ash Shaddādah, Jisr ash Shadadi, Shaddādī, Shedadi, Tell Shedadi. Al Ḩasakah, NE Syria
Ash Shaddādah *see* Ash Shadādah
Ash Sharah *97 B7* *var.* Esh Sharā. *mountain range* W Jordan
Ash Shāriqah *98 D4* *Eng.* Sharjah. Ash Shāriqah, NE United Arab Emirates
Ash Shawbak *97 B7* Ma'ān, W Jordan
Ash Shiḩr *99 C6* SE Yemen
Asia *90* *continent*
Asinara *74 A4* *island* W Italy
Asipovichy *85 D6* *Rus.* Osipovichi. Mahilyowskaya Voblasts', C Belarus
Aşkale *95 E3* Erzurum, NE Turkey
Askersund *63 C6* Örebro, C Sweden
Asmara *see* Asmera
Asmera *50 C4* *var.* Asmara. *country capital* (Eritrea) C Eritrea
Aspadana *see* Eşfahān
Asphaltites, Lacus *see* Dead Sea
Aspinwall *see* Colón
Assab *see* 'Aseb
As Sabkhah *96 D2* *var.* Sabkha. Ar Raqqah, NE Syria
Assad, Lake *see* Asad, Buḩayrat al
Aş Şafāwī *97 C6* Al Mafraq, N Jordan
Aş Şaḩrā' ash Sharqīyah *see* Sahara el Sharqîya
As Salamīyah *see* Salamīyah
'Assal, Lac *46 E4* *lake* C Djibouti
As Salţ *97 B6* *var.* Salt. Al Balqā', NW Jordan
Assamaka *see* Assamakka
Assamakka *53 F2* *var.* Assamaka. Agadez, NW Niger
As Samāwah *98 B3* *var.* Samawa. Al Muthanná, S Iraq
Assenede *65 B5* Oost-Vlaanderen, NW Belgium
Assiout *see* Asyūţ
Assiut *see* Asyūţ
Assling *see* Jesenice
Assouan *see* Aswān
Assu *see* Açu
Assuan *see* Aswān
As Sukhnah *96 C3* *var.* Sukhne, *Fr.* Soukhné. Ḩimş, C Syria
As Sulaymānīyah *98 C3* *var.* Sulaimaniya, *Kurd.* Slēmānī. As Sulaymānīyah, NE Iraq
As Sulayyil *99 B5* Ar Riyāḑ, S Saudi Arabia
Aş Şuwār *96 D2* *var.* Şuwār. Dayr az Zawr, E Syria
As Suwaydā' *97 B5* *var.* El Suweida, Es Suweida, Suweida, *Fr.* Soueida. As Suwaydā', SW Syria
As Suways *see* Suez
Asta Colonia *see* Asti
Astacus *see* İzmit
Astana *92 C4* *prev.* Akmola, Akmolinsk, Tselinograd, Aqmola. *country capital* (Kazakhstan) Akmola, N Kazakhstan
Asta Pompeia *see* Asti
Astarabad *see* Gorgān
Asterābād *see* Gorgān
Asti *74 A2* *anc.* Asta Colonia, Asta Pompeia, Hasta Colonia, Hasta Pompeia. Piemonte, NW Italy
Astigi *see* Ecija
Astipálaia *see* Astypálaia
Astorga *70 C1* *anc.* Asturica Augusta. Castilla-León, N Spain
Astrabad *see* Gorgān
Astrakhan' *89 C7* Astrakhanskaya Oblast', SW Russian Federation
Asturias *70 C1* *autonomous community* NW Spain
Asturias *see* Oviedo
Asturica Augusta *see* Astorga
Astypálaia *83 D7* *var.* Astipálaia, *It.* Stampalia. *island* Kykládes, Greece, Aegean Sea
Asunción *42 D2* *country capital* (Paraguay) Central, S Paraguay
Aswān *50 B2* *var.* Assouan, Assuan, Aswân; *anc.* Syene. SE Egypt
Aswân *see* Aswān
Asyūţ *50 B2* *var.* Assiout, Assiut, Asyût, Siut; *anc.* Lycopolis. C Egypt
Asyût *see* Asyūţ
Atacama Desert *42 B2* *Eng.* Atacama Desert. *desert* N Chile
Atacama Desert *see* Atacama, Desierto de
Atafu Atoll *123 E3* *island* NW Tokelau
Atamyrat *100 D3* *prev.* Kerki. Lebap Welaýaty, E Turkmenistan
Aţâr *52 C2* Adrar, W Mauritania
Atas Bogd *104 D3* *mountain* SW Mongolia
Atascadero *25 B7* California, W USA
Atatürk Baraji *95 E4* *reservoir* S Turkey
Atbara *50 C3* *var.* 'Aţbārah. River Nile, NE Sudan
'Aţbārah/'Aţbarah, Nahr *see* Atbara
Atbasar *92 C4* Akmola, N Kazakhstan
Atchison *23 F4* Kansas, C USA
Aternum *see* Pescara
Ath *65 B6* *var.* Aat. Hainaut, SW Belgium
Athabasca *15 E5* Alberta, SW Canada
Athabasca *15 E5* *var.* Athabaska. *river* Alberta, SW Canada
Athabasca, Lake *15 F4* *lake* Alberta/Saskatchewan, SW Canada
Athabaska *see* Athabasca
Athenae *see* Athína
Athens *21 E2* Georgia, SE USA
Athens *18 D4* Ohio, N USA
Athens *27 G3* Texas, SW USA
Athens *see* Athína
Atherton *126 D3* Queensland, NE Australia
Athína *83 C6* *Eng.* Athens, *prev.* Athínai; *anc.* Athenae. *country capital* (Greece) Attikí, C Greece
Athínai *see* Athína
Athlone *67 B5* *Ir.* Baile Átha Luain. C Ireland
Ath Thawrah *see* Madīnat ath Thawrah
Ati *54 C3* Batha, C Chad
Atikokan *16 B4* Ontario, S Canada
Atka *93 G3* Magadanskaya Oblast', E Russian Federation
Atka *14 A3* Atka Island, Alaska, USA
Atlanta *20 D2* *state capital* Georgia, SE USA
Atlanta *27 H2* Texas, SW USA
Atlantic City *19 F4* New Jersey, NE USA
Atlantic-Indian Basin *45 D7* *undersea basin* SW Indian Ocean
Atlantic-Indian Ridge *47 B8* *undersea ridge* SW Indian Ocean
Atlantic Ocean *44 B4* *ocean*
Atlas Mountains *48 C2* *mountain range* NW Africa
Atlasovo *93 H3* Kamchatskaya Oblast', E Russian Federation
Atlas Saharien *48 D2* *var.* Saharan Atlas. *mountain range* Algeria/Morocco
Atlas, Tell *see* Atlas Tellien
Atlas Tellien *80 C3* *Eng.* Tell Atlas. *mountain range* N Algeria
Atlin *14 D4* British Columbia, W Canada
Aţ Ţafīlah *97 B7* *var.* Et Tafila, Tafila. Aţ Ţafīlah, W Jordan
Aţ Ţā'if *99 B5* Makkah, W Saudi Arabia
Attaleia/Attalia *see* Antalya
At Tall al Abyaḑ *96 C2* *var.* Tall al Abyaḑ, Tell Abyad, *Fr.* Tell Abiad. Ar Raqqah, N Syria
Aţ Ţanf *96 D4* Ḩimş, S Syria
Attapu *see* Samakhixai
Attawapiskat *16 C3* Ontario, C Canada
Attawapiskat *16 C3* *river* Ontario, S Canada
At Tibnī *96 D2* *var.* Tibnī. Dayr az Zawr, NE Syria
Attopeu *see* Samakhixai
Attu Island *14 A2* *island* Aleutian Islands, Alaska, USA
Atyrau *92 B4* *prev.* Gur'yev. Atyrau, W Kazakhstan
Aubagne *69 D6* *anc.* Albania. Bouches-du-Rhône, SE France
Aubange *65 D8* Luxembourg, SE Belgium
Aubervilliers *68 E1* Seine-St-Denis, Île-de-France, N France Europe
Auburn *24 B2* Washington, NW USA
Auch *69 B6* *Lat.* Augusta Auscorum, Elimberrum. Gers, S France
Auckland *128 D2* Auckland, North Island, New Zealand
Auckland Islands *120 C5* *island group* S New Zealand
Audern *see* Audru
Audincourt *68 E4* Doubs, E France
Audru *84 D2* *Ger.* Audern. Pärnumaa, SW Estonia
Augathella *127 D5* Queensland, E Australia
Augsbourg *see* Augsburg
Augsburg *73 C6* *Fr.* Augsbourg; *anc.* Augusta Vindelicorum. Bayern, S Germany
Augusta *125 A7* Western Australia
Augusta *21 E2* Georgia, SE USA
Augusta *19 G2* *state capital* Maine, NE USA
Augusta *see* London
Augusta Auscorum *see* Auch
Augusta Emerita *see* Mérida
Augusta Praetoria *see* Aosta
Augusta Trajana *see* Stara Zagora
Augusta Treverorum *see* Trier
Augusta Vangionum *see* Worms
Augusta Vindelicorum *see* Augsburg
Augustobona Tricassium *see* Troyes
Augustodurum *see* Bayeux
Augustoritum Lemovicensium *see* Limoges
Augustów *76 E2* *Rus.* Avgustov. Podlaskie, NE Poland
Aulie Ata/Auliye-Ata *see* Taraz
Aunglan *114 B4* *var.* Allanmyo, Myaydo. Magway, C Myanmar (Burma)
Auob *56 B4* *var.* Oup. *river* Namibia/South Africa
Aurangābād *112 D5* Mahārāshtra, C India
Auray *68 A3* Morbihan, NW France
Aurelia Aquensis *see* Baden-Baden
Aurelianum *see* Orléans
Aurès, Massif de l' *80 C4* *mountain range* NE Algeria
Aurillac *69 C5* Cantal, C France
Aurium *see* Ourense
Aurora *37 F2* NW Guyana
Aurora *22 D4* Colorado, C USA
Aurora *18 B3* Illinois, N USA
Aurora *23 G5* Missouri, C USA
Aurora *see* Maéwo, Vanuatu
Aus *56 B4* Karas, SW Namibia
Ausa *see* Vic
Aussig *see* Ústí nad Labem
Austin *23 G3* Minnesota, N USA
Austin *27 G3* *state capital* Texas, SW USA
Australes, Archipel des *see* Australes, Îles
Australes et Antarctiques Françaises, Terres *see* French Southern and Antarctic Territories
Australes, Îles *121 F4* *var.* Archipel des Australes, Îles Tubuai, Tubuai Islands, *Eng.* Austral Islands. *island group* SW French Polynesia
Austral Fracture Zone *121 H4* *tectonic feature* S Pacific Ocean
Australia *120 A4* *off.* Commonwealth of Australia. *country*
Australia, Commonwealth of *see* Australia
Australian Alps *127 C7* *mountain range* SE Australia
Australian Capital Territory *127 D7* *prev.* Federal Capital Territory. *territory* SE Australia
Australie, Bassin Nord de l' *see* North Australian Basin
Austral Islands *see* Australes, Îles
Austrava *see* Ostrov
Austria *73 D7* *off.* Republic of Austria, *Ger.* Österreich. *country* C Europe
Austria, Republic of *see* Austria
Autesiodorum *see* Auxerre
Autissiodorum *see* Auxerre
Autricum *see* Chartres
Auvergne *69 C5* *cultural region* C France
Auxerre *68 C4* *anc.* Autesiodorum, Autissiodorum. Yonne, C France
Avaricum *see* Bourges
Avarua *123 G5* *dependent territory capital* (Cook Islands) Rarotonga, S Cook Islands
Avasfelsőfalu *see* Negrești-Oaș
Ávdira *82 C3* Anatolikí Makedonía kai Thráki, NE Greece
Aveiro *70 B2* *anc.* Talabriga. Aveiro, W Portugal
Avela *see* Ávila
Avellino *75 D5* *anc.* Abellinum. Campania, S Italy
Avenio *see* Avignon
Avesta *63 C6* Dalarna, C Sweden
Aveyron *69 C6* *river* S France
Avezzano *74 C4* Abruzzo, C Italy
Avgustov *see* Augustów
Aviemore *66 C3* N Scotland, United Kingdom
Avignon *69 D6* *anc.* Avenio. Vaucluse, SE France
Ávila *70 D3* *var.* Avila; *anc.* Abela, Abula, Abyla, Avela. Castilla-León, C Spain
Avilés *70 C1* Asturias, NW Spain
Avranches *68 B3* Manche, N France
Avveel *see* Ivalo, Finland
Avvil *see* Ivalo
Awaji-shima *109 C6* *island* SW Japan
Āwash *51 D5* Āfar, NE Ethiopia
Awbārī *49 F3* SW Libya
Ax *see* Dax
Axel *65 B5* Zeeland, SW Netherlands
Axel Heiberg Island *15 E1* *var.* Axel Heiburg. *island* Nunavut, N Canada
Axel Heiburg *see* Axel Heiberg Island
Axiós *see* Vardar
Ayacucho *38 D4* Ayacucho, S Peru
Ayagoz *92 C5* *var.* Ayaguz, *Kaz.* Ayakoz. *river* E Kazakhstan
Ayamonte *70 C4* Andalucía, S Spain
Ayaviri *39 E4* Puno, S Peru
Aydarko'l Ko'li *101 E2* *Rus.* Ozero Aydarkul'. *lake* C Uzbekistan
Aydarkul', Ozero *see* Aydarko'l Ko'li
Aydın *94 A4* *var.* Aïdin; *anc.* Tralles Aydin. Aydın, SW Turkey
Ayers Rock *see* Uluru
Ayeyarwady *see* Irrawaddy
Ayiá *see* Agiá
Áyios Evstrátios *see* Ágios Efstrátios
Áyios Nikólaos *see* Ágios Nikólaos
Ayorou *53 E3* Tillabéri, W Niger
'Ayoûn el 'Atroûs *52 D3* *var.* Aïoun el Atrous, Aïoun el Atroûss. Hodh el Gharbi, SE Mauritania
Ayr *66 C4* W Scotland, United Kingdom
Ayteke Bi *92 B4* *Kaz.* Zhangaqazaly; *prev.* Novokazalinsk. Kzylorda, SW Kazakhstan
Aytos *82 E2* Burgas, E Bulgaria
Ayutthaya *115 C5* *var.* Phra Nakhon Si Ayutthaya. Phra Nakhon Si Ayutthaya, C Thailand
Ayvalık *94 A3* Balıkesir, W Turkey
Azahar, Costa del *71 F3* *coastal region* E Spain
Azaouâd *53 E3* *desert* C Mali
Azärbaycan/Azärbaycan Respublikasī *see* Azerbaijan
A'zāz *96 B2* Ḩalab, NW Syria
Azerbaijan *95 G2* *off.* Azerbaijani Republic, *Az.* Azärbaycan, Azärbaycan Respublikası; *prev.* Azerbaijan SSR. *country* SE Asia
Azerbaijani Republic *see* Azerbaijan
Azerbaijan SSR *see* Azerbaijan
Azimabad *see* Patna
Azizie *see* Telish
Azogues *38 B2* Cañar, S Ecuador
Azores *70 A4* *var.* Açores, Ilhas dos Açores, *Port.* Arquipélago dos Açores. *island group* Portugal, NE Atlantic Ocean
Azores-Biscay Rise *58 A3* *undersea rise* E Atlantic Ocean
Azotos/Azotus *see* Ashdod
Azoum, Bahr *54 C3* *seasonal river* SE Chad
Azov, Sea of *81 H1* *Rus.* Azovskoye More, *Ukr.* Azovs'ke More. *sea* NE Black Sea
Azovs'ke More/Azovskoye More *see* Azov, Sea of
Azraq, Wāḩat al *97 C6* *oasis* N Jordan
Aztec *26 C1* New Mexico, SW USA
Azuaga *70 C4* Extremadura, W Spain
Azuero, Península de *31 F5* *peninsula* S Panama
Azul *43 D5* Buenos Aires, E Argentina
Azur, Côte d' *69 E6* *coastal region* SE France
'Azza *see* Gaza
Az Zagāzīq *50 B1* *var.* Az Zaqāzīq *var.* Zagazig. N Egypt
Az Zaqāzīq *see* Az Zagāzīq
Az Zarqā' *97 B6* NW Jordan
Az Zāwiyah *49 F2* *var.* Zawia. NW Libya
Az Zilfī *98 B4* Ar Riyāḑ, N Saudi Arabia

B

Baalbek *96 B4* *var.* Ba'labakk; *anc.* Heliopolis. E Lebanon
Baardheere *51 D6* *var.* Bardere, *It.* Bardera. Gedo, SW Somalia
Baarle-Hertog *65 C5* Antwerpen, N Belgium
Baarn *64 C3* Utrecht, C Netherlands
Babadag *86 D5* Tulcea, SE Romania
Babahoyo *38 B2* *prev.* Bodegas. Los Ríos, C Ecuador
Bābā, Kūh-e *101 E4* *mountain range* C Afghanistan
Babayevo *88 B4* Vologodskaya Oblast', NW Russian Federation
Babeldaob *122 A1* *var.* Babeldaop, Babelthuap. *island* N Palau
Babeldaop *see* Babeldaob
Bab el Mandeb *99 B7* *strait* Gulf of Aden/Red Sea
Babelthuap *see* Babeldaob
Babian Jiang *see* Black River
Babruysk *85 D7* *Rus.* Bobruysk. Mahilyowskaya Voblasts', E Belarus
Babuyan Channel *117 E1* *channel* N Philippines
Babuyan Islands *117 E1* *island group* N Philippines
Bacabal *41 F2* Maranhão, E Brazil
Bacău *86 C4* *Hung.* Bákó. Bacău, NE Romania
Băc Bô, Vinh *see* Tongking, Gulf of
Băc Giang *114 D3* Ha Băc, N Vietnam
Bacheykava *85 D5* *Rus.* Bocheykovo. Vitsyebskaya Voblasts', N Belarus
Back *15 F3* *river* Nunavut, N Canada
Bačka Palanka *78 D3* *prev.* Palanka. Serbia, NW Serbia
Bačka Topola *78 D3* *Hung.* Topolya; *prev. Hung.* Bácstopolya. Vojvodina, N Serbia
Bac Liêu *115 D6* *var.* Vinh Loi. Minh Hai, S Vietnam
Bacolod *103 E4* *off.* Bacolod City. Negros, C Philippines
Bacolod City *see* Bacolod
Bácsszenttamás *see* Srbobran
Bácstopolya *see* Bačka Topola
Bactra *see* Balkh
Badajoz *70 C4* *anc.* Pax Augusta. Extremadura, W Spain
Baden-Baden *73 B6* *anc.* Aurelia Aquensis. Baden-Württemberg, SW Germany
Bad Freienwalde *72 D3* Brandenburg, NE Germany
Badger State *see* Wisconsin
Bad Hersfeld *72 B4* Hessen, C Germany
Bad Homburg *see* Bad Homburg vor der Höhe
Bad Homburg vor der Höhe *73 B5* *var.* Bad Homburg. Hessen, W Germany
Bad Ischl *73 D7* Oberösterreich, N Austria
Bad Krozingen *73 A6* Baden-Württemberg, SW Germany
Badlands *22 D2* *physical region* North Dakota/South Dakota, N USA
Badu Island *126 C1* *island* Queensland, NE Australia
Bad Vöslau *73 E6* Niederösterreich, NE Austria
Baeterrae/Baeterrae Septimanorum *see* Béziers
Baetic Cordillera/Baetic Mountains *see* Béticos, Sistemas
Bafatá *52 C4* C Guinea-Bissau
Baffin Bay *15 G2* *bay* Canada/Greenland
Baffin Island *15 G2* *island* Nunavut, NE Canada
Bafing *52 C3* *river* W Africa
Bafoussam *54 A4* Ouest, W Cameroon
Bafra *94 D2* Samsun, N Turkey
Bāft *98 D4* Kermān, S Iran
Bagaces *30 D4* Guanacaste, NW Costa Rica
Bagdad *see* Baghdād
Bagé *41 E5* Rio Grande do Sul, S Brazil
Baghdād *98 B3* *var.* Bagdad, *Eng.* Baghdad. *country capital* (Iraq) Baghdād, C Iraq
Baghdad *see* Baghdād
Baghlān *101 E3* Baghlān, NE Afghanistan
Bago *114 B4* *var.* Pegu. Bago, SW Myanmar (Burma)
Bagoé *52 D4* *river* Côte d'Ivoire/Mali
Bagrationovsk *84 A4* *Ger.* Preussisch Eylau. Kaliningradskaya Oblast', W Russian Federation
Bagrax Hu *see* Bosten Hu
Baguio *117 E1* *off.* Baguio City. Luzon, N Philippines
Baguio City *see* Baguio
Bagzane, Monts *53 F3* *mountain* N Niger
Bahama Islands *see* Bahamas
Bahamas *32 C2* *off.* Commonwealth of the Bahamas. *country* N West Indies
Bahamas *13 D6* *var.* Bahama Islands. *island group* N West Indies
Bahamas, Commonwealth of the *see* Bahamas
Baharly *100 C3* *var.* Bäherden, *Rus.* Bakharden; *prev.* Bakherden. Ahal Welaýaty, C Turkmenistan
Bahāwalpur *112 C2* Punjab, E Pakistan
Bäherden *see* Baharly
Bahia *41 F3* *off.* Estado da Bahia. *region* E Brazil
Bahia *41 F3* *off.* Estado da Bahia. *state* E Brazil
Bahía Blanca *43 C5* Buenos Aires, E Argentina
Bahia, Estado da *see* Bahia
Bahir Dar *50 C4* *var.* Bahr Dar, Bahrdar Giyorgis. Āmara, N Ethiopia
Bahraich *113 E3* Uttar Pradesh, N India
Bahrain *98 C4* *off.* State of Bahrain, Dawlat al Bahrayn, *Ar.* Al Baḩrayn, *prev.* Bahrein; *anc.* Tylos, Tyros. *country* SW Asia
Bahrain, State of *see* Bahrain
Bahrayn, Dawlat al *see* Bahrain
Bahr Dar/Bahrdar Giyorgis *see* Bahir Dar
Bahrein *see* Bahrain
Bahr el, Azraq *see* Blue Nile
Bahr Tabariya, Sea of *see* Tiberias, Lake
Bahushewsk *85 E6* *Rus.* Bogushëvsk. Vitsyebskaya Voblasts', NE Belarus
Baia Mare *86 B3* *Ger.* Frauenbach, *Hung.* Nagybánya; *prev.* Neustadt. Maramureș, NW Romania
Baia Sprie *86 B3* *Ger.* Mittelstadt, *Hung.* Felsőbánya. Maramureș, NW Romania
Baïbokoum *54 B4* Logone-Oriental, SW Chad
Baidoa *see* Baydhabo
Baie-Comeau *17 E3* Québec, SE Canada
Baikal, Lake *93 E4* *Eng.* Lake Baikal. *lake* S Russian Federation
Baikal, Lake *see* Baykal, Ozero
Baile Átha Cliath *see* Dublin
Baile Átha Luain *see* Athlone
Bailén *70 D4* Andalucía, S Spain
Baile na Mainistreach *see* Newtownabbey
Băilești *86 B5* Dolj, SW Romania
Ba Illi *54 B3* Chari-Baguirmi, SW Chad
Bainbridge *20 D3* Georgia, SE USA
Bā'ir *see* Bāyir
Baireuth *see* Bayreuth
Bairiki *122 D2* *country capital* (Kiribati) Tarawa, NW Kiribati
Bairnsdale *127 C7* Victoria, SE Australia
Baishan *107 E3* *prev.* Hunjiang. Jilin, NE China
Baiyin *106 B4* Gansu, C China
Baja *77 C7* Bács-Kiskun, S Hungary
Baja California *26 A4* *Eng.* Lower California. *peninsula* NW Mexico
Baja California Norte *28 B2* *state* NW Mexico
Bajo Boquete *see* Boquete
Bajram Curri *79 D5* Kukës, N Albania
Bakala *54 C4* Ouaka, C Central African Republic
Bakan *see* Shimonoseki
Baker *24 C3* Oregon, NW USA
Baker and Howland Islands *123 E2* *US unincorporated territory* W Polynesia
Baker Lake *15 F3* Nunavut, N Canada
Bakersfield *25 C7* California, W USA
Bakharden *see* Baharly
Bakhchisaray *see* Bakhchysaray
Bakhchysaray *87 F5* *Rus.* Bakhchisaray. Respublika Krym, S Ukraine
Bakherden *see* Baharly
Bakhmach *87 F1* Chernihivs'ka Oblast', N Ukraine
Bākhtarān *see* Kermānshāh
Bakı *95 H2* *Eng.* Baku. *country capital* (Azerbaijan) E Azerbaijan
Bákó *see* Bacău
Bakony *77 C7* *Eng.* Bakony Mountains, *Ger.* Bakonywald. *mountain range* W Hungary
Bakony Mountains/Bakonywald *see* Bakony
Baku *see* Bakı
Bakwanga *see* Mbuji-Mayi
Balabac Island *107 C8* *island* W Philippines
Balabac, Selat *see* Balabac Strait
Balabac Strait *116 D2* *var.* Selat Balabac. *strait* Malaysia/Philippines
Ba'labakk *see* Baalbek
Balaguer *71 F2* Cataluña, NE Spain
Balakovo *89 C6* Saratovskaya Oblast', W Russian Federation
Bālā Morghāb *100 D4* Laghmān, NW Afghanistan
Balashov *89 B6* Saratovskaya Oblast', W Russian Federation
Balasore *see* Bāleshwar
Balaton, Lake *77 C7* *var.* Lake Balaton, *Ger.* Plattensee. *lake* W Hungary
Balaton, Lake *see* Balaton
Balbina, Represa *40 D1* *reservoir* NW Brazil
Balboa *31 G4* Panamá, C Panama
Balcarce *43 D5* Buenos Aires, E Argentina
Balclutha *129 B7* Otago, South Island, New Zealand
Baldy Mountain *22 C1* *mountain* Montana, NW USA

Bâle – Bergara

Bâle see Basel
Balearic Plain see Algerian Basin
Baleares Major see Mallorca
Balearic Islands 71 G3 Eng. Balearic Islands. island group Spain, W Mediterranean Sea
Balearic Islands see Baleares, Islas
Balearis Minor see Menorca
Baleine, Rivière à la 17 E2 river Québec, E Canada
Balen 65 C5 Antwerpen, N Belgium
Bāleshwar 113 F4 prev. Balasore. Orissa, E India
Bălgrad see Alba Iulia
Bali 116 D5 island C Indonesia
Balıkesir 94 A3 Balıkesir, W Turkey
Balīkh, Nahr 96 C2 river N Syria
Balikpapan 116 D4 Borneo, C Indonesia
Balkanabat 100 B2 Rus. Nebitdag. Balkan Welaýaty, W Turkmenistan
Balkan Mountains 82 C2 Bul./SCr. Stara Planina. mountain range Bulgaria/Serbia
Balkh 101 E3 anc. Bactra. Balkh, N Afghanistan
Balkhash 92 C5 Kaz. Balqash. Karaganda, SE Kazakhstan
Balkhash, Lake see Balkhash, Ozero
Balkhash, Ozero 92 C5 Eng. Lake Balkhash, Kaz. Balqash. lake SE Kazakhstan
Balladonia 125 C6 Western Australia
Ballarat 127 C7 Victoria, SE Australia
Balleny Islands 132 B5 island group Antarctica
Ballinger 27 F3 Texas, SW USA
Balochistān see Baluchistān
Balqash see Balkhash/Balkhash, Ozero
Balş 86 B5 Olt, S Romania
Balsas 41 F2 Maranhão, E Brazil
Balsas, Río 29 E5 var. Río Mexcala. river S Mexico
Bal'shavik 85 D7 Rus. Bol'shevik. Homyel'skaya Voblasts', SE Belarus
Balta 86 D3 Odes'ka Oblast', SW Ukraine
Bălţi 86 D3 Rus. Bel'tsy. N Moldova
Baltic Port see Paldiski
Baltic Sea 63 C7 Ger. Ostee, Rus. Baltiskoye More. sea N Europe
Baltimore 19 F4 Maryland, NE USA
Baltischport/Baltiski see Paldiski
Baltiskoye More see Baltic Sea
Baltkrievija see Belarus
Baluchistān 112 B3 var. Balochistān, Beluchistan. province SW Pakistan
Balvi 84 D4 Balvi, NE Latvia
Balykchy 101 G2 Kir. Ysyk-Köl; prev. Issyk-Kul', Rybach'ye. Issyk-Kul'skaya Oblast', NE Kyrgyzstan
Balzers 72 E2 S Liechtenstein
Bam 98 E4 Kermān, SE Iran
Bamako 52 D4 country capital (Mali) Capital District, SW Mali
Bambari 54 C4 Ouaka, C Central African Republic
Bamberg 73 C5 Bayern, SE Germany
Bamenda 54 A4 Nord-Ouest, W Cameroon
Banaba 122 D2 var. Ocean Island. island Tungaru, W Kiribati
Banaras see Vārānasi
Bandaaceh 116 A3 var. Banda Atjeh; prev. Koetaradja, Kutaradja, Kutaraja. Sumatera, W Indonesia
Banda Atjeh see Bandaaceh
Banda, Laut see Banda Sea
Bandama 52 D5 var. Bandama Fleuve. river S Côte d'Ivoire
Bandama Fleuve see Bandama
Bandar 'Abbās see Bandar-e 'Abbās
Bandarbeyla 51 E5 var. Bender Beila, Bender Beyla. Bari, NE Somalia
Bandar-e 'Abbās 98 D4 var. Bandar 'Abbās; prev. Gombroon. Hormozgān, S Iran
Bandar-e Būshehr 98 C4 var. Būshehr, Eng. Bushire. Būshehr, S Iran
Bandar-e Kangān 98 D4 var. Kangān. Būshehr, S Iran
Bandar-e Khamīr 98 D4 Hormozgān, S Iran
Bandar-e Langeh see Bandar-e Lengeh
Bandar-e Lengeh 98 D4 var. Bandar-e Langeh, Lingeh. Hormozgān, S Iran
Bandar Kassim see Boosaaso
Bandar Lampung 116 C4 var. Bandarlampung, Tanjungkarang-Telukbetung; prev. Tandjoengkarang, Tanjungkarang, Teloekbetoeng, Telukbetung. Sumatera, W Indonesia
Bandarlampung see Bandar Lampung
Bandar Maharani see Muar
Bandar Masulipatnam see Machilīpatnam
Bandar Penggaram see Batu Pahat
Bandar Seri Begawan 116 D3 prev. Brunei Town. country capital (Brunei) N Brunei
Banda Sea 117 F5 var. Laut Banda. sea E Indonesia
Bandiagara 53 E3 Mopti, C Mali
Bandırma 94 A3 var. Penderma. Balıkesir, NW Turkey
Bandjarmasin see Banjarmasin
Bandoeng see Bandung
Bandundu 55 C6 prev. Banningville. Bandundu, W Dem. Rep. Congo
Bandung 116 C5 prev. Bandoeng. Jawa, C Indonesia
Bangalore 110 C2 var. Bengalooru. state capital Karnātaka, S India
Bangassou 54 D4 Mbomou, SE Central African Republic
Banggai, Kepulauan 117 E4 island group C Indonesia
Banghāzī 49 G2 Eng. Bengazi, Benghazi, It. Bengasi. NE Libya
Bangka, Pulau 116 C4 island W Indonesia
Bangkok see Ao Krung Thep
Bangkok, Bight of see Krung Thep, Ao
Bangladesh 113 G3 off. People's Republic of Bangladesh; prev. East Pakistan. country S Asia
Bangladesh, People's Republic of see Bangladesh
Bangor 67 C6 NW Wales, United Kingdom
Bangor 67 B5 Ir. Beannchar. E Northern Ireland, United Kingdom
Bangor 19 G2 Maine, NE USA
Bang Pla Soi see Chon Buri
Bangui 55 B5 country capital (Central African Republic) Ombella-Mpoko, SW Central African Republic
Bangweulu, Lake 51 B8 var. Lake Bengweulu. lake N Zambia
Ban Hat Yai see Hat Yai
Ban Hin Heup 114 C4 Viangchan, C Laos
Ban Houayxay/Ban Houei Sai see Houayxay
Ban Hua Hin 115 C6 var. Hua Hin. Prachuap Khiri Khan, SW Thailand
Bani 52 D3 river S Mali
Banias see Bāniyās
Banijska Palanka see Glina
Banī Suwayf 50 B2 var. Beni Suef. N Egypt
Bāniyās 96 B3 var. Banias, Baniyas, Paneas. Ţarţūs, W Syria
Banjak, Kepulauan see Banyak, Kepulauan
Banja Luka 78 B3 Republika Srpska, NW Bosnia and Herzegovina
Banjarmasin 116 D4 prev. Bandjarmasin. Borneo, C Indonesia
Banjul 52 B3 prev. Bathurst. country capital (Gambia) W Gambia
Banks, Îles see Banks Islands
Banks Island 15 E2 island Northwest Territories, NW Canada
Banks Islands 122 D4 Fr. Îles Banks. island group N Vanuatu
Banks Lake 24 B1 reservoir Washington, NW USA
Banks Peninsula 129 C6 peninsula South Island, New Zealand
Banks Strait 127 C8 strait SW Tasman Sea
Bānkura 113 F4 West Bengal, NE India
Ban Mak Khaeng see Udon Thani
Banmo see Bhamo
Banningville see Bandundu
Bañolas see Banyoles
Ban Pak Phanang see Pak Phanang
Ban Sichon see Sichon
Banská Bystrica 77 C6 Ger. Neusohl, Hung. Besztercebánya. Banskobystricky Kraj, C Slovakia
Bantry Bay 67 A7 Ir. Bá Bheanntraí. bay SW Ireland
Banya 82 E2 Burgas, E Bulgaria
Banyak, Kepulauan 116 A3 prev. Kepulauan Banjak. island group NW Indonesia
Banyo 54 B4 Adamaoua, NW Cameroon
Banyoles 71 G2 var. Bañolas. Cataluña, NE Spain
Banzare Seamounts 119 C7 seamount range S Indian Ocean
Banzart see Bizerte
Baoji 106 B4 var. Pao-chi, Paoki. Shaanxi, C China
Baoro 54 B4 Nana-Mambéré, W Central African Republic
Baoshan 106 A6 var. Pao-shan. Yunnan, SW China
Baotou 105 F3 var. Pao-t'ou, Paotow. Nei Mongol Zizhiqu, N China
Ba'qūbah 98 B3 var. Qubba. Diyālá, C Iraq
Baquerizo Moreno see Puerto Baquerizo Moreno
Bar 79 C5 It. Antivari. S Montenegro
Baraawe 51 D6 It. Brava. Shabeellaha Hoose, S Somalia
Bārāmati 112 C5 Mahārāshtra, W India
Baranavichy 85 B6 Pol. Baranowicze, Rus. Baranovichi. Brestskaya Voblasts', SW Belarus
Baranovichi/Baranowicze see Baranavichy
Barbados 33 G1 country SE West Indies
Barbastro 71 F2 Aragón, NE Spain
Barbate de Franco 70 C5 Andalucía, S Spain
Barbuda 33 G3 island N Antigua and Barbuda
Barcaldine 126 C4 Queensland, E Australia
Barcarozsnyó see Râşnov
Barcău see Berettyó
Barce see Al Marj
Barcelona 71 G2 anc. Barcino, Barcinona. Cataluña, E Spain
Barcelona 37 E2 Anzoátegui, NE Venezuela
Barcino/Barcinona see Barcelona
Barcoo see Cooper Creek
Barcs 77 C7 Somogy, SW Hungary
Bardaï 54 C1 Borkou-Ennedi-Tibesti, N Chad
Bardejov 77 D5 Ger. Bartfeld, Hung. Bártfa. Presovský Kraj, E Slovakia
Bardera/Bardere see Baardheere
Barduli see Barletta
Bareilly 113 E3 var. Bareli. Uttar Pradesh, N India
Bareli see Bareilly
Barendrecht 64 C4 Zuid-Holland, SW Netherlands
Barentin 68 C3 Seine-Maritime, N France
Barentsburg 61 G2 Spitsbergen, W Svalbard
Barentsevo More/Barents Havet see Barents Sea
Barentsøya 61 G2 island E Svalbard
Barents Sea 88 C2 Nor. Barents Havet, Rus. Barentsevo More. sea Arctic Ocean
Bar Harbor 19 H2 Mount Desert Island, Maine, NE USA
Bari 75 E5 var. Bari delle Puglie; anc. Barium. Puglia, SE Italy
Bāridah see Al Bāridah
Bari delle Puglie see Bari
Barikot see Barīkowţ
Barīkowţ 101 F4 var. Barikot. Konar, NE Afghanistan
Barillas 30 A2 var. Santa Cruz Barillas. Huehuetenango, NW Guatemala
Barinas 36 C2 Barinas, W Venezuela
Barisal 113 G4 Barisal, S Bangladesh
Barisan, Pegunungan 116 B4 mountain range Sumatera, W Indonesia
Barito, Sungai 116 D4 river Borneo, C Indonesia
Barium see Bari
Barka see Al Marj
Barkly Tableland 126 B3 plateau Northern Territory/Queensland, N Australia
Bârlad 86 D4 prev. Bîrlad. Vaslui, E Romania
Barlavento, Ilhas de 52 A2 var. Windward Islands. island group N Cape Verde
Bar-le-Duc 68 D3 var. Bar-sur-Ornain. Meuse, NE France
Barlee, Lake 125 B6 lake Western Australia
Barlee Range 124 A4 mountain range Western Australia
Barletta 75 D5 anc. Barduli. Puglia, SE Italy
Barlinek 76 B3 Ger. Berlinchen. Zachodnio-pomorskie, NW Poland
Barmen-Elberfeld see Wuppertal
Barmouth 67 C6 NW Wales, United Kingdom
Barnaul 92 D4 Altayskiy Kray, C Russian Federation
Barnet 67 A7 United Kingdom
Barnstaple 67 C7 SW England, United Kingdom
Baroda see Vadodara
Baroghil Pass 101 F3 var. Kowtal-e Barowghīl. pass Afghanistan/Pakistan
Baron'ki 85 E7 Rus. Boron'ki. Mahilyowskaya Voblasts', E Belarus
Barowghīl, Kowtal-e see Baroghil Pass
Barquisimeto 36 C2 Lara, NW Venezuela
Barra 66 B3 island NW Scotland, United Kingdom
Barra de Río Grande 31 E3 Región Autónoma Atlántico Sur, E Nicaragua
Barranca 38 C3 Lima, W Peru
Barrancabermeja 36 B2 Santander, N Colombia
Barranquilla 36 B1 Atlántico, N Colombia
Barreiro 70 B4 Setúbal, W Portugal
Barrier Range 127 C6 hill range New South Wales, SE Australia
Barrow 14 D2 Alaska, USA
Barrow 67 B6 Ir. An Bhearú. river SE Ireland
Barrow-in-Furness 67 C5 NW England, United Kingdom
Barrow Island 124 A4 island Western Australia
Barstow 25 C7 California, W USA
Bar-sur-Ornain see Bar-le-Duc
Bartang 101 F3 river SE Tajikistan
Bartenstein see Bartoszyce
Bártfa/Bartfeld see Bardejov
Bartica 37 F3 N Guyana
Bartın 94 C2 Bartın, NW Turkey
Bartlesville 27 G1 Oklahoma, C USA
Bartoszyce 76 D2 Ger. Bartenstein. Warmińsko-mazurskie, NE Poland
Baruun-Urt 105 F2 Sühbaatar, E Mongolia
Barú, Volcán 31 E5 var. Volcán de Chiriquí. volcano W Panama
Barwon River 127 D5 river New South Wales, SE Australia
Barysaw 85 D6 Rus. Borisov. Minskaya Voblasts', NE Belarus
Basarabeasca 86 D4 Rus. Bessarabka. SE Moldova
Basel 73 A7 Eng. Basle, Fr. Bâle. Basel-Stadt, NW Switzerland
Basilan 117 E3 island Sulu Archipelago, SW Philippines
Basle see Basel
Basra see Al Başrah
Bassano del Grappa 74 C2 Veneto, NE Italy
Bassein see Pathein
Basseterre 33 G4 country capital (Saint Kitts and Nevis) Saint Kitts, Saint Kitts and Nevis
Basse-Terre 33 G3 dependent territory capital (Guadeloupe) Basse Terre, SW Guadeloupe
Basse Terre 33 G4 island W Guadeloupe
Bassikounou 52 D3 Hodh ech Chargui, SE Mauritania
Bass, Îlots de see Marotiri
Bass Strait 127 C7 strait SE Australia
Bassum 72 B3 Niedersachsen, NW Germany
Bastia 69 E7 Corse, France, C Mediterranean Sea
Bastogne 65 D7 Luxembourg, SE Belgium
Bastrop 20 B2 Louisiana, S USA
Bastyn' 85 B7 Rus. Bostyn'. Brestskaya Voblasts', SW Belarus
Basuo see Dongfang
Basutoland see Lesotho
Bata 55 A5 NW Equatorial Guinea
Batae Coritanorum see Leicester
Batajnica 78 D3 Vojvodina, N Serbia
Batangas 117 E2 off. Batangas City. Luzon, N Philippines
Batangas City see Batangas
Batavia see Jakarta
Bătdâmbâng 115 C5 prev. Battambang. Bătdâmbâng, NW Cambodia
Batéké, Plateaux 55 B6 plateau S Congo
Bath 67 D7 hist. Akermanceaster; anc. Aquae Calidae, Aquae Solis. SW England, United Kingdom
Bathinda 112 D2 Punjab, NW India
Bathsheba 33 G1 E Barbados
Bathurst 127 D6 New South Wales, SE Australia
Bathurst 17 F4 New Brunswick, SE Canada
Bathurst see Banjul
Bathurst Island 124 D2 island Northern Territory, N Australia
Bathurst Island 15 F2 island Parry Islands, Nunavut, N Canada
Batin, Wadi al 98 C4 dry watercourse SW Asia
Batman 95 E4 var. İluh. Batman, SE Turkey
Batna 49 E2 NE Algeria
Baton Rouge 20 B3 state capital Louisiana, S USA
Batroûn 96 A4 var. Al Batrūn. N Lebanon
Battambang see Bătdâmbâng
Batticaloa 110 D3 Eastern Province, E Sri Lanka
Battipaglia 75 D5 Campania, S Italy
Battle Born State see Nevada
Bat'umi 95 F2 W Georgia
Batu Pahat 116 B3 prev. Bandar Penggaram. Johor, Peninsular Malaysia
Bauchi 53 G4 Bauchi, NE Nigeria
Bauer Basin 131 F3 undersea basin E Pacific Ocean
Bauska 84 C3 Ger. Bauske. Bauska, S Latvia
Bauske see Bauska
Bautzen 72 D4 Lus. Budyšin. Sachsen, E Germany
Bauzanum see Bolzano
Bavaria see Bayern
Bavarian Alps 73 C7 Ger. Bayrische Alpen. mountain range Austria/Germany
Bavière see Bayern
Bavispe, Río 28 C2 river NW Mexico
Bawīţī 50 B2 var. Bawîţi. N Egypt
Bawîţi see Bawīţī
Bawku 53 E4 N Ghana
Bayamo 32 C3 Granma, E Cuba
Bayan Har Shan 104 D4 var. Bayan Khar. mountain range C China
Bayanhongor 104 D2 Bayanhongor, C Mongolia
Bayan Khar see Bayan Har Shan
Bayano, Lago 31 G4 lake E Panama
Bay City 18 C3 Michigan, N USA
Bay City 27 G4 Texas, SW USA
Baydhabo 51 D6 var. Baydhowa, Isha Baydhabo, It. Baidoa. Bay, SW Somalia
Baydhowa see Baydhabo
Bayern 73 C6 Eng. Bavaria, Fr. Bavière. state SE Germany
Bayeux 68 B3 anc. Augustodurum. Calvados, N France
Bāyir 97 C7 var. Bā'ir. Ma'ān, S Jordan
Bay Islands 30 C1 Eng. Bay Islands. island group N Honduras
Bay Islands see Bahía, Islas de la
Baymak 89 D6 Respublika Bashkortostan, W Russian Federation
Bayonne 69 A6 anc. Lapurdum. Pyrénées-Atlantiques, SW France
Bayou State see Mississippi
Bayram-Ali see Baýramaly
Baýramaly 100 D3 var. Bayramaly; prev. Bayram-Ali. Mary Welaýaty, S Turkmenistan
Bayreuth 73 C5 var. Baireuth. Bayern, SE Germany
Bayrische Alpen see Bavarian Alps
Bayrūt see Beyrouth
Bay State see Massachusetts
Baysun see Boysun
Bayt Laḩm see Bethlehem
Baytown 27 H4 Texas, SW USA
Baza 71 E4 Andalucía, S Spain
Bazargic see Dobrich
Bazin see Pezinok
Beagle Channel 43 C8 channel Argentina/Chile
Béal Feirste see Belfast
Beannchar see Bangor, Northern Ireland, UK
Bear Island see Bjørnøya
Bear Lake 24 E4 lake Idaho/Utah, NW USA
Beas de Segura 71 E4 Andalucía, S Spain
Beata, Isla 33 E3 island SW Dominican Republic
Beatrice 23 F4 Nebraska, C USA
Beaufort Sea 14 D2 sea Arctic Ocean
Beaufort-Wes see Beaufort West
Beaufort West 56 C5 Afr. Beaufort-Wes. Western Cape, SW South Africa
Beaumont 27 H3 Texas, SW USA
Beaune 68 D4 Côte d'Or, C France
Beauvais 68 C3 anc. Bellovacum, Caesaromagus. Oise, N France
Beaver Island 18 C2 island Michigan, N USA
Beaver Lake 27 H1 reservoir Arkansas, C USA
Beaver River 27 F1 river Oklahoma, C USA
Beaver State see Oregon
Beāwar 112 C3 Rājasthān, N India
Bečej 78 D3 Ger. Altbetsche, Hung. Óbecse, Rácz-Becse; prev. Magyar-Becse, Stari Bečej. Vojvodina, N Serbia
Béchar 48 D2 prev. Colomb-Béchar. W Algeria
Beckley 18 D5 West Virginia, NE USA
Bécs see Wien
Bedford 67 D6 E England, United Kingdom
Bedum 64 E1 Groningen, NE Netherlands
Beehive State see Utah
Be'er Menuha 97 B7 prev. Be'ér Menuẖa. Southern, S Israel
Be'ér Menuẖa see Be'er Menuha
Beernem 65 A5 West-Vlaanderen, NW Belgium
Beersheba see Be'er Sheva
Be'er Sheva 97 A7 var. Beersheba, Ar. Bir es Saba; prev. Be'ér Sheva'. Southern, S Israel
Be'ér Sheva' see Be'er Sheva
Beesel 65 D5 Limburg, SE Netherlands
Beeville 27 G4 Texas, SW USA
Bega 127 D7 New South Wales, SE Australia
Begoml' see Byahoml'
Begovat see Bekobod
Behagle see Laï
Behar see Bihār
Beibu Wan see Tongking, Gulf of
Beida see Al Bayḑā'
Beihai 106 B6 Guangxi Zhuangzu Zizhiqu, S China
Beijing 106 C3 var. Pei-ching, Eng. Peking; prev. Pei-p'ing. country capital (China) Beijing Shi, E China
Beilen 64 E2 Drenthe, NE Netherlands
Beira 57 E3 Sofala, C Mozambique
Beirut see Beyrouth
Beit Lekhem see Bethlehem
Beiuş 86 B3 Hung. Belényes. Bihor, NW Romania
Beja 70 B4 anc. Pax Julia. Beja, SE Portugal
Béjar 70 C3 Castilla-León, N Spain
Bejraburi see Phetchaburi
Bekabad see Bekobod
Békás see Bicaz
Bek-Budi see Qarshi
Békéscsaba 77 D7 Rom. Bichiş-Ciaba. Békés, SE Hungary
Bekobod 101 E2 Rus. Bekabad; prev. Begovat. Toshkent Viloyati, E Uzbekistan
Bela Crkva 78 E3 Ger. Weisskirchen, Hung. Fehértemplom. Vojvodina, W Serbia
Belarus 85 B6 off. Republic of Belarus, var. Belorussia, Latv. Baltkrievija; prev. Belorussian SSR, Rus. Belorusskaya SSR. country E Europe
Belarus, Republic of see Belarus
Belau see Palau
Belaya Tserkov' see Bila Tserkva
Bełchatów 76 C4 var. Belchatow. Łódzski, C Poland
Belchatow see Bełchatów
Belcher, Îles see Belcher Islands
Belcher Islands 16 C2 Fr. Îles Belcher. island group Nunavut, SE Canada
Beledweyne 51 D5 var. Belet Huen, It. Belet Uen. Hiiraan, C Somalia
Belém 41 F1 var. Pará. state capital Pará, N Brazil
Belén 30 D4 Rivas, SW Nicaragua
Belen 26 D2 New Mexico, SW USA
Belényes see Beiuş
Belet Huen/Belet Uen see Beledweyne
Belfast 67 B5 Ir. Béal Feirste. national capital E Northern Ireland, United Kingdom
Belfield 22 D2 North Dakota, N USA
Belfort 68 E4 Territoire-de-Belfort, E France
Belgard see Białogard
Belgaum 110 B1 Karnātaka, W India
Belgian Congo see Congo (Democratic Republic of)
België/Belgique see Belgium
Belgium 65 B6 off. Kingdom of Belgium, Dut. België, Fr. Belgique. country NW Europe
Belgium, Kingdom of see Belgium
Belgorod 89 A6 Belgorodskaya Oblast', W Russian Federation
Belgrano II 132 A2 Argentinian research station Antarctica
Belice see Belize/Belize City
Beligrad see Berat
Beli Manastir 78 C3 Hung. Pélmonostor; prev. Monostor. Osijek-Baranja, NE Croatia
Bélinga 55 B5 Ogooué-Ivindo, NE Gabon
Belitung, Pulau 116 C4 island W Indonesia
Belize 30 B1 Sp. Belice; prev. British Honduras, Colony of Belize. country Central America
Belize 30 B1 river Belize/Guatemala
Belize see Belize City
Belize City 30 C1 var. Belize, Sp. Belice. Belize, NE Belize
Belize, Colony of see Belize
Beljak see Villach
Belkofski 14 B3 Alaska, USA
Belle Île 68 A4 island NW France
Belle Isle, Strait of 17 G3 strait Newfoundland and Labrador, E Canada
Bellenz see Bellinzona
Belleville 18 B4 Illinois, N USA
Bellevue 23 F4 Iowa, C USA
Bellevue 24 B2 Washington, NW USA
Bellingham 24 B1 Washington, NW USA
Belling Hausen Mulde see Southeast Pacific Basin
Bellingshausen Abyssal Plain see Bellingshausen Plain
Bellingshausen Plain 131 F5 var. Bellingshausen Abyssal Plain. abyssal plain SE Pacific Ocean
Bellingshausen Sea 132 A3 sea Antarctica
Bellinzona 73 B8 Ger. Bellenz. Ticino, S Switzerland
Bello 36 B2 Antioquia, W Colombia
Bello Horizonte see Belo Horizonte
Bellovacum see Beauvais
Bellville 56 B5 Western Cape, SW South Africa
Belmopan 30 C1 country capital (Belize) Cayo, C Belize
Belogradchik 82 B1 Vidin, NW Bulgaria
Belo Horizonte 41 F4 prev. Bello Horizonte. state capital Minas Gerais, SE Brazil
Belomorsk 88 B3 Respublika Kareliya, NW Russian Federation
Beloretsk 89 D6 Respublika Bashkortostan, W Russian Federation
Belorussia/Belorussian SSR see Belarus
Belorusskaya Gryada see Byelaruskaya Hrada
Belorusskaya SSR see Belarus
Beloshchel'ye see Nar'yan-Mar
Belostok see Białystok
Belovár see Bjelovar
Beloye More 88 C3 Eng. White Sea. sea NW Russian Federation
Belozërsk 88 B4 Vologodskaya Oblast', NW Russian Federation
Belton 27 G3 Texas, SW USA
Bel'tsy see Bălţi
Beluchistan see Baluchistān
Belukha, Gora 92 D5 mountain Kazakhstan/Russian Federation
Belynichi see Byalynichy
Belyy, Ostrov 92 D2 island N Russian Federation
Bemaraha 57 F3 var. Plateau du Bemaraha. mountain range W Madagascar
Bemaraha, Plateau du see Bemaraha
Bemidji 23 F1 Minnesota, N USA
Bemmel 64 D4 Gelderland, SE Netherlands
Benaco see Garda, Lago di
Benares see Vārānasi
Benavente 70 D2 Castilla-León, N Spain
Bend 24 B3 Oregon, NW USA
Bender see Tighina
Bender Beila/Bender Beyla see Bandarbeyla
Bender Cassim/Bender Qaasim see Boosaaso
Bendern 72 E1 NW Liechtenstein Europe
Bendery see Tighina
Bendigo 127 C7 Victoria, SE Australia
Beneschau see Benešov
Beneški Zaliv see Venice, Gulf of
Benešov 77 B5 Ger. Beneschau. Středočeský Kraj, W Czech Republic
Benevento 75 D5 anc. Beneventum, Malventum. Campania, S Italy
Beneventum see Benevento
Bengal, Bay of 102 C4 bay N Indian Ocean
Bengalooru see Bangalore
Bengasi see Banghāzī
Bengazi see Banghāzī
Bengbu 106 D5 var. Peng-pu. Anhui, E China
Benghazi see Banghāzī
Bengkulu 116 B4 prev. Bengkoeloe, Benkoelen, Benkulen. Sumatera, W Indonesia
Benguela 56 A2 var. Benguella. Benguela, W Angola
Benguella see Benguela
Bengweulu, Lake see Bangweulu, Lake
Ben Hope 66 B2 mountain N Scotland, United Kingdom
Beni 55 E5 Nord-Kivu, NE Dem. Rep. Congo
Benidorm 71 F4 País Valenciano, SE Spain
Beni-Mellal 48 C2 C Morocco
Benin 53 F4 off. Republic of Benin; prev. Dahomey. country W Africa
Benin, Bight of 53 F5 gulf W Africa
Benin City 53 F5 Edo, SW Nigeria
Benin, Republic of see Benin
Beni, Río 39 E3 river N Bolivia
Beni Suef see Banī Suwayf
Ben Nevis 66 C3 mountain N Scotland, United Kingdom
Bénoué see Benue
Benson 26 B3 Arizona, SW USA
Bent Jbaïl 97 A5 var. Bint Jubayl. S Lebanon
Benton 20 B1 Arkansas, C USA
Benue 54 B4 Fr. Bénoué. river Cameroon/Nigeria
Beograd 78 D3 Eng. Belgrade. Serbia, N Serbia
Berane 79 D5 prev. Ivangrad. E Montenegro
Berat 79 C6 var. Berati, SCr. Beligrad. Berat, C Albania
Berătău see Berettyó
Berati see Berat
Berau, Teluk 117 G4 var. MacCluer Gulf. bay Papua, E Indonesia
Berbera 50 D4 Sahil, NW Somalia
Berbérati 55 B5 Mambéré-Kadéï, SW Central African Republic
Berck-Plage 68 C2 Pas-de-Calais, N France
Berdichev see Berdychiv
Berdyans'k 87 G4 Rus. Berdyansk; prev. Osipenko. Zaporiz'ka Oblast', SE Ukraine
Berdychiv 86 D2 Rus. Berdichev. Zhytomyrs'ka Oblast', N Ukraine
Beregovo/Beregszász see Berehove
Berehove 86 B3 Cz. Berehovo, Hung. Beregszász, Rus. Beregovo. Zakarpats'ka Oblast', W Ukraine
Berehovo see Berehove
Bereket 100 B2 prev. Rus. Gazandzhyk, Kazandzhik, Turkm. Gazanjyk. Balkan Welaýaty, W Turkmenistan
Beretău see Berettyó
Berettyó 77 D7 Rom. Barcău; prev. Berătău, Beretău. river Hungary/Romania
Berettyóújfalu 77 D6 Hajdú-Bihar, E Hungary
Berezhany 86 C2 Pol. Brzeżany. Ternopil's'ka Oblast', W Ukraine
Berezina see Byerezino
Berezniki 89 D5 Permskaya Oblast', NW Russian Federation
Berga 71 G2 Cataluña, NE Spain
Bergamo 74 B2 anc. Bergomum. Lombardia, N Italy
Bergara 71 E1 País Vasco, N Spain

Bramaputra – Caprivizipfel

Bramaputra *see* Brahmaputra
Brampton *16 D5* Ontario, S Canada
Branco, Rio *34 C3 river* N Brazil
Brandberg *56 A3 mountain* NW Namibia
Brandenburg *72 C3 var.* Brandenburg an der Havel. Brandenburg, NE Germany
Brandenburg an der Havel *see* Brandenburg
Brandon *15 F5* Manitoba, S Canada
Braniewo *76 D2 Ger.* Braunsberg. Warmińsko-mazurskie, N Poland
Brasil *see* Brazil
Brasília *41 F3 country capital* (Brazil) Distrito Federal, C Brazil
Brasil, República Federativa do *see* Brazil
Braşov *86 C4 Ger.* Kronstadt, *Hung.* Brassó; *prev.* Oraşul Stalin. Braşov, C Romania
Brassó *see* Braşov
Bratislava *77 C6 Ger.* Pressburg, *Hung.* Pozsony. *country capital* (Slovakia) Bratislavský Kraj, W Slovakia
Bratsk *93 E4* Irkutskaya Oblast', C Russian Federation
Brattia *see* Brač
Braunsberg *see* Braniewo
Braunschweig *72 C4 Eng./Fr.* Brunswick. Niedersachsen, N Germany
Brava *see* Baraawe
Brava, Costa *71 H2 coastal region* NE Spain
Bravo del Norte, Río/Bravo, Río *see* Grande, Rio
Bravo, Río *28 C1 river* Mexico/USA North America
Brawley *25 D8* California, W USA
Brazil *40 C2 off.* Federative Republic of Brazil, *Port.* República Federativa do Brasil, *Sp.* Brasil; *prev.* United States of Brazil. *country* South America
Brazil Basin *45 C5 var.* Brazilian Basin, Brazil'skaya Kotlovina. *undersea basin* W Atlantic Ocean
Brazil, Federative Republic of *see* Brazil
Brazilian Basin *see* Brazil Basin
Brazilian Highlands *see* Central, Planalto
Brazil'skaya Kotlovina *see* Brazil Basin
Brazil, United States of *see* Brazil
Brazos River *27 G3 river* Texas, SW USA
Brazza *see* Brač
Brazzaville *55 B6 country capital* (Congo) Capital District, S Congo
Brčko *78 C3* Republika Srpska, NE Bosnia and Herzegovina
Brecht *65 C5* Antwerpen, N Belgium
Brecon Beacons *67 C6 mountain range* S Wales, United Kingdom
Breda *64 C4* Noord-Brabant, S Netherlands
Bree *65 D5* Limburg, NE Belgium
Bregalnica *79 E6 river* E FYR Macedonia
Bregenz *35 B7 anc.* Brigantium. Vorarlberg, W Austria
Bregovo *82 B1* Vidin, NW Bulgaria
Bremen *72 B3 Fr.* Brême. Bremen, NW Germany
Bremerhaven *72 B3* Bremen, NW Germany
Bremerton *24 B2* Washington, NW USA
Brenham *27 G3* Texas, SW USA
Brenner, Col du/Brennero, Passo del *see* Brenner Pass
Brenner Pass *74 C1 var.* Brenner Sattel, *Fr.* Col du Brenner, *Ger.* Brennerpass, *It.* Passo del Brennero. *pass* Austria/Italy
Brennerpass *see* Brenner Pass
Brenner Sattel *see* Brenner Pass
Brescia *74 B2 anc.* Brixia. Lombardia, N Italy
Breslau *see* Wrocław
Bressanone *74 C1 Ger.* Brixen. Trentino-Alto Adige, N Italy
Brest *85 A6 Pol.* Brześć nad Bugiem, *Rus.* Brest-Litovsk; *prev.* Brześć Litewski. Brestskaya Voblasts', SW Belarus
Brest *68 A3* Finistère, NW France
Brest-Litovsk *see* Brest
Bretagne *68 A3 Eng.* Brittany, *Lat.* Britannia Minor. *cultural region* NW France
Brewster, Kap *see* Kangikajik
Brewton *20 C3* Alabama, S USA
Brezhnev *see* Naberezhnyye Chelny
Brezovo *82 D2 prev.* Abrashlare. Plovdiv, C Bulgaria
Bria *54 D4* Haute-Kotto, C Central African Republic
Briançon *69 D5 anc.* Brigantio. Hautes-Alpes, SE France
Bricgstow *see* Bristol
Bridgeport *19 F3* Connecticut, NE USA
Bridgetown *33 G2 country capital* (Barbados) SW Barbados
Bridlington *67 D5* E England, United Kingdom
Bridport *67 D7* S England, United Kingdom
Brieg *see* Brzeg
Brig *73 A7 Fr.* Brigue, *It.* Briga. Valais, SW Switzerland
Briga *see* Brig
Brigantio *see* Briançon
Brigantium *see* Bregenz
Brigham City *22 B3* Utah, W USA
Brighton *67 E7* SE England, United Kingdom
Brighton *22 D4* Colorado, C USA
Brigue *see* Brig
Brindisi *75 E5 anc.* Brundisium, Brundusium. Puglia, SE Italy
Briovera *see* St-Lô
Brisbane *127 E5 state capital* Queensland, E Australia
Bristol *67 D7 anc.* Bricgstow. SW England, United Kingdom
Bristol *19 F3* Connecticut, NE USA
Bristol *18 D5* Tennessee, S USA
Bristol Bay *14 B3 bay* Alaska, USA
Bristol Channel *67 C7 inlet* England/Wales, United Kingdom
Britain *58 C3 var.* Great Britain. *island* United Kingdom
Britannia Minor *see* Bretagne
British Columbia *14 D4 Fr.* Colombie-Britannique. *province* SW Canada
British Guiana *see* Guyana
British Honduras *see* Belize
British Indian Ocean Territory *119 B5 UK dependent territory* C Indian Ocean
British Isles *67 island group* NW Europe
British North Borneo *see* Sabah
British Solomon Islands Protectorate *see* Solomon Islands
British Virgin Islands *33 F3 var.* Virgin Islands. *UK dependent territory* E West Indies
Brittany *see* Bretagne
Briva Curretia *see* Brive-la-Gaillarde
Briva Isarae *see* Pontoise
Brive *see* Brive-la-Gaillarde
Brive-la-Gaillarde *69 C5 prev.* Brive; *anc.* Briva Curretia. Corrèze, C France
Brixen *see* Bressanone
Brixia *see* Brescia
Brno *77 B5 Ger.* Brünn. Jihomoravský Kraj, SE Czech Republic
Broceni *84 B3* Saldus, SW Latvia
Brod/Bród *see* Slavonski Brod
Brodeur Peninsula *15 F2 peninsula* Baffin Island, Nunavut, NE Canada
Brod na Savi *see* Slavonski Brod
Brodnica *76 C3 Ger.* Buddenbrock. Kujawski-pomorskie, C Poland
Broek-in-Waterland *64 C3* Noord-Holland, C Netherlands
Broken Arrow *27 G1* Oklahoma, C USA
Broken Bay *126 E1 bay* New South Wales, SE Australia
Broken Hill *127 B6* New South Wales, SE Australia
Broken Ridge *119 D6 undersea plateau* S Indian Ocean
Bromberg *see* Bydgoszcz
Bromley *67 B8* United Kingdom
Brookhaven *20 B3* Mississippi, S USA
Brookings *23 F3* South Dakota, N USA
Brooks Range *14 D2 mountain range* Alaska, USA
Brookton *125 B6* Western Australia
Broome *124 B3* Western Australia
Broomfield *22 D4* Colorado, C USA
Broucsella *see* Brussel/Bruxelles
Brovary *87 E2* Kyyivs'ka Oblast', N Ukraine
Brownfield *27 E2* Texas, SW USA
Brownsville *27 G5* Texas, SW USA
Brownwood *27 F3* Texas, SW USA
Brozha *85 D7* Mahilyowskaya Voblasts', E Belarus
Bruges *see* Brugge
Brugge *65 A5 Fr.* Bruges. West-Vlaanderen, NW Belgium
Brummen *64 D3* Gelderland, E Netherlands
Brundisium/Brundusium *see* Brindisi
Brunei *116 D3 off.* Brunei Darussalam, *Mal.* Negara Brunei Darussalam. *country* SE Asia
Brunei Darussalam *see* Brunei
Brunei Town *see* Bandar Seri Begawan
Brünn *see* Brno
Brunner, Lake *129 C5 lake* South Island, New Zealand
Brunswick *21 E3* Georgia, SE USA
Brunswick *see* Braunschweig
Brusa *see* Bursa
Brus Laguna *30 D2* Gracias a Dios, E Honduras
Brussa *see* Bursa
Brussel *65 C6 var.* Brussels, *Fr.* Bruxelles, *Ger.* Brüssel; *anc.* Broucsella. *country capital* (Belgium) Brussels, C Belgium
Brüssel/Brussels *see* Brussel/Bruxelles
Brüx *see* Most
Bruxelles *see* Brussel
Bryan *27 G3* Texas, SW USA
Bryansk *89 A5* Bryanskaya Oblast', W Russian Federation
Brzeg *76 C4 Ger.* Brieg; *anc.* Civitas Altae Ripae. Opolskie, S Poland
Brześć Litewski/Brześć nad Bugiem *see* Brest
Brzeżany *see* Berezhany
Bucaramanga *36 B2* Santander, N Colombia
Buchanan *52 C5 prev.* Grand Bassa. SW Liberia
Buchanan, Lake *27 F3 reservoir* Texas, SW USA
Bucharest *see* Bucureşti
Buckeye State *see* Ohio
Bu Craa *see* Bou Craa
Bucureşti *86 C5 Eng.* Bucharest, *Ger.* Bukarest, *prev.* Altenburg; *anc.* Cetatea Damboviţei. *country capital* (Romania) Bucureşti, S Romania
Buda-Kashalyova *85 D7 Rus.* Buda-Koshelëvo. Homyel'skaya Voblasts', SE Belarus
Buda-Koshelëvo *see* Buda-Kashalyova
Budapest *77 C6 off.* Budapest Főváros, *SCr.* Budimpešta. *country capital* (Hungary) Pest, N Hungary
Budapest Főváros *see* Budapest
Budaun *112 D3* Uttar Pradesh, N India
Buddenbrock *see* Brodnica
Budimpešta *see* Budapest
Budweis *see* České Budějovice
Budyšin *see* Bautzen
Buena Park *24 E2* California, W USA North America
Buenaventura *36 A3* Valle del Cauca, W Colombia
Buena Vista *39 G4* Santa Cruz, C Bolivia
Buena Vista *71 H5* S Gibraltar Europe
Buenos Aires *42 D4 hist.* Santa Maria del Buen Aire. *country capital* (Argentina) Buenos Aires, E Argentina
Buenos Aires *31 E5* Puntarenas, SE Costa Rica
Buenos Aires, Lago *43 B6 var.* Lago General Carrera. *lake* Argentina/Chile
Buffalo *19 E3* New York, NE USA
Buffalo Narrows *15 F4* Saskatchewan, C Canada
Buff Bay *32 B5* E Jamaica
Buftea *86 C5* Ilfov, S Romania
Bug *59 E3 Bel.* Zakhodni Buh, *Eng.* Western Bug, *Rus.* Zapadnyy Bug, *Ukr.* Zakhidnyy Buh. *river* E Europe
Buga *36 B3* Valle del Cauca, W Colombia
Bughotu *see* Santa Isabel
Buguruslan *89 D6* Orenburgskaya Oblast', W Russian Federation
Buitenzorg *see* Bogor
Bujalance *70 D4* Andalucía, S Spain
Bujanovac *79 E5* SE Serbia
Bujnurd *see* Bojnūrd
Bujumbura *51 B7 prev.* Usumbura. *country capital* (Burundi) W Burundi
Bukarest *see* Bucureşti
Bukavu *55 E6 prev.* Costermansville. Sud-Kivu, E Dem. Rep. Congo
Bukhara *see* Buxoro
Bukoba *51 B6* Kagera, NW Tanzania
Bülach *73 B7* Zürich, NW Switzerland
Bulawayo *56 D3* Matabeleland North, SW Zimbabwe
Bulgan *105 E2* Bulgan, N Mongolia
Bulgaria *82 C2 off.* Republic of Bulgaria, *Bul.* Bŭlgariya; *prev.* People's Republic of Bulgaria. *country* SE Europe
Bulgaria, People's Republic of *see* Bulgaria
Bulgaria, Republic of *see* Bulgaria
Bŭlgariya *see* Bulgaria
Bullion State *see* Missouri
Bull Shoals Lake *20 B1 reservoir* Arkansas/ Missouri, C USA
Bulukumba *117 E4 prev.* Boeloekoemba. Sulawesi, C Indonesia
Bumba *55 D5* Equateur, N Dem. Rep. Congo
Bunbury *125 A7* Western Australia
Bundaberg *126 E4* Queensland, E Australia
Bungo-suido *109 B7 strait* SW Japan
Bunia *55 E5* Orientale, NE Dem. Rep. Congo
Bünyan *94 D3* Kayseri, C Turkey
Buraida *see* Buraydah
Buraydah *98 B4 var.* Buraida. Al Qaşim, N Saudi Arabia
Burdigala *see* Bordeaux
Burdur *94 B4 var.* Buldur. Burdur, SW Turkey
Burdur Gölü *94 B4 salt lake* SW Turkey
Burë *50 C4* Āmara, N Ethiopia
Burgas *82 E2 var.* Bourgas. Burgas, E Bulgaria
Burgaski Zaliv *82 E2 gulf* E Bulgaria
Burgos *70 D2* Castilla-León, N Spain
Burgundy *see* Bourgogne
Burhan Budai Shan *104 D4 mountain range* C China
Buriram *115 D5 var.* Buri Ram, Puriramya. Buri Ram, E Thailand
Buri Ram *see* Buriram
Burjassot *71 F3* País Valenciano, E Spain
Burkburnett *27 F2* Texas, SW USA
Burketown *126 B3* Queensland, NE Australia
Burkina *see* Burkina Faso
Burkina Faso *53 E4 off.* Burkina Faso; *var.* Burkina; *prev.* Upper Volta. *country* W Africa
Burley *24 D4* Idaho, NW USA
Burlington *23 G4* Iowa, C USA
Burlington *19 F2* Vermont, NE USA
Burma *see* Myanmar
Burnie *127 C8* Tasmania, SE Australia
Burns *24 C3* Oregon, NW USA
Burnside *15 F3 river* Nunavut, NW Canada
Burnsville *23 F2* Minnesota, N USA
Burrel *79 D6 var.* Burreli. Dibër, C Albania
Burreli *see* Burrel
Burriana *71 F3* País Valenciano, E Spain
Bursa *94 B3 var.* Brussa, *prev.* Brusa; *anc.* Prusa. Bursa, NW Turkey
Būr Saʻīd *50 B1 var.* Port Said. N Egypt
Burtnieks *84 C3 var.* Burtnieks Ezers. *lake* N Latvia
Burtnieks Ezers *see* Burtnieks
Burundi *51 B7 off.* Republic of Burundi; *prev.* Kingdom of Burundi, Urundi. *country* C Africa
Burundi, Kingdom of *see* Burundi
Burundi, Republic of *see* Burundi
Buru, Pulau *117 F4 prev.* Boeroe. *island* E Indonesia
Busan *see* Pusan
Buşayrah *96 D3* Dayr az Zawr, E Syria
Büshehr/Bushire *see* Bandar-e Büshehr
Busra *see* Al Başrah, Iraq
Busselton *125 A7* Western Australia
Bussora *see* Al Başrah
Buta *55 D5* Orientale, N Dem. Rep. Congo
Butembo *55 E5* Nord-Kivu, NE Dem. Rep. Congo
Butler *19 E4* Pennsylvania, NE USA
Buton, Pulau *117 E4 var.* Pulau Butung; *prev.* Boetoeng. *island* C Indonesia
Bütow *see* Bytów
Butte *22 B2* Montana, NW USA
Butterworth *116 B3* Pinang, Peninsular Malaysia
Button Islands *17 E1 island group* Nunavut, NE Canada
Butuan *117 F2 off.* Butuan City. Mindanao, S Philippines
Butuan City *see* Butuan
Butung, Pulau *see* Buton, Pulau
Butuntum *see* Bitonto
Buulobarde *51 D5 var.* Buulo Berde. Hiiraan, C Somalia
Buulo Berde *see* Buulobarde
Buur Gaabo *51 D6* Jubbada Hoose, S Somalia
Buxoro *100 D2 var.* Bokhara, *Rus.* Bukhara. Buxoro Viloyati, C Uzbekistan
Buynaksk *89 B8* Respublika Dagestan, SW Russian Federation
Büyükağrı Dağı *95 F3 var.* Aghri Dagh, Agri Dagi, Koh I Noh, Masis, *Eng.* Great Ararat, Mount Ararat. *mountain* E Turkey
Büyükmenderes Nehri *94 A4 river* SW Turkey
Buzău *86 C4* Buzău, SE Romania
Büzmeýin *see* Abadan
Buzuluk *89 D6* Orenburgskaya Oblast', W Russian Federation
Byahoml' *85 D5 Rus.* Begoml'. Vitsyebskaya Voblasts', N Belarus
Byalynichy *85 D6 Rus.* Belynichi. Mahilyowskaya Voblasts', E Belarus
Byan Tumen *see* Choybalsan
Bydgoszcz *76 C3 Ger.* Bromberg. Kujawski-pomorskie, C Poland
Byelaruskaya Hrada *85 B6 Rus.* Belorusskaya Gryada. *ridge* N Belarus
Byerezino *85 D6 Rus.* Berezina. *river* C Belarus
Byron Island *see* Nikunau
Bystrovka *see* Kemin
Bytča *77 C5* Žilinský Kraj, N Slovakia
Bytom *77 C5 Ger.* Beuthen. Śląskie, S Poland
Bytów *76 C2 Ger.* Bütow. Pomorskie, N Poland
Byuzmeyin *see* Abadan
Byval'ki *85 D8* Homyel'skaya Voblasts', SE Belarus
Byzantium *see* İstanbul

C

Caála *56 B2 var.* Kaala, Robert Williams, *Port.* Vila Robert Williams. Huambo, C Angola
Caazapá *42 D3* Caazapá, S Paraguay
Caballo Reservoir *26 C3 reservoir* New Mexico, SW USA
Cabañaquinta *70 D1* Asturias, N Spain
Cabanatuan *117 E1 off.* Cabanatuan City. Luzon, N Philippines
Cabanatuan City *see* Cabanatuan
Cabillonum *see* Chalon-sur-Saône
Cabimas *36 C1* Zulia, NW Venezuela
Cabinda *56 A1 var.* Kabinda. Cabinda, NW Angola
Cabinda *56 A1 var.* Kabinda. *province* NW Angola
Cahora Bassa, Albufeira de *56 D2 var.* Lake Cabora Bassa. *reservoir* NW Mozambique
Cabora Bassa, Lake *see* Cahora Bassa, Albufeira de
Caborca *28 B1* Sonora, NW Mexico
Cabot Strait *17 G4 strait* E Canada
Cabo Verde, Ilhas do *see* Cape Verde
Cabras, Ilha das *54 E2 island* S Sao Tome and Principe, Africa, E Atlantic Ocean
Cabrera *71 G3 river* NW Spain
Cáceres *70 C3 Ar.* Qazris. Extremadura, W Spain
Cachimbo, Serra do *41 E2 mountain range* C Brazil
Caconda *56 B2* Huíla, C Angola
Čadca *77 C5 Hung.* Csaca. Žilinský Kraj, N Slovakia
Cadillac *18 C2* Michigan, N USA
Cadiz *117 E2 off.* Cadiz City. Negros, C Philippines
Cádiz *70 C5 anc.* Gades, Gadier, Gadir, Gadire. Andalucía, SW Spain
Cadiz City *see* Cadiz
Cádiz, Golfo de *70 B5 Eng.* Gulf of Cadiz. *gulf* Portugal/Spain
Cadiz, Gulf of *see* Cádiz, Golfo de
Cadurcum *see* Cahors
Caen *68 B3* Calvados, N France
Caene/Caenepolis *see* Qinā
Caerdydd *see* Cardiff
Caer Glou *see* Gloucester
Caer Gybi *see* Holyhead
Caerleon *see* Chester
Caer Luel *see* Carlisle
Caesaraugusta *see* Zaragoza
Caesarea Mazaca *see* Kayseri
Caesarobriga *see* Talavera de la Reina
Caesarodunum *see* Tours
Caesaromagus *see* Beauvais
Caesena *see* Cesena
Cafayate *42 C2* Salta, N Argentina
Cagayan de Oro *117 E2 off.* Cagayan de Oro City. Mindanao, S Philippines
Cagayan de Oro City *see* Cagayan de Oro
Cagliari *75 A6 anc.* Caralis. Sardegna, Italy, C Mediterranean Sea
Caguas *33 F3* E Puerto Rico
Cahors *69 C5 anc.* Cadurcum. Lot, S France
Cahul *86 D4 Rus.* Kagul. S Moldova
Caicos Passage *32 D2 strait* Bahamas/Turks and Caicos Islands
Caiffa *see* Hefa
Cailungo *74 E1* N San Marino
Caiphas *see* Hefa
Cairns *126 D3* Queensland, NE Australia
Cairo *50 B2 var.* El Qâhira, *Ar.* Al Qāhirah. *country capital* (Egypt) N Egypt
Caisleán an Bharraigh *see* Castlebar
Cajamarca *38 B3 prev.* Caxamarca. Cajamarca, NW Peru
Čakovec *78 B2 Ger.* Csakathurn, *Hung.* Csáktornya; *prev. Ger.* Tschakathurn. Medimurje, N Croatia
Calabar *53 G5* Cross River, S Nigeria
Calabozo *36 D2* Guárico, C Venezuela
Calafat *86 B5* Dolj, SW Romania
Calafate *see* El Calafate
Calahorra *71 E2* La Rioja, N Spain
Calais *68 C2* Pas-de-Calais, N France
Calais *19 H2* Maine, NE USA
Calais, Pas de *see* Dover, Strait of
Calama *42 B2* Antofagasta, N Chile
Călăras *see* Călăraşi
Călăraşi *86 D3 var.* Călăras, *Rus.* Kalarash. C Moldova
Călăraşi *86 C5* Călăraşi, SE Romania
Calatayud *71 E2* Aragón, NE Spain
Calbayog *117 E2 off.* Calbayog City. Samar, C Philippines
Calbayog City *see* Calbayog
Calcutta *see* Kolkatta
Caldas da Rainha *70 B3* Leiria, W Portugal
Caldera *42 B3* Atacama, N Chile
Caldwell *24 C3* Idaho, NW USA
Caledonia *30 C1* Corozal, N Belize
Caleta Olivia *43 B6* Santa Cruz, SE Argentina
Calgary *15 E5* Alberta, SW Canada
Cali *36 B3* Valle del Cauca, W Colombia
Calicut *110 C2 var.* Kozhikode. Kerala, SW India
California *25 B7 off.* State of California, *also known as* El Dorado, The Golden State. *state* W USA
California, Golfo de *28 B2 Eng.* Gulf of California; *prev.* Sea of Cortez. *gulf* W Mexico
California, Gulf of *see* California, Golfo de
Călimăneşti *86 B4* Vâlcea, SW Romania
Calisia *see* Kalisz
Callabonna, Lake *127 B5 lake* South Australia
Callao *38 C4* Callao, W Peru
Callatis *see* Mangalia
Callosa de Segura *71 F4* País Valenciano, E Spain
Calmar *see* Kalmar
Caloundra *127 E5* Queensland, E Australia
Caltanissetta *75 C7* Sicilia, Italy, C Mediterranean Sea
Caluula *50 E4* Bari, NE Somalia
Camabatela *56 B1* Cuanza Norte, NW Angola
Camacupa *56 B2 var.* General Machado, *Port.* Vila General Machado. Bié, C Angola
Camagüey *32 C2 prev.* Puerto Príncipe. Camagüey, C Cuba
Camagüey, Archipiélago de *32 C2 island group* C Cuba
Camana *39 E4 var.* Camaná. Arequipa, SW Peru
Camargue *69 D6 physical region* SE France
Ca Mau *115 D6 var.* Quan Long. Minh Hai, S Vietnam
Cambay, Gulf of *see* Khambhāt, Gulf of
Camberia *see* Chambéry
Cambodia *115 D5 off.* Kingdom of Cambodia, *var.* Democratic Kampuchea, Roat Kampuchea, *Cam.* Kampuchea; *prev.* People's Democratic Republic of Kampuchea. *country* SE Asia
Cambodia, Kingdom of *see* Cambodia
Cambrai *68 C2 Flem.* Kambryk, *prev.* Cambray; *anc.* Cameracum. Nord, N France
Cambray *see* Cambrai
Cambrian Mountains *67 C6 mountain range* C Wales, United Kingdom
Cambridge *32 A4* W Jamaica
Cambridge *128 D3* Waikato, North Island, New Zealand
Cambridge *67 E6 Lat.* Cantabrigia. E England, United Kingdom
Cambridge *19 F4* Maryland, NE USA
Cambridge *18 D4* Ohio, NE USA
Cambridge Bay *15 F3 var.* Ikaluktutiak. Victoria Island, Nunavut, NW Canada
Camden *20 B2* Arkansas, C USA
Camellia State *see* Alabama
Cameracum *see* Cambrai
Cameroon *54 A4 off.* Republic of Cameroon, *Fr.* Cameroun. *country* W Africa
Cameroon, Republic of *see* Cameroon
Cameroun *see* Cameroon
Camocim *41 F2* Ceará, E Brazil
Camopi *37 H3* E French Guiana
Campamento *30 C2* Olancho, C Honduras
Campania *75 D5 Eng.* Champagne. *region* S Italy
Campbell, Cape *129 D5 headland* South Island, New Zealand
Campbell Island *120 D5 island* S New Zealand
Campbell Plateau *120 D5 undersea plateau* SW Pacific Ocean
Campbell River *14 D5* Vancouver Island, British Columbia, SW Canada
Campeche *29 G4* Campeche, SE Mexico
Campeche, Bahía de *29 F4 Eng.* Bay of Campeche. *bay* E Mexico
Campeche, Bay of *see* Campeche, Bahía de
Câm Pha *114 E3* Quang Ninh, N Vietnam
Câmpina *86 C4 prev.* Cîmpina. Prahova, SE Romania
Campina Grande *41 G2* Paraíba, E Brazil
Campinas *41 F4* São Paulo, S Brazil
Campobasso *75 D5* Molise, C Italy
Campo Criptana *see* Campo de Criptana
Campo de Criptana *71 E3 var.* Campo Criptana. Castilla-La Mancha, C Spain
Campo dos Goitacazes *see* Campos
Campo Grande *41 E4 state capital* Mato Grosso do Sul, SW Brazil
Campos *41 F4 var.* Campo dos Goitacazes. Rio de Janeiro, SE Brazil
Câmpulung *86 B4 prev.* Câmpulung-Muşcel, Cîmpulung. Argeş, S Romania
Câmpulung-Muşcel *see* Câmpulung
Campus Stellae *see* Santiago
Cam Ranh *115 E6* Khanh Hoa, S Vietnam
Canada *12 B4 country* N North America
Canada Basin *12 C2 undersea basin* Arctic Ocean
Canadian River *27 E2 river* SW USA
Çanakkale *94 A3 var.* Dardanelli; *prev.* Chanak, Kale Sultanie. Çanakkale, W Turkey
Cananea *28 B1* Sonora, NW Mexico
Canarreos, Archipiélago de los *32 B2 island group* W Cuba
Canary Islands *48 A2 Eng.* Canary Islands. *island group* Spain, NE Atlantic Ocean
Canary Islands *see* Canarias, Islas
Cañas *30 D4* Guanacaste, NW Costa Rica
Canaveral, Cape *21 E4 headland* Florida, SE USA
Canavieiras *41 G3* Bahia, E Brazil
Canberra *120 C4 country capital* (Australia) Australian Capital Territory, SE Australia
Cancún *29 H3* Quintana Roo, SE Mexico
Candia *see* Irákleio
Canea *see* Chaniá
Cangzhou *106 D4* Hebei, E China
Caniapiscau *17 E2 river* Québec, E Canada
Caniapiscau, Réservoir de *16 D3 reservoir* Québec, C Canada
Canik Dağları *94 D2 mountain range* N Turkey
Canillo *69 A7* Canillo, C Andorra Europe
Çankırı *94 C3 var.* Chankiri; *anc.* Gangra, Germanicopolis. Çankın, N Turkey
Cannanore *110 B2 var.* Kannur. Kerala, SW India
Cannes *69 D6* Alpes-Maritimes, SE France
Canoas *41 E5* Rio Grande do Sul, S Brazil
Canon City *22 C5* Colorado, C USA
Cantabria *70 D1 autonomous community* N Spain
Cantábrica, Cordillera *70 C1 mountain range* N Spain
Cantabrigia *see* Cambridge
Cantaura *37 E2* Anzoátegui, NE Venezuela
Canterbury *67 E7 hist.* Cantwaraburh; *anc.* Durovernum, *Lat.* Cantuaria. SE England, United Kingdom
Canterbury Bight *129 C6 bight* South Island, New Zealand
Canterbury Plains *129 C6 plain* South Island, New Zealand
Cân Thơ *115 E6* Cân Thơ, S Vietnam
Canton *20 B2* Mississippi, S USA
Canton *18 D4* Ohio, N USA
Canton *see* Guangzhou
Canton Island *see* Kanton
Cantuaria/Cantwaraburh *see* Canterbury
Canyon *27 E2* Texas, SW USA
Cao Bằng *114 D3 var.* Caobang. Cao Bằng, N Vietnam
Caobang *see* Cao Bằng
Cap-Breton, Île du *see* Cape Breton Island
Cape Barren Island *127 C8 island* Furneaux Group, Tasmania, SE Australia
Cape Basin *47 B7 undersea basin* S Atlantic Ocean
Cape Breton Island *17 G4 Fr.* Île du Cap-Breton. *island* Nova Scotia, SE Canada
Cape Charles *19 F5* Virginia, NE USA
Cape Coast *53 E5 prev.* Cape Coast Castle. S Ghana
Cape Coast Castle *see* Cape Coast
Cape Girardeau *23 H5* Missouri, C USA
Capelle aan den IJssel *64 C4* Zuid-Holland, SW Netherlands
Cape Palmas *see* Harper
Cape Saint Jacques *see* Vung Tau
Cape Town *56 B5 var.* Ekapa, *Afr.* Kaapstad, Kapstad. *country capital* (South Africa-legislative capital) Western Cape, SW South Africa
Cape Verde *52 A2 off.* Republic of Cape Verde, *Port.* Cabo Verde, Ilhas do Cabo Verde. *country* E Atlantic Ocean
Cape Verde Basin *44 C4 undersea basin* E Atlantic Ocean
Cape Verde Plain *44 C4 abyssal plain* E Atlantic Ocean
Cape Verde, Republic of *see* Cape Verde
Cape York Peninsula *126 C2 peninsula* Queensland, N Australia
Cap-Haïtien *32 D3 var.* Le Cap. N Haiti
Capira *31 G5* Panamá, C Panama
Capitán Arturo Prat *132 A2 Chilean research station* South Shetland Islands, Antarctica
Capitán Pablo Lagerenza *42 D1 var.* Mayor Pablo Lagerenza. Chaco, N Paraguay
Capodistria *see* Koper
Capri *75 C5 island* S Italy
Caprivi Concession *see* Caprivi Strip
Caprivi Strip *56 C3 Ger.* Caprivizipfel; *prev.* Caprivi Concession. *cultural region* NE Namibia
Caprivizipfel *see* Caprivi Strip

Cap Saint-Jacques – Chinese Empire

Cap Saint-Jacques *see* Vung Tau
Caquetá, Río *36 C5 var.* Rio Japurá, Yapurá. *river* Brazil/Colombia
Caquetá, Río *see* Japurá, Rio
CAR *see* Central African Republic
Caracal *86 B5* Olt, S Romania
Caracaraí *40 D1* Rondônia, W Brazil
Caracas *36 D1 country capital* (Venezuela) Distrito Federal, N Venezuela
Caralis *see* Cagliari
Caratasca, Laguna de *31 E2 lagoon* NE Honduras
Carballiño *see* O Carballiño
Carbondale *18 B5* Illinois, N USA
Carbonia *75 A6 var.* Carbonia Centro. Sardegna, Italy, C Mediterranean Sea
Carbonia Centro *see* Carbonia
Carcaso *see* Carcassonne
Carcassonne *69 C6 anc.* Carcaso. Aude, S France
Cardamomes, Chaîne des *see* Krâvanh, Chuŏr Phnum
Cardamom Mountains *see* Krâvanh, Chuŏr Phnum
Cárdenas *32 B2* Matanzas, W Cuba
Cardiff *67 C7 Wel.* Caerdydd. *national capital* S Wales, United Kingdom
Cardigan Bay *67 C6 bay* W Wales, United Kingdom
Carei *86 B3 Ger.* Gross-Karol, Karol, *Hung.* Nagykároly; *prev.* Careii-Mari. Satu Mare, NW Romania
Careii-Mari *see* Carei
Carey, Lake *125 B6 lake* Western Australia
Cariaco *37 E1* Sucre, NE Venezuela
Caribbean Sea *32 C4 sea* W Atlantic Ocean
Caribrod *see* Dimitrovgrad
Carlisle *66 C4 anc.* Caer Luel, Luguvallium, Luguvallum. NW England, United Kingdom
Carlow *67 B6 Ir.* Ceatharlach. SE Ireland
Carlsbad *26 D3* New Mexico, SW USA
Carlsbad *see* Karlovy Vary
Carlsberg Ridge *118 B4 undersea ridge* S Arabian Sea
Carlsruhe *see* Karlsruhe
Carmana/Carmania *see* Kermān
Carmarthen *67 C6* SW Wales, United Kingdom
Carmaux *69 C6* Tarn, S France
Carmel *18 C4* Indiana, N USA
Carmelita *30 B1* Petén, N Guatemala
Carmen *29 G4 var.* Ciudad del Carmen. Campeche, SE Mexico
Carmona *70 C4* Andalucía, S Spain
Carmona *see* Uíge
Carnaro *see* Kvarner
Carnarvon *125 A5* Western Australia
Carnegie, Lake *125 B5 salt lake* Western Australia
Car Nicobar *111 F3 island* Nicobar Islands, India, NE Indian Ocean
Caroạo, Ilha *54 E1 island* N Sao Tome and Principe, Africa, E Atlantic Ocean
Carolina *41 F2* Maranhão, E Brazil
Caroline Island *see* Millennium Island
Caroline Islands *122 B2 island group* C Micronesia
Carolopois *see* Châlons-en-Champagne
Caroní, Río *37 E3 river* E Venezuela
Caronium *see* A Coruña
Carora *36 C1* Lara, N Venezuela
Carpathian Mountains *59 E4 var.* Carpathians, *Cz./Pol.* Karpaty, *Ger.* Karpaten. *mountain range* E Europe
Carpathians *see* Carpathian Mountains
Carpathos/Carpathus *see* Kárpathos
Carpaţii Meridionalii *86 B4 var.* Alpi Transilvaniei, Carpaţii Sudici, *Eng.* South Carpathians, Transylvanian Alps, *Ger.* Südkarpaten, Transsylvanische Alpen, *Hung.* Déli-Kárpátok, Erdélyi-Havasok. *mountain range* C Romania
Carpaţii Sudici *see* Carpaţii Meridionalii
Carpentaria, Gulf of *126 B2 gulf* N Australia
Carpi *74 C2* Emilia-Romagna, N Italy
Carrara *74 B3* Toscana, C Italy
Carson City *25 C5 state capital* Nevada, W USA
Carson Sink *25 C5 salt flat* Nevada, W USA
Carstensz, Puntjak *see* Jaya, Puncak
Cartagena *36 B1 var.* Cartagena de los Indes. Bolívar, NW Colombia
Cartagena *71 F4 anc.* Carthago Nova. Murcia, SE Spain
Cartagena de los Indes *see* Cartagena
Cartago *31 E4* Cartago, C Costa Rica
Carthage *23 F5* Missouri, C USA
Carthago Nova *see* Cartagena
Cartwright *17 F2* Newfoundland and Labrador, E Canada
Carúpano *37 E1* Sucre, NE Venezuela
Carusbur *see* Cherbourg
Caruthersville *23 H5* Missouri, C USA
Cary *21 F1* North Carolina, SE USA
Casablanca *48 C2 Ar.* Dar-el-Beida. NW Morocco
Casa Grande *26 B2* Arizona, SW USA
Cascade Range *24 B3 mountain range* Oregon/Washington, NW USA
Cascadia Basin *12 A4 undersea basin* NE Pacific Ocean
Cascais *70 B4* Lisboa, C Portugal
Caserta *75 D5* Campania, S Italy
Casey *132 D4 Australian research station* Antarctica
Čáslav *77 B5 Ger.* Tschaslau. Střední Čechy, C Czech Republic
Casper *22 C3* Wyoming, C USA
Caspian Depression *89 B7 Kaz.* Kaspīy Mangy Oypaty, *Rus.* Prikaspiyskaya Nizmennost'. *depression* Kazakhstan/Russian Federation
Caspian Sea *92 A4 Az.* Xäzär Dänizi, *Kaz.* Kaspiy Tengizi, *Per.* Baḩr-e Khazar, Daryā-ye Khazar, *Rus.* Kaspiyskoye More. *inland sea* Asia/Europe
Cassai *see* Kasai
Cassel *see* Kassel
Castamoni *see* Kastamonu
Casteggio *74 B2* Lombardia, N Italy
Castelló de la Plana *see* Castellón de la Plana
Castellón *see* Castellón de la Plana
Castellón de la Plana *71 F3 var.* Castellón, *Cat.* Castelló de la Plana. País Valenciano, E Spain
Castelnaudary *69 C6* Aude, S France
Castelo Branco *70 C3* Castelo Branco, C Portugal
Castelsarrasin *69 B6* Tarn-et-Garonne, S France
Castelvetrano *75 C7* Sicilia, Italy, C Mediterranean Sea
Castilla-La Mancha *71 E3 autonomous community* NE Spain
Castilla-León *70 C2 var.* Castillia y Leon. *autonomous community* NW Spain
Castillia y Leon *see* Castilla-León
Castlebar *67 A5 Ir.* Caisleán an Bharraigh. W Ireland
Castleford *67 D5* N England, United Kingdom
Castle Harbour *20 B5 inlet* Bermuda, NW Atlantic Ocean
Castra Regina *see* Regensburg
Castricum *64 C3* Noord-Holland, W Netherlands
Castries *33 F1 country capital* (Saint Lucia) N Saint Lucia
Castro *43 B6* Los Lagos, W Chile
Castrovillari *75 D6* Calabria, SW Italy
Castuera *70 D4* Extremadura, W Spain
Caswell Sound *129 A7 sound* South Island, New Zealand
Catacamas *30 D2* Olancho, C Honduras
Catacaos *38 B3* Piura, NW Peru
Catalan Bay *71 H4 bay* E Gibraltar, Mediterranean Sea
Cataluña *71 G2* N Spain
Catamarca *see* San Fernando del Valle de Catamarca
Catania *75 D7* Sicilia, Italy, C Mediterranean Sea
Catanzaro *75 D6* Calabria, SW Italy
Catarroja *71 F3* País Valenciano, E Spain
Cat Island *32 C1 island* C Bahamas
Catskill Mountains *19 F3 mountain range* New York, NE USA
Cattaro *see* Kotor
Cauca, Río *36 B2 river* N Colombia
Caucasia *36 B2* Antioquia, NW Colombia
Caucasus *59 G4 Rus.* Kavkaz. *mountain range* Georgia/Russian Federation
Caura, Río *37 E3 river* C Venezuela
Cavaia *see* Kavajë
Cavalla *52 D5 var.* Cavally, Cavally Fleuve. *river* Côte d'Ivoire/Liberia
Cavally/Cavally Fleuve *see* Cavalla
Caviana de Fora, Ilha *41 E1 var.* Ilha Caviana. *island* N Brazil
Caviana, Ilha *see* Caviana de Fora, Ilha
Cawnpore *see* Kānpur
Caxamarca *see* Cajamarca
Caxito *56 B1* Bengo, NW Angola
Cayenne *37 H3 dependent territory/ arrondissement capital* (French Guiana) NE French Guiana
Cayes *32 D3 var.* Les Cayes. SW Haiti
Cayman Brac *32 B3 island* E Cayman Islands
Cayman Islands *32 B3 UK dependent territory* W West Indies
Cayo *see* San Ignacio
Cay Sal *32 B2 islet* SW Bahamas
Cazin *78 B3* Federacija Bosna I Hercegovina, NW Bosnia and Herzegovina
Cazorla *71 E4* Andalucía, S Spain
Ceadâr-Lunga *see* Ciadîr-Lunga
Ceará *41 F2 off.* Estado do Ceará. *region* C Brazil
Ceará *41 F2 off.* Estado do Ceará. *state* C Brazil
Ceará *see* Fortaleza
Ceara Abyssal Plain *see* Ceará Plain
Ceará, Estado do *see* Ceará
Ceará Plain *34 E3 var.* Ceara Abyssal Plain. *abyssal plain* W Atlantic Ocean
Ceatharlach *see* Carlow
Cébaco, Isla *31 F5 island* SW Panama
Cebu *117 E2 off.* Cebu City. Cebu, C Philippines
Cebu City *see* Cebu
Čechy *see* Bohemia
Cecina *74 B3* Toscana, C Italy
Cedar City *22 A5* Utah, W USA
Cedar Falls *23 G3* Iowa, C USA
Cedar Lake *16 A2 lake* Manitoba, C Canada
Cedar Rapids *23 G3* Iowa, C USA
Cedros, Isla *28 A2 island* W Mexico
Ceduna *127 A6* South Australia
Cefalù *75 C7 anc.* Cephaloedium. Sicilia, Italy, C Mediterranean Sea
Celebes *see* Sulawesi
Celebes Sea *117 E3 Ind.* Laut Sulawesi. *sea* Indonesia/Philippines
Celje *73 E7 Ger.* Cilli. C Slovenia
Celldömölk *77 C6* Vas, W Hungary
Celle *72 B3 var.* Zelle. Niedersachsen, N Germany
Celovec *see* Klagenfurt
Celtic Sea *67 B7 Ir.* An Mhuir Cheilteach. *sea* SW British Isles
Celtic Shelf *58 B3 continental shelf* E Atlantic Ocean
Cenderawasih, Teluk *117 G4 var.* Teluk Irian, Teluk Sarera. *bay* W Pacific Ocean
Cenon *69 B5* Gironde, SW France
Centennial State *see* Colorado
Centrafricaine, République *see* Central African Republic
Central African Republic *54 C4 var.* République Centrafricaine, *abbrev.* CAR; *prev.* Ubangi-Shari, Oubangui-Chari, Territoire de l'Oubangui-Chari. *country* C Africa
Central, Cordillera *36 B3 mountain range* W Colombia
Cordillera Central *33 E3 mountain range* C Dominican Republic
Cordillera Central *31 F5 mountain range* C Panama
Central, Cordillera *117 E1 mountain range* Luzon, N Philippines
Central Group *see* Inner Islands
Centralia *24 B2* Washington, NW USA
Central Indian Ridge *see* Mid-Indian Ridge
Central Makran Range *112 A3 mountain range* W Pakistan
Central Pacific Basin *120 D1 undersea basin* C Pacific Ocean
Central, Planalto *41 F3 var.* Brazilian Highlands. *mountain range* E Brazil
Central Provinces and Berar *see* Madhya Pradesh
Central Range *122 B3 mountain range* NW Papua New Guinea
Central Russian Upland *see* Srednerusskaya Vozvyshennost'
Central Siberian Plateau *92 D3 var.* Central Siberian Uplands, *Eng.* Central Siberian Plateau. *mountain range* N Russian Federation
Central Siberian Plateau/Central Siberian Uplands *see* Srednesibirskoye Ploskogor'ye
Central, Sistema *70 D3 mountain range* C Spain
Central Valley *25 B6 valley* California, W USA
Centum Cellae *see* Civitavecchia
Ceos *see* Tziá
Cephaloedium *see* Cefalù
Ceram *see* Seram, Pulau
Ceram Sea *117 F4 Ind.* Laut Seram. *sea* E Indonesia
Cerasus *see* Giresun
Cereté *36 B2* Córdoba, NW Colombia
Cergy-Pontoise *see* Pontoise
Cerignola *75 D5* Puglia, SE Italy
Çerkeş *94 C2* Çankin, N Turkey
Cernăuţi *see* Chernivtsi
Cernay *68 E4* Haut-Rhin, NE France
Cerro de Pasco *38 C3* Pasco, C Peru
Cervera *71 F2* Cataluña, NE Spain
Cervino, Monte *see* Matterhorn
Cesena *74 C3 anc.* Caesena. Emilia-Romagna, N Italy
Cēsis *84 D3 Ger.* Wenden. Cēsis, C Latvia
Česká Republika *see* Czech Republic
České Budějovice *77 B5 Ger.* Budweis. Jihočeský Kraj, S Czech Republic
Český Krumlov *77 A5 var.* Böhmisch-Krumau, *Ger.* Krummau. Jihočeský Kraj, S Czech Republic
Český Les *see* Bohemian Forest
Cetatea Damboviţei *see* Bucureşti
Cetinje *79 C5 It.* Cettigne. S Montenegro
Cette *see* Sète
Cettigne *see* Cetinje
Ceuta *48 C2 enclave* Spain, N Africa
Cévennes *69 C6 mountain range* S France
Ceyhan *94 D4* Adana, S Turkey
Ceylanpınar *95 E4* Şanlıurfa, SE Turkey
Ceylon *see* Sri Lanka
Ceylon Plain *102 B4 abyssal plain* N Indian Ocean
Ceyre to the Caribs *see* Marie-Galante
Chachapoyas *38 B2* Amazonas, NW Peru
Chachevichy *85 D6 Rus.* Chechevichi. Mahilyowskaya Voblasts', E Belarus
Chaco *see* Gran Chaco
Chad *54 C3 off.* Republic of Chad, *Fr.* Tchad. *country* C Africa
Chad, Lake *54 B3 Fr.* Lac Tchad. *lake* C Africa
Chad, Republic of *see* Chad
Chadron *22 D3* Nebraska, C USA
Chadyr-Lunga *see* Ciadîr-Lunga
Chagai Hills *112 A2 var.* Chāh Gay. *mountain range* Afghanistan/Pakistan
Chaghasarāy *see* Asadābād
Chagos-Laccadive Plateau *102 B4 undersea plateau* N Indian Ocean
Chagos Trench *119 C5 trench* N Indian Ocean
Chāh Gay *see* Chāgai Hills
Chaillu, Massif du *55 B6 mountain range* C Gabon
Chain Ridge *118 B4 undersea ridge* W Indian Ocean
Chajul *30 B2* Quiché, W Guatemala
Chakhānsūr *100 D5* Nīmrūz, SW Afghanistan
Chala *38 D4* Arequipa, SW Peru
Chalatenango *30 C3* Chalatenango, N El Salvador
Chalcidice *see* Chalkidikí
Chalcis *see* Chalkída
Chalki *83 E7 island* Dodekánisa, Greece, Aegean Sea
Chalkída *83 C5 var.* Halkida, *prev.* Khalkís; *anc.* Chalcis. Evvoia, E Greece
Chalkidikí *82 C4 var.* Khalkidhikí; *anc.* Chalcidice. *peninsula* NE Greece
Challans *68 B4* Vendée, NW France
Challapata *39 F4* Oruro, SW Bolivia
Challenger Deep *130 B3 trench* W Pacific Ocean
Challenger Fracture Zone *131 F4 tectonic feature* SE Pacific Ocean
Châlons-en-Champagne *68 D3 prev.* Châlons-sur-Marne, *hist.* Arcae Remorum; *anc.* Carolopois. Marne, NE France
Châlons-sur-Marne *see* Châlons-en-Champagne
Chalon-sur-Saône *68 D4 anc.* Cabillonum. Saône-et-Loire, C France
Cha Mai *see* Thung Song
Chaman *112 B2* Baluchistān, SW Pakistan
Chambéry *69 D5 anc.* Camberia. Savoie, E France
Champagne *68 D3 cultural region* N France
Champagne *see* Campania
Champaign *18 B4* Illinois, N USA
Champasak *115 D5* Champasak, S Laos
Champlain, Lake *19 F2 lake* Canada/USA
Champotón *29 G4* Campeche, SE Mexico
Chanak *see* Çanakkale
Chañaral *42 B3* Atacama, N Chile
Chan-chiang/Chanchiang *see* Zhanjiang
Chandeleur Islands *20 C3 island group* Louisiana, S USA
Chandīgarh *112 D2 state capital* Punjab, N India
Chandrapur *113 E5* Mahārāshtra, C India
Changan *see* Xi'an, Shaanxi, C China
Changane *57 E3 river* S Mozambique
Changchun *106 D3 var.* Ch'angch'un, Ch'ang-ch'un; *prev.* Hsinking. *province capital* Jilin, NE China
Ch'angch'un/Ch'ang-ch'un *see* Changchun
Changkiakow *see* Zhangjiakou
Chang, Ko *115 C6 island* S Thailand
Changsha *106 C5 var.* Ch'angsha, Ch'ang-sha. *province capital* Hunan, S China
Ch'angsha/Ch'ang-sha *see* Changsha
Changzhi *106 C4* Shanxi, C China
Chaniá *83 C7 var.* Hania, Khaniá, *Eng.* Canea; *anc.* Cydonia. Kríti, Greece, E Mediterranean Sea
Chañi, Nevado de *42 B2 mountain* NW Argentina
Chankiri *see* Çankırı
Channel Islands *67 C8 Fr.* Iles Normandes. *island group* S English Channel
Channel Islands *25 B8 island group* California, W USA
Channel-Port aux Basques *17 G4* Newfoundland and Labrador, SE Canada
Channel, The *see* English Channel
Channel Tunnel *68 C2 tunnel* France/United Kingdom
Chantabun/Chantaburi *see* Chanthaburi
Chantada *70 C1* Galicia, NW Spain
Chanthaburi *115 C6 var.* Chantabun, Chantaburi. Chantaburi, S Thailand
Chanute *23 F5* Kansas, C USA
Chaouèn *see* Chefchaouen
Chaoyang *106 D3* Liaoning, NE China
Chapala, Lago de *28 D4 lake* C Mexico
Chapan, Gora *100 B3 mountain* C Turkmenistan
Chapayevsk *89 C6* Samarskaya Oblast', W Russian Federation
Chaplynka *87 F4* Khersons'ka Oblast', S Ukraine
Chapra *see* Chhapra
Charcot Seamounts *58 B3 seamount range* E Atlantic Ocean
Chardzhev *see* Türkmenabat
Chardzhou/Chardzhui *see* Türkmenabat
Charente *69 B5 cultural region* W France
Charente *69 B5 river* W France
Chari *54 B3 var.* Shari. *river* Central African Republic/Chad
Chārīkār *101 E4* Parvān, NE Afghanistan
Charity *37 F2* NW Guyana
Chärjew *see* Türkmenabat
Charkhlik/Charkhliq *see* Ruoqiang
Charleroi *65 C7* Hainaut, S Belgium
Charlesbourg *17 E4* Québec, SE Canada
Charles de Gaulle *68 E1* (Paris) Seine-et-Marne, N France
Charles Island *16 D1 island* Nunavut, NE Canada
Charles Island *see* Santa María, Isla
Charleston *21 F2* South Carolina, SE USA
Charleston *18 D5 state capital* West Virginia, NE USA
Charleville *127 D5* Queensland, E Australia
Charleville-Mézières *68 D3* Ardennes, N France
Charlie-Gibbs Fracture Zone *44 C2 tectonic feature* N Atlantic Ocean
Charlotte *21 E1* North Carolina, SE USA
Charlotte Amalie *33 F3 prev.* Saint Thomas. *dependent territory capital* (Virgin Islands (US)) Saint Thomas, N Virgin Islands (US)
Charlotte Harbor *21 E5 inlet* Florida, SE USA
Charlottenhof *see* Aegviidu
Charlottesville *19 E5* Virginia, NE USA
Charlottetown *17 F4 province capital* Prince Edward Island, Prince Edward Island, SE Canada
Charlotte Town *see* Roseau, Dominica
Charsk *see* Shar
Charters Towers *126 D3* Queensland, NE Australia
Chartres *68 C3 anc.* Autricum, Civitas Carnutum. Eure-et-Loir, C France
Chashniki *85 D5* Vitsyebskaya Voblasts', N Belarus
Châteaubriant *68 B4* Loire-Atlantique, NW France
Châteaudun *68 C3* Eure-et-Loir, C France
Châteauroux *68 C4 prev.* Indreville. Indre, C France
Château-Thierry *68 C3* Aisne, N France
Châtelet *65 C7* Hainaut, S Belgium
Châtelherault *see* Châtellerault
Châtellerault *68 B4 var.* Châtelherault. Vienne, W France
Chatham Island *see* San Cristóbal, Isla
Chatham Island Rise *see* Chatham Rise
Chatham Islands *121 E5 island group* New Zealand, SW Pacific Ocean
Chatham Rise *120 D5 var.* Chatham Island Rise. *undersea rise* S Pacific Ocean
Chatkal Range *101 F2 Rus.* Chatkal'skiy Khrebet. *mountain range* Kyrgyzstan/Uzbekistan
Chatkal'skiy Khrebet *see* Chatkal Range
Chāttagām *see* Chittagong
Chattahoochee River *20 D3 river* SE USA
Chattanooga *20 D1* Tennessee, S USA
Chatyr-Tash *101 G2* Narynskaya Oblast', C Kyrgyzstan
Châu Đốc *115 D6 var.* Chauphu, Chau Phu. An Giang, S Vietnam
Chauk *114 A3* Magway, W Myanmar (Burma)
Chaumont *68 D4 prev.* Chaumont-en-Bassigny. Haute-Marne, N France
Chaumont-en-Bassigny *see* Chaumont
Chau Phu *see* Châu Đốc
Chausy *see* Chavusy
Chaves *70 C2 anc.* Aquae Flaviae. Vila Real, N Portugal
Chávez, Isla *see* Santa Cruz, Isla
Chavusy *85 E6 Rus.* Chausy. Mahilyowskaya Voblasts', E Belarus
Chaykovskiy *89 D5* Permskaya Oblast', NW Russian Federation
Cheb *77 A5 Ger.* Eger. Karlovarský Kraj, W Czech Republic
Cheboksary *89 C5* Chuvashskaya Respublika, W Russian Federation
Cheboygan *18 C2* Michigan, N USA
Chechaouèn *see* Chefchaouen
Chech, Erg *52 D1 desert* Algeria/Mali
Chechevichi *see* Chachevichy
Che-chiang *see* Zhejiang
Cheduba Island *114 A4 island* W Myanmar (Burma)
Chefchaouen *48 C2 var.* Chaouèn, Chechaouèn, *Sp.* Xauen. N Morocco
Chefoo *see* Yantai
Cheju-do *107 E4 Jap.* Saishū; *prev.* Quelpart. *island* S South Korea
Cheju Strait *107 E4 Eng.* Cheju Strait. *strait* S South Korea
Cheju Strait *see* Cheju-haehyŏp
Chekiang *see* Zhejiang
Cheleken *see* Hazar
Chelkar *see* Shalkar
Chelm *76 E4 Rus.* Kholm. Lubelskie, SE Poland
Chełmno *76 C3 Ger.* Culm, Kulm. Kujawski-pomorskie, C Poland
Chełmża *76 C3 Ger.* Culmsee, Kulmsee. Kujawski-pomorskie, C Poland
Cheltenham *67 D6* C England, United Kingdom
Chelyabinsk *92 C3* Chelyabinskaya Oblast', C Russian Federation
Chemnitz *72 D4 prev.* Karl-Marx-Stadt. Sachsen, E Germany
Chemulpo *see* Inch'ŏn
Chenāb *112 C2 river* India/Pakistan
Chengchiatun *see* Liaoyuan
Ch'eng-chou/Chengchow *see* Zhengzhou
Chengde *106 D3 var.* Jehol. Hebei, E China
Chengdu *106 B5 var.* Chengtu, Ch'eng-tu. *province capital* Sichuan, C China
Chenghsien *see* Zhengzhou
Chengtu/Ch'eng-tu *see* Chengdu
Chennai *110 D2 prev.* Madras. *state capital* Tamil Nādu, S India
Chenstokhov *see* Częstochowa
Chen Xian/Chenxian/Chen Xiang *see* Chenzhou
Chenzhou *106 C6 var.* Chenxian, Chen Xian, Chen Xiang. Hunan, S China
Chepelare *82 C3* Smolyan, S Bulgaria
Chepén *38 B3* La Libertad, C Peru
Cher *68 C4 river* C France
Cherbourg *68 B3 anc.* Carusbur. Manche, N France
Cherepovets *88 B4* Vologodskaya Oblast', NW Russian Federation
Chergui, Chott ech *48 D2 salt lake* NW Algeria
Cherikov *see* Cherykaw
Cherkassy *see* Cherkasy
Cherkasy *87 E2 Rus.* Cherkassy. Cherkas'ka Oblast', C Ukraine
Cherkessk *89 B7* Karachayevo-Cherkesskaya Respublika, SW Russian Federation
Chernigov *see* Chernihiv
Chernihiv *87 E1 Rus.* Chernigov. Chernihivs'ka Oblast', NE Ukraine
Chernivtsi *86 C3 Ger.* Czernowitz, *Rom.* Cernăuţi, *Rus.* Chernovtsy. Chernivets'ka Oblast', W Ukraine
Cherno More *see* Black Sea
Chernomorskoye *see* Chornomors'ke
Chernovtsy *see* Chernivtsi
Chernoye More *see* Black Sea
Chernyakhovsk *84 A4 Ger.* Insterburg. Kaliningradskaya Oblast', W Russian Federation
Cherry Hill *19 F4* New Jersey, NE USA
Cherski Range *see* Cherskogo, Khrebet
Cherskiy *93 G2* Respublika Sakha (Yakutiya), NE Russian Federation
Cherskogo, Khrebet *93 F2 var.* Cherski Range. *mountain range* NE Russian Federation
Cherso *see* Cres
Cherven' *see* Chervyen'
Chervonograd *see* Chervonohrad
Chervonohrad *86 C2 Rus.* Chervonograd. L'vivs'ka Oblast', NW Ukraine
Chervyen' *85 D6 Rus.* Cherven'. Minskaya Voblasts', C Belarus
Cherykaw *85 E7 Rus.* Cherikov. Mahilyowskaya Voblasts', E Belarus
Chesapeake Bay *19 F5 inlet* NE USA
Chesha Bay *see* Chëshskaya Guba
Chëshskaya Guba *133 D5 var.* Archangel Bay, Chesha Bay, Dvina Bay. *bay* NW Russian Federation
Chester *67 C6 Wel.* Caerleon, *hist.* Legaceaster, *Lat.* Deva, Devana Castra. C England, United Kingdom
Chetumal *29 H4 var.* Payo Obispo. Quintana Roo, SE Mexico
Cheviot Hills *66 D4 hill range* England/Scotland, United Kingdom
Cheyenne *22 D4 state capital* Wyoming, C USA
Cheyenne River *22 D3 river* South Dakota/Wyoming, N USA
Chezdi-Oşorheiu *see* Târgu Secuiesc
Chhapra *113 F3 prev.* Chapra. Bihār, N India
Chhattīsgarh *113 E4 cultural region* E India
Chiai *106 D6 var.* Chia-i, Chiayi, Kiayi, Jiayi, *Jap.* Kagi. C Taiwan
Chia-i *see* Chiai
Chiang-hsi *see* Jiangxi
Chiang Mai *114 B4 var.* Chiangmai, Chiengmai, Kiangmai. Chiang Mai, NW Thailand
Chiangmai *see* Chiang Mai
Chiang Rai *114 C3 var.* Chianpai, Chienrai, Muang Chiang Rai. Chiang Rai, NW Thailand
Chiang-su *see* Jiangsu
Chianning/Chian-ning *see* Nanjing
Chianpai *see* Chiang Rai
Chianti *74 C3 cultural region* C Italy
Chiapa *see* Chiapa de Corzo
Chiapa de Corzo *29 G5 var.* Chiapa. Chiapas, SE Mexico
Chiayi *see* Chiai
Chiba *108 B1 var.* Tiba. Chiba, Honshū, S Japan
Chibougamau *16 D3* Québec, SE Canada
Chicago *18 B3* Illinois, N USA
Ch'i-ch'i-ha-erh *see* Qiqihar
Chickasha *27 G2* Oklahoma, C USA
Chiclayo *38 B3* Lambayeque, NW Peru
Chico *25 B5* California, W USA
Chico, Río *43 B7 river* SE Argentina
Chico, Río *43 B6 river* S Argentina
Chicoutimi *17 E4* Québec, SE Canada
Chiengmai *see* Chiang Mai
Chienrai *see* Chiang Rai
Chiesanuova *74 D2* SW San Marino
Chieti *74 D4 var.* Teate. Abruzzo, C Italy
Chifeng *105 G2 var.* Ulanhad. Nei Mongol Zizhiqu, N China
Chigirin *see* Chyhyryn
Chih-fu *see* Yantai
Chihli *see* Hebei
Chihli, Gulf of *see* Bo Hai
Chihuahua *28 C2* Chihuahua, NW Mexico
Childress *27 F2* Texas, SW USA
Chile *42 B3 off.* Republic of Chile. *country* SW South America
Chile Basin *35 A5 undersea basin* E Pacific Ocean
Chile Chico *43 B6* Aisén, W Chile
Chile, Republic of *see* Chile
Chile Rise *35 A7 undersea rise* SE Pacific Ocean
Chilia-Nouă *see* Kiliya
Chililabombwe *56 D2* Copperbelt, C Zambia
Chi-lin *see* Jilin
Chillán *43 B5* Bío Bío, C Chile
Chillicothe *18 D4* Ohio, N USA
Chill Mhantáin, Sléibhte *see* Wicklow Mountains
Chiloé, Isla de *43 A6 var.* Isla Grande de Chiloé. *island* W Chile
Chilpancingo *29 E5 var.* Chilpancingo de los Bravos. Guerrero, S Mexico
Chilpancingo de los Bravos *see* Chilpancingo
Chilung *106 D6 var.* Keelung, *Jap.* Kirun, Kirun'; *prev. Sp.* Santissima Trinidad. N Taiwan
Chimán *31 G5* Panamá, E Panama
Chimbay *see* Chimboy
Chimborazo *38 A1 volcano* C Ecuador
Chimbote *38 C3* Ancash, W Peru
Chimboy *100 D1 Rus.* Chimbay. Qoraqalpog'iston Respublikasi, NW Uzbekistan
Chimkent *see* Shymkent
Chimoio *57 E3* Manica, C Mozambique
China *102 C2 off.* People's Republic of China, *Chin.* Chung-hua Jen-min Kung-ho-kuo, Zhonghua Renmin Gongheguo; *prev.* Chinese Empire. *country* E Asia
Chi-nan/Chinan *see* Jinan
Chinandega *30 C3* Chinandega, NW Nicaragua
China, People's Republic of *see* China
China, Republic of *see* Taiwan
Chincha Alta *38 D4* Ica, SW Peru
Chin-chiang *see* Quanzhou
Chin-chou/Chinchow *see* Jinzhou
Chindwin *see* Chindwinn
Chindwinn *114 B2 var.* Chindwin. *river* N Myanmar (Burma)
Chinese Empire *see* China

Creston – Dmitriyevsk

Creston *23 F4* Iowa, C USA
Crestview *20 D3* Florida, SE USA
Crete *see* Kríti
Créteil *68 E2* Val-de-Marne, N France
Crete, Sea of/Creticum, Mare *see* Kritikó Pélagos
Creuse *68 B4 river* C France
Crewe *67 D6* C England, United Kingdom
Crexa *see* Cres
Crikvenica *78 A3 It.* Cirquenizza; *prev.* Cirkvenica, Crjkvenica. Primorje-Gorski Kotar, NW Croatia
Crimea *59 F4 peninsula* SE Ukraine Europe
Cristóbal *31 G4* Colón, C Panama
Cristóbal Colón, Pico *36 B1 mountain* N Colombia
Cristur/Cristuru Săcuiesc *see* Cristuru Secuiesc
Cristuru Secuiesc *86 C4 prev.* Cristur, Cristuru Săcuiesc, Sitaş Cristuru, *Ger.* Kreutz, *Hung.* Székelykeresztúr, Szitás-Keresztúr. Harghita, C Romania
Crjkvenica *see* Crikvenica
Crna Gora *see* Montenegro
Crna Reka *79 D6 river* S FYR Macedonia
Crni Drim *see* Black Drin
Croatia *78 B3 off.* Republic of Croatia, *Ger.* Kroatien, *SCr.* Hrvatska. *country* SE Europe
Croatia, Republic of *see* Croatia
Crocodile *see* Limpopo
Croia *see* Krujë
Croker Island *124 E2 island* Northern Territory, N Australia
Cromwell *129 B7* Otago, South Island, New Zealand
Crooked Island *32 D2 island* SE Bahamas
Crooked Island Passage *32 D2 channel* SE Bahamas
Crookston *23 F1* Minnesota, N USA
Crossen *see* Krosno Odrzańskie
Croton/Crotona *see* Crotone
Crotone *75 E6 var.* Cotrone; *anc.* Croton, Crotona. Calabria, SW Italy
Croydon *67 A8* SE England, United Kingdom
Crozet Basin *119 B6 undersea basin* S Indian Ocean
Crozet Islands *119 B7 island group* French Southern and Antarctic Territories
Crozet Plateau *119 B7 var.* Crozet Plateaus. *undersea plateau* SW Indian Ocean
Crozet Plateaus *see* Crozet Plateau
Crystal Brook *127 B6* South Australia
Csaca *see* Čadca
Csakathurn/Csáktornya *see* Čakovec
Csíkszereda *see* Miercurea-Ciuc
Csorna *77 C6* Győr-Moson-Sopron, NW Hungary
Csurgó *77 C7* Somogy, SW Hungary
Cuando *56 C2 var.* Kwando. *river* S Africa
Cuango *see* Kwango
Cuanza *56 B1 var.* Kwanza. *river* C Angola
Cuauhtémoc *28 C2* Chihuahua, N Mexico
Cuautla *29 E4* Morelos, S Mexico
Cuba *32 B2 off.* Republic of Cuba. *country* W West Indies
Cubal *56 B2* Benguela, W Angola
Cubango *56 B2 var.* Kuvango, *Port.* Vila Artur de Paiva, Vila da Ponte. Huíla, SW Angola
Cubango *56 B2 var.* Kavango, Kavengo, Kubango, Okavango, Okavanggo. *river* S Africa
Cuba, Republic of *see* Cuba
Cúcuta *36 C2 var.* San José de Cúcuta. Norte de Santander, N Colombia
Cuddapah *110 C2* Andhra Pradesh, S India
Cuenca *38 B2* Azuay, S Ecuador
Cuenca *71 E3 anc.* Conca. Castilla-La Mancha, C Spain
Cuera *see* Chur
Cuernavaca *29 E4* Morelos, S Mexico
Cuiabá *41 E3 prev.* Cuyabá. *state capital* Mato Grosso, SW Brazil
Cúige *see* Connaught
Cúige Laighean *see* Leinster
Cúige Mumhan *see* Munster
Cuijck *64 D4* Noord-Brabant, SE Netherlands
Cúil Raithin *see* Coleraine
Cuito *56 B2 var.* Kwito. *river* SE Angola
Cukai *116 B3 var.* Chukai, Kemaman. Terengganu, Peninsular Malaysia
Cularo *see* Grenoble
Culiacán *28 C3 var.* Culiacán Rosales, Culiacán-Rosales. Sinaloa, C Mexico
Culiacán-Rosales/Culiacán Rosales *see* Culiacán
Cullera *71 F3* País Valenciano, E Spain
Cullman *20 C2* Alabama, S USA
Culm *see* Chełmno
Culmsee *see* Chełmża
Cumaná *37 E1* Sucre, NE Venezuela
Cumbal, Nevado de *36 A4 elevation* S Colombia
Cumberland *19 E4* Maryland, NE USA
Cumberland Plateau *20 D1 plateau* E USA
Cumberland Sound *15 H3 inlet* Baffin Island, Nunavut, NE Canada
Cumpas *28 B2* Sonora, NW Mexico
Cuneo *74 A2 Fr.* Coni. Piemonte, NW Italy
Cunnamulla *127 C5* Queensland, E Australia
Ćuprija *78 E4* Serbia, E Serbia
Curaçao *33 E5 island* Netherlands Antilles
Curia Rhaetorum *see* Chur
Curicó *42 B4* Maule, C Chile
Curieta *see* Krk
Curitiba *41 E4 prev.* Curytiba. *state capital* Paraná, S Brazil
Curtbunar *see* Tervel
Curtea de Argeş *86 C4 var.* Curtea-de-Arges. Argeş, S Romania
Curtea-de-Arges *see* Curtea de Argeş
Curtici *86 A4 Ger.* Kurtitsch, *Hung.* Kürtös. Arad, W Romania
Curtis Island *126 E4 island* Queensland, SE Australia
Curytiba *see* Curitiba
Curzola *see* Korčula
Cusco *39 E4 var.* Cuzco. Cusco, C Peru
Cusset *69 C5* Allier, C France
Cutch, Gulf of *see* Kachchh, Gulf of
Cuttack *113 F4* Orissa, E India
Cuvier Plateau *119 E6 undersea plateau* E Indian Ocean
Cuxhaven *72 B2* Niedersachsen, NW Germany
Cuyabá *see* Cuiabá
Cuyuni, Río *see* Cuyuni River
Cuyuni River *37 F3 var.* Río Cuyuni. *river* Guyana/Venezuela
Cuzco *see* Cusco
Cyclades *see* Kykládes
Cydonia *see* Chaniá
Cymru *see* Wales
Cyprus *80 C4 off.* Republic of Cyprus, *Gk.* Kypros, *Turk.* Kıbrıs, Kıbrıs Cumhuriyeti. *country* E Mediterranean Sea
Cyprus, Republic of *see* Cyprus
Cythnos *see* Kýthnos
Czech Republic *77 A5 Cz.* Česká Republika. *country* C Europe
Czenstochau *see* Częstochowa
Czernowitz *see* Chernivtsi
Częstochowa *76 C4 Ger.* Czenstochau, Tschenstochau, *Rus.* Chenstokhov. Śląskie, S Poland
Człuchów *76 C3 Ger.* Schlochau. Pomorskie, NW Poland

D

Dabajuro *36 C1* Falcón, NW Venezuela
Dabeiba *36 B2* Antioquia, NW Colombia
Dąbrowa Tarnowska *77 D5* Małopolskie, S Poland
Dabryn' *85 C8 Rus.* Dobryn'. Homyel'skaya Voblasts', SE Belarus
Dacca *see* Dhaka
Daegu *see* Taegu
Dagana *52 B3* N Senegal
Dagda *84 D4* Krāslava, SE Latvia
Dagden *see* Hiiumaa
Dagenham *67 B8* United Kingdom
Dağliq Quarabağ *see* Nagorno-Karabakh
Dagö *see* Hiiumaa
Dagupan *117 E1 off.* Dagupan City. Luzon, N Philippines
Dagupan City *see* Dagupan
Da Hinggan Ling *105 G1 Eng.* Great Khingan Range. *mountain range* NE China
Dahm, Ramlat *99 B6 desert* NW Yemen
Dahomey *see* Benin
Daihoku *see* T'aipei
Daimiel *70 D3* Castilla-La Mancha, C Spain
Daimoniá *83 B7* Pelopónnisos, S Greece
Dainan *see* T'ainan
Daingin, Bá an *see* Dingle Bay
Dairen *see* Dalian
Dakar *52 B3 country capital* (Senegal) W Senegal
Dakhla *see* Ad Dakhla
Dakoro *53 G3* Maradi, S Niger
Đakovica *see* Gjakovë
Đakovo *78 C3 var.* Djakovo, *Hung.* Diakovár. Osijek-Baranja, E Croatia
Dakshin *see* Deccan
Dalain Hob *104 D3 var.* Ejin Qi. Nei Mongol Zizhiqu, N China
Dalai Nor *see* Hulun Nur
Dalaman *94 A4* Muğla, SW Turkey
Dalandzadgad *105 E3* Ömnögovĭ, S Mongolia
Đa Lat *115 E6* Lâm Đông, S Vietnam
Dalby *127 D5* Queensland, E Australia
Dale City *19 E4* Virginia, NE USA
Dalhart *27 E1* Texas, SW USA
Dali *106 A6 var.* Xiaguan. Yunnan, SW China
Dalian *106 D4 var.* Dairen, Dalien, Jay Dairen, Lüda, Ta-lien, *Rus.* Dalny. Liaoning, NE China
Dalien *see* Dalian
Dallas *27 G2* Texas, SW USA
Dalmacija *78 B4 Eng.* Dalmatia, *Ger.* Dalmatien, *It.* Dalmazia. *cultural region* S Croatia
Dalmatia/Dalmatien/Dalmazia *see* Dalmacija
Dalny *see* Dalian
Dalton *20 D1* Georgia, SE USA
Dálvvadis *see* Jokkmokk
Daly Waters *126 A2* Northern Territory, N Australia
Damachava *85 A6 var.* Damachova, *Pol.* Domaczewo, *Rus.* Domachëvo. Brestskaya Voblasts', SW Belarus
Damachova *see* Damachava
Damān *112 C4* Damān and Diu, W India
Damara *54 C4* Ombella-Mpoko, S Central African Republic
Damas *see* Dimashq
Damasco *see* Dimashq
Damascus *see* Dimashq
Damavand, Qolleh-ye *98 D3 mountain* N Iran
Damietta *see* Dumyāt
Dammām *see* Ad Dammān
Damoûr *97 A5 var.* Ad Dāmūr. W Lebanon
Dampier *124 A4* Western Australia
Dampier, Selat *117 F4 strait* Papua, E Indonesia
Damqawt *99 D6 var.* Damqut. E Yemen
Damqut *see* Damqawt
Damxung *104 C5 var.* Gongtang. Xizang Zizhiqu, W China
Danakil Desert *50 D4 var.* Afar Depression, Danakil Plain. *desert* E Africa
Danakil Plain *see* Danakil Desert
Danané *52 D5* W Côte d'Ivoire
Đă Năng *115 E5 prev.* Tourane. Quang Nam-Đa Năng, C Vietnam
Danborg *see* Daneborg
Dandong *106 D3 var.* Tan-tung; *prev.* An-tung. Liaoning, NE China
Daneborg *61 E3 var.* Danborg. Tunu, N Greenland
Dänew *see* Galkynyş
Dangara *see* Danghara
Dangerous Archipelago *see* Tuamotu, Îles
Danghara *101 E3 Rus.* Dangara. SW Tajikistan
Danghe Nanshan *104 D3 mountain range* W China
Dang Raek, Phanom/Dangrek, Chaîne des *see* Dângrêk, Chuŏr Phnum
Dangrek, Chuor Phnum *115 D5 var.* Phanom Dang Raek, Phanom Dong Rak, *Fr.* Chaîne des Dangrek. *mountain range* Cambodia/Thailand
Dangriga *30 C1 prev.* Stann Creek. Stann Creek, E Belize
Danish West Indies *see* Virgin Islands (US)
Danlí *30 D2* El Paraíso, S Honduras
Danmark *see* Denmark
Danmarksstraedet *see* Denmark Strait
Dannenberg *72 C3* Niedersachsen, N Germany
Dannevirke *128 D4* Manawatu-Wanganui, North Island, New Zealand
Dantzig *see* Gdańsk
Danube *59 E4 Bul.* Dunav, *Cz.* Dunaj, *Ger.* Donau, *Hung.* Duna, *Rom.* Dunărea. *river* C Europe
Danubian Plain *see* Dunavska Ravnina
Danum *see* Doncaster
Danville *19 E5* Virginia, NE USA
Danxian/Dan Xian *see* Danzhou
Danzhou *106 C7 prev.* Danxian, Dan Xian, Nada. Hainan, S China
Danzig *see* Gdańsk
Danziger Bucht *see* Danzig, Gulf of
Danzig, Gulf of *76 C2 var.* Gulf of Gdańsk, *Ger.* Danziger Bucht, *Pol.* Zakota Gdańska, *Rus.* Gdan'skaya Bukhta. *gulf* N Poland
Daqm *see* Duqm
Dar'ā *97 B5 var.* Der'a, *Fr.* Déraa. Dar'ā, SW Syria
Darabani *86 C3* Botoşani, NW Romania
Daraut-Kurgan *see* Daroot-Korgon
Dardanelles *94 A2 Eng.* Dardanelles. *strait* NW Turkey
Dardanelles *see* Çanakkale Boğazı
Dardanelli *see* Çanakkale
Dar-el-Beida *see* Casablanca
Dar es Salaam *51 C7* Dar es Salaam, E Tanzania
Darfield *129 C6* Canterbury, South Island, New Zealand
Darfur *50 A4 var.* Darfur Massif. *cultural region* W Sudan
Darfur Massif *see* Darfur
Darhan *105 E2* Darhan Uul, N Mongolia
Darién, Golfo del *see* Darien, Gulf of
Darien, Gulf of *36 A2 Sp.* Golfo del Darién. *gulf* S Caribbean Sea
Darien, Isthmus of *see* Panama, Istmo de
Darién, Serranía del *31 H5 mountain range* Colombia/Panama
Dario *see* Ciudad Darío
Dariorigum *see* Vannes
Darjeeling *see* Dārjiling
Dārjiling *113 F3 prev.* Darjeeling. West Bengal, NE India
Darling River *127 C6 river* New South Wales, SE Australia
Darlington *67 D5* N England, United Kingdom
Darmstadt *73 B5* Hessen, SW Germany
Darnah *49 G2 var.* Dérna. NE Libya
Darnley, Cape *132 D2 cape* Antarctica
Daroca *71 E2* Aragón, NE Spain
Daroot-Korgon *101 F3 var.* Daraut-Kurgan. Oshskaya Oblast', SW Kyrgyzstan
Dartford *67 B8* SE England, United Kingdom
Dartmoor *67 C7 moorland* SW England, United Kingdom
Dartmouth *17 F4* Nova Scotia, SE Canada
Darvaza *see* Derweze, Turkmenistan
Darwin *124 D2 prev.* Palmerston, Port Darwin. *territory capital* Northern Territory, N Australia
Darwin, Isla *38 A4 island* Galápagos, Galapagos Islands, W Ecuador
Dashhowuz *see* Daşoguz
Dashkawka *85 D6 Rus.* Dashkovka. Mahilyowskaya Voblasts', E Belarus
Dashkovka *see* Dashkawka
Daşoguz *100 C2 Rus.* Dashkhovuz, *Turkm.* Dashhowuz; *prev.* Tashauz. Daşoguz Welaýaty, N Turkmenistan
Đa, Sông *see* Black River
Datong *106 C3 var.* Tatung, Ta-t'ung. Shanxi, C China
Daugava *see* Western Dvina
Daugavpils *84 D4 Ger.* Dünaburg; *prev. Rus.* Dvinsk. Daugvapils, SE Latvia
Daung Kyun *115 B6 island* S Myanmar (Burma)
Dauphiné *69 D5 cultural region* E France
Dāvangere *110 C2* Karnātaka, W India
Davao *117 F3 off.* Davao City. Mindanao, S Philippines
Davao City *see* Davao
Davao Gulf *117 F3 gulf* Mindanao, S Philippines
Davenport *23 G3* Iowa, C USA
David *31 E5* Chiriquí, W Panama
Davie Ridge *119 A5 undersea ridge* W Indian Ocean
Davis *132 D3 Australian research station* Antarctica
Davis Sea *132 D3 sea* Antarctica
Davis Strait *60 B3 strait* Baffin Bay/Labrador Sea
Dawei *115 B5 var.* Tavoy, Htawei. Tanintharyi, S Myanmar (Burma)
Dawlat Qaṭar *see* Qatar
Dax *69 B6 var.* Ax; *anc.* Aquae Augustae, Aquae Tarbelicae. Landes, SW France
Dayr az Zawr *96 D3 var.* Deir ez Zor. Dayr az Zawr, E Syria
Dayton *18 C4* Ohio, N USA
Daytona Beach *21 E4* Florida, SE USA
De Aar *56 C5* Northern Cape, C South Africa
Dead Sea *97 B6 var.* Bahret Lut, Lacus Asphaltites, *Ar.* Al Baḥr al Mayyit, Baḥrat Lūt, *Heb.* Yam HaMelaḥ. *salt lake* Israel/Jordan
Deán Funes *42 C3* Córdoba, C Argentina
Death Valley *25 C7 valley* California, W USA
Deatnu *62 D2 Fin.* Tenojoki, *Nor.* Tana. *river* Finland/Norway
Debar *79 D6 Ger.* Dibra, *Turk.* Debre. W FYR Macedonia
De Behagle *see* Laï
Dębica *77 D5* Podkarpackie, SE Poland
De Bildt *see* De Bilt
De Bilt *64 C3 var.* De Bildt. Utrecht, C Netherlands
Dębno *76 B3* Zachodnio-pomorskie, NW Poland
Debre *see* Debar
Debrecen *77 D6 Ger.* Debreczin, *Rom.* Debreţin; *prev.* Debreczen. Hajdú-Bihar, E Hungary
Debreczen/Debreczin *see* Debrecen
Debreţin *see* Debrecen
Decatur *20 C1* Alabama, S USA
Decatur *18 B4* Illinois, N USA
Deccan *112 D5 Hind.* Dakshin. *plateau* C India
Děčín *76 B4 Ger.* Tetschen. Ústecký Kraj, NW Czech Republic
Dedeagaç/Dedeagach *see* Alexandroúpoli
Dedemsvaart *64 E3* Overijssel, E Netherlands
Dee *66 C3 river* NE Scotland, United Kingdom
Deering *14 C2* Alaska, USA
Deés *see* Dej
Deggendorf *73 D6* Bayern, SE Germany
Değirmenlik *80 C5 Gk.* Kythréa. N Cyprus
Deh Bīd *see* Şafāshahr
Dehli *see* Delhi
Deh Shū *100 D5 var.* Deshu. Helmand, S Afghanistan
Deinze *65 B5* Oost-Vlaanderen, NW Belgium
Deir ez Zor *see* Dayr az Zawr
Deirgeirt, Loch *see* Derg, Lough
Dej *86 B3 Hung.* Dés; *prev.* Deés. Cluj, NW Romania
De Jouwer *see* Joure
Dekéleia *see* Dhekélia
Dékoa *54 C4* Kémo, C Central African Republic
De Land *21 E4* Florida, SE USA
Delano *25 C7* California, W USA
Delārām *100 D5* Nīmrūz, SW Afghanistan
Delaware *18 D4* Ohio, N USA
Delaware *19 F4 off.* State of Delaware, *also known as* Blue Hen State, Diamond State, First State. *state* NE USA
Delft *64 B4* Zuid-Holland, W Netherlands
Delfzijl *64 E1* Groningen, NE Netherlands
Delgo *50 B3* Northern, N Sudan
Delhi *112 D3 var.* Dehli, *Hind.* Dilli, *hist.* Shahjahanabad. *union territory capital* Delhi, N India
Delicias *28 D2 var.* Ciudad Delicias. Chihuahua, N Mexico
Déli-Kárpátok *see* Carpaţii Meridionalii
Delmenhorst *72 B3* Niedersachsen, NW Germany
Del Rio *27 F4* Texas, SW USA
Deltona *21 E4* Florida, SE USA
Demba *55 D6* Kasai-Occidental, C Dem. Rep. Congo
Dembia *54 D4* Mbomou, SE Central African Republic
Demchok *104 A5 var.* Dêmqog. *disputed region* China/India
Demerara Plain *34 C2 abyssal plain* W Atlantic Ocean
Deming *26 C3* New Mexico, SW USA
Demmin *72 C2* Mecklenburg-Vorpommern, NE Germany
Demopolis *20 C2* Alabama, S USA
Dêmqog *104 A5 var.* Demchok. China/India
Denali *see* McKinley, Mount
Denau *see* Denov
Dender *65 B6 Fr.* Dendre. *river* W Belgium
Dendre *see* Dender
Denekamp *64 E3* Overijssel, E Netherlands
Den Haag *see* 's-Gravenhage
Denham *125 A5* Western Australia
Den Ham *64 E3* Overijssel, E Netherlands
Den Helder *64 C2* Noord-Holland, NW Netherlands
Dénia *71 F4* País Valenciano, E Spain
Deniliquin *127 C7* New South Wales, SE Australia
Denison *23 F3* Iowa, C USA
Denison *27 G2* Texas, SW USA
Denizli *94 B4* Denizli, SW Turkey
Denmark *63 A7 off.* Kingdom of Denmark, *Dan.* Danmark; *anc.* Hafnia. *country* N Europe
Denmark, Kingdom of *see* Denmark
Denmark Strait *60 D4 var.* Danmarksstraedet. *strait* Greenland/Iceland
Dennery *33 F1* E Saint Lucia
Denov *101 E3 Rus.* Denau. Surkhondaryo Viloyati, S Uzbekistan
Denpasar *116 D5 prev.* Paloe. Bali, C Indonesia
Denton *27 G2* Texas, SW USA
D'Entrecasteaux Islands *122 B3 island group* SE Papua New Guinea
Denver *22 D4 state capital* Colorado, C USA
Der'a/Derá/Déraa *see* Dar'ā
Dera Ghāzi Khān *112 C2 var.* Dera Ghāzikhān. Punjab, C Pakistan
Dera Ghāzikhān *see* Dera Ghāzi Khān
Đeravica *79 D5 mountain* S Serbia
Derbent *89 B8* Respublika Dagestan, SW Russian Federation
Derby *67 D6* C England, United Kingdom
Derelí *see* Gónnoi
Dergachi *see* Derhachi
Derg, Lough *67 A6 Ir.* Loch Deirgeirt. *lake* W Ireland
Derhachi *87 G2 Rus.* Dergachi. Kharkivs'ka Oblast', E Ukraine
De Ridder *20 A3* Louisiana, S USA
Dérna *see* Darnah
Derry *see* Londonderry
Dertosa *see* Tortosa
Derventa *78 B3* Republika Srpska, N Bosnia and Herzegovina
Derweze *100 C2 Rus.* Darvaza. Ahal Welaýaty, C Turkmenistan
Dés *see* Dej
Deschutes River *24 B3 river* Oregon, NW USA
Desē *50 C4 var.* Desse, *It.* Dessie. Āmara, N Ethiopia
Deseado, Río *43 B7 river* S Argentina
Desertas, Ilhas *48 A2 island group* Madeira, Portugal, NE Atlantic Ocean
Deshu *see* Deh Shū
Des Moines *23 F3 state capital* Iowa, C USA
Desna *87 E2 river* Russian Federation/Ukraine
Dessau *72 C4* Sachsen-Anhalt, E Germany
Desse *see* Desē
Dessie *see* Desē
Destêrro *see* Florianópolis
Detroit *18 D3* Michigan, N USA
Detroit Lakes *23 F2* Minnesota, N USA
Deurne *65 D5* Noord-Brabant, SE Netherlands
Deutschendorf *see* Poprad
Deutsch-Eylau *see* Iława
Deutsch Krone *see* Wałcz
Deutschland/Deutschland, Bundesrepublik *see* Germany
Deutsch-Südwestafrika *see* Namibia
Deva *86 B4 Ger.* Diemrich, *Hung.* Déva. Hunedoara, W Romania
Déva *see* Deva
Deva *see* Chester
Devana *see* Aberdeen
Devana Castra *see* Chester
Đevđelija *see* Gevgelija
Deventer *64 D3* Overijssel, E Netherlands
Devils Lake *23 E1* North Dakota, N USA
Devoll *see* Devollit, Lumi i
Devollit, Lumi i *79 D6 var.* Devoll. *river* SE Albania
Devon Island *15 F2 prev.* North Devon Island. *island* Parry Islands, Nunavut, NE Canada
Devonport *127 C8* Tasmania, SE Australia
Devrek *94 C2* Zonguldak, N Turkey
Dexter *23 H5* Missouri, C USA
Deynau *see* Galkynyş
Dezfūl *98 C3 var.* Dizful. Khūzestān, SW Iran
Dezhou *106 D4* Shandong, E China
Dhaka *113 G4 prev.* Dacca. *country capital* (Bangladesh) Dhaka, C Bangladesh
Dhanbād *113 F4* Jhārkhand, NE India
Dhekélia *80 C5 Eng.* Dhekelia, *Gk.* Dekéleia. *UK air base* SE Cyprus
see Dhekélia
Dhidhimótikhon *see* Didymóteicho
Dhíkti Ori *see* Díkti
Dhodhekánisos *see* Dodekánisa
Dhomokós *see* Domokós
Dhráma *see* Dráma
Dhrepanon, Akrotírio *see* Drépano, Akrotírio
Dhún na nGall, Bá *see* Donegal Bay
Dhuusa Marreeb *51 E5 var.* Dusa Marreb, *It.* Dusa Mareb. Galguduud, C Somalia
Diakovár *see* Đakovo
Diamantina, Chapada *41 F3 mountain range* E Brazil
Diamantina Fracture Zone *119 E6 tectonic feature* E Indian Ocean
Diamond State *see* Delaware
Diarbekr *see* Diyarbakır
Dibio *see* Dijon
Dibra *see* Debar
Dibrugarh *113 H3* Assam, NE India
Dickinson *22 D2* North Dakota, N USA
Dicle *see* Tigris
Didimotiho *see* Didymóteicho
Didymóteicho *82 D3 var.* Dhidhimótikhon, Didimotiho. Anatolikí Makedonía kai Thráki, NE Greece
Diedenhofen *see* Thionville
Diekirch *65 D7* Diekirch, C Luxembourg
Diemrich *see* Deva
Điên Biên *114 D3 var.* Bien Bien, Dien Bien Phu. Lai Châu, N Vietnam
Dien Bien Phu *see* Điên Biên
Diepenbeek *65 D6* Limburg, NE Belgium
Diepholz *72 B3* Niedersachsen, NW Germany
Dieppe *68 C2* Seine-Maritime, N France
Dieren *64 D4* Gelderland, E Netherlands
Differdange *65 D8* Luxembourg, SW Luxembourg
Digne *69 D6 var.* Digne-les-Bains. Alpes-de-Haute-Provence, SE France
Digne-les-Bains *see* Digne
Digoel *see* Digul, Sungai
Digoin *68 C4* Saône-et-Loire, C France
Digul, Sungai *117 H5 prev.* Digoel. *river* Papua, E Indonesia
Dihang *see* Brahmaputra
Dijlah *see* Tigris
Dijon *68 D4 anc.* Dibio. Côte d'Or, C France
Dikhil *50 D4* SW Djibouti
Dikson *92 D2* Taymyrskiy (Dolgano-Nenetskiy) Avtonomnyy Okrug, N Russian Federation
Dikti *83 D8 var.* Dhíkti Ori. *mountain range* Kríti, Greece, E Mediterranean Sea
Dili *117 F5 var.* Dilli, Dilly. *country capital* (East Timor) N East Timor
Dilia *53 G3 var.* Dillia. *river* SE Niger
Di Linh *115 E6* Lâm Đông, S Vietnam
Dilli *see* Dili, East Timor
Dilli *see* Delhi, India
Dillia *see* Dilia
Dilling *50 B4 var.* Ad Dalanj. Southern Kordofan, C Sudan
Dillon *22 B2* Montana, NW USA
Dilly *see* Dili
Dilolo *55 D7* Katanga, S Dem. Rep. Congo
Dimashq *97 B5 var.* Ash Shām, Esh Sham, *Eng.* Damascus, *Fr.* Damas, *It.* Damasco. *country capital* (Syria) Dimashq, SW Syria
Dimitrovgrad *82 D3* Khaskovo, S Bulgaria
Dimitrovgrad *89 C6 prev.* Caribrod. Serbia, SE Serbia
Dimitrovo *see* Pernik
Dimovo *82 B1* Vidin, NW Bulgaria
Dinajpur *113 F3* Rajshahi, NW Bangladesh
Dinan *68 B3* Côtes d'Armor, NW France
Dinant *65 C7* Namur, S Belgium
Dinar *94 B4* Afyon, SW Turkey
Dinara *see* Dinaric Alps
Dinaric Alps *78 C4 var.* Dinara. *mountain range* Bosnia and Herzegovina/Croatia
Dindigul *110 C3* Tamil Nādu, SE India
Dingle Bay *67 A6 Ir.* Bá an Daingin. *bay* SW Ireland
Dinguiraye *52 C4* N Guinea
Diourbel *52 B3* W Senegal
Dirē Dawa *51 D5* Dirē Dawa, E Ethiopia
Dirk Hartog Island *125 A5 island* Western Australia
Dirschau *see* Tczew
Disappointment, Lake *124 C4 salt lake* Western Australia
Discovery Bay *32 B4* Middlesex, Jamaica, Greater Antilles, C Jamaica Caribbean Sea
Disko Bugt *see* Qeqertarsuup Tunua
Dispur *113 G3 state capital* Assam, NE India
Divinópolis *41 F4* Minas Gerais, SE Brazil
Divo *52 D5* S Côte d'Ivoire
Divodurum Mediomatricum *see* Metz
Diyarbakır *95 E4 var.* Diarbekr; *anc.* Amida. Diyarbakır, SE Turkey
Dizful *see* Dezfūl
Djailolo *see* Halmahera, Pulau
Djajapura *see* Jayapura
Djakarta *see* Jakarta
Djakovo *see* Đakovo
Djambala *55 B6* Plateaux, C Congo
Djambi *see* Jambi
Djambi *see* Hari, Batang
Djanet *49 E4 prev.* Fort Charlet. SE Algeria
Djéblé *see* Jablah
Djelfa *48 D2 var.* El Djelfa. N Algeria
Djéma *54 D4* Haut-Mbomou, E Central African Republic
Djember *see* Jember
Djérablous *see* Jarābulus
Djerba *49 F2 var.* Djerba, Jazīrat Jarbah. *island* E Tunisia
Djerba *see* Jerba, Île de
Djérem *54 B4 river* C Cameroon
Djevdjelija *see* Gevgelija
Djibouti *50 D4 var.* Jibuti. *country capital* (Djibouti) E Djibouti
Djibouti *50 D4 off.* Republic of Djibouti, *var.* Jibuti; *prev.* French Somaliland, French Territory of the Afars and Issas, *Fr.* Côte Française des Somalis, Territoire Français des Afars et des Issas. *country* E Africa
Djibouti, Republic of *see* Djibouti
Djokjakarta *see* Yogyakarta
Djourab, Erg du *54 C2 desert* N Chad
Djúpivogur *61 E5* Austurland, SE Iceland
Dmitriyevsk *see* Makiyivka

E

F

Fort-Foureau – Glens Falls

Fort-Foureau see Kousséri
Fort Frances 16 B4 Ontario, S Canada
Fort Good Hope 15 E3 var. Rádeyilikóé. Northwest Territories, NW Canada
Fort Gouraud see Fdérik
Forth 66 C4 river C Scotland, United Kingdom
Forth, Firth of 66 C4 estuary E Scotland, United Kingdom
Fortín General Eugenio Garay see General Eugenio A. Garay
Fort Jameson see Chipata
Fort-Lamy see Ndjamena
Fort Lauderdale 21 F5 Florida, SE USA
Fort Liard 15 E4 var. Liard. Northwest Territories, W Canada
Fort Madison 23 G4 Iowa, C USA
Fort McMurray 15 E4 Alberta, C Canada
Fort McPherson 14 D3 var. McPherson. Northwest Territories, NW Canada
Fort Morgan 22 D4 Colorado, C USA
Fort Myers 21 E5 Florida, SE USA
Fort Nelson 15 E4 British Columbia, W Canada
Fort Peck Lake 22 C1 reservoir Montana, NW USA
Fort Pierce 21 F4 Florida, SE USA
Fort Providence 15 E4 var. Providence. Northwest Territories, W Canada
Fort-Repoux see Akjoujt
Fort Rosebery see Mansa
Fort Rousset see Owando
Fort-Royal see Fort-de-France
Fort St. John 15 E4 British Columbia, W Canada
Fort Scott 23 F5 Kansas, C USA
Fort Severn 16 C2 Ontario, C Canada
Fort-Shevchenko 92 A4 Mangistau, W Kazakhstan
Fort-Sibut see Sibut
Fort Simpson 15 E4 var. Simpson. Northwest Territories, W Canada
Fort Smith 15 E4 Northwest Territories, W Canada
Fort Smith 20 B1 Arkansas, C USA
Fort Stockton 27 E3 Texas, SW USA
Fort-Trinquet see Bir Mogreïn
Fort Vermilion 15 E4 Alberta, W Canada
Fort Victoria see Masvingo
Fort Walton Beach 20 C3 Florida, SE USA
Fort Wayne 18 C4 Indiana, N USA
Fort William 66 C3 N Scotland, United Kingdom
Fort Worth 27 G2 Texas, SW USA
Fort Yukon 14 D3 Alaska, USA
Forum Alieni see Ferrara
Forum Livii see Forlì
Fossa Claudia see Chioggia
Fougamou 55 A6 Ngounié, C Gabon
Fougères 68 B3 Ille-et-Vilaine, NW France
Fou-hsin see Fuxin
Foulwind, Cape 129 B5 headland South Island, New Zealand
Foumban 54 A4 Ouest, NW Cameroon
Fou-shan see Fushun
Foveaux Strait 129 A8 strait S New Zealand
Foxe Basin 15 G3 sea Nunavut, N Canada
Fox Glacier 129 B6 West Coast, South Island, New Zealand
Fraga 71 F2 Aragón, NE Spain
Fram Basin 133 C3 var. Amundsen Basin. undersea basin Arctic Ocean
France 68 B4 off. French Republic, It./Sp. Francia; prev. Gaul, Gaule, Lat. Gallia. country W Europe
Franceville 55 B6 var. Massoukou, Masuku. Haut-Ogooué, E Gabon
Francfort see Frankfurt am Main
Franche-Comté 68 D4 cultural region E France
Francia see France
Francis Case, Lake 23 E3 reservoir South Dakota, N USA
Francisco Escárcega 29 G4 Campeche, SE Mexico
Francistown 56 D3 North East, NE Botswana
Franconian Jura see Fränkische Alb
Frankenalb see Fränkische Alb
Frankenstein/Frankenstein in Schlesien see Ząbkowice Śląskie
Frankfort 18 C5 state capital Kentucky, S USA
Frankfort on the Main see Frankfurt am Main
Frankfurt see Frankfurt am Main, Germany
Frankfurt see Słubice, Poland
Frankfurt am Main 73 B5 var. Frankfurt, Fr. Francfort; prev. Eng. Frankfort on the Main. Hessen, SW Germany
Frankfurt an der Oder 72 D3 Brandenburg, E Germany
Fränkische Alb 73 C6 var. Frankenalb, Eng. Franconian Jura. mountain range S Germany
Franklin 20 C1 Tennessee, S USA
Franklin D. Roosevelt Lake 24 C1 reservoir Washington, NW USA
Franz Josef Land 92 D1 Eng. Franz Josef Land. island group N Russian Federation
Franz Josef Land see Frantsa-Iosifa, Zemlya
Fraserburgh 66 D3 NE Scotland, United Kingdom
Fraser Island 126 E4 var. Great Sandy Island. island Queensland, E Australia
Frauenbach see Baia Mare
Frauenburg see Saldus, Latvia
Fredericksburg 19 E5 Virginia, NE USA
Fredericton 17 F4 province capital New Brunswick, SE Canada
Frederikshåb see Paamiut
Fredrikshald see Halden
Fredrikstad 63 B6 Østfold, S Norway
Freeport 32 C1 Grand Bahama Island, N Bahamas
Freeport 27 H4 Texas, SW USA
Free State see Maryland
Freetown 52 C4 country capital (Sierra Leone) W Sierra Leone
Freiburg see Freiburg im Breisgau, Germany
Freiburg im Breisgau 73 A6 var. Freiburg, Fr. Fribourg-en-Brisgau. Baden-Württemberg, SW Germany
Freiburg in Schlesien see Świebodzice
Fremantle 125 A6 Western Australia
Fremont 23 F4 Nebraska, C USA
French Guiana 37 H3 var. Guiana, Guyane. French overseas department N South America
French Guinea see Guinea
French Polynesia 121 F4 French overseas territory S Pacific Ocean
French Republic see France
French Somaliland see Djibouti
French Southern and Antarctic Territories 119 B7 Fr. Terres Australes et Antarctiques Françaises. French overseas territory S Indian Ocean
French Sudan see Mali
French Territory of the Afars and Issas see Djibouti
French Togoland see Togo
Fresnillo 28 D3 var. Fresnillo de González Echeverría. Zacatecas, C Mexico
Fresnillo de González Echeverría see Fresnillo
Fresno 25 C6 California, W USA
Frías 42 C3 Catamarca, N Argentina
Fribourg-en-Brisgau see Freiburg im Breisgau
Friedek-Mistek see Frýdek-Místek
Friedrichshafen 73 B7 Baden-Württemberg, S Germany
Friendly Islands see Tonga
Frisches Haff see Vistula Lagoon
Frobisher Bay 60 B3 inlet Baffin Island, Nunavut, NE Canada
Frobisher Bay see Iqaluit
Frohavet 62 B4 sound C Norway
Frome, Lake 127 B6 salt lake South Australia
Frontera 29 G4 Tabasco, SE Mexico
Frontignan 69 C6 Hérault, S France
Frostviken see Kvarnbergsvattnet
Frøya 62 A4 island W Norway
Frumentum see Formentera
Frunze see Bishkek
Frýdek-Místek 77 C5 Ger. Friedek-Mistek. Moravskoslezský Kraj, E Czech Republic
Fu-chien see Fujian
Fu-chou see Fuzhou
Fuengirola 70 D5 Andalucía, S Spain
Fuerte Olimpo 42 D2 var. Olimpo. Alto Paraguay, NE Paraguay
Fuerte, Río 26 C5 river C Mexico
Fuerteventura 48 B3 island Islas Canarias, Spain, NE Atlantic Ocean
Fuhkien see Fujian
Fu-hsin see Fuxin
Fuji 109 D6 var. Huzi. Shizuoka, Honshū, S Japan
Fujian 106 D6 var. Fu-chien, Fuhkien, Fukien, Min, Fujian Sheng. province SE China
Fujian Sheng see Fujian
Fuji, Mount/Fujiyama see Fuji-san
Fuji-san 109 C6 var. Fujiyama, Eng. Mount Fuji. mountain Honshū, SE Japan
Fukang 104 C2 Xinjiang Uygur Zizhiqu, W China
Fukien see Fujian
Fukui 109 C6 var. Hukui. Fukui, Honshū, SW Japan
Fukuoka 109 A7 var. Hukuoka, hist. Najima. Fukuoka, Kyūshū, SW Japan
Fukushima 108 D4 var. Hukusima. Fukushima, Honshū, C Japan
Fulda 73 B5 Hessen, C Germany
Funafuti see Fongafale
Funafuti Atoll 123 E3 atoll C Tuvalu
Funchal 48 A2 Madeira, Portugal, NE Atlantic Ocean
Fundy, Bay of 17 F5 bay Canada/USA
Fünen see Fyn
Fünfkirchen see Pécs
Furnes see Veurne
Fürth 73 C5 Bayern, S Germany
Furukawa 108 D4 var. Hurukawa, Ōsaki. Miyagi, Honshū, C Japan
Fusan see Pusan
Fushë Kosovë 79 D5 Serb. Kosovo Polje. C Kosovo
Fushun 106 D3 var. Fou-shan, Fu-shun. Liaoning, NE China
Fu-shun see Fushun
Fusin see Fuxin
Füssen 73 C7 Bayern, S Germany
Futog 78 D3 Vojvodina, NW Serbia
Futuna, Île 123 E4 island S Wallis and Futuna
Fuxin 106 D3 var. Fou-hsin, Fu-hsin, Fusin. Liaoning, NE China
Fuzhou 106 D6 var. Foochow, Fu-chou. province capital Fujian, SE China
Fyn 63 B8 Ger. Fünen. island C Denmark
FYR Macedonia/FYROM see Macedonia, FYR
Fyzabad see Feyzābād

G

Gaafu Alifu Atoll see North Huvadhu Atoll
Gaalkacyo 51 E5 var. Galka'yo, It. Galcaio. Mudug, C Somalia
Gabela 56 B2 Cuanza Sul, W Angola
Gaberones see Gaborone
Gabès 49 E2 var. Qābis. E Tunisia
Gabès, Golfe de 49 F2 Ar. Khalīj Qābis. gulf E Tunisia
Gabon 55 B6 off. Gabonese Republic. country C Africa
Gabonese Republic see Gabon
Gaborone 56 C4 prev. Gaberones. country capital (Botswana) South East, SE Botswana
Gabrovo 82 D2 Gabrovo, N Bulgaria
Gadag 110 C1 Karnātaka, W India
Gades/Gadier/Gadir/Gadire see Cádiz
Gadsden 20 D2 Alabama, S USA
Gaeta 75 C5 Lazio, C Italy
Gaeta, Golfo di 75 C5 var. Gulf of Gaeta. gulf C Italy
Gaeta, Gulf of see Gaeta, Golfo di
Gäfle see Gävle
Gafsa 49 E2 var. Qafşah. W Tunisia
Gagnoa 52 D5 C Côte d'Ivoire
Gagra 95 E1 NW Georgia
Gaillac 69 C6 var. Gaillac-sur-Tarn. Tarn, S France
Gaillac-sur-Tarn see Gaillac
Gaillimh see Galway
Gaillimhe, Cuan na see Galway Bay
Gainesville 21 E3 Florida, SE USA
Gainesville 20 D2 Georgia, SE USA
Gainesville 27 G2 Texas, SW USA
Lake Gairdner 127 A6 salt lake South Australia
Gaizina Kalns see Gaiziņkalns
Gaiziņkalns 84 C3 var. Gaizina Kalns. mountain E Latvia
Galán, Cerro 42 B3 mountain NW Argentina
Galanta 77 C6 Hung. Galánta. Trnavský Kraj, W Slovakia
Galapagos Fracture Zone 131 E3 tectonic feature E Pacific Ocean
Galapagos Islands 131 F3 var. Islas de los Galápagos, Eng. Galapagos Islands, Tortoise Islands. island group Ecuador, E Pacific Ocean
Galapagos Islands see Colón, Archipiélago de
Galápagos, Islas de los see Colón, Archipiélago de
Galapagos Rise 131 F3 undersea rise E Pacific Ocean
Galashiels 66 C4 SE Scotland, United Kingdom
Galați 86 D4 Ger. Galatz. Galați, E Romania
Galatz see Galați
Galcaio see Gaalkacyo
Galesburg 18 B3 Illinois, N USA
Galicia 70 B1 anc. Gallaecia. autonomous community NW Spain
Galicia Bank 58 B4 undersea bank E Atlantic Ocean
Galilee, Sea of see Tiberias, Lake
Galka'yo see Gaalkacyo
Galkynyş 100 D3 prev. Rus. Deynau, Dyanev, Turkm. Dänew. Lebap Welaýaty, NE Turkmenistan
Gallaecia see Galicia
Galle 110 D4 prev. Point de Galle. Southern Province, SW Sri Lanka
Gallego Rise 131 F3 undersea rise E Pacific Ocean
Gallegos see Río Gallegos
Gallia see France
Gallipoli 75 E6 Puglia, SE Italy
Gällivare 62 C3 Lapp. Váhtjer. Norrbotten, N Sweden
Gallup 26 C1 New Mexico, SW USA
Galtat-Zemmour 48 B3 C Western Sahara
Galveston 27 H4 Texas, SW USA
Galway 67 A5 Ir. Gaillimh. W Ireland
Galway Bay 67 A6 Ir. Cuan na Gaillimhe. bay W Ireland
Gámas see Kaamanen
Gambell 14 C2 Saint Lawrence Island, Alaska, USA
Gambia 52 B3 off. Republic of The Gambia, The Gambia. country W Africa
Gambia 52 C3 Fr. Gambie. river W Africa
Gambia, Republic of The see Gambia
Gambia, The see Gambia
Gambie see Gambia
Gambier, Îles 121 G4 island group E French Polynesia
Gamboma 55 B6 Plateaux, E Congo
Gamlakarleby see Kokkola
Gan 110 B5 Addu Atoll, C Maldives
Gan see Gansu, China
Gan see Jiangxi, China
Ganaane see Juba
Gäncä 95 G2 Rus. Gyandzha; prev. Kirovabad, Yelisavetpol. W Azerbaijan
Gand see Gent
Gandajika 55 D7 Kasai-Oriental, S Dem. Rep. Congo
Gander 17 G3 Newfoundland and Labrador, SE Canada
Gāndhīdhām 112 C4 Gujarāt, W India
Gandía 71 F3 País Valenciano, E Spain
Ganges 113 F3 Ben. Padma. river Bangladesh/India
Ganges Cone see Ganges Fan
Ganges Fan 118 D3 var. Ganges Cone. undersea fan N Bay of Bengal
Ganges, Mouths of the 113 G4 delta Bangladesh/India
Gangra see Çankırı
Gangtok 113 F3 state capital Sikkim, N India
Gansos, Lago dos see Goose Lake
Gansu 106 B4 var. Gan, Gansu Sheng, Kansu. province N China
Gansu Sheng see Gansu
Gantsevichi see Hantsavichy
Ganzhou 106 D6 Jiangxi, S China
Gao 53 E3 Gao, E Mali
Gaocheng see Litang
Gaoual 52 C4 N Guinea
Gaoxiong see Kaohsiung
Gap 69 D5 anc. Vapincum. Hautes-Alpes, SE France
Gaplaňgyr Platosy 100 C2 Rus. Plato Kaplangky. ridge Turkmenistan/Uzbekistan
Gar see Gar Xincun
Garabil Belentligi 100 D3 Rus. Vozvyshennost' Karabil'. mountain range S Turkmenistan
Garabogaz Aylagy 100 B2 Rus. Zaliv Kara-Bogaz-Gol. bay NW Turkmenistan
Garachiné 31 G5 Darién, SE Panama
Garagum 100 C3 var. Garagumy, Qara Qum, Eng. Black Sand Desert, Kara Kum; prev. Peski Karakumy. desert C Turkmenistan
Garagum Canal 100 D3 var. Kara Kum Canal, Rus. Karagumskiy Kanal, Karakumskiy Kanal. canal C Turkmenistan
Garagumy see Garagum
Gara Khitrino 82 D2 Shumen, NE Bulgaria
Gárassavon see Kaaresuvanto
Garda, Lago di 74 C2 var. Benaco, Eng. Lake Garda, Ger. Gardasee. lake NE Italy
Garda, Lake see Garda, Lago di
Gardasee see Garda, Lago di
Garden City 23 E5 Kansas, C USA
Garden State, The see New Jersey
Gardner Island see Nikumaroro
Garegegasnjárga see Karigasniemi
Gargždai 84 B3 Klaipėda, W Lithuania
Garissa 51 D6 Coast, E Kenya
Garland 27 G2 Texas, SW USA
Garoe see Garoowe
Garonne 69 B5 anc. Garumna. river S France
Garoowe 51 E5 var. Garoe. Nugaal, N Somalia
Garoua 54 B4 var. Garua. Nord, N Cameroon
Garry Lake 15 F3 lake Nunavut, N Canada
Garsen 51 D6 Coast, S Kenya
Garua see Garoua
Garumna see Garonne
Garwolin 76 D4 Mazowieckie, E Poland
Gar Xincun 104 A4 prev. Gar. Xizang Zizhiqu, W China
Gary 18 B3 Indiana, N USA
Garzón 36 B4 Huila, S Colombia
Gasan-Kuli see Esenguly
Gascogne 69 B6 Eng. Gascony. cultural region S France
Gascony see Gascogne
Gascoyne River 125 A5 river Western Australia
Gaspé 17 F3 Québec, SE Canada
Gaspé, Péninsule de 17 E4 var. Péninsule de la Gaspésie. peninsula Québec, SE Canada
Gaspésie, Péninsule de la see Gaspé, Péninsule de
Gastonia 21 E1 North Carolina, SE USA
Gastoúni 83 B6 Dytikí Ellás, S Greece
Gatchina 88 B4 Leningradskaya Oblast', NW Russian Federation
Gatineau 16 D4 Québec, SE Canada
Gatooma see Kadoma
Gatún, Lake 31 F4 reservoir C Panama
Gauhāti see Guwāhāti
Gauja 84 D3 Ger. Aa. river Estonia/Latvia
Gaul/Gaule see France
Gauteng see Johannesburg, South Africa
Gāvbandī 98 D4 Hormozgān, S Iran
Gávdos 83 C8 island SE Greece
Gavere 65 B6 Oost-Vlaanderen, NW Belgium
Gävle 63 C6 var. Gäfle; prev. Gefle. Gävleborg, C Sweden
Gawler 127 B6 South Australia
Gaya 113 F3 Bihār, N India
Gaya see Kyjov
Gayndah 127 E5 Queensland, E Australia
Gaysin see Haysyn
Gaza 97 A6 Ar. Ghazzah, Heb. 'Azza. NE Gaza Strip
Gaz-Achak see Gazojak
Gazandzhyk/Gazanjyk see Bereket
Gaza Strip 97 A7 Ar. Qita Ghazzah. disputed region SW Asia
Gaziantep 94 D4 var. Gazi Antep; prev. Aintab, Antep. Gaziantep, S Turkey
Gazi Antep see Gaziantep
Gazimağusa 80 D5 var. Famagusta, Gk. Ammóchostos. E Cyprus
Gazimağusa Körfezi 80 C5 var. Famagusta Bay, Gk. Kólpos Ammóchostos. bay E Cyprus
Gazli 100 D2 Buxoro Viloyati, C Uzbekistan
Gazojak 100 D2 Rus. Gaz-Achak. Lebap Welaýaty, NE Turkmenistan
Gbanga 52 D5 var. Gbarnga. N Liberia
Gbarnga see Gbanga
Gdańsk 76 C2 Fr. Dantzig, Ger. Danzig. Pomorskie, N Poland
Gdan'skaya Bukhta/Gdańsk, Gulf of see Danzig, Gulf of
Gdańska, Zakota see Danzig, Gulf of
Gdingen see Gdynia
Gdynia 76 C2 Ger. Gdingen. Pomorskie, N Poland
Gedaref 50 C4 var. Al Qaḍārif, El Gedaref. Gedaref, E Sudan
Gediz 94 B3 Kütahya, W Turkey
Gediz Nehri 94 A3 river W Turkey
Geel 65 C5 var. Gheel. Antwerpen, N Belgium
Geelong 127 C7 Victoria, SE Australia
Ge'e'mu see Golmud
Gefle see Gävle
Geilo 63 A5 Buskerud, S Norway
Gejiu 106 B6 var. Kochiu. Yunnan, S China
Gëkdepe see Gökdepe
Gela 75 C7 prev. Terranova di Sicilia. Sicilia, Italy, C Mediterranean Sea
Geldermalsen 64 C4 Gelderland, C Netherlands
Geleen 65 D6 Limburg, SE Netherlands
Gelib see Jilib
Gellinsor 51 E5 Mudug, C Somalia
Gembloux 65 C6 Namur, Belgium
Gemena 55 C5 Equateur, NW Dem. Rep. Congo
Gem of the Mountains see Idaho
Gemona del Friuli 74 D2 Friuli-Venezia Giulia, NE Italy
Gem State see Idaho
Genalë Wenz see Juba
Genck see Genk
General Alvear 42 B4 Mendoza, W Argentina
General Carrera, Lago see Buenos Aires, Lago
General Eugenio A. Garay 42 C1 var. Fortín General Eugenio Garay; prev. Yrendagüé. Nueva Asunción, NW Paraguay
General José F.Uriburu see Zárate
General Machado see Camacupa
General Santos 117 F3 off. General Santos City. Mindanao, S Philippines
General Santos City see General Santos
Gênes see Genova
Geneva see Genève
Geneva, Lake 73 A7 Fr. Lac de Genève, Lac Léman, le Léman, Ger. Genfer See. lake France/Switzerland
Genève 73 A7 Eng. Geneva, Ger. Genf, It. Ginevra. Genève, SW Switzerland
Genève, Lac de see Geneva, Lake
Genf see Genève
Genfer See see Geneva, Lake
Genichesk see Heniches'k
Genk 65 D6 var. Genck. Limburg, NE Belgium
Gennep 64 D4 Limburg, SE Netherlands
Genoa see Genova
Genoa, Gulf of 74 A3 Eng. Gulf of Genoa. gulf NW Italy
Genoa, Gulf of see Genova, Golfo di
Genova 80 D1 Eng. Genoa; anc. Genua, Fr. Gênes. Liguria, NW Italy
Genovesa, Isla 38 B5 var. Tower Island. island Galapagos Islands, Ecuador, E Pacific Ocean
Gent 65 B5 Eng. Ghent, Fr. Gand. Oost-Vlaanderen, NW Belgium
Genua see Genova
Geok-Tepe see Gökdepe
George 56 C5 Western Cape, S South Africa
George 60 A4 river Newfoundland and Labrador/Québec, E Canada
George, Lake 21 E3 lake Florida, SE USA
Georgenburg see Jurbarkas
Georges Bank 13 D5 undersea bank W Atlantic Ocean
George Sound 129 A7 sound South Island, New Zealand
Georges River 126 D2 river New South Wales, E Australia
Georgetown 37 F2 country capital (Guyana) N Guyana
George Town 32 C2 Great Exuma Island, C Bahamas
George Town 32 B3 var. Georgetown. dependent territory capital (Cayman Islands) Grand Cayman, SW Cayman Islands
George Town 116 B3 var. Penang, Pinang. Pinang, Peninsular Malaysia
Georgetown 21 F2 South Carolina, SE USA
Georgetown see George Town
George V Land 132 C4 physical region Antarctica
Georgia 95 F2 off. Republic of Georgia, Geor. Sak'art'velo, Rus. Gruzinskaya SSR, Gruziya. country SW Asia
Georgia 20 D2 off. State of Georgia, also known as Empire State of the South, Peach State. state SE USA
Georgian Bay 18 D2 lake bay Ontario, S Canada
Georgia, Republic of see Georgia
Georgia, Strait of 24 A1 strait British Columbia, W Canada
Georgi Dimitrov see Kostenets
Georgiu-Dezh see Liski
Georg von Neumayer 132 A2 German research station Antarctica
Gera 72 C4 Thüringen, E Germany
Geráki 83 B6 Pelopónnisos, S Greece
Geraldine 129 B6 Canterbury, South Island, New Zealand
Geraldton 125 A6 Western Australia
Geral, Serra 35 D5 mountain range S Brazil
Gerede 94 C2 Bolu, N Turkey
Gereshk 100 D5 Helmand, SW Afghanistan
Gering 22 D3 Nebraska, C USA
German East Africa see Tanzania
Germanicopolis see Çankırı
Germanicum, Mare/German Ocean see North Sea
German Southwest Africa see Namibia
Germany 72 B4 off. Federal Republic of Germany, Bundesrepublik Deutschland, Ger. Deutschland. country N Europe
Germany, Federal Republic of see Germany
Geroliménas 83 B7 Pelopónnisos, S Greece
Gerona see Girona
Gerpinnes 65 C7 Hainaut, S Belgium
Gerunda see Girona
Gerze 94 D2 Sinop, N Turkey
Gesoriacum see Boulogne-sur-Mer
Gessoriacum see Boulogne-sur-Mer
Getafe 70 D3 Madrid, C Spain
Gevaş 95 F3 Van, SE Turkey
Gevgeli see Gevgelija
Gevgelija 79 E6 var. Đevđelija, Djevdjelija, Turk. Gevgeli. SE Macedonia
Ghaba see Al Ghābah
Ghana 53 E5 off. Republic of Ghana. country W Africa
Ghanzi 56 C3 var. Khanzi. Ghanzi, W Botswana
Gharandal 97 B7 Al'Aqabah, SW Jordan
Gharbt, Jabal al see Liban, Jebel
Ghardaïa 48 D2 N Algeria
Gharvān see Gharyān
Gharyān 49 F2 var. Gharvān. NW Libya
Ghawdex see Gozo
Ghaznī 101 E4 var. Ghazni. Ghaznī, E Afghanistan
Ghazzah see Gaza
Gheel see Geel
Ghent see Gent
Gheorgheni 86 C4 prev. Gheorghieni, Sîn-Miclăuş, Ger. Niklasmarkt, Hung. Gyergyószentmiklós. Harghita, C Romania
Gheorghieni see Gheorgheni
Ghūdara 101 F3 var. Gudara, Rus. Kudara. SE Tajikistan
Ghurdaqah see Hurghada
Ghūrīān 100 D4 Herāt, W Afghanistan
Giamame see Jamaame
Giannitsá 82 B4 var. Yiannitsá. Kentrikí Makedonía, N Greece
Gibraltar 71 G4 UK dependent territory SW Europe
Gibraltar, Bay of 71 G5 bay Gibraltar/Spain Europe Mediterranean Sea Atlantic Ocean
Gibraltar, Détroit de/Gibraltar, Estrecho de see Gibraltar, Strait of
Gibraltar, Strait of 70 C5 Fr. Détroit de Gibraltar, Sp. Estrecho de Gibraltar. strait Atlantic Ocean/Mediterranean Sea
Gibson Desert 125 B5 desert Western Australia
Giedraičiai 85 C5 Utena, E Lithuania
Giessen 73 B5 Hessen, W Germany
Gifu 109 C6 var. Gihu. Gifu, Honshū, SW Japan
Giganta, Sierra de la 28 B3 mountain range NW Mexico
Gihu see Gifu
G'ijduvon 100 D2 Rus. Gizhduvon. Buxoro Viloyati, C Uzbekistan
Gijón 70 D1 var. Xixón. Asturias, NW Spain
Gila River 26 A2 river Arizona, SW USA
Gilbert Islands see Tungaru
Gilbert River 126 C3 river Queensland, NE Australia
Gilf Kebir Plateau see Haḍabat al Jilf al Kabīr
Gillette 22 D3 Wyoming, C USA
Gilolo see Halmahera, Pulau
Gilroy 25 B6 California, W USA
Gimie, Mount 33 F1 mountain C Saint Lucia
Gimma see Jīma
Ginevra see Genève
Gingin 125 A6 Western Australia
Giohar see Jawhar
Gipeswic see Ipswich
Girardot 36 B3 Cundinamarca, C Colombia
Giresun 95 E2 var. Kerasunt; anc. Cerasus, Pharnacia. Giresun, NE Turkey
Girgenti see Agrigento
Girin see Jilin
Girne 80 C5 Gk. Kerýneia, Kyrenia. N Cyprus
Giron see Kiruna
Girona 71 G2 var. Gerona; anc. Gerunda. Cataluña, NE Spain
Gisborne 128 E3 Gisborne, North Island, New Zealand
Gissar Range 101 E3 Rus. Gissarskiy Khrebet. mountain range Tajikistan/Uzbekistan
Gissarskiy Khrebet see Gissar Range
Githio see Gýtheio
Giulianova 74 D4 Abruzzi, C Italy
Giumri see Gyumri
Giurgiu 86 C5 Giurgiu, S Romania
Giza 50 B1 var. Al Jīzah, El Gîza, Gizeh. N Egypt
Gizhduvon see G'ijduvon
Giżycko 76 D2 Ger. Lötzen. Warmińsko-Mazurskie, NE Poland
Gjakovë 79 D5 Serb. Đakovica. W Kosovo
Gjilan 79 D5 Serb. Gnjilane. E Kosovo
Gjinokastër see Gjirokastër
Gjirokastër 79 C7 var. Gjirokastra; prev. Gjinokastër, Gk. Argyrokastron, It. Argirocastro. Gjirokastër, S Albania
Gjirokastra see Gjirokastër
Gjoa Haven 15 F3 var. Uqsuqtuuq. King William Island, Nunavut, NW Canada
Gjøvik 63 B5 Oppland, S Norway
Glace Bay 17 G4 Cape Breton Island, Nova Scotia, SE Canada
Gladstone 126 E4 Queensland, E Australia
Glåma 63 B5 var. Glommen. river S Norway
Glasgow 66 C4 S Scotland, United Kingdom
Glavn'a Morava see Velika Morava
Glazov 89 D5 Udmurtskaya Respublika, NW Russian Federation
Gleiwitz see Gliwice
Glendale 26 B2 Arizona, SW USA
Glendive 22 D2 Montana, NW USA
Glens Falls 19 F3 New York, NE USA

Glevum – Hagåtña

Glevum see Gloucester
Glina 78 B3 var. Banijska Palanka. Sisak-Moslavina, NE Croatia
Glittertind 63 A5 mountain S Norway
Gliwice 77 C5 Ger. Gleiwitz. Śląskie, S Poland
Globe 26 B2 Arizona, SW USA
Globino see Hlobyne
Glogau see Głogów
Głogów 76 B4 Ger. Glogau, Glogow. Dolnośląskie, SW Poland
Glogow see Głogów
Glomma see Gláma
Glommen see Gláma
Gloucester 67 D6 hist. Caer Glou, Lat. Glevum. C England, United Kingdom
Głowno 76 D4 Łódź, C Poland
Glubokoye see Hlybokaye
Glukhov see Hlukhiv
Gnesen see Gniezno
Gniezno 76 C3 Ger. Gnesen. Weilkopolskie, C Poland
Gnjilane see Gjilan
Gobabis 56 B3 Omaheke, E Namibia
Gobi 104 D3 desert China/Mongolia
Gobō 109 C6 Wakayama, Honshū, SW Japan
Godāvari 102 B3 var. Godavari. river C India
Godavari see Godāvari
Godhavn see Qeqertarsuaq
Godhra 112 C4 Gujarāt, W India
Göding see Hodonín
Godoy Cruz 42 B4 Mendoza, W Argentina
Godthaab/Godthåb see Nuuk
Godwin Austen, Mount see K2
Goede Hoop, Kaap de see Good Hope, Cape of
Goeie Hoop, Kaap die see Good Hope, Cape of
Goeree 64 B4 island SW Netherlands
Goes 65 B5 Zeeland, SW Netherlands
Goettingen see Göttingen
Gogebic Range 18 B1 hill range Michigan/Wisconsin, N USA
Goiânia 41 E3 prev. Goyania. state capital Goiás, C Brazil
Goiás 41 E3 off. Estado de Goiás; prev. Goiaz, Goyaz. region C Brazil
Goiás 41 E3 off. Estado de Goiás; prev. Goiaz, Goyaz. state C Brazil
Goiás, Estado de see Goiás
Goiaz see Goiás
Goidhoo Atoll see Horsburgh Atoll
Gojōme 108 D4 Akita, Honshū, NW Japan
Gökçeada 82 D4 var. Imroz Adasi, Gk. Imbros. island NW Turkey
Gökdepe 100 C3 Rus. Gëkdepe, Geok-Tepe. Ahal Welaýaty, C Turkmenistan
Göksun 94 D4 Kahramanmaraş, C Turkey
Gol 63 A5 Buskerud, S Norway
Golan Heights 97 B5 Ar. Al Jawlān, Heb. HaGolan. mountain range SW Syria
Golaya Pristan see Hola Prystan'
Gołdap 76 E2 Ger. Goldap. Warmińsko-Mazurskie, NE Poland
Gold Coast 127 E5 cultural region Queensland, E Australia
Golden Bay 128 C4 bay South Island, New Zealand
Golden State, The see California
Goldingen see Kuldīga
Goldsboro 21 F1 North Carolina, SE USA
Goleniów 76 B3 Ger. Gollnow. Zachodnio-pomorskie, NW Poland
Gollnow see Goleniów
Golmo see Golmud
Golmud 104 D4 var. Ge'e'mu, Golmo, Chin. Ko-erh-mu. Qinghai, C China
Golovanevsk see Holovanivs'k
Golub-Dobrzyń 76 C3 Kujawski-pomorskie, C Poland
Goma 55 E6 Nord-Kivu, NE Dem. Rep. Congo
Gombi 53 H4 Adamawa, E Nigeria
Gombroon see Bandar-e 'Abbās
Gomel' see Homyel'
Gomera 48 A3 island Islas Canarias, Spain, NE Atlantic Ocean
Gómez Palacio 28 D3 Durango, C Mexico
Gonaïves 32 D3 var. Les Gonaïves. N Haiti
Gonâve, Île de la 32 D3 island C Haiti
Gondar see Gonder
Gonder 50 C4 var. Gondar. Āmara, NW Ethiopia
Gondia 113 E4 Mahārāshtra, C India
Gonggar 104 C5 var. Gyixong. Xizang Zizhiqu, W China
Gongola 53 G4 river E Nigeria
Gongtang see Damxung
Gonni/Gónnos see Gónnoi
Gónnoi 82 B4 var. Gonni, Gónnos; prev. Derelí. Thessalía, C Greece
Good Hope, Cape of 56 B5 Afr. Kaap de Goede Hoop, Kaap die Goeie Hoop. headland SW South Africa
Goodland 22 D4 Kansas, C USA
Goondiwindi 127 D5 Queensland, E Australia
Goor 64 E3 Overijssel, E Netherlands
Goose Green 43 D7 var. Prado del Ganso. East Falkland, Falkland Islands
Goose Lake 24 B4 var. Lago dos Gansos. lake California/Oregon, W USA
Gopher State see Minnesota
Göppingen 73 B6 Baden-Württemberg, SW Germany
Góra Kalwaria 92 D4 Mazowieckie, C Poland
Gorakhpur 113 E3 Uttar Pradesh, N India
Gorany see Harany
Goražde 78 C4 Federacija Bosna I Hercegovina, SE Bosnia and Herzegovina
Gorbovichi see Harbavichy
Goré 54 C4 Logone-Oriental, S Chad
Gorē 51 C5 Oromīya, C Ethiopia
Gore 129 B7 Southland, South Island, New Zealand
Gorgān 98 D2 var. Astarabad, Astrabad, Gurgan, prev. Asterābād; anc. Hyrcania. Golestān, N Iran
Gori 95 F2 C Georgia
Gorinchem 64 C4 var. Gorkum. Zuid-Holland, C Netherlands
Goris 95 G3 SE Armenia
Gorki see Horki
Gor'kiy see Nizhniy Novgorod
Gorkum see Gorinchem
Görlitz 72 D4 Sachsen, E Germany
Görlitz see Zgorzelec
Gorlovka see Horlivka
Gorna Dzhumaya see Blagoevgrad
Gornja Mužlja see Mužlja
Gornji Milanovac 78 C4 Serbia, C Serbia
Gorodets see Haradzyets
Gorodishche see Horodyshche
Gorodnya see Horodnya
Gorodok see Haradok
Gorodok/Gorodok Yagellonski see Horodok
Gorontalo 117 E4 Sulawesi, C Indonesia
Gorontalo, Teluk see Tomini, Gulf of
Gorssel 64 D3 Gelderland, E Netherlands
Goryn see Horyn'
Gorzów Wielkopolski 76 B3 Ger. Landsberg, Landsberg an der Warthe. Lubuskie, W Poland
Gosford 127 D6 New South Wales, SE Australia
Goshogawara 108 D3 var. Gosyogawara. Aomori, Honshū, C Japan
Gospić 78 A3 Lika-Senj, C Croatia
Gostivar 79 D6 W FYR Macedonia
Gosyogawara see Goshogawara
Göteborg 63 B7 Eng. Gothenburg. Västra Götaland, S Sweden
Gotel Mountains 53 G5 mountain range E Nigeria
Gotha 72 C4 Thüringen, C Germany
Gothenburg see Göteborg
Gotland 63 C7 island SE Sweden
Goto-retto 109 A7 island group SW Japan
Gotska Sandön 84 B1 island SE Sweden
Gōtsu 109 B6 var. Gôtu. Shimane, Honshū, SW Japan
Göttingen 72 B4 var. Goettingen. Niedersachsen, C Germany
Gottschee see Kočevje
Gottwaldov see Zlín
Gôtu see Gōtsu
Gouda 64 C4 Zuid-Holland, C Netherlands
Gough Fracture Zone 45 C6 tectonic feature S Atlantic Ocean
Gough Island 47 B8 island Tristan da Cunha, S Atlantic Ocean
Gouin, Réservoir 16 D4 reservoir Québec, SE Canada
Goulburn 127 D6 New South Wales, SE Australia
Goundam 53 E3 Tombouctou, NW Mali
Gouré 53 G3 Zinder, SE Niger
Goverla, Gora see Hoverla, Hora
Governador Valadares 41 F4 Minas Gerais, SE Brazil
Govi Altayn Nuruu 105 E3 mountain range S Mongolia
Goya 42 D3 Corrientes, NE Argentina
Goyania see Goiânia
Goyaz see Goiás
Goz Beïda 54 C3 Ouaddaï, SE Chad
Gozo 75 C8 var. Ghawdex. island N Malta
Graciosa 70 A5 var. Ilha Graciosa. island Azores, Portugal, NE Atlantic Ocean
Graciosa, Ilha see Graciosa
Gradačac 78 C3 Federacija Bosna I Hercegovina, N Bosnia and Herzegovina
Gradaús, Serra dos 41 E3 mountain range C Brazil
Gradiška see Bosanska Gradiška
Grafton 127 E5 New South Wales, SE Australia
Grafton 23 E1 North Dakota, N USA
Graham Land 132 A2 physical region Antarctica
Grajewo 76 E3 Podlaskie, NE Poland
Grampian Mountains 66 C3 mountain range C Scotland, United Kingdom
Gran see Esztergom, Hungary
Granada 30 D3 Granada, SW Nicaragua
Granada 70 D5 Andalucía, S Spain
Gran Canaria 48 A3 var. Grand Canary. island Islas Canarias, Spain, NE Atlantic Ocean
Gran Chaco 42 D2 var. Chaco. lowland plain South America
Grand Bahama Island 32 B1 island N Bahamas
Grand Banks of Newfoundland 12 E4 undersea basin NW Atlantic Ocean
Grand Bassa see Buchanan
Grand Canary see Gran Canaria
Grand Canyon 26 A1 canyon Arizona, SW USA
Grand Canyon State see Arizona
Grand Cayman 32 B3 island SW Cayman Islands
Grand Duchy of Luxembourg see Luxembourg
Grande, Bahía 43 B7 bay S Argentina
Grande-Comore see Ngazidja
Grande de Chiloé, Isla see Chiloé, Isla de
Grande Prairie 15 E4 Alberta, W Canada
Grand Erg Occidental 48 D3 desert W Algeria
Grand Erg Oriental 49 E3 desert Algeria/Tunisia
Rio Grande 29 E2 var. Río Bravo, Sp. Río Bravo del Norte, Bravo del Norte. river Mexico/USA
Grande Terre 33 G3 island E West Indies
Grand Falls 17 G3 Newfoundland, Newfoundland and Labrador, SE Canada
Grand Forks 23 E1 North Dakota, N USA
Grandichi see Hrandzichy
Grand Island 23 E4 Nebraska, C USA
Grand Junction 22 C4 Colorado, C USA
Grand Paradis see Gran Paradiso
Grand Rapids 18 C3 Michigan, N USA
Grand Rapids 23 F1 Minnesota, N USA
Grand-Saint-Bernard, Col du see Great Saint Bernard Pass
Grand-Santi 37 G3 W French Guiana
Granite State see New Hampshire
Gran Lago see Nicaragua, Lago de
Gran Malvina see West Falkland
Gran Paradiso 74 A2 Fr. Grand Paradis. mountain NW Italy
Gran San Bernardo, Passo di see Great Saint Bernard Pass
Gran Santiago see Santiago
Grants 26 C2 New Mexico, SW USA
Grants Pass 24 B4 Oregon, NW USA
Granville 68 B3 Manche, N France
Gratianopolis see Grenoble
Gratz see Graz
Graudenz see Grudziądz
Graulhet 69 C6 Tarn, S France
Grave 64 D4 Noord-Brabant, SE Netherlands
Grayling 14 C2 Alaska, USA
Graz 73 E7 prev. Gratz. Steiermark, SE Austria
Great Abaco 32 C1 var. Abaco Island. island N Bahamas
Great Alfold see Great Hungarian Plain
Great Ararat see Büyükağrı Dağı
Great Australian Bight 125 D7 bight S Australia
Great Barrier Island 128 D2 island N New Zealand
Great Barrier Reef 126 D2 reef Queensland, NE Australia
Great Basin 25 C5 basin W USA
Great Bear Lake 15 E3 Fr. Grand Lac de l'Ours. lake Northwest Territories, NW Canada
Great Belt 63 B8 var. Store Bælt, Eng. Great Belt, Storebelt. channel Baltic Sea/Kattegat
Great Belt see Storebælt
Great Bend 23 E5 Kansas, C USA
Great Britain see Britain
Great Dividing Range 126 D4 mountain range NE Australia
Greater Antilles 32 D3 island group West Indies
Greater Caucasus 95 G2 mountain range Azerbaijan/Georgia/Russian Federation Asia/Europe
Greater Sunda Islands 102 D5 var. Sunda Islands. island group Indonesia
Great Exhibition Bay 128 C1 inlet North Island, New Zealand
Great Exuma Island 32 C2 island C Bahamas
Great Falls 22 B1 Montana, NW USA
Great Grimsby see Grimsby
Great Hungarian Plain 77 C7 var. Great Alfold, Plain of Hungary, Hung. Alföld. plain SE Europe
Great Inagua 32 D2 var. Inagua Islands. island S Bahamas
Great Indian Desert see Thar Desert
Great Khingan Range see Da Hinggan Ling
Great Lake see Tônlé Sap
Great Lakes 13 C5 lakes Ontario, Canada/USA
Great Lakes State see Michigan
Great Meteor Seamount see Great Meteor Tablemount
Great Meteor Tablemount 44 B3 var. Great Meteor Seamount. seamount E Atlantic Ocean
Great Nicobar 111 G3 island Nicobar Islands, India, NE Indian Ocean
Great Plain of China 103 E2 plain E China
Great Plains 23 E3 var. High Plains. plains Canada/USA
Great Rift Valley 51 C5 var. Rift Valley. depression Asia/Africa
Great Ruaha 51 C7 river S Tanzania
Great Saint Bernard Pass 74 A1 Fr. Col du Grand-Saint-Bernard, It. Passo del Gran San Bernardo. pass Italy/Switzerland
Great Salt Desert see Kavīr, Dasht-e
Great Salt Lake 22 A3 salt lake Utah, W USA
Great Salt Lake Desert 22 A4 plain Utah, W USA
Great Sand Sea 49 H3 desert Egypt/Libya
Great Sandy Desert 124 C4 desert Western Australia
Great Sandy Desert see Ar Rub 'al Khālī
Great Sandy Island see Fraser Island
Great Slave Lake 15 E4 Fr. Grand Lac des Esclaves. lake Northwest Territories, NW Canada
Great Socialist People's Libyan Arab Jamahiriya see Libya
Great Sound 20 A5 sound Bermuda, NW Atlantic Ocean
Great Victoria Desert 125 C5 desert South Australia/Western Australia
Great Wall of China 106 C4 ancient monument N China Asia
Great Yarmouth 67 E6 var. Yarmouth. E England, United Kingdom
Grebenka see Hrebinka
Gredos, Sierra de 70 D3 mountain range W Spain
Greece 83 A5 off. Hellenic Republic, Gk. Ellás; anc. Hellas. country SE Europe
Greeley 22 D4 Colorado, C USA
Green Bay 18 B2 Wisconsin, N USA
Green Bay 18 B2 lake bay Michigan/Wisconsin, N USA
Greeneville 21 E1 Tennessee, S USA
Greenland 60 D3 Dan. Grønland, Inuit Kalaallit Nunaat. Danish external territory NE North America
Greenland Sea 61 F2 sea Arctic Ocean
Green Mountains 19 G2 mountain range Vermont, NE USA
Green Mountain State see Vermont
Greenock 66 C4 W Scotland, United Kingdom
Green River 22 B3 Wyoming, C USA
Green River 18 C5 river Kentucky, C USA
Green River 22 B4 river Utah, W USA
Greensboro 21 F1 North Carolina, SE USA
Greenville 20 B2 Mississippi, S USA
Greenville 21 F1 North Carolina, SE USA
Greenville 21 E1 South Carolina, SE USA
Greenville 27 G2 Texas, SW USA
Greenwich 67 B8 United Kingdom
Greenwood 20 B2 Mississippi, S USA
Greenwood 21 E2 South Carolina, SE USA
Gregory Range 126 C3 mountain range Queensland, E Australia
Greifenberg/Greifenberg in Pommern see Gryfice
Greifswald 72 D2 Mecklenburg-Vorpommern, NE Germany
Grenada 20 C2 Mississippi, S USA
Grenada 33 G5 country SE West Indies
Grenadines, The 33 H4 island group Grenada/St Vincent and the Grenadines
Grenoble 69 D5 anc. Cularo, Gratianopolis. Isère, E France
Gresham 24 B3 Oregon, NW USA
Grevená 82 B4 Dytikí Makedonía, N Greece
Grevenmacher 65 E8 Grevenmacher, E Luxembourg
Greymouth 129 B5 West Coast, South Island, New Zealand
Grey Range 127 C5 mountain range New South Wales/Queensland, E Australia
Greytown see San Juan del Norte
Griffin 20 D2 Georgia, SE USA
Grimari 54 C4 Ouaka, C Central African Republic
Grimsby 67 E5 prev. Great Grimsby. E England, United Kingdom
Grobin see Grobiņa
Grobiņa 84 B3 Ger. Grobin. Liepāja, W Latvia
Gródek Jagielloński see Horodok
Grodno see Hrodna
Grodzisk Wielkopolski 76 B3 Wielkopolskie, C Poland
Groesbeek 64 D4 Gelderland, SE Netherlands
Grójec 76 D4 Mazowieckie, C Poland
Groningen 64 E1 Groningen, NE Netherlands
Grønland see Greenland
Groote Eylandt 126 B2 island Northern Territory, N Australia
Grootfontein 56 B3 Otjozondjupa, N Namibia
Groot Karasberge 56 B4 mountain range S Namibia
Gros Islet 33 F1 N Saint Lucia
Grossa, Isola see Dugi Otok
Grossbetschkerek see Zrenjanin
Grosse Morava see Velika Morava
Grosser Sund see Suur Väin
Grosseto 74 B4 Toscana, C Italy
Grossglockner 73 C7 mountain W Austria
Grosskanizsa see Nagykanizsa
Gross-Karol see Carei
Grosskikinda see Kikinda
Grossmichel see Michalovce
Gross-Schlatten see Abrud
Grosswardein see Oradea
Groznyy 89 B8 Chechenskaya Respublika, SW Russian Federation
Grudovo see Sredets
Grudziądz 76 C3 Ger. Graudenz. Kujawsko-pomorskie, C Poland
Grums 63 B6 Värmland, C Sweden
Grünberg/Grünberg in Schlesien see Zielona Góra
Grüneberg see Zielona Góra
Gruzinskaya SSR/Gruziya see Georgia
Gryazi 89 B6 Lipetskaya Oblast', W Russian Federation
Gryfice 76 B2 Ger. Greifenberg, Greifenberg in Pommern. Zachodnio-pomorskie, NW Poland
Guabito 31 E4 Bocas del Toro, NW Panama
Guadalajara 28 D4 Jalisco, C Mexico
Guadalajara 71 E3 Ar. Wad Al-Hajarah; anc. Arriaca. Castilla-La Mancha, C Spain
Guadalcanal 122 C3 island C Solomon Islands
Guadalquivir 70 D4 river W Spain
Guadalupe 28 D3 Zacatecas, C Mexico
Guadalupe Peak 26 D3 mountain Texas, SW USA
Guadalupe River 27 G4 river SW USA
Guadarrama, Sierra de 71 E2 mountain range C Spain
Guadeloupe 33 H3 French overseas department E West Indies
Guadiana 70 C4 river Portugal/Spain
Guadix 71 E4 Andalucía, S Spain
Guaimaca 30 C2 Francisco Morazán, C Honduras
Guajira, Península de la 36 B1 peninsula N Colombia
Gualaco 30 D2 Olancho, C Honduras
Gualán 30 B2 Zacapa, C Guatemala
Gualdicciolo 74 D1 NW San Marino
Gualeguaychú 42 D4 Entre Ríos, E Argentina
Guam 122 B1 US unincorporated territory W Pacific Ocean
Guamúchil 28 C3 Sinaloa, C Mexico
Guanabacoa 32 B2 La Habana, W Cuba
Guanajuato 29 E4 Guanajuato, C Mexico
Guanare 36 C2 Portuguesa, N Venezuela
Guanare, Río 36 D2 river W Venezuela
Guangdong 106 C6 var. Guangdong Sheng, Kuang-tung, Kwangtung, Yue. province S China
Guangdong Sheng see Guangdong
Guangju see Kwangju
Guangxi see Guangxi Zhuangzu Zizhiqu
Guangxi Zhuangzu Zizhiqu 106 C6 var. Guangxi, Gui, Kuang-hsi, Kwangsi, Eng. Kwangsi Chuang Autonomous Region. autonomous region S China
Guangyuan 106 B5 var. Kuang-yuan, Kwangyuan. Sichuan, C China
Guangzhou 106 C6 var. Kuang-chou, Kwangchow, Eng. Canton. province capital Guangdong, S China
Guantánamo 32 D3 Guantánamo, SE Cuba
Guantánamo, Bahía de 32 D3 Eng. Guantanamo Bay. US military base SE Cuba
Guantanamo Bay see Guantánamo, Bahía de
Guaporé, Rio 40 D3 var. Río Iténez. river Bolivia/Brazil
Guarda 70 C3 Guarda, N Portugal
Guarumal 31 F5 Veraguas, S Panama
Guasave 28 C3 Sinaloa, C Mexico
Guatemala 30 A2 off. Republic of Guatemala. country Central America
Guatemala Basin 13 B7 undersea basin E Pacific Ocean
Guatemala City see Ciudad de Guatemala
Guatemala, Republic of see Guatemala
Guaviare 34 B2 off. Comisaría Guaviare. province S Colombia
Guaviare, Comisaría see Guaviare
Guaviare, Río 36 D3 river E Colombia
Guayanas, Macizo de las see Guiana Highlands
Guayaquil 38 A2 var. Santiago de Guayaquil. Guayas, SW Ecuador
Guayaquil, Golfo de 38 A2 var. Gulf of Guayaquil. gulf SW Ecuador
Guayaquil, Gulf of see Guayaquil, Golfo de
Guaymas 28 B2 Sonora, NW Mexico
Gubadag 100 C2 Turkm. Tel'man; prev. Tel'mansk. Daşoguz Welaýaty, N Turkmenistan
Guben 72 D4 var. Wilhelm-Pieck-Stadt. Brandenburg, E Germany
Gudara see Ghŭdara
Gudaut'a 95 E1 NW Georgia
Guéret 68 C4 Creuse, C France
Guernsey 67 D8 island Channel Islands, NW Europe
Guerrero Negro 28 A2 Baja California Sur, NW Mexico
Gui see Guangxi Zhuangzu Zizhiqu
Guiana see French Guiana
Guiana Highlands 40 D1 var. Macizo de las Guayanas. mountain range N South America
Guiba see Juba
Guidder see Guider
Guider 54 B4 var. Guidder. Nord, N Cameroon
Guidimouni 53 G3 Zinder, S Niger
Guildford 67 D7 SE England, United Kingdom
Guilin 106 C6 var. Kuei-lin, Kweilin. Guangxi Zhuangzu Zizhiqu, S China
Guimarães 70 B2 var. Guimaráes. Braga, N Portugal
Guimaráes see Guimarães
Guinea 52 C4 off. Republic of Guinea, var. Guinée; prev. French Guinea, People's Revolutionary Republic of Guinea. country W Africa
Guinea Basin 47 A5 undersea basin E Atlantic Ocean
Guinea-Bissau 52 B4 off. Republic of Guinea-Bissau, Fr. Guinée-Bissau, Port. Guiné-Bissau; prev. Portuguese Guinea. country W Africa
Guinea-Bissau, Republic of see Guinea-Bissau
Guinea, Gulf of 46 B4 Fr. Golfe de Guinée. gulf E Atlantic Ocean
Guinea, People's Revolutionary Republic of see Guinea
Guinea, Republic of see Guinea
Guiné-Bissau see Guinea-Bissau
Guinée see Guinea
Guinée-Bissau see Guinea-Bissau
Guinée, Golfe de see Guinea, Gulf of
Güiria 37 E1 Sucre, NE Venezuela
Guiyang 106 B6 var. Kuei-Yang, Kuei-yang, Kueyang, Kweiyang; prev. Kweichu. province capital Guizhou, S China
Guizhou 106 B6 Guangdong, SE China
Gujarāt 112 C4 var. Gujerat. cultural region W India
Gujerat see Gujarāt
Gujrānwāla 112 D2 Punjab, NE Pakistan
Gujrāt 112 D2 Punjab, E Pakistan
Gulbarga 110 C1 Karnātaka, C India
Gulbene 84 D3 Ger. Alt-Schwanenburg. Gulbene, NE Latvia
Gulf of Liaotung see Liaodong Wan
Gulfport 20 C3 Mississippi, S USA
Gulf, The 98 C4 var. Persian Gulf, Ar. Khalīj al 'Arabī, Per. Khalīj-e Fars. gulf SW Asia
Gulistan see Guliston
Guliston 101 E2 Rus. Gulistan. Sirdaryo Viloyati, E Uzbekistan
Gulja see Yining
Gulkana 14 D3 Alaska, USA
Gulu 51 B6 N Uganda
Gulyantsi 82 C1 Pleven, N Bulgaria
Guma see Pishan
Gumbinnen see Gusev
Gumpolds see Humpolec
Gümülcine/Gümüljina see Komotiní
Gümüşane see Gümüşhane
Gümüşhane 95 E3 var. Gümüşane, Gumushkhane. Gümüşhane, NE Turkey
Gumushkhane see Gümüşhane
Güney Doğu Toroslar 95 E4 mountain range SE Turkey
Gunnbjørn Fjeld 60 D4 var. Gunnbjörns Bjerge. mountain C Greenland
Gunnbjörns Bjerge see Gunnbjørn Fjeld
Gunnedah 127 D6 New South Wales, SE Australia
Gunnison 22 C5 Colorado, C USA
Gurbansoltan Eje 100 C2 prev. Ýylanly, Rus. Il'yaly. Daşoguz Welaýaty, N Turkmenistan
Gurbantünggüt Shamo 104 B2 desert W China
Gurgan see Gorgān
Guri, Embalse de 37 E2 reservoir E Venezuela
Gurkfeld see Krško
Gurktaler Alpen 73 D7 mountain range S Austria
Gürün 94 D3 Sivas, C Turkey
Gur'yev/Gur'yevskaya Oblast' see Atyrau
Gusau 53 G4 Zamfara, NW Nigeria
Gusev 84 B4 Ger. Gumbinnen. Kaliningradskaya Oblast', W Russian Federation
Gustavus 14 D4 Alaska, USA
Güstrow 72 C3 Mecklenburg-Vorpommern, NE Germany
Guta/Gúta see Kolárovo
Gütersloh 72 B4 Nordrhein-Westfalen, W Germany
Gutta see Kolárovo
Guttstadt see Dobre Miasto
Guwāhāti 113 G3 prev. Gauhāti. Assam, NE India
Guyana 37 F3 off. Co-operative Republic of Guyana; prev. British Guiana. country N South America
Guyana, Co-operative Republic of see Guyana
Guyane see French Guiana
Guymon 27 E1 Oklahoma, C USA
Güzelyurt 80 C5 Gk. Kólpos Mórfu, Morphou. W Cyprus
Gvardeysk 84 A4 Ger. Tapaiu. Kaliningradskaya Oblast', W Russian Federation
Gwādar 112 A3 var. Gwadur. Baluchistān, SW Pakistan
Gwadur see Gwādar
Gwalior 112 D3 Madhya Pradesh, C India
Gwanda 56 D3 Matabeleland South, SW Zimbabwe
Gwy see Wye
Gyandzha see Gäncä
Gyangzê 104 C5 Xizang Zizhiqu, W China
Gyaring Co 104 C5 lake W China
Gyêgu see Yushu
Gyergyószentmiklós see Gheorgheni
Gyixong see Gonggar
Gympie 127 E5 Queensland, E Australia
Gyomaendrőd 77 D7 Békés, SE Hungary
Gyöngyös 77 D6 Heves, NE Hungary
Győr 77 C6 Ger. Raab, Lat. Arrabona. Győr-Moson-Sopron, NW Hungary
Gýtheio 83 B6 var. Githio; prev. Yíthion. Pelopónnisos, S Greece
Gyulafehérvár see Alba Iulia
Gyumri 95 F2 var. Giumri, Rus. Kumayri; prev. Aleksandropol', Leninakan. W Armenia
Gyzyrlabat see Serdar

H

Haabai see Ha'apai Group
Haacht 65 C6 Vlaams Brabant, C Belgium
Haaksbergen 64 E3 Overijssel, E Netherlands
Ha'apai Group 123 F4 var. Haabai. island group C Tonga
Haapsalu 84 D2 Ger. Hapsal. Läänemaa, W Estonia
Ha'Arava see 'Arabah, Wādī al
Haarlem 64 C3 prev. Harlem. Noord-Holland, W Netherlands
Haast 129 B6 West Coast, South Island, New Zealand
Hachijo-jima 109 D6 island Izu-shotō, SE Japan
Hachinohe 108 D3 Aomori, Honshū, C Japan
Haḑabat al Jilf al Kabīr 50 A2 var. Gilf Kebir Plateau. plateau SW Egypt
Hadama see Nazrēt
Hadejia 53 G4 Jigawa, N Nigeria
Hadejia 53 G3 river N Nigeria
Hadera 97 A6 var. Khadera; prev. Ḩadera. Haifa, C Israel
Ḩadera see Hadera
Hadhdhunmathi Atoll 110 A5 atoll S Maldives
Ha Đông 114 D3 var. Hadong. Ha Tây, N Vietnam
Hadong see Ha Đông
Hadramaut see Ḩaḑramawt
Ḩaḑramawt 99 C6 Eng. Hadramaut. mountain range S Yemen
Hadrianopolis see Edirne
Haerbin/Haerhpin/Ha-erh-pin see Harbin
Hafnia see Denmark
Hafnia see København
Hafren see Severn
Hafun, Ras see Xaafuun, Raas
Hagåtña 122 B1, var. Agaña. dependent territory capital (Guam) NW Guam

Hagerstown – Hrandzichy

Hagerstown 19 E4 Maryland, NE USA
Ha Giang 114 D3 Ha Giang, N Vietnam
Hagios Evstrátios see Ágios Efstrátios
HaGolan see Golan Heights
Hagondange 68 D3 Moselle, NE France
Haguenau 68 E3 Bas-Rhin, NE France
Haibowan see Wuhai
Haicheng 106 D3 Liaoning, NE China
Haidarabad see Hyderābād
Haifa see Hefa
Haifa, Bay of see Mifrats Hefa
Haifong see Hai Phong
Haikou 106 C7 var. Hai-k'ou, Hoihow, Fr. Hoï-Hao. province capital Hainan, S China
Hai-k'ou see Haikou
Ḩā'il 98 B4 Ḩā'il, NW Saudi Arabia
Hailuoto 62 D4 Swe. Karlö. island W Finland
Hainan 106 B7 var. Hainan Sheng, Qiong. province S China
Hainan Dao 106 C7 island S China
Hainan Sheng see Hainan
Hainasch see Ainaži
Haines 14 D4 Alaska, USA
Hainichen 72 D4 Sachsen, E Germany
Hai Phong 114 D3 var. Haifong, Haiphong. N Vietnam
Haiphong see Hai Phong
Haiti 32 D3 off. Republic of Haiti. country C West Indies
Haiti, Republic of see Haiti
Haiya 50 C3 Red Sea, NE Sudan
Hajdúhadház 77 D6 Hajdú-Bihar, E Hungary
Hajîne see Abū Ḩardān
Hajnówka 76 E3 Ger. Hermhausen. Podlaskie, NE Poland
Hakodate 108 D3 Hokkaidō, NE Japan
Hal see Halle
Ḩalab 96 B2 Eng. Aleppo, Fr. Alep; anc. Beroea. Ḩalab, NW Syria
Ḩalāniyāt, Juzur al 99 D6 var. Jazā'ir Bin Ghalfān, Eng. Kuria Muria Islands. island group S Oman
Halberstadt 72 C4 Sachsen-Anhalt, C Germany
Halden 63 B6 prev. Fredrikshald. Østfold, S Norway
Halfmoon Bay 129 A8 var. Oban. Stewart Island, Southland, New Zealand
Haliacmon see Aliákmonas
Halifax 17 F4 province capital Nova Scotia, SE Canada
Halkida see Chalkída
Halle 65 B6 Fr. Hal. Vlaams Brabant, C Belgium
Halle 72 C4 var. Halle an der Saale. Sachsen-Anhalt, C Germany
Halle an der Saale see Halle
Halle-Neustadt 72 C4 Sachsen-Anhalt, C Germany
Halley 132 B2 UK research station Antarctica
Hall Islands 120 B2 island group C Micronesia
Halls Creek 124 C3 Western Australia
Halmahera, Laut see Halmahera Sea
Halmahera, Pulau 117 F3 prev. Djailolo, Gilolo, Jailolo. island E Indonesia
Halmahera Sea 117 F4 Ind. Laut Halmahera. sea E Indonesia
Halmstad 63 B7 Halland, S Sweden
Hälsingborg see Helsingborg
Hamada 109 B6 Shimane, Honshū, SW Japan
Hamadān 98 C3 anc. Ecbatana. Hamadān, W Iran
Ḩamāh 96 B3 var. Hama; anc. Epiphania, Bibl. Hamath. Ḩamāh, W Syria
Hamamatsu 109 D6 var. Hamamatu. Shizuoka, Honshū, S Japan
Hamamatu see Hamamatsu
Hamar 63 B5 prev. Storhammer. Hedmark, S Norway
Hamath see Ḩamāh
Hamburg 72 B3 Hamburg, N Germany
Hamd, Wadi al 98 A4 dry watercourse W Saudi Arabia
Hämeenlinna 63 D5 Swe. Tavastehus. Etelä-Suomi, S Finland
HaMela h, Yam see Dead Sea
Hamersley Range 124 A4 mountain range Western Australia
Hamhŭng 107 E3 C North Korea
Hami 104 C3 var. Ha-mi, Uigh. Kumul, Qomul. Xinjiang Uygur Zizhiqu, NW China
Ha-mi see Hami
Hamilton 20 A5 dependent territory capital (Bermuda) C Bermuda
Hamilton 16 D5 Ontario, S Canada
Hamilton 128 D3 Waikato, North Island, New Zealand
Hamilton 66 C4 S Scotland, United Kingdom
Hamilton 20 C2 Alabama, S USA
Hamim, Wadi al 49 G2 river NE Libya
Hamïs Musait see Khamīs Mushayt
Hamm 72 B4 var. Hamm in Westfalen. Nordrhein-Westfalen, W Germany
Ḩammāmāt, Khalīj al see Hammamet, Golfe de
Hammamet, Golfe de 80 D3 Ar. Khalīj al Ḩammāmāt. gulf NE Tunisia
Hammar, Hawr al 98 C3 lake SE Iraq
Hamm in Westfalen see Hamm
Hampden 129 B7 Otago, South Island, New Zealand
Hampstead 67 A7 Maryland, USA
Ħamrun 80 B5 C Malta
Hāmūn, Daryācheh-ye see Şāberī, Hāmūn-e/ Sīstān, Daryācheh-ye
Hamwih see Southampton
Hâncești see Hincești
Hancewicze see Hantsavichy
Handan 106 C4 var. Han-tan. Hebei, E China
Haneda 108 A2 (Tōkyō) Tōkyō, Honshū, S Japan
HaNegev 97 A7 Eng. Negev. desert S Israel
Hanford 25 C6 California, W USA
Hangayn Nuruu 104 D2 mountain range C Mongolia
Hang-chou/Hangchow see Hangzhou
Hangö see Hanko
Hangzhou 106 D5 var. Hang-chou, Hangchow. province capital Zhejiang, SE China
Hania see Chaniá
Hanka, Lake see Khanka, Lake
Hanko 63 D6 Swe. Hangö. Etelä-Suomi, SW Finland
Han-kou/Han-k'ou/Hankow see Wuhan
Hanmer Springs 129 C5 Canterbury, South Island, New Zealand
Hannibal 23 G4 Missouri, C USA
Hannover 72 B3 Eng. Hanover. Niedersachsen, NW Germany
Hanöbukten 63 B7 bay S Sweden
Ha Nôi 114 D3 Eng. Hanoi, Fr. Hanoï. country capital (Vietnam) N Vietnam
Hanover see Hannover
Han Shui 105 E4 river C China
Han-tan see Handan
Hantsavichy 85 B6 Pol. Hancewicze, Rus. Gantsevichi. Brestskaya Voblasts', SW Belarus
Hanyang see Wuhan
Hanzhong 106 B5 Shaanxi, C China
Hāora 113 F4 prev. Howrah. West Bengal, NE India
Haparanda 62 D4 Norrbotten, N Sweden
Hapsal see Haapsalu
Haradok 85 E5 Rus. Gorodok. Vitsyebskaya Voblasts', N Belarus
Haradzyets 85 B6 Rus. Gorodets. Brestskaya Voblasts', SW Belarus
Haramachi 108 D4 Fukushima, Honshū, E Japan
Harany 85 D5 Rus. Gorany. Vitsyebskaya Voblasts', N Belarus
Harare 56 D3 prev. Salisbury. country capital (Zimbabwe) Mashonaland East, NE Zimbabwe
Harbavichy 85 E6 Rus. Gorbovichi. Mahilyowskaya Voblasts', E Belarus
Harbel 52 C5 W Liberia
Harbin 107 E2 var. Haerbin, Ha-erh-pin, Kharbin; prev. Haerhpin, Pingkiang, Pinkiang. province capital Heilongjiang, NE China
Hardangerfjorden 63 A6 fjord S Norway
Hardangervidda 63 A6 plateau S Norway
Hardenberg 64 E3 Overijssel, E Netherlands
Harelbeke 65 A6 var. Harlebeke. West-Vlaanderen, W Belgium
Harem see Ḩārim
Haren 64 E2 Groningen, NE Netherlands
Hārer 51 D5 E Ethiopia
Hargeisa see Hargeysa
Hargeysa 51 D5 var. Hargeisa. Woqooyi Galbeed, NW Somalia
Hariana see Haryāna
Hari, Batang 116 B4 prev. Djambi. river Sumatera, W Indonesia
Ḩārim 96 B2 var. Harem. Idlib, W Syria
Harima-nada 109 B6 sea S Japan
Harirud 101 E4 var. Tedzhen, Turkm. Tejen. river Afghanistan/Iran
Harlan 23 F3 Iowa, C USA
Harlebeke see Harelbeke
Harlem see Haarlem
Harlingen 64 D2 Fris. Harns. Friesland, N Netherlands
Harlingen 27 G5 Texas, SW USA
Harlow 67 E6 E England, United Kingdom
Harney Basin 24 B4 basin Oregon, NW USA
Härnösand 63 C5 var. Hernösand. Västernorrland, C Sweden
Harns see Harlingen
Harper 52 D5 var. Cape Palmas. NE Liberia
Harricana 16 D3 river Québec, SE Canada
Harris 66 B3 physical region NW Scotland, United Kingdom
Harrisburg 19 E4 state capital Pennsylvania, NE USA
Harrisonburg 19 E4 Virginia, NE USA
Harrison, Cape 17 F2 headland Newfoundland and Labrador, E Canada
Harris Ridge see Lomonosov Ridge
Harrogate 67 D5 N England, United Kingdom
Hârșova 86 D5 prev. Hirsova. Constanța, SE Romania
Harstad 62 C2 Troms, N Norway
Hartford 19 G3 state capital Connecticut, NE USA
Hartlepool 67 D5 N England, United Kingdom
Harunabad see Eslāmābād
Har Us Gol 104 C2 lake Hovd, W Mongolia
Har Us Nuur 104 C2 lake NW Mongolia
Harwich 67 E6 E England, United Kingdom
Haryāna 112 D2 var. Hariana. cultural region N India
Hashemite Kingdom of Jordan see Jordan
Hasselt 65 C6 Limburg, NE Belgium
Hassetché see Al Ḩasakah
Hasta Colonia/Hasta Pompeia see Asti
Hastings 128 E4 Hawke's Bay, North Island, New Zealand
Hastings 67 E7 SE England, United Kingdom
Hastings 23 E4 Nebraska, C USA
Hațeg 86 B4 Ger. Wallenthal, Hung. Hátszeg; prev. Hatzeg, Hötzing. Hunedoara, SW Romania
Hátszeg see Hațeg
Hattem 64 D3 Gelderland, E Netherlands
Hatteras, Cape 21 G1 headland North Carolina, SE USA
Hatteras Plain 13 D6 abyssal plain W Atlantic Ocean
Hattiesburg 20 C3 Mississippi, S USA
Hatton Bank see Hatton Ridge
Hatton Ridge 58 B2 var. Hatton Bank. undersea ridge N Atlantic Ocean
Hat Yai 115 C7 var. Ban Hat Yai. Songkhla, SW Thailand
Hatzeg see Hațeg
Hatzfeld see Jimbolia
Haugesund 63 A6 Rogaland, S Norway
Haukeligrend 63 A6 Telemark, S Norway
Haukivesi 63 E5 lake SE Finland
Hauraki Gulf 128 D2 gulf North Island, N New Zealand
Hauroko, Lake 129 A7 lake South Island, New Zealand
Haut Atlas 48 C2 Eng. High Atlas. mountain range C Morocco
Hautes Fagnes 65 D6 Ger. Hohes Venn. mountain range E Belgium
Hauts Plateaux 48 D2 plateau Algeria/Morocco
Hauzenberg 73 D6 Bayern, SE Germany
Havana 13 D6 Illinois, N USA
Havana see La Habana
Havant 67 D7 S England, United Kingdom
Havelock 21 F1 North Carolina, SE USA
Havelock North 128 E4 Hawke's Bay, North Island, New Zealand
Haverfordwest 67 C6 SW Wales, United Kingdom
Havířov 77 C5 Moravskoslezský Kraj, E Czech Republic
Havre 22 C1 Montana, NW USA
Havre see le Havre
Havre-St-Pierre 17 F3 Québec, E Canada
Hawai'i 25 A8 off. State of Hawai'i, also known as Aloha State, Paradise of the Pacific, var. Hawaii. state USA, C Pacific Ocean
Hawai'i 25 B8 var. Hawaii. island Hawaiian Islands, USA, C Pacific Ocean
Hawaiian Islands 130 D2 prev. Sandwich Islands. island group Hawaii, USA
Hawaiian Ridge 130 H4 undersea ridge N Pacific Ocean
Hawea, Lake 129 B6 lake South Island, New Zealand
Hawera 128 D4 Taranaki, North Island, New Zealand
Hawick 66 C4 SE Scotland, United Kingdom
Hawke Bay 128 E4 bay North Island, New Zealand
Hawkeye State see Iowa
Hawlêr see Arbīl
Hawthorne 25 C6 Nevada, W USA
Hay 127 C6 New South Wales, SE Australia
HaYarden see Jordan
Hayastani Hanrapetut'yun see Armenia
Hayes 16 B2 river Manitoba, C Canada
Hay River 15 E4 Northwest Territories, W Canada
Hays 23 E5 Kansas, C USA
Haysyn 86 D3 Rus. Gaysin. Vinnyts'ka Oblast', C Ukraine
Hazar 100 B2 prev. Rus. Cheleken. Balkan Welaýaty, W Turkmenistan
Heard and McDonald Islands 119 B7 Australian external territory S Indian Ocean
Hearst 16 C4 Ontario, S Canada
Heart of Dixie see Alabama
Heathrow 67 A8 (London) SE England, United Kingdom
Hebei 106 C4 var. Hebei Sheng, Hopeh, Hopei, Ji; prev. Chihli. province E China
Hebei Sheng see Hebei
Hebron 97 A6 var. Al Khalīl, El Khalil, Heb. Hevron; anc. Kiriath-Arba. S West Bank
Heemskerk 64 C3 Noord-Holland, W Netherlands
Heerde 64 D3 Gelderland, E Netherlands
Heerenveen 64 D2 Fris. It Hearrenfean. Friesland, N Netherlands
Heerhugowaard 64 C2 Noord-Holland, NW Netherlands
Heerlen 65 D6 Limburg, SE Netherlands
Heerwegen see Polkowice
Hefa 97 A5 var. Haifa, hist. Caiffa, Caiphas; anc. Sycaminum. Haifa, N Israel
Hefa, Mifraz see Mifrats Hefa
Hefei 106 D5 var. Hofei, hist. Luchow. province capital Anhui, E China
Hegang 107 E2 Heilongjiang, NE China
Hei see Heilongjiang
Heide 72 B2 Schleswig-Holstein, N Germany
Heidelberg 73 B5 Baden-Württemberg, SW Germany
Heidenheim see Heidenheim an der Brenz
Heidenheim an der Brenz 73 B6 var. Heidenheim. Baden-Württemberg, S Germany
Hei-ho see Nagqu
Heilbronn 73 B6 Baden-Württemberg, SW Germany
Heiligenbeil see Mamonovo
Heilongjiang 106 D2 var. Hei, Heilongjiang Sheng, Hei-lung-chiang, Heilungkiang. province NE China
Heilong Jiang see Amur
Heilongjiang Sheng see Heilongjiang
Heiloo 64 C3 Noord-Holland, NW Netherlands
Heilsberg see Lidzbark Warmiński
Hei-lung-chiang/Heilungkiang see Heilongjiang
Heimdal 63 B5 Sør-Trøndelag, S Norway
Heinaste see Ainaži
Hekimhan 94 D3 Malatya, C Turkey
Helena 22 B2 state capital Montana, NW USA
Helensville 128 D2 Auckland, North Island, New Zealand
Helgoland Bay see Helgoländer Bucht
Helgoländer Bucht 72 A2 var. Helgoland Bay, Heligoland Bight. bay NW Germany
Heligoland Bight see Helgoländer Bucht
Heliopolis see Baalbek
Hellas see Greece
Hellenic Republic see Greece
Hellevoetsluis 64 B4 Zuid-Holland, SW Netherlands
Hellín 71 E4 Castilla-La Mancha, C Spain
Darya-ye Helmand 100 D5 var. Rūd-e Hīrmand. river Afghanistan/Iran
Helmantica see Salamanca
Helmond 65 D5 Noord-Brabant, S Netherlands
Helsingborg 63 B7 prev. Hälsingborg. Skåne, S Sweden
Helsingfors see Helsinki
Helsinki 63 D6 Swe. Helsingfors. country capital (Finland) Etelä-Suomi, S Finland
Heltau see Cisnădie
Helvetia see Switzerland
Henan 106 C5 var. Henan Sheng, Honan, Yu. province C China
Henderson 18 B5 Kentucky, S USA
Henderson 25 D7 Nevada, W USA
Henderson 27 H3 Texas, SW USA
Hendū Kosh see Hindu Kush
Hengchow see Hengyang
Hengduan Shan 106 A5 mountain range SW China
Hengelo 64 E3 Overijssel, E Netherlands
Hengnan see Hengyang
Hengyang 106 C6 var. Hengnan, Heng-yang; prev. Hengchow. Hunan, S China
Heng-yang see Hengyang
Heniches'k 87 F4 Rus. Genichesk. Khersons'ka Oblast', S Ukraine
Hennebont 68 A3 Morbihan, NW France
Henrique de Carvalho see Saurimo
Henzada see Hinthada
Herakleion see Irákleio
Herāt 100 D4 var. Herat; anc. Aria. Herāt, W Afghanistan
Heredia 31 E4 Heredia, C Costa Rica
Hereford 27 E2 Texas, SW USA
Herford 72 B4 Nordrhein-Westfalen, NW Germany
Héristal see Herstal
Herk-de-Stad 65 C6 Limburg, NE Belgium
Herlen Gol/Herlen He see Kerulen
Hermannstadt see Sibiu
Hermansverk 63 A5 Sogn Og Fjordane, S Norway
Hermhausen see Hajnówka
Hermiston 24 C2 Oregon, NW USA
Hermon, Mount 97 B5 Ar. Jabal ash Shaykh. mountain S Syria
Hermosillo 28 B2 Sonora, NW Mexico
Hermoupolis see Ermoúpoli
Hernösand see Härnösand
Herrera del Duque 70 D3 Extremadura, W Spain
Herselt 65 C5 Antwerpen, C Belgium
Herstal 65 D6 Fr. Héristal. Liège, E Belgium
Herzogenbusch see 's-Hertogenbosch
Hesse see Hessen
Hessen 73 B5 Eng./Fr. Hesse. state C Germany
Hevron see Hebron
Heydebrech see Kędzierzyn-Kozle
Heydekrug see Šilutė
Heywood Islands 124 C3 island group Western Australia
Hibbing 23 F1 Minnesota, N USA
Hibernia see Ireland
Hidalgo del Parral 28 C2 var. Parral. Chihuahua, N Mexico
Hida-sanmyaku 109 C5 mountain range Honshū, S Japan
Hierosolyma see Jerusalem
Hierro 48 A3 var. Ferro. island Islas Canarias, Spain, NE Atlantic Ocean
High Atlas see Haut Atlas
High Plains see Great Plains
High Point 21 E1 North Carolina, SE USA
Hiiumaa 84 C2 Ger. Dagden, Swe. Dagö. island W Estonia
Hikurangi 128 D2 Northland, North Island, New Zealand
Hildesheim 72 B4 Niedersachsen, N Germany
Hilla see Al Ḩillah
Hillaby, Mount 33 G1 mountain N Barbados
Hill Bank 30 C1 Orange Walk, N Belize
Hillegom 64 C3 Zuid-Holland, W Netherlands
Hilo 25 B8 Hawaii, USA, C Pacific Ocean
Hilton Head Island 21 E2 South Carolina, SE USA
Hilversum 64 C3 Noord-Holland, C Netherlands
Himalaya/Himalaya Shan see Himalayas
Himalayas 113 E2 var. Himalaya, Chin. Himalaya Shan. mountain range S Asia
Himeji 109 C6 var. Himezi. Hyōgo, Honshū, SW Japan
Himezi see Himeji
Ḩimş 96 B4 var. Homs; anc. Emesa. Ḩimş, C Syria
Hincești 86 D4 var. Hâncești; prev. Kotovsk. C Moldova
Hinchinbrook Island 126 D3 island Queensland, NE Australia
Hinds 129 C6 Canterbury, South Island, New Zealand
Hindu Kush 101 F4 Per. Hendū Kosh. mountain range Afghanistan/Pakistan
Hinesville 21 E3 Georgia, SE USA
Hinnøya 62 C3 Lapp. Iinnasuolu. island C Norway
Hinson Bay 20 A5 bay W Bermuda W Atlantic Ocean
Hinthada 114 B4 var. Henzada. Ayeyarwady, SW Myanmar (Burma)
Hios see Chíos
Hirfanlı Barajı 94 C3 reservoir C Turkey
Hīrmand, Rūd-e see Helmand, Daryā-ye
Hirosaki 108 D3 Aomori, Honshū, C Japan
Hiroshima 109 B6 var. Hirosima. Hiroshima, Honshū, SW Japan
Hirschberg/Hirschberg im Riesengebirge/ Hirschberg in Schlesien see Jelenia Góra
Hirson 68 D3 Aisne, N France
Hirşova see Hârșova
Hispalis see Sevilla
Hispana/Hispania see Spain
Hispaniola 34 B1 island Dominion Republic/Haiti
Hitachi 109 D5 var. Hitati. Ibaraki, Honshū, S Japan
Hitati see Hitachi
Hitra 62 A4 prev. Hitteren. island S Norway
Hitteren see Hitra
Hjälmaren 63 C6 Eng. Lake Hjalmar. lake C Sweden
Hjalmar, Lake see Hjälmaren
Hjørring 63 B7 Nordjylland, N Denmark
Hkakabo Razi 114 B1 mountain Myanmar (Burma)/China
Hlobyne 87 F2 Rus. Globino. Poltavs'ka Oblast', NE Ukraine
Hlukhiv 87 F1 Rus. Glukhov. Sums'ka Oblast', NE Ukraine
Hlybokaye 85 D5 Rus. Glubokoye. Vitsyebskaya Voblasts', N Belarus
Hoa Binh 114 D3 Hoa Binh, N Vietnam
Hoang Lien Son 114 D3 mountain range N Vietnam
Hobart 127 C8 prev. Hobarton, Hobart Town. state capital Tasmania, SE Australia
Hobarton/Hobart Town see Hobart
Hobbs 27 E3 New Mexico, SW USA
Hobro 63 A7 Nordjylland, N Denmark
Hô Chi Minh 115 E6 var. Ho Chi Minh City; prev. Saigon. S Vietnam
Ho Chi Minh City see Hô Chi Minh
Hodeida see Al Ḩudaydah
Hódmezővásárhely 77 D7 Csongrád, SE Hungary
Hodna, Chott El 80 C4 var. Chott el-Hodna, Ar. Shatt al-Hodna. salt lake N Algeria
Hodna, Chott el-/Hodna, Shatt al- see Hodna, Chott El
Hodonín 77 C5 Ger. Göding. Jihomoravský Kraj, SE Czech Republic
Hoei see Huy
Hoey see Huy
Hof 73 C5 Bayern, SE Germany
Hofei see Hefei
Hōfu 109 B7 Yamaguchi, Honshū, SW Japan
Hofuf see Al Hufūf
Hogoley Islands see Chuuk Islands
Hohensalza see Inowrocław
Hohenstadt see Zábřeh
Hohes Venn see Hautes Fagnes
Hohe Tauern 73 C7 mountain range W Austria
Hohhot 105 F3 var. Huhehot, Huhohaote, Mong. Kukukhoto; prev. Kweisui, Kwesui. Nei Mongol Zizhiqu, N China
Hôi An 115 E5 prev. Faifo. Quang Nam-Đa Nāng, C Vietnam
Hoï-Hao/Hoihow see Haikou
Hokianga Harbour 128 C2 inlet SE Tasman Sea
Hokitika 129 B5 West Coast, South Island, New Zealand
Hokkaido 108 C2 prev. Ezo, Yeso, Yezo. island NE Japan
Hola Prystan' 87 E4 Rus. Golaya Pristan. Khersons'ka Oblast', S Ukraine
Holbrook 26 B2 Arizona, SW USA
Holetown 33 G1 prev. Jamestown. W Barbados
Holguín 32 C2 Holguín, SE Cuba
Hollabrunn 73 E6 Niederösterreich, NE Austria
Holland see Netherlands
Hollandia see Jayapura
Holly Springs 20 C1 Mississippi, S USA
Holman 15 E3 Victoria Island, Northwest Territories, N Canada
Holmsund 62 D4 Västerbotten, N Sweden
Holon 97 A6 var. Kholon; prev. Ḩolon. Tel Aviv, C Israel
Ḩolon see Holon
Holovanivs'k 87 E3 Rus. Golovanevsk. Kirovohrads'ka Oblast', C Ukraine
Holstebro 63 A7 Ringkøbing, W Denmark
Holsteinborg/Holsteinsborg/Holstenborg/ Holstensborg see Sisimiut
Holyhead 67 C5 Wel. Caer Gybi. NW Wales, United Kingdom
Hombori 53 E3 Mopti, S Mali
Homs see Al Khums, Libya
Homs see Ḩimş
Homyel' 85 D7 Rus. Gomel'. Homyel'skaya Voblasts', SE Belarus
Honan see Luoyang, China
Honan see Henan, China
Hondo 27 F4 Texas, SW USA
Hondo see Honshū
Honduras 30 C2 off. Republic of Honduras. country Central America
Honduras, Golfo de see Honduras, Gulf of
Honduras, Gulf of 30 C2 Sp. Golfo de Honduras. gulf W Caribbean Sea
Honduras, Republic of see Honduras
Hønefoss 63 B6 Buskerud, S Norway
Honey Lake 25 B5 lake California, W USA
Hon Gai see Hông Gai
Hongay see Hông Gai
Hông Gai 114 E3 var. Hon Gai, Hongay. Quang Ninh, N Vietnam
Hông Hà, Sông see Red River
Hong Kong 106 A1 Chin. Xianggang. Hong Kong, S China
Hong Kong Island 106 B2 island S China Asia
Honiara 122 C3 country capital (Solomon Islands) Guadalcanal, C Solomon Islands
Honjō 108 D4 var. Honzyô, Yurihonjō. Akita, Honshū, C Japan
Honolulu 25 A8 state capital O'ahu, Hawaii, USA, C Pacific Ocean
Honshu 109 E5 var. Hondo, Honsyû. island SW Japan
Honsyû see Honshū
Honte see Westerschelde
Honzyô see Honjō
Hoogeveen 64 E2 Drenthe, NE Netherlands
Hoogezand-Sappemeer 64 E2 Groningen, NE Netherlands
Hoorn 64 C2 Noord-Holland, NW Netherlands
Hoosier State see Indiana
Hopa 95 E2 Artvin, NE Turkey
Hope 14 C3 British Columbia, SW Canada
Hopedale 17 F2 Newfoundland and Labrador, NE Canada
Hopeh/Hopei see Hebei
Hopkinsville 18 B5 Kentucky, S USA
Horasan 95 F3 Erzurum, NE Turkey
Horizon Deep 130 D4 trench W Pacific Ocean
Horki 85 E6 Rus. Gorki. Mahilyowskaya Voblasts', E Belarus
Horlivka 87 G3 Rom. Adâncata, Rus. Gorlovka. Donets'ka Oblast', E Ukraine
Hormoz, Tangeh-ye see Hormuz, Strait of
Hormuz, Strait of 98 D4 var. Strait of Ormuz, Per. Tangeh-ye Hormoz. strait Iran/Oman
Cape Horn 43 C8 Eng. Cape Horn. headland S Chile
Horn, Cape see Hornos, Cabo de
Hornsby 126 E1 New South Wales, SE Australia
Horodnya 87 E1 Rus. Gorodnya. Chernihivs'ka Oblast', NE Ukraine
Horodok 86 B2 Pol. Gródek Jagielloński, Rus. Gorodok, Gorodok Yagellonski. L'vivs'ka Oblast', NW Ukraine
Horodyshche 87 E2 Rus. Gorodishche. Cherkas'ka Oblast', C Ukraine
Horoshiri-dake 108 D2 var. Horosiri Dake. mountain Hokkaidō, N Japan
Horosiri Dake see Horoshiri-dake
Horsburgh Atoll 110 A4 var. Goidhoo Atoll. atoll N Maldives
Horseshoe Bay 20 A5 bay W Bermuda W Atlantic Ocean
Horseshoe Seamounts 58 A4 seamount range E Atlantic Ocean
Horsham 127 B7 Victoria, SE Australia
Horst 65 D5 Limburg, SE Netherlands
Horten 63 B6 Vestfold, S Norway
Horyn' 85 B7 Rus. Goryn. river NW Ukraine
Hosingen 65 D7 Diekirch, NE Luxembourg
Hospitalet see L'Hospitalet de Llobregat
Hotan 104 B4 var. Khotan, Chin. Ho-t'ien. Xinjiang Uygur Zizhiqu, NW China
Ho-t'ien see Hotan
Hoting 62 C4 Jämtland, C Sweden
Hot Springs 20 B1 Arkansas, C USA
Hötzing see Hațeg
Houayxay 114 C3 var. Ban Houayxay. Bokèo, N Laos
Houghton 18 B1 Michigan, N USA
Houilles 69 B5 Yvelines, Île-de-France, N France Europe
Houlton 19 H1 Maine, NE USA
Houma 20 B3 Louisiana, S USA
Houston 27 H4 Texas, SW USA
Hovd 104 C2 var. Khovd, Kobdo; prev. Jirgalanta. Hovd, W Mongolia
Hove 67 E7 SE England, United Kingdom
Hoverla, Hora 86 C3 Rus. Gora Goverla. mountain W Ukraine
Hovsgol, Lake see Hövsgöl Nuur
Hövsgöl Nuur 104 D1 var. Lake Hovsgol. lake N Mongolia
Howa, Ouadi see Howar, Wādi
Howar, Wadi 50 A3 var. Ouadi Howa. river Chad/Sudan
Howrah see Hāora
Hoy 66 C2 island N Scotland, United Kingdom
Hoyerswerda 72 D4 Lus. Wojerecy. Sachsen, E Germany
Hpa-an 114 B4 var. Pa-an. Kayin State, S Myanmar (Burma)
Hpyu see Phyu
Hradec Králové 77 B5 Ger. Königgrätz. Královéhradecký Kraj, N Czech Republic
Hrandzichy 85 B5 Rus. Grandichi. Hrodzyenskaya Voblasts', W Belarus

K

Klamath Mountains – Kutai

Klamath Mountains 24 A4 mountain range California/Oregon, W USA
Klang 116 B3 var. Kelang; prev. Port Swettenham. Selangor, Peninsular Malaysia
Klarälven 63 B6 river Norway/Sweden
Klatovy 77 A5 Ger. Klattau. Plzeňský Kraj, W Czech Republic
Klattau see Klatovy
Klausenburg see Cluj-Napoca
Klazienaveen 64 E2 Drenthe, NE Netherlands
Kleines Ungarisches Tiefland see Little Alföld
Klein Karas 56 B4 Karas, S Namibia
Kleinwardein see Kisvárda
Kleisoúra 83 A5 Ípeiros, W Greece
Klerksdorp 56 D4 North-West, N South Africa
Klimavichy 85 E7 Rus. Klimovichi. Mahilyowskaya Voblasts', E Belarus
Klimovichi see Klimavichy
Klintsy 89 A5 Bryanskaya Oblast', W Russian Federation
Klisura 82 C2 Plovdiv, C Bulgaria
Ključ 78 B3 Federacija Bosna I Hercegovina, NW Bosnia and Herzegovina
Kłobuck 76 C4 Śląskie, S Poland
Klosters 73 B7 Graubünden, SE Switzerland
Kluang see Keluang
Kluczbork 76 C4 Ger. Kreuzburg, Kreuzburg in Oberschlesien. Opolskie, S Poland
Klyuchevskaya Sopka, Vulkan 93 H3 volcano E Russian Federation
Knin 78 B4 Šibenik-Knin, S Croatia
Knjaževac 78 E4 Serbia, E Serbia
Knokke-Heist 65 A5 West-Vlaanderen, NW Belgium
Knoxville 20 D1 Tennessee, S USA
Knud Rasmussen Land 60 D1 physical region N Greenland
Kobdo see Hovd
Kōbe 109 C6 Hyōgo, Honshū, SW Japan
København 63 B7 Eng. Copenhagen; anc. Hafnia. country capital (Denmark) Sjælland, København, E Denmark
Kobenni 52 D3 Hodh el Gharbi, S Mauritania
Koblenz 73 A5 prev. Coblenz, Fr. Coblence; anc. Confluentes. Rheinland-Pfalz, W Germany
Kobrin see Kobryn
Kobryn 85 A6 Rus. Kobrin. Brestskaya Voblasts', SW Belarus
K'obulet'i 95 F2 W Georgia
Kočani 79 E6 NE FYR Macedonia
Kočevje 73 D8 Ger. Gottschee. S Slovenia
Koch Bihār 113 G3 West Bengal, NE India
Kochchi Cochin/Kochi
Kōchi 109 B7 var. Kôti. Kōchi, Shikoku, SW Japan
Kochiu see Gejiu
Kodiak 14 C3 Kodiak Island, Alaska, USA
Kodiak Island 14 C3 island Alaska, USA
Koedoes see Kudus
Koeln see Köln
Koepang see Kupang
Ko-erh-mu see Golmud
Koetai see Mahakam, Sungai
Koetaradja see Bandaaceh
Kōfu 109 D5 var. Kôhu. Yamanashi, Honshū, S Japan
Kogarah 126 E2 New South Wales, E Australia
Kogon 100 D2 Rus. Kagan. Buxoro Viloyati, C Uzbekistan
Kőhalom see Rupea
Kohīma 113 H3 state capital Nāgāland, E India
Koh I Noh see Büyükağrı Dağı
Kohtla-Järve 84 E2 Ida-Virumaa, NE Estonia
Kôhu see Kōfu
Kokand see Qo'qon
Kokchetav see Kokshetau
Kokkola 62 D4 Swe. Karleby; prev. Swe. Gamlakarleby. Länsi-Suomi, W Finland
Koko 53 F4 Kebbi, W Nigeria
Kokomo 18 C4 Indiana, N USA
Koko Nor see Qinghai, China
Koko Nor see Qinghai Hu, China
Kokrines 14 C2 Alaska, USA
Kokshaal-Tau 101 G2 Rus. Khrebet Kakshaal-Too. mountain range China/Kyrgyzstan
Kokshetau 92 C4 Kaz. Kökshetaū; prev. Kokchetav. Kokshetau, N Kazakhstan
Kökshetaū see Kokshetau
Koksijde 65 A5 West-Vlaanderen, W Belgium
Koksoak 16 D2 river Québec, E Canada
Kokstad 56 D5 KwaZulu/Natal, E South Africa
Kolaka 117 E4 Sulawesi, C Indonesia
K'o-la-ma-i see Karamay
Kola Peninsula see Kol'skiy Poluostrov
Kolari 62 D3 Lappi, NW Finland
Kolárovo 77 C6 Ger. Gutta; prev. Guta, Hung. Gúta. Nitriansky Kraj, SW Slovakia
Kolberg see Kołobrzeg
Kolda 52 C3 S Senegal
Kolding 63 A7 Vejle, C Denmark
Kölen 59 E1 Nor. Kjølen. mountain range Norway/Sweden
Kolguyev, Ostrov 88 C2 island NW Russian Federation
Kolhāpur 110 B1 Mahārāshtra, SW India
Kolhumadulu 110 A5 var. Thaa Atoll. atoll S Maldives
Kolín 77 B5 Ger. Kolin. Střední Čechy, C Czech Republic
Kolka 84 C2 Talsi, NW Latvia
Kolkasrags 84 C2 prev. Eng. Cape Domesnes. headland NW Latvia
Kolkatta 113 G4 prev. Calcutta. West Bengal, N India
Kolmar see Colmar
Köln 72 A4 var. Koeln, Eng./Fr. Cologne, prev. Cöln; anc. Colonia Agrippina, Oppidum Ubiorum. Nordrhein-Westfalen, W Germany
Koło 76 C3 Wielkopolskie, C Poland
Kołobrzeg 76 B2 Ger. Kolberg. Zachodnio-pomorskie, NW Poland
Kolokani 52 D3 Koulikoro, W Mali
Kolomea see Kolomyya
Kolomna 89 B5 Moskovskaya Oblast', W Russian Federation
Kolomyya 86 C3 Ger. Kolomea. Ivano-Frankivs'ka Oblast', W Ukraine
Kolosjoki see Nikel'
Kolozsvár see Cluj-Napoca
Kolpa 78 A2 Ger. Kulpa, SCr. Kupa. river Croatia/Slovenia
Kolpino 88 B4 Leningradskaya Oblast', NW Russian Federation
Kólpos Mórfu see Güzelyurt
Kol'skiy Poluostrov 88 C2 Eng. Kola Peninsula. peninsula NW Russian Federation
Kolwezi 55 D7 Katanga, S Dem. Rep. Congo
Kolyma 93 G2 river NE Russian Federation
Komatsu 109 C5 var. Komatu. Ishikawa, Honshū, SW Japan
Komatu see Komatsu
Kommunizm, Qullai see Ismoili Somoní, Qullai
Komoé 53 E4 var. Komoé Fleuve. river E Côte d'Ivoire
Komoé Fleuve see Komoé
Komotau see Chomutov
Komotiní 82 D3 var. Gümüljina, Turk. Gümülcine. Anatolikí Makedonía kai Thráki, NE Greece
Kompong see Kâmpóng Chhnăng
Kompong Cham see Kâmpóng Cham
Kompong Som see Kâmpóng Saôm
Kompong Speu see Kâmpóng Spoe
Komrat see Comrat
Komsomolets, Ostrov 93 E1 island Severnaya Zemlya, N Russian Federation
Komsomol'sk-na-Amure 93 G4 Khabarovskiy Kray, SE Russian Federation
Kondolovo 82 E3 Burgas, E Bulgaria
Kondopoga 88 B3 Respublika Kareliya, NW Russian Federation
Kondoz 101 E3 Pash. Kunduz. province NE Afghanistan
Köneürgenç 100 C2 var. Köneürgench, Rus. Këneurgench; prev. Kunya-Urgench. Daşoguz Welaýaty, N Turkmenistan
Kong Christian IX Land 60 D4 Eng. King Christian IX Land. physical region SE Greenland
Kong Frederik IX Land 60 C3 physical region SW Greenland
Kong Frederik VIII Land 61 E2 Eng. King Frederik VIII Land. physical region NE Greenland
Kong Frederik VI Kyst 60 C4 Eng. King Frederik VI Coast. physical region SE Greenland
Kong Karls Land 61 G2 Eng. King Charles Islands. island group SE Svalbard
Kongo see Congo (river)
Kongolo 55 D6 Katanga, E Dem. Rep. Congo
Kongor 51 B5 Jonglei, E South Sudan
Kong Oscar Fjord 61 E3 fjord E Greenland
Kongsberg 63 B6 Buskerud, S Norway
Kông, Tônle 115 E5 var. Xê Kong. river Cambodia/Laos
Kong, Xê see Kông, Tônle
Königgrätz see Hradec Králové
Königshütte see Chorzów
Konin 76 C3 Ger. Kuhnau. Weilkopolskie, C Poland
Koninkrijk der Nederlanden see Netherlands
Konispol 79 C7 var. Konispoli. Vlorë, S Albania
Konispoli see Konispol
Kónitsa 82 A4 Ípeiros, W Greece
Konitz see Chojnice
Konjic 78 C4 Federacija Bosna I Hercegovina, S Bosnia and Herzegovina
Konosha 88 C4 Arkhangel'skaya Oblast', NW Russian Federation
Konotop 87 F1 Sums'ka Oblast', NE Ukraine
Konstantinovka see Kostyantynivka
Konstanz 73 B7 var. Constanz, Eng. Constance, hist. Kostnitz; anc. Constantia. Baden-Württemberg, S Germany
Konstanza see Constanța
Konya 94 C4 var. Konieh, prev. Konia; anc. Iconium. Konya, C Turkey
Kopaonik 79 D5 mountain range S Serbia
Kopar see Koper
Koper 73 D8 It. Capodistria; prev. Kopar. SW Slovenia
Köpetdag Gershi 100 C3 mountain range Iran/Turkmenistan
Köpetdag Gershi/Kopetdag, Khrebet see Koppeh Dāgh
Koppeh Dāgh 98 D2 Rus. Khrebet Kopetdag, Turkm. Köpetdag Gershi. mountain range Iran/Turkmenistan
Kopreinitz see Koprivnica
Koprivnica 78 B2 Ger. Kopreinitz, Hung. Kaproncza. Koprivnica-Križevci, N Croatia
Köprülü see Veles
Koptsevichi see Kaptsevichy
Kopyl' see Kapyl'
Korat see Nakhon Ratchasima
Korat Plateau 114 D4 plateau E Thailand
Korba 113 E4 Chhattīsgarh, C India
Korça see Korçë
Korçë 79 D6 var. Korça, Gk. Korytsa, It. Corriza; prev. Koritsa. Korçë, SE Albania
Korčula 78 B4 It. Curzola; anc. Corcyra Nigra. island S Croatia
Korea Bay 105 G3 bay China/North Korea
Korea, Democratic People's Republic of see North Korea
Korea, Republic of see South Korea
Korea Strait 109 A7 Jap. Chōsen-kaikyō, Kor. Taehan-haehyŏp. channel Japan/South Korea
Korhogo 52 D4 N Côte d'Ivoire
Kórinthos 83 B6 anc. Corinthus Eng. Corinth. Pelopónnisos, S Greece
Korinthiakós Kólpos 83 B5 Eng. Gulf of Corinth; anc. Corinthiacus Sinus. gulf C Greece
Koritsa see Korçë
Kōriyama 109 D5 Fukushima, Honshū, C Japan
Korla 104 C3 Chin. K'u-erh-lo. Xinjiang Uygur Zizhiqu, NW China
Körmend 77 B7 Vas, W Hungary
Koróni 83 B6 Pelopónnisos, S Greece
Koror 122 A2 (Palau) Oreor, N Palau
Kőrös see Križevci
Korosten' 86 D1 Zhytomyrs'ka Oblast', NW Ukraine
Koro Toro 54 C2 Borkou-Ennedi-Tibesti, N Chad
Korsovka see Kārsava
Kortrijk 65 A6 Fr. Courtrai. West-Vlaanderen, W Belgium
Koryak Range 93 H2 var. Koryakskiy Khrebet, Eng. Koryak Range. mountain range NE Russian Federation
Koryak Range see Koryakskoye Nagor'ye
Koryakskiy Khrebet see Koryakskoye Nagor'ye
Koryazhma 88 C4 Arkhangel'skaya Oblast', NW Russian Federation
Korytsa see Korçë
Kos 83 E6 Kos, Dodekánisa, Greece, Aegean Sea
Kos 83 E6 It. Coo; anc. Cos. island Dodekánisa, Greece, Aegean Sea
Ko-saki 109 A7 headland Nagasaki, Tsushima, SW Japan
Kościan 76 B4 Ger. Kosten. Wielkopolskie, C Poland
Kościerzyna 76 C2 Pomorskie, NW Poland
Kosciusko, Mount see Kosciuszko, Mount
Kosciuszko, Mount 127 C7 prev. Mount Kosciusko. mountain New South Wales, SE Australia
K'o-shih see Kashi
Koshikijima-retto 109 A8 var. Kosikizima Rettô. island group SW Japan
Kōshū see Kwangju
Košice 77 D6 Ger. Kaschau, Hung. Kassa. Košický Kraj, E Slovakia
Kosikizima Rettô see Koshikijima-rettō
Köslin see Koszalin
Koson 101 E3 Rus. Kasan. Qashqadaryo Viloyati, S Uzbekistan
Kosovo 79 D5 prev. Autonomous Province of Kosovo and Metohija. country SE Europe
Kosovo and Metohija, Autonomous Province of see Kosovo
Kosovo Polje see Fushë Kosovë
Kosovska Mitrovica see Mitrovicë
Kosrae 122 C2 prev. Kusaie. island Caroline Islands, E Micronesia
Kossou, Lac de 52 D5 lake C Côte d'Ivoire
Kostanay 92 C4 var. Kustanay, Kaz. Qostanay. Kostanay, N Kazakhstan
Kosten see Kościan
Kostenets 82 C2 prev. Georgi Dimitrov. Sofiya, W Bulgaria
Kostnitz see Konstanz
Kostroma 88 B4 Kostromskaya Oblast', NW Russian Federation
Kostyantynivka 87 G3 Rus. Konstantinovka. Donets'ka Oblast', SE Ukraine
Kostyukovichi see Kastsyukovichy
Kostyukovka see Kastsyukowka
Koszalin 76 B2 Ger. Köslin. Zachodnio-pomorskie, NW Poland
Kota 112 D3 prev. Kotah. Rājasthān, N India
Kota Baharu see Kota Bharu
Kota Bahru see Kota Bharu
Kotabaru see Jayapura
Kota Bharu 116 B3 var. Kota Baharu, Kota Bahru. Kelantan, Peninsular Malaysia
Kotaboemi see Kotabumi
Kotabumi 116 B4 prev. Kotaboemi. Sumatera, W Indonesia
Kotah see Kota
Kota Kinabalu 116 D3 prev. Jesselton. Sabah, East Malaysia
Kotel'nyy, Ostrov 93 E2 island Novosibirskiye Ostrova, N Russian Federation
Kotka 63 E5 Etelä-Suomi, S Finland
Kotlas 88 C4 Arkhangel'skaya Oblast', NW Russian Federation
Kotonu see Cotonou
Kotor 79 C5 It. Cattaro. SW Montenegro
Kotovs'k 86 D3 Rus. Kotovsk. Odes'ka Oblast', SW Ukraine
Kotovsk see Hîncești
Kottbus see Cottbus
Kotto 54 D4 river Central African Republic/Dem. Rep. Congo
Kotuy 93 E2 river N Russian Federation
Koudougou 53 E4 C Burkina
Koulamoutou 55 B6 Ogooué-Lolo, C Gabon
Koulikoro 52 D3 Koulikoro, SW Mali
Koumra 54 C4 Moyen-Chari, S Chad
Kourou 37 H3 N French Guiana
Kousseir see Al Quṣayr
Kousséri 54 B3 prev. Fort-Foureau. Extrême-Nord, NE Cameroon
Koutiala 52 D4 Sikasso, S Mali
Kouvola 63 E5 Etelä-Suomi, S Finland
Kovel' 86 C1 Pol. Kowel. Volyns'ka Oblast', NW Ukraine
Kovno see Kaunas
Koweit see Kuwait
Kowel see Kovel'
Kowloon 106 A2 Hong Kong, S China
Kowno see Kaunas
Kozáni 82 B4 Dytikí Makedonía, N Greece
Kozara 78 B3 mountain range NW Bosnia and Herzegovina
Kozarska Dubica see Bosanska Dubica
Kozu-shima 109 D6 island E Japan
Kozyatyn 86 D2 Rus. Kazatin. Vinnyts'ka Oblast', C Ukraine
Kpalimé 53 E5 var. Palimé. SW Togo
Krâchéh 115 D6 prev. Kratie. Krâchéh, E Cambodia
Kragujevac 78 D4 Serbia, C Serbia
Krainburg see Kranj
Kra, Isthmus of 115 B6 isthmus Malaysia/Thailand
Krakau see Kraków
Kraków 77 D5 Eng. Cracow, Ger. Krakau; anc. Cracovia. Małopolskie, S Poland
Krâlănh 115 D5 Siĕmréab, NW Cambodia
Kraljevo 78 D4 prev. Rankovićevo. Serbia, C Serbia
Kramators'k 87 G3 Rus. Kramatorsk. Donets'ka Oblast', SE Ukraine
Kramatorsk see Kramators'k
Kramfors 63 C5 Västernorrland, C Sweden
Kranéa see Kraniá
Kraniá 82 B4 var. Kranéa. Dytikí Makedonía, N Greece
Kranj 73 D7 Ger. Krainburg. NW Slovenia
Kranz see Zelenogradsk
Krāslava 84 D4 Krāslava, SE Latvia
Krasnaye 85 C5 Rus. Krasnoye. Minskaya Voblasts', C Belarus
Krasnoarmeysk 89 C6 Saratovskaya Oblast', W Russian Federation
Krasnodar 89 A7 prev. Ekaterinodar, Yekaterinodar. Krasnodarskiy Kray, SW Russian Federation
Krasnodon 87 H3 Luhans'ka Oblast', E Ukraine
Krasnogor see Kallaste
Krasnogvardeyskoye see Krasnohvardiys'ke
Krasnohvardiys'ke 87 F4 Rus. Krasnogvardeyskoye. Respublika Krym, S Ukraine
Krasnokamensk 93 F4 Chitinskaya Oblast', S Russian Federation
Krasnokamsk 89 D5 Permskaya Oblast', W Russian Federation
Krasnoperekops'k 87 F4 Rus. Krasnoperekopsk. Respublika Krym, S Ukraine
Krasnoperekopsk see Krasnoperekops'k
Krasnostav see Krasnystaw
Krasnovodsk see Türkmenbaşy
Krasnovodskiy Zaliv see Türkmenbasy Aylagy
Krasnowodsk Aylagy see Türkmenbasy Aylagy
Krasnoyarsk 92 D4 Krasnoyarskiy Kray, S Russian Federation
Krasnoye see Krasnaye
Krasnystaw 76 E4 Rus. Krasnostav. Lubelskie, SE Poland
Krasnyy Kut 89 C6 Saratovskaya Oblast', W Russian Federation
Krasnyy Luch 87 H3 prev. Krindachevka. Luhans'ka Oblast', E Ukraine
Kratie see Krâchéh
Krâvanh, Chuŏr Phnum 115 C6 Eng. Cardamom Mountains, Fr. Chaîne des Cardamomes. mountain range W Cambodia
Krefeld 72 A4 Nordrhein-Westfalen, W Germany
Kreisstadt see Krosno Odrzańskie
Kremenchug see Kremenchuk
Kremenchugskoye Vodokhranilishche/ Kremenchuk Reservoir see Kremenchuts'ke Vodoskhovyshche
Kremenchuk 87 F2 Rus. Kremenchug. Poltavs'ka Oblast', NE Ukraine
Kremenchuk Reservoir 87 F2 Eng. Kremenchuk Reservoir, Rus. Kremenchugskoye Vodokhranilishche. reservoir C Ukraine
Kremenets' 86 C2 Pol. Krzemieniec, Rus. Kremenets. Ternopil's'ka Oblast', W Ukraine
Kremennaya see Kreminna
Kreminna 87 G2 Rus. Kremennaya. Luhans'ka Oblast', E Ukraine
Kresena see Kresna
Kresna 82 C3 var. Kresena. Blagoevgrad, SW Bulgaria
Kretikon Delagos see Kritikó Pélagos
Kretinga 84 B3 Ger. Krottingen. Klaipėda, NW Lithuania
Kreutz see Cristuru Secuiesc
Kreuz see Križevci, Croatia
Kreuz see Risti, Estonia
Kreuzburg/Kreuzburg in Oberschlesien see Kluczbork
Krichëv see Krychaw
Krievija see Russian Federation
Krindachevka see Krasnyy Luch
Krishna 110 C1 prev. Kistna. river C India
Krishnagiri 110 C2 Tamil Nādu, SE India
Kristiania see Oslo
Kristiansand 63 A6 var. Christiansand. Vest-Agder, S Norway
Kristianstad 63 B7 Skåne, S Sweden
Kristiansund 62 A4 var. Christiansund. Møre og Romsdal, S Norway
Kríti 83 C7 Eng. Crete. island Greece, Aegean Sea
Kritikó Pélagos 83 D7 var. Kretikon Delagos, Eng. Sea of Crete; anc. Mare Creticum. sea Greece, Aegean Sea
Krivoy Rog see Kryvyy Rih
Križevci 78 B2 Ger. Kreuz, Hung. Kőrös. Varaždin, NE Croatia
Krk 78 A3 It. Veglia; anc. Curieta. island NW Croatia
Kroatien see Croatia
Krolevets' 87 F1 Rus. Krolevets. Sums'ka Oblast', NE Ukraine
Krolevets see Krolevets'
Królewska Huta see Chorzów
Kronach 73 C5 Bayern, E Germany
Kronstadt see Brașov
Kroonstad 56 D4 Free State, C South Africa
Kropotkin 89 A7 Krasnodarskiy Kray, SW Russian Federation
Krosno 77 D5 Ger. Krossen. Podkarpackie, SE Poland
Krosno Odrzańskie 76 B3 Ger. Crossen, Kreisstadt. Lubuskie, W Poland
Krossen see Krosno
Krottingen see Kretinga
Krško 73 E8 Ger. Gurkfeld; prev. Videm-Krško. E Slovenia
Krugloye see Kruhlaye
Kruhlaye 85 D6 Rus. Krugloye. Mahilyowskaya Voblasts', E Belarus
Kruja see Krujë
Krujë 79 C6 var. Kruja, It. Croia. Durrës, C Albania
Krummau see Český Krumlov
Krung Thep, Ao 115 C5 var. Bight of Bangkok. bay S Thailand
Krung Thep Mahanakhon see Ao Krung Thep
Krupki 85 D6 Minskaya Voblasts', C Belarus
Krušné Hory see Erzgebirge
Krychaw 85 E7 Rus. Krichëv. Mahilyowskaya Voblasts', E Belarus
Kryms'ki Hory 87 F5 mountain range S Ukraine
Kryms'kyy Pivostriv 87 F5 peninsula S Ukraine
Krynica 77 D5 Ger. Tannenhof. Małopolskie, S Poland
Kryve Ozero 87 E3 Odes'ka Oblast', SW Ukraine
Kryvyy Rih 87 F3 Rus. Krivoy Rog. Dnipropetrovs'ka Oblast', SE Ukraine
Krzemieniec see Kremenets'
Ksar al Kabir see Ksar-el-Kebir
Ksar al Soule see Er-Rachidia
Ksar-el-Kebir 48 C2 var. Alcázar, Ksar al Kabir, Ksar-el-Kébir, Ar. Al-Kasr al-Kebir, Al-Qsar al-Kbir, Sp. Alcazarquivir. NW Morocco
Ksar-el-Kébir see Ksar-el-Kebir
Kuala Dungun see Dungun
Kuala Lumpur 116 B3 country capital (Malaysia) Kuala Lumpur, Peninsular Malaysia
Kuala Terengganu 116 B3 var. Kuala Trengganu. Terengganu, Peninsular Malaysia
Kualatungkal 116 B4 Sumatera, W Indonesia
Kuang-chou see Guangzhou
Kuang-hsi see Guangxi Zhuangzu Zizhiqu
Kuang-tung see Guangdong
Kuang-yuan see Guangyuan
Kuantan 116 B3 Pahang, Peninsular Malaysia
Kuba see Quba
Kuban' 87 G5 var. Hypanis. river SW Russian Federation
Kubango see Cubango/Okavango
Kuching 116 C3 prev. Sarawak. Sarawak, East Malaysia
Kūchnay Darweyshān 100 D5 Helmand, S Afghanistan
Kuçova see Kuçovë
Kuçovë 79 C6 var. Kuçova; prev. Qyteti Stalin. Berat, C Albania
Kudara see Ghŭdara
Kudus 116 C5 prev. Koedoes. Jawa, C Indonesia
Kuei-lin see Guilin
Kuei-Yang/Kuei-yang see Guiyang
K'u-erh-lo see Korla
Kueyang see Guiyang
Kugaaruk 15 G3 prev. Pelly Bay. Nunavut, N Canada
Kugluktuk 31 E3 var. Qurlurtuuq; prev. Coppermine. Nunavut, NW Canada
Kuhmo 62 E4 Oulu, E Finland
Kuhnau see Konin
Kūhnö see Kihnu
Kuibyshev see Kuybyshevskoye Vodokhranilishche
Kuito 56 B2 Port. Silva Porto. Bié, C Angola
Kuji 108 D3 var. Kuzi. Iwate, Honshū, C Japan
Kukës 79 D5 var. Kukësi. Kukës, NE Albania
Kukësi see Kukës
Kukong see Shaoguan
Kukukhoto see Hohhot
Kula Kangri 113 G3 var. Kulhakangri. mountain Bhutan/China
Kuldīga 84 B3 Ger. Goldingen. Kuldīga, W Latvia
Kuldja see Yining
Kulhakangri see Kula Kangri
Kullorsuaq 60 D2 var. Kuvdlorssuak. Kitaa, C Greenland
Kulm see Chełmno
Kulmsee see Chełmża
Kŭlob 101 F3 Rus. Kulyab. SW Tajikistan
Kulpa see Kolpa
Kulu 94 C3 Konya, W Turkey
Kulunda Steppe 92 C4 Kaz. Qulyndy Zhazyghy, Rus. Kulundinskaya Ravnina. grassland Kazakhstan/Russian Federation
Kulundinskaya Ravnina see Kulunda Steppe
Kulyab see Kŭlob
Kum see Qom
Kuma 89 B7 river SW Russian Federation
Kumamoto 109 A7 Kumamoto, Kyūshū, SW Japan
Kumanova see Kumanovo
Kumanovo 79 E5 Turk. Kumanova. N Macedonia
Kumasi 53 E5 prev. Coomassie. C Ghana
Kumayri see Gyumri
Kumba 55 A5 Sud-Ouest, W Cameroon
Kumertau 89 D6 Respublika Bashkortostan, W Russian Federation
Kumillā see Comilla
Kumo 53 G4 Gombe, E Nigeria
Kumon Range 114 B2 mountain range N Myanmar (Burma)
Kumul see Hami
Kunashiri see Kunashir, Ostrov
Kunashir, Ostrov 108 E1 var. Kunashiri. island Kuril'skiye Ostrova, SE Russian Federation
Kunda 84 E2 Lääne-Virumaa, NE Estonia
Kunduz see Kondoz
Kunene 47 C6 var. Kunene. river Angola/Namibia
Kunene see Cunene
Kungsbacka 63 B7 Halland, S Sweden
Kungur 89 D5 Permskaya Oblast', NW Russian Federation
Kunlun Mountains see Kunlun Shan
Kunlun Shan 104 B4 Eng. Kunlun Mountains. mountain range NW China
Kunming 106 B6 var. K'un-ming; prev. Yunnan. province capital Yunnan, SW China
K'un-ming see Kunming
Kununurra 124 D3 Western Australia
Kunya-Urgench see Köneürgenç
Kuopio 63 E5 Itä-Suomi, C Finland
Kupa see Kolpa
Kupang 117 E5 prev. Koepang. Timor, C Indonesia
Kup"yans'k 87 G2 Rus. Kupyansk. Kharkivs'ka Oblast', E Ukraine
Kupyansk see Kup"yans'k
Kür see Kura
Kura 95 H3 Az. Kür, Geor. Mtkvari, Turk. Kura Nehri. river SW Asia
Kura Nehri see Kura
Kurashiki 109 B6 var. Kurasiki. Okayama, Honshū, SW Japan
Kurasiki see Kurashiki
Kurdistan 95 F4 cultural region SW Asia
Kŭrdzhali 82 D3 var. Kirdzhali. Kŭrdzhali, S Bulgaria
Kure 109 B7 Hiroshima, Honshū, SW Japan
Küre Dağları 94 C2 mountain range N Turkey
Kuressaare 84 C2 Ger. Arensburg; prev. Kingissepp. Saaremaa, W Estonia
Kureyka 90 D2 river N Russian Federation
Kurgan-Tyube see Qŭrghonteppa
Kuria Muria Islands see Ḩalāniyāt, Juzur al
Kurile Islands 93 H4 Eng. Kurile Islands. island group SE Russian Federation
Kurile Islands see Kuril'skiye Ostrova
Kurile-Kamchatka Depression see Kurile Trench
Kurile Trench 91 F3 var. Kurile-Kamchatka Depression. trench NW Pacific Ocean
Kuril'sk 108 E1 Jap. Shana. Kuril'skiye Ostrova, Sakhalinskaya Oblats', SE Russian Federation
Ku-ring-gai 126 E1 New South Wales, E Australia
Kurisches Haff see Courland Lagoon
Kurkund see Kilingi-Nõmme
Kurnool 110 C1 var. Karnul. Andhra Pradesh, S India
Kursk 89 A6 Kurskaya Oblast', W Russian Federation
Kurskiy Zaliv see Courland Lagoon
Kuršumlija 79 D5 Serbia, S Serbia
Kurtbunar see Tervel
Kurtitsch/Kürtös see Curtici
Kuruktag 104 C3 mountain range NW China
Kurume 109 A7 Fukuoka, Kyūshū, SW Japan
Kurupukari 37 F3 C Guyana
Kusaie see Kosrae
Kushiro 108 D2 var. Kusiro. Hokkaidō, NE Japan
Kushka see Serhetabat
Kusiro see Kushiro
Kuskokwim Mountains 14 C3 mountain range Alaska, USA
Kustanay see Kostanay
Küstence/Küstendje see Constanța
Kütahya 94 B3 prev. Kutaia. Kütahya, W Turkey
Kutai see Mahakam, Sungai

Liaoyuan – Macedonia

Liaoyuan *107 E3* var. Dongliao, Shuang-liao, Jap. Chengchiatun. Jilin, NE China
Liard see Fort Liard
Liban see Lebanon
Liban, Jebel *96 B4* Ar. Jabal al Gharbt, Jabal Lubnān, Eng. Mount Lebanon. mountain range C Lebanon
Libau see Liepāja
Libby *22 A1* Montana, NW USA
Liberal *23 E5* Kansas, C USA
Liberalitas Julia see Évora
Liberec *76 B4* Ger. Reichenberg. Liberecký Kraj, N Czech Republic
Liberia *30 D4* Guanacaste, NW Costa Rica
Liberia *52 C5* off. Republic of Liberia. country W Africa
Liberia, Republic of see Liberia
Libian Desert see Libyan Desert
Lībīyah, Aş Şaḩrā' al see Libyan Desert
Libourne *69 B5* Gironde, SW France
Libreville *55 A5* country capital (Gabon) Estuaire, NW Gabon
Libya *49 F3* off. Great Socialist People's Libyan Arab Jamahiriya, Ar. Al Jamāhīrīyah al 'Arabīyah al Lībīyah ash Sha'bīyah al Ishtirākīy; prev. Libyan Arab Republic. country N Africa
Libyan Arab Republic see Libya
Libyan Desert *49 H4* var. Libian Desert, Ar. Aş Şahrā' al Lībīyah. desert N Africa
Libyan Plateau *81 F4* var. Aḍ Diffah. plateau Egypt/Libya
Lichtenfels *73 C5* Bayern, SE Germany
Lichtenvoorde *64 E4* Gelderland, E Netherlands
Lichuan *106 C5* Hubei, C China
Lida *85 B5* Hrodzyenskaya Voblasts', W Belarus
Lidhorikíon see Lidoríki
Lidköping *63 B6* Västra Götaland, S Sweden
Lidokhorikion see Lidoríki
Lidoríki *83 B5* prev. Lidhorikíon, Lidokhorikion. Stereá Ellás, C Greece
Lidzbark Warmiński *76 D2* Ger. Heilsberg. Olsztyn, N Poland
Liechtenstein *72 D1* off. Principality of Liechtenstein. country C Europe
Liechtenstein, Principality of see Liechtenstein
Liège *65 D6* Dut. Luik, Ger. Lüttich. Liège, E Belgium
Liegnitz see Legnica
Lienz *73 D7* Tirol, W Austria
Liepāja *84 B3* Ger. Libau. Liepāja, W Latvia
Lietuva see Lithuania
Lievenhof see Līvāni
Liezen *73 D7* Steiermark, C Austria
Liffey *67 B6* river Ireland
Lifou *122 D5* island Îles Loyauté, E New Caledonia
Liger see Loire
Ligure, Appennino *74 A2* Eng. Ligurian Mountains. mountain range NW Italy
Ligure, Mar see Ligurian Sea
Ligurian Mountains see Ligure, Appennino
Ligurian Sea *74 A3* Fr. Mer Ligurienne, It. Mar Ligure. sea N Mediterranean Sea
Ligurienne, Mer see Ligurian Sea
Lihu'e *25 A7* var. Lihue. Kaua'i, Hawaii, USA
Lihue see Lihu'e
Lihula *84 D2* Ger. Leal. Läänemaa, W Estonia
Liivi Laht see Riga, Gulf of
Likasi *55 D7* prev. Jadotville. Shaba, SE Dem. Rep. Congo
Liknes *63 A6* Vest-Agder, S Norway
Lille *68 C2* var. l'Isle, Dut. Rijssel, Flem. Ryssel, prev. Lisle; anc. Insula. Nord, N France
Lillehammer *63 B5* Oppland, S Norway
Lillestrøm *63 B6* Akershus, S Norway
Lilongwe *57 E2* country capital (Malawi) Central, W Malawi
Lilybaeum see Marsala
Lima *38 C4* country capital (Peru) Lima, W Peru
Limanowa *77 D5* Małopolskie, S Poland
Limassol see Lemesós
Limerick *67 A6* Ir. Luimneach. Limerick, SW Ireland
Limín Vathéos see Sámos
Límnos *81 F3* anc. Lemnos. island E Greece
Limoges *69 C5* anc. Augustoritum Lemovicensium, Lemovices. Haute-Vienne, C France
Limón *31 E4* var. Puerto Limón. Limón, E Costa Rica
Limón *30 D2* Colón, NE Honduras
Limonum see Poitiers
Limousin *69 C5* cultural region C France
Limoux *69 C6* Aude, S France
Limpopo *56 D3* var. Crocodile. river S Africa
Linares *42 B4* Maule, C Chile
Linares *29 E3* Nuevo León, NE Mexico
Linares *70 D4* Andalucía, S Spain
Lincoln *67 D5* anc. Lindum, Lindum Colonia. E England, United Kingdom
Lincoln *19 H2* Maine, NE USA
Lincoln *23 F4* state capital Nebraska, C USA
Lincoln Sea *12 D2* sea Arctic Ocean
Linden *37 F3* E Guyana
Líndhos see Líndos
Lindi *51 D8* Lindi, SE Tanzania
Líndos *83 E7* var. Líndhos. Ródos, Dodekánisa, Greece, Aegean Sea
Lindum/Lindum Colonia see Lincoln
Line Islands *123 G3* island group E Kiribati
Lingeh see Bandar-e Lengeh
Lingen *72 A3* var. Lingen an der Ems. Niedersachsen, NW Germany
Lingen an der Ems see Lingen
Lingga, Kepulauan *116 B4* island group W Indonesia
Linköping *63 C6* Östergötland, S Sweden
Linz *73 D6* anc. Lentia. Oberösterreich, N Austria
Lion, Golfe du *69 C7* Eng. Gulf of Lion, Gulf of Lions; anc. Sinus Gallicus. gulf S France
Lion, Gulf of/Lions, Gulf of see Lion, Golfe du
Liozno see Lyozna
Lipari *75 D6* island Isole Eolie, S Italy
Lipari Islands/Lipari, Isole see Eolie, Isole
Lipetsk *89 B5* Lipetskaya Oblast', W Russian Federation
Lipno *76 C3* Kujawsko-pomorskie, C Poland
Lipova *86 A4* Hung. Lippa. Arad, W Romania
Lipovets see Lypovets'
Lippa see Lipova
Lipsia/Lipsk see Leipzig
Lira *51 B6* N Uganda
Lisala *55 C5* Equateur, N Dem. Rep. Congo
Lisboa *70 B4* Eng. Lisbon; anc. Felicitas Julia, Olisipo. country capital (Portugal) Lisboa, W Portugal
Lisbon see Lisboa
Lisichansk see Lysychans'k
Lisieux *68 B3* anc. Noviomagus. Calvados, N France
Liski *89 B6* prev. Georgiu-Dezh. Voronezhskaya Oblast', W Russian Federation
Lisle/l'Isle see Lille
Lismore *127 E5* New South Wales, SE Australia
Lissa see Vis, Croatia
Lissa see Leszno, Poland
Lisse *64 C3* Zuid-Holland, W Netherlands
Litang *106 A5* var. Gaocheng. Sichuan, C China
Lītani, Nahr el *97 B5* var. Nahr al Litant. river C Lebanon
Litant, Nahr al see Lītani, Nahr el
Litauen see Lithuania
Lithgow *127 D6* New South Wales, SE Australia
Lithuania *84 B4* off. Republic of Lithuania, Ger. Litauen, Lith. Lietuva, Pol. Litwa, Rus. Litva; prev. Lithuanian SSR, Rus. Litovskaya SSR. country NE Europe
Lithuanian SSR see Lithuania
Lithuania, Republic of see Lithuania
Litóchoro *82 B4* var. Litohoro, Litókhoron. Kentrikí Makedonía, N Greece
Litohoro/Litókhoron see Litóchoro
Litovskaya SSR see Lithuania
Little Alföld *77 C6* Ger. Kleines Ungarisches Tiefland, Hung. Kisalföld, Slvk. Podunajská Rovina. plain Hungary/Slovakia
Little Andaman *111 F2* island Andaman Islands, India, NE Indian Ocean
Little Barrier Island *128 D2* island N New Zealand
Little Bay *71 H5* bay Alboran Sea, Mediterranean Sea
Little Cayman *32 B3* island E Cayman Islands
Little Falls *23 F2* Minnesota, N USA
Littlefield *27 E2* Texas, SW USA
Little Inagua *32 D2* var. Inagua Islands. island S Bahamas
Little Minch, The *66 B3* strait NW Scotland, United Kingdom
Little Missouri River *22 D2* river NW USA
Little Nicobar *111 G3* island Nicobar Islands, India, NE Indian Ocean
Little Rhody see Rhode Island
Little Rock *20 B1* state capital Arkansas, C USA
Little Saint Bernard Pass *69 D5* Fr. Col du Petit St-Bernard, It. Colle del Piccolo San Bernardo. pass France/Italy
Little Sound *20 A5* bay Bermuda, NW Atlantic Ocean
Littleton *22 D4* Colorado, C USA
Littoria see Latina
Litva/Litwa see Lithuania
Liu-chou/Liuchow see Liuzhou
Liuzhou *106 C6* var. Liu-chou, Liuchow. Guangxi Zhuangzu Zizhiqu, S China
Livanátai see Livanátes
Livanátes *83 B5* prev. Livanátai. Stereá Ellás, C Greece
Līvāni *84 D4* Ger. Lievenhof. Preiļi, SE Latvia
Liverpool *17 F5* Nova Scotia, SE Canada
Liverpool *67 C5* NW England, United Kingdom
Livingston *22 B2* Montana, NW USA
Livingston *27 H3* Texas, SW USA
Livingstone *56 C3* var. Maramba. Southern, S Zambia
Livingstone Mountains *129 A7* mountain range South Island, New Zealand
Livno *78 B4* Federicija Bosna I Hercegovina, SW Bosnia and Herzegovina
Livojoki *62 D4* river C Finland
Livonia *18 D3* Michigan, N USA
Livorno *74 B3* Eng. Leghorn. Toscana, C Italy
Lixian Jiang see Black River
Lixoúri *83 A5* prev. Lixoúrion. Kefallinía, Iónia Nisiá, Greece, C Mediterranean Sea
Lixoúrion see Lixoúri
Lizarra see Estella
Ljouwert see Leeuwarden
Ljubelj see Loibl Pass
Ljubljana *73 D7* Ger. Laibach, It. Lubiana; anc. Aemona, Emona. country capital (Slovenia) C Slovenia
Ljungby *63 B7* Kronoberg, S Sweden
Ljusdal *63 C5* Gävleborg, C Sweden
Ljusnan *63 C5* river C Sweden
Llanelli *67 C6* prev. Llanelly. SW Wales, United Kingdom
Llanelly see Llanelli
Llanes *70 D1* Asturias, N Spain
Llanos *36 D2* physical region Colombia/Venezuela
Lleida *71 F2* Cast. Lérida; anc. Ilerda. Cataluña, NE Spain
Llucmajor *71 G3* Mallorca, Spain, W Mediterranean Sea
Loaita Island *106 C8* island W Spratly Islands
Loanda see Luanda
Lobatse *56 C4* var. Lobatsi. Kgatleng, SE Botswana
Lobatsi see Lobatse
Löbau *72 D4* Sachsen, E Germany
Lobito *56 B2* Benguela, W Angola
Lob Nor see Lop Nur
Lobositz see Lovosice
Loburi see Lop Buri
Locarno *73 B8* Ger. Luggarus. Ticino, S Switzerland
Lochem *64 E3* Gelderland, E Netherlands
Lockport *19 E3* New York, NE USA
Lodja *55 D6* Kasai-Oriental, C Dem. Rep. Congo
Lodwar *51 C6* Rift Valley, NW Kenya
Łódź *76 D4* Rus. Lodz. Łódź, C Poland
Loei *114 C4* var. Loey, Muang Loei. Loei, C Thailand
Loey see Loei
Lofoten *62 B3* var. Lofoten Islands. island group C Norway
Lofoten Islands see Lofoten
Logan *22 B3* Utah, W USA
Logan, Mount *14 D3* mountain Yukon Territory, W Canada
Logroño *71 E1* anc. Vareia, Lat. Juliobriga. La Rioja, N Spain
Loibl Pass *73 D7* Ger. Loiblpass, Slvn. Ljubelj. pass Austria/Slovenia
Loiblpass see Loibl Pass
Loikaw *114 B4* Kayah State, C Myanmar (Burma)
Loire *68 B4* var. Liger. river C France
Loja *38 B2* Loja, S Ecuador
Lokitaung *51 C5* Rift Valley, NW Kenya
Lokoja *53 G4* Kogi, C Nigeria
Loksa *84 E2* Ger. Loxa. Harjumaa, NW Estonia
Lolland *63 B8* prev. Laaland. island S Denmark
Lom *82 C1* prev. Lom-Palanka. Montana, NW Bulgaria
Lomami *55 D6* river C Dem. Rep. Congo
Lomas *38 D4* Arequipa, SW Peru
Lomas de Zamora *42 D4* Buenos Aires, E Argentina
Lombardia *74 B2* Eng. Lombardy. region N Italy
Lombardy see Lombardia
Lombok, Pulau *116 D5* island Nusa Tenggara, C Indonesia
Lomé *53 F5* country capital (Togo) S Togo
Lomela *55 D6* Kasai-Oriental, C Dem. Rep. Congo
Lommel *65 C5* Limburg, N Belgium
Lomond, Loch *66 B4* lake C Scotland, United Kingdom
Lomonosov Ridge *133 B3* var. Harris Ridge, Rus. Khrebet Homonsova. undersea ridge Arctic Ocean
Lomonsova, Khrebet see Lomonosov Ridge
Lom-Palanka see Lom
Lompoc *25 B7* California, W USA
Lom Sak *114 C4* var. Muang Lom Sak. Phetchabun, C Thailand
Łomża *76 D3* Rus. Lomzha. Podlaskie, NE Poland
Lomzha see Łomża
Loncoche *43 B5* Araucanía, C Chile
Londinium see London
London *67 A7* anc. Augusta, Lat. Londinium. country capital (United Kingdom) SE England, United Kingdom
London *16 C5* Ontario, S Canada
London *18 C5* Kentucky, S USA
Londonderry *66 B4* var. Derry, Ir. Doire. NW Northern Ireland, United Kingdom
Londonderry, Cape *124 C2* cape Western Australia
Londrina *41 E4* Paraná, S Brazil
Lone Star State see Texas
Long Bay *21 F2* bay W Jamaica
Long Beach *25 C7* California, W USA
Longford *67 B5* Ir. An Longfort. Longford, C Ireland
Long Island *32 D2* island C Bahamas
Long Island *19 G4* island New York, NE USA
Longlac *16 C3* Ontario, S Canada
Longmont *22 D4* Colorado, C USA
Longreach *126 C4* Queensland, E Australia
Long Strait *93 G1* Eng. Long Strait. strait NE Russian Federation
Long Strait see Longa, Proliv
Longview *27 H3* Texas, SW USA
Longview *24 B2* Washington, NW USA
Long Xuyên *115 D6* var. Longxuyen. An Giang, S Vietnam
Longxuyen see Long Xuyên
Longyan *106 D6* Fujian, SE China
Longyearbyen *61 G2* dependent territory capital (Svalbard) Spitsbergen, W Svalbard
Lons-le-Saunier *68 D4* anc. Ledo Salinarius. Jura, E France
Lop Buri *115 C5* var. Loburi. Lop Buri, C Thailand
Lop Nor see Lop Nur
Lop Nur *104 C3* var. Lob Nor, Lop Nor, Lo-pu Po. seasonal lake NW China
Loppersum *64 E1* Groningen, NE Netherlands
Lo-pu Po see Lop Nur
Lorca *71 E4* Ar. Lurka; anc. Eliocroca, Lat. Illurco. Murcia, S Spain
Lord Howe Island *120 C4* island E Australia
Lord Howe Rise *120 C4* undersea rise SW Pacific Ocean
Loreto *28 B3* Baja California Sur, NW Mexico
Lorient *68 A3* prev. l'Orient. Morbihan, NW France
l'Orient see Lorient
Lorn, Firth of *66 B4* inlet W Scotland, United Kingdom
Loro Sae see East Timor
Lörrach *73 A7* Baden-Württemberg, S Germany
Lorraine *68 D3* cultural region NE France
Los Alamos *26 C1* New Mexico, SW USA
Los Amates *30 B2* Izabal, E Guatemala
Los Ángeles *43 B5* Bío Bío, C Chile
Los Angeles *25 C7* California, W USA
Losanna see Lausanne
Lošinj *78 A3* Ger. Lussin, It. Lussino. island W Croatia
Loslau see Wodzisław Śląski
Los Mochis *28 C3* Sinaloa, C Mexico
Losonc/Losontz see Lučenec
Los Roques, Islas *36 D1* island group N Venezuela
Lot *69 B5* cultural region S France
Lot *69 B5* river S France
Lotagipi Swamp *51 C5* wetland Kenya/South Sudan
Lötzen see Giżycko
Loualaba see Lualaba
Louangnamtha *114 C3* var. Luong Nam Tha. Louang Namtha, N Laos
Louangphabang *102 D3* var. Louangphrabang, Luang Prabang. Louangphabang, N Laos
Louangphrabang see Louangphabang
Loubomo see Dolisie
Loudéac *68 A3* Côtes d'Armor, NW France
Loudi *106 C5* Hunan, S China
Louga *52 B3* NW Senegal
Louisiade Archipelago *122 B4* island group SE Papua New Guinea
Louisiana *20 A2* off. State of Louisiana, also known as Creole State, Pelican State. state S USA
Louisville *18 C5* Kentucky, S USA
Louisville Ridge *121 E4* undersea ridge S Pacific Ocean
Loup River *23 E4* river Nebraska, C USA
Lourdes *69 B6* Hautes-Pyrénées, S France
Lourenço Marques see Maputo
Louth *67 E5* E England, United Kingdom
Loutrá *82 C4* Kentrikí Makedonía, N Greece
Louvain see Leuven
Louvain-la Neuve *65 C6* Walloon Brabant, C Belgium
Louviers *68 C3* Eure, N France
Lovech *82 C2* Lovech, N Bulgaria
Loveland *22 D4* Colorado, C USA
Lovosice *76 A4* Ger. Lobositz. Ustecký Kraj, NW Czech Republic
Lóvua *56 C1* Moxico, E Angola
Lowell *19 G3* Massachusetts, NE USA
Löwen see Leuven
Lower California see Baja California
Lower Hutt *129 D5* Wellington, North Island, New Zealand
Lower Lough Erne *67 A5* lake SW Northern Ireland, United Kingdom
Lower Red Lake *23 F1* lake Minnesota, N USA
Lower Rhine see Neder Rijn
Lower Tunguska see Nizhnyaya Tunguska
Lowestoft *67 E6* E England, United Kingdom
Loxa see Loksa
Lo-yang see Luoyang
Loyauté, Îles *122 D5* island group S New Caledonia
Loyev see Loyew
Loyew *85 D8* Rus. Loyev. Homyel'skaya Voblasts', SE Belarus
Loznica *78 C3* Serbia, W Serbia
Lu see Shandong, China
Lualaba *55 D6* Fr. Loualaba. river SE Dem. Rep. Congo
Luanda *56 A1* var. Loanda, Port. São Paulo de Loanda. country capital (Angola) Luanda, NW Angola
Luang Prabang see Louangphabang
Luang, Thale *115 C7* lagoon S Thailand
Luangua, Rio see Luangwa
Luangwa *51 B8* var. Aruângua, Rio Luangua. river Mozambique/Zambia
Luanshya *56 D2* Copperbelt, C Zambia
Luarca *70 C1* Asturias, N Spain
Lubaczów *77 E5* var. Lúbaczów. Podkarpackie, SE Poland
L'uban' *76 B4* Leningradskaya Oblast', Russian Federation
Lubānas Ezers see Lubāns
Lubango *56 B2* Port. Sá da Bandeira. Huíla, SW Angola
Lubāns *84 D4* var. Lubānas Ezers. lake E Latvia
Lubao *55 D6* Kasai-Oriental, C Dem. Rep. Congo
Lübben *72 D4* Brandenburg, E Germany
Lübbenau *72 D4* Brandenburg, E Germany
Lubbock *27 E2* Texas, SW USA
Lübeck *72 C2* Schleswig-Holstein, N Germany
Lubelska, Wyżyna *76 E4* plateau SE Poland
Lüben see Lubin
Lubiana see Ljubljana
Lubin *76 B4* Ger. Lüben. Dolnośląskie, SW Poland
Lublin *76 E4* Rus. Lyublin. Lubelskie, E Poland
Lubliniec *76 C4* Śląskie, S Poland
Lubnān, Jabal see Liban, Jebel
Lubny *87 F2* Poltavs'ka Oblast', NE Ukraine
Lubsko *76 B4* Ger. Sommerfeld. Lubuskie, W Poland
Lubumbashi *55 E8* prev. Élisabethville. Shaba, SE Dem. Rep. Congo
Lubutu *55 D6* Maniema, E Dem. Rep. Congo
Luca see Lucca
Lucan *67 B5* Ir. Leamhcán. Dublin, E Ireland
Lucanian Mountains see Lucano, Appennino
Lucano, Appennino *75 D5* Eng. Lucanian Mountains. mountain range S Italy
Lucapa *56 C1* var. Lukapa. Lunda Norte, NE Angola
Lucca *74 B3* anc. Luca. Toscana, C Italy
Lucea *32 A4* W Jamaica
Lucena *117 E1* off. Lucena City. Luzon, N Philippines
Lucena *70 D4* Andalucía, S Spain
Lucena City see Lucena
Lučenec *77 D6* Ger. Losontz, Hung. Losonc. Banskobystrický Kraj, C Slovakia
Lucentum see Alicante
Lucerna/Lucerne see Luzern
Luchow see Hefei
Łuck see Luts'k
Lucknow *113 E3* var. Lakhnau. state capital Uttar Pradesh, N India
Lüda see Dalian
Luda Kamchiya *82 D2* river E Bulgaria
Ludasch see Luduş
Lüderitz *56 B4* prev. Angra Pequena. Karas, SW Namibia
Ludhiāna *112 D2* Punjab, N India
Ludington *18 C2* Michigan, N USA
Ludsan see Ludza
Luduş *86 B4* Ger. Ludasch, Hung. Marosludas. Mureş, C Romania
Ludvika *63 C6* Dalarna, C Sweden
Ludwigsburg *73 B6* Baden-Württemberg, SW Germany
Ludwigsfelde *72 D3* Brandenburg, NE Germany
Ludwigshafen *73 B5* var. Ludwigshafen am Rhein. Rheinland-Pfalz, W Germany
Ludwigshafen am Rhein see Ludwigshafen
Ludwigslust *72 C3* Mecklenburg-Vorpommern, N Germany
Ludza *84 D4* Ger. Ludsan. Ludza, E Latvia
Luebo *55 C6* Kasai-Occidental, SW Dem. Rep. Congo
Luena *56 C2* var. Lwena, Port. Luso. Moxico, E Angola
Lufira *55 E7* river SE Dem. Rep. Congo
Lufkin *27 H3* Texas, SW USA
Luga *88 A4* Leningradskaya Oblast', NW Russian Federation
Lugano *73 B8* Ger. Lauis. Ticino, S Switzerland
Lugansk see Luhans'k
Lugdunum see Lyon
Lugdunum Batavorum see Leiden
Lugenda, Rio *57 E2* river N Mozambique
Luggarus see Locarno
Lugh Ganana see Luuq
Lugo *70 C1* anc. Lugus Augusti. Galicia, NW Spain
Lugoj *86 A4* Ger. Lugosch, Hung. Lugos. Timiş, W Romania
Lugos/Lugosch see Lugoj
Lugus Augusti see Lugo
Luguvallium/Luguvallum see Carlisle
Luhans'k *87 H3* Rus. Lugansk; prev. Voroshilovgrad. Luhans'ka Oblast', E Ukraine
Luimneach see Limerick
Lukapa see Lucapa
Lukenie *55 C6* river C Dem. Rep. Congo
Lukovit *82 C2* Lovech, N Bulgaria
Łuków *76 E4* Ger. Bogendorf. Lubelskie, E Poland
Lukuga *55 D7* river SE Dem. Rep. Congo
Luleå *62 D4* Norrbotten, N Sweden
Luleälven *62 C3* river N Sweden
Lulonga *55 C5* river NW Dem. Rep. Congo
Lulua *55 D7* river S Dem. Rep. Congo
Luluabourg see Kananga
Lumber State see Maine
Lumbo *57 F2* Nampula, NE Mozambique
Lumsden *129 A7* Southland, South Island, New Zealand
Lund *63 B7* Skåne, S Sweden
Lüneburg *72 C3* Niedersachsen, N Germany
Lunga, Isola see Dugi Otok
Lungkiang see Qiqihar
Lungué-Bungo *56 C2* var. Lungwebungu. river Angola/Zambia
Lungwebungu see Lungué-Bungo
Luninets see Luninyets
Łuniniec see Luninyets
Luninyets *85 B7* Pol. Łuniniec, Rus. Luninets. Brestskaya Voblasts', SW Belarus
Lunteren *64 D4* Gelderland, C Netherlands
Luong Nam Tha see Louangnamtha
Luoyang *106 C4* var. Honan, Lo-yang. Henan, C China
Lupatia see Altamura
Lúrio *57 F2* Nampula, NE Mozambique
Lúrio, Rio *57 E2* river NE Mozambique
Lurka see Lorca
Lusaka *56 D2* country capital (Zambia) Lusaka, SE Zambia
Lushnja see Lushnjë
Lushnjë *79 C6* var. Lushnja. Fier, C Albania
Luso see Luena
Lussin/Lussino see Lošinj
Lūt, Baḩrat/Lut, Bahret see Dead Sea
Lut, Dasht-e *98 D3* var. Kavīr-e Lūt. desert E Iran
Lutetia/Lutetia Parisiorum see Paris
Lūt, Kavīr-e see Lūt, Dasht-e
Luton *67 D6* E England, United Kingdom
Łutselk'e *15 F4* prev. Snowdrift. Northwest Territories, W Canada
Luts'k *86 C1* Pol. Łuck, Rus. Lutsk. Volyns'ka Oblast', NW Ukraine
Lutsk see Luts'k
Lüttich see Liège
Lutzow-Holm Bay *132 C2* var. Lutzow-Holm Bay. bay Antarctica
Lutzow-Holm Bay see Lützow Holmbukta
Luuq *51 D6* It. Lugh Ganana. Gedo, SW Somalia
Luvua *55 D7* river SE Dem. Rep. Congo
Luwego *51 C8* river S Tanzania
Luxembourg *65 D8* country capital (Luxembourg) Luxembourg, S Luxembourg
Luxembourg *65 D8* off. Grand Duchy of Luxembourg, var. Lëtzebuerg, Luxemburg. country NW Europe
Luxemburg see Luxembourg
Luxor *50 B2* Ar. Al Uqşur. E Egypt
Luza *88 C4* Kirovskaya Oblast', NW Russian Federation
Luz, Costa de la *70 C5* coastal region SW Spain
Luzern *73 B7* Fr. Lucerne, It. Lucerna. Luzern, C Switzerland
Luzon *117 E1* island N Philippines
Luzon Strait *103 E3* strait Philippines/Taiwan
L'viv *86 B2* Ger. Lemberg, Pol. Lwów, Rus. L'vov. L'vivs'ka Oblast', W Ukraine
L'vov see L'viv
Lwena see Luena
Lwów see L'viv
Lyakhavichy *85 B6* Rus. Lyakhovichi. Brestskaya Voblasts', SW Belarus
Lyakhovichi see Lyakhavichy
Lyallpur see Faisalābād
Lyangar see Langar
Lyck see Ełk
Lycksele *62 C4* Västerbotten, N Sweden
Lycopolis see Asyūţ
Lyel'chytsy *85 C7* Rus. Lel'chitsy. Homyel'skaya Voblasts', SE Belarus
Lyepyel' *85 D5* Rus. Lepel'. Vitsyebskaya Voblasts', N Belarus
Lyme Bay *67 C7* bay S England, United Kingdom
Lynchburg *19 E5* Virginia, NE USA
Lynn see King's Lynn
Lynn Lake *15 F4* Manitoba, C Canada
Lynn Regis see King's Lynn
Lyon *69 D5* Eng. Lyons; anc. Lugdunum. Rhône, E France
Lyons see Lyon
Lyozna *85 E6* Rus. Liozno. Vitsyebskaya Voblasts', NE Belarus
Lypovets' *86 D2* Rus. Lipovets. Vinnyts'ka Oblast', C Ukraine
Lys see Leie
Lysychans'k *87 H3* Rus. Lisichansk. Luhans'ka Oblast', E Ukraine
Lyttelton *129 C6* South Island, New Zealand
Lyublin see Lublin
Lyubotin see Lyubotyn
Lyubotyn *87 G2* Rus. Lyubotin. Kharkivs'ka Oblast', E Ukraine
Lyulyakovo *82 E2* prev. Keremitlik. Burgas, E Bulgaria
Lyusina *85 B6* Rus. Lyusino. Brestskaya Voblasts', SW Belarus
Lyusino see Lyusina

M

Maale see Male'
Ma'ān *97 B7* Ma'ān, SW Jordan
Maardu *84 D2* Ger. Maart. Harjumaa, NW Estonia
Ma'aret-en-Nu'man see Ma'arrat an Nu'mān
Ma'arrat an Nu'mān *96 B3* var. Ma'aret-en-Nu'man, Fr. Maarret enn Naamâne. Idlib, NW Syria
Maarret enn Naamâne see Ma'arrat an Nu'mān
Maart see Maardu
Maas see Meuse
Maaseik *65 D5* prev. Maeseyck. Limburg, NE Belgium
Maastricht *65 D6* var. Maestricht; anc. Traiectum ad Mosam, Traiectum Tungorum. Limburg, SE Netherlands
Macao *107 C6* Chin. Aomen, Port. Macau. Guangdong, SE China
Macapá *41 E1* state capital Amapá, N Brazil
Macarsca see Makarska
Macassar see Makassar
Macău see Makó, Hungary
Macau see Macao
MacCluer Gulf see Berau, Teluk
Macdonnell Ranges *124 D4* mountain range Northern Territory, C Australia
Macedonia see Macedonia, FYR

Macedonia, FYR – Masai Steppe

Macedonia, FYR 79 D6 off. the Former Yugoslav Republic of Macedonia, var. Macedonia, Mac. Makedonija, abbrev. FYR Macedonia, FYROM. country SE Europe
Macedonia, the Former Yugoslav Republic of see Macedonia, FYR
Maceió 41 G3 state capital Alagoas, E Brazil
Machachi 38 B1 Pichincha, C Ecuador
Machala 38 B2 El Oro, SW Ecuador
Machanga 57 E3 Sofala, E Mozambique
Machilīpatnam 110 D1 var. Bandar Masulipatnam. Andhra Pradesh, E India
Machiques 36 C2 Zulia, NW Venezuela
Macías Nguema Biyogo see Bioco, Isla de
Măcin 86 D5 Tulcea, SE Romania
Mackay 126 D4 Queensland, NE Australia
Mackay, Lake 124 C4 salt lake Northern Territory/Western Australia
Mackenzie 15 E3 river Northwest Territories, NW Canada
Mackenzie Bay 132 D3 bay Antarctica
Mackenzie Mountains 14 D3 mountain range Northwest Territories, NW Canada
Macleod, Lake 124 A4 lake Western Australia
Macomb 18 A4 Illinois, N USA
Macomer 75 A5 Sardegna, Italy, C Mediterranean Sea
Mâcon 69 D5 anc. Matisco, Matisco Ædourum. Saône-et-Loire, C France
Macon 20 D2 Georgia, SE USA
Macon 23 G4 Missouri, C USA
Macquarie Ridge 132 C5 undersea ridge SW Pacific Ocean
Macuspana 29 G4 Tabasco, SE Mexico
Ma'dabā 97 B6 var. Mādabā, Madeba; anc. Medeba. Ma'dabā, NW Jordan
Mādabā see Ma'dabā
Madagascar 57 F3 off. Democratic Republic of Madagascar, Malg. Madagasikara; prev. Malagasy Republic. country W Indian Ocean
Madagascar 57 F3 island W Indian Ocean
Madagascar Basin 47 E7 undersea basin W Indian Ocean
Madagascar, Democratic Republic of see Madagascar
Madagascar Plateau 47 E7 var. Madagascar Ridge, Madagascar Rise, Rus. Madagaskarskiy Khrebet. undersea plateau W Indian Ocean
Madagascar Rise/Madagascar Ridge see Madagascar Plateau
Madagasikara see Madagascar
Madagaskarskiy Khrebet see Madagascar Plateau
Madang 122 B3 Madang, N Papua New Guinea
Madanīyīn see Médenine
Mađarska see Hungary
Made 64 C4 Noord-Brabant, S Netherlands
Madeba see Ma'dabā
Madeira 48 A2 var. Ilha de Madeira. island Madeira, Portugal, NE Atlantic Ocean
Madeira, Ilha de see Madeira
Madeira Plain 44 C3 abyssal plain E Atlantic Ocean
Madeira, Rio 40 D2 var. Río Madera. river Bolivia/Brazil
Madeleine, Îles de la 17 F4 Eng. Magdalen Islands. island group Québec, E Canada
Madera 25 B6 California, W USA
Madera, Río see Madeira, Rio
Madhya Pradesh 113 E4 prev. Central Provinces and Berar. cultural region C India
Madīnat ath Thawrah 96 C2 var. Ath Thawrah. Ar Raqqah, N Syria
Madioen see Madiun
Madison 23 F3 South Dakota, N USA
Madison 18 B3 state capital Wisconsin, N USA
Madiun 116 D5 prev. Madioen. Jawa, C Indonesia
Madoera see Madura, Pulau
Madona 84 D4 Ger. Modohn. Madona, E Latvia
Madras see Chennai
Madras see Tamil Nādu
Madre de Dios, Río 39 E3 river Bolivia/Peru
Madre del Sur, Sierra 29 E5 mountain range S Mexico
Madre, Laguna 29 F3 lagoon NE Mexico
Madre, Laguna 27 G5 lagoon Texas, SW USA
Madre Occidental, Sierra 28 C3 var. Western Sierra Madre. mountain range C Mexico
Madre Oriental, Sierra 29 E3 var. Eastern Sierra Madre. mountain range C Mexico
Madre, Sierra 30 B2 var. Sierra de Soconusco. mountain range Guatemala/Mexico
Madrid 70 D3 country capital (Spain) Madrid, C Spain
Madura see Madurai
Madurai 110 C3 prev. Madura, Mathurai. Tamil Nādu, S India
Madura, Pulau 116 D5 prev. Madoera. island C Indonesia
Maebashi 109 D5 var. Maebasi, Mayebashi. Gunma, Honshū, S Japan
Maebasi see Maebashi
Mae Nam Khong see Mekong
Mae Nam Nan 114 C4 river NW Thailand
Mae Nam Yom 114 C4 river W Thailand
Maeseyck see Maaseik
Maestricht see Maastricht
Maéwo 122 D4 prev. Aurora. island C Vanuatu
Mafia 51 D7 island E Tanzania
Mafraq/Muḥāfaẓat al Mafraq see Al Mafraq
Magadan 93 G3 Magadanskaya Oblast', E Russian Federation
Magallanes see Punta Arenas
Magallanes, Estrecho de see Magellan, Strait of
Magangué 36 B2 Bolívar, N Colombia
Magdalena 39 F3 Beni, N Bolivia
Magdalena 28 B1 Sonora, NW Mexico
Isla Magdalena 28 B3 island NW Mexico
Magdalena, Río 36 B2 river C Colombia
Magdalen Islands see Madeleine, Îles de la
Magdeburg 72 C4 Sachsen-Anhalt, C Germany
Magelang 116 C5 Jawa, C Indonesia
Magellan, Strait of 43 B8 Sp. Estrecho de Magallanes. strait Argentina/Chile
Mageroy see Magerøya
Magerøya 62 D1 var. Mageroy, Lapp. Máhkarávju. island N Norway
Maggiore, Lago see Maggiore, Lake
Maggiore, Lake 74 B1 It. Lago Maggiore. lake Italy/Switzerland
Maglaj 78 C3 Federacija Bosna I Hercegovina, N Bosnia and Herzegovina
Maglie 75 E6 Puglia, SE Italy
Magna 22 B4 Utah, W USA
Magnesia see Manisa
Magnitogorsk 92 B4 Chelyabinskaya Oblast', C Russian Federation
Magnolia State see Mississippi
Magṭa' Laḥjar 52 C3 var. Magta Lahjar, Magta' Lahjar, Magtá Lahjar. Brakna, SW Mauritania
Magway 114 A3 var. Magwe. Magway, W Myanmar (Burma)
Magyar-Becse see Bečej
Magyarkanizsa see Kanjiža
Magyarország see Hungary
Mahajanga 57 F2 var. Majunga. Mahajanga, NW Madagascar
Mahakam, Sungai 116 D4 var. Koetai, Kutai. river Borneo, C Indonesia
Mahalapye 56 D3 var. Mahalatswe. Central, SE Botswana
Mahalatswe see Mahalapye
Māhān 98 D3 Kermān, E Iran
Mahanādi 113 F4 river E India
Mahārāshtra 112 D5 cultural region W India
Mahbés see El Mahbas
Mahbūbnagar 112 D5 Andhra Pradesh, C India
Mahdia 49 F2 var. Al Mahdīyah, Mehdia. NE Tunisia
Mahé 57 H1 island Inner Islands, NE Seychelles
Mahia Peninsula 128 E4 peninsula North Island, New Zealand
Mahilyow 85 D6 Rus. Mogilëv. Mahilyowskaya Voblasts', E Belarus
Máhkarávju see Magerøya
Mahmūd-e 'Erāqī see Maḥmūd-e Rāqī
Maḥmūd-e Rāqī 101 E4 var. Mahmūd-e 'Erāqī. Kāpīsā, NE Afghanistan
Mahón 71 H3 Cat. Maó, Eng. Port Mahon; anc. Portus Magonis. Menorca, Spain, W Mediterranean Sea
Mähren see Moravia
Mährisch-Weisskirchen see Hranice
Maicao 36 C1 La Guajira, N Colombia
Mai Ceu/Mai Chio see Maych'ew
Maidstone 67 E7 SE England, United Kingdom
Maiduguri 53 H4 Borno, NE Nigeria
Mailand see Milano
Maimāna see Meymaneh
Main 73 B5 river C Germany
Mai-Ndombe, Lac 55 C6 prev. Lac Léopold II. lake W Dem. Rep. Congo
Maine 19 G2 off. State of Maine, also known as Lumber State, Pine Tree State. state NE USA
Maine 68 B3 cultural region NW France
Maine, Gulf of 19 H2 gulf NE USA
Mainland 66 C2 island N Scotland, United Kingdom
Mainland 66 D1 island NE Scotland, United Kingdom
Mainz 73 B5 Fr. Mayence. Rheinland-Pfalz, SW Germany
Maio 52 A3 var. Mayo. island Ilhas de Sotavento, SE Cape Verde
Maisur see Mysore, India
Maisur see Karnātaka, India
Maizhokunggar 104 C5 Xizang Zizhiqu, W China
Majorca see Mallorca
Mājro see Majuro Atoll
Majunga see Mahajanga
Majuro Atoll 122 D2 var. Mājro. atoll Ratak Chain, SE Marshall Islands
Makale see Mek'elē
Makarov Basin 133 B3 undersea basin Arctic Ocean
Makarska 78 B4 It. Macarsca. Split-Dalmacija, SE Croatia
Makasar see Makassar
Makasar, Selat see Makassar Straits
Makassar 117 E4 var. Macassar, Makasar; prev. Ujungpandang. Sulawesi, C Indonesia
Makassar Straits 116 D4 Ind. Makasar Selat. strait C Indonesia
Makay 57 F3 var. Massif du Makay. mountain range SW Madagascar
Makay, Massif du see Makay
Makedonija see Macedonia, FYR
Makeni 52 C4 C Sierra Leone
Makeyevka see Makiyivka
Makhachkala 92 A4 prev. Petrovsk-Port. Respublika Dagestan, SW Russian Federation
Makin 122 D2 prev. Pitt Island. atoll Tungaru, W Kiribati
Makira see San Cristobal
Makiyivka 87 G3 Rus. Makeyevka; prev. Dmitriyevsk. Donets'ka Oblast', E Ukraine
Makkah 99 A5 Eng. Mecca. Makkah, W Saudi Arabia
Makkovik 17 F2 Newfoundland and Labrador, NE Canada
Makó 77 D7 Rom. Macău. Csongrád, SE Hungary
Makoua 55 B5 Cuvette, C Congo
Makran Coast 98 E4 coastal region SE Iran
Makrany 85 A6 Rus. Mokrany. Brestskaya Voblasts', SW Belarus
Mākū 98 B2 Āžarbāyjān-e Gharbī, NW Iran
Makurdi 53 G4 Benue, C Nigeria
Mala see Malaita, Solomon Islands
Malabār Coast 110 B3 coast SW India
Malabo 55 A5 prev. Santa Isabel. country capital (Equatorial Guinea) Isla de Bioco, NW Equatorial Guinea
Malaca see Málaga
Malacca, Strait of 116 B3 Ind. Selat Malaka. strait Indonesia/Malaysia
Malacka see Malacky
Malacky 77 C6 Hung. Malacka. Bratislavský Kraj, W Slovakia
Maladzyechna 85 C5 Pol. Molodeczno, Rus. Molodechno. Minskaya Voblasts', C Belarus
Málaga 70 D5 anc. Malaca. Andalucía, S Spain
Malagarasi River 51 B7 river W Tanzania Africa
Malagasy Republic see Madagascar
Malaita 122 C3 var. Mala. island N Solomon Islands
Malakal 51 B5 Upper Nile, NE South Sudan
Malakula see Malekula
Malang 116 D5 Jawa, C Indonesia
Malange see Malanje
Malanje 56 B1 var. Malange. Malanje, NW Angola
Mälaren 63 C6 lake C Sweden
Malatya 95 E4 anc. Melitene. Malatya, SE Turkey
Mala Vyska 87 E3 Rus. Malaya Viska. Kirovohrads'ka Oblast', S Ukraine
Malawi 57 E1 off. Republic of Malaŵi; prev. Nyasaland, Nyasaland Protectorate. country S Africa
Malawi, Lake see Nyasa, Lake
Malaŵi, Republic of see Malawi
Malaya Viska see Mala Vyska
Malay Peninsula 102 D4 peninsula Malaysia/Thailand
Malaysia 116 B3 off. Malaysia, var. Federation of Malaysia; prev. the separate territories of Federation of Malaya, Sarawak and Sabah (North Borneo) and Singapore. country SE Asia
Malaysia, Federation of see Malaysia
Malbork 76 C2 Ger. Marienburg, Marienburg in Westpreussen. Pomorskie, N Poland
Malchin 72 C3 Mecklenburg-Vorpommern, N Germany
Malden 23 H5 Missouri, C USA
Malden Island 123 G3 prev. Independence Island. atoll E Kiribati
Maldives 110 A4 off. Maldivian Divehi, Republic of Maldives. country N Indian Ocean
Maldives, Republic of see Maldives
Maldivian Divehi see Maldives
Male' 110 B4 Div. Maale. country capital (Maldives) Male' Atoll, C Maldives
Male' Atoll 110 B4 var. Kaafu Atoll. atoll C Maldives
Malekula 122 D4 var. Malakula; prev. Mallicolo. island W Vanuatu
Malesína 83 C5 Stereá Ellás, E Greece
Malheur Lake 24 C3 lake Oregon, NW USA
Mali 53 E3 off. Republic of Mali, Fr. République du Mali; prev. French Sudan, Sudanese Republic. country W Africa
Malik, Wadi al see Milk, Wadi el
Mali Kyun 115 B5 var. Tavoy Island. island Mergui Archipelago, S Myanmar (Burma)
Malin see Malyn
Malindi 51 D7 Coast, SE Kenya
Malines see Mechelen
Mali, Republic of see Mali
Mali, République du see Mali
Malkiye see Al Mālikīyah
Malko Tŭrnovo 82 E3 Burgas, E Bulgaria
Mallaig 66 B3 N Scotland, United Kingdom
Mallawī 50 B2 var. Mallawi. C Egypt
Mallawi see Mallawī
Mallicolo see Malekula
Mallorca 71 G3 Eng. Majorca; anc. Baleares Major. island Islas Baleares, Spain, W Mediterranean Sea
Malmberget 62 C3 Lapp. Malmivaara. Norrbotten, N Sweden
Malmédy 65 D6 Liège, E Belgium
Malmivaara see Malmberget
Malmö 63 B7 Skåne, S Sweden
Maļoeļap see Maloelap Atoll
Maloelap Atoll 122 D1 var. Maļoeļap. atoll E Marshall Islands
Małopolska, Wyżyna 76 D4 plateau S Poland
Malozemel'skaya Tundra 88 D3 physical region NW Russian Federation
Malta 84 D4 Rēzekne, SE Latvia
Malta 22 C1 Montana, NW USA
Malta 75 C8 off. Republic of Malta. country C Mediterranean Sea
Malta 75 C8 island Malta, C Mediterranean Sea
Malta, Canale di see Malta Channel
Malta Channel 75 C8 It. Canale di Malta. strait Italy/Malta
Malta, Republic of see Malta
Maluku 117 F4 Dut. Molukken, Eng. Moluccas; prev. Spice Islands. island group E Indonesia
Maluku, Laut see Molucca Sea
Malung 63 B6 Dalarna, C Sweden
Malventum see Benevento
Malvina, Isla Gran see West Falkland
Malvinas, Islas see Falkland Islands
Malyn 86 D2 Rus. Malin. Zhytomyrs'ka Oblast', N Ukraine
Malyy Kavkaz see Lesser Caucasus
Mamberamo, Sungai 117 H4 river Papua, E Indonesia
Mambij see Manbij
Mamonovo 84 A4 Ger. Heiligenbeil. Kaliningradskaya Oblast', W Russian Federation
Mamoré, Rio 39 F3 river Bolivia/Brazil
Mamou 52 C4 W Guinea
Mamoudzou 57 F2 dependent territory capital (Mayotte) C Mayotte
Mamuno 56 C3 Ghanzi, W Botswana
Manacor 71 G3 Mallorca, Spain, W Mediterranean Sea
Manado 117 F3 prev. Menado. Sulawesi, C Indonesia
Managua 30 D3 country capital (Nicaragua) Managua, W Nicaragua
Managua, Lake 30 C3 var. Xolotlán. lake W Nicaragua
Manakara 57 G4 Fianarantsoa, SE Madagascar
Manama see Al Manāmah
Mananjary 57 G3 Fianarantsoa, SE Madagascar
Manáos see Manaus
Manapouri, Lake 129 A7 lake South Island, New Zealand
Manar see Mannar
Manas, Gora 101 E2 mountain Kyrgyzstan/Uzbekistan
Manaus 40 D2 prev. Manáos. state capital Amazonas, NW Brazil
Manavgat 94 B4 Antalya, SW Turkey
Manbij 96 C2 var. Mambij, Fr. Membidj. Ḥalab, N Syria
Manchester 67 D5 Lat. Mancunium. NW England, United Kingdom
Manchester 19 G3 New Hampshire, NE USA
Man-chou-li see Manzhouli
Manchurian Plain 103 E1 plain NE China
Máncio Lima see Japiim
Mancunium see Manchester
Mand see Mand, Rūd-e
Mandalay 114 B3 Mandalay, C Myanmar (Burma)
Mandan 23 E2 North Dakota, N USA
Mandeville 32 B5 C Jamaica
Mándra 83 C6 Attikí, C Greece
Rud-e Mand 98 D4 var. Mand. river S Iran
Mandurah 125 A6 Western Australia
Manduria 75 E5 Puglia, SE Italy
Mandya 110 C2 Karnātaka, C India
Manfredonia 75 D5 Puglia, SE Italy
Mangai 55 C6 Bandundu, W Dem. Rep. Congo
Mangaia 123 G5 island group S Cook Islands
Mangalia 86 D5 anc. Callatis. Constanța, SE Romania
Mangalmé 54 C3 Guéra, SE Chad
Mangalore 110 B2 Karnātaka, W India
Mangaung see Bloemfontein
Mango see Sansanné-Mango, Togo
Mangoky 57 F3 river W Madagascar
Manhattan 23 F4 Kansas, C USA
Manicouagan, Réservoir 16 D3 lake Québec, E Canada
Manihiki 123 G4 atoll N Cook Islands
Manihiki Plateau 121 E3 undersea plateau C Pacific Ocean
Maniitsoq 60 C3 var. Manîtsoq, Dan. Sukkertoppen. Kitaa, S Greenland
Manila 117 E1 off. City of Manila. country capital (Philippines) Luzon, N Philippines
Manila, City of see Manila
Manisa 94 A3 var. Manissa, prev. Saruhan; anc. Magnesia. Manisa, W Turkey
Manissa see Manisa
Manitoba 15 F5 province S Canada
Manitoba, Lake 15 F5 lake Manitoba, S Canada
Manitoulin Island 16 C4 island Ontario, S Canada
Manîtsoq see Maniitsoq
Manizales 36 B3 Caldas, W Colombia
Manjimup 125 A7 Western Australia
Mankato 23 F3 Minnesota, N USA
Manlleu 71 G2 Cataluña, NE Spain
Manly 126 E1 Iowa, C USA
Manmād 112 C5 Mahārāshtra, W India
Mannar 110 C3 var. Manar. Northern Province, NW Sri Lanka
Mannar, Gulf of 110 C3 gulf India/Sri Lanka
Mannheim 73 B5 Baden-Württemberg, SW Germany
Manono 55 E7 Shaba, SE Dem. Rep. Congo
Manosque 69 D6 Alpes-de-Haute-Provence, SE France
Manra 123 F3 prev. Sydney Island. atoll Phoenix Islands, C Kiribati
Mansa 56 D2 prev. Fort Rosebery. Luapula, N Zambia
Mansel Island 15 G3 island Nunavut, NE Canada
Mansfield 18 D4 Ohio, N USA
Manta 38 A2 Manabí, W Ecuador
Manteca 25 B6 California, W USA
Mantoue see Mantova
Mantova 74 B2 Eng. Mantua, Fr. Mantoue. Lombardia, NW Italy
Mantua see Mantova
Manuae 123 G4 island S Cook Islands
Manukau see Manurewa
Manurewa 128 D3 var. Manukau. Auckland, North Island, New Zealand
Manzanares 71 E3 Castilla-La Mancha, C Spain
Manzanillo 32 C3 Granma, E Cuba
Manzanillo 28 D4 Colima, SW Mexico
Manzhouli 105 F1 var. Man-chou-li. Nei Mongol Zizhiqu, N China
Mao 54 B3 Kanem, W Chad
Maó see Mahón
Maoke, Pegunungan 117 H4 Dut. Sneeuw-gebergte, Eng. Snow Mountains. mountain range Papua, E Indonesia
Maoming 106 C6 Guangdong, S China
Mapmaker Seamounts 103 H2 seamount range N Pacific Ocean
Maputo 56 D4 prev. Lourenço Marques. country capital (Mozambique) Maputo, S Mozambique
Marabá 41 F2 Pará, NE Brazil
Maracaibo 36 C1 Zulia, NW Venezuela
Maracaibo, Gulf of see Venezuela, Golfo de
Maracaibo, Lago de 36 C2 var. Lake Maracaibo. inlet NW Venezuela
Maracaibo, Lake see Maracaibo, Lago de
Maracay 36 D2 Aragua, N Venezuela
Marada see Marādah
Marādah 49 G3 var. Marada. N Libya
Maradi 53 G3 Maradi, S Niger
Maragha see Marāgheh
Marāgheh 98 C2 var. Maragha. Āžarbāyjān-e Khāvarī, NW Iran
Marajó, Baía de 41 F1 bay N Brazil
Marajó, Ilha de 41 E1 island N Brazil
Marakesh see Marrakech
Maramba see Livingstone
Maranhão 41 F2 off. Estado do Maranhão. state E Brazil
Maranhão 41 F2 off. Estado do Maranhão. region E Brazil
Maranhão, Estado do see Maranhão
Marañón, Río 38 B2 river N Peru
Marathon 16 C4 Ontario, S Canada
Marathón see Marathónas
Marathónas 83 C5 prev. Marathón. Attikí, C Greece
Märäzä 95 H2 Rus. Maraza. E Azerbaijan
Maraza see Märäzä
Marbella 70 D5 Andalucía, S Spain
Marble Bar 124 B4 Western Australia
Marburg see Marburg an der Lahn, Germany
Marburg see Maribor, Slovenia
Marburg an der Lahn 72 B4 hist. Marburg. Hessen, W Germany
March see Morava
Marche 74 C3 Eng. Marches. region C Italy
Marche 69 C5 cultural region C France
Marche-en-Famenne 65 C7 Luxembourg, SE Belgium
Marchena, Isla 38 B5 var. Bindloe Island. island Galapagos Islands, Ecuador, E Pacific Ocean
Marches see Marche
Mar Chiquita, Laguna 42 C3 lake C Argentina
Marcounda see Markounda
Mardān 112 C1 North-West Frontier Province, N Pakistan
Mar del Plata 43 D5 Buenos Aires, E Argentina
Mardin 95 E4 Mardin, SE Turkey
Maré 122 D5 island Îles Loyauté, E New Caledonia
Marea Neagră see Black Sea
Mareeba 126 D3 Queensland, NE Australia
Marek see Dupnitsa
Marganets see Marhanets'
Margarita, Isla de 37 E1 island N Venezuela
Margate 67 E7 prev. Mergate. SE England, United Kingdom
Margherita see Jamaame
Margherita, Lake 51 C5 Eng. Lake Margherita, It. Abbaia. lake SW Ethiopia
Margherita, Lake see Ābaya Hāyk'
Marghita 86 B3 Hung. Margitta. Bihor, NW Romania
Margitta see Marghita
Marhanets' 87 F3 Rus. Marganets. Dnipropetrovs'ka Oblast', E Ukraine
María Cleofas, Isla 28 C4 island C Mexico
Maria Island 127 C8 island Tasmania, SE Australia
María Madre, Isla 28 C4 island C Mexico
María Magdalena, Isla 28 C4 island C Mexico
Mariana Trench 103 G4 trench W Pacific Ocean
Mariánské Lázně 77 A5 Ger. Marienbad. Karlovarský Kraj, W Czech Republic
Marías, Islas 28 C4 island group C Mexico
Maria-Theresiopel see Subotica
Maribor 73 E7 Ger. Marburg. NE Slovenia
Marica see Maritsa
Maridi 51 B5 W Equatoria, S South Sudan
Marie Byrd Land 132 A3 physical region Antarctica
Marie-Galante 33 G4 var. Ceyre to the Caribs. island SE Guadeloupe
Marienbad see Mariánské Lázně
Marienburg see Alūksne, Latvia
Marienburg see Malbork, Poland
Marienburg in Westpreussen see Malbork
Marienhausen see Viļaka
Mariental 56 B4 Hardap, SW Namibia
Marienwerder see Kwidzyń
Mariestad 63 B6 Västra Götaland, S Sweden
Marietta 20 D2 Georgia, SE USA
Marijampolė 84 B4 prev. Kapsukas. Marijampolė, S Lithuania
Marília 41 E4 São Paulo, S Brazil
Marín 70 B1 Galicia, NW Spain
Mar'ina Gorka see Mar"ina Horka
Mar"ina Horka 85 C6 Rus. Mar'ina Gorka. Minskaya Voblasts', C Belarus
Maringá 41 E4 Paraná, S Brazil
Marion 23 G3 Iowa, C USA
Marion 18 D4 Ohio, N USA
Marion, Lake 21 E2 reservoir South Carolina, SE USA
Mariscal Estigarribia 42 D2 Boquerón, NW Paraguay
Maritsa 82 D3 var. Marica, Gk. Évros, Turk. Meriç; anc. Hebrus. river SW Europe
Maritzburg see Pietermaritzburg
Mariupol' 87 G4 prev. Zhdanov. Donets'ka Oblast', SE Ukraine
Marka 51 D6 var. Merca. Shabeellaha Hoose, S Somalia
Markham, Mount 132 B4 mountain Antarctica
Markounda 54 C4 var. Marcounda. Ouham, NW Central African Republic
Marktredwitz 73 C5 Bayern, E Germany
Marlborough 126 D4 Queensland, E Australia
Marmanda see Marmande
Marmande 69 B5 anc. Marmanda. Lot-et-Garonne, SW France
Sea of Marmara 94 A2 Eng. Sea of Marmara. sea NW Turkey
Marmara, Sea of see Marmara Denizi
Marmaris 94 A4 Muğla, SW Turkey
Marne 68 C3 cultural region N France
Marne 68 D3 river N France
Maro 54 C4 Moyen-Chari, S Chad
Maroantsetra 57 G2 Toamasina, NE Madagascar
Maromokotro 57 G2 mountain N Madagascar
Maroni 37 G3 Dut. Marowijne. river French Guiana/Suriname
Maroshevíz see Toplița
Marosludas see Luduș
Marosvásárhely see Târgu Mureș
Marotiri 121 F4 var. Îlots de Bass, Morotiri. island group Îles Australes, SW French Polynesia
Maroua 54 B3 Extrême-Nord, N Cameroon
Marowijne see Maroni
Marquesas Fracture Zone 131 E3 fracture zone E Pacific Ocean
Marquette 18 B1 Michigan, N USA
Marrakech 48 C2 var. Marakesh, Eng. Marrakesh; prev. Morocco. W Morocco
Marrakesh see Marrakech
Marrawah 127 C8 Tasmania, SE Australia
Marree 127 B5 South Australia
Marsá al Burayqah 49 G3 var. Al Burayqah. N Libya
Marsabit 51 C6 Eastern, N Kenya
Marsala 75 B7 anc. Lilybaeum. Sicilia, Italy, C Mediterranean Sea
Marsberg 72 B4 Nordrhein-Westfalen, W Germany
Marseille 69 D6 Eng. Marseilles; anc. Massilia. Bouches-du-Rhône, SE France
Marseilles see Marseille
Marshall 23 F2 Minnesota, N USA
Marshall 27 H2 Texas, SW USA
Marshall Islands 122 C1 off. Republic of the Marshall Islands. country W Pacific Ocean
Marshall Islands, Republic of the see Marshall Islands
Marshall Seamounts 103 H3 seamount range SW Pacific Ocean
Marsh Harbour 32 C1 Great Abaco, W Bahamas
Martaban 114 B4 var. Moktama. Mon State, S Myanmar (Burma)
Martha's Vineyard 19 G3 island Massachusetts, NE USA
Martigues 69 D6 Bouches-du-Rhône, SE France
Martin 77 C5 Ger. Sankt Martin, Hung. Turócszentmárton; prev. Turčianský Svätý Martin. Žilinský Kraj, N Slovakia
Martinique 33 G4 French overseas department E West Indies
Martinique Channel see Martinique Passage
Martinique Passage 33 G4 var. Dominica Channel, Martinique Channel. channel Dominica/Martinique
Marton 128 D4 Manawatu-Wanganui, North Island, New Zealand
Martos 70 D4 Andalucía, S Spain
Marungu 55 E7 mountain range SE Dem. Rep. Congo
Mary 100 D3 prev. Merv. Mary Welaýaty, S Turkmenistan
Maryborough 127 D4 Queensland, E Australia
Maryborough see Port Laoise
Mary Island see Kanton
Maryland 19 E5 off. State of Maryland, also known as America in Miniature, Cockade State, Free State, Old Line State. state NE USA
Maryland, State of see Maryland
Maryville 23 F4 Missouri, C USA
Maryville 20 D1 Tennessee, S USA
Masai Steppe 51 C7 grassland NW Tanzania

Masaka – Mitumba, Chaîne des/Mitumba Range

Masaka 51 B6 SW Uganda
Masallı 95 H3 *Rus.* Masally. S Azerbaijan
Masally *see* Masallı
Masasi 51 C8 Mtwara, SE Tanzania
Masawa/Massawa *see* Mits'iwa
Masaya 30 D3 Masaya, W Nicaragua
Mascarene Basin 119 B5 *undersea basin* W Indian Ocean
Mascarene Islands 57 H4 *island group* W Indian Ocean
Mascarene Plain 119 B5 *abyssal plain* W Indian Ocean
Mascarene Plateau 119 B5 *undersea plateau* W Indian Ocean
Maseru 56 D4 *country capital* (Lesotho) W Lesotho
Mas-ha 97 D7 W West Bank Asia
Mashhad 98 E2 *var.* Meshed. Khorāsān-Razavī, NE Iran
Masindi 51 B6 W Uganda
Masira *see* Maşīrah, Jazīrat
Masira, Gulf of *see* Maşīrah, Khalīj
Maşīrah, Jazīrat 99 E5 *var.* Masīra. *island* E Oman
Maşīrah, Khalīj 99 E5 *var.* Gulf of Masira. *bay* E Oman
Masis *see* Büyükağrı Dağı
Maskat *see* Masqaţ
Mason City 23 F3 Iowa, C USA
Masqaţ 99 E5 *var.* Maskat, *Eng.* Muscat. *country capital* (Oman) NE Oman
Massa 74 B3 Toscana, C Italy
Massachusetts 19 G3 *off.* Commonwealth of Massachusetts, *also known as* Bay State, Old Bay State, Old Colony State. *state* NE USA
Massenya 54 B3 Chari-Baguirmi, SW Chad
Massif Central 69 C5 *plateau* C France
Massilia *see* Marseille
Massoukou *see* Franceville
Mastanli *see* Momchilgrad
Masterton 129 D5 Wellington, North Island, New Zealand
Masty 85 B5 *Rus.* Mosty. Hrodzyenskaya Voblasts', W Belarus
Masuda 109 B6 Shimane, Honshū, SW Japan
Masuku *see* Franceville
Masvingo 56 D3 *prev.* Fort Victoria, Nyanda, Victoria. Masvingo, SE Zimbabwe
Maşyāf 96 B3 *Fr.* Misiaf. Ḩamāh, C Syria
Matadi 55 B6 Bas-Congo, W Dem. Rep. Congo
Matagalpa 30 D3 Matagalpa, C Nicaragua
Matale 110 D3 Central Province, C Sri Lanka
Matam 52 C3 NE Senegal
Matamata 128 D3 Waikato, North Island, New Zealand
Matamoros 28 D3 Coahuila, NE Mexico
Matamoros 29 E2 Tamaulipas, C Mexico
Matane 17 E4 Québec, SE Canada
Matanzas 32 B2 Matanzas, NW Cuba
Matara 110 D4 Southern Province, S Sri Lanka
Mataram 116 D5 Pulau Lombok, C Indonesia
Mataró 71 G2 *anc.* Illuro. Cataluña, E Spain
Mataura 129 B7 Southland, South Island, New Zealand
Mataura 129 B7 *river* South Island, New Zealand
Mata Uta *see* Matā'utu
Matā'utu 123 E4 *var.* Mata Uta. *dependent territory capital* (Wallis and Futuna) Île Uvea, Wallis and Futuna
Matera 75 E5 Basilicata, S Italy
Mathurai *see* Madurai
Matianus *see* Orūmīyeh, Daryācheh-ye
Matías Romero 29 F5 Oaxaca, SE Mexico
Matisco/Matisco Ædourum *see* Mâcon
Mato Grosso 41 E3 *off.* Estado de Mato Grosso; *prev.* Matto Grosso. *state* W Brazil
Mato Grosso 41 E3 *off.* Estado de Mato Grosso; *prev.* Matto Grosso. *region* W Brazil
Mato Grosso do Sul 41 E4 *off.* Estado de Mato Grosso do Sul. *region* S Brazil
Mato Grosso do Sul 41 E4 *off.* Estado de Mato Grosso do Sul. *state* S Brazil
Mato Grosso do Sul, Estado de *see* Mato Grosso do Sul
Mato Grosso, Estado de *see* Mato Grosso
Mato Grosso, Planalto de 34 C4 *plateau* C Brazil
Matosinhos 70 B2 *prev.* Matozinhos. Porto, NW Portugal
Matozinhos *see* Matosinhos
Matsue 109 B6 *var.* Matsuye, Matue. Shimane, Honshū, SW Japan
Matsumoto 109 C5 *var.* Matumoto. Nagano, Honshū, S Japan
Matsuyama 109 B7 *var.* Matuyama. Ehime, Shikoku, SW Japan
Matsuye *see* Matsue
Matterhorn 73 A8 *It.* Monte Cervino. *mountain* Italy/Switzerland
Matthews Ridge 37 F2 N Guyana
Matthew Town 32 D2 Great Inagua, S Bahamas
Matto Grosso *see* Mato Grosso
Matucana 38 C4 Lima, W Peru
Matue *see* Matsue
Matumoto *see* Matsumoto
Maturín 37 E2 Monagas, NE Venezuela
Matuyama *see* Matsuyama
Mau 113 E3 *var.* Maunāth Bhanjan. Uttar Pradesh, N India
Maui 25 B8 *island* Hawai'i, USA, C Pacific Ocean
Maun 56 C3 North-West, C Botswana
Maunāth Bhanjan *see* Mau
Mauren 72 E1 NE Liechtenstein Europe
Maurice *see* Mauritius
Mauritania 52 C2 *off.* Islamic Republic of Mauritania, *Ar.* Mūrītānīyah. *country* W Africa
Mauritania, Islamic Republic of *see* Mauritania
Mauritius 57 H3 *off.* Republic of Mauritius, *Fr.* Maurice. *country* W Indian Ocean
Mauritius 119 B5 *island* W Indian Ocean
Mauritius, Republic of *see* Mauritius
Mawlamyaing *see* Mawlamyine
Mawlamyine 114 B4 *var.* Mawlamyaing, Moulmein. Mon State, S Myanmar (Burma)
Mawson 132 D2 *Australian research station* Antarctica
Mayadin *see* Al Mayādīn
Mayaguana 32 D2 *island* SE Bahamas
Mayaguana Passage 32 D2 *passage* SE Bahamas
Mayagüez 33 F3 W Puerto Rico
Mayamey 98 D2 Semnān, N Iran
Maya Mountains 30 B2 *Sp.* Montañas Mayas. *mountain range* Belize/Guatemala
Mayas, Montañas *see* Maya Mountains
Maych'ew 50 C4 *var.* Mai Chio, *It.* Mai Ceu. Tigray, N Ethiopia
Maydān Shahr *see* Meydān Shahr
Mayebashi *see* Maebashi
Mayence *see* Mainz
Mayfield 129 B6 Canterbury, South Island, New Zealand
Maykop 89 A7 Respublika Adygeya, SW Russian Federation
Maymana *see* Meymaneh
Maymyo *see* Pyin-Oo-Lwin
Mayo *see* Maio
Mayor Island 128 D3 *island* NE New Zealand
Mayor Pablo Lagerenza *see* Capitán Pablo Lagerenza
Mayotte 57 F2 *French territorial collectivity* E Africa
May Pen 32 B5 C Jamaica
Mayyit, Al Baḩr al *see* Dead Sea
Mazabuka 56 D2 Southern, S Zambia
Mazaca *see* Kayseri
Mazagan *see* El-Jadida
Mazār-e Sharīf 101 E3 *var.* Mazār-i Sharif. Balkh, N Afghanistan
Mazār-i Sharif *see* Mazār-e Sharīf
Mazatlán 28 C3 Sinaloa, C Mexico
Mažeikiai 84 B3 Telšiai, NW Lithuania
Mazirbe 84 C2 Talsi, NW Latvia
Mazra'a *see* Al Mazra'ah
Mazury 76 D3 *physical region* NE Poland
Mazyr 85 C7 *Rus.* Mozyr'. Homyel'skaya Voblasts', SE Belarus
Mbabane 56 D4 *country capital* (Swaziland) NW Swaziland
Mbacké *see* Mbaké
Mbaïki 55 C5 *var.* M'Baiki. Lobaye, SW Central African Republic
M'Baiki *see* Mbaïki
Mbaké 52 B3 *var.* Mbacké. W Senegal
Mbala 56 D1 *prev.* Abercorn. Northern, NE Zambia
Mbale 51 C6 E Uganda
Mbandaka 55 C5 *prev.* Coquilhatville. Equateur, NW Dem. Rep. Congo
M'Banza Congo 56 B1 *var.* Mbanza Congo; *prev.* São Salvador, São Salvador do Congo. Dem. Rep. Congo, NW Angola
Mbanza-Ngungu 55 B6 Bas-Congo, W Dem. Rep. Congo
Mbarara 51 B6 SW Uganda
Mbé 54 B4 Nord, N Cameroon
Mbeya 51 C7 Mbeya, SW Tanzania
Mbomou/M'Bomu/Mbomu *see* Bomu
Mbour 52 B3 W Senegal
Mbuji-Mayi 55 D7 *prev.* Bakwanga. Kasai-Oriental, S Dem. Rep. Congo
McAlester 27 G2 Oklahoma, C USA
McAllen 27 G5 Texas, SW USA
McCamey 27 E3 Texas, SW USA
McClintock Channel 15 F2 *channel* Nunavut, N Canada
McComb 20 B3 Mississippi, S USA
McCook 23 E4 Nebraska, C USA
McKean Island 123 E3 *island* Phoenix Islands, C Kiribati
Mount McKinley 14 C3 *var.* Denali. *mountain* Alaska, USA
McKinley Park 14 C3 Alaska, USA
McMinnville 24 B3 Oregon, NW USA
McMurdo 132 B4 *US research station* Antarctica
McPherson 23 E5 Kansas, C USA
McPherson *see* Fort McPherson
Mdantsane 56 D5 Eastern Cape, SE South Africa
Mead, Lake 25 D6 *reservoir* Arizona/Nevada, W USA
Mecca *see* Makkah
Mechelen 65 C5 *Eng.* Mechlin, *Fr.* Malines. Antwerpen, C Belgium
Mechlin *see* Mechelen
Mecklenburger Bucht 72 C2 *bay* N Germany
Mecsek 77 C7 *mountain range* SW Hungary
Medan 116 B3 Sumatera, E Indonesia
Medeba *see* Ma'dabā
Medellín 36 B3 Antioquia, NW Colombia
Médenine 49 F2 *var.* Madanīyīn. SE Tunisia
Medeshamstede *see* Peterborough
Medford 24 B4 Oregon, NW USA
Medgidia 86 D5 Constanţa, SE Romania
Medgyes *see* Mediaş
Mediaş 86 B4 *Ger.* Mediasch, *Hung.* Medgyes. Sibiu, C Romania
Mediasch *see* Mediaş
Medicine Hat 15 F5 Alberta, SW Canada
Medina *see* Al Madīnah
Medinaceli 71 E2 Castilla-León, N Spain
Medina del Campo 70 D2 Castilla-León, N Spain
Medinat Israel *see* Israel
Mediolanum *see* Saintes, France
Mediolanum *see* Milano, Italy
Mediomatrica *see* Metz
Mediterranean Sea 80 D3 *Fr.* Mer Méditerranée. *sea* Africa/Asia/Europe
Méditerranée, Mer *see* Mediterranean Sea
Médoc 69 B5 *cultural region* SW France
Medvezh'yegorsk 88 B3 Respublika Kareliya, NW Russian Federation
Meekatharra 125 B5 Western Australia
Meemu Atoll *see* Mulakatholhu
Meerssen 65 D6 *var.* Mersen. Limburg, SE Netherlands
Meerut 112 D2 Uttar Pradesh, N India
Megáli Préspa, Límni *see* Prespa, Lake
Meghālaya 91 G3 *cultural region* NE India
Mehdia *see* Mahdia
Meheso *see* Mī'ēso
Me Hka *see* Nmai Hka
Mehrīz 98 D3 Yazd, C Iran
Mehtar Lām 101 F4 *var.* Mehtarlām, Meterlam, Metharlam, Metharlam. Laghmān, E Afghanistan
Mehtarlām *see* Mehtar Lām
Meiktila 114 B3 Mandalay, C Myanmar (Burma)
Méjico *see* Mexico
Mejillones 42 B2 Antofagasta, N Chile
Mek'elē 50 C4 *var.* Makale. Tigray, N Ethiopia
Mékhé 52 B3 NW Senegal
Mekong 102 D3 *var.* Lan-ts'ang Chiang, *Cam.* Mékôngk, *Chin.* Lancang Jiang, *Lao.* Mènam Khong, *Th.* Mae Nam Khong, *Tib.* Dza Chu, *Vtn.* Sông Tiên Giang. *river* SE Asia
Mékôngk *see* Mekong
Mekong, Mouths of the 115 E6 *delta* S Vietnam
Melaka 116 B3 *var.* Malacca. Melaka, Peninsular Malaysia
Melaka, Selat *see* Malacca, Strait of
Melanesia 122 D3 *island group* W Pacific Ocean
Melanesian Basin 120 C2 *undersea basin* W Pacific Ocean
Melbourne 127 C7 *state capital* Victoria, SE Australia
Melbourne 21 E4 Florida, SE USA
Meleda *see* Mljet
Melghir, Chott 49 E2 *var.* Chott Melrhir. *salt lake* E Algeria
Melilla 58 B5 *anc.* Rusaddir, Russadir. Melilla, Spain, N Africa
Melilla 48 D2 *enclave* Spain, N Africa
Melita 15 F5 Manitoba, S Canada
Melita *see* Mljet
Melitene *see* Malatya
Melitopol' 87 F4 Zaporiz'ka Oblast', SE Ukraine
Melle 65 B5 Oost-Vlaanderen, NW Belgium
Mellerud 63 B6 Västra Götaland, S Sweden
Mellieħa 80 B5 E Malta
Mellizo Sur, Cerro 43 A7 *mountain* S Chile
Melo 42 E4 Cerro Largo, NE Uruguay
Melodunum *see* Melun
Melrhir, Chott *see* Melghir, Chott
Melsungen 72 B4 Hessen, C Germany
Melun 68 C3 *anc.* Melodunum. Seine-et-Marne, N France
Melville Bay/Melville Bugt *see* Qimusseriarsuaq
Melville Island 124 D2 *island* Northern Territory, N Australia
Melville Island 15 E2 *island* Parry Islands, Northwest Territories, NW Canada
Melville, Lake 17 F2 *lake* Newfoundland and Labrador, E Canada
Melville Peninsula 15 G3 *peninsula* Nunavut, NE Canada
Melville Sound *see* Viscount Melville Sound
Membidj *see* Manbij
Memel *see* Neman, NE Europe
Memel *see* Klaipeda, Lithuania
Memmingen 73 B6 Bayern, S Germany
Memphis 20 C1 Tennessee, S USA
Menaam *see* Menaldum
Menado *see* Manado
Ménaka 53 F3 Goa, E Mali
Menaldum 64 D1 *Fris.* Menaam. Friesland, N Netherlands
Mènam Khong *see* Mekong
Mendaña Fracture Zone 131 F4 *fracture zone* E Pacific Ocean
Mende 69 C5 *anc.* Mimatum. Lozère, S France
Mendeleyev Ridge 133 B2 *undersea ridge* Arctic Ocean
Mendocino Fracture Zone 130 D2 *fracture zone* NE Pacific Ocean
Mendoza 42 B4 Mendoza, W Argentina
Menemen 94 A3 İzmir, W Turkey
Menengiyn Tal 105 F2 *plain* E Mongolia
Menongue 56 B2 *var.* Vila Serpa Pinto, *Port.* Serpa Pinto. Cuando Cubango, C Angola
Menorca 71 H3 *Eng.* Minorca; *anc.* Balearis Minor. *island* Islas Baleares, Spain, W Mediterranean Sea
Mentawai, Kepulauan 116 A4 *island group* W Indonesia
Meppel 64 D2 Drenthe, NE Netherlands
Meran *see* Merano
Merano 74 C1 *Ger.* Meran. Trentino-Alto Adige, N Italy
Merca *see* Marka
Mercedes 42 D3 Corrientes, NE Argentina
Mercedes 42 D4 Soriano, SW Uruguay
Meredith, Lake 27 E1 *reservoir* Texas, SW USA
Merefa 87 G2 Kharkivs'ka Oblast', E Ukraine
Mergate *see* Margate
Mergui *see* Myeik
Mergui Archipelago 115 B6 *island group* S Myanmar (Burma)
Mérida 29 H3 Yucatán, SW Mexico
Mérida 70 C4 *anc.* Augusta Emerita. Extremadura, W Spain
Mérida 36 C2 Mérida, W Venezuela
Meridian 20 C2 Mississippi, S USA
Mérignac 69 B5 Gironde, SW France
Merín, Laguna *see* Mirim Lagoon
Merkulovichi *see* Myerkulavichy
Merowe 50 B3 Northern, N Sudan
Merredin 125 B6 Western Australia
Mersen *see* Meerssen
Mersey 67 D5 *river* NW England, United Kingdom
Mersin 94 C4 *var.* İçel. İçel, S Turkey
Mērsrags 84 C3 Talsi, NW Latvia
Meru 51 C6 Eastern, C Kenya
Merv *see* Mary
Merzifon 94 D2 Amasya, N Turkey
Merzig 73 A5 Saarland, SW Germany
Mesa 26 B2 Arizona, SW USA
Meseritz *see* Międzyrzecz
Meshed *see* Mashhad
Mesopotamia 35 C5 *var.* Mesopotamia Argentina. *physical region* NE Argentina
Mesopotamia Argentina *see* Mesopotamia
Messalo, Rio 57 E2 *var.* Mualo. *river* NE Mozambique
Messana/Messene *see* Messina
Messina *see* Musina
Messina, Strait of *see* Messina, Stretto di
Messina, Stretto di 75 D7 *Eng.* Strait of Messina. *strait* SW Italy
Messíni 83 B6 Pelopónnisos, S Greece
Mesta *see* Néstos
Mestghanem *see* Mostaganem
Mestia 95 F1 *var.* Mestiya. N Georgia
Mestiya *see* Mestia
Mestre 74 C2 Veneto, NE Italy
Metairie 20 B3 Louisiana, S USA
Metán 42 C2 Salta, N Argentina
Metapán 30 B2 Santa Ana, NW El Salvador
Meta, Río 36 D3 *river* Colombia/Venezuela
Meterlam *see* Mehtar Lām
Methariam/Metharlam *see* Mehtar Lām
Metis *see* Metz
Metković 78 B4 Dubrovnik-Neretva, SE Croatia
Métsovo 82 B4 *prev.* Métsovon. Ípeiros, C Greece
Métsovon *see* Métsovo
Metz 68 D3 *anc.* Divodurum Mediomatricum, Mediomatrica, Metis. Moselle, NE France
Meulaboh 116 A3 Sumatera, W Indonesia
Meuse 65 C6 *Dut.* Maas. *river* W Europe
Mexcala, Río *see* Balsas, Río
Mexicali 28 A1 Baja California Norte, NW Mexico
Mexicanos, Estados Unidos *see* Mexico
México 29 E4 *var.* Ciudad de México, *Eng.* Mexico City. *country capital* (Mexico) México, C Mexico
Mexico 23 G4 Missouri, C USA
Mexico 28 C3 *off.* United Mexican States, *var.* Méjico, México, *Sp.* Estados Unidos Mexicanos. *country* N Central America
México *see* Mexico
Mexico City *see* México
México, Golfo de *see* Mexico, Gulf of
Mexico, Gulf of 29 F2 *Sp.* Golfo de México. *gulf* W Atlantic Ocean
Meyadine *see* Al Mayādīn
Meydān Shahr 101 E4 *var.* Maydān Shahr. Vardak, E Afghanistan
Meymaneh 100 D3 *var.* Maimāna, Maymana. Fāryāb, NW Afghanistan
Mezen' 88 D3 *river* NW Russian Federation
Mezőtúr 77 D7 Jász-Nagykun-Szolnok, E Hungary
Mġarr 80 A5 Gozo, N Malta
Miadzioł Nowy *see* Myadzyel
Miahuatlán 29 F5 *var.* Miahuatlán de Porfirio Díaz. Oaxaca, SE Mexico
Miahuatlán de Porfirio Díaz *see* Miahuatlán
Miami 21 F5 Florida, SE USA
Miami 27 G1 Oklahoma, C USA
Miami Beach 21 F5 Florida, SE USA
Mīāneh 98 C2 *var.* Miyāneh. Āẕarbāyjān-e Sharqī, NW Iran
Mianyang 106 B5 Sichuan, C China
Miastko 76 C2 *Ger.* Rummelsburg in Pommern. Pomorskie, N Poland
Mi Chai *see* Nong Khai
Michalovce 77 E5 *Ger.* Grossmichel, *Hung.* Nagymihály. Košický Kraj, E Slovakia
Michigan 18 C1 *off.* State of Michigan, *also known as* Great Lakes State, Lake State, Wolverine State. *state* N USA
Michigan, Lake 18 C2 *lake* N USA
Michurin *see* Tsarevo
Michurinsk 89 B5 Tambovskaya Oblast', W Russian Federation
Micoud 33 F2 SE Saint Lucia
Micronesia 122 B1 *off.* Federated States of Micronesia. *country* W Pacific Ocean
Micronesia 122 C1 *island group* W Pacific Ocean
Micronesia, Federated States of *see* Micronesia
Mid-Atlantic Cordillera *see* Mid-Atlantic Ridge
Mid-Atlantic Ridge 44 C3 *var.* Mid-Atlantic Cordillera, Mid-Atlantic Rise, Mid-Atlantic Swell. *undersea ridge* Atlantic Ocean
Mid-Atlantic Rise/Mid-Atlantic Swell *see* Mid-Atlantic Ridge
Middelburg 65 B5 Zeeland, SW Netherlands
Middelharnis 64 B4 Zuid-Holland, SW Netherlands
Middelkerke 65 A5 West-Vlaanderen, W Belgium
Middle America Trench 13 B7 *trench* E Pacific Ocean
Middle Andaman 111 F2 *island* Andaman Islands, India, NE Indian Ocean
Middle Atlas 48 C2 *Eng.* Middle Atlas. *mountain range* N Morocco
Middle Atlas *see* Moyen Atlas
Middleburg Island *see* 'Eua
Middle Congo *see* Congo (Republic of)
Middlesboro 18 C5 Kentucky, S USA
Middlesbrough 67 D5 N England, United Kingdom
Middletown 19 F4 New Jersey, NE USA
Middletown 19 F3 New York, NE USA
Mid-Indian Basin 119 C5 *undersea basin* N Indian Ocean
Mid-Indian Ridge 119 C5 *var.* Central Indian Ridge. *undersea ridge* C Indian Ocean
Midland 16 D5 Ontario, S Canada
Midland 18 C3 Michigan, N USA
Midland 27 E3 Texas, SW USA
Mid-Pacific Mountains 130 C2 *var.* Mid-Pacific Seamounts. *seamount range* NW Pacific Ocean
Mid-Pacific Seamounts *see* Mid-Pacific Mountains
Midway Islands 130 D2 *US territory* C Pacific Ocean
Miechów 77 D5 Małopolskie, S Poland
Międzyrzec Podlaski 76 E3 Lubelskie, E Poland
Międzyrzecz 76 B3 *Ger.* Meseritz. Lubuskie, W Poland
Mielec 77 D5 Podkarpackie, SE Poland
Miercurea-Ciuc 86 C4 *Ger.* Szeklerburg, *Hung.* Csíkszereda. Harghita, C Romania
Mieres del Camín *see* Mieres del Camino
Mieres del Camino 70 D1 *var.* Mieres del Camín. Asturias, NW Spain
Mī'ēso 51 D5 *var.* Meheso, Miesso. Oromīya, C Ethiopia
Miesso *see* Mī'ēso
Mifrats Hefa 97 A5 *Eng.* Bay of Haifa; *prev.* MifrazHefa. *bay* N Israel
Miguel Asua 28 D3 *var.* Miguel Auza. Zacatecas, C Mexico
Miguel Auza *see* Miguel Asua
Mijdrecht 64 C3 Utrecht, C Netherlands
Mikashevichi *see* Mikashevichy
Mikashevichy 85 C7 *Pol.* Mikaszewicze, *Rus.* Mikashevichi. Brestskaya Voblasts', SW Belarus
Mikaszewicze *see* Mikashevichy
Mikhaylovgrad *see* Montana
Mikhaylovka 89 B6 Volgogradskaya Oblast', SW Russian Federation
Míkonos *see* Mýkonos
Mikre 82 C2 Lovech, N Bulgaria
Mikun' 88 D4 Respublika Komi, NW Russian Federation
Mikuni-sanmyaku 109 D5 *mountain range* Honshū, N Japan Asia
Mikura-jima 109 D6 *island* E Japan
Milagro 38 B2 Guayas, SW Ecuador
Milan *see* Milano
Milange 57 E2 Zambézia, NE Mozambique
Milano 74 B2 *Eng.* Milan, *Ger.* Mailand; *anc.* Mediolanum. Lombardia, N Italy
Milas 94 A4 Muğla, SW Turkey
Milashavichy 85 C7 *Rus.* Milashevichi. Homyel'skaya Voblasts', SE Belarus
Milashevichi *see* Milashavichy
Mildura 127 C6 Victoria, SE Australia
Mile *see* Mili Atoll
Miles 127 D5 Queensland, E Australia
Miles City 22 C2 Montana, NW USA
Milford *see* Milford Haven
Milford Haven 67 C6 *prev.* Milford. SW Wales, United Kingdom
Milford Sound 129 A6 Southland, South Island, New Zealand
Milford Sound 129 A6 *inlet* South Island, New Zealand
Milḩ, Baḩr al *see* Razāzah, Buḩayrat ar
Mili Atoll 122 D2 *var.* Mile. *atoll* Ratak Chain, SE Marshall Islands
Mil'kovo 93 H3 Kamchatskaya Oblast', E Russian Federation
Milk River 15 E5 Alberta, SW Canada
Milk River 22 C1 *river* Montana, NW USA
Milk, Wadi el 66 B4 *var.* Wadi al Malik. *river* C Sudan
Milledgeville 21 E2 Georgia, SE USA
Mille Lacs Lake 23 F2 *lake* Minnesota, N USA
Millennium Island 121 F3 *prev.* Caroline Island, Thornton Island. *atoll* Line Islands, E Kiribati
Millerovo 89 B6 Rostovskaya Oblast', SW Russian Federation
Mílos 83 C7 *island* Kykládes, Greece, Aegean Sea
Milton 129 B7 Otago, South Island, New Zealand
Milton Keynes 67 D6 SE England, United Kingdom
Milwaukee 18 B3 Wisconsin, N USA
Mimatum *see* Mende
Min *see* Fujian
Mīnā' Qābūs 118 B3 NE Oman
Minas Gerais 41 F3 *off.* Estado de Minas Gerais. *state* E Brazil
Minas Gerais 41 F3 *off.* Estado de Minas Gerais. *region* E Brazil
Minas Gerais, Estado de *see* Minas Gerais
Minatitlán 29 F4 Veracruz-Llave, E Mexico
Minbu 114 A3 Magway, W Myanmar (Burma)
Minch, The 66 B3 *var.* North Minch. *strait* NW Scotland, United Kingdom
Mindanao 117 F2 *island* S Philippines
Mindanao Sea *see* Bohol Sea
Mindelheim 73 C6 Bayern, S Germany
Mindello *see* Mindelo
Mindelo 52 A2 *var.* Mindello; *prev.* Porto Grande. São Vicente, N Cape Verde
Minden 72 B4 *anc.* Minthun. Nordrhein-Westfalen, NW Germany
Mindoro 117 E2 *island* N Philippines
Mindoro Strait 117 E2 *strait* W Philippines
Mineral Wells 27 F2 Texas, SW USA
Mingäçevir 95 G2 *Rus.* Mingechaur, Mingechevir. C Azerbaijan
Mingechaur/Mingechevir *see* Mingäçevir
Mingora *see* Saidu Sharif
Minho 70 B2 *former province* N Portugal
Minho 70 B2 *Sp.* Miño. *river* Portugal/Spain
Minho, Rio *see* Miño
Minicoy Island 110 B3 *island* SW India
Minius *see* Miño
Minna 53 G4 Niger, C Nigeria
Minneapolis 23 F2 Minnesota, N USA
Minnesota 23 F2 *off.* State of Minnesota, *also known as* Gopher State, New England of the West, North Star State. *state* N USA
Miño 70 B2 *var.* Mino, Minius, *Port.* Rio Minho. *river* Portugal/Spain
Miño *see* Minho, Rio
Minorca *see* Menorca
Minot 23 E1 North Dakota, N USA
Minsk 85 C6 *country capital* (Belarus) Minskaya Voblasts', C Belarus
Minskaya Wzvyshsha 85 C6 *mountain range* C Belarus
Mińsk Mazowiecki 76 D3 *var.* Nowo-Minsk. Mazowieckie, C Poland
Minthun *see* Minden
Minto, Lac 16 D2 *lake* Québec, C Canada
Minya *see* Al Minyā
Miraflores 28 C3 Baja California Sur, NW Mexico
Miranda de Ebro 71 E1 La Rioja, N Spain
Mirgorod *see* Myrhorod
Miri 116 D3 Sarawak, East Malaysia
Mirim Lagoon 41 E5 *var.* Lake Mirim, *Sp.* Laguna Merín. *lagoon* Brazil/Uruguay
Mirim, Lake *see* Mirim Lagoon
Mírina *see* Mýrina
Mīrjāveh 98 E4 Sīstān va Balūchestān, SE Iran
Mirny 132 C3 *Russian research station* Antarctica
Mirnyy 93 F3 Respublika Sakha (Yakutiya), NE Russian Federation
Mīrpur Khās 112 B3 Sind, SE Pakistan
Mirtoan Sea *see* Mirtóo Pélagos
Mirtóo Pélagos 83 C6 *Eng.* Mirtoan Sea; *anc.* Myrtoum Mare. *sea* S Greece
Misiaf *see* Maşyāf
Miskito Coast *see* Mosquito Coast
Miskitos, Cayos 31 E2 *island group* NE Nicaragua
Miskolc 77 D6 Borsod-Abaúj-Zemplén, NE Hungary
Misool, Pulau 117 F4 *island* Maluku, E Indonesia
Mişrātah 49 F2 *var.* Misurata. NW Libya
Mission 27 G5 Texas, SW USA
Mississippi 20 B2 *off.* State of Mississippi, *also known as* Bayou State, Magnolia State. *state* SE USA
Mississippi Delta 20 B4 *delta* Louisiana, S USA
Mississippi River 13 C6 *river* C USA
Missoula 22 B1 Montana, NW USA
Missouri 23 F5 *off.* State of Missouri, *also known as* Bullion State, Show Me State. *state* C USA
Missouri River 23 E3 *river* C USA
Mistassini, Lac 16 D3 *lake* Québec, SE Canada
Mistelbach an der Zaya 73 E6 Niederösterreich, NE Austria
Misti, Volcán 39 E4 *volcano* S Peru
Misurata *see* Mişrātah
Mitau *see* Jelgava
Mitchell 127 D5 Queensland, E Australia
Mitchell 23 E3 South Dakota, N USA
Mitchell, Mount 21 E1 *mountain* North Carolina, SE USA
Mitchell River 126 C2 *river* Queensland, NE Australia
Mi Tho *see* My Tho
Mitilíni *see* Mytilíni
Mito 109 D5 Ibaraki, Honshū, S Japan
Mitrovica/Mitrovicë *see* Kosovska Mitrovica, Serbia
Mitrovica/Mitrowitz *see* Sremska Mitrovica, Serbia
Mitrovicë 79 D5 *Serb.* Mitrovica, Kosovska Mitrovica, Titova Mitrovica. N Kosovo
Mits'iwa 50 C4 *var.* Masawa, Massawa. E Eritrea
Mitspe Ramon 97 A7 *prev.* Mizpe Ramon. Southern, S Israel
Mittelstadt *see* Baia Sprie
Mitú 36 C4 Vaupés, SE Colombia
Mitumba, Chaîne des/Mitumba Range *see* Mitumba, Monts

Nagara Svarga – Niort

Nagara Svarga see Nakhon Sawan
Nagasaki 109 A7 Nagasaki, Kyūshū, SW Japan
Nagato 109 A7 Yamaguchi, Honshū, SW Japan
Nāgercoil 110 C3 Tamil Nādu, SE India
Nagorno-Karabakh 95 G3 var. Nagorno-Karabakhskaya Avtonomnaya Oblast, Arm. Lerrnayin Gharabakh, Az. Dağliq Quarabağ, Rus. Nagornyy Karabakh. former autonomous region SW Azerbaijan
Nagorno- Karabakhskaya Avtonomnaya Oblast see Nagorno-Karabakh
Nagornyy Karabakh see Nagorno-Karabakh
Nagoya 109 C6 Aichi, Honshū, SW Japan
Nāgpur 112 D4 Mahārāshtra, C India
Nagqu 104 C5 Chin. Na-Ch'ii; prev. Hei-ho. Xizang Zizhiqu, W China
Nagybánya see Baia Mare
Nagybecskerek see Zrenjanin
Nagydisznód see Cisnădie
Nagyenyed see Aiud
Nagykálló 77 E6 Szabolcs-Szatmár-Bereg, E Hungary
Nagykanizsa 77 C7 Ger. Grosskanizsa. Zala, SW Hungary
Nagykároly see Carei
Nagykikinda see Kikinda
Nagykőrös 77 D7 Pest, C Hungary
Nagymihály see Michalovce
Nagysurány see Šurany
Nagyszalonta see Salonta
Nagyszeben see Sibiu
Nagyszentmiklós see Sânnicolau Mare
Nagyszöllös see Vynohradiv
Nagyszombat see Trnava
Nagytapolcsány see Topoľčany
Nagyvárad see Oradea
Naha 108 A3 Okinawa, Okinawa, SW Japan
Nahariya 97 A5 prev. Nahariyya. Northern, N Israel
Nahariyya see Nahariya
Nahuel Huapí, Lago 43 B5 lake W Argentina
Nain 17 F2 Newfoundland and Labrador, NE Canada
Nā'īn 98 D3 Eşfahān, C Iran
Nairobi 47 E5 country capital (Kenya) Nairobi Area, S Kenya
Nairobi 51 C6 Nairobi Area, S Kenya
Naissus see Niš
Najaf see An Najaf
Najima see Fukuoka
Najin 107 E3 NE North Korea
Najrān 99 B6 var. Abā as Su'ūd. Najrān, S Saudi Arabia
Nakambé see White Volta
Nakamura 109 B7 var. Shimanto. Kōchi, Shikoku, SW Japan
Nakatsugawa 109 C6 var. Nakatugawa. Gifu, Honshū, SW Japan
Nakatugawa see Nakatsugawa
Nakhichevan' see Naxçıvan
Nakhodka 93 G5 Primorskiy Kray, SE Russian Federation
Nakhon Pathom 115 C5 var. Nagara Pathom, Nakorn Pathom. Nakhon Pathom, W Thailand
Nakhon Ratchasima 115 C5 var. Khorat, Korat. Nakhon Ratchasima, E Thailand
Nakhon Sawan 115 C5 var. Muang Nakhon Sawan, Nagara Svarga. Nakhon Sawan, W Thailand
Nakhon Si Thammarat 115 C7 var. Nagara Sridharmaraj, Nakhon Sithamnaraj. Nakhon Si Thammarat, SW Thailand
Nakhon Sithamnaraj see Nakhon Si Thammarat
Nakorn Pathom see Nakhon Pathom
Nakuru 51 C6 Rift Valley, SW Kenya
Nal'chik 89 B8 Kabardino-Balkarskaya Respublika, SW Russian Federation
Nālūt 49 F2 NW Libya
Namakan Lake 18 A1 lake Canada/USA
Namangan 101 F2 Namangan Viloyati, E Uzbekistan
Nambala 56 D2 Central, C Zambia
Nam Co 104 C5 lake W China
Nam Định 114 D3 Nam Ha, N Vietnam
Namib Desert 56 B3 desert W Namibia
Namibe 56 A2 Port. Moçâmedes, Mossâmedes. Namibe, SW Angola
Namibia 56 B3 off. Republic of Namibia, var. South West Africa, Afr. Suidwes-Afrika, Ger. Deutsch-Südwestafrika; prev. German Southwest Africa, South-West Africa. country S Africa
Namibia, Republic of see Namibia
Namnetes see Nantes
Namo see Namu Atoll
Nam Ou 114 C3 river N Laos
Nampa 24 D3 Idaho, NW USA
Nampula 57 E2 Nampula, NE Mozambique
Namsos 62 B4 Nord-Trøndelag, C Norway
Nam Tha 114 C4 river N Laos
Namu Atoll 122 D2 var. Namo. atoll Ralik Chain, C Marshall Islands
Namur 65 C6 Dut. Namen. Namur, SE Belgium
Namyit Island 106 C8 island S Spratly Islands
Nan 114 C4 var. Muang Nan. Nan, NW Thailand
Nanaimo 14 D5 Vancouver Island, British Columbia, SW Canada
Nanchang 106 C5 var. Nan-ch'ang, Nanch'ang-hsien. province capital Jiangxi, S China
Nan-ch'ang see Nanchang
Nanch'ang-hsien see Nanchang
Nan-ching see Nanjing
Nancy 68 D3 Meurthe-et-Moselle, NE France
Nandaime 30 D3 Granada, SW Nicaragua
Nānded 112 D5 Mahārāshtra, C India
Nandi see Nadi
Nándorhgy see Oţelu Roşu
Nandyāl 110 C1 Andhra Pradesh, E India
Nan Hai see South China Sea
Naniwa see Ōsaka
Nanjing 106 D5 var. Nan-ching, Nanking; prev. Chianning, Chian-ning, Kiang-ning, Jiangsu. province capital Jiangsu, E China
Nanking see Nanjing
Nanning 106 B6 var. Nan-ning; prev. Yung-ning. Guangxi Zhuangzu Zizhiqu, S China
Nan-ning see Nanning
Nanortalik 60 C5 Kitaa, S Greenland
Nanpan Jiang 114 D2 river S China
Nanping 106 D6 var. Nan-p'ing; prev. Yenping. Fujian, SE China
Nan-p'ing see Nanping
Nansei-shotō 108 A2 Eng. Ryukyu Islands. island group SW Japan
Nansei Syotō Trench see Ryukyu Trench
Nansen Basin 133 C4 undersea basin Arctic Ocean
Nansen Cordillera 133 B3 var. Arctic Mid Oceanic Ridge, Nansen Ridge. seamount range Arctic Ocean
Nansen Ridge see Nansen Cordillera
Nansha Qundao see Spratly Islands
Nanterre 68 D1 Hauts-de-Seine, N France
Nantes 68 B4 Bret. Naoned; anc. Condivincum, Namnetes. Loire-Atlantique, NW France
Nantucket Island 19 G3 island Massachusetts, NE USA
Nanumaga 123 E3 var. Nanumanga. atoll NW Tuvalu
Nanumanga see Nanumaga
Nanumea Atoll 123 E3 atoll NW Tuvalu
Nanyang 106 C5 var. Nan-yang. Henan, C China
Nan-yang see Nanyang
Naoned see Nantes
Napa 25 B6 California, W USA
Napier 128 E4 Hawke's Bay, North Island, New Zealand
Naples 21 E5 Florida, SE USA
Naples see Napoli
Napo 34 A3 province NE Ecuador
Napoléon-Vendée see la Roche-sur-Yon
Napoli 75 C5 Eng. Naples, Ger. Neapel; anc. Neapolis. Campania, S Italy
Napo, Río 38 C1 river Ecuador/Peru
Naracoorte 127 B7 South Australia
Naradhivas see Narathiwat
Narathiwat 115 C7 var. Naradhivas. Narathiwat, SW Thailand
Narbada see Narmada
Narbo Martius see Narbonne
Narbonne 69 C6 anc. Narbo Martius. Aude, S France
Narborough Island see Fernandina, Isla
Nares Abyssal Plain see Nares Plain
Nares Plain 13 E6 var. Nares Abyssal Plain. abyssal plain NW Atlantic Ocean
Nares Stræde see Nares Strait
Nares Strait 60 D1 Dan. Nares Stræde. strait Canada/Greenland
Narew 76 E3 river E Poland
Narmada 102 B3 var. Narbada. river C India
Narova see Narva
Narovlya see Narowlya
Narowlya 85 C8 Rus. Narovlya. Homyel'skaya Voblasts', SE Belarus
Närpes 63 D5 Fin. Närpiö. Länsi-Suomi, W Finland
Närpiö see Närpes
Narrabri 127 D6 New South Wales, SE Australia
Narrogin 125 B6 Western Australia
Narva 84 E2 Ida-Virumaa, NE Estonia
Narva 84 E2 prev. Narova. river Estonia/Russian Federation
Narva Bay 84 E2 Est. Narva Laht, Ger. Narwa-Bucht, Rus. Narvskiy Zaliv. bay Estonia/Russian Federation
Narva Laht see Narva Bay
Narva Reservoir 84 E2 Est. Narva Veehoidla, Rus. Narvskoye Vodokhranilishche. reservoir Estonia/Russian Federation
Narva Veehoidla see Narva Reservoir
Narvik 62 C3 Nordland, C Norway
Narvskiy Zaliv see Narva Bay
Narvskoye Vodokhranilishche see Narva Reservoir
Narwa-Bucht see Narva Bay
Nar'yan-Mar 88 D3 prev. Beloshchel'ye, Dzerzhinskiy. Nenetskiy Avtonomnyy Okrug, NW Russian Federation
Naryn 101 G2 Narynskaya Oblast', C Kyrgyzstan
Nassau 32 C1 country capital (Bahamas) New Providence, N Bahamas
Năsăud 86 B3 Ger. Nussdorf, Hung. Naszód. Bistriţa-Năsăud, N Romania
Nase see Naze
Nāshik 112 C5 prev. Nāsik. Mahārāshtra, W India
Nashua 19 G3 New Hampshire, NE USA
Nashville 20 C1 state capital Tennessee, S USA
Näsijärvi 63 D5 lake SW Finland
Nāsik see Nāshik
Nasir, Buhayrat/Nâşir,Buheiret see Nasser, Lake
Nāsiri see Ahvāz
Nasiriya see An Nāşirīyah
Nasser, Lake 50 B3 var. Buhayrat Nasir, Buḩayrat Nāşir, Buḩeiret Nâşir. lake Egypt/Sudan
Naszód see Năsăud
Nata 56 C3 Central, NE Botswana
Natal 41 G2 state capital Rio Grande do Norte, E Brazil
Natal Basin 119 A6 var. Mozambique Basin. undersea basin W Indian Ocean
Natanya see Netanya
Natchez 20 B3 Mississippi, S USA
Natchitoches 20 A2 Louisiana, S USA
Nathanya see Netanya
Natitingou 53 F4 NW Benin
Natsrat see Natzrat
Natuna Islands see Natuna, Kepulauan
Natuna, Kepulauan 102 D4 var. Natuna Islands. island group W Indonesia
Naturaliste Plateau 119 E6 undersea plateau E Indian Ocean
Natzrat 97 A5 var. Natsrat, Ar. En Nazira, Eng. Nazareth; prev. Naẓerat. Northern, N Israel
Naugard see Nowogard
Naujamiestis 84 C4 Panevėžys, C Lithuania
Nauru 122 D2 off. Republic of Nauru; prev. Pleasant Island. country W Pacific Ocean
Nauru, Republic of see Nauru
Nauta 38 C2 Loreto, N Peru
Navahrudak 85 C6 Pol. Nowogródek, Rus. Novogrudok. Hrodzyenskaya Voblasts', W Belarus
Navanagar see Jāmnagar
Navapolatsk 85 D5 Rus. Novopolotsk. Vitsyebskaya Voblasts', N Belarus
Navarra 71 E2 Eng./Fr. Navarre. autonomous community N Spain
Navarre see Navarra
Navassa Island 32 C3 US unincorporated territory C West Indies
Navoi see Navoiy
Navoiy 101 E2 Rus. Navoi. Navoiy Viloyati, C Uzbekistan
Navojoa 28 C2 Sonora, NW Mexico
Navolat see Navolato
Navolato 28 C3 var. Navolat. Sinaloa, C Mexico
Návpaktos see Náfpaktos
Návplion see Náfplio
Nawabashah see Nawābshāh
Nawābshāh 112 B3 var. Nawabashah. Sind, S Pakistan
Naxçıvan 95 G3 Rus. Nakhichevan'. SW Azerbaijan
Náxos 83 D6 var. Naxos. Náxos, Kykládes, Greece, Aegean Sea
Náxos 83 D6 island Kykládes, Greece, Aegean Sea
Nayoro 108 D2 Hokkaidō, NE Japan
Nay Pyi Taw 114 B4 country capital Myanmar (Burma)) Mandalay, C Myanmar (Burma)
Nazareth see Natzrat
Nazca 38 D4 Ica, S Peru
Nazca Ridge 35 A5 undersea ridge E Pacific Ocean
Naze 108 B3 var. Nase. Kagoshima, Amami-ōshima, SW Japan
Naẓerat see Natzrat
Nazilli 94 A4 Aydın, SW Turkey
Nazrēt 51 C5 var. Adama, Hadama. Oromīya, C Ethiopia
N'Dalatando 56 B1 Port. Salazar, Vila Salazar. Cuanza Norte, NW Angola
Ndélé 54 C4 Bamingui-Bangoran, N Central African Republic
Ndendé 55 B6 Ngounié, S Gabon
Ndindi 55 A6 Nyanga, S Gabon
Ndjamena 54 B3 var. N'Djamena; prev. Fort-Lamy. country capital (Chad) Chari-Baguirmi, W Chad
N'Djamena see Ndjamena
Ndjolé 55 A5 Moyen-Ogooué, W Gabon
Ndola 56 D2 Copperbelt, C Zambia
Ndzouani see Anjouan
Neagh, Lough 67 B5 lake E Northern Ireland, United Kingdom
Néa Moudanía 82 C4 var. Néa Moudhaniá. Kentrikí Makedonía, N Greece
Néa Moudhaniá see Néa Moudanía
Neapel see Napoli
Neápoli 82 B4 prev. Neápolis. Dytikí Makedonía, N Greece
Neápoli 83 D8 Kríti, Greece, E Mediterranean Sea
Neápoli 83 C7 Pelopónnisos, S Greece
Neápolis see Neápoli, Greece
Neapolis see Napoli, Italy
Neapolis see Nablus, West Bank
Near Islands 14 A2 island group Aleutian Islands, Alaska, USA
Néa Zíchni 82 C3 var. Néa Zíkhni; prev. Néa Zíkhna. Kentrikí Makedonía, NE Greece
Néa Zíkhna/Néa Zíkhni see Néa Zíchni
Nebaj 30 B2 Quiché, W Guatemala
Nebitdag see Balkanabat
Neblina, Pico da 40 C1 mountain NW Brazil
Nebraska 22 D4 off. State of Nebraska, also known as Blackwater State, Cornhusker State, Tree Planters State. state C USA
Nebraska City 23 F4 Nebraska, C USA
Neches River 27 H3 river Texas, SW USA
Neckar 73 B6 river SW Germany
Necochea 43 D5 Buenos Aires, E Argentina
Nederland see Netherlands
Neder Rijn 64 D4 Eng. Lower Rhine. river C Netherlands
Nederweert 65 D5 Limburg, SE Netherlands
Neede 64 E3 Gelderland, E Netherlands
Neerpelt 65 D5 Limburg, NE Belgium
Neftekamsk 89 D5 Respublika Bashkortostan, W Russian Federation
Neftezavodsk see Seýdi
Negara Brunei Darussalam see Brunei
Negēlē 51 D5 var. Negelli, It. Neghelli. Oromīya, C Ethiopia
Negelli see Negēlē
Negev see HaNegev
Neghelli see Negēlē
Negomane 57 E2 var. Negomano. Cabo Delgado, N Mozambique
Negomano see Negomane
Negombo 110 C3 Western Province, SW Sri Lanka
Negotin 78 E4 Serbia, E Serbia
Negra, Punta 38 A3 headland NW Peru
Negreşti see Negreşti-Oaş
Negreşti-Oaş 86 B3 Hung. Avasfelsőfalu; prev. Negreşti. Satu Mare, NE Romania
Negro, Río 43 C5 river E Argentina
Negro, Río 40 D1 river N South America
Negro, Río 42 D4 river Brazil/Uruguay
Negros 117 E2 island C Philippines
Nehbandān 98 E3 Khorāsān, E Iran
Neijiang 106 B5 Sichuan, C China
Neiva 36 B3 Huila, S Colombia
Nellore 110 D2 Andhra Pradesh, E India
Nelson 129 C5 Nelson, South Island, New Zealand
Nelson 15 G4 river Manitoba, C Canada
Néma 52 D3 Hodh ech Chargui, SE Mauritania
Neman 84 B4 Ger. Ragnit. Kaliningradskaya Oblast', W Russian Federation
Neman 84 A4 Bel. Nyoman, Ger. Memel, Lith. Nemunas, Pol. Niemen. river NE Europe
Nemausus see Nîmes
Neméa 83 B6 Pelopónnisos, S Greece
Nemetocenna see Arras
Nemours 68 C3 Seine-et-Marne, N France
Nemunas see Neman
Nemuro 108 E2 Hokkaidō, NE Japan
Neochóri 83 B5 Dytikí Ellás, C Greece
Nepal 113 E3 off. Nepal. country S Asia
Nepal see Nepal
Nereta 84 C4 Aizkraukle, S Latvia
Neretva 78 C4 river Bosnia and Herzegovina/Croatia
Neris 85 C5 Bel. Viliya, Pol. Wilia; prev. Pol. Wilja. river Belarus/Lithuania
Neris see Viliya
Nerva 70 C4 Andalucía, S Spain
Neryungri 93 F4 Respublika Sakha (Yakutiya), NE Russian Federation
Neskaupstadhur 61 E5 Austurland, E Iceland
Ness, Loch 66 C3 lake N Scotland, United Kingdom
Nesterov see Zhovkva
Néstos 82 C3 Bul. Mesta, Turk. Kara Su. river Bulgaria/Greece
Nesvizh see Nyasvizh
Netanya 97 A6 var. Natanya, Nathanya. Central, C Israel
Netherlands 64 C3 off. Kingdom of the Netherlands, var. Holland, Dut. Koninkrijk der Nederlanden, Nederland. country NW Europe
Netherlands Antilles 33 E5 prev. Dutch West Indies. Dutch autonomous region S Caribbean Sea
Netherlands East Indies see Indonesia
Netherlands Guiana see Suriname
Netherlands, Kingdom of the see Netherlands
Netherlands New Guinea see Papua
Nettilling Lake 15 G3 lake Baffin Island, Nunavut, N Canada
Netze see Noteć
Neu Amerika see Puławy
Neubrandenburg 72 D3 Mecklenburg-Vorpommern, NE Germany
Neuchâtel 73 A7 Ger. Neuenburg. Neuchâtel, W Switzerland
Neuchâtel, Lac de 73 A7 Ger. Neuenburger See. lake W Switzerland
Neuenburger See see Neuchâtel, Lac de
Neufchâteau 65 D8 Luxembourg, SE Belgium
Neugradisk see Nova Gradiška
Neuhof see Zgierz
Neukuhren see Pionerskiy
Neumarkt see Târgu Secuiesc, Covasna, Romania
Neumarkt see Târgu Mureş
Neumoldowa see Moldova Nouă
Neumünster 72 B2 Schleswig-Holstein, N Germany
Neunkirchen 73 A5 Saarland, SW Germany
Neuquén 43 B5 Neuquén, SE Argentina
Neuruppin 72 C3 Brandenburg, NE Germany
Neusalz an der Oder see Nowa Sól
Neu Sandec see Nowy Sącz
Neusatz see Novi Sad
Neusiedler See 73 E6 Hung. Fertő. lake Austria/Hungary
Neusohl see Banská Bystrica
Neustadt see Baia Mare, Maramureş, Romania
Neustadt an der Haardt see Neustadt an der Weinstrasse
Neustadt an der Weinstrasse 73 B5 prev. Neustadt an der Haardt, hist. Niewenstat; anc. Nova Civitas. Rheinland-Pfalz, SW Germany
Neustadtl see Novo mesto
Neustettin see Szczecinek
Neustrelitz 72 D3 Mecklenburg-Vorpommern, NE Germany
Neutra see Nitra
Neu-Ulm 73 B6 Bayern, S Germany
Neuwied 73 A5 Rheinland-Pfalz, W Germany
Neuzen see Terneuzen
Nevada 25 C5 off. State of Nevada, also known as Battle Born State, Sagebrush State, Silver State. state W USA
Nevada, Sierra 70 D5 mountain range S Spain
Nevada, Sierra 25 C6 mountain range W USA
Nevers 68 C4 anc. Noviodunum. Nièvre, C France
Neves 54 E2 São Tomé, S Sao Tome and Principe, Africa
Nevinnomyssk 89 B7 Stavropol'skiy Kray, SW Russian Federation
Nevşehir 94 C3 var. Nevshehr. Nevşehir, C Turkey
Newala 51 C8 Mtwara, SE Tanzania
New Albany 18 C5 Indiana, N USA
New Amsterdam 37 G3 E Guyana
Newark 19 F4 New Jersey, NE USA
New Bedford 19 G3 Massachusetts, NE USA
Newberg 24 B3 Oregon, NW USA
New Bern 21 F1 North Carolina, SE USA
New Braunfels 27 G4 Texas, SW USA
Newbridge 67 B6 Ir. An Droichead Nua. Kildare, C Ireland
New Britain 122 B3 island E Papua New Guinea
New Brunswick 17 E4 Fr. Nouveau-Brunswick. province SE Canada
New Caledonia 122 D4 var. Kanaky, Fr. Nouvelle-Calédonie. French overseas territory SW Pacific Ocean
New Caledonia 122 C5 island SW Pacific Ocean
New Caledonia Basin 120 C4 undersea basin W Pacific Ocean
Newcastle 127 D6 New South Wales, SE Australia
Newcastle see Newcastle upon Tyne
Newcastle upon Tyne 66 D4 var. Newcastle, hist. Monkchester, Lat. Pons Aelii. NE England, United Kingdom
New Delhi 112 D3 country capital (India) Delhi, N India
New England of the West see Minnesota
Newfoundland 17 G3 Fr. Terre-Neuve. island Newfoundland and Labrador, SE Canada
Newfoundland and Labrador 17 F2 Fr. Terre Neuve. province E Canada
Newfoundland Basin 44 B3 undersea feature NW Atlantic Ocean
New Georgia Islands 122 C3 island group NW Solomon Islands
New Glasgow 17 F4 Nova Scotia, SE Canada
New Goa see Panaji
New Guinea 122 A3 Dut. Nieuw Guinea, Ind. Irian. island Indonesia/Papua New Guinea
New Hampshire 19 F2 off. State of New Hampshire, also known as Granite State. state NE USA
New Haven 19 G3 Connecticut, NE USA
New Hebrides see Vanuatu
New Iberia 20 B3 Louisiana, S USA
New Ireland 122 C3 island NE Papua New Guinea
New Jersey 19 F4 off. State of New Jersey, also known as The Garden State. state NE USA
Newman 124 B4 Western Australia
Newmarket 67 E6 E England, United Kingdom
New Mexico 26 C2 off. State of New Mexico, also known as Land of Enchantment, Sunshine State. state SW USA
New Orleans 20 B3 Louisiana, S USA
New Plymouth 128 C4 Taranaki, North Island, New Zealand
Newport 67 C7 SE Wales, United Kingdom
Newport 18 C4 Kentucky, S USA
Newport 19 G2 Vermont, NE USA
Newport News 19 F5 Virginia, NE USA
New Providence 32 C1 island N Bahamas
Newquay 67 C7 SW England, United Kingdom
Newry 67 B5 Ir. An tIúr. SE Northern Ireland, United Kingdom
New Sarum see Salisbury
New Siberian Islands see Novosibirskiye Ostrova
New South Wales 127 C6 state SE Australia
Newton 23 G3 Iowa, C USA
Newton 23 F5 Kansas, C USA
Newtownabbey 67 B5 Ir. Baile na Mainistreach. E Northern Ireland, United Kingdom
New Ulm 23 F2 Minnesota, N USA
New York 19 F4 New York, NE USA
New York 19 F3 state NE USA
New Zealand 128 A4 country SW Pacific Ocean
Neyveli 110 C2 Tamil Nādu, SE India
Nezhin see Nizhyn
Ngangze Co 104 B5 lake W China
Ngaoundéré 54 B4 var. N'Gaoundéré. Adamaoua, N Cameroon
N'Gaoundéré see Ngaoundéré
Ngazidja 57 F2 Fr. Grande-Comore. island NW Comoros
N'Giva 56 B3 var. Ondjiva, Port. Vila Pereira de Eça. Cunene, S Angola
Ngo 55 B6 Plateaux, SE Congo
Ngoko 55 B5 river Cameroon/Congo
Ngourti 53 H3 Diffa, E Niger
Nguigmi 53 H3 var. N'Guigmi. Diffa, SE Niger
N'Guigmi see Nguigmi
N'Gunza see Sumbe
Nguru 53 G3 Yobe, NE Nigeria
Nha Trang 115 E6 Khanh Hoa, S Vietnam
Niagara Falls 16 D5 Ontario, S Canada
Niagara Falls 19 E3 New York, NE USA
Niagara Falls 18 D3 waterfall Canada/USA
Niamey 53 F3 country capital (Niger) Niamey, SW Niger
Niangay, Lac 53 E3 lake E Mali
Nia-Nia 55 E5 Orientale, NE Dem. Rep. Congo
Nias, Pulau 116 A3 island W Indonesia
Nicaea see Nice
Nicaragua 30 D3 off. Republic of Nicaragua. country Central America
Nicaragua, Lago de 30 D4 var. Cocibolca, Gran Lago, Eng. Lake Nicaragua. lake S Nicaragua
Nicaragua, Lake see Nicaragua, Lago de
Nicaragua, Republic of see Nicaragua
Nicaria see Ikaría
Nice 69 D6 It. Nizza; anc. Nicaea. Alpes-Maritimes, SE France
Nicephorium see Ar Raqqah
Nicholas II Land see Severnaya Zemlya
Nicholls Town 32 C1 Andros Island, NW Bahamas
Nicobar Islands 102 B4 island group India, E Indian Ocean
Nicosia 80 C5 Gk. Lefkosía, Turk. Lefkoşa. country capital (Cyprus) C Cyprus
Nicoya 30 D4 Guanacaste, W Costa Rica
Nicoya, Golfo de 30 D5 gulf W Costa Rica
Nicoya, Península de 30 D4 peninsula NW Costa Rica
Nida 84 A3 Ger. Nidden. Klaipėda, SW Lithuania
Nidaros see Trondheim
Nidden see Nida
Nidzica 76 D3 Ger. Niedenburg. Warmińsko-Mazurskie, NE Poland
Niedenburg see Nidzica
Niedere Tauern 77 A6 mountain range C Austria
Niemen see Neman
Nieśwież see Nyasvizh
Nieuw Amsterdam 37 G3 Commewijne, NE Suriname
Nieuw-Bergen 64 D4 Limburg, SE Netherlands
Nieuwegein 64 C4 Utrecht, C Netherlands
Nieuw Guinea see New Guinea
Nieuw Nickerie 37 G3 Nickerie, NW Suriname
Niewenstat see Neustadt an der Weinstrasse
Niğde 94 C4 Niğde, C Turkey
Niger 53 F3 off. Republic of Niger. country W Africa
Niger 53 F4 river W Africa
Nigeria 53 F4 off. Federal Republic of Nigeria. country W Africa
Nigeria, Federal Republic of see Nigeria
Niger, Mouths of the 53 F5 delta S Nigeria
Niger, Republic of see Niger
Nihon see Japan
Niigata 109 D5 Niigata, Honshū, C Japan
Niihama 109 B7 Ehime, Shikoku, SW Japan
Ni'ihau 25 A7 var. Niihau. island Hawai'i, USA, C Pacific Ocean
Nii-jima 109 D6 island E Japan
Nijkerk 64 D3 Gelderland, C Netherlands
Nijlen 65 C5 Antwerpen, N Belgium
Nijmegen 64 D4 Ger. Nimwegen; anc. Noviomagus. Gelderland, SE Netherlands
Nikaria see Ikaría
Nikel' 88 C2 Finn. Kolosjoki. Murmanskaya Oblast', NW Russian Federation
Nikiniki 117 E5 Timor, S Indonesia
Niklasmarkt see Gheorgheni
Nikolainkaupunki see Vaasa
Nikolayev see Mykolayiv
Nikol'sk see Ussuriysk
Nikol'sk-Ussuriyskiy see Ussuriysk
Nikopol' 87 F3 Dnipropetrovs'ka Oblast', SE Ukraine
Nikšić 79 C5 C Montenegro
Nikumaroro 123 E3 ; prev. Gardner Island. atoll Phoenix Islands, C Kiribati
Nikunau 123 E3 var. Nukunau; prev. Byron Island. atoll Tungaru, W Kiribati
Nile 50 B2 former province NW Uganda
Nile 46 D3 Ar. Nahr an Nīl. river N Africa
Nile Delta 50 B1 delta N Egypt
Nīl, Nahr an see Nile
Nîmes 69 C6 anc. Nemausus, Nismes. Gard, S France
Nimwegen see Nijmegen
Nine Degree Channel 110 B3 channel India/Maldives
Ninetyeast Ridge 119 D5 undersea feature E Indian Ocean
Ninety Mile Beach 128 C1 beach North Island, New Zealand
Ningbo 106 D5 var. Ning-po, Yin-hsien; prev. Ninghsien. Zhejiang, SE China
Ning-hsia see Ningxia
Ninghsien see Ningbo
Ning-po see Ningbo
Ningsia/Ningsia Hui/Ningsia Hui Autonomous Region see Ningxia
Ningxia 106 B4 off. Ningxia Huizu Zizhiqu, var. Ning-hsia, Ningsia, Eng. Ningsia Hui, Ningsia Hui Autonomous Region. autonomous region N China
Ningxia Huizu Zizhiqu see Ningxia
Nio see Íos
Niobrara River 23 E3 river Nebraska/Wyoming, C USA
Nioro 52 D3 var. Nioro du Sahel. Kayes, W Mali
Nioro du Sahel see Nioro
Niort 68 B4 Deux-Sèvres, W France

O

P

Parsons – Pontoise

Parsons 23 F5 Kansas, C USA
Pasadena 25 C7 California, W USA
Pasadena 27 H4 Texas, SW USA
Paşcani 86 C3 Hung. Páskán. Iaşi, NE Romania
Pasco 24 C2 Washington, NW USA
Pascua, Isla de 131 F4 var. Rapa Nui, Easter Island. island E Pacific Ocean
Pasewalk 72 D3 Mecklenburg-Vorpommern, NE Germany
Pashkeni see Bolyarovo
Pasinler 95 F3 Erzurum, NE Turkey
Páskán see Paşcani
Pasłęk 76 D2 Ger. Preußisch Holland. Warmińsko-Mazurskie, NE Poland
Pasni 112 A3 Baluchistān, SW Pakistan
Paso de Indios 43 B6 Chubut, S Argentina
Passarowitz see Požarevac
Passau 73 D6 Bayern, SE Germany
Passo Fundo 41 E5 Rio Grande do Sul, S Brazil
Pastavy 85 C5 Pol. Postawy, Rus. Postavy. Vitsyebskaya Voblasts', NW Belarus
Pastaza, Río 38 B2 river Ecuador/Peru
Pasto 36 A4 Nariño, SW Colombia
Pasvalys 84 C4 Panevėžys, N Lithuania
Patagonia 35 B7 physical region Argentina/Chile
Patalung see Phatthalung
Patani see Pattani
Patavium see Padova
Patea 128 D4 Taranaki, North Island, New Zealand
Paterson 19 F3 New Jersey, NE USA
Pathein 114 A4 var. Bassein. Ayeyarwady, SW Myanmar (Burma)
Pátmos 83 D6 island Dodekánisa, Greece, Aegean Sea
Patna 113 F3 var. Azimabad. state capital Bihār, N India
Patnos 95 F3 Ağrı, E Turkey
Patos, Lagoa dos 41 E5 lagoon S Brazil
Pátra 83 B5 Eng. Patras; prev. Pátrai. Dytikí Elláda, S Greece
Pátrai/Patras see Pátra
Pattani 115 C7 var. Patani. Pattani, SW Thailand
Pattaya 115 C5 Chon Buri, S Thailand
Patuca, Río 30 D2 river E Honduras
Pau 69 B6 Pyrénées-Atlantiques, SW France
Paulatuk 15 E3 Northwest Territories, NW Canada
Paungde 114 B4 Bago, C Myanmar (Burma)
Pautalia see Kyustendil
Pavia 74 B2 anc. Ticinum. Lombardia, N Italy
Pāvilosta 84 B3 Liepāja, W Latvia
Pavlikeni 82 D2 Veliko Tŭrnovo, N Bulgaria
Pavlodar 92 C4 Pavlodar, NE Kazakhstan
Pavlograd see Pavlohrad
Pavlohrad 87 G3 Rus. Pavlograd. Dnipropetrovs'ka Oblast', E Ukraine
Pawai, Pulau 116 A2 island SW Singapore Asia
Pawn 114 B3 river C Myanmar (Burma)
Pax Augusta see Badajoz
Pax Julia see Beja
Paxoí 83 A5 island Iónia Nisiá, Greece, C Mediterranean Sea
Payo Obispo see Chetumal
Paysandú 42 D4 Paysandú, W Uruguay
Pazar 95 E2 Rize, NE Turkey
Pazardzhik 82 C3 prev. Tatar Pazardzhik. Pazardzhik, SW Bulgaria
Peace Garden State see North Dakota
Peach State see Georgia
Pearl Islands 31 G5 Eng. Pearl Islands. island group SE Panama
Pearl Islands see Perlas, Archipiélago de las
Pearl Lagoon see Perlas, Laguna de
Pearl River 20 B3 river Louisiana/Mississippi, S USA
Pearsall 27 F4 Texas, SW USA
Peawanuk 16 C2 river Ontario, S Canada
Peć see Pejë
Pechora 88 D3 Respublika Komi, NW Russian Federation
Pechora 88 D3 river NW Russian Federation
Pechora Sea see Pechorskoye More
Pechorskoye More 88 D2 Eng. Pechora Sea. sea NW Russian Federation
Pecos 27 E3 Texas, SW USA
Pecos River 27 E3 river New Mexico/Texas, SW USA
Pécs 77 C7 Ger. Fünfkirchen, Lat. Sopianae. Baranya, SW Hungary
Pedra Lume 52 A3 Sal, NE Cape Verde
Pedro Cays 32 C3 island group Greater Antilles, S Jamaica North America N Caribbean Sea W Atlantic Ocean
Pedro Juan Caballero 42 D2 Amambay, E Paraguay
Peer 65 D5 Limburg, NE Belgium
Pegasus Bay 129 C6 bay South Island, New Zealand
Pegu see Bago
Pehuajó 42 C4 Buenos Aires, E Argentina
Pei-ching see Beijing/Beijing Shi
Peine 72 B3 Niedersachsen, C Germany
Pei-p'ing see Beijing/Beijing Shi
Peipsi Järv/Peipus-See see Peipus, Lake
Peipus, Lake 84 E3 Est. Peipsi Järv, Ger. Peipus-See, Rus. Chudskoye Ozero. lake Estonia/Russian Federation
Peiraías 83 C6 prev. Piraiévs, Eng. Piraeus. Attikí, C Greece
Pejë 79 D5 Serb. Peć. W Kosovo
Pèk 114 D4 var. Xieng Khouang; prev. Xiangkhoang. Xiangkhoang, N Laos
Pekalongan 116 C4 Jawa, C Indonesia
Pekanbaru 116 B3 var. Pakanbaru. Sumatera, W Indonesia
Pekin 18 B4 Illinois, N USA
Peking see Beijing/Beijing Shi
Pelagie 75 B8 island group SW Italy
Pelagosa see Palagruža
Pelican State see Louisiana
Pelly Bay see Kugaaruk
Pélmonostor see Beli Manastir
Peloponnese 83 B6 var. Morea, Eng. Peloponnese; anc. Peloponnesus. peninsula S Greece
Peloponnese/Peloponnesus see Pelopónnisos
Pematangsiantar 116 B3 Sumatera, W Indonesia
Pemba 57 F2 prev. Port Amelia, Porto Amélia. Cabo Delgado, NE Mozambique
Pemba 51 D7 island E Tanzania
Pembroke 16 D4 Ontario, SE Canada
Penang see Pinang, Pulau, Peninsular Malaysia
Penang see George Town
Penas, Golfo de 43 A7 gulf S Chile
Penderma see Bandırma
Pendleton 24 C3 Oregon, NW USA
Pend Oreille, Lake 24 D2 lake Idaho, NW USA
Peneius see Pineiós
Peng-pu see Bengbu
Penibético, Sistema see Béticos, Sistemas
Peniche 70 B3 Leiria, W Portugal
Peninsular State see Florida
Penninae, Alpes/Pennine, Alpi see Pennine Alps
Pennine Alps 73 A8 Fr. Alpes Pennines, It. Alpi Pennine, Lat. Alpes Penninae. mountain range Italy/Switzerland
Pennine Chain see Pennines
Pennines 67 D5 var. Pennine Chain. mountain range N England, United Kingdom
Pennines, Alpes see Pennine Alps
Pennsylvania 19 E4 off. Commonwealth of Pennsylvania, also known as Keystone State. state NE USA
Penobscot River 19 G2 river Maine, NE USA
Penong 127 A6 South Australia
Penonomé 31 F5 Coclé, C Panama
Penrhyn 123 G3 atoll N Cook Islands
Penrhyn Basin 121 F3 undersea feature C Pacific Ocean
Penrith 126 D1 New South Wales, SE Australia
Penrith 67 D5 NW England, United Kingdom
Pensacola 20 C3 Florida, SE USA
Pentecost 122 D4 Fr. Pentecôte. island C Vanuatu
Pentecôte see Pentecost
Penza 89 C6 Penzenskaya Oblast', W Russian Federation
Penzance 67 C7 SW England, United Kingdom
Peoria 18 B4 Illinois, N USA
Perchtoldsdorf 73 E6 Niederösterreich, NE Austria
Percival Lakes 124 C4 lakes Western Australia
Perdido, Monte 71 F1 mountain NE Spain
Perece Vela Basin see West Mariana Basin
Pereira 36 B3 Risaralda, W Colombia
Peremyshl see Przemyśl
Pergamino 42 C4 Buenos Aires, E Argentina
Périgueux 69 C5 anc. Vesuna. Dordogne, SW France
Perito Moreno 43 B6 Santa Cruz, S Argentina
Perlas, Laguna de 31 E3 Eng. Pearl Lagoon. lagoon E Nicaragua
Perleberg 72 C3 Brandenburg, N Germany
Perlepe see Prilep
Perm' 92 C3 prev. Molotov. Permskaya Oblast', NW Russian Federation
Pernambuco 41 G2 off. Estado de Pernambuco. state E Brazil
Pernambuco 41 G2 off. Estado de Pernambuco. region E Brazil
Pernambuco see Recife
Pernambuco Abyssal Plain see Pernambuco Plain
Pernambuco, Estado de see Pernambuco
Pernambuco Plain 45 C5 var. Pernambuco Abyssal Plain. undersea feature E Atlantic Ocean
Pernau see Pärnu
Pernauer Bucht see Pärnu Laht
Pērnava see Pärnu
Pernik 82 B2 prev. Dimitrovo. Pernik, W Bulgaria
Pernov see Pärnu
Perote 29 F4 Veracruz-Llave, E Mexico
Pérouse see Perugia
Perovsk see Kzylorda
Perpignan 69 C6 Pyrénées-Orientales, S France
Perryton 27 F1 Texas, SW USA
Perryville 23 H5 Missouri, C USA
Persia see Iran
Perth 125 A6 state capital Western Australia
Perth 66 C4 C Scotland, United Kingdom
Perth Basin 119 E6 undersea feature SE Indian Ocean
Peru 38 C3 off. Republic of Peru. country W South America
Peru see Beru
Peru Basin 45 A5 undersea feature E Pacific Ocean
Peru-Chile Trench 34 A4 undersea feature E Pacific Ocean
Perugia 74 C4 Fr. Pérouse; anc. Perusia. Umbria, C Italy
Perugia, Lake of see Trasimeno, Lago
Peru, Republic of see Peru
Perusia see Perugia
Péruwelz 65 B6 Hainaut, SW Belgium
Pervomays'k 87 E3 prev. Ol'viopol'. Mykolayivs'ka Oblast', S Ukraine
Pervyy Kuril'skiy Proliv 93 H3 strait E Russian Federation
Pesaro 74 C3 anc. Pisaurum. Marche, C Italy
Pescara 74 D4 anc. Aternum, Ostia Aterni. Abruzzo, C Italy
Peshāwar 112 C1 North-West Frontier Province, N Pakistan
Peshkopi 79 C6 var. Peshkopia, Peshkopija. Dibër, NE Albania
Peshkopia/Peshkopija see Peshkopi
Pessac 69 B5 Gironde, SW France
Petach-Tikva see Petah Tikva
Petah Tikva 97 A6 var. Petach-Tikva, Petah Tiqva, Petakh Tikva; prev. Petaḥ Tiqwa. Tel Aviv, C Israel
Petaḥ Tiqwa see Petah Tikva
Petakh Tikva/Petah Tiqva see Petah Tikva
Pétange 65 D8 Luxembourg, SW Luxembourg
Petchaburi see Phetchaburi
Peterborough 127 B6 South Australia
Peterborough 16 D5 Ontario, SE Canada
Peterborough 67 E6 prev. Medeshamstede. E England, United Kingdom
Peterhead 66 D3 NE Scotland, United Kingdom
Peter I Øy 132 A3 Norwegian dependency Antarctica
Petermann Bjerg 61 E3 mountain C Greenland
Petersburg 19 E5 Virginia, NE USA
Peters Mine 37 F3 var. Peter's Mine. N Guyana
Petit St-Bernard, Col du see Little Saint Bernard Pass
Peto 29 H4 Yucatán, SE Mexico
Petoskey 18 C2 Michigan, N USA
Petra see Wādī Mūsā
Petrich 82 C3 Blagoevgrad, SW Bulgaria
Petrikau see Piotrków Trybunalski
Petrikov see Pyetrykaw
Petrinja 78 B3 Sisak-Moslavina, C Croatia
Petroaleksandrovsk see To'rtkok'l
Petrodvorets 88 A4 Fin. Pietarhovi. Leningradskaya Oblast', NW Russian Federation
Petrograd see Sankt-Peterburg
Petrokov see Piotrków Trybunalski
Petropavl see Petropavlovsk
Petropavlovsk 92 C4 Kaz. Petropavl. Severnyy Kazakhstan, N Kazakhstan
Petropavlovsk-Kamchatskiy 93 H3 Kamchatskaya Oblast', E Russian Federation
Petroşani 86 B4 var. Petroşeni, Ger. Petroschen, Hung. Petrozsény. Hunedoara, W Romania
Petroschen/Petroşeni see Petroşani
Petroskoi see Petrozavodsk
Petrovgrad see Zrenjanin
Petrovsk-Port see Makhachkala
Petrozavodsk 92 B2 Fin. Petroskoi. Respublika Kareliya, NW Russian Federation
Petrozsény see Petroşani
Pettau see Ptuj
Pevek 93 G1 Chukotskiy Avtonomnyy Okrug, NE Russian Federation
Pezinok 77 C6 Ger. Bösing, Hung. Bazin. Bratislavský Kraj, W Slovakia
Pforzheim 73 B6 Baden-Württemberg, SW Germany
Pfungstadt 73 B5 Hessen, W Germany
Phangan, Ko 115 C6 island SW Thailand
Phang-Nga 115 B7 var. Pang-Nga, Phangnga. Phangnga, SW Thailand
Phangnga see Phang-Nga
Phan Rang/Phanrang see Phan Rang-Thap Cham
Phan Rang-Thap Cham 115 E6 var. Phanrang, Phan Rang, Phan Rang Thap Cham. Ninh Thuân, S Vietnam
Phan Thiêt 115 E6 Binh Thuân, S Vietnam
Pharnacia see Giresun
Pharus see Hvar
Phatthalung 115 C7 var. Padalung, Patalung. Phatthalung, SW Thailand
Phayao 114 C4 var. Muang Phayao. Phayao, NW Thailand
Phenix City 20 D2 Alabama, S USA
Phet Buri see Phetchaburi
Phetchaburi 115 C5 var. Bejraburi, Petchaburi, Phet Buri. Phetchaburi, SW Thailand
Philadelphia 19 F4 Pennsylvania, NE USA
Philadelphia see 'Ammān
Philippine Basin 103 F3 undersea feature W Pacific Ocean
Philippine Islands 117 E1 island group W Pacific Ocean
Philippines 117 E1 off. Republic of the Philippines. country SE Asia
Philippine Sea 103 F3 sea W Pacific Ocean
Philippines, Republic of the see Philippines
Philippine Trench 120 A1 undersea feature W Philippine Sea
Philippopolis see Plovdiv
Phitsanulok 114 C4 var. Bisnulok, Muang Phitsanulok, Pitsanulok. Phitsanulok, C Thailand
Phlórina see Flórina
Phnom Penh see Phnum Penh
Phnum Penh 115 D6 var. Phnom Penh. country capital (Cambodia) Phnum Penh, S Cambodia
Phoenix 26 B2 state capital Arizona, SW USA
Phoenix Islands 123 E3 island group C Kiribati
Phôngsali 114 C3 var. Phong Saly. Phôngsali, N Laos
Phong Saly see Phôngsali
Phrae 114 C4 var. Muang Phrae, Prae. Phrae, NW Thailand
Phra Nakhon Si Ayutthaya see Ayutthaya
Phra Thong, Ko 115 B6 island SW Thailand
Phuket 115 B7 var. Bhuket, Puket, Mal. Ujung Salang; prev. Junkseylon, Salang. Phuket, SW Thailand
Phuket, Ko 115 B7 island SW Thailand
Phumĭ Kâmpóng Trâbêk 115 D5 prev. Phum Kompong Trabek. Kâmpóng Thum, C Cambodia
Phumĭ Sâmraông 115 D5 prev. Phum Samrong. Siĕmréab, NW Cambodia
Phum Kompong Trabek see Phumĭ Kâmpóng Trâbêk
Phum Samrong see Phumĭ Sâmraông
Phu Vinh see Tra Vinh
Phyu 114 B4 var. Hpyu, Pyu. Bago, C Myanmar (Burma)
Piacenza 74 B2 Fr. Paisance; anc. Placentia. Emilia-Romagna, N Italy
Piatra-Neamţ 86 C4 Hung. Karácsonkő. Neamţ, NE Romania
Piauhy see Piauí
Piauí 41 F2 off. Estado do Piauí; prev. Piauhy. state E Brazil
Piauí 41 F2 off. Estado do Piauí; prev. Piauhy. region E Brazil
Piauí, Estado do see Piauí
Picardie 68 C3 Eng. Picardy. cultural region N France
Picardy see Picardie
Piccolo San Bernardo, Colle di see Little Saint Bernard Pass
Pichilemu 42 B4 Libertador, C Chile
Pico 70 A5 var. Ilha do Pico. island Azores, Portugal, NE Atlantic Ocean
Pico, Ilha do see Pico
Picos 41 F2 Piauí, E Brazil
Picton 129 C5 Marlborough, South Island, New Zealand
Piedmont see Piemonte
Piedras Negras 29 E2 var. Ciudad Porfirio Díaz. Coahuila, NE Mexico
Pielavesi 62 D4 lake C Finland
Pielinen 62 E4 var. Pielisjärvi. lake E Finland
Pielisjärvi see Pielinen
Piemonte 74 A2 Eng. Piedmont. region NW Italy
Pierre 23 E3 state capital South Dakota, N USA
Piešťany 77 C6 Ger. Pistyan, Hung. Pöstyén. Tranavský Kraj, W Slovakia
Pietarhovi see Petrodvorets
Pietari see Sankt-Peterburg
Pietarsaari see Jakobstad
Pietermaritzburg 56 C5 var. Maritzburg. KwaZulu/Natal, E South Africa
Pietersburg see Polokwane
Pigs, Bay of see Cochinos, Bahía de
Pihkva Järv see Pskov, Lake
Pijijiapán 29 G5 Chiapas, SE Mexico
Pikes Peak 22 C5 mountain Colorado, C USA
Pikeville 18 D5 Kentucky, S USA
Pikinni see Bikini Atoll
Piła 76 B3 Ger. Schneidemühl. Wielkopolskie, C Poland
Pilar 42 D3 var. Villa del Pilar. Ñeembucú, S Paraguay
Pilcomayo, Rio 35 C5 river C South America
Pilos see Pýlos
Pilsen see Plzeň
Pilzno see Plzeň
Pinang see Pinang, Pulau, Peninsular Malaysia
Pinang see George Town
Pinang, Pulau 116 B3 var. Penang, Pinang; prev. Prince of Wales Island. island Peninsular Malaysia
Pinar del Río 32 A2 Pinar del Río, W Cuba
Píndhos/Píndhos Óros see Píndos
Pindus Mountains 82 A4 var. Píndhos Óros, Eng. Pindus Mountains; prev. Píndhos. mountain range C Greece
Pindus Mountains see Píndos
Pine Bluff 20 B2 Arkansas, C USA
Pine Creek 124 D2 Northern Territory, N Australia
Pinega 88 C3 river NW Russian Federation
Pineiós 82 B4 var. Piniós; anc. Peneius. river C Greece
Pineland 27 H3 Texas, SW USA
Pínes, Akrotírio 82 C4 var. Akrotírio Pínnes. headland N Greece
Pines, The Isle of the see Juventud, Isla de la
Pine Tree State see Maine
Pingdingshan 106 C4 Henan, C China
Pingkiang see Harbin
Ping, Mae Nam 114 B4 river W Thailand
Piniós see Pineiós
Pinkiang see Harbin
Pínnes, Akrotírio see Pínes, Akrotírio
Pinos, Isla de see Juventud, Isla de la
Pinotepa Nacional 29 F5 var. Santiago Pinotepa Nacional. Oaxaca, SE Mexico
Pinsk 85 B7 Pol. Pińsk. Brestskaya Voblasts', SW Belarus
Pinta, Isla 38 A5 var. Abingdon. island Galapagos Islands, Ecuador, E Pacific Ocean
Piombino 74 B3 Toscana, C Italy
Pioneer Mountains 24 D3 mountain range Montana, N USA North America
Pionerskiy 84 A4 Ger. Neukuhren. Kaliningradskaya Oblast', W Russian Federation
Piotrków Trybunalski 76 D4 Ger. Petrikau, Rus. Petrokov. Łodzkie, C Poland
Piraeus/Piraiévs see Peiraías
Pírgos see Pýrgos
Pirineos see Pyrenees
Piripiri 41 F2 Piauí, E Brazil
Pirna 72 D4 Sachsen, E Germany
Pirot 79 E5 Serbia, SE Serbia
Piryatin see Pyryatyn
Pisa 74 B3 var. Pisae. Toscana, C Italy
Pisae see Pisa
Pisaurum see Pesaro
Pisco 38 D4 Ica, SW Peru
Písek 77 A5 Budějovický Kraj, S Czech Republic
Pishan 104 A3 var. Guma. Xinjiang Uygur Zizhiqu, NW China
Pishpek see Bishkek
Pistoia 74 B3 anc. Pistoria, Pistoriæ. Toscana, C Italy
Pistoria/Pistoriæ see Pistoia
Pistyan see Piešťany
Pisz 76 D3 Ger. Johannisburg. Warmińsko-Mazurskie, NE Poland
Pita 52 C4 NW Guinea
Pitalito 36 B4 Huila, S Colombia
Pitcairn Island 121 G4 island S Pitcairn Islands
Pitcairn Islands 121 G4 UK dependent territory C Pacific Ocean
Piteå 62 D4 Norrbotten, N Sweden
Piteşti 86 B5 Argeş, S Romania
Pitsanulok see Phitsanulok
Pitt Island see Makin
Pittsburg 23 F5 Kansas, C USA
Pittsburgh 19 E4 Pennsylvania, NE USA
Pittsfield 19 F3 Massachusetts, NE USA
Piura 38 B2 Piura, NW Peru
Pivdennyy Buh 87 E3 Rus. Yuzhnyy Bug. river S Ukraine
Placentia see Piacenza
Placetas 32 B2 Villa Clara, C Cuba
Plainview 27 E2 Texas, SW USA
Planeta Rica 36 B2 Córdoba, NW Colombia
Planken 72 E1 C Liechtenstein Europe
Plano 27 G2 Texas, SW USA
Plasencia 70 C3 Extremadura, W Spain
Plate, River 42 D4 var. River Plate. estuary Argentina/Uruguay
Plate, River see Plata, Río de la
Platinum 14 C3 Alaska, USA
Plattensee see Balaton
Platte River 23 E4 river Nebraska, C USA
Plattsburgh 19 F2 New York, NE USA
Plauen 73 C5 var. Plauen im Vogtland. Sachsen, E Germany
Plauen im Vogtland see Plauen
Pļaviņas 84 D4 Ger. Stockmannshof. Aizkraukle, S Latvia
Plây Cu 115 E5 var. Pleiku. Gia Lai, C Vietnam
Pleasant Island see Nauru
Pleiku see Plây Cu
Plenty, Bay of 128 E3 bay North Island, New Zealand
Plérin 68 A3 Côtes d'Armor, NW France
Plesetsk 88 C3 Arkhangel'skaya Oblast', NW Russian Federation
Pleshchenitsy see Plyeshchanitsy
Pleskau see Pskov
Pleskauer See see Pskov, Lake
Pleskava see Pskov
Pleszew 76 C4 Wielkopolskie, C Poland
Pleven 82 C2 prev. Plevna. Pleven, N Bulgaria
Plevlja/Plevlje see Pljevlja
Plevna see Pleven
Pljevlja 78 C4 prev. Plevlja, Plevlje. N Montenegro
Ploce see Ploče
Ploče 78 B4 It. Plocce; prev. Kardeljevo. Dubrovnik-Neretva, SE Croatia
Płock 76 D3 Ger. Plozk. Mazowieckie, C Poland
Plöcken Pass 73 C7 Ger. Plöckenpass, It. Passo di Monte Croce Carnico. pass SW Austria
Plöckenpass see Plöcken Pass
Ploești see Ploiești
Ploiești 86 C5 prev. Ploești. Prahova, SE Romania
Plomári 83 D5 prev. Plomárion. Lésvos, E Greece
Plomárion see Plomári
Płońsk 76 D3 Mazowieckie, C Poland
Plovdiv 82 C3 prev. Eumolpias; anc. Evmolpia, Philippopolis, Lat. Trimontium. Plovdiv, C Bulgaria
Plozk see Płock
Plungė 84 B3 Telšiai, W Lithuania
Plyeshchanitsy 85 D5 Rus. Pleshchenitsy. Minskaya Voblasts', N Belarus
Plymouth 33 G3 dependent territory capital (Montserrat) SW Montserrat
Plymouth 67 C7 SW England, United Kingdom
Plzeň 77 A5 Ger. Pilsen, Pol. Pilzno. Plzeňský Kraj, W Czech Republic
Po 58 D4 river N Italy
Pobedy, Pik 104 B3 Chin. Tomür Feng. mountain China/Kyrgyzstan
Po, Bocche del see Po, Foci del
Pocahontas 20 B1 Arkansas, C USA
Pocatello 24 E4 Idaho, NW USA
Pochinok 89 A5 Smolenskaya Oblast', W Russian Federation
Pocking 73 D6 Bayern, SE Germany
Poděbrady 77 B5 Ger. Podiebrad. Středočeský Kraj, C Czech Republic
Podgorica 79 C5 prev. Titograd. country capital (Montenegro) S Montenegro
Podiebrad see Poděbrady
Podil's'ka Vysochina 86 D3 plateau W Ukraine
Podium Anicensis see le Puy
Podol'sk 89 B5 Moskovskaya Oblast', W Russian Federation
Podravska Slatina see Slatina
Podujevë 79 D5 Serb. Podujevo. N Kosovo
Podujevo see Podujevë
Podunajská Rovina see Little Alföld
Poetovio see Ptuj
Pogradec 79 D6 var. Pogradeci. Korçë, SE Albania
Pogradeci see Pogradec
Pohjanlahti see Bothnia, Gulf of
Pohnpei 122 C2 prev. Ponape Ascension Island. island E Micronesia
Poictiers see Poitiers
Poinsett, Cape 132 D4 headland Antarctica
Point de Galle see Galle
Pointe-à-Pitre 33 G3 Grande Terre, C Guadeloupe
Pointe-Noire 55 B6 Kouilou, S Congo
Point Lay 14 C2 Alaska, USA
Poitiers 68 B4 prev. Poictiers; anc. Limonum. Vienne, W France
Poitou 68 B4 cultural region W France
Pokharā 113 E3 Western, C Nepal
Pokrovka see Kyzyl-Suu
Pokrovs'ke 87 G3 Rus. Pokrovskoye. Dnipropetrovs'ka Oblast', E Ukraine
Pokrovskoye see Pokrovs'ke
Pola see Pula
Pola de Lena 70 D1 Asturias, N Spain
Poland 76 B4 off. Republic of Poland, var. Polish Republic, Pol. Polska, Rzeczpospolita Polska; prev. Pol. Polska Rzeczpospolita Ludowa, The Polish People's Republic. country C Europe
Poland, Republic of see Poland
Polatlı 94 C3 Ankara, C Turkey
Polatsk 85 D5 Rus. Polotsk. Vitsyebskaya Voblasts', N Belarus
Pol-e Khomrī 101 E4 var. Pul-i-Khumri. Baghlān, NE Afghanistan
Poli see Pólis
Polikastro/Políkastron see Polýkastro
Polikrayshte 82 D2 Veliko Tŭrnovo, N Bulgaria
Pólis 80 C5 var. Poli. W Cyprus
Polish People's Republic, The see Poland
Polish Republic see Poland
Polkowice 76 B4 Ger. Heerwegen. Dolnośląskie, W Poland
Pollença 71 G3 Mallorca, Spain, W Mediterranean Sea
Pologi see Polohy
Polohy 87 G3 Rus. Pologi. Zaporiz'ka Oblast', SE Ukraine
Polokwane 56 D4 prev. Pietersburg. Limpopo, NE South Africa
Polonne 86 D2 Rus. Polonnoye. Khmel'nyts'ka Oblast', NW Ukraine
Polonnoye see Polonne
Polotsk see Polatsk
Polska/Polska, Rzeczpospolita/Polska Rzeczpospolita Ludowa see Poland
Polsko Kosovo 82 D2 Ruse, N Bulgaria
Poltava 87 F2 Poltavs'ka Oblast', NE Ukraine
Poltoratsk see Aşgabat
Põlva 84 E3 Ger. Põlwe. Põlvamaa, SE Estonia
Põlwe see Põlva
Polyarnyy 88 C2 Murmanskaya Oblast', NW Russian Federation
Polýkastro 82 B3 var. Polikastro; prev. Políkastron. Kentrikí Makedonía, N Greece
Polynesia 121 F4 island group C Pacific Ocean
Pomeranian Bay 72 D2 Ger. Pommersche Bucht, Pol. Zatoka Pomorska. bay Germany/Poland
Pomir, Dar"yoi see Pamir/Pāmīr, Daryā-ye
Pommersche Bucht see Pomeranian Bay
Pomorska, Zatoka see Pomeranian Bay
Pomorskiy Proliv 88 D2 strait NW Russian Federation
Po, Mouth of the 74 C2 var. Bocche del Po. river NE Italy
Pompaelo see Pamplona
Pompano Beach 21 F5 Florida, SE USA
Ponape Ascension Island see Pohnpei
Ponca City 27 G1 Oklahoma, C USA
Ponce 33 F3 C Puerto Rico
Pondicherry 110 C2 var. Puduchcheri, Fr. Pondichéry. Pondicherry, SE India
Ponferrada 70 C1 Castilla-León, NW Spain
Poniatowa 76 E4 Lubelskie, E Poland
Pons Aelii see Newcastle upon Tyne
Pons Vetus see Pontevedra
Ponta Delgada 70 B5 São Miguel, Azores, Portugal, NE Atlantic Ocean
Ponta Grossa 41 E4 Paraná, S Brazil
Pontarlier 68 D4 Doubs, E France
Ponteareas 70 B2 Galicia, NW Spain
Ponte da Barca 70 B2 Viana do Castelo, N Portugal
Pontevedra 70 B1 anc. Pons Vetus. Galicia, NW Spain
Pontiac 18 D3 Michigan, N USA
Pontianak 116 C4 Borneo, C Indonesia
Pontisarae see Pontoise
Pontivy 68 A3 Morbihan, NW France
Pontoise 68 C3 anc. Briva Isarae, Cergy-Pontoise, Pontisarae. Val-d'Oise, N France

Ponziane Island – Quetzalcoalco

Ponziane Island 75 C5 island C Italy
Poole 67 D7 S England, United Kingdom
Poona see Pune
Poopó, Lago 39 F4 var. Lago Pampa Aullagas. lake W Bolivia
Popayán 36 B4 Cauca, SW Colombia
Poperinge 65 A6 West-Vlaanderen, W Belgium
Poplar Bluff 23 G5 Missouri, C USA
Popocatépetl 29 E4 volcano S Mexico
Popper see Poprad
Poprad 77 D5 Ger. Deutschendorf, Hung. Poprád. Prešovský Kraj, E Slovakia
Poprád 77 D5 Ger. Popper, Hung. Poprád. river Poland/Slovakia
Porbandar 112 B4 Gujarāt, W India
Porcupine Plain 58 B3 undersea feature E Atlantic Ocean
Pordenone 74 C2 anc. Portenau. Friuli-Venezia Giulia, NE Italy
Poreč 78 A2 It. Parenzo. Istra, NW Croatia
Porech'ye see Parechcha
Pori 63 D5 Swe. Björneborg. Länsi-Suomi, SW Finland
Porirua 129 D5 Wellington, North Island, New Zealand
Porkhov 88 A4 Pskovskaya Oblast', W Russian Federation
Porlamar 37 E1 Nueva Esparta, NE Venezuela
Póros 83 C6 Póros, S Greece
Póros 83 A5 Kefallinía, Iónia Nisiá, Greece, C Mediterranean Sea
Pors see Porsangenfijorden
Porsangenfijorden 62 D2 Lapp. Pors. fjord N Norway
Porsgrunn 63 B6 Telemark, S Norway
Portachuelo 39 G4 Santa Cruz, C Bolivia
Portadown 67 B5 Ir. Port An Dúnáin. S Northern Ireland, United Kingdom
Portalegre 70 C3 anc. Ammaia, Amoea. Portalegre, E Portugal
Port Alexander 14 D4 Baranof Island, Alaska, USA
Port Alfred 56 D5 Eastern Cape, S South Africa
Port Amelia see Pemba
Port An Dúnáin see Portadown
Port Angeles 24 B1 Washington, NW USA
Port Antonio 32 B5 NE Jamaica
Port Arthur 27 H4 Texas, SW USA
Port Augusta 127 B6 South Australia
Port-au-Prince 32 D3 country capital (Haiti) C Haiti
Port Blair 111 F2 Andaman and Nicobar Islands, SE India
Port Charlotte 21 E4 Florida, SE USA
Port Darwin see Darwin
Port d'Envalira 69 B8 E Andorra Europe
Port Douglas 126 D3 Queensland, NE Australia
Port Elizabeth 56 C5 Eastern Cape, S South Africa
Portenau see Pordenone
Porterville 25 C7 California, W USA
Port-Étienne see Nouâdhibou
Port Florence see Kisumu
Port-Francqui see Ilebo
Port-Gentil 55 A6 Ogooué-Maritime, W Gabon
Port Harcourt 53 G5 Rivers, S Nigeria
Port Hardy 14 D5 Vancouver Island, British Columbia, SW Canada
Port Harrison see Inukjuak
Port Hedland 124 B4 Western Australia
Port Huron 18 D3 Michigan, N USA
Portimão 70 B4 var. Vila Nova de Portimão. Faro, S Portugal
Port Jackson 126 E1 harbour New South Wales, E Australia
Portland 127 B7 Victoria, SE Australia
Portland 19 G2 Maine, NE USA
Portland 24 B3 Oregon, NW USA
Portland 27 G4 Texas, SW USA
Portland Bight 32 B5 bay S Jamaica
Portlaoighise see Port Laoise
Port Laoise 67 B6 var. Portlaoise, Ir. Portlaoighise; prev. Maryborough. C Ireland
Portlaoise see Port Laoise
Port Lavaca 27 G4 Texas, SW USA
Port Lincoln 127 A6 South Australia
Port Louis 57 H3 country capital (Mauritius) NW Mauritius
Port-Lyautey see Kénitra
Port Macquarie 127 E6 New South Wales, SE Australia
Port Mahon see Mahón
Portmore 32 B5 C Jamaica
Port Moresby 122 B3 country capital (Papua New Guinea) Central/National Capital District, SW Papua New Guinea
Port Natal see Durban
Porto 70 B2 Eng. Oporto; anc. Portus Cale. Porto, NW Portugal
Porto Alegre 41 E5 var. Pôrto Alegre. state capital Rio Grande do Sul, S Brazil
Porto Alegre 54 E2 São Tomé, S Sao Tome and Principe, Africa
Porto Alexandre see Tombua
Porto Amélia see Pemba
Porto Bello see Portobelo
Portobelo 31 G4 var. Porto Bello, Puerto Bello. Colón, N Panama
Port O'Connor 27 G4 Texas, SW USA
Porto Edda see Sarandë
Portoferraio 74 B4 Toscana, C Italy
Port-of-Spain 33 H5 country capital (Trinidad and Tobago) Trinidad, Trinidad and Tobago
Porto Grande see Mindelo
Portogruaro 74 C2 Veneto, NE Italy
Porto-Novo 53 F5 country capital (Benin) S Benin
Porto Rico see Puerto Rico
Porto Santo 48 A2 var. Ilha do Porto Santo. island Madeira, Portugal, NE Atlantic Ocean
Porto Santo, Ilha do see Porto Santo
Porto Torres 75 A5 Sardegna, Italy, C Mediterranean Sea
Porto Velho 40 D2 var. Velho. state capital Rondônia, W Brazil
Portoviejo 38 A2 var. Puertoviejo. Manabí, W Ecuador
Port Pirie 127 B6 South Australia
Port Rex see East London
Port Said see Būr Sa'īd
Portsmouth 67 D7 S England, United Kingdom
Portsmouth 19 G3 New Hampshire, NE USA
Portsmouth 18 D4 Ohio, N USA
Portsmouth 19 F5 Virginia, NE USA
Port Stanley see Stanley
Port Sudan 50 C3 Red Sea, NE Sudan
Port Swettenham see Klang/Pelabuhan Klang
Port Talbot 67 C7 S Wales, United Kingdom
Portugal 70 B3 off. Portuguese Republic. country SW Europe
Portuguese East Africa see Mozambique
Portuguese Guinea see Guinea-Bissau
Portuguese Republic see Portugal
Portuguese Timor see East Timor
Portuguese West Africa see Angola
Portus Cale see Porto
Portus Magnus see Almería
Portus Magonis see Mahón
Port-Vila 122 D4 var. Vila. country capital (Vanuatu) Éfaté, C Vanuatu
Porvenir 39 E3 Pando, NW Bolivia
Porvenir 43 B8 Magallanes, S Chile
Porvoo 63 E6 Swe. Borgå. Etelä-Suomi, S Finland
Porzecze see Parechcha
Posadas 42 D3 Misiones, NE Argentina
Poschega see Požega
Posen see Poznań
Posnania see Poznań
Postavy/Postawy see Pastavy
Posterholt 65 D5 Limburg, SE Netherlands
Postojna 73 D8 Ger. Adelsberg, It. Postumia. SW Slovenia
Postumia see Postojna
Pöstyén see Piešt'any
Potamós 83 C7 Antikýthira, S Greece
Potentia see Potenza
Potenza 75 D5 anc. Potentia. Basilicata, S Italy
P'ot'i 95 F2 W Georgia
Potiskum 53 G4 Yobe, NE Nigeria
Potomac River 19 E5 river NE USA
Potosí 39 F4 Potosí, S Bolivia
Potsdam 72 D3 Brandenburg, NE Germany
Potwar Plateau 112 C2 plateau NE Pakistan
Poŭthĭsăt 115 D6 prev. Pursat. Poŭthĭsăt, W Cambodia
Po, Valle del see Po Valley
Po Valley 74 C2 It. Valle del Po. valley N Italy
Považská Bystrica 77 C5 Ger. Waagbistritz, Hung. Vágbeszterce. Trenčiansky Kraj, W Slovakia
Poverty Bay 128 E4 inlet North Island, New Zealand
Póvoa de Varzim 70 B2 Porto, NW Portugal
Powder River 22 D2 river Montana/Wyoming, NW USA
Powell 22 C2 Wyoming, C USA
Powell, Lake 22 B5 lake Utah, W USA
Požarevac 78 D4 Ger. Passarowitz. Serbia, NE Serbia
Poza Rica 29 F4 var. Poza Rica de Hidalgo. Veracruz-Llave, E Mexico
Poza Rica de Hidalgo see Poza Rica
Požega 78 D4 prev. Slavonska Požega, Ger. Poschega, Hung. Pozsega. Požega-Slavonija, NE Croatia
Požega 78 D4 Serbia
Poznań 76 C3 Ger. Posen, Posnania. Wielkolpolskie, C Poland
Pozoblanco 70 D4 Andalucía, S Spain
Pozsega see Požega
Pozsony see Bratislava
Pozzallo 75 C8 Sicilia, Italy, C Mediterranean Sea
Prachatice 77 A5 Ger. Prachatitz. Jihočeský Kraj, S Czech Republic
Prachatitz see Prachatice
Prado del Ganso see Goose Green
Prae see Phrae
Prag/Praga/Prague see Praha
Praha 77 A5 Eng. Prague, Ger. Prag, Pol. Praga. country capital (Czech Republic) Středočeský Kraj, NW Czech Republic
Praia 52 A3 country capital (Cape Verde) Santiago, S Cape Verde
Prairie State see Illinois
Prathet Thai see Thailand
Prato 74 B3 Toscana, C Italy
Pratt 23 E5 Kansas, C USA
Prattville 20 D2 Alabama, S USA
Pravda 82 D1 prev. Dogrular. Silistra, NE Bulgaria
Pravia 70 C1 Asturias, N Spain
Preny see Prienai
Prenzlau 72 D3 Brandenburg, NE Germany
Prerau see Přerov
Přerov 77 C5 Ger. Prerau. Olomoucký Kraj, E Czech Republic
Preschau see Prešov
Prescott 26 B2 Arizona, SW USA
Preševo 79 D5 Serbia, SE Serbia
Presidente Epitácio 41 E4 São Paulo, S Brazil
Presidente Stroessner see Ciudad del Este
Prešov 77 D5 var. Preschau, Ger. Eperies, Hung. Eperjes. Prešovský Kraj, E Slovakia
Prespa, Lake 79 D6 Alb. Liqen i Prespës, Gk. Límni Megáli Préspa, Limni Prespa, Mac. Prespansko Ezero, Serb. Prespansko Jezero. lake SE Europe
Prespa, Limni/Prespansko Ezero/Prespansko Jezero/Prespës, Liqen i see Prespa, Lake
Presque Isle 19 H1 Maine, NE USA
Pressburg see Bratislava
Preston 67 D5 NW England, United Kingdom
Prestwick 66 C4 W Scotland, United Kingdom
Pretoria 56 D4 see also Tshwane; var. Epitoli. country capital (South Africa-administrative capital) Gauteng, NE South Africa
Preussisch Eylau see Bagrationovsk
Preußisch Holland see Pasłęk
Preussisch-Stargard see Starogard Gdański
Préveza 83 A5 Ípeiros, W Greece
Pribilof Islands 14 A3 island group Alaska, USA
Priboj 78 C4 Serbia, W Serbia
Price 22 B4 Utah, W USA
Prichard 20 C3 Alabama, S USA
Priekulė 84 B3 Ger. Prökuls. Klaipėda, W Lithuania
Prienai 85 B5 Pol. Preny. Kaunas, S Lithuania
Prieska 56 C4 Northern Cape, C South Africa
Prijedor 78 B3 Republika Srpska, NW Bosnia and Herzegovina
Prijepolje 78 D4 Serbia, W Serbia
Prikaspiyskaya Nizmennost' see Caspian Depression
Prilep 79 D6 Turk. Perlepe. S FYR Macedonia
Priluki see Pryluky
Primorsk 84 A4 Ger. Fischhausen. Kaliningradskaya Oblast', W Russian Federation
Primorsko 82 E2 prev. Keupriya. Burgas, E Bulgaria
Primorsk/Primorskoye see Prymors'k
Prince Albert 15 F5 Saskatchewan, S Canada
Prince Edward Island 17 F4 Fr. Île-du Prince-Édouard. province SE Canada
Prince Edward Islands 47 E8 island group S South Africa
Prince George 15 E5 British Columbia, SW Canada
Prince of Wales Island 126 B1 island Queensland, E Australia
Prince of Wales Island 15 F2 island Queen Elizabeth Islands, Nunavut, NW Canada
Prince of Wales Island see Pinang, Pulau
Prince Patrick Island 15 E2 island Parry Islands, Northwest Territories, NW Canada
Prince Rupert 14 D4 British Columbia, SW Canada
Prince's Island see Príncipe
Princess Charlotte Bay 126 C2 bay Queensland, NE Australia
Princess Elizabeth Land 132 C3 physical region Antarctica
Príncipe 55 A5 var. Príncipe Island, Eng. Prince's Island. island N Sao Tome and Principe
Príncipe Island see Príncipe
Prinzapolka 31 E3 Región Autónoma Atlántico Norte, NE Nicaragua
Pripet 85 C7 Bel. Prypyats', Ukr. Pryp"yat'. river Belarus/Ukraine
Pripet Marshes 85 B7 wetland Belarus/Ukraine
Prishtinë 79 D5 Eng. Pristina, Serb. Priština. C Kosovo
Pristina see Prishtinë
Priština see Prishtinë
Privas 69 D5 Ardèche, E France
Privolzhskaya Vozvyshennost' 59 G3 var. Volga Uplands. mountain range W Russian Federation
Prizren 79 D5 S Kosovo
Probolinggo 116 D5 Jawa, C Indonesia
Probstberg see Wyszków
Progreso 29 H3 Yucatán, SE Mexico
Prokhladnyy 89 B8 Kabardino-Balkarskaya Respublika, SW Russian Federation
Prokletije see North Albanian Alps
Prökuls see Priekulė
Prokuplje 79 D5 Serbia, SE Serbia
Prome see Pyay
Promyshlennyy 88 E3 Respublika Komi, NW Russian Federation
Prościejów see Prostějov
Proskurov see Khmel 'nyts'kyy
Prossnitz see Prostějov
Prostějov 77 C5 Ger. Prossnitz, Pol. Prościejów. Olomoucký Kraj, E Czech Republic
Provence 69 D6 cultural region SE France
Providence 19 G3 state capital Rhode Island, NE USA
Providence see Fort Providence
Providencia, Isla de 31 F3 island NW Colombia, Caribbean Sea
Provideniya 133 B1 Chukotskiy Avtonomnyy Okrug, NE Russian Federation
Provo 22 B4 Utah, W USA
Prudhoe Bay 14 D2 Alaska, USA
Prusa see Bursa
Pruszków 76 D3 Ger. Kaltdorf. Mazowieckie, C Poland
Prut 86 D4 Ger. Pruth. river E Europe
Pruth see Prut
Pružana see Pruzhany
Pruzhany 85 B6 Pol. Prużana. Brestskaya Voblasts', SW Belarus
Prychornomor'ska Nyzovyna see Black Sea Lowland
Prydniprovs'ka Nyzovyna/Prydnyaprowskaya Nizina see Dnieper Lowland
Prydz Bay 132 D3 bay Antarctica
Pryluky 87 E2 Rus. Priluki. Chernihivs'ka Oblast', NE Ukraine
Prymors'k 87 G4 Rus. Primorsk; prev. Primorskoye. Zaporiz'ka Oblast', SE Ukraine
Pryp"yat'/Prypyats' see Pripet
Przemyśl 77 E5 Rus. Peremyshl. Podkarpackie, C Poland
Przheval'sk see Karakol
Psará 83 D5 island E Greece
Psel 87 F2 Rus. Psël. river Russian Federation/ Ukraine
Psël see Psel
Pskov 92 B2 Ger. Pleskau, Latv. Pleskava. Pskovskaya Oblast', W Russian Federation
Pskov, Lake 84 E3 Est. Pihkva Järv, Ger. Pleskauer See, Rus. Pskovskoye Ozero. lake Estonia/ Russian Federation
Pskovskoye Ozero see Pskov, Lake
Ptich' see Ptsich
Ptsich 85 C7 Rus. Ptich'. Homyel'skaya Voblasts', SE Belarus
Ptsich 85 C7 Rus. Ptich'. river SE Belarus
Ptuj 73 E7 Ger. Pettau; anc. Poetovio. NE Slovenia
Pucallpa 38 C3 Ucayali, C Peru
Puck 76 C2 Pomorskie, N Poland
Pudasjärvi 62 D4 Oulu, C Finland
Puebla 29 F4 var. Puebla de Zaragoza. Puebla, S Mexico
Puebla de Zaragoza see Puebla
Pueblo 22 D5 Colorado, C USA
Puerto Acosta 39 E4 La Paz, W Bolivia
Puerto Aisén 43 B6 Aisén, S Chile
Puerto Ángel 29 F5 Oaxaca, SE Mexico
Puerto Argentino see Stanley
Puerto Ayacucho 36 D3 Amazonas, SW Venezuela
Puerto Baquerizo Moreno 38 B5 var. Baquerizo Moreno. Galapagos Islands, Ecuador, E Pacific Ocean
Puerto Barrios 30 C2 Izabal, E Guatemala
Puerto Bello see Portobelo
Puerto Berrío 36 B2 Antioquia, C Colombia
Puerto Cabello 36 D1 Carabobo, N Venezuela
Puerto Cabezas 31 E2 var. Bilwi. Región Autónoma Atlántico Norte, NE Nicaragua
Puerto Carreño 36 D3 Vichada, E Colombia
Puerto Cortés 30 C2 Cortés, NW Honduras
Puerto Cumarebo 36 C1 Falcón, N Venezuela
Puerto Deseado 43 C7 Santa Cruz, SE Argentina
Puerto Escondido 29 F5 Oaxaca, SE Mexico
Puerto Gallegos see Río Gallegos
Puerto Inírida 36 D3 var. Obando. Guainía, E Colombia
Puerto La Cruz 37 E1 Anzoátegui, NE Venezuela
Puerto Lempira 31 E2 Gracias a Dios, E Honduras
Puerto Limón see Limón
Puertollano 70 D4 Castilla-La Mancha, C Spain
Puerto López 36 C1 La Guajira, N Colombia
Puerto Maldonado 39 E3 Madre de Dios, E Peru
Puerto México see Coatzacoalcos
Puerto Montt 43 B5 Los Lagos, C Chile
Puerto Natales 43 B7 Magallanes, S Chile
Puerto Obaldía 31 H5 Kuna Yala, NE Panama
Puerto Plata 33 E3 var. San Felipe de Puerto Plata. N Dominican Republic
Puerto Presidente Stroessner see Ciudad del Este
Puerto Princesa 117 E2 off. Puerto Princesa City. Palawan, W Philippines
Puerto Princesa City see Puerto Princesa
Puerto Príncipe see Camagüey
Puerto Rico 33 F3 off. Commonwealth of Puerto Rico; prev. Porto Rico. US commonwealth territory C West Indies
Puerto Rico 34 B1 island C West Indies
Puerto Rico, Commonwealth of see Puerto Rico
Puerto Rico Trench 34 B1 trench NE Caribbean Sea
Puerto San José see San José
Puerto San Julián 43 B7 var. San Julián. Santa Cruz, SE Argentina
Puerto Suárez 39 H4 Santa Cruz, E Bolivia
Puerto Vallarta 28 D4 Jalisco, SW Mexico
Puerto Varas 43 B5 Los Lagos, C Chile
Puerto Viejo 31 E4 Heredia, NE Costa Rica
Puertoviejo see Portoviejo
Puget Sound 24 B1 sound Washington, NW USA
Puglia 75 E5 var. Le Puglie, Eng. Apulia. region SE Italy
Pukaki, Lake 129 B6 lake South Island, New Zealand
Pukekohe 128 D3 Auckland, North Island, New Zealand
Puket see Phuket
Pukhavichy 85 C6 Rus. Pukhovichi. Minskaya Voblasts', C Belarus
Pukhovichi see Pukhavichy
Pula 78 A3 It. Pola; prev. Pulj. Istra, NW Croatia
Pulaski 18 D5 Virginia, NE USA
Puławy 76 D4 Ger. Neu Amerika. Lubelskie, E Poland
Pul-i-Khumri see Pol-e Khomrī
Pulj see Pula
Pullman 24 C2 Washington, NW USA
Pułtusk 76 D3 Mazowieckie, C Poland
Puná, Isla 38 A2 island SW Ecuador
Pune 112 C5 prev. Poona. Mahārāshtra, W India
Punjab 112 C2 prev. West Punjab, Western Punjab. province E Pakistan
Puno 39 E4 Puno, SE Peru
Punta Alta 43 C5 Buenos Aires, E Argentina
Punta Arenas 43 B8 prev. Magallanes. Magallanes, S Chile
Punta Gorda 30 C2 Toledo, SE Belize
Punta Gorda 31 E4 Región Autónoma Atlántico Sur, SE Nicaragua
Puntarenas 30 D4 Puntarenas, W Costa Rica
Punto Fijo 36 C1 Falcón, N Venezuela
Pupuya, Nevado 39 E4 mountain W Bolivia
Puri 113 F5 var. Jagannath. Orissa, E India
Puriramya see Buriram
Purmerend 64 C3 Noord-Holland, C Netherlands
Pursat see Poŭthĭsăt, Poŭthĭsăt, W Cambodia
Purus, Rio 40 C2 var. Río Purús. river Brazil/Peru
Pusan 107 E4 off. Pusan-gwangyŏksi, var. Busan, Jap. Fusan. SE South Korea
Pusan-gwangyŏksi see Pusan
Pushkino see Biläsuvar
Püspökladány 77 D6 Hajdú-Bihar, E Hungary
Putorana, Gory/Putorana Mountains see Putorana, Plato
Putorana Mountains 93 E3 var. Gory Putorana, Eng. Putorana Mountains. mountain range N Russian Federation
Putrajaya 116 B3 country capital (Malaysia) Kuala Lumpur, Peninsular Malaysia
Puttalam 110 C3 North Western Province, W Sri Lanka
Puttgarden 72 C2 Schleswig-Holstein, N Germany
Putumayo, Río 36 B5 var. Içá, Rio. river NW South America
Puurmani 84 D2 Ger. Talkhof. Jõgevamaa, E Estonia
Pyatigorsk 89 B7 Stavropol'skiy Kray, SW Russian Federation
Pyatikhatki see P"yatykhatky
P"yatykhatky 87 F3 Rus. Pyatikhatki. Dnipropetrovs'ka Oblast', E Ukraine
Pyay 114 B4 var. Prome, Pye. Bago, C Myanmar (Burma)
Pye see Pyay
Pyetrykaw 85 C7 Rus. Petrikov. Homyel'skaya Voblasts', SE Belarus
Pyinmana 114 B4 country capital (Myanmar (Burma)) Mandalay, C Myanmar (Burma)
Pyin-Oo-Lwin 114 B3 var. Maymyo. Mandalay, C Myanmar (Burma)
Pýlos 83 B6 var. Pilos. Pelopónnisos, S Greece
P'yŏngyang 107 E3 var. P'yŏngyang-si, Eng. Pyongyang. country capital (North Korea) SW North Korea
P'yŏngyang-si see P'yŏngyang
Pyramid Lake 25 C5 lake Nevada, W USA
Pyrenaei Montes see Pyrenees
Pyrenees 80 B2 Fr. Pyrénées, Sp. Pirineos; anc. Pyrenaei Montes. mountain range SW Europe
Pýrgos 83 B6 var. Pírgos. Dytikí Elláts, S Greece
Pyritz see Pyrzyce
Pyryatyn 87 E2 Rus. Piryatin. Poltavs'ka Oblast', NE Ukraine
Pyrzyce 76 B3 Ger. Pyritz. Zachodnio-pomorskie, NW Poland
Pyu see Phyu
Pyuntaza 114 B4 Bago, SW Myanmar (Burma)

Q

Qā' al Jafr 97 C7 lake S Jordan
Qaanaaq 60 D1 var. Qânâq, Dan. Thule. Avannaarsua, N Greenland
Qabātiya 97 E6 N West Bank Asia
Qābis see Gabès
Qābis, Khalīj see Gabès, Golfe de
Qacentina see Constantine
Qafṣah see Gafsa
Qagan Us see Dulan
Qahremānshahr see Kermānshāh
Qaidam Pendi 104 C4 basin C China
Qal'aikhum 101 F3 Rus. Kalaikhum. S Tajikistan
Qalāt 101 E5 Per. Kalāt. Zābol, S Afghanistan
Qal'at Bīshah 99 B5 'Asīr, SW Saudi Arabia
Qalqiliya see Qalqīlya
Qalqīlya 97 D6 var. Qalqiliya. Central, W West Bank Asia
Qamdo 104 D5 Xizang Zizhiqu, W China
Qamishly see Al Qāmishlī
Qânâq see Qaanaaq
Qaqortoq 60 C4 Dan. Julianehåb. Kitaa, S Greenland
Qaraghandy/Qaraghandy Oblysy see Karaganda
Qara Qum see Garagum
Qarataū see Karatau, Zhambyl, Kazakhstan
Qarkilik see Ruoqiang
Qarokŭl 101 F3 Rus. Karakul'. E Tajikistan
Qarqannah, Juzur see Kerkenah, Îles de
Qars see Kars
Qarshi 101 E3 Rus. Karshi; prev. Bek-Budi. Qashqadaryo Viloyati, S Uzbekistan
Qasigianguit see Qasigiannguit
Qasigiannguit 60 C3 var. Qasigianguit, Dan. Christianshåb. Kitaa, C Greenland
Qaṣr al Farāfirah 50 B2 var. Qasr Farâfra. W Egypt
Qasr Farâfra see Qaṣr al Farāfirah
Qaṭanā 97 B5 var. Katana. Dimashq, S Syria
Qatar 98 C4 off. State of Qatar, Ar. Dawlat Qaṭar. country SW Asia
Qatar, State of see Qatar
Qattara Depression see Qaṭṭārah, Munkhafaḍ al
Qaṭṭâra, Monkhafad el see Qaṭṭārah, Munkhafaḍ al
Qaṭṭārah, Munkhafaḍ al 50 A1 var. Monkhafad el Qaṭṭâra, Eng. Qattara Depression. desert NW Egypt
Qausuittuq see Resolute
Qazaqstan/Qazaqstan Respublikasy see Kazakhstan
Qazimämmäd 95 H3 Rus. Kazi Magomed. SE Azerbaijan
Qazris see Cáceres
Qazvīn 98 C2 var. Kazvin. Qazvīn, N Iran
Qena see Qinā
Qeqertarssuaq see Qeqertarsuaq
Qeqertarsuaq 60 C3 var. Qeqertarssuaq, Dan. Godhavn. Kitaa, S Greenland
Qeqertarsuaq 60 C3 island W Greenland
Qeqertarsuup Tunua 60 C3 Dan. Disko Bugt. inlet W Greenland
Qerveh see Qorveh
Qeshm 98 D4 var. Jazīreh-ye Qeshm, Qeshm Island. island S Iran
Qeshm Island/Qeshm, Jazīreh-ye see Qeshm
Qilian Shan 104 D3 var. Kilien Mountains. mountain range N China
Qimusseriarsuaq 60 C2 Dan. Melville Bugt, Eng. Melville Bay. bay NW Greenland
Qinā 50 B2 var. Qena; anc. Caene, Caenepolis. E Egypt
Qing see Qinghai
Qingdao 106 D4 var. Ching-Tao, Ch'ing-tao, Tsingtao, Tsintao, Ger. Tsingtau. Shandong, E China
Qinghai 104 C4 var. Chinghai, Koko Nor, Qing, Qinghai Sheng, Tsinghai. province C China
Qinghai Hu 104 D4 var. Ch'ing Hai, Tsing Hai, Mong. Koko Nor. lake C China
Qinghai Sheng see Qinghai
Qingzang Gaoyuan 104 B4 var. Xizang Gaoyuan, Eng. Plateau of Tibet. plateau W China
Qinhuangdao 106 D3 Hebei, E China
Qinzhou 106 B6 Guangxi Zhuangzu Zizhiqu, S China
Qiong see Hainan
Qiqihar 106 D2 var. Ch'i-ch'i-ha-erh, Tsitsihar; prev. Lungkiang. Heilongjiang, NE China
Qira 104 B4 Xinjiang Uygur Zizhiqu, NW China
Qita Ghazzah see Gaza Strip
Qitai 104 C3 Xinjiang Uygur Zizhiqu, NW China
Qīzān see Jīzān
Qizil Orda see Kzylorda
Qizil Qum/Qizilqum see Kyzyl Kum
Qizilrabot 101 G3 Rus. Kyzylrabot. SE Tajikistan
Qogir Feng see K2
Qom 98 C3 var. Kum, Qum. Qom, N Iran
Qomolangma Feng see Everest, Mount
Qomul see Hami
Qo'qon 101 F2 var. Khokand, Rus. Kokand. Farg'ona Viloyati, E Uzbekistan
Qorveh 98 C3 var. Qerveh, Qurveh. Kordestān, W Iran
Qostanay/Qostanay Oblysy see Kostanay
Qoubaïyât 96 B4 var. Al Qubayyāt. N Lebanon
Qoussantîna see Constantine
Quang Ngai 115 E5 var. Quangngai, Quang Nghia. Quang Ngai, C Vietnam
Quangngai see Quang Ngai
Quang Nghia see Quang Ngai
Quan Long see Ca Mau
Quanzhou 106 D6 var. Ch'uan-chou, Tsinkiang; prev. Chin-chiang. Fujian, SE China
Quanzhou 106 C6 Guangxi Zhuangzu Zizhiqu, S China
Qu'Appelle 15 F5 river Saskatchewan, S Canada
Quarles, Pegunungan 117 E4 mountain range Sulawesi, C Indonesia
Quarnero see Kvarner
Quartu Sant' Elena 75 A6 Sardegna, Italy, C Mediterranean Sea
Quba 95 H2 Rus. Kuba. N Azerbaijan
Qubba see Ba'qūbah
Québec 17 E4 var. Quebec. province capital Québec, SE Canada
Québec 16 D3 var. Quebec. province SE Canada
Queen Charlotte Islands 14 C5 Fr. Îles de la Reine-Charlotte. island group British Columbia, SW Canada
Queen Charlotte Sound 14 C5 sea area British Columbia, W Canada
Queen Elizabeth Islands 15 E1 Fr. Îles de la Reine-Élisabeth. island group Nunavut, N Canada
Queensland 126 B4 state N Australia
Queenstown 129 B7 Otago, South Island, New Zealand
Queenstown 56 D5 Eastern Cape, S South Africa
Quelimane 57 E3 var. Kilimane, Kilmain, Quilimane. Zambézia, NE Mozambique
Quelpart see Cheju-do
Quepos 31 E4 Puntarenas, S Costa Rica
Que Que see Kwekwe
Quera see Chur
Querétaro 29 E4 Querétaro de Arteaga, C Mexico
Quesada 31 E4 var. Ciudad Quesada, San Carlos. Alajuela, N Costa Rica
Quetta 112 B2 Baluchistān, SW Pakistan
Quetzalcoalco see Coatzacoalcos

Rottweil – San Juan Bautista

Rottweil *73 B6* Baden-Württemberg, S Germany
Rotuma *123 E4 island* NW Fiji Oceania S Pacific Ocean
Roubaix *68 C2* Nord, N France
Rouen *68 C3 anc.* Rotomagus. Seine-Maritime, N France
Roulers *see* Roeselare
Roumania *see* Romania
Round Rock *27 G3* Texas, SW USA
Rourkela *see* Rāulakela
Rousselaere *see* Roeselare
Roussillon *69 C6 cultural region* S France
Rouyn-Noranda *16 D4* Québec, SE Canada
Rovaniemi *62 D3* Lappi, N Finland
Rovigno *see* Rovinj
Rovigo *74 C2* Veneto, NE Italy
Rovinj *78 A3 It.* Rovigno. Istra, NW Croatia
Rovno *see* Rivne
Rovuma, Rio *57 F2 var.* Ruvuma. *river* Mozambique/Tanzania
Rovuma, Rio *see* Ruvuma
Równe *see* Rivne
Roxas City *117 E2* Panay Island, C Philippines
Royale, Isle *18 B1 island* Michigan, N USA
Royan *69 B5* Charente-Maritime, W France
Rozdol'ne *87 F4 Rus.* Razdolnoye. Respublika Krym, S Ukraine
Rožňava *77 D6 Ger.* Rosenau, *Hung.* Rozsnyó. Košický Kraj, E Slovakia
Rózsahegy *see* Ružomberok
Rozsnyó *see* Râşnov, Romania
Rozsnyó *see* Rožňava, Slovakia
Ruanda *see* Rwanda
Ruapehu, Mount *128 D4 volcano* North Island, New Zealand
Ruapuke Island *129 B8 island* SW New Zealand
Ruatoria *128 E3* Gisborne, North Island, New Zealand
Ruawai *128 D2* Northland, North Island, New Zealand
Rubezhnoye *see* Rubizhne
Rubizhne *87 H3 Rus.* Rubezhnoye. Luhans'ka Oblast', E Ukraine
Ruby Mountains *25 D5 mountain range* Nevada, W USA
Rucava *84 B3* Liepāja, SW Latvia
Rudensk *see* Rudzyensk
Rūdiškės *85 B5* Vilnius, S Lithuania
Rudnik *82 E2* Varna, E Bulgaria
Rudny *see* Rudnyy
Rudnyy *92 C4 var.* Rudny. Kostanay, N Kazakhstan
Rudolf, Lake *see* Turkana, Lake
Rudolfswert *see* Novo mesto
Rudzyensk *85 C6 Rus.* Rudensk. Minskaya Voblasts', C Belarus
Rufiji *51 C7 river* E Tanzania
Rufino *42 C4* Santa Fe, C Argentina
Rugāji *84 D4* Balvi, E Latvia
Rügen *72 D2 headland* NE Germany
Ruggell *72 E1* N Liechtenstein Europe
Ruhja *see* Rūjiena
Ruhnu *84 C2 var.* Ruhnu Saar, *Swe.* Runö. *island* SW Estonia
Ruhnu Saar *see* Ruhnu
Rujen *see* Rūjiena
Rūjiena *84 D3 Est.* Ruhja, *Ger.* Rujen. Valmiera, N Latvia
Rukwa, Lake *51 B7 lake* SE Tanzania
Rum *see* Rhum
Ruma *78 D3* Vojvodina, N Serbia
Rumadiya *see* Ar Ramādī
Rumania/Rumänien *see* Romania
Rumbek *51 B5* El Buhayrat, C South Sudan
Rum Cay *32 D2 island* C Bahamas
Rumia *76 C2* Pomorskie, N Poland
Rummah, Wādī ar *see* Rimah, Wādī ar
Rummelsburg in Pommern *see* Miastko
Rumuniya/Rumŭniya/Rumunjska *see* Romania
Runanga *129 B5* West Coast, South Island, New Zealand
Rundu *56 C3 var.* Runtu. Okavango, NE Namibia
Runö *see* Ruhnu
Runtu *see* Rundu
Ruoqiang *104 C3 var.* Jo-ch'iang, *Uigh.* Charkhlik, Charkhliq, Qarkilik. Xinjiang Uygur Zizhiqu, NW China
Rupea *86 C4 Ger.* Reps, *Hung.* Kőhalom; *prev.* Cohalm. Braşov, C Romania
Rupel *65 B5 river* N Belgium
Rupella *see* la Rochelle
Rupert, Rivière de *16 D3 river* Québec, C Canada
Rusaddir *see* Melilla
Ruschuk/Rusçuk *see* Ruse
Ruse *82 D1 var.* Ruschuk, Rustchuk, *Turk.* Rusçuk. Ruse, N Bulgaria
Rusaddir *see* Melilla
Russellville *20 A1* Arkansas, C USA
Russia *see* Russian Federation
Russian America *see* Alaska
Russian Federation *90 D2 off.* Russian Federation, *var.* Russia, *Latv.* Krievija, *Rus.* Rossiyskaya Federatsiya. *country* Asia/Europe
Rustaq *see* Ar Rustāq
Rust'avi *95 G2* SE Georgia
Rustchuk *see* Ruse
Ruston *20 B2* Louisiana, S USA
Rutanzige, Lake *see* Edward, Lake
Rutba *see* Ar Ruṭbah
Rutlam *see* Ratlām
Rutland *19 F2* Vermont, NE USA
Rutog *104 A4 var.* Rutög, Rutok. Xizang Zizhiqu, W China
Rutok *see* Rutog
Ruvuma *see* Rovuma, Rio
Ruwenzori *55 E5 mountain range* Dem. Rep. Congo/Uganda
Ruzhany *85 B6* Brestskaya Voblasts', SW Belarus
Ružomberok *77 C5 Ger.* Rosenberg, *Hung.* Rózsahegy. Žilinský Kraj, N Slovakia
Rwanda *51 B6 off.* Rwandese Republic; *prev.* Ruanda. *country* C Africa
Rwandese Republic *see* Rwanda
Ryazan' *89 B5* Ryazanskaya Oblast', W Russian Federation
Rybach'ye *see* Balykchy
Rybinsk *88 B4 prev.* Andropov. Yaroslavskaya Oblast', W Russian Federation
Rybnik *77 C5* Śląskie, S Poland
Rybnitsa *see* Rîbniţa
Ryde *126 E1* United Kingdom
Ryki *76 D4* Lubelskie, E Poland
Rykovo *see* Yenakiyeve
Rypin *76 C3* Kujawsko-pomorskie, C Poland
Ryssel *see* Lille
Rysy *77 C5 mountain* S Poland
Ryukyu Islands *see* Nansei-shotō
Ryukyu Trench *103 F3 var.* Nansei Syotō Trench. *trench* S East China Sea
Rzeszów *77 E5* Podkarpackie, SE Poland
Rzhev *88 B4* Tverskaya Oblast', W Russian Federation

S

Saale *72 C4 river* C Germany
Saalfeld *73 C5 var.* Saalfeld an der Saale. Thüringen, C Germany
Saalfeld an der Saale *see* Saalfeld
Saarbrücken *73 A6 Fr.* Sarrebruck. Saarland, SW Germany
Sääre *84 C2 var.* Sjar. Saaremaa, W Estonia
Saare *see* Saaremaa
Saaremaa *84 C2 Ger.* Oesel, Ösel; *prev.* Saare. *island* W Estonia
Saariselkä *62 D2 Lapp.* Suoločielgi. Lappi, N Finland
Sab' Ābār *96 C4 var.* Sab'a Biyar, Sa'b Bi'ār. Ḥimṣ, C Syria
Sab'a Biyar *see* Sab' Ābār
Šabac *78 D3* Serbia, W Serbia
Sabadell *71 G2* Cataluña, E Spain
Sabah *116 D3 prev.* British North Borneo, North Borneo. *state* East Malaysia
Sabanalarga *36 B1* Atlántico, N Colombia
Sabaneta *36 C1* Falcón, N Venezuela
Sabaria *see* Szombathely
Sab'atayn, Ramlat as *99 C6 desert* C Yemen
Sabaya *39 F4* Oruro, S Bolivia
Sa'b Bi'ār *see* Sab' Ābār
Saberi, Hamun-e *100 C5 var.* Daryācheh-ye Hāmun, Daryācheh-ye Sīstān. *lake* Afghanistan/Iran
Sabhā *49 F3* C Libya
Sabi *see* Save
Sabinas *29 E2* Coahuila, NE Mexico
Sabinas Hidalgo *29 E2* Nuevo León, NE Mexico
Sabine River *27 H3 river* Louisiana/Texas, SW USA
Sabkha *see* As Sabkhah
Sable, Cape *21 E5 headland* Florida, SE USA
Sable Island *17 G4 island* Nova Scotia, SE Canada
Ṣabyā *99 B6* Jīzān, SW Saudi Arabia
Sabzawar *see* Sabzevār
Sabzevār *98 D2 var.* Sabzawar. Khorāsān-Razavī, NE Iran
Sachsen *72 D4 Eng.* Saxony, *Fr.* Saxe. *state* E Germany
Sachs Harbour *15 E2 var.* Ikaahuk. Banks Island, Northwest Territories, N Canada
Sächsisch-Reen/Sächsisch-Regen *see* Reghin
Sacramento *25 B5 state capital* California, W USA
Sacramento Mountains *26 D2 mountain range* New Mexico, SW USA
Sacramento River *25 B5 river* California, W USA
Sacramento Valley *25 B5 valley* California, W USA
Sá da Bandeira *see* Lubango
Ṣa'dah *99 B6* NW Yemen
Sado *109 C5 var.* Sadoga-shima. *island* C Japan
Sadoga-shima *see* Sado
Saena Julia *see* Siena
Safad *see* Tsefat
Ṣafāqis *see* Sfax
Ṣafāshahr *98 D3 var.* Deh Bīd. Fārs, C Iran
Safed *see* Tsefat
Säffle *63 B6* Värmland, C Sweden
Safford *26 C3* Arizona, SW USA
Safi *48 B2* W Morocco
Selseleh-ye Safīd Kuh *100 D4 Eng.* Paropamisus Range. *mountain range* W Afghanistan
Sagaing *114 B3* Sagaing, C Myanmar (Burma)
Sagami-nada *109 D6 inlet* SW Japan
Sagan *see* Żagań
Sāgar *112 D4 prev.* Saugor. Madhya Pradesh, C India
Sagarmāthā *see* Everest, Mount
Sagebrush State *see* Nevada
Saghez *see* Saqqez
Saginaw *18 C3* Michigan, N USA
Saginaw Bay *18 D2 lake bay* Michigan, N USA
Sagua la Grande *32 B2* Villa Clara, C Cuba
Sagunto *71 F3 Cat.* Sagunt, *Ar.* Murviedro; *anc.* Saguntum. País Valenciano, E Spain
Sagunt/Saguntum *see* Sagunto
Sahara *46 B3 desert* Libya/Algeria
Sahara el Gharbiya *see* Ṣaḥrā' al Gharbīyah
Saharan Atlas *see* Atlas Saharien
Sahel *52 D3 physical region* C Africa
Sāḥilīyah, Jibāl as *96 B3 mountain range* NW Syria
Sāhīwāl *112 C2 prev.* Montgomery. Punjab, E Pakistan
Ṣaḥrā' al Gharbīyah *50 B2 var.* Sahara el Gharbîya, *Eng.* Western Desert. *desert* C Egypt
Saïda *97 A5 var.* Ṣaydā, Sayida; *anc.* Sidon. W Lebanon
Sa'īdābād *see* Sīrjān
Saidpur *113 G3 var.* Syedpur. Rajshahi, NW Bangladesh
Saidu Sharif *112 C1 var.* Mingora, Mongora. North-West Frontier Province, N Pakistan
Saigon *see* Hô Chi Minh
Saimaa *63 E5 lake* SE Finland
St Albans *67 E6 anc.* Verulamium. E England, United Kingdom
Saint Albans *18 D5* West Virginia, NE USA
St Andrews *66 C4* E Scotland, United Kingdom
Saint Anna Trough *see* Svyataya Anna Trough
St. Ann's Bay *32 B4* C Jamaica
St. Anthony *17 G3* Newfoundland and Labrador, SE Canada
Saint Augustine *21 E3* Florida, SE USA
St Austell *67 C7* SW England, United Kingdom
St.Botolph's Town *see* Boston
St-Brieuc *68 A3* Côtes d'Armor, NW France
St. Catharines *16 D5* Ontario, S Canada
St-Chamond *69 D5* Loire, E France
Saint Christopher and Nevis, Federation of *see* Saint Kitts and Nevis
Saint Christopher-Nevis *see* Saint Kitts and Nevis
Saint Clair, Lake *18 D3 var.* Lac à L'Eau Claire. *lake* Canada/USA
St-Claude *69 D5 anc.* Condate. Jura, E France
Saint Cloud *23 F2* Minnesota, N USA
Saint Croix *33 F3 island* S Virgin Islands (US)
Saint Croix River *18 A2 river* Minnesota/Wisconsin, N USA
St David's Island *20 B5 island* E Bermuda
St-Denis *57 G4 dependent territory capital* (Réunion) NW Réunion
St-Dié *68 E4* Vosges, NE France
St-Egrève *69 D5* Isère, E France
Sainte Marie, Cap *see* Vohimena, Tanjona
Saintes *69 B5 anc.* Mediolanum. Charente-Maritime, W France
St-Étienne *69 D5* Loire, E France
St-Flour *69 C5* Cantal, C France
St-Gall/Saint Gall/St. Gallen *see* Sankt Gallen
St-Gaudens *69 B6* Haute-Garonne, S France
Saint George *127 D5* Queensland, E Australia
St George *20 B4* N Bermuda
Saint George *22 A5* Utah, W USA
St. George's *33 G5 country capital* (Grenada) SW Grenada
St-Georges *17 E4* Québec, SE Canada
St-Georges *37 H3* E French Guiana
Saint George's Channel *67 B6 channel* Ireland/Wales, United Kingdom
St George's Island *20 B4 island* E Bermuda
Saint Helena *47 B6 UK dependent territory* C Atlantic Ocean
St Helier *67 D8 dependent territory capital* (Jersey) S Jersey, Channel Islands
St.Iago de la Vega *see* Spanish Town
Saint Ignace *18 C2* Michigan, N USA
St-Jean, Lac *17 E4 lake* Québec, SE Canada
Saint Joe River *24 D2 river* Idaho, NW USA North America
St. John *17 F4* New Brunswick, SE Canada
Saint-John *see* Saint John
Saint John River *19 H1 Fr.* Saint-John. *river* Canada/USA
St John's *33 G3 country capital* (Antigua and Barbuda) Antigua, Antigua and Barbuda
St. John's *17 H3 province capital* Newfoundland and Labrador, E Canada
Saint Joseph *23 F4* Missouri, C USA
St Julian's *80 B5* N Malta
St Kilda *66 A3 island* NW Scotland, United Kingdom
Saint Kitts and Nevis *33 F3 off.* Federation of Saint Christopher and Nevis, *var.* Saint Christopher-Nevis. *country* E West Indies
St-Laurent *see* St-Laurent-du-Maroni
St-Laurent-du-Maroni *37 H3 var.* St-Laurent. NW French Guiana
St-Laurent, Fleuve *see* St. Lawrence
St. Lawrence *17 E4 Fr.* Fleuve St-Laurent. *river* Canada/USA
St. Lawrence, Gulf of *17 F3 gulf* NW Atlantic Ocean
Saint Lawrence Island *14 B2 island* Alaska, USA
St-Lô *68 B3 anc.* Briovera, Laudus. Manche, N France
St-Louis *68 E4* Haut-Rhin, NE France
Saint Louis *52 B3* NW Senegal
Saint Louis *23 G4* Missouri, C USA
Saint Lucia *33 E1 country* SE West Indies
Saint Lucia Channel *33 H4 channel* Martinique/Saint Lucia
St-Malo *68 B3* Ille-et-Vilaine, NW France
St-Malo, Golfe de *68 A3 gulf* NW France
Saint Martin *see* Sint Maarten
St.Matthew's Island *see* Zadetkyi Kyun
St.Matthias Group *122 B3 island group* NE Papua New Guinea
St. Moritz *73 B7 Ger.* Sankt Moritz, *Rmsch.* San Murezzan. Graubünden, SE Switzerland
St-Nazaire *68 A4* Loire-Atlantique, NW France
Saint Nicholas *see* São Nicolau
Saint-Nicolas *see* Sint-Niklaas
St-Omer *68 C2* Pas-de-Calais, N France
Saint Paul *23 F2 state capital* Minnesota, N USA
St-Paul, Île *119 C6 var.* St.Paul Island. *island* Île St-Paul, NE French Southern and Antarctic Territories Antarctica Indian Ocea
St.Paul Island *see* St-Paul, Île
St Peter Port *67 D8 dependent territory capital* (Guernsey) C Guernsey, Channel Islands
Saint Petersburg *21 E4* Florida, SE USA
Saint Petersburg *see* Sankt-Peterburg
St-Pierre and Miquelon *17 G4 Fr.* Îles St-Pierre et Miquelon. *French territorial collectivity* NE North America
St-Quentin *68 C3* Aisne, N France
Saint Thomas *see* São Tomé, Sao Tome and Principe
Saint Thomas *see* Charlotte Amalie, Virgin Islands (US)
Saint Ubes *see* Setúbal
Saint Vincent *33 G4 island* N Saint Vincent and the Grenadines
Saint Vincent *see* São Vicente
Saint Vincent and the Grenadines *33 H4 country* SE West Indies
Saint Vincent, Cape *see* São Vicente, Cabo de
Saint Vincent Passage *33 H4 passage* Saint Lucia/Saint Vincent and the Grenadines
Saint Yves *see* Setúbal
Saipan *120 B1 island/country capital* (Northern Mariana Islands) S Northern Mariana Islands
Saishū *see* Cheju-do
Sajama, Nevado *39 F4 mountain* W Bolivia
Sajószentpéter *77 D6* Borsod-Abaúj-Zemplén, NE Hungary
Sakākah *98 B4* Al Jawf, NW Saudi Arabia
Sakakawea, Lake *22 D1 reservoir* North Dakota, N USA
Sak'art'velo *see* Georgia
Sakata *108 D4* Yamagata, Honshū, C Japan
Sakhalin *93 G4 var.* Sakhalin. *island* SE Russian Federation
Sakhalin *see* Sakhalin, Ostrov
Sakhon Nakhon *see* Sakon Nakhon
Şäki *95 G2 Rus.* Sheki; *prev.* Nukha. NW Azerbaijan
Saki *see* Saky
Sakishima-shoto *108 A3 var.* Sakisima Syotô. *island group* SW Japan
Sakisima Syotô *see* Sakishima-shotō
Sakiz *see* Saqqez
Sakiz-Adasi *see* Chíos
Sakon Nakhon *114 D4 var.* Muang Sakon Nakhon, Sakhon Nakhon. Sakon Nakhon, E Thailand
Saky *87 F5 Rus.* Saki. Respublika Krym, S Ukraine
Sal *52 A3 island* Ilhas de Barlavento, NE Cape Verde
Sala *63 C6* Västmanland, C Sweden
Salacgrīva *84 C3 Est.* Salatsi. Limbaži, N Latvia
Sala Consilina *75 D5* Campania, S Italy
Salado, Río *40 D5 river* E Argentina
Salado, Río *42 C3 river* C Argentina
Ṣalālah *99 D6* SW Oman
Salamá *30 B2* Baja Verapaz, C Guatemala
Salamanca *42 B4* Coquimbo, C Chile
Salamanca *70 D2 anc.* Helmantica, Salmantica. Castilla-León, NW Spain
Salamīyah *96 B3 var.* As Salamīyah. Ḥamāh, W Syria
Salang *see* Phuket
Salantai *84 B3* Klaipėda, NW Lithuania
Salatsi *see* Salacgrīva
Salavan *115 D5 var.* Saravan, Saravane. Salavan, S Laos
Salavat *89 D6* Respublika Bashkortostan, W Russian Federation
Sala y Gomez *131 F4 island* Chile, E Pacific Ocean
Sala y Gomez Fracture Zone *see* Sala y Gomez Ridge
Sala y Gomez Ridge *131 G4 var.* Sala y Gomez Fracture Zone. *fracture zone* SE Pacific Ocean
Salazar *see* N'Dalatando
Šalčininkai *85 C5* Vilnius, SE Lithuania
Salduba *see* Zaragoza
Saldus *84 B3 Ger.* Frauenburg. Saldus, W Latvia
Sale *127 C7* Victoria, SE Australia
Salé *48 C2* NW Morocco
Salekhard *92 D3 prev.* Obdorsk. Yamalo-Nenetskiy Avtonomnyy Okrug, N Russian Federation
Salem *110 C2* Tamil Nādu, SE India
Salem *24 B3 state capital* Oregon, NW USA
Salerno *75 D5 anc.* Salernum. Campania, S Italy
Salerno, Gulf of *75 C5 Eng.* Gulf of Salerno. *gulf* S Italy
Salerno, Gulf of *see* Salerno, Golfo di
Salernum *see* Salerno
Salihorsk *85 C7 Rus.* Soligorsk. Minskaya Voblasts', S Belarus
Salima *57 E2* Central, C Malawi
Salina *23 E5* Kansas, C USA
Salina Cruz *29 F5* Oaxaca, SE Mexico
Salinas *38 A2* Guayas, W Ecuador
Salinas *25 B6* California, W USA
Salisbury *67 D7 var.* New Sarum. S England, United Kingdom
Salisbury *see* Harare
Sállan *see* Sørøya
Sallyana *see* Salyān
Salmantica *see* Salamanca
Salmon River *24 D3 river* Idaho, NW USA
Salmon River Mountains *24 D3 mountain range* Idaho, NW USA
Salo *63 D6* Länsi-Suomi, SW Finland
Salon-de-Provence *69 D6* Bouches-du-Rhône, SE France
Salonica/Salonika *see* Thessaloníki
Salonta *86 A3 Hung.* Nagyszalonta. Bihor, W Romania
Sal'sk *89 B7* Rostovskaya Oblast', SW Russian Federation
Salt *see* As Salt
Salta *42 C2* Salta, NW Argentina
Saltash *67 C7* SW England, United Kingdom
Saltillo *29 E3* Coahuila, NE Mexico
Salt Lake City *22 B4 state capital* Utah, W USA
Salto *42 D4* Salto, N Uruguay
Salton Sea *25 D8 lake* California, W USA
Salvador *41 G3 prev.* São Salvador. *state capital* Bahia, E Brazil
Salween *102 C2 Bur.* Thanlwin, *Chin.* Nu Chiang, Nu Jiang. *river* SE Asia
Salyān *113 E3 var.* Sallyana. Mid Western, W Nepal
Salzburg *73 D6 anc.* Juvavum. Salzburg, N Austria
Salzgitter *72 C4 prev.* Watenstedt-Salzgitter. Niedersachsen, C Germany
Salzwedel *72 C3* Sachsen-Anhalt, N Germany
Šamac *see* Bosanski Šamac
Samakhixai *115 E5 var.* Attapu, Attopeu. Attapu, S Laos
Samalayuca *28 C1* Chihuahua, N Mexico
Samar *117 F2 island* C Philippines
Samara *92 B3 prev.* Kuybyshev. Samarskaya Oblast', W Russian Federation
Samarang *see* Semarang
Samarinda *116 D4* Borneo, C Indonesia
Samarkand *see* Samarqand
Samarkandski/Samarkandskoye *see* Temirtau
Samarobriva *see* Amiens
Samarqand *101 E2 Rus.* Samarkand. Samarqand Viloyati, C Uzbekistan
Samawa *see* As Samāwah
Sambalpur *113 F4* Orissa, E India
Sambava *57 G2* Antsiranana, NE Madagascar
Sambir *86 B2 Rus.* Sambor. L'vivs'ka Oblast', NW Ukraine
Sambor *see* Sambir
Sambre *68 D2 river* Belgium/France
Samfya *56 D2* Luapula, N Zambia
Saminatal *72 E2 valley* Austria/Liechtenstein Europe
Samnān *see* Semnān
Sam Neua *see* Xam Nua
Samoa *123 E4 off.* Independent State of Western Samoa, *var.* Sāmoa; *prev.* Western Samoa. *country* W Polynesia
Sāmoa *see* Samoa
Samoa Basin *121 E3 undersea basin* W Pacific Ocean
Samobor *78 A2* Zagreb, N Croatia
Sámos *83 E6 prev.* Limín Vathéos. Sámos, Dodekánisa, Greece, Aegean Sea
Sámos *83 D6 island* Dodekánisa, Greece, Aegean Sea
Samothrace *see* Samothráki
Samothráki *82 D4* Samothráki, NE Greece
Samothraki *82 C4 anc.* Samothrace. *island* NE Greece
Sampit *116 C4* Borneo, C Indonesia
Samsun *94 D2 anc.* Amisus. Samsun, N Turkey
Samtredia *95 F2* W Georgia
Samui, Ko *115 C6 island* SW Thailand
Samut Prakan *115 C5 var.* Muang Samut Prakan, Paknam. Samut Prakan, C Thailand
San *52 D3* Ségou, C Mali
San *77 E5 river* SE Poland
Ṣan'ā' *99 B6 Eng.* Sana. *country capital* (Yemen) W Yemen
Sana *78 B3 river* NW Bosnia and Herzegovina
Sanae *132 B2 South African research station* Antarctica
Sanaga *55 B5 river* C Cameroon
San Ambrosio, Isla *35 A5 Eng.* San Ambrosio Island. *island* W Chile
San Ambrosio Island *see* San Ambrosio, Isla
Sanandaj *98 C3 prev.* Sinneh. Kordestān, W Iran
San Andrés, Isla de *31 F3 island* NW Colombia, Caribbean Sea
San Andrés Tuxtla *29 F4 var.* Tuxtla. Veracruz-Llave, E Mexico
San Angelo *27 F3* Texas, SW USA
San Antonio *30 B2* Toledo, S Belize
San Antonio *42 B4* Valparaíso, C Chile
San Antonio *27 F4* Texas, SW USA
San Antonio Oeste *43 C5* Río Negro, E Argentina
San Antonio River *27 G4 river* Texas, SW USA
Sanāw *99 C6 var.* Sanaw. NE Yemen
San Benedicto, Isla *28 B4 island* W Mexico
San Benito *30 B1* Petén, N Guatemala
San Benito *27 G5* Texas, SW USA
San Bernardino *25 C7* California, W USA
San Blas *28 C3* Sinaloa, C Mexico
San Blas, Cape *20 D3 headland* Florida, SE USA
San Blas, Cordillera de *31 G4 mountain range* NE Panama
San Carlos *30 D4* Río San Juan, S Nicaragua
San Carlos *26 B2* Arizona, SW USA
San Carlos *see* Quesada, Costa Rica
San Carlos de Ancud *see* Ancud
San Carlos de Bariloche *43 B5* Río Negro, SW Argentina
San Carlos del Zulia *36 C2* Zulia, W Venezuela
San Clemente Island *25 B8 island* Channel Islands, California, W USA
San Cristóbal *36 C2* Táchira, W Venezuela
San Cristobal *122 C4 var.* Makira. *island* SE Solomon Islands
San Cristóbal *see* San Cristóbal de Las Casas
San Cristóbal de Las Casas *29 G5 var.* San Cristóbal. Chiapas, SE Mexico
San Cristóbal, Isla *38 B5 var.* Chatham Island. *island* Galapagos Islands, Ecuador, E Pacific Ocean
Sancti Spíritus *32 B2* Sancti Spíritus, C Cuba
Sandakan *116 D3* Sabah, East Malaysia
Sandalwood Island *see* Sumba, Pulau
Sandanski *82 C3 prev.* Sveti Vrach. Blagoevgrad, SW Bulgaria
Sanday *66 D2 island* NE Scotland, United Kingdom
Sanders *26 C2* Arizona, SW USA
Sand Hills *22 D3 mountain range* Nebraska, C USA
San Diego *25 C8* California, W USA
Sandnes *63 A6* Rogaland, S Norway
Sandomierz *76 D4 Rus.* Sandomir. Świętokrzyskie, C Poland
Sandomir *see* Sandomierz
Sandoway *see* Thandwe
Sandpoint *24 C1* Idaho, NW USA
Sand Springs *27 G1* Oklahoma, C USA
Sandusky *18 D3* Ohio, N USA
Sandvika *63 A6* Akershus, S Norway
Sandviken *63 C6* Gävleborg, C Sweden
Sandwich Island *see* Efate
Sandwich Islands *see* Hawaiian Islands
Sandy Bay *71 H5* Saskatchewan, C Canada
Sandy City *22 B4* Utah, W USA
Sandy Lake *16 B3 lake* Ontario, C Canada
San Esteban *30 D2* Olancho, C Honduras
San Eugenio/San Eugenio del Cuareim *see* Artigas
San Felipe *36 D1* Yaracuy, NW Venezuela
San Felipe de Puerto Plata *see* Puerto Plata
San Félix, Isla *35 A5 Eng.* San Felix Island. *island* W Chile
San Felix Island *see* San Félix, Isla
San Fernando *70 C5 prev.* Isla de León. Andalucía, S Spain
San Fernando *33 H5* Trinidad, Trinidad and Tobago
San Fernando *24 D1* California, W USA
San Fernando *36 D2 var.* San Fernando de Apure. Apure, C Venezuela
San Fernando de Apure *see* San Fernando
San Fernando del Valle de Catamarca *42 C3 var.* Catamarca. Catamarca, NW Argentina
San Fernando de Monte Cristi *see* Monte Cristi
San Francisco *25 B6* California, W USA
San Francisco del Oro *28 C2* Chihuahua, N Mexico
San Francisco de Macorís *33 E3* C Dominican Republic
San Fructuoso *see* Tacuarembó
San Gabriel *38 B1* Carchi, N Ecuador
San Gabriel Mountains *24 E1 mountain range* California, USA
Sangihe, Kepulauan *see* Sangir, Kepulauan
Sangir, Kepulauan *117 F3 var.* Kepulauan Sangihe. *island group* N Indonesia
Sāngli *110 B1* Mahārāshtra, W India
Sangmélima *55 B5* Sud, S Cameroon
Sangre de Cristo Mountains *26 D1 mountain range* Colorado/New Mexico, C USA
San Ignacio *30 B1 prev.* Cayo, El Cayo. Cayo, W Belize
San Ignacio *39 F3* Beni, N Bolivia
San Ignacio *28 B2* Baja California Sur, NW Mexico
San Joaquin Valley *25 B7 valley* California, W USA
San Jorge, Golfo *43 C6 var.* Gulf of San Jorge. *gulf* S Argentina
San Jorge, Gulf of *see* San Jorge, Golfo
San José *31 E4 country capital* (Costa Rica) San José, C Costa Rica
San José *39 G3 var.* San José de Chiquitos. Santa Cruz, E Bolivia
San José *30 B3 var.* Puerto San José. Escuintla, S Guatemala
San Jose *25 B6* California, W USA
San José *see* San José del Guaviare, Colombia
San José de Chiquitos *see* San José
San José de Cúcuta *see* Cúcuta
San José del Guaviare *36 C4 var.* San José. Guaviare, S Colombia
San Juan *42 B4* San Juan, W Argentina
San Juan *33 F3 dependent territory capital* (Puerto Rico) NE Puerto Rico
San Juan *see* San Juan de los Morros
San Juan Bautista *42 D3* Misiones, S Paraguay

San Juan Bautista – Sevastopol'

San Juan Bautista see Villahermosa
San Juan Bautista Tuxtepec see Tuxtepec
San Juan de Alicante 71 F4 País Valenciano, E Spain
San Juan del Norte 31 E4 var. Greytown. Río San Juan, SE Nicaragua
San Juan de los Morros 36 D2 var. San Juan. Guárico, N Venezuela
San Juanito, Isla 28 C4 island C Mexico
San Juan Mountains 26 D1 mountain range Colorado, C USA
San Juan, Río 31 E4 river Costa Rica/Nicaragua
San Juan River 26 C1 river Colorado/Utah, W USA
San Julián see Puerto San Julián
Sankt-Bartholomäi see Palamuse
Sankt Gallen 73 B7 var. St. Gallen, Eng. Saint Gall, Fr. St-Gall. Sankt Gallen, NE Switzerland
Sankt-Georgen see Sfântu Gheorghe
Sankt-Jakobi see Pärnu-Jaagupi, Pärnumaa, Estonia
Sankt Martin see Martin
Sankt Moritz see St. Moritz
Sankt-Peterburg 88 B4 prev. Leningrad, Petrograd, Eng. Saint Petersburg, Fin. Pietari. Leningradskaya Oblast', NW Russian Federation
Sankt Pölten 73 E6 Niederösterreich, N Austria
Sankt Veit am Flaum see Rijeka
Sankuru 55 D6 river C Dem. Rep. Congo
Şanlıurfa 95 E4 prev. Sanli Urfa, Urfa; anc. Edessa. şanlıurfa, S Turkey
Sanli Urfa see Şanlıurfa
San Lorenzo 39 G5 Tarija, S Bolivia
San Lorenzo 38 A1 Esmeraldas, N Ecuador
San Lorenzo, Isla 38 C4 island W Peru
Sanlúcar de Barrameda 70 C5 Andalucía, S Spain
San Luis 42 C4 San Luis, C Argentina
San Luis 30 B2 Petén, NE Guatemala
San Luis 28 A1 var. San Luis Río Colorado. Sonora, NW Mexico
San Luis Obispo 25 B7 California, W USA
San Luis Potosí 29 E3 San Luis Potosí, C Mexico
San Luis Río Colorado see San Luis
San Marcos 30 A2 San Marcos, W Guatemala
San Marcos 27 G4 Texas, SW USA
San Marcos de Arica see Arica
San Marino 74 E1 country capital (San Marino) C San Marino
San Marino 74 D1 off. Republic of San Marino. country S Europe
San Marino, Republic of see San Marino
San Martín 132 A2 Argentinian research station Antarctica
San Mateo 37 E2 Anzoátegui, NE Venezuela
San Matías 39 H3 Santa Cruz, E Bolivia
San Matías, Gulf of 43 C5 var. Gulf of San Matías. gulf E Argentina
San Matías, Gulf of see San Matías, Golfo
Sanmenxia 106 C4 var. Shan Xian. Henan, C China
Sânmiclăuş Mare see Sânnicolau Mare
San Miguel 30 C3 San Miguel, SE El Salvador
San Miguel 28 D2 Coahuila, N Mexico
San Miguel de Ibarra see Ibarra
San Miguel de Tucumán 42 C3 var. Tucumán. Tucumán, N Argentina
San Miguelito 31 G4 Panamá, C Panama
San Miguel, Río 39 G3 river E Bolivia
San Murezzan see St. Moritz
Sannār see Sennar
Sânnicolaul-Mare see Sânnicolau Mare
Sânnicolau Mare 86 A4 var. Sânnicolaul-Mare, Hung. Nagyszentmiklós; prev. Sânmiclăuş Mare, Sînnicolau Mare. Timiş, W Romania
Sanok 77 E5 Podkarpackie, SE Poland
San Pablo 39 F5 Potosí, S Bolivia
San Pedro 30 C1 Corozal, NE Belize
San-Pédro 52 D5 S Côte d'Ivoire
San Pedro 28 D3 var. San Pedro de las Colonias. Coahuila, NE Mexico
San Pedro de la Cueva 28 C2 Sonora, NW Mexico
San Pedro de las Colonias see San Pedro
San Pedro de Lloc 38 B3 La Libertad, NW Peru
San Pedro Mártir, Sierra 28 A1 mountain range NW Mexico
San Pedro Sula 30 C2 Cortés, NW Honduras
San Rafael 42 B4 Mendoza, W Argentina
San Rafael Mountains 25 C7 mountain range California, W USA
San Ramón de la Nueva Orán 42 C2 Salta, N Argentina
San Remo 74 A3 Liguria, NW Italy
San Salvador 30 B3 country capital (El Salvador) San Salvador, SW El Salvador
San Salvador 32 D2 prev. Watlings Island. island E Bahamas
San Salvador de Jujuy 42 C2 var. Jujuy. Jujuy, N Argentina
San Salvador, Isla 38 A4 island Ecuador
Sansanné-Mango 53 E4 var. Mango. N Togo
Sansepolcro 74 C3 Toscana, C Italy
San Severo 75 D5 Puglia, SE Italy
Santa Ana 39 F3 Beni, N Bolivia
Santa Ana 30 B3 Santa Ana, NW El Salvador
Santa Ana 24 D2 California, W USA
Santa Ana de Coro see Coro
Santa Ana Mountains 24 E2 mountain range California, W USA
Santa Barbara 28 C2 Chihuahua, N Mexico
Santa Barbara 25 C7 California, W USA
Santa Catalina Island 25 B8 island Channel Islands, California, W USA
Santa Catarina 41 E5 off. Estado de Santa Catarina. region S Brazil
Santa Catarina 41 E5 off. Estado de Santa Catarina. state S Brazil
Santa Catarina, Estado de see Santa Catarina
Santa Clara 32 B2 Villa Clara, C Cuba
Santa Clarita 24 D1 California, USA
Santa Comba 70 B1 Galicia, NW Spain
Santa Cruz 54 E2 São Tomé, S Sao Tome and Principe, Africa
Santa Cruz 25 B6 California, W USA
Santa Cruz 39 G4 department E Bolivia
Santa Cruz Barillas see Barillas
Santa Cruz del Quiché 30 B2 Quiché, W Guatemala
Santa Cruz de Tenerife 48 A3 Tenerife, Islas Canarias, Spain, NE Atlantic Ocean
Santa Cruz, Isla 38 B5 var. Indefatigable Island, Isla Chávez. island Galapagos Islands, Ecuador, E Pacific Ocean
Santa Cruz Islands 122 D3 island group E Solomon Islands
Santa Cruz, Río 43 B7 river S Argentina
Santa Elena 30 B1 Cayo, W Belize
Santa Fe 42 C4 Santa Fe, C Argentina
Santa Fe 26 D1 state capital New Mexico, SW USA
Santa Fe see Bogotá
Santa Fe de Bogotá see Bogotá
Santa Genoveva 28 B3 mountain NW Mexico
Santa Isabel 122 C3 var. Bughotu. island N Solomon Islands
Santa Isabel see Malabo
Santa Lucia Range 25 B7 mountain range California, W USA
Santa Margarita, Isla 28 B3 island NW Mexico
Santa Maria 41 E5 Rio Grande do Sul, S Brazil
Santa Maria 25 B7 California, USA
Santa Maria 70 A5 island Azores, Portugal, NE Atlantic Ocean
Santa María del Buen Aire see Buenos Aires
Santa María, Isla 38 A5 var. Isla Floreana, Charles Island. island Galapagos Islands, Ecuador, E Pacific Ocean
Santa Marta 36 B1 Magdalena, N Colombia
Santa Maura see Lefkáda
Santa Monica 24 D1 California, W USA
Santana 54 E2 São Tomé, C Sao Tome and Principe, Africa
Santander 70 D1 Cantabria, N Spain
Santarém 41 E2 Pará, N Brazil
Santarém 70 B3 anc. Scalabis. Santarém, W Portugal
Santa Rosa 42 C4 La Pampa, C Argentina
Santa Rosa see Santa Rosa de Copán
Santa Rosa de Copán 30 C2 var. Santa Rosa. Copán, W Honduras
Santa Rosa Island 25 B8 island California, W USA
Sant Carles de la Rápida see Sant Carles de la Ràpita
Sant Carles de la Ràpita 71 F3 var. Sant Carles de la Rápida. Cataluña, NE Spain
Santiago 42 B4 var. Gran Santiago. country capital (Chile) Santiago, C Chile
Santiago 33 E3 var. Santiago de los Caballeros. N Dominican Republic
Santiago 31 F5 Veraguas, S Panama
Santiago 70 B1 var. Santiago de Compostela, Eng. Compostella; anc. Campus Stellae. Galicia, NW Spain
Santiago 52 A3 var. São Tiago. island Ilhas de Sotavento, S Cape Verde
Santiago see Santiago de Cuba, Cuba
Santiago de Compostela see Santiago
Santiago de Cuba 32 C3 var. Santiago. Santiago de Cuba, E Cuba
Santiago de Guayaquil see Guayaquil
Santiago del Estero 42 C3 Santiago del Estero, C Argentina
Santiago de los Caballeros see Santiago, Dominican Republic
Santiago de los Caballeros see Ciudad de Guatemala, Guatemala
Santiago Pinotepa Nacional see Pinotepa Nacional
Santiago, Río 38 B2 river N Peru
Santi Quaranta see Sarandë
Santissima Trinidad see Chilung
Sant Julià de Lòria 69 A8 Sant Julià de Lòria, SW Andorra Europe
Santo see Espiritu Santo
Santo Antão 52 A2 island Ilhas de Barlavento, N Cape Verde
Santo António 54 E1 Príncipe, N Sao Tome and Principe, Africa
Santo Domingo 33 D3 prev. Ciudad Trujillo. country capital (Dominican Republic) SE Dominican Republic
Santo Domingo de los Colorados 38 B1 Pichincha, NW Ecuador
Santo Domingo Tehuantepec see Tehuantepec
San Tomé de Guayana see Ciudad Guayana
Santos 41 F4 São Paulo, S Brazil
Santos Plateau 35 D5 undersea plateau SW Atlantic Ocean
Santo Tomé 42 D3 Corrientes, NE Argentina
Santo Tomé de Guayana see Ciudad Guayana
San Valentín, Cerro 43 A6 mountain S Chile
San Vicente 30 C3 San Vicente, C El Salvador
São Francisco, Rio 41 F3 river E Brazil
Sao Hill 51 C7 Iringa, S Tanzania
São João da Madeira 70 B2 Aveiro, N Portugal
São Jorge 70 A5 island Azores, Portugal, NE Atlantic Ocean
São Luís 41 F2 state capital Maranhão, NE Brazil
São Mandol see São Manuel, Rio
São Manuel, Rio 41 E3 var. São Mandol, Teles Pirés. river C Brazil
São Marcos, Baía de 41 F1 bay N Brazil
São Miguel 70 A5 island Azores, Portugal, NE Atlantic Ocean
Saona, Isla 33 E3 island SE Dominican Republic
Saône 69 D5 river E France
São Nicolau 52 A3 Eng. Saint Nicholas. island Ilhas de Barlavento, N Cape Verde
São Paulo 41 E4 state capital São Paulo, S Brazil
São Paulo 41 E4 off. Estado de São Paulo. state S Brazil
São Paulo 41 E4 off. Estado de São Paulo. region S Brazil
São Paulo de Loanda see Luanda
São Paulo, Estado de see São Paulo
São Pedro do Rio Grande do Sul see Rio Grande
São Roque, Cabo de 41 G2 headland E Brazil
São Salvador see Salvador, Brazil
São Salvador/São Salvador do Congo see M'Banza Congo, Angola
São Tiago see Santiago
São Tomé 55 A5 country capital (Sao Tome and Principe) São Tomé, S Sao Tome and Principe
São Tomé 54 E2 Eng. Saint Thomas. island S Sao Tome and Principe
Sao Tome and Principe 54 D1 off. Democratic Republic of Sao Tome and Principe. country E Atlantic Ocean
Sao Tome and Principe, Democratic Republic of see Sao Tome and Principe
São Tomé, Pico de 54 D2 mountain São Tomé, C Sao Tome and Principe, Africa
São Vicente 52 A3 Eng. Saint Vincent. island Ilhas de Barlavento, N Cape Verde
São Vicente, Cabo de 70 B5 Eng. Cape Saint Vincent, Port. Cabode São Vicente. cape S Portugal
São Vicente, Cabo de see São Vicente, Cabo de
Sápai see Sápes
Sapele 53 F5 Delta, S Nigeria
Sápes 82 D3 var. Sápai. Anatolikí Makedonía kai Thráki, NE Greece
Sapir 97 B7 prev. Sappir. Southern, S Israel
Sa Pobla 71 G3 Mallorca, Spain, W Mediterranean Sea
Sappir see Sapir
Sapporo 108 D2 Hokkaidō, NE Japan
Sapri 75 D6 Campania, S Italy
Sapulpa 27 G1 Oklahoma, C USA
Saqqez 98 C2 var. Saghez, Sakiz, Saqqiz. Kordestān, NW Iran
Saqqiz see Saqqez
Sara Buri 115 C5 var. Saraburi. Saraburi, C Thailand
Saraburi see Sara Buri
Saragossa see Zaragoza
Saragt see Sarahs
Saraguro 38 B2 Loja, S Ecuador
Sarahs 100 D3 var. Saragt, Rus. Serakhs. Ahal Welaýaty, S Turkmenistan
Sarajevo 78 C4 country capital (Bosnia and Herzegovina) Federacija Bosna I Hercegovina, SE Bosnia and Herzegovina
Sarakhs 98 E2 Khorāsān-Razavī, NE Iran
Saraktash 89 D6 Orenburgskaya Oblast', W Russian Federation
Saran' 92 C4 Kaz. Saran. Karaganda, C Kazakhstan
Saranda see Sarandë
Sarandë 79 C7 var. Saranda, It. Porto Edda; prev. Santi Quaranta. Vlorë, S Albania
Saransk 89 C5 Respublika Mordoviya, W Russian Federation
Sarasota 21 E4 Florida, SE USA
Saratov 92 B3 Saratovskaya Oblast', W Russian Federation
Saravan/Saravane see Salavan
Sarawak 116 D3 state East Malaysia
Sarawak see Kuching
Sarcelles 68 D1 Val-d'Oise, Île-de-France, N France Europe
Sardegna 75 A5 Eng. Sardinia. island Italy, C Mediterranean Sea
Sardinia see Sardegna
Sarera, Teluk see Cenderawasih, Teluk
Sargasso Sea 44 B4 sea W Atlantic Ocean
Sargodha 112 C2 Punjab, NE Pakistan
Sarh 54 C4 prev. Fort-Archambault. Moyen-Chari, S Chad
Sārī 98 D2 var. Sari, Sāri. Māzandarān, N Iran
Saría 83 E7 island SE Greece
Sarıkamış 95 F3 Kars, NE Turkey
Sarikol Range 101 G3 Rus. Sarykol'skiy Khrebet. mountain range China/Tajikistan
Sark 67 D8 Fr. Sercq. island Channel Islands
Şarkışla 94 D3 Sivas, C Turkey
Sarmiento 43 B6 Chubut, S Argentina
Sarnia 16 C5 Ontario, S Canada
Sarny 86 C1 Rivnens'ka Oblast', NW Ukraine
Sarochyna 85 D5 Rus. Sorochino. Vitsyebskaya Voblasts', N Belarus
Sarov 89 C5 prev. Sarova. Respublika Mordoviya, SW Russian Federation
Sarova see Sarov
Sarpsborg 63 B6 Østfold, S Norway
Sarrebruck see Saarbrücken
Sartène 69 E7 Corse, France, C Mediterranean Sea
Sarthe 68 B4 river N France
Sárti 82 C4 Kentrikí Makedonía, N Greece
Saruhan see Manisa
Saryarqa see Kazakhskiy Melkosopochnik
Sarykol'skiy Khrebet see Sarikol Range
Sary-Tash 101 F2 Oshskaya Oblast', SW Kyrgyzstan
Saryyesik-Atyrau, Peski 101 G1 desert E Kazakhstan
Sasebo 109 A7 Nagasaki, Kyūshū, SW Japan
Saskatchewan 15 F5 province SW Canada
Saskatchewan 15 F5 river Manitoba/ Saskatchewan, C Canada
Saskatoon 15 F5 Saskatchewan, S Canada
Sasovo 89 B5 Ryazanskaya Oblast', W Russian Federation
Sassandra 52 D5 S Côte d'Ivoire
Sassandra 52 D5 var. Ibo, Sassandra Fleuve. river S Côte d'Ivoire
Sassandra Fleuve see Sassandra
Sassari 75 A5 Sardegna, Italy, C Mediterranean Sea
Sassenheim 64 C3 Zuid-Holland, W Netherlands
Sassnitz 72 D2 Mecklenburg-Vorpommern, NE Germany
Sathmar see Satu Mare
Sátoraljaújhely 77 D6 Borsod-Abaúj-Zemplén, NE Hungary
Satpura Range 112 D4 mountain range C India
Satsuma-Sendai see Sendai
Satsunan-shotō 108 A3 island group Nansei-shotō, SW Japan Asia
Sattanen 62 D3 Lappi, NE Finland
Satu Mare 86 B3 Ger. Sathmar, Hung. Szatmárrnémeti. Satu Mare, NW Romania
Sau see Sava
Saudi Arabia 99 B5 off. Kingdom of Saudi Arabia, Al 'Arabīyah as Su'ūdīyah, Ar. Al Mamlakah al 'Arabīyah as Su'ūdīyah. country SW Asia
Saudi Arabia, Kingdom of see Saudi Arabia
Sauer see Sûre
Saugor see Sāgar
Saulkrasti 84 C3 Rīga, C Latvia
Sault Sainte Marie 16 C4 Michigan, N USA
Sault Sainte Marie 18 C1 Michigan, N USA
Sault Ste. Marie 16 C4 Ontario, S Canada
Saumur 68 B4 Maine-et-Loire, NW France
Saurimo 56 C1 Port. Henrique de Carvalho, Vila Henrique de Carvalho. Lunda Sul, NE Angola
Sava 85 E6 Mahilyowskaya Voblasts', E Belarus
Sava 78 B3 Eng. Save, Ger. Sau, Hung. Száva. river SE Europe
Savá 30 D2 Colón, N Honduras
Savai'i 123 E4 island NW Samoa
Savannah 21 E2 Georgia, SE USA
Savannah River 21 E2 river Georgia/South Carolina, SE USA
Savannakhét see Khanthabouli
Savanna-La-Mar 32 A5 W Jamaica
Savaria see SzombathelySave see Sava
Save, Rio 57 E3 var. Sabi. river Mozambique/ Zimbabwe
Saverne 68 E3 var. Zabern; anc. Tres Tabernae. Bas-Rhin, NE France
Savigliano 74 A2 Piemonte, NW Italy
Savigsivik see Savissivik
Savinski see Savinskiy
Savinskiy 88 C3 var. Savinski. Arkhangel'skaya Oblast', NW Russian Federation
Savissivik 60 D1 var. Savigsivik. Avannaarsua, N Greenland
Savoie 69 D5 cultural region E France
Savona 74 A2 Liguria, NW Italy
Savu Sea 117 E5 Ind. Laut Sawu. sea S Indonesia
Sawakin see Suakin
Sawdirī see Sodiri
Sawhāj 50 B2 var. Sawhāj var. Sohâg, Suliag. C Egypt
Sawhāj see Sawhāj
Şawqirah 99 D6 var. Suqrah. S Oman
Sawu, Laut see Savu Sea
Saxe see Sachsen
Saxony see Sachsen
Sayaboury see Xaignabouli
Sayanskiy Khrebet 90 D3 mountain range S Russian Federation
Saýat 100 D3 Rus. Sayat. Lebap Welaýaty, E Turkmenistan
Sayaxché 30 B2 Petén, N Guatemala
Şaydā/Sayida see Saïda
Sayhūt 99 D6 E Yemen
Saynshand 105 E2 Dornogovĭ, SE Mongolia
Sayre 19 E3 Pennsylvania, NE USA
Say'ūn 99 C6 var. Saywūn. C Yemen
Saywūn see Say'ūn
Scalabis see Santarém
Scandinavia 44 D2 geophysical region NW Europe
Scarborough 67 D5 N England, United Kingdom
Scarpanto see Kárpathos
Scebeli see Shebeli
Schaan 72 E1 W Liechtenstein Europe
Schaerbeek 65 C6 Brussels, C Belgium
Schaffhausen 73 B7 Fr. Schaffhouse. Schaffhausen, N Switzerland
Schaffhouse see Schaffhausen
Schagen 64 C2 Noord-Holland, NW Netherlands
Schaulen see Šiauliai
Schebschi Mountains see Shebshi Mountains
Scheessel 72 B3 Niedersachsen, NW Germany
Schefferville 17 E2 Québec, E Canada
Schelde see Scheldt
Scheldt 65 B5 Dut. Schelde, Fr. Escaut. river W Europe
Schell Creek Range 25 D5 mountain range Nevada, W USA
Schenectady 19 F3 New York, NE USA
Schertz 27 G4 Texas, SW USA
Schiermonnikoog 64 D1 Fris. Skiermûntseach. island Waddeneilanden, N Netherlands
Schijndel 64 D4 Noord-Brabant, S Netherlands
Schil see Jiu
Schiltigheim 68 E3 Bas-Rhin, NE France
Schivelbein see Świdwin
Schleswig 72 B2 Schleswig-Holstein, N Germany
Schleswig-Holstein 72 B2 state N Germany
Schlettstadt see Sélestat
Schlochau see Człuchów
Schneekoppe see Sněžka
Schneidemühl see Piła
Schoden see Skuodas
Schönebeck 72 C4 Sachsen-Anhalt, C Germany
Schönlanke see Trzcianka
Schooten see Schoten
Schoten 65 C5 var. Schooten. Antwerpen, N Belgium
Schouwen 64 B4 island SW Netherlands
Schwabenalb see Schwäbische Alb
Schwäbische Alb 73 B6 var. Schwabenalb, Eng. Swabian Jura. mountain range S Germany
Schwandorf 73 C5 Bayern, SE Germany
Schwaz 73 C7 Tirol, W Austria
Schweidnitz see Świdnica
Schweinfurt 73 B5 Bayern, SE Germany
Schweiz see Switzerland
Schwerin 72 C3 Mecklenburg-Vorpommern, N Germany
Schwertberg see Świecie
Schwiebus see Świebodzin
Schwyz 73 B7 var. Schwiz. Schwyz, C Switzerland
Schyl see Jiu
Scio see Chíos
Scoresby Sound/Scoresbysund see Ittoqqortoormiit
Scoresby Sund see Kangertittivaq
Scotia Sea 35 C8 sea SW Atlantic Ocean
Scotland 66 C3 cultural region Scotland, U K
Scott Base 132 B4 NZ research station Antarctica
Scott Island 132 B5 island Antarctica
Scottsbluff 22 D3 Nebraska, C USA
Scottsboro 20 D1 Alabama, S USA
Scottsdale 26 B2 Arizona, SW USA
Scranton 19 F3 Pennsylvania, NE USA
Scrobesbyrig' see Shrewsbury
Scupi see Skopje
Scutari see Shkodër
Scutari, Lake 79 C5 Alb. Liqeni i Shkodrës, SCr. Skadarsko Jezero. lake Albania/Montenegro
Scyros see Skýros
Searcy 20 B1 Arkansas, C USA
Seattle 24 B2 Washington, NW USA
Sébaco 30 D3 Matagalpa, W Nicaragua
Sebaste/Sebastia see Sivas
Sebastían Vizcaíno, Bahía 28 A2 bay NW Mexico
Sebastopol see Sevastopol'
Sebenico see Šibenik
Sechura, Bahía de 38 A3 bay NW Peru
Secunderābād 112 D5 var. Sikandarabad. Andhra Pradesh, C India
Sedan 68 D3 Ardennes, N France
Seddon 129 D5 Marlborough, South Island, New Zealand
Seddonville 129 C5 West Coast, South Island, New Zealand
Sédhiou 52 B3 SW Senegal
Sedlez see Siedlce
Sedona 26 B2 Arizona, SW USA
Sedunum see Sion
Seeland see Sjælland
Seenu Atoll see Addu Atoll
Seesen 72 B4 Niedersachsen, C Germany
Segestica see Sisak
Segezha 88 B3 Respublika Kareliya, NW Russian Federation
Seghedin see Szeged
Segna see Senj
Segodunum see Rodez
Ségou 52 D3 var. Segu. Ségou, C Mali
Segovia 70 D2 Castilla-León, C Spain
Segoviao Wangkí see Coco, Río
Segu see Ségou
Séguédine 53 H2 Agadez, NE Niger
Seguin 27 G4 Texas, SW USA
Segura 71 E4 river S Spain
Seinäjoki 63 D5 Swe. Östermyra. Länsi-Suomi, W Finland
Seine 68 D1 river N France
Seine, Baie de la 68 B3 bay N France
Sekondi see Sekondi-Takoradi
Sekondi-Takoradi 53 E5 var. Sekondi. S Ghana
Selânik see Thessaloníki
Selenga 105 E1 Mong. Selenge Mörön. river Mongolia/Russian Federation
Selenge Mörön see Selenga
Sélestat 68 E4 Ger. Schlettstadt. Bas-Rhin, NE France
Seleucia see Silifke
Selfoss 61 E5 Sudhurland, SW Iceland
Sélibabi 52 C3 var. Sélibaby. Guidimaka, S Mauritania
Sélibaby see Sélibabi
Selma 25 C6 California, W USA
Selway River 24 D2 river Idaho, NW USA North America
Selwyn Range 126 B3 mountain range Queensland, C Australia
Selzaete see Zelzate
Semarang 116 C5 var. Samarang. Jawa, C Indonesia
Sembé 55 B5 Sangha, NW Congo
Semendria see Smederevo
Semey see Semipalatinsk
Semezhevo see Syemyezhava
Seminole 27 E3 Texas, SW USA
Seminole, Lake 20 D3 reservoir Florida/Georgia, SE USA
Semipalatinsk 92 D4 Kaz. Semey. Vostochnyy Kazakhstan, E Kazakhstan
Semnān 98 D3 var. Samnān. Semnān, N Iran
Semois 65 C8 river SE Belgium
Sendai 109 A8 var. Satsuma-Sendai. Kagoshima, Kyūshū, SW Japan
Sendai 108 D4 Miyagi, Honshū, C Japan
Sendai-wan 108 D4 bay E Japan
Senec 77 C6 Ger. Wartberg, Hung. Szenc; prev. Szempcz. Bratislavský Kraj, W Slovakia
Senegal 52 B3 off. Republic of Senegal, Fr. Sénégal. country W Africa
Senegal 52 C3 Fr. Sénégal. river W Africa
Senegal, Republic of see Senegal
Senftenberg 72 D4 Brandenburg, E Germany
Senia see Senj
Senica 77 C6 Ger. Senitz, Hung. Szenice. Trnavský Kraj, W Slovakia
Seniça see Sjenica
Senitz see Senica
Senj 78 A3 Ger. Zengg, It. Segna; anc. Senia. Lika-Senj, NW Croatia
Senja 62 C2 prev. Senjen. island N Norway
Senjen see Senja
Senkaku-shoto 108 A3 island group SW Japan
Senlis 68 C3 Oise, N France
Sennar 50 C4 var. Sannār. Sinnar, C Sudan
Senones see Sens
Sens 68 C3 anc. Agendicum, Senones. Yonne, C France
Sensburg see Mrągowo
Sên, Stœng 115 D5 river C Cambodia
Senta 78 D3 Hung. Zenta. Vojvodina, N Serbia
Seo de Urgel see La See d'Urgel
Seoul see Sŏul
Şepşi-Sângeorz/Sepsiszentgyőrgy see Sfântu Gheorghe
Sept-Îles 17 E3 Québec, SE Canada
Seraing 65 D6 Liège, E Belgium
Serakhs see Sarahs
Seram, Laut see Ceram Sea
Pulau Seram 117 F4 var. Serang, Eng. Ceram. island Maluku, E Indonesia
Serang 116 C5 Jawa, C Indonesia
Serang see Seram, Pulau
Serasan, Selat 116 C3 strait Indonesia/Malaysia
Serbia 78 D4 off. Federal Republic of Serbia; prev. Yugoslavia, SCr. Jugoslavija. country SE Europe
Serbia, Federal Republic of see Serbia
Sercq see Sark
Serdar 100 C2 prev. Rus. Gyzyrlabat, Kizyl-Arvat. Balkan Welaýaty, W Turkmenistan
Serdica see Sofiya
Serdobol' see Sortavala
Serenje 56 D2 Central, E Zambia
Seres see Sérres
Seret/Sereth see Siret
Serhetabat 100 D4 prev. Rus. Gushgy, Kushka. Mary Welaýaty, S Turkmenistan
Sérifos 83 C6 anc. Seriphos. island Kykládes, Greece, Aegean Sea
Seriphos see Sérifos
Serov 92 C3 Sverdlovskaya Oblast', C Russian Federation
Serowe 56 D3 Central, SE Botswana
Serpa Pinto see Menongue
Serpent's Mouth, The 37 F2 Sp. Boca de la Serpiente. strait Trinidad and Tobago/Venezuela
Serpiente, Boca de la see Serpent's Mouth, The
Serpukhov 89 B5 Moskovskaya Oblast', W Russian Federation
Sérrai see Sérres
Serrana, Cayo de 31 F2 island group NW Colombia South America
Serranilla, Cayo de 31 F2 island group NW Colombia South America Caribbean Sea
Serravalle 74 E1 N San Marino
Sérres 82 C3 var. Seres; prev. Sérrai. Kentrikí Makedonía, NE Greece
Sesdlets see Siedlce
Sesto San Giovanni 74 B2 Lombardia, N Italy
Sesvete 78 B2 Zagreb, N Croatia
Setabis see Xàtiva
Sète 69 C6 prev. Cette. Hérault, S France
Setesdal 63 A6 valley S Norway
Sétif 49 E2 var. Stif. N Algeria
Setté Cama 55 A6 Ogooué-Maritime, SW Gabon
Setúbal 70 B4 Eng. Saint Ubes, Saint Yves. Setúbal, W Portugal
Setúbal, Baía de 70 B4 bay W Portugal
Seul, Lac 16 B3 lake Ontario, S Canada
Sevan 95 G2 C Armenia
Sevana Lich 95 G3 Eng. Lake Sevan, Rus. Ozero Sevan. lake E Armenia
Sevan, Lake/Sevan, Ozero see Sevana Lich
Sevastopol' 87 F5 Eng. Sebastopol. Respublika Krym, S Ukraine

Severn – Sohâg

Severn 16 B2 river Ontario, S Canada
Severn 67 D6 Wel. Hafren. river England/Wales, United Kingdom
Severnaya Dvina 88 C4 var. Northern Dvina. river NW Russian Federation
Severnaya Zemlya 93 E2 var. Nicholas II Land. island group N Russian Federation
Severnyy 88 E3 Respublika Komi, NW Russian Federation
Severodonetsk see Syeverodonets'k
Severodvinsk 88 C3 prev. Molotov, Sudostroy. Arkhangel'skaya Oblast', NW Russian Federation
Severomorsk 88 C2 Murmanskaya Oblast', NW Russian Federation
Seversk 92 D4 Tomskaya Oblast', C Russian Federation
Sevier Lake 22 A4 lake Utah, W USA
Sevilla 70 C4 Eng. Seville; anc. Hispalis. Andalucía, SW Spain
Seville see Sevilla
Sevlievo 82 D2 Gabrovo, N Bulgaria
Sevluš/Sevlyush see Vynohradiv
Seward's Folly see Alaska
Seychelles 57 G1 off. Republic of Seychelles. country W Indian Ocean
Seychelles, Republic of see Seychelles
Seydhisfjördhur 61 E5 Austurland, E Iceland
Seýdi 100 D2 Rus. Seydi; prev. Neftezavodsk. Lebap Welaýaty, E Turkmenistan
Seyhan see Adana
Sfákia see Chóra Sfakíon
Sfântu Gheorghe 86 C4 Ger. Sankt-Georgen, Hung. Sepsiszentgyőrgy; prev. Şepşi-Sângeorz, Sfîntu Gheorghe. Covasna, C Romania
Sfax 49 F2 Ar. Şafāqis. E Tunisia
Sfîntu Gheorghe see Sfântu Gheorghe
's-Gravenhage 64 B4 var. Den Haag, Eng. The Hague, Fr. La Haye. country capital (Netherlands-seat of government) Zuid-Holland, W Netherlands
's-Gravenzande 64 B4 Zuid-Holland, W Netherlands
Shaan/Shaanxi Sheng see Shaanxi
Shaanxi 106 B5 var. Shaan, Shaanxi Sheng, Shan-hsi, Shenshi, Shensi. province C China
Shabani see Zvishavane
Shabeelle, Webi see Shebeli
Shache 104 A3 var. Yarkant. Xinjiang Uygur Zizhiqu, NW China
Shacheng see Huailai
Shackleton Ice Shelf 132 D3 ice shelf Antarctica
Shaddādī see Ash Shadādah
Shāhābād see Eslāmābād
Sha Hi see Orūmīyeh, Daryācheh-ye
Shahjahanabad see Delhi
Shahr-e Kord 98 C3 var. Shahr Kord. Chahār Maḩall va Bakhtīārī, C Iran
Shahr Kord see Shahr-e Kord
Shāhrūd 98 D2 prev. Emāmrūd, Emāmshahr. Semnān, N Iran
Shalkar 92 B4 var. Chelkar. Aktyubinsk, W Kazakhstan
Shām, Bādiyat ash see Syrian Desert
Shana see Kuril'sk
Shandī see Shendi
Shandong 106 D4 var. Lu, Shandong Sheng, Shantung. province E China
Shandong Sheng see Shandong
Shanghai 106 D5 var. Shang-hai. Shanghai Shi, E China
Shangrao 106 D5 Jiangxi, S China
Shan-hsi see Shaanxi, China
Shan-hsi see Shanxi, China
Shannon 67 A6 Ir. An tSionainn. river W Ireland
Shan Plateau 114 B3 plateau E Myanmar (Burma)
Shansi see Shanxi
Shantar Islands see Shantarskiye Ostrova
Shantarskiye Ostrova 93 G3 Eng. Shantar Islands. island group E Russian Federation
Shantou 106 D6 var. Shan-t'ou, Swatow. Guangdong, S China
Shan-t'ou see Shantou
Shantung see Shandong
Shanxi 106 C4 var. Jin, Shan-hsi, Shansi, Shanxi Sheng. province C China
Shan Xian see Sanmenxia
Shanxi Sheng see Shanxi
Shaoguan 106 C6 var. Shao-kuan, Cant. Kukong; prev. Ch'u-chiang. Guangdong, S China
Shao-kuan see Shaoguan
Shaqrā' 98 B4 Ar Riyāḑ, C Saudi Arabia
Shaqrā see Shuqrah
Shar 92 D5 var. Charsk. Vostochnyy Kazakhstan, E Kazakhstan
Shari 108 D2 Hokkaidō, NE Japan
Shari see Chari
Sharjah see Ash Shāriqah
Shark Bay 125 A5 bay Western Australia
Sharqī, Al Jabal ash/Sharqi, Jebel esh see Anti-Lebanon
Shashe 56 D3 var. Shashi. river Botswana/ Zimbabwe
Shashi see Shashe
Shatskiy Rise 103 G1 undersea rise N Pacific Ocean
Shawnee 27 G1 Oklahoma, C USA
Shaykh, Jabal ash see Hermon, Mount
Shchadryn 85 D7 Rus. Shchedrin. Homyel'skaya Voblasts', SE Belarus
Shchedrin see Shchadryn
Shcheglovsk see Kemerovo
Shchëkino 89 B5 Tul'skaya Oblast', W Russian Federation
Shchors 87 E1 Chernihivs'ka Oblast', N Ukraine
Shchuchin see Shchuchyn
Shchuchinsk 92 C4 prev. Shchuchye. Akmola, N Kazakhstan
Shchuchye see Shchuchinsk
Shchuchyn 85 B5 Pol. Szczuczyn Nowogródzki, Rus. Shchuchin. Hrodzyenskaya Voblasts', W Belarus
Shebekino 89 A6 Belgorodskaya Oblast', W Russian Federation
Shebelē Wenz, Wabē see Shebeli
Shebeli 51 D5 Amh. Wabē Shebelē Wenz, It. Scebeli, Som. Webi Shabeelle. river Ethiopia/ Somalia
Sheberghān 101 E3 var. Shibarghān, Shiberghan, Shiberghān. Jowzjān, N Afghanistan
Sheboygan 18 B2 Wisconsin, N USA
Shebshi Mountains 54 A4 var. Schebschi Mountains. mountain range E Nigeria
Shechem see Nablus
Shedadi see Ash Shadādah
Sheffield 67 D5 N England, United Kingdom
Shekhem see Nablus
Sheki see Şäki
Shelby 22 B1 Montana, NW USA
Sheldon 23 F3 Iowa, C USA
Shelekhov Gulf see Shelikhova, Zaliv
Shelikhova, Zaliv 93 G2 Eng. Shelekhov Gulf. gulf E Russian Federation
Shendi 50 C4 var. Shandī. River Nile, NE Sudan
Shengking see Liaoning
Shenking see Liaoning
Shenshi/Shensi see Shaanxi
Shenyang 106 D3 Chin. Shen-yang, Eng. Moukden, Mukden; prev. Fengtien. province capital Liaoning, NE China
Shen-yang see Shenyang
Shepetivka 86 D2 Rus. Shepetovka. Khmel'nyts'ka Oblast', NW Ukraine
Shepetovka see Shepetivka
Shepparton 127 C7 Victoria, SE Australia
Sherbrooke 17 E4 Québec, SE Canada
Shereik 50 C3 River Nile, N Sudan
Sheridan 22 C2 Wyoming, C USA
Sherman 27 G2 Texas, SW USA
's-Hertogenbosch 64 C4 Fr. Bois-le-Duc, Ger. Herzogenbusch. Noord-Brabant, S Netherlands
Shetland Islands 66 D1 island group NE Scotland, United Kingdom
Shevchenko see Aktau
Shibarghān see Sheberghān
Shiberghan/Shiberghān see Sheberghān
Shibetsu 108 D2 var. Sibetu. Hokkaidō, NE Japan
Shibh Jazirat Sīnā' see Sinai
Shibushi-wan 109 B8 bay SW Japan
Shigatse see Xigazê
Shih-chia-chuang/Shihmen see Shijiazhuang
Shihezi 104 C2 Xinjiang Uygur Zizhiqu, NW China
Shiichi see Shyichy
Shijiazhuang 106 C4 var. Shih-chia-chuang; prev. Shihmen. province capital Hebei, E China
Shikārpur 112 B3 Sind, S Pakistan
Shikoku 109 C7 var. Sikoku. island SW Japan
Shikoku Basin 103 F2 var. Sikoku Basin. undersea basin N Philippine Sea
Shikotan, Ostrov 108 E2 Jap. Shikotan-tō. island NE Russian Federation
Shikotan-tō see Shikotan, Ostrov
Shilabo 51 D5 Sumalē, E Ethiopia
Shiliguri 113 F3 prev. Siliguri. West Bengal, NE India
Shilka 93 F4 river S Russian Federation
Shillong 113 G3 state capital Meghālaya, NE India
Shimanto see Nakamura
Shimbir Berris see Shimbiris
Shimbiris 50 E4 var. Shimbir Berris. mountain N Somalia
Shimoga 110 C2 Karnātaka, W India
Shimonoseki 109 A7 var. Simonoseki, hist. Akamagaseki, Bakan. Yamaguchi, Honshū, SW Japan
Shinano-gawa 109 C5 var. Sinano Gawa. river Honshū, C Japan
Shīndand 100 D4 Herāt, W Afghanistan
Shingū 109 C6 var. Singû. Wakayama, Honshū, SW Japan
Shinjō 108 D4 var. Sinzyô. Yamagata, Honshū, C Japan
Shinyanga 51 C7 Shinyanga, NW Tanzania
Shiprock 26 C1 New Mexico, SW USA
Shīrāz 98 D4 var. Shīrāz. Fārs, S Iran
Shishchitsy see Shyshchytsy
Shivpuri 112 D3 Madhya Pradesh, C India
Shizugawa 108 D4 Miyagi, Honshū, NE Japan
Shizuoka 109 D6 var. Sizuoka. Shizuoka, Honshū, S Japan
Shklov see Shklow
Shklow 85 D6 Rus. Shklov. Mahilyowskaya Voblasts', E Belarus
Shkodër 79 C5 var. Shkodra, It. Scutari, SCr. Skadar. Shkodër, NW Albania
Shkodra see Shkodër
Shkodrës, Liqeni i see Scutari, Lake
Shkumbinit, Lumi i 79 C6 var. Shkumbi, Shkumbin. river C Albania
Shkumbi/Shkumbin see Shkumbinit, Lumi i
Sholāpur see Solāpur
Shostka 87 F1 Sums'ka Oblast', NE Ukraine
Show Low 26 B2 Arizona, SW USA
Show Me State see Missouri
Shpola 87 E3 Cherkas'ka Oblast', N Ukraine
Shqipëria/Shqipërisë, Republika e see Albania
Shreveport 20 A2 Louisiana, S USA
Shrewsbury 67 D6 hist. Scrobesbyrig'. W England, United Kingdom
Shu 92 C5 Kaz. Shū. Zhambyl, SE Kazakhstan
Shuang-liao see Liaoyuan
Shū, Kazakhstan see Shu
Shumagin Islands 14 B3 island group Alaska, USA
Shumen 82 D2 Shumen, NE Bulgaria
Shumilina 85 E5 Rus. Shumilino. Vitsyebskaya Voblasts', NE Belarus
Shumilino see Shumilina
Shunsen see Ch'unch'ŏn
Shuqrah 99 B7 var. Shaqrā. SW Yemen
Shwebo 114 B3 Sagaing, C Myanmar (Burma)
Shyichy 85 C7 Rus. Shiichi. Homyel'skaya Voblasts', SE Belarus
Shymkent 92 B5 prev. Chimkent. Yuzhnyy Kazakhstan, S Kazakhstan
Shyshchytsy 85 C6 Rus. Shishchitsy. Minskaya Voblasts', C Belarus
Siam see Thailand
Siam, Gulf of see Thailand, Gulf of
Sian see Xi'an
Siang see Brahmaputra
Siangtan see Xiangtan
Šiauliai 84 B4 Ger. Schaulen. Šiauliai, N Lithuania
Siazan' see Siyäzän
Sibay 89 D6 Respublika Bashkortostan, W Russian Federation
Šibenik 78 B4 It. Sebenico. Šibenik-Knin, S Croatia
Siberia 93 E3 var. Siberia. physical region NE Russian Federation
Siberia see Sibir'
Siberoet see Siberut, Pulau
Siberut, Pulau 116 A4 prev. Siberoet. island Kepulauan Mentawai, W Indonesia
Sibi 112 B2 Baluchistān, SW Pakistan
Sibiti 55 B6 Lékoumou, S Congo
Sibiu 86 B4 Ger. Hermannstadt, Hung. Nagyszeben. Sibiu, C Romania
Sibolga 116 B3 Sumatera, W Indonesia
Sibu 116 D3 Sarawak, East Malaysia
Sibut 54 C4 prev. Fort-Sibut. Kémo, S Central African Republic
Sibuyan Sea 117 E2 sea W Pacific Ocean
Sichon 115 C6 var. Ban Sichon, Si Chon. Nakhon Si Thammarat, SW Thailand
Si Chon see Sichon
Sichuan 106 B5 var. Chuan, Sichuan Sheng, Ssu-ch'uan, Szechuan, Szechwan. province C China
Sichuan Pendi 106 B5 basin C China
Sichuan Sheng see Sichuan
Sicilian Channel see Sicily, Strait of
Sicily 75 C7 Eng. Sicily; anc. Trinacria. island Italy, C Mediterranean Sea
Sicily, Strait of 75 B7 var. Sicilian Channel. strait C Mediterranean Sea
Sicuani 39 E4 Cusco, S Peru
Sidári 82 A4 Kérkyra, Iónia Nisiá, Greece, C Mediterranean Sea
Sidas 116 C4 Borneo, C Indonesia
Siderno 75 D7 Calabria, SW Italy
Sidhirókastron see Sidirókastro
Sîdi Barrâni 50 A1 NW Egypt
Sidi Bel Abbès 48 D2 var. Sidi bel Abbès, Sidi-Bel-Abbès. NW Algeria
Sidirókastro 82 C3 prev. Sidhirókastron. Kentrikí Makedonía, NE Greece
Sidley, Mount 132 B4 mountain Antarctica
Sidney 22 D1 Montana, NW USA
Sidney 22 D4 Nebraska, C USA
Sidney 18 C4 Ohio, N USA
Sidon see Saïda
Sidra see Surt
Sidra/Sidra, Gulf of see Surt, Khalīj, N Libya
Siebenbürgen see Transylvania
Siedlce 76 E3 Ger. Sedlez, Rus. Sesdlets. Mazowieckie, C Poland
Siegen 72 B4 Nordrhein-Westfalen, W Germany
Siemiatycze 76 E3 Podlaskie, NE Poland
Siena 74 B3 Fr. Sienne; anc. Saena Julia. Toscana, C Italy
Sienne see Siena
Sieradz 76 C4 Sieradz, C Poland
Sierpc 76 D3 Mazowieckie, C Poland
Sierra Leone 52 C4 off. Republic of Sierra Leone. country W Africa
Sierra Leone Basin 44 C4 undersea basin E Atlantic Ocean
Sierra Leone, Republic of see Sierra Leone
Sierra Leone Ridge see Sierra Leone Rise
Sierra Leone Rise 44 C4 var. Sierra Leone Ridge, Sierra Leone Schwelle. undersea rise E Atlantic Ocean
Sierra Leone Schwelle see Sierra Leone Rise
Sierra Vista 26 B3 Arizona, SW USA
Sífnos 83 C6 anc. Siphnos. island Kykládes, Greece, Aegean Sea
Sigli 116 A3 Sumatera, W Indonesia
Siglufjördhur 61 E4 Nordhurland Vestra, N Iceland
Signal Peak 26 A2 mountain Arizona, SW USA
Signan see Xi'an
Signy 132 A2 UK research station South Orkney Islands, Antarctica
Siguatepeque 30 C2 Comayagua, W Honduras
Siguiri 52 D4 NE Guinea
Sihanoukville see Kâmpóng Saôm
Siilinjärvi 62 E4 Itä-Suomi, C Finland
Siirt 95 F4 var. Sert; anc. Tigranocerta. Siirt, SE Turkey
Sikandarabad see Secunderābād
Sikasso 52 D4 Sikasso, S Mali
Sikeston 23 H5 Missouri, C USA
Sikhote-Alin', Khrebet 93 G4 mountain range SE Russian Federation
Siking see Xi'an
Siklós 77 C7 Baranya, SW Hungary
Sikoku see Shikoku
Sikoku Basin see Shikoku Basin
Šilalė 84 B4 Tauragė, W Lithuania
Silchar 113 G3 Assam, NE India
Silesia 76 B4 physical region SW Poland
Silifke 94 C4 anc. Seleucia. İçel, S Turkey
Siliguri see Shiliguri
Siling Co 104 C5 lake W China
Silinhot see Xilinhot
Silistra 82 E1 var. Silistria; anc. Durostorum. Silistra, NE Bulgaria
Silistria see Silistra
Sillamäe 84 E2 Ger. Sillamäggi. Ida-Virumaa, NE Estonia
Sillamäggi see Sillamäe
Sillein see Žilina
Šilutė 84 B4 Ger. Heydekrug. Klaipėda, W Lithuania
Silvan 95 E4 Dıyarbakır, SE Turkey
Silva Porto see Kuito
Silver State see Colorado
Silver State see Nevada
Simanichy 85 C7 Rus. Simonichi. Homyel'skaya Voblasts', SE Belarus
Simav 94 B3 Kütahya, W Turkey
Simav Çayı 94 A3 river NW Turkey
Simbirsk see Ul'yanovsk
Simeto 75 C7 river Sicilia, Italy, C Mediterranean Sea
Simeulue, Pulau 116 A3 island NW Indonesia
Simferopol' 87 F5 Respublika Krym, S Ukraine
Simitla 82 C3 Blagoevgrad, SW Bulgaria
Şimlăul Silvaniei/Şimleul Silvaniei see Şimleu Silvaniei
Şimleu Silvaniei 86 B3 Hung. Szilágysomlyó; prev. Şimlăul Silvaniei, Şimleul Silvaniei. Sălaj, NW Romania
Simonichi see Simanichy
Simonoseki see Shimonoseki
Simpelveld 65 D6 Limburg, SE Netherlands
Simplon Pass 73 B8 pass S Switzerland
Simpson see Fort Simpson
Simpson Desert 126 B4 desert Northern Territory/ South Australia
Sinai 50 C2 var. Sinai Peninsula, Ar. Shibh Jazirat Sīnā', Sīnā. physical region NE Egypt
Sinaia 86 C4 Prahova, SE Romania
Sinano Gawa see Shinano-gawa
Sinā/Sinai Peninsula see Sinai
Sincelejo 36 B2 Sucre, NW Colombia
Sind 112 B3 var. Sindh. province SE Pakistan
Sindelfingen 73 B6 Baden-Württemberg, SW Germany
Sindh see Sind
Sindi 84 D2 Ger. Zintenhof. Pärnumaa, SW Estonia
Sines 70 B4 Setúbal, S Portugal
Singan see Xi'an
Singapore 116 B3 country capital (Singapore) S Singapore
Singapore 116 A1 off. Republic of Singapore. country SE Asia
Singapore, Republic of see Singapore
Singen 73 B6 Baden-Württemberg, S Germany
Singida 51 C7 Singida, C Tanzania
Singkang 117 E4 Sulawesi, C Indonesia
Singkawang 116 C3 Borneo, C Indonesia
Singora see Songkhla
Singû see Shingū
Sining see Xining
Siniscola 75 A5 Sardegna, Italy, C Mediterranean Sea
Sinj 78 B4 Split-Dalmacija, SE Croatia
Sinkiang/Sinkiang Uighur Autonomous Region see Xinjiang Uygur Zizhiqu
Sinnamarie see Sinnamary
Sinnamary 37 H3 var. Sinnamarie. N French Guiana
Sinneh see Sanandaj
Sînnicolau Mare see Sânnicolau Mare
Sinoe, Lacul see Sinoie, Lacul
Sinoie, Lacul 86 D5 prev. Lacul Sinoe. lagoon SE Romania
Sinop 94 D2 anc. Sinope. Sinop, N Turkey
Sinope see Sinop
Sinsheim 73 B6 Baden-Württemberg, SW Germany
Sint Maarten 33 G3 Eng. Saint Martin. island N Netherlands Antilles
Sint-Michielsgestel 64 C4 Noord-Brabant, S Netherlands
Sîn-Miclăuş see Gheorgheni
Sint-Niklaas 65 B5 Fr. Saint-Nicolas. Oost-Vlaanderen, N Belgium
Sint-Pieters-Leeuw 65 B6 Vlaams Brabant, C Belgium
Sintra 70 B3 prev. Cintra. Lisboa, W Portugal
Sinujiif 51 E5 Nugaal, NE Somalia
Sinus Aelaniticus see Aqaba, Gulf of
Sinus Gallicus see Lion, Golfe du
Sinyang see Xinyang
Sinzyô see Shinjō
Sion 73 A7 Ger. Sitten; anc. Sedunum. Valais, SW Switzerland
Sioux City 23 F3 Iowa, C USA
Sioux Falls 23 F3 South Dakota, N USA
Sioux State see North Dakota
Siphnos see Sífnos
Siping 106 D3 var. Ssu-p'ing, Szeping; prev. Ssu-p'ing-chieh. Jilin, NE China
Siple, Mount 132 A4 mountain Siple Island, Antarctica
Siquirres 31 E4 Limón, E Costa Rica
Siracusa 75 D7 Eng. Syracuse. Sicilia, Italy, C Mediterranean Sea
Sir Edward Pellew Group 126 B2 island group Northern Territory, NE Australia
Siret 86 C3 var. Siretul, Ger. Sereth, Rus. Seret. river Romania/Ukraine
Siretul see Siret
Siria see Syria
Sirikit Reservoir 114 C4 lake N Thailand
Sīrjān 98 D4 prev. Sa'īdābād. Kermān, S Iran
Sirna see Sýrna
Şırnak 95 F4 Şırnak, SE Turkey
Síros see Sýros
Sirte see Surt
Sirti, Gulf of see Surt, Khalīj
Sisak 78 B3 var. Siscia, Ger. Sissek, Hung. Sziszek; anc. Segestica. Sisak-Moslavina, C Croatia
Siscia see Sisak
Sisimiut 60 C3 var. Holsteinborg, Holsteinsborg, Holstenborg, Holstensborg. Kitaa, S Greenland
Sissek see Sisak
Sīstān, Daryācheh-ye see Şāberī, Hāmūn-e
Sitaș Cristuru see Cristuru Secuiesc
Siteía 83 D8 var. Sitía. Kríti, Greece, E Mediterranean Sea
Sitges 71 G2 Cataluña, NE Spain
Sitía see Siteía
Sittang see Sittoung
Sittard 65 D5 Limburg, SE Netherlands
Sitten see Sion
Sittoung 114 B4 var. Sittang. river S Myanmar (Burma)
Sittwe 114 A3 var. Akyab. Rakhine State, W Myanmar (Burma)
Siuna 30 D3 Región Autónoma Atlántico Norte, NE Nicaragua
Siut see Asyūţ
Sivas 94 D3 anc. Sebastia, Sebaste. Sivas, C Turkey
Siverek 95 E4 Şanlıurfa, S Turkey
Siwa see Sīwah
Sīwah 50 A2 var. Siwa. NW Egypt
Six Counties, The see Northern Ireland
Six-Fours-les-Plages 69 D6 Var, SE France
Siyäzän 95 H2 Rus. Siazan'. NE Azerbaijan
Sjar see Sääre
Sjenica 79 D5 Turk. Seniça. Serbia, SW Serbia
Skadar see Shkodër
Skadarsko Jezero see Scutari, Lake
Skagerak see Skagerrak
Skagerrak 63 A6 var. Skagerak. channel N Europe
Skagit River 24 B1 river Washington, NW USA
Skalka 62 C3 lake N Sweden
Skarżysko-Kamienna 76 D4 Świętokrzyskie, C Poland
Skaudvilė 84 B4 Tauragė, SW Lithuania
Skegness 67 E6 E England, United Kingdom
Skellefteå 62 D4 Västerbotten, N Sweden
Skellefteälven 62 C4 river N Sweden
Ski 63 B6 Akershus, S Norway
Skíathos 83 C5 Skíathos, Vóreies Sporádes, Greece, Aegean Sea
Skidal' 85 B5 Rus. Skidel'. Hrodzyenskaya Voblasts', W Belarus
Skidel' see Skidal'
Skiermûntseach see Schiermonnikoog
Skierniewice 76 D3 Łódzkie, C Poland
Skiftet 84 C1 strait Finland Atlantic Ocean Baltic Sea Gulf of Bothnia/Gulf of Finland
Skíros see Skýros
Skópelos 83 C5 Skópelos, Vóreies Sporádes, Greece, Aegean Sea
Skopje 79 D6 var. Üsküb, Turk. Üsküp, prev. Skoplje; anc. Scupi. country capital (FYR Macedonia) N FYR Macedonia
Skoplje see Skopje
Skovorodino 93 F4 Amurskaya Oblast', SE Russian Federation
Skuodas 84 B3 Ger. Schoden, Pol. Szkudy. Klaipėda, NW Lithuania
Skye, Isle of 66 B3 island NW Scotland, United Kingdom
Skylge see Terschelling
Skýros 83 C5 var. Skíros. Skýros, Vóreies Sporádes, Greece, Aegean Sea
Skýros 83 C5 var. Skíros; anc. Scyros. island Vóreies Sporádes, Greece, Aegean Sea
Slagelse 63 B7 Vestsjælland, E Denmark
Slatina 78 C3 Hung. Szlatina; prev. Podravska Slatina. Virovitica-Podravina, NE Croatia
Slatina 86 B5 Olt, S Romania
Slavgorod see Slawharad
Slavonski Brod 78 C3 Ger. Brod, Hung. Bród; prev. Brod, Brod na Savi. Brod-Posavina, NE Croatia
Slavuta 86 C2 Khmel'nyts'ka Oblast', NW Ukraine
Slavyansk see Slov"yans'k
Slawharad 85 E7 Rus. Slavgorod. Mahilyowskaya Voblasts', E Belarus
Sławno 76 C2 Zachodnio-pomorskie, NW Poland
Slēmānī see As Sulaymānīyah
Sliema 80 B5 N Malta
Sligo 67 A5 Ir. Sligeach. Sligo, NW Ireland
Sliven 82 D2 var. Slivno. Sliven, C Bulgaria
Slivnitsa 82 B2 Sofiya, W Bulgaria
Slivno see Sliven
Slobozia 86 C5 Ialomiţa, SE Romania
Slonim 85 B6 Pol. Słonim. Hrodzyenskaya Voblasts', W Belarus
Słonim see Slonim
Slovakia 77 C6 off. Slovenská Republika, Ger. Slowakei, Hung. Szlovákia, Slvk. Slovensko. country C Europe
Slovak Ore Mountains see Slovenské rudohorie
Slovenia 73 D8 off. Republic of Slovenia, Ger. Slowenien, Slvn. Slovenija. country SE Europe
Slovenia, Republic of see Slovenia
Slovenija see Slovenia
Slovenská Republika see Slovakia
Slovenské rudohorie 77 D6 Eng. Slovak Ore Mountains, Ger. Slowakisches Erzgebirge, Ungarisches Erzgebirge. mountain range C Slovakia
Slovensko see Slovakia
Slov"yans'k 87 G3 Rus. Slavyansk. Donets'ka Oblast', E Ukraine
Slowakei see Slovakia
Slowakisches Erzgebirge see Slovenské rudohorie
Slowenien see Slovenia
Słubice 76 B3 Ger. Frankfurt. Lubuskie, W Poland
Sluch 86 D1 river NW Ukraine
Słupsk 76 C2 Ger. Stolp. Pomorskie, N Poland
Slutsk 85 C6 Minskaya Voblasts', S Belarus
Smallwood Reservoir 17 F2 lake Newfoundland and Labrador, S Canada
Smara 48 B3 var. Es Semara. N Western Sahara
Smarhon' 85 C5 Pol. Smorgonie, Rus. Smorgon'. Hrodzyenskaya Voblasts', W Belarus
Smederevo 78 D4 Ger. Semendria. Serbia, N Serbia
Smederevska Palanka 78 D4 Serbia, C Serbia
Smela see Smila
Smila 87 E2 Rus. Smela. Cherkas'ka Oblast', C Ukraine
Smilten see Smiltene
Smiltene 84 D3 Ger. Smilten. Valka, N Latvia
Smøla 62 A4 island W Norway
Smolensk 89 A5 Smolenskaya Oblast', W Russian Federation
Smorgon'/Smorgonie see Smarhon'
Smyrna see İzmir
Snake 12 B4 river Yukon Territory, NW Canada
Snake River 24 C3 river NW USA
Snake River Plain 24 D4 plain Idaho, NW USA
Sneek 64 D2 Friesland, N Netherlands
Sneeuw-gebergte see Maoke, Pegunungan
Sněžka 76 B4 Ger. Schneekoppe, Pol. Śnieżka. mountain N Czech Republic/Poland
Śniardwy, Jezioro 76 D2 Ger. Spirdingsee. lake NE Poland
Sniečkus see Visaginas
Śnieżka see Sněžka
Snina 77 E5 Hung. Szinna. Prešovský Kraj, E Slovakia
Snowdonia 67 C6 mountain range NW Wales, United Kingdom
Snowdrift see Łutselk'e
Snow Mountains see Maoke, Pegunungan
Snyder 27 F3 Texas, SW USA
Sobradinho, Barragem de see Sobradinho, Represa de
Sobradinho, Represa de 41 F2 var. Barragem de Sobradinho. reservoir E Brazil
Sochi 89 A7 Krasnodarskiy Kray, SW Russian Federation
Société, Îles de la/Society Islands see Société, Archipel de la
Society Islands 123 G4 var. Archipel de Tahiti, Îles de la Société, Eng. Society Islands. island group W French Polynesia
Soconusco, Sierra de see Madre, Sierra
Socorro 26 D2 New Mexico, SW USA
Socorro, Isla 28 B5 island W Mexico
Socotra see Suquţrā
Soc Trăng 115 D6 var. Khanh Hung. Soc Trăng, S Vietnam
Socuéllamos 71 E3 Castilla-La Mancha, C Spain
Sodankylä 62 D3 Lappi, N Finland
Sodari see Sodiri
Söderhamn 63 C5 Gävleborg, C Sweden
Södertälje 63 C6 Stockholm, C Sweden
Sodiri 50 B4 var. Sawdirī, Sodari. Northern Kordofan, C Sudan
Soekaboemi see Sukabumi
Soemba see Sumba, Pulau
Soengaipenoeh see Sungaipenuh
Soerabaja see Surabaya
Soerakarta see Surakarta
Sofia see Sofiya
Sofiya 82 C2 var. Sophia, Eng. Sofia, Lat. Serdica. country capital (Bulgaria) (Bulgaria) Sofiya-Grad, W Bulgaria
Sogamoso 36 B3 Boyacá, C Colombia
Sognefjorden 63 A5 fjord NE North Sea
Sohâg see Sawhāj

Suways, Qanāt as – Teseney

Suways, Qanāt as see Suez Canal
Suweida see As Suwaydā'
Suzhou 106 D5 var. Soochow, Su-chou, Suchow; prev. Wuhsien. Jiangsu, E China
Svalbard 61 E1 Norwegian dependency Arctic Ocean
Svartisen 62 C3 glacier C Norway
Svay Riĕng 115 D6 Svay Riĕng, S Cambodia
Sveg 63 B5 Jämtland, C Sweden
Svenstavik 63 C5 Jämtland, C Sweden
Sverdlovsk see Yekaterinburg
Sverige see Sweden
Sveti Vrach see Sandanski
Svetlogorsk see Svyetlahorsk
Svetlograd 89 B7 Stavropol'skiy Kray, SW Russian Federation
Svetlovodsk see Svitlovods'k
Svetozarevo see Jagodina
Svilengrad 82 D3 prev. Mustafa-Pasha. Khaskovo, S Bulgaria
Svitlovods'k 87 F3 Rus. Svetlovodsk. Kirovohrads'ka Oblast', C Ukraine
Svizzera see Switzerland
Svobodnyy 93 G4 Amurskaya Oblast', SE Russian Federation
Svyataya Anna Trough 133 C4 var. Saint Anna Trough. trough N Kara Sea
Svyetlahorsk 85 D7 Rus. Svetlogorsk. Homyel'skaya Voblasts', SE Belarus
Swabian Jura see Schwäbische Alb
Swakopmund 56 B3 Erongo, W Namibia
Swan Islands 31 E1 island group NE Honduras North America
Swansea 67 C7 Wel. Abertawe. S Wales, United Kingdom
Swarzędz 76 C3 Poznań, W Poland
Swatow see Shantou
Swaziland 56 D4 off. Kingdom of Swaziland. country S Africa
Swaziland, Kingdom of see Swaziland
Sweden 62 B4 off. Kingdom of Sweden, Swe. Sverige. country N Europe
Sweden, Kingdom of see Sweden
Sweetwater 27 F3 Texas, SW USA
Świdnica 76 B4 Ger. Schweidnitz. Wałbrzych, SW Poland
Świdwin 76 B2 Ger. Schivelbein. Zachodnio-pomorskie, NW Poland
Świebodzice 76 B4 Ger. Freiburg in Schlesien, Swiebodzice. Walbrzych, SW Poland
Świebodzin 76 B3 Ger. Schwiebus. Lubuskie, W Poland
Świecie 76 C3 Ger. Schwertberg. Kujawsko-pomorskie, C Poland
Swindon 67 D7 S England, United Kingdom
Swinemünde see Świnoujście
Świnoujście 76 B2 Ger. Swinemünde. Zachodnio-pomorskie, NW Poland
Swiss Confederation see Switzerland
Switzerland 73 A7 off. Swiss Confederation, Fr. La Suisse, Ger. Schweiz, It. Svizzera; anc. Helvetia. country C Europe
Sycaminum see Hefa
Sydenham Island see Nonouti
Sydney 126 D1 state capital New South Wales, SE Australia
Sydney 17 G4 Cape Breton Island, Nova Scotia, SE Canada
Sydney Island see Manra
Syedpur see Saidpur
Syemyezhava 85 C6 Rus. Semezhevo. Minskaya Voblasts', C Belarus
Syene see Aswān
Syeverodonets'k 87 H3 Rus. Severodonetsk. Luhans'ka Oblast', E Ukraine
Syktyvkar 88 D4 prev. Ust'-Sysol'sk. Respublika Komi, NW Russian Federation
Sylhet 113 G3 Sylhet, NE Bangladesh
Synel'nykove 87 G3 Dnipropetrovs'ka Oblast', E Ukraine
Syowa 132 C2 Japanese research station Antarctica
Syracuse 19 E3 New York, NE USA
Syracuse see Siracusa
Syrdar'ya 92 B4 Sirdaryo Viloyati, E Uzbekistan
Syria 96 B3 off. Syrian Arab Republic, var. Siria, Syrie, Ar. Al-Jumhūrīyah al-'Arabīyah as-Sūrīyah, Sūrīya. country SW Asia
Syrian Arab Republic see Syria
Syrian Desert 97 D5 Ar. Al Hamad, Bādiyat ash Shām. desert SW Asia
Syrie see Syria
Sýrna 83 E7 var. Sirna. island Kykládes, Greece, Aegean Sea
Sýros 83 C6 var. Síros. island Kykládes, Greece, Aegean Sea
Syulemeshlii see Sredets
Syvash, Zaliv see Syvash, Zatoka
Syvash, Zatoka 87 F4 Rus. Zaliv Syvash. inlet S Ukraine
Syzran' 89 C6 Samarskaya Oblast', W Russian Federation
Szabadka see Subotica
Szamotuły 76 B3 Poznań, W Poland
Szászrégen see Reghin
Szatmárrnémeti see Satu Mare
Száva see Sava
Szczecin 76 B3 Eng./Ger. Stettin. Zachodnio-pomorskie, NW Poland
Szczecinek 76 B2 Ger. Neustettin. Zachodnio-pomorskie, NW Poland
Szczeciński, Zalew 76 A2 var. Stettiner Haff, Ger. Oderhaff. bay Germany/Poland
Szczuczyn Nowogródzki see Shchuchyn
Szczytno 76 D3 Ger. Ortelsburg. Warmińsko-Mazurskie, NE Poland
Szechuan/Szechwan see Sichuan
Szeged 77 D7 Ger. Szegedin, Rom. Seghedin. Csongrád, SE Hungary
Szegedin see Szeged
Székelykeresztúr see Cristuru Secuiesc
Székesfehérvár 77 C6 Ger. Stuhlweissenberg; anc. Alba Regia. Fejér, W Hungary
Szeklerburg see Miercurea-Ciuc
Szekler Neumarkt see Târgu Secuiesc
Szekszárd 77 C7 Tolna, S Hungary
Szempcz/Szenc see Senec
Szenice see Senica
Szenttamás see Srbobran
Szeping see Siping
Szilágysomlyó see Şimleu Silvaniei
Szinna see Snina
Sziszek see Sisak
Szitás-Keresztúr see Cristuru Secuiesc
Szkudy see Skuodas
Szlatina see Slatina
Szlovákia see Slovakia
Szolnok 77 D6 Jász-Nagykun-Szolnok, C Hungary
Szombathely 77 B6 Ger. Steinamanger; anc. Sabaria, Savaria. Vas, W Hungary
Szprotawa 76 B4 Ger. Sprottau. Lubuskie, W Poland
Sztálinváros see Dunaújváros
Szucsava see Suceava

T

Tabariya, Bahrat see Tiberias, Lake
Table Rock Lake 27 G1 reservoir Arkansas/Missouri, C USA
Tábor 77 B5 Jihočeský Kraj, S Czech Republic
Tabora 51 B7 Tabora, W Tanzania
Tabrīz 98 C2 var. Tebriz; anc. Tauris. Āžarbāyjān-e Sharqī, NW Iran
Tabuaeran 123 G2 prev. Fanning Island. atoll Line Islands, E Kiribati
Tabūk 98 A4 Tabūk, NW Saudi Arabia
Täby 63 C6 Stockholm, C Sweden
Tachau see Tachov
Tachov 77 A5 Ger. Tachau. Plveňský Kraj, W Czech Republic
Tacloban 117 F2 off. Tacloban City. Leyte, C Philippines
Tacloban City see Tacloban
Tacna 39 E4 Tacna, SE Peru
Tacoma 24 B2 Washington, NW USA
Tacuarembó 42 D4 prev. San Fructuoso. Tacuarembó, C Uruguay
Tademait, Plateau du 48 D3 plateau C Algeria
Tadmor/Tadmur see Tudmur
Tādpatri 110 C2 Andhra Pradesh, E India
Tadzhikistan see Tajikistan
Taegu 107 E4 off. Taegu-gwangyŏksi, var. Daegu, Jap. Taikyū. SE South Korea
Taegu-gwangyŏksi see Taegu
Taehan-haehyŏp see Korea Strait
Taehan Min'guk see South Korea
Taejŏn 107 E4 off. Taejŏn-gwangyŏksi, Jap. Taiden. C South Korea
Taejŏn-gwangyŏksi see Taejŏn
Tafassâsset, Ténéré du 53 G2 desert N Niger
Tafila/Ţafilah, Muḩāfaẓat aṭ see Aṭ Ṭafilah
Taganrog 89 A7 Rostovskaya Oblast', SW Russian Federation
Taganrog, Gulf of 87 G4 Rus. Taganrogskiy Zaliv, Ukr. Tahanroz'ka Zatoka. gulf Russian Federation/Ukraine
Taganrogskiy Zaliv see Taganrog, Gulf of
Taguatinga 41 F3 Tocantins, C Brazil
Tagus 70 C3 Port. Rio Tejo, Sp. Río Tajo. river Portugal/Spain
Tagus Plain 58 A4 abyssal plain E Atlantic Ocean
Tahanroz'ka Zatoka see Taganrog, Gulf of
Tahat 49 E4 mountain SE Algeria
Tahiti 123 H4 island Îles du Vent, W French Polynesia
Tahiti, Archipel de see Société, Archipel de la
Tahlequah 27 G1 Oklahoma, C USA
Tahoe, Lake 25 B5 lake California/Nevada, W USA
Tahoua 53 F3 Tahoua, W Niger
Taichū see T'aichung
T'aichung 106 D6 Jap. Taichū; prev. Taiwan. C Taiwan
Taiden see Taejŏn
Taieri 129 B7 river South Island, New Zealand
Taihape 128 D4 Manawatu-Wanganui, North Island, New Zealand
Taihoku see T'aipei
Taikyū see Taegu
Tailem Bend 127 B7 South Australia
T'ainan 106 D6 Jap. Tainan; prev. Dainan. S Taiwan
T'aipei 106 D6 Jap. Taihoku; prev. Daihoku. country capital (Taiwan) (Taiwan) N Taiwan
Taiping 116 B3 Perak, Peninsular Malaysia
Taiwan 106 D6 off. Republic of China, var. Formosa, Formo'sa. country E Asia
Taiwan see T'aichung
T'aiwan Haihsia/Taiwan Haixia see Taiwan Strait
Taiwan Strait 106 D6 var. Formosa Strait, Chin. T'aiwan Haihsia, Taiwan Haixia. strait China/Taiwan
Taiyuan 106 C4 var. T'ai-yuan, T'ai-yüan; prev. Yangku. province capital Shanxi, C China
T'ai-yuan/T'ai-yüan see Taiyuan
Ta'izz 99 B7 SW Yemen
Tajikistan 101 E3 off. Republic of Tajikistan, Rus. Tadzhikistan, Taj. Jumhurii Tojikiston; prev. Tajik S.S.R. country C Asia
Tajikistan, Republic of see Tajikistan
Tajik S.S.R see Tajikistan
Tajo, Río see Tagus
Tak 114 C4 var. Rahaeng. Tak, W Thailand
Takao see Kaohsiung
Takaoka 109 C5 Toyama, Honshū, SW Japan
Takapuna 128 D2 Auckland, North Island, New Zealand
Takhiatash see Taxiatosh
Takhtakupyr see Taxtako'pir
Takikawa 108 D2 Hokkaidō, NE Japan
Takla Makan Desert see Taklimakan Shamo
Taklimakan Shamo 104 B3 Eng. Takla Makan Desert. desert NW China
Takow see Kaohsiung
Takutea 123 G4 island S Cook Islands
Talabriga see Aveiro, Portugal
Talabriga see Talavera de la Reina, Spain
Talachyn 85 D6 Rus. Tolochin. Vitsyebskaya Voblasts', NE Belarus
Talamanca, Cordillera de 31 E5 mountain range S Costa Rica
Talara 38 B2 Piura, NW Peru
Talas 101 F2 Talasskaya Oblast', NW Kyrgyzstan
Talaud, Kepulauan 117 F3 island group E Indonesia
Talavera de la Reina 70 D3 anc. Caesarobriga, Talabriga. Castilla-La Mancha, C Spain
Talca 42 B4 Maule, C Chile
Talcahuano 43 B5 Bío Bío, C Chile
Taldykorgan 92 C5 Kaz. Taldyqorghan; prev. Taldy-Kurgan. Taldykorgan, SE Kazakhstan
Taldy-Kurgan/Taldyqorghan see Taldykorgan
Ta-lien see Dalian
Taliq-an see Tāloqān
Tal'ka 85 C6 Minskaya Voblasts', C Belarus
Talkhof see Puurmani
Tallahassee 20 D3 prev. Muskogean. state capital Florida, SE USA
Tall al Abyaḍ see At Tall al Abyaḍ
Tallin see Tallinn
Tallinn 84 D2 Ger. Reval, Rus. Tallin; prev. Revel. country capital (Estonia) (Estonia) Harjumaa, NW Estonia
Tall Kalakh 96 B4 var. Tell Kalakh. Ḩimş, C Syria
Tallulah 20 B2 Louisiana, S USA
Talnakh 92 D3 Taymyrskiy (Dolgano-Nenetskiy) Avtonomnyy Okrug, N Russian Federation
Tal'ne 87 E3 Rus. Tal'noye. Cherkas'ka Oblast', C Ukraine
Tal'noye see Tal'ne
Taloga 27 F1 Oklahoma, C USA
Tāloqān 101 E3 var. Taliq-an. Takhār, NE Afghanistan
Talsen see Talsi
Talsi 84 C3 Ger. Talsen. Talsi, NW Latvia
Taltal 42 B2 Antofagasta, N Chile
Talvik 62 D2 Finnmark, N Norway
Tamabo, Banjaran 116 D3 mountain range East Malaysia
Tamale 53 E4 C Ghana
Tamana 123 E3 prev. Rotcher Island. atoll Tungaru, W Kiribati
Tamanrasset 49 E4 var. Tamenghest. S Algeria
Tamar 67 C7 river SW England, United Kingdom
Tamar see Tudmur
Tamatave see Toamasina
Tamazunchale 29 E4 San Luis Potosí, C Mexico
Tambacounda 52 C3 SE Senegal
Tambov 89 B6 Tambovskaya Oblast', W Russian Federation
Tambura 51 B5 W Equatoria, SW South Sudan
Tamchaket see Tâmchekkeṭ
Tâmchekkeṭ 52 C3 var. Tamchaket. Hodh el Gharbi, S Mauritania
Tamenghest see Tamanrasset
Tamil Nādu 110 C3 prev. Madras. cultural region SE India
Tam Ky 115 E5 Quang Nam-Ɖa Nāng, C Vietnam
Tammerfors see Tampere
Tampa 21 E4 Florida, SE USA
Tampa Bay 21 E4 bay Florida, SE USA
Tampere 63 D5 Swe. Tammerfors. Länsi-Suomi, W Finland
Tampico 29 E3 Tamaulipas, C Mexico
Tamworth 127 D6 New South Wales, SE Australia
Tanabe 109 C7 Wakayama, Honshū, SW Japan
Tana Bru 62 D2 Finnmark, N Norway
T'ana Hāyk' 50 C4 var. Lake Tana. lake NW Ethiopia
Tanais see Don
Tana, Lake see T'ana Hāyk'
Tanami Desert 124 D3 desert Northern Territory, N Australia
Tananarive see Antananarivo
Ţăndărei 86 D5 Ialomiţa, SE Romania
Tandil 43 D5 Buenos Aires, E Argentina
Tandjoengkarang see Bandar Lampung
Tanega-shima 109 B8 island Nansei-shotō, SW Japan
Tanen Taunggyi see Tane Range
Tane Range 114 B4 Bur. Tanen Taunggyi. mountain range W Thailand
Tanezrouft 48 D4 desert Algeria/Mali
Ṭanf, Jabal aṭ 96 D4 mountain SE Syria
Tanga 51 C7 Tanga, E Tanzania
Tanganyika and Zanzibar see Tanzania
Tanganyika, Lake 51 B7 lake E Africa
Tanger 48 C2 var. Tangiers, Tangier, Fr./Ger. Tangerk, Sp. Tánger; anc. Tingis. NW Morocco
Tangerk see Tanger
Tanggula Shan 104 C4 mountain W China
Tangier see Tanger
Tangiers see Tanger
Tangra Yumco 104 B5 var. Tangro Tso. lake W China
Tangro Tso see Tangra Yumco
Tangshan 106 D3 var. T'ang-shan. Hebei, E China
T'ang-shan see Tangshan
Tanimbar, Kepulauan 117 F5 island group Maluku, E Indonesia
Tanjungkarang/Tanjungkarang-Telukbetung see Bandar Lampung
Tanna 122 D4 island S Vanuatu
Tannenhof see Krynica
Tan-Tan 48 B3 SW Morocco
Tan-tung see Dandong
Tanzania 51 C7 off. United Republic of Tanzania, Swa. Jamhuri ya Muungano wa Tanzania; prev. German East Africa, Tanganyika and Zanzibar. country E Africa
Tanzania, Jamhuri ya Muungano wa see Tanzania
Tanzania, United Republic of see Tanzania
Taoudenit see Taoudenni
Taoudenni 53 E2 var. Taoudenit. Tombouctou, N Mali
Tapa 84 E2 Ger. Taps. Lääne-Virumaa, NE Estonia
Tapachula 29 G5 Chiapas, SE Mexico
Tapaiu see Gvardeysk
Tapajós, Rio 41 E2 var. Tapajóz. river NW Brazil
Tapajóz see Tapajós, Rio
Taps see Tapa
Ţarābulus 49 F2 var. Ţarābulus al Gharb, Eng. Tripoli. country capital (Libya) (Libya) NW Libya
Ţarābulus al Gharb see Ţarābulus
Tarābulus/Ţarābulus ash Shām see Tripoli
Taraclia 86 D4 Rus. Tarakilya. S Moldova
Tarakilya see Taraclia
Taranaki, Mount 128 C4 var. Egmont. volcano North Island, New Zealand
Tarancón 71 E3 Castilla-La Mancha, C Spain
Taranto 75 E5 var. Tarentum. Puglia, SE Italy
Taranto, Gulf of 75 E6 Eng. Gulf of Taranto. gulf S Italy
Taranto, Gulf of see Taranto, Golfo di
Tarapoto 38 C2 San Martín, N Peru
Tarare 69 D5 Rhône, E France
Tarascon 69 D6 Bouches-du-Rhône, SE France
Tarawa 122 D2 atoll Tungaru, W Kiribati
Taraz 92 C5 prev. Aulie Ata, Auliye-Ata, Dzhambul, Zhambyl. Zhambyl, S Kazakhstan
Tarazona 71 E2 Aragón, NE Spain
Tarbes 69 B6 anc. Bigorra. Hautes-Pyrénées, S France
Tarcoola 127 A6 South Australia
Taree 127 D6 New South Wales, SE Australia
Tarentum see Taranto
Târgovişte 86 C5 prev. Tîrgovişte. Dâmboviţa, S Romania
Targu Jiu 86 B4 prev. Tîrgu Jiu. Gorj, W Romania
Târgul-Neamţ see Târgu-Neamţ
Târgul-Săcuiesc see Târgu Secuiesc
Târgu Mureş 86 B4 prev. Oşorhei, Tîrgu Mures, Ger. Neumarkt, Hung. Marosvásárhely. Mureş, C Romania
Târgu-Neamţ 86 C3 var. Târgul-Neamţ; prev. Tîrgu-Neamţ. Neamţ, NE Romania
Târgu Ocna 86 C4 Hung. Aknavásár; prev. Tîrgu Ocna. Bacău, E Romania
Târgu Secuiesc 86 C4 Ger. Neumarkt, Szekler Neumarkt, Hung. Kezdivásárhely; prev. Chezdi-Oşorheiu, Târgul-Săcuiesc, Tîrgu Secuiesc. Covasna, E Romania
Tar Heel State see North Carolina
Tarija 39 G5 Tarija, S Bolivia
Tarīm 99 C6 C Yemen
Tarim Basin see Tarim Pendi
Tarim Pendi 102 C2 Eng. Tarim Basin. basin NW China
Tarim He 104 B3 river NW China
Tarma 38 C3 Junín, C Peru
Tarn 69 C6 cultural region S France
Tarn 69 C6 river S France
Tarnobrzeg 76 D4 Podkarpackie, SE Poland
Tarnopol see Ternopil'
Tarnów 77 D5 Małopolskie, S Poland
Tarraco see Tarragona
Tarragona 71 G2 anc. Tarraco. Cataluña, E Spain
Tarrasa see Terrassa
Tàrrega 71 F2 var. Tarrega. Cataluña, NE Spain
Tarsatica see Rijeka
Tarsus 94 C4 İçel, S Turkey
Tartous/Tartouss see Ţarţūs
Tartu 84 D3 Ger. Dorpat; prev. Rus. Yurev, Yury'ev. Tartumaa, SE Estonia
Ţarţūs 96 A3 off. Muḩāfaẓat Ţarţūs, var. Tartous, Tartus. governorate W Syria
Ţarţūs, Muḩāfaẓat see Ţarţūs
Ta Ru Tao, Ko 115 B7 island S Thailand Asia
Tarvisio 74 D2 Friuli-Venezia Giulia, NE Italy
Tarvisium see Treviso
Tashauz see Daşoguz
Tashi Chho Dzong see Thimphu
Tashkent see Toshkent
Tash-Kömür see Tash-Kumyr
Tash-Kumyr 101 F2 Kir. Tash-Kömür. Dzhalal-Abadskaya Oblast', W Kyrgyzstan
Tashqurghan see Kholm
Tasikmalaja see Tasikmalaya
Tasikmalaya 116 C5 prev. Tasikmalaja. Jawa, C Indonesia
Tasman Basin 120 C5 var. East Australian Basin. undersea basin S Tasman Sea
Tasman Bay 129 C5 inlet South Island, New Zealand
Tasmania 127 B8 prev. Van Diemen's Land. state SE Australia
Tasmania 130 B4 island SE Australia
Tasman Plateau 120 C5 var. South Tasmania Plateau. undersea plateau SW Tasman Sea
Tasman Sea 120 C5 sea SW Pacific Ocean
Tassili-n-Ajjer 49 E4 plateau E Algeria
Tatabánya 77 C6 Komárom-Esztergom, NW Hungary
Tatar Pazardzhik see Pazardzhik
Tathlīth 99 B5 'Asīr, S Saudi Arabia
Tatra Mountains 77 D5 Ger. Tatra, Hung. Tátra, Pol./Slvk. Tatry. mountain range Poland/Slovakia
Tatra/Tátra see Tatra Mountains
Tatry see Tatra Mountains
Ta-t'ung/Tatung see Datong
Tatvan 95 F3 Bitlis, SE Turkey
Ta'ū 123 F4 var. Tau. island Manua Islands, E American Samoa
Taukum, Peski 101 G1 desert SE Kazakhstan
Taumarunui 128 D4 Manawatu-Wanganui, North Island, New Zealand
Taungdwingyi 114 B3 Magway, C Myanmar (Burma)
Taunggyi 114 B3 Shan State, C Myanmar (Burma)
Taungoo 114 B4 Bago, C Myanmar (Burma)
Taunton 67 C7 SW England, United Kingdom
Taupo 128 D3 Waikato, North Island, New Zealand
Taupo, Lake 128 D3 lake North Island, New Zealand
Tauragė 84 B4 Ger. Tauroggen. Tauragė, SW Lithuania
Tauranga 128 D3 Bay of Plenty, North Island, New Zealand
Tauris see Tabrīz
Tauroggen see Tauragė
Taurus Mountains see Toros Dağları
Tavas 94 B4 Denizli, SW Turkey
Tavastehus see Hämeenlinna
Tavira 70 C5 Faro, S Portugal
Tavoy see Dawei
Tavoy Island see Mali Kyun
Ta Waewae Bay 129 A7 bay South Island, New Zealand
Tawakoni, Lake 27 G2 reservoir Texas, SW USA
Tawau 116 D3 Sabah, East Malaysia
Ṭawkar see Tokar
Tawzar see Tozeur
Taxco 29 E4 var. Taxco de Alarcón. Guerrero, S Mexico
Taxco de Alarcón see Taxco
Taxiatosh 100 C2 Rus. Takhiatash. Qoraqalpog'iston Respublikasi, W Uzbekistan
Taxtako'pir 100 D1 Rus. Takhtakupyr. Qoraqalpog'iston Respublikasi, NW Uzbekistan
Tay 66 C3 river C Scotland, United Kingdom
Taylor 27 G3 Texas, SW USA
Taymā' 98 A4 Tabūk, NW Saudi Arabia
Taymyr, Ozero 93 E2 lake N Russian Federation
Taymyr, Poluostrov 93 E2 peninsula N Russian Federation
Taz 92 D3 river N Russian Federation
T'bilisi 95 G2 Eng. Tiflis. country capital (Georgia) (Georgia) SE Georgia
Tchad see Chad
Tchad, Lac see Chad, Lake
Tchien see Zwedru
Tchongking see Chongqing
Tczew 76 C2 Ger. Dirschau. Pomorskie, N Poland
Te Anau 129 A7 Southland, South Island, New Zealand
Te Anau, Lake 129 A7 lake South Island, New Zealand
Teapa 29 G4 Tabasco, SE Mexico
Teate see Chieti
Tebingtinggi 116 B3 Sumatera, N Indonesia
Tebriz see Tabrīz
Techirghiol 86 D5 Constanţa, SE Romania
Tecomán 28 D4 Colima, SW Mexico
Tecpan 29 E5 var. Tecpan de Galeana. Guerrero, S Mexico
Tecpan de Galeana see Tecpan
Tecuci 86 C4 Galaţi, E Romania
Tedzhen see Harīrūd/Tejen
Tedzhen see Tejen
Tees 67 D5 river N England, United Kingdom
Tefé 40 D2 Amazonas, N Brazil
Tegal 116 C4 Jawa, C Indonesia
Tegelen 65 D5 Limburg, SE Netherlands
Tegucigalpa 30 C3 country capital (Honduras) (Honduras) Francisco Morazán, SW Honduras
Teheran see Tehrān
Tehrān 98 C3 var. Teheran. country capital (Iran) (Iran) Tehrān, N Iran
Tehuacán 29 F4 Puebla, S Mexico
Tehuantepec 29 F5 var. Santo Domingo Tehuantepec. Oaxaca, SE Mexico
Tehuantepec, Golfo de 29 F5 var. Gulf of Tehuantepec. gulf S Mexico
Tehuantepec, Gulf of see Tehuantepec, Golfo de
Tehuantepec, Isthmus of see Tehuantepec, Istmo de
Tehuantepec, Istmo de 29 F5 var. Isthmus of Tehuantepec. isthmus SE Mexico
Tejen 100 C3 Rus. Tedzhen. Ahal Welaýaty, S Turkmenistan
Tejen see Harīrūd
Tejo, Rio see Tagus
Te Kao 128 C1 Northland, North Island, New Zealand
Tekax 29 H4 var. Tekax de Álvaro Obregón. Yucatán, SE Mexico
Tekax de Álvaro Obregón see Tekax
Tekeli 92 C5 Almaty, SE Kazakhstan
Tekirdağ 94 A2 It. Rodosto; anc. Bisanthe, Raidestos, Rhaedestus. Tekirdağ, NW Turkey
Te Kuiti 128 D3 Waikato, North Island, New Zealand
Tela 30 C2 Atlántida, NW Honduras
Telanaipura see Jambi
Tel Aviv-Jaffa see Tel Aviv-Yafo
Tel Aviv-Yafo 97 A6 var. Tel Aviv-Jaffa. Tel Aviv, C Israel
Teles Pirés see São Manuel, Rio
Telish 82 C2 prev. Azizie. Pleven, N Bulgaria
Tell Abiad/Tell Abyad see At Tall al Abyaḍ
Tell Kalakh see Tall Kalakh
Tell Shedadi see Ash Shadādah
Tel'man/Tel'mansk see Gubadag
Teloekbetoeng see Bandar Lampung
Telo Martius see Toulon
Telschen see Telšiai
Telšiai 84 B3 Ger. Telschen. Telšiai, NW Lithuania
Telukbetung see Bandar Lampung
Temerin 78 D3 Vojvodina, N Serbia
Temeschburg/Temeschwar see Timişoara
Temesvár/Temeswar see Timişoara
Temirtau 92 C4 prev. Samarkandski, Samarkandskoye. Karaganda, C Kazakhstan
Tempio Pausania 75 A5 Sardegna, Italy, C Mediterranean Sea
Temple 27 G3 Texas, SW USA
Temuco 43 B5 Araucanía, C Chile
Temuka 129 B6 Canterbury, South Island, New Zealand
Tenasserim 115 B6 Tanintharyi, S Myanmar (Burma)
Ténenkou 52 D3 Mopti, C Mali
Ténéré 53 G3 physical region C Niger
Tenerife 48 A3 island Islas Canarias, Spain, NE Atlantic Ocean
Tengger Shamo 105 E3 desert N China
Tengréla 52 D4 var. Tingréla. N Côte d'Ivoire
Tenkodogo 53 E4 S Burkina
Tennant Creek 126 A3 Northern Territory, C Australia
Tennessee 20 C1 off. State of Tennessee, also known as The Volunteer State. state SE USA
Tennessee River 20 C1 river S USA
Tenos see Tínos
Tepelena see Tepelenë
Tepelenë 79 C7 var. Tepelena, It. Tepeleni. Gjirokastër, S Albania
Tepeleni see Tepelenë
Tepic 28 D4 Nayarit, C Mexico
Teplice 76 A4 Ger. Teplitz; prev. Teplice-Šanov, Teplitz-Schönau. Ústecký Kraj, NW Czech Republic
Teplice-Šanov/Teplitz/Teplitz-Schönau see Teplice
Tequila 28 D4 Jalisco, SW Mexico
Teraina 123 G2 prev. Washington Island. atoll Line Islands, E Kiribati
Teramo 74 C4 anc. Interamna. Abruzzi, C Italy
Tercan 95 E3 Erzincan, NE Turkey
Terceira 70 A5 var. Ilha Terceira. island Azores, Portugal, NE Atlantic Ocean
Terceira, Ilha see Terceira
Terekhovka see Tsyerakhowka
Teresina 41 F2 var. Therezina. state capital Piauí, NE Brazil
Termez see Termiz
Termia see Kýthnos
Términos, Laguna de 29 G4 lagoon SE Mexico
Termiz 101 E3 Rus. Termez. Surkhondaryo Viloyati, S Uzbekistan
Termoli 74 D4 Molise, C Italy
Terneuzen 65 B5 var. Neuzen. Zeeland, SW Netherlands
Terni 74 C4 anc. Interamna Nahars. Umbria, C Italy
Ternopil' 86 C2 Pol. Tarnopol, Rus. Ternopol'. Ternopil's'ka Oblast', W Ukraine
Ternopol' see Ternopil'
Terracina 75 C5 Lazio, C Italy
Terranova di Sicilia see Gela
Terranova Pausania see Olbia
Terrassa 71 G2 Cast. Tarrasa. Cataluña, E Spain
Terre Adélie 132 C4 physical region Antarctica
Terre Haute 18 B4 Indiana, N USA
Terre Neuve see Newfoundland and Labrador
Terschelling 64 C1 Fris. Skylge. island Waddeneilanden, N Netherlands
Teruel 71 F3 anc. Turba. Aragón, E Spain
Tervel 82 E1 prev. Kurtbunar, Rom. Curtbunar. Dobrich, NE Bulgaria
Tervueren see Tervuren
Tervuren 65 C6 var. Tervueren. Vlaams Brabant, C Belgium
Teseney 50 C4 var. Tessenei. W Eritrea

Tschakathurn – Vangaindrano

Tschakathurn see Čakovec
Tschaslau see Čáslav
Tschenstochau see Częstochowa
Tsefat 97 B5 var. Safed, Ar. Safad; prev. Ẕefat. Northern, N Israel
Tselinograd see Astana
Tsetsen Khan see Öndörhaan
Tsetserleg 104 D2 Arhangay, C Mongolia
Tshela 55 B6 Bas-Congo, W Dem. Rep. Congo
Tshikapa 55 C7 Kasai-Occidental, SW Dem. Rep. Congo
Tshuapa 55 D6 river C Dem. Rep. Congo
Tshwane 56 D4 see also Pretoria; var. Epitoli. country capital (South Africa-administrative capital) Gauteng, NE South Africa
Tsinan see Jinan
Tsing Hai see Qinghai Hu, China
Tsinghai see Qinghai, China
Tsingtao/Tsingtau see Qingdao
Tsinkiang see Quanzhou
Tsintao see Qingdao
Tsitsihar see Qiqihar
Tsu 109 C6 var. Tu. Mie, Honshū, SW Japan
Tsugaru-kaikyo 108 C3 strait N Japan
Tsumeb 56 B3 Otjikoto, N Namibia
Tsuruga 109 C6 var. Turuga. Fukui, Honshū, SW Japan
Tsuruoka 108 D4 var. Turuoka. Yamagata, Honshū, C Japan
Tsushima 109 A7 var. Tsushima-tō, Tusima. island group SW Japan
Tsushima-tō see Tsushima
Tsyerakhowka 85 D8 Rus. Terekhovka. Homyel'skaya Voblasts', SE Belarus
Tsyurupinsk see Tsyurupyns'k
Tsyurupyns'k 87 E4 Rus. Tsyurupinsk. Khersons'ka Oblast', S Ukraine
Tu see Tsu
Tuamotu, Archipel des see Tuamotu, Îles
Tuamotu Fracture Zone 121 H3 fracture zone E Pacific Ocean
Tuamotu, Îles 123 H4 var. Archipel des Tuamotu, Dangerous Archipelago, Tuamotu Islands. island group N French Polynesia
Tuamotu Islands see Tuamotu, Îles
Tuapi 31 E2 Región Autónoma Atlántico Norte, NE Nicaragua
Tuapse 89 A7 Krasnodarskiy Kray, SW Russian Federation
Tuba City 26 B1 Arizona, SW USA
Tubbergen 64 E3 Overijssel, E Netherlands
Tubeke see Tubize
Tubize 65 B6 Dut. Tubeke. Walloon Brabant, C Belgium
Tubmanburg 52 C5 NW Liberia
Ţubruq 49 H2 Eng. Tobruk, It. Tobruch. NE Libya
Tubuai, Îles/Tubuai Islands see Australes, Îles
Tucker's Town 20 B5 E Bermuda
Tuckum see Tukums
Tucson 26 B3 Arizona, SW USA
Tucumán see San Miguel de Tucumán
Tucumcari 27 E2 New Mexico, SW USA
Tucupita 37 E2 Delta Amacuro, NE Venezuela
Tucuruí, Represa de 41 F2 reservoir NE Brazil
Tudela 71 E2 Basq. Tutera; anc. Tutela. Navarra, N Spain
Tudmur 96 C3 var. Tadmur, Tamar, Gk. Palmyra, Bibl. Tadmor. Ḥimṣ, C Syria
Tuguegarao 117 E1 Luzon, N Philippines
Tuktoyaktuk 15 E3 Northwest Territories, NW Canada
Tukums 84 C3 Ger. Tuckum. Tukums, W Latvia
Tula 89 B5 Tul'skaya Oblast', W Russian Federation
Tulancingo 29 E4 Hidalgo, C Mexico
Tulare Lake Bed 25 C7 salt flat California, W USA
Tulcán 38 B1 Carchi, N Ecuador
Tulcea 86 D5 Tulcea, E Romania
Tul'chin see Tul'chyn
Tul'chyn 86 D3 Rus. Tul'chin. Vinnyts'ka Oblast', C Ukraine
Tuléar see Toliara
Tulia 27 E2 Texas, SW USA
Ţūlkarm 97 D7 West Bank, Israel
Tulle 69 C5 anc. Tutela. Corrèze, C France
Tulln 73 E6 var. Oberhollabrunn. Niederösterreich, NE Austria
Tully 126 D3 Queensland, NE Australia
Tulsa 27 G1 Oklahoma, C USA
Tuluá 36 B3 Valle del Cauca, W Colombia
Tulun 93 E4 Irkutskaya Oblast', S Russian Federation
Tumaco 36 A4 Nariño, SW Colombia
Tumba, Lac see Ntomba, Lac
Tumbes 38 A2 Tumbes, NW Peru
Tumkūr 110 C2 Karnātaka, W India
Tumuc-Humac Mountains 41 E1 var. Serra Tumucumaque. mountain range N South America
Tumucumaque, Serra see Tumuc-Humac Mountains
Tunca Nehri see Tundzha
Tunduru 51 C8 Ruvuma, S Tanzania
Tundzha 82 D3 Turk. Tunca Nehri. river Bulgaria/Turkey
Tungabhadra Reservoir 110 C2 lake S India
Tungaru 123 E2 prev. Gilbert Islands. island group W Kiribati
T'ung-shan see Xuzhou
Tungsten 14 D4 Northwest Territories, W Canada
Tung-t'ing Hu see Dongting Hu
Tunis 49 E1 var. Tūnis. country capital (Tunisia) (Tunisia) NE Tunisia
Tunis, Golfe de 80 D3 Ar. Khalīj Tūnis. gulf NE Tunisia
Tunisia 49 F2 off. Tunisian Republic, Ar. Al Jumhūrīyah at Tūnisīyah, Fr. République Tunisienne. country N Africa
Tunisian Republic see Tunisia
Tunisienne, République see Tunisia
Tūnisīyah, Al Jumhūrīyah at see Tunisia
Tūnis, Khalīj see Tunis, Golfe de
Tunja 36 B3 Boyacá, C Colombia
Tuong Buong see Tương Đương
Tương Đương 114 D4 var. Tuong Buong. Nghê An, N Vietnam
Tüp see Tyup
Tupelo 20 C2 Mississippi, S USA
Tupiza 39 G5 Potosí, S Bolivia
Turabah 99 B5 Makkah, W Saudi Arabia
Turangi 128 D4 Waikato, North Island, New Zealand
Turan Lowland 100 C2 var. Turan Plain, Kaz. Turan Oypaty, Rus. Turanskaya Nizmennost', Turk. Turan Pesligi, Uzb. Turan Pasttekisligi. plain C Asia
Turan Oypaty/Turan Pesligi/Turan Plain/Turanskaya Nizmennost' see Turan Lowland
Turan Pasttekisligi see Turan Lowland
Ţurayf 98 A3 Al Ḥudūd ash Shamālīyah, NW Saudi Arabia
Turba see Teruel
Turbat 112 A3 Baluchistān, SW Pakistan
Turčianský Svätý Martin see Martin
Turda 86 B4 Ger. Thorenburg, Hung. Torda. Cluj, NW Romania
Turek 76 C3 Wielkopolskie, C Poland
Turfan see Turpan
Turin see Torino
Turkana, Lake 51 C6 var. Lake Rudolf. lake N Kenya
Turkestan 92 B5 Kaz. Türkistan. Yuzhnyy Kazakhstan, S Kazakhstan
Turkey 94 B3 off. Republic of Turkey, Turk. Türkiye Cumhuriyeti. country SW Asia
Turkey, Republic of see Turkey
Turkish Republic of Northern Cyprus 80 D5 disputed territory Cyprus
Türkistan see Turkestan
Türkiye Cumhuriyeti see Turkey
Türkmenabat 100 D3 prev. Rus. Chardzhev, Chardzhou, Chardzhui, Lenin-Turkmenski, Turkm. Chärjew. Lebap Welaýaty, E Turkmenistan
Türkmen Aylagy 100 B2 Rus. Turkmenskiy Zaliv. lake gulf W Turkmenistan
Turkmenbashi see Türkmenbaşy
Türkmenbaşy 100 B2 Rus. Turkmenbashi; prev. Krasnovodsk. Balkan Welaýaty, W Turkmenistan
Türkmenbasy Aylagy 100 A2 prev. Rus. Krasnovodskiy Zaliv, Turkm. Krasnowodsk Aylagy. lake Gulf W Turkmenistan
Turkmenistan 100 B2 ; prev. Turkmenskaya Soviet Socialist Republic. country C Asia
Turkmenskaya Soviet Socialist Republic see Turkmenistan
Turkmenskiy Zaliv see Türkmen Aylagy
Turks and Caicos Islands 33 E2 UK dependent territory N West Indies
Turku 63 D6 Swe. Åbo. Länsi-Suomi, SW Finland
Turlock 25 B6 California, W USA
Turnagain, Cape 128 D4 headland North Island, New Zealand
Turnau see Turnov
Turnhout 65 C5 Antwerpen, N Belgium
Turnov 76 B4 Ger. Turnau. Liberecký Kraj, N Czech Republic
Tŭrnovo see Veliko Tŭrnovo
Turnu Măgurele 86 B5 var. Turnu-Măgurele. Teleorman, S Romania
Turnu Severin see Drobeta-Turnu Severin
Turócszentmárton see Martin
Turoni see Tours
Turpan 104 C3 var. Turfan. Xinjiang Uygur Zizhiqu, NW China
Turpan Depression see Turpan Pendi
Turpan Pendi 104 C3 Eng. Turpan Depression. depression NW China
Turpentine State see North Carolina
Türtkŭl/Turtkul' see To'rtkok'l
Turuga see Tsuruga
Turuoka see Tsuruoka
Tuscaloosa 20 C2 Alabama, S USA
Tuscan Archipelago see Toscano, Archipelago
Tuscany see Toscana
Tusima see Tsushima
Tutela see Tulle, France
Tutela see Tudela, Spain
Tutera see Tudela
Tuticorin 110 C3 Tamil Nādu, SE India
Tutrakan 82 D1 Silistra, NE Bulgaria
Tutuila 123 F4 island W American Samoa
Tuvalu 123 E3 prev. Ellice Islands. country SW Pacific Ocean
Tuwayq, Jabal 99 C5 mountain range C Saudi Arabia
Tuxpan 28 D4 Jalisco, C Mexico
Tuxpán 29 F4 var. Tuxpán de Rodríguez Cano. Veracruz-Llave, E Mexico
Tuxpán de Rodríguez Cano see Tuxpán
Tuxtepec 29 F4 var. San Juan Bautista Tuxtepec. Oaxaca, S Mexico
Tuxtla 29 G5 var. Tuxtla Gutiérrez. Chiapas, SE Mexico
Tuxtla see San Andrés Tuxtla
Tuxtla Gutiérrez see Tuxtla
Tuy Hoa 115 E5 Phu Yên, S Vietnam
Tuz, Lake 94 C3 lake C Turkey
Tver' 88 B4 prev. Kalinin. Tverskaya Oblast', W Russian Federation
Tverya 97 B5 var. Tiberias; prev. Teverya. Northern, N Israel
Twin Falls 24 D4 Idaho, NW USA
Tyan'-Shan' see Tien Shan
Tychy 77 D5 Ger. Tichau. Śląskie, S Poland
Tyler 27 G3 Texas, SW USA
Tylos see Bahrain
Tympáki 83 C8 var. Timbaki; prev. Timbákion. Kríti, Greece, E Mediterranean Sea
Tynda 93 F4 Amurskaya Oblast', SE Russian Federation
Tyne 66 D4 river N England, United Kingdom
Tyôsi see Chōshi
Tyras see Dniester
Tyre see Soûr
Tyrnau see Trnava
Týrnavos 82 B4 var. Tírnavos. Thessalía, C Greece
Tyrol see Tirol
Tyros see Bahrain
Tyrrhenian Sea 75 B6 It. Mare Tirreno. sea N Mediterranean Sea
Tyumen' 92 C3 Tyumenskaya Oblast', C Russian Federation
Tyup 101 G2 Kir. Tüp. Issyk-Kul'skaya Oblast', NE Kyrgyzstan
Tywyn 67 C6 W Wales, United Kingdom
Tzekung see Zigong
Tziá 83 C6 prev. Kéa, Kéos; anc. Ceos. island Kykládes, Greece, Aegean Sea

U

UAE see United Arab Emirates
Uanle Uen see Wanlaweyn
Uaupés, Rio see Vaupés, Río
Ubangi-Shari see Central African Republic
Ube 109 B7 Yamaguchi, Honshū, SW Japan
Ubeda 71 E4 Andalucía, S Spain
Uberaba 41 F4 Minas Gerais, SE Brazil
Uberlândia 41 F4 Minas Gerais, SE Brazil
Ubol Rajadhani/Ubol Ratchathani see Ubon Ratchathani
Ubon Ratchathani 115 D5 var. Muang Ubon, Ubol Rajadhani, Ubol Ratchathani, Udon Ratchathani. Ubon Ratchathani, E Thailand
Ubrique 70 D5 Andalucía, S Spain
Ubsu-Nur, Ozero see Uvs Nuur
Ucayali, Río 38 D3 river C Peru
Uchiura-wan 108 D3 bay NW Pacific Ocean
Uchkuduk see Uchquduq
Uchquduq 100 D2 Rus. Uchkuduk. Navoiy Viloyati, N Uzbekistan
Uchtagan Gumy/Uchtagan, Peski see Uçtagan Gumy
Uçtagan Gumy 100 C2 var. Uchtagan Gumy, Rus. Peski Uchtagan. desert NW Turkmenistan
Udaipur 112 C3 prev. Oodeypore. Rājasthān, N India
Uddevalla 63 B6 Västra Götaland, S Sweden
Udine 74 D2 anc. Utina. Friuli-Venezia Giulia, NE Italy
Udintsev Fracture Zone 132 A5 tectonic feature S Pacific Ocean
Udipi see Udupi
Udon Ratchathani see Ubon Ratchathani
Udon Thani 114 C4 var. Ban Mak Khaeng, Udorndhani. Udon Thani, N Thailand
Udorndhani see Udon Thani
Udupi 110 B2 var. Udipi. Karnātaka, SW India
Uele 55 D5 var. Welle. river NE Dem. Rep. Congo
Uelzen 72 C3 Niedersachsen, N Germany
Ufa 89 D6 Respublika Bashkortostan, W Russian Federation
Ugāle 84 C2 Ventspils, NW Latvia
Uganda 51 B6 off. Republic of Uganda. country E Africa
Uganda, Republic of see Uganda
Uhorshchyna see Hungary
Uhuru Peak see Kilimanjaro
Uíge 56 B1 Port. Carmona, Vila Marechal Carmona. Uíge, NW Angola
Uinta Mountains 22 B4 mountain range Utah, W USA
Uitenhage 56 C5 Eastern Cape, S South Africa
Uithoorn 64 C3 Noord-Holland, C Netherlands
Ujda see Oujda
Ujelang Atoll 122 C1 var. Wujlān. atoll Ralik Chain, W Marshall Islands
Újgradiska see Nova Gradiška
Újmoldova see Moldova Nouă
Ujungpandang see Makassar
Ujung Salang see Phuket
Újvidék see Novi Sad
UK see United Kingdom
Ukhta 92 C3 Respublika Komi, NW Russian Federation
Ukiah 25 B5 California, W USA
Ukmergė 84 C4 Pol. Wiłkomierz. Vilnius, C Lithuania
Ukraine 86 C2 off. Ukraine, Rus. Ukraina, Ukr. Ukrayina; prev. Ukrainian Soviet Socialist Republic, Ukrainskay S.S.R. country SE Europe
Ukraine see Ukraine
Ukrainian Soviet Socialist Republic see Ukraine
Ukrainskay S.S.R/Ukrayina see Ukraine
Ulaanbaatar 105 E2 Eng. Ulan Bator; prev. Urga. country capital (Mongolia) (Mongolia) Töv, C Mongolia
Ulaangom 104 C2 Uvs, NW Mongolia
Ulan Bator see Ulaanbaatar
Ulanhad see Chifeng
Ulan-Ude 93 E4 prev. Verkhneudinsk. Respublika Buryatiya, S Russian Federation
Uleälv see Oulujoki
Uleträsk see Oulujärvi
Ulft 64 E4 Gelderland, E Netherlands
Ullapool 66 C3 N Scotland, United Kingdom
Ulm 73 B6 Baden-Württemberg, S Germany
Ulsan 107 E4 Jap. Urusan. SE South Korea
Ulster 67 B5 province Northern Ireland, United Kingdom/Ireland
Ulungur Hu 104 B2 lake NW China
Uluru 125 D5 var. Ayers Rock. monolith Northern Territory, C Australia
Ulyanivka 87 E3 Rus. Ul'yanovka. Kirovohrads'ka Oblast', C Ukraine
Ul'yanovka see Ulyanivka
Ul'yanovsk 89 C5 prev. Simbirsk. Ul'yanovskaya Oblast', W Russian Federation
Umán 29 H3 Yucatán, SE Mexico
Uman' 87 E3 Rus. Uman. Cherkas'ka Oblast', C Ukraine
Uman see Uman'
Umanak/Umanaq see Uummannaq
'Umān, Khalīj see Oman, Gulf of
'Umān, Salṭanat see Oman
Umbrian-Machigian Mountains see Umbro-Marchigiano, Appennino
Umbro-Marchigiano, Appennino 74 C3 Eng. Umbrian-Machigian Mountains. mountain range C Italy
Umeå 62 C4 Västerbotten, N Sweden
Umeälven 62 C4 river N Sweden
Umiat 14 D2 Alaska, USA
Umm Buru 50 A4 Western Darfur, W Sudan
Umm Durmān see Omdurman
Umm Ruwaba 50 C4 var. Umm Ruwābah, Um Ruwāba. Northern Kordofan, C Sudan
Umm Ruwābah see Umm Ruwaba
Umnak Island 14 A3 island Aleutian Islands, Alaska, USA
Um Ruwāba see Umm Ruwaba
Umtali see Mutare
Umtata 56 D5 Eastern Cape, SE South Africa
Una 78 B3 river Bosnia and Herzegovina/Croatia
Unac 78 B3 river W Bosnia and Herzegovina
Unalaska Island 14 A3 island Aleutian Islands, Alaska, USA
'Unayzah 98 B4 var. Anaiza. Al Qaṣīm, C Saudi Arabia
Unci see Almería
Uncía 39 F4 Potosí, C Bolivia
Uncompahgre Peak 22 B5 mountain Colorado, C USA
Undur Khan see Öndörhaan
Ungaria see Hungary
Ungarisches Erzgebirge see Slovenské rudohorie
Ungarn see Hungary
Ungava Bay 17 E1 bay Québec, E Canada
Ungava Peninsula 16 D1 peninsula Québec, SE Canada
Ungeny see Ungheni
Ungheni 86 D3 Rus. Ungeny. W Moldova
Unguja see Zanzibar
Üngüz Angyrsyndaky Garagum 100 C2 Rus. Zaunguzskiye Garagumy. desert N Turkmenistan
Ungvár see Uzhhorod
Unimak Island 14 B3 island Aleutian Islands, Alaska, USA
Union 21 E1 South Carolina, SE USA
Union City 20 C1 Tennessee, S USA
Union of Myanmar see Myanmar
United Arab Emirates 99 C5 Ar. Al Imārāt al 'Arabīyah al Muttaḥidah, abbrev. UAE; prev. Trucial States. country SW Asia
United Arab Republic see Egypt
United Kingdom 67 B5 off. United Kingdom of Great Britain and Northern Ireland, abbrev. UK. country NW Europe
United Kingdom of Great Britain and Northern Ireland see United Kingdom
United Mexican States see Mexico
United Provinces see Uttar Pradesh
United States of America 13 B5 off. United States of America, var. America, The States, abbrev. U.S., USA. country North America
Unst 66 D1 island NE Scotland, United Kingdom
Ünye 94 D2 Ordu, W Turkey
Upala 30 D4 Alajuela, NW Costa Rica
Upata 37 E2 Bolívar, E Venezuela
Upemba, Lac 55 D7 lake SE Dem. Rep. Congo
Upernavik 60 C2 var. Upernivik. Kitaa, C Greenland
Upernivik see Upernavik
Upington 56 C4 Northern Cape, W South Africa
'Upolu 123 F4 island SE Samoa
Upper Klamath Lake 24 A4 lake Oregon, NW USA
Upper Lough Erne 67 A5 lake SW Northern Ireland, United Kingdom
Upper Red Lake 23 F1 lake Minnesota, N USA
Upper Volta see Burkina
Uppsala 63 C6 Uppsala, C Sweden
Uqsuqtuuq see Gjoa Haven
Ural 90 B3 Kaz. Zayyq. river Kazakhstan/Russian Federation
Ural Mountains see Ural'skiye Gory
Ural'sk 92 B3 Kaz. Oral. Zapadnyy Kazakhstan, NW Kazakhstan
Ural'skiye Gory 92 C3 var. Ural'skiy Khrebet, Eng. Ural Mountains. mountain range Kazakhstan/Russian Federation
Ural'skiy Khrebet see Ural'skiye Gory
Uraricoera 40 D1 Roraima, N Brazil
Ura-Tyube see Üroteppa
Urbandale 23 F3 Iowa, C USA
Urdunn see Jordan
Uren' 89 C5 Nizhegorodskaya Oblast', W Russian Federation
Urga see Ulaanbaatar
Urganch 100 D2 Rus. Urgench; prev. Novo-Urgench. Xorazm Viloyati, W Uzbekistan
Urgench see Urganch
Urgut 101 E3 Samarqand Viloyati, C Uzbekistan
Urmia, Lake see Orūmīyeh, Daryācheh-ye
Uroševac see Ferizaj
Üroteppa 101 E2 Rus. Ura-Tyube. NW Tajikistan
Uruapan 29 E4 var. Uruapan del Progreso. Michoacán, SW Mexico
Uruapan del Progreso see Uruapan
Uruguai, Rio see Uruguay
Uruguay 42 D4 off. Oriental Republic of Uruguay; prev. La Banda Oriental. country E South America
Uruguay 42 D3 var. Rio Uruguai, Río Uruguay. river E South America
Uruguay, Oriental Republic of see Uruguay
Uruguay, Río see Uruguay
Urumchi see Ürümqi
Urumi Yeh see Orūmīyeh, Daryācheh-ye
Ürümqi 104 C3 var. Tihwa, Urumchi, Urumqi, Urumtsi, Wu-lu-k'o-mu-shi, Wu-lu-mu-ch'i; prev. Ti-hua. Xinjiang Uygur Zizhiqu, NW China
Urumtsi see Ürümqi
Urundi see Burundi
Urup, Ostrov 93 H4 island Kuril'skiye Ostrova, SE Russian Federation
Urusan see Ulsan
Urziceni 86 C5 Ialomiţa, SE Romania
Usa 88 E3 river NW Russian Federation
Uşak 94 B3 prev. Ushak. Uşak, W Turkey
Ushak see Uşak
Ushant see Ouessant, Île d'
Ushuaia 43 B8 Tierra del Fuego, S Argentina
Usinsk 88 E3 Respublika Komi, NW Russian Federation
Üsküb/Üsküp see Skopje
Usmas Ezers 84 B3 lake NW Latvia
Usol'ye-Sibirskoye 93 E4 Irkutskaya Oblast', C Russian Federation
Ussel 69 C5 Corrèze, C France
Ussuriysk 93 G5 prev. Nikol'sk, Nikol'sk-Ussuriyskiy, Voroshilov. Primorskiy Kray, SE Russian Federation
Ustica 75 B6 island S Italy
Ust'-Ilimsk 93 E4 Irkutskaya Oblast', C Russian Federation
Ústí nad Labem 76 A4 Ger. Aussig. Ústecký Kraj, NW Czech Republic
Ustinov see Izhevsk
Ustka 76 C2 Ger. Stolpmünde. Pomorskie, N Poland
Ust'-Kamchatsk 93 H2 Kamchatskaya Oblast', E Russian Federation
Ust'-Kamenogorsk 92 D5 Kaz. Öskemen. Vostochnyy Kazakhstan, E Kazakhstan
Ust'-Kut 93 E4 Irkutskaya Oblast', C Russian Federation
Ust'-Olenëk 93 E3 Respublika Sakha (Yakutiya), NE Russian Federation
Ustrzyki Dolne 77 E5 Podkarpackie, SE Poland
Ust'-Sysol'sk see Syktyvkar
Ust Urt see Ustyurt Plateau
Ustyurt Plateau 100 B1 var. Ust Urt, Uzb. Ustyurt Platosi. plateau Kazakhstan/Uzbekistan
Ustyurt Platosi see Ustyurt Plateau
Usulután 30 C3 Usulután, SE El Salvador
Usumacinta, Río 30 B1 river Guatemala/Mexico
Usumbura see Bujumbura
U.S./USA see United States of America
Utah 22 B4 off. State of Utah, also known as Beehive State, Mormon State. state W USA
Utah Lake 22 B4 lake Utah, W USA
Utena 84 C4 Utena, E Lithuania
Utica 19 F3 New York, NE USA
Utina see Udine
Utrecht 64 C4 Lat. Trajectum ad Rhenum. Utrecht, C Netherlands
Utsunomiya 109 D5 var. Utunomiya. Tochigi, Honshū, S Japan
Uttarakhand 113 E2 cultural region N India
Uttar Pradesh 113 E3 prev. United Provinces, United Provinces of Agra and Oudh. cultural region N India
Utunomiya see Utsunomiya
Uulu 84 D2 Pärnumaa, SW Estonia
Uummannaq 60 C3 var. Umanak, Umanaq. Kitaa, C Greenland
Uummannarsuaq see Nunap Isua
Uvalde 27 F4 Texas, SW USA
Uvaravichy 85 D7 Rus. Uvarovichi. Homyel'skaya Voblasts', SE Belarus
Uvarovichi see Uvaravichy
Uvea, Île 123 E4 island N Wallis and Futuna
Uvs Nuur 104 C1 var. Ozero Ubsu-Nur. lake Mongolia/Russian Federation
'Uwaynāt, Jabal al 66 A3 var. Jebel Uweinat. mountain Libya/Sudan
Uweinat, Jebel see 'Uwaynāt, Jabal al
Uyo 53 G5 Akwa Ibom, S Nigeria
Uyuni 39 F5 Potosí, W Bolivia
Uzbekistan 100 D2 off. Republic of Uzbekistan. country C Asia
Uzbekistan, Republic of see Uzbekistan
Uzhgorod see Uzhhorod
Uzhhorod 86 B2 Rus. Uzhgorod; prev. Ungvár. Zakarpats'ka Oblast', W Ukraine
Užice 78 D4 prev. Titovo Užice. Serbia, W Serbia

V

Vaal 56 D4 river C South Africa
Vaals 65 D6 Limburg, SE Netherlands
Vaasa 63 D5 Swe. Vasa; prev. Nikolainkaupunki. Länsi-Suomi, W Finland
Vaassen 64 D3 Gelderland, E Netherlands
Vác 77 C6 Ger. Waitzen. Pest, N Hungary
Vadodara 112 C4 prev. Baroda. Gujarāt, W India
Vaduz 72 E2 country capital (Liechtenstein) (Liechtenstein) W Liechtenstein
Vág see Váh
Vágbeszterce see Považská Bystrica
Váh 77 C5 Ger. Waag, Hung. Vág. river W Slovakia
Váhtjer see Gällivare
Väinameri 84 C2 prev. Muhu Väin, Ger. Moon-Sund. sea E Baltic Sea
Vajdahunyad see Hunedoara
Valachia see Wallachia
Valday 88 B4 Novgorodskaya Oblast', W Russian Federation
Valdecañas, Embalse de 70 D3 reservoir W Spain
Valdepeñas 71 E4 Castilla-La Mancha, C Spain
Valdés, Península 43 C6 peninsula SE Argentina
Valdez 14 C3 Alaska, USA
Valdia see Weldiya
Valdivia 43 B5 Los Lagos, C Chile
Val-d'Or 16 D4 Québec, SE Canada
Valdosta 21 E3 Georgia, SE USA
Valence 69 D5 anc. Valentia, Valentia Julia, Ventia. Drôme, E France
Valencia 71 F3 País Valenciano, E Spain
Valencia 24 D1 California, USA
Valencia 36 D1 Carabobo, N Venezuela
Valencia, Gulf of 71 F3 var. Gulf of Valencia. gulf E Spain
Valencia, Gulf of see Valencia, Golfo de
Valencia/València see País Valenciano
Valenciennes 68 D2 Nord, N France
Valentia see Valence, France
Valentia see País Valenciano
Valentia Julia see Valence
Valentine State see Oregon
Valera 36 C2 Trujillo, NW Venezuela
Valetta see Valletta
Valga 84 D3 Ger. Walk, Latv. Valka. Valgamaa, S Estonia
Valira 69 A8 river Andorra/Spain Europe
Valjevo 78 C4 Serbia, W Serbia
Valjok see Válljohka
Valka 84 D3 Ger. Walk. Valka, N Latvia
Valka see Valga
Valkenswaard 65 D5 Noord-Brabant, S Netherlands
Valladolid 29 H3 Yucatán, SE Mexico
Valladolid 70 D2 Castilla-León, NW Spain
Vall D'Uxó see La Vall d'Uixó
Valle de La Pascua 36 D2 Guárico, N Venezuela
Valledupar 36 B1 Cesar, N Colombia
Vallejo 25 B6 California, W USA
Vallenar 42 B3 Atacama, N Chile
Valletta 75 C8 prev. Valetta. country capital (Malta) (Malta) E Malta
Valley City 23 E2 North Dakota, N USA
Válljohka 62 D2 var. Valjok. Finnmark, N Norway
Valls 71 G2 Cataluña, NE Spain
Valmiera 84 D3 Est. Volmari, Ger. Wolmar. Valmiera, N Latvia
Valona see Vlorë
Valozhyn 85 C5 Pol. Wołożyn, Rus. Volozhin. Minskaya Voblasts', C Belarus
Valparaíso 42 B4 Valparaíso, C Chile
Valparaiso 18 C3 Indiana, N USA
Valverde del Camino 70 C4 Andalucía, S Spain
Van 95 F3 Van, E Turkey
Vanadzor 95 F2 prev. Kirovakan. N Armenia
Vancouver 14 D5 British Columbia, SW Canada
Vancouver 24 B3 Washington, NW USA
Vancouver Island 14 D5 island British Columbia, SW Canada
Vanda see Vantaa
Van Diemen Gulf 124 D2 gulf Northern Territory, N Australia
Van Diemen's Land see Tasmania
Vaner, Lake see Vänern
Vänern 63 B6 Eng. Lake Vaner; prev. Lake Vener. lake S Sweden
Vangaindrano 57 G4 Fianarantsoa, SE Madagascar

Van Gölü – Wan

Van Gölü *95 F3 Eng.* Lake Van; *anc.* Thospitis. *salt lake* E Turkey
Van Horn *26 D3* Texas, SW USA
Van, Lake *see* Van Gölü
Vannes *68 A3 anc.* Dariorigum. Morbihan, NW France
Vantaa *63 D6 Swe.* Vanda. Etelä-Suomi, S Finland
Vanua Levu *123 E4 island* N Fiji
Vanuatu *122 C4 off.* Republic of Vanuatu; *prev.* New Hebrides. *country* SW Pacific Ocean
Vanuatu, Republic of *see* Vanuatu
Van Wert *18 C4* Ohio, N USA
Vapincum *see* Gap
Varakļāni *84 D4* Madona, C Latvia
Vārānasi *113 E3 prev.* Banaras, Benares, *hist.* Kasi. Uttar Pradesh, N India
Varangerfjorden *62 E2 Lapp.* Várjjatvuotna. *fjord* N Norway
Varangerhalvøya *62 D2 Lapp.* Várnjárga. *peninsula* N Norway
Varannó *see* Vranov nad Topl'ou
Varasd *see* Varaždin
Varaždin *78 B2 Ger.* Warasdin, *Hung.* Varasd. Varaždin, N Croatia
Varberg *63 B7* Halland, S Sweden
Vardar *79 E6 Gk.* Axiós. *river* FYR Macedonia/Greece
Varde *63 A7* Ribe, W Denmark
Vareia *see* Logroño
Varėna *85 B5 Pol.* Orany. Alytus, S Lithuania
Varese *74 B2* Lombardia, N Italy
Vârful Moldoveanu *86 B4 var.* Moldoveanul; *prev.* Vîrful Moldoveanu. *mountain* C Romania
Várjjatvuotna *see* Varangerfjorden
Varkaus *63 E5* Itä-Suomi, C Finland
Varna *82 E2 prev.* Stalin; *anc.* Odessus. Varna, E Bulgaria
Varnenski Zaliv *82 E2 prev.* Stalinski Zaliv. *bay* E Bulgaria
Várnjárga *see* Varangerhalvøya
Varshava *see* Warszawa
Vasa *see* Vaasa
Vasilikí *83 A5* Lefkáda, Iónia Nisiá, Greece, C Mediterranean Sea
Vasilishki *85 B5 Pol.* Wasiliszki. Hrodzyenskaya Voblasts', W Belarus
Vasil'kov *see* Vasyl'kiv
Vaslui *86 D4* Vaslui, C Romania
Västerås *63 C6* Västmanland, C Sweden
Vasyl'kiv *87 E2 var.* Vasil'kov. Kyyivs'ka Oblast', N Ukraine
Vaté *see* Efate
Vatican City *75 A7 off.* Vatican City. *country* S Europe
Vatnajökull *61 E5 glacier* SE Iceland
Vatter, Lake *see* Vättern
Vättern *63 B6 Eng.* Lake Vatter; *prev.* Lake Vetter. *lake* S Sweden
Vaughn *26 D2* New Mexico, SW USA
Vaupés, Río *36 C4 var.* Rio Uaupés. *river* Brazil/Colombia
Vava'u Group *123 E4 island group* N Tonga
Vavuniya *110 D3* Northern Province, N Sri Lanka
Vawkavysk *85 B6 Pol.* Wołkowysk, *Rus.* Volkovysk. Hrodzyenskaya Voblasts', W Belarus
Växjö *63 C7 var.* Vexiö. Kronoberg, S Sweden
Vaygach, Ostrov *88 E2 island* NW Russian Federation
Veendam *64 E2* Groningen, NE Netherlands
Veenendaal *64 D4* Utrecht, C Netherlands
Vega *62 B4 island* C Norway
Veglia *see* Krk
Veisiejai *85 B5* Alytus, S Lithuania
Vejer de la Frontera *70 C5* Andalucía, S Spain
Veldhoven *65 D5* Noord-Brabant, S Netherlands
Velebit *78 A3 mountain range* C Croatia
Velenje *73 E7 Ger.* Wöllan. N Slovenia
Veles *79 E6 Turk.* Köprülü. C FYR Macedonia
Velho *see* Porto Velho
Velika Kikinda *see* Kikinda
Velika Morava *78 D4 var.* Glavn'a Morava, Morava, *Ger.* Grosse Morava. *river* C Serbia
Velikaya *91 G2 river* NE Russian Federation
Veliki Bečkerek *see* Zrenjanin
Velikiye Luki *88 A4* Pskovskaya Oblast', W Russian Federation
Velikiy Novgorod *88 B4 prev.* Novgorod. Novgorodskaya Oblast', W Russian Federation
Veliko Tŭrnovo *82 D2 prev.* Tirnovo, Trnovo, Tŭrnovo. Veliko Tŭrnovo, N Bulgaria
Velingrad *82 C3* Pazardzhik, C Bulgaria
Vel'ký Krtíš *77 D6* Banskobystrický Kraj, C Slovakia
Vellore *110 C2* Tamil Nādu, SE India
Velobriga *see* Viana do Castelo
Velsen *see* Velsen-Noord
Velsen-Noord *64 C3 var.* Velsen. Noord-Holland, W Netherlands
Vel'sk *88 C4 var.* Velsk. Arkhangel'skaya Oblast', NW Russian Federation
Velykyy Tokmak *see* Tokmak
Vendôme *68 C4* Loir-et-Cher, C France
Venedig *see* Venezia
Vener, Lake *see* Vänern
Venetia *see* Venezia
Venezia *74 C2 Eng.* Venice, *Fr.* Venise, *Ger.* Venedig; *anc.* Venetia. Veneto, NE Italy
Venezia, Golfo di *see* Venice, Gulf of
Venezuela *36 D2 off.* Republic of Venezuela; *prev.* Estados Unidos de Venezuela, United States of Venezuela. *country* N South America
Venezuela, Estados Unidos de *see* Venezuela
Venezuela, Gulf of *36 C1 Eng.* Gulf of Maracaibo, Gulf of Venezuela. *gulf* NW Venezuela
Venezuela, Gulf of *see* Venezuela, Golfo de
Venezuelan Basin *34 B1 undersea basin* E Caribbean Sea
Venezuela, Republic of *see* Venezuela
Venezuela, United States of *see* Venezuela
Venice *20 C4* Louisiana, S USA
Venice *see* Venezia
Venice, Gulf of *74 C2 It.* Golfo di Venezia, *Slvn.* Beneški Zaliv. *gulf* N Adriatic Sea
Venise *see* Venezia
Venlo *65 D5 prev.* Venloo. Limburg, SE Netherlands
Venloo *see* Venlo
Venta *84 B3 Ger.* Windau. *river* Latvia/Lithuania
Venta Belgarum *see* Winchester
Ventia *see* Valence
Ventimiglia *74 A3* Liguria, NW Italy
Ventspils *84 B2 Ger.* Windau. Ventspils, NW Latvia
Vera *42 D3* Santa Fe, C Argentina
Veracruz *29 F4 var.* Veracruz Llave. Veracruz-Llave, E Mexico
Veracruz Llave *see* Veracruz
Vercellae *see* Vercelli
Vercelli *74 A2 anc.* Vercellae. Piemonte, NW Italy
Verdal *see* Verdalsøra
Verdalsøra *62 B4 var.* Verdal. Nord-Trøndelag, C Norway
Verde, Cabo *see* Cape Verde
Verde, Costa *70 D1 coastal region* N Spain
Verden *72 B3* Niedersachsen, NW Germany
Veria *see* Véroia
Verkhnedvinsk *see* Vyerkhnyadzvinsk
Verkhneudinsk *see* Ulan-Ude
Verkhoyanskiy Khrebet *93 F3 mountain range* NE Russian Federation
Vermillion *23 F3* South Dakota, N USA
Vermont *19 F2 off.* State of Vermont, *also known as* Green Mountain State. *state* NE USA
Vernal *22 B4* Utah, W USA
Vernon *27 F2* Texas, SW USA
Verőcze *see* Virovitica
Véroia *82 B4 var.* Veria, Vérroia, *Turk.* Karaferiye. Kentrikí Makedonía, N Greece
Verona *74 C2* Veneto, NE Italy
Vérroia *see* Véroia
Versailles *68 D1* Yvelines, N France
Versecz *see* Vršac
Verulamium *see* St Albans
Verviers *65 D6* Liège, E Belgium
Vesdre *65 D6 river* E Belgium
Veselinovo *82 D2* Shumen, NE Bulgaria
Vesontio *see* Besançon
Vesoul *68 D4 anc.* Vesulium, Vesulum. Haute-Saône, E France
Vesterålen *62 B2 island group* N Norway
Vestfjorden *62 C3 fjord* C Norway
Vestmannaeyjar *61 E5* Sudhurland, S Iceland
Vesulium/Vesulum *see* Vesoul
Vesuna *see* Périgueux
Vesuvio *75 D5 Eng.* Vesuvius. *volcano* S Italy
Vesuvius *see* Vesuvio
Veszprém *77 C7 Ger.* Veszprim. Veszprém, W Hungary
Veszprim *see* Veszprém
Vetrino *82 E2* Varna, E Bulgaria
Vetrino *see* Vyetryna
Vetter, Lake *see* Vättern
Veurne *65 A5 var.* Furnes. West-Vlaanderen, W Belgium
Vexiö *see* Växjö
Viacha *39 F4* La Paz, W Bolivia
Viana de Castelo *see* Viana do Castelo
Viana do Castelo *70 B2 var.* Viana de Castelo; *anc.* Velobriga. Viana do Castelo, NW Portugal
Vianen *64 C4* Utrecht, C Netherlands
Viangchan *114 C4 Eng./Fr.* Vientiane. *country capital* (Laos) (Laos) C Laos
Viangphoukha *114 C3 var.* Vieng Pou Kha. Louang Namtha, N Laos
Viareggio *74 B3* Toscana, C Italy
Viborg *63 A7* Viborg, NW Denmark
Vic *71 G2 var.* Vich; *anc.* Ausa, Vicus Ausonensis. Cataluña, NE Spain
Vicentia *see* Vicenza
Vicenza *74 C2 anc.* Vicentia. Veneto, NE Italy
Vich *see* Vic
Vichy *69 C5* Allier, C France
Vicksburg *20 B2* Mississippi, S USA
Victoria *57 H1 country capital* (Seychelles) (Seychelles) Mahé, SW Seychelles
Victoria *14 D5 province capital* Vancouver Island, British Columbia, SW Canada
Victoria *80 A5 var.* Rabat. Gozo, NW Malta
Victoria *27 G4* Texas, SW USA
Victoria *127 C7 state* SE Australia
Victoria *see* Masvingo, Zimbabwe
Victoria Bank *see* Vitória Seamount
Victoria de Durango *see* Durango
Victoria de las Tunas *see* Las Tunas
Victoria Falls *56 C3* Matabeleland North, W Zimbabwe
Victoria Falls *56 C2 waterfall* Zambia/Zimbabwe
Victoria Falls *see* Iguaçu, Salto do
Victoria Island *15 F3 island* Northwest Territories/Nunavut, NW Canada
Victoria, Lake *51 B6 var.* Victoria Nyanza. *lake* E Africa
Victoria Land *132 C4 physical region* Antarctica
Victoria Nyanza *see* Victoria, Lake
Victoria River *124 D3 river* Northern Territory, N Australia
Victorville *25 C7* California, W USA
Vicus Ausonensis *see* Vic
Vicus Elbii *see* Viterbo
Vidalia *21 E2* Georgia, SE USA
Videm-Krško *see* Krško
Vídeň *see* Wien
Vidin *82 B1 anc.* Bononia. Vidin, NW Bulgaria
Vidzy *85 C5* Vitsyebskaya Voblasts', NW Belarus
Viedma *43 C5* Río Negro, E Argentina
Vieja, Sierra *26 D3 mountain range* Texas, SW USA
Vieng Pou Kha *see* Viangphoukha
Vienna *see* Wien, Austria
Vienna *see* Vienne, France
Vienne *69 D5 anc.* Vienna. Isère, E France
Vienne *68 B4 river* W France
Vientiane *see* Viangchan
Vientos, Paso de los *see* Windward Passage
Vierzon *68 C4* Cher, C France
Viesīte *84 C4 Ger.* Eckengraf. Jēkabpils, S Latvia
Vietnam *114 D4 off.* Socialist Republic of Vietnam, *Vtn.* Công Hoa Xa Hôi Chu Nghia Việt Nam. *country* SE Asia
Vietnam, Socialist Republic of *see* Vietnam
Vietri *see* Viêt Tri
Viêt Tri *114 D3 var.* Vietri. Vinh Phu, N Vietnam
Vieux Fort *33 F2* S Saint Lucia
Vigo *70 B2* Galicia, NW Spain
Viipuri *see* Vyborg
Vijayawāda *110 D1 prev.* Bezwada. Andhra Pradesh, SE India
Vila *see* Port-Vila
Vila Artur de Paiva *see* Cubango
Vila da Ponte *see* Cubango
Vila de João Belo *see* Xai-Xai
Vila de Mocímboa da Praia *see* Mocímboa da Praia
Vila do Conde *70 B2* Porto, NW Portugal
Vila do Zumbo *56 D2 prev.* Vila do Zumbu, Zumbo. Tete, NW Mozambique
Vila do Zumbu *see* Vila do Zumbo
Vilafranca del Penedès *71 G2 var.* Villafranca del Panadés. Cataluña, NE Spain
Vila General Machado *see* Camacupa
Vila Henrique de Carvalho *see* Saurimo
Viļaka *84 D4 Ger.* Marienhausen. Balvi, NE Latvia
Vilalba *70 C1* Galicia, NW Spain
Vila Marechal Carmona *see* Uíge
Vila Nova de Gaia *70 B2* Porto, NW Portugal
Vila Nova de Portimão *see* Portimão
Vila Pereira de Eça *see* N'Giva
Vila Real *70 C2 var.* Vila Rial. Vila Real, N Portugal
Vila Rial *see* Vila Real
Vila Robert Williams *see* Caála
Vila Salazar *see* N'Dalatando
Vila Serpa Pinto *see* Menongue
Vileyka *see* Vilyeyka
Vilhelmina *62 C4* Västerbotten, N Sweden
Vilhena *40 D3* Rondônia, W Brazil
Vília *83 C5* Attikí, C Greece
Viliya *85 C5 Lith.* Neris. *river* W Belarus
Viliya *see* Neris
Viljandi *84 D2 Ger.* Fellin. Viljandimaa, S Estonia
Vilkaviškis *84 B4 Pol.* Wyłkowyszki. Marijampolė, SW Lithuania
Villa Acuña *28 D2 var.* Ciudad Acuña. Coahuila, NE Mexico
Villa Bella *39 F2* Beni, N Bolivia
Villacarrillo *71 E4* Andalucía, S Spain
Villa Cecilia *see* Ciudad Madero
Villach *73 D7 Slvn.* Beljak. Kärnten, S Austria
Villacidro *75 A5* Sardegna, Italy, C Mediterranean Sea
Villa Concepción *see* Concepción
Villa del Pilar *see* Pilar
Villafranca de los Barros *70 C4* Extremadura, W Spain
Villafranca del Panadés *see* Vilafranca del Penedès
Villahermosa *29 G4 prev.* San Juan Bautista. Tabasco, SE Mexico
Villajoyosa *71 F4 Cat.* La Vila Joíosa. País Valenciano, E Spain
Villa María *42 C4* Córdoba, C Argentina
Villa Martín *39 F5* Potosí, SW Bolivia
Villa Mercedes *42 C4* San Juan, Argentina
Villanueva *28 D3* Zacatecas, C Mexico
Villanueva de la Serena *70 C3* Extremadura, W Spain
Villanueva de los Infantes *71 E4* Castilla-La Mancha, C Spain
Villarrica *42 D2* Guairá, SE Paraguay
Villavicencio *36 B3* Meta, C Colombia
Villaviciosa *70 D1* Asturias, N Spain
Villazón *39 G5* Potosí, S Bolivia
Villena *71 F4* País Valenciano, E Spain
Villeurbanne *69 D5* Rhône, E France
Villingen-Schwenningen *73 B6* Baden-Württemberg, S Germany
Villmanstrand *see* Lappeenranta
Vilna *see* Vilnius
Vilnius *85 C5 Pol.* Wilno, *Ger.* Wilna; *prev. Rus.* Vilna. *country capital* (Lithuania) (Lithuania) Vilnius, SE Lithuania
Vil'shanka *87 E3 Rus.* Olshanka. Kirovohrads'ka Oblast', C Ukraine
Vilvoorde *65 C6 Fr.* Vilvorde. Vlaams Brabant, C Belgium
Vilvorde *see* Vilvoorde
Vilyeyka *85 C5 Pol.* Wilejka, *Rus.* Vileyka. Minskaya Voblasts', NW Belarus
Vilyuy *93 F3 river* NE Russian Federation
Viña del Mar *42 B4* Valparaíso, C Chile
Vinaròs *71 F3* País Valenciano, E Spain
Vincennes *18 B4* Indiana, N USA
Vindhya Mountains *see* Vindhya Range
Vindhya Range *112 D4 var.* Vindhya Mountains. *mountain range* N India
Vindobona *see* Wien
Vineland *19 F4* New Jersey, NE USA
Vinh *114 D4* Nghê An, N Vietnam
Vinh Loi *see* Bac Liêu
Vinishte *82 C2* Montana, NW Bulgaria
Vinita *27 G1* Oklahoma, C USA
Vinkovci *78 C3 Ger.* Winkowitz, *Hung.* Vinkovcze. Vukovar-Srijem, E Croatia
Vinkovcze *see* Vinkovci
Vinnitsa *see* Vinnytsya
Vinnytsya *86 D2 Rus.* Vinnitsa. Vinnyts'ka Oblast', C Ukraine
Vinogradov *see* Vynohradiv
Vinson Massif *132 A3 mountain* Antarctica
Viranşehir *95 E4* Şanlıurfa, SE Turkey
Vîrful Moldoveanu *see* Vârful Moldoveanu
Virginia *23 G1* Minnesota, N USA
Virginia *19 E5 off.* Commonwealth of Virginia, *also known as* Mother of Presidents, Mother of States, Old Dominion. *state* NE USA
Virginia Beach *19 F5* Virginia, NE USA
Virgin Islands *see* British Virgin Islands
Virgin Islands (US) *33 F3 var.* Virgin Islands of the United States; *prev.* Danish West Indies. *US unincorporated territory* E West Indies
Virgin Islands of the United States *see* Virgin Islands (US)
Virôchey *115 E5* Rôtânôkiri, NE Cambodia
Virovitica *78 C2 Ger.* Virovititz, *Hung.* Verőcze; *prev. Ger.* Werowitz. Virovitica-Podravina, NE Croatia
Virovititz *see* Virovitica
Virton *65 D8* Luxembourg, SE Belgium
Virtsu *84 D2 Ger.* Werder. Läänemaa, W Estonia
Vis *78 B4 It.* Lissa; *anc.* Issa. *island* S Croatia
Vis *see* Fish
Visaginas *84 C4 prev.* Sniečkus. Utena, E Lithuania
Visākhapatnam *113 E5 var.* Vishakhapatnam. Andhra Pradesh, SE India
Visalia *25 C6* California, W USA
Visby *63 C7 Ger.* Wisby. Gotland, SE Sweden
Viscount Melville Sound *15 F2 prev.* Melville Sound. *sound* Northwest Territories, N Canada
Visé *65 D6* Liège, E Belgium
Viseu *70 C2 prev.* Vizeu. Viseu, N Portugal
Vishakhapatnam *see* Visākhapatnam
Vislinskiy Zaliv *see* Vistula Lagoon
Visoko *78 C4* Federacija Bosna I Hercegovina, C Bosnia and Herzegovina
Visttasjohka *62 D3 river* N Sweden
Vistula *76 C2 Eng.* Vistula, *Ger.* Weichsel. *river* C Poland
Vistula *see* Wisła
Vistula Lagoon *76 C2 Ger.* Frisches Haff, *Pol.* Zalew Wiślany, *Rus.* Vislinskiy Zaliv. *lagoon* Poland/Russian Federation
Vitebsk *see* Vitsyebsk
Viterbo *74 C4 anc.* Vicus Elbii. Lazio, C Italy
Viti *see* Fiji
Viti Levu *123 E4 island* W Fiji
Vitim *93 F4 river* C Russian Federation
Vitória *41 F4 state capital* Espírito Santo, SE Brazil
Vitoria *see* Vitoria-Gasteiz
Vitoria Bank *see* Vitória Seamount
Vitória da Conquista *41 F3* Bahia, E Brazil
Vitoria-Gasteiz *71 E1 var.* Vitoria, *Eng.* Vittoria. País Vasco, N Spain
Vitória Seamount *45 B5 var.* Victoria Bank, Vitoria Bank. *seamount* C Atlantic Ocean
Vitré *68 B3* Ille-et-Vilaine, NW France
Vitsyebsk *85 E5 Rus.* Vitebsk. Vitsyebskaya Voblasts', NE Belarus
Vittoria *75 C7* Sicilia, Italy, C Mediterranean Sea
Vittoria *see* Vitoria-Gasteiz
Vizcaya, Golfo de *see* Biscay, Bay of
Vizianagaram *113 E5 var.* Vizianagram. Andhra Pradesh, E India
Vizianagram *see* Vizianagaram
Vjosës, Lumi i *79 C7 var.* Vijosa, Vijosë, *Gk.* Aóos. *river* Albania/Greece
Vlaanderen *see* Flanders
Vlaardingen *64 B4* Zuid-Holland, SW Netherlands
Vladikavkaz *89 B8 prev.* Dzaudzhikau, Ordzhonikidze. Respublika Severnaya Osetiya, SW Russian Federation
Vladimir *89 B5* Vladimirskaya Oblast', W Russian Federation
Vladimirovka *see* Yuzhno-Sakhalinsk
Vladimir-Volynskiy *see* Volodymyr-Volyns'kyy
Vladivostok *93 G5* Primorskiy Kray, SE Russian Federation
Vlagtwedde *64 E2* Groningen, NE Netherlands
Vlasotince *79 E5* Serbia, SE Serbia
Vlieland *64 C1 Fris.* Flylân. *island* Waddeneilanden, N Netherlands
Vlijmen *64 C4* Noord-Brabant, S Netherlands
Vlissingen *65 B5 Eng.* Flushing, *Fr.* Flessingue. Zeeland, SW Netherlands
Vlodava *see* Włodawa
Vlonë/Vlora *see* Vlorë
Vlorë *79 C7 prev.* Vlonë, *It.* Valona, Vlora. Vlorë, SW Albania
Vlotslavsk *see* Włocławek
Vöcklabruck *73 D6* Oberösterreich, NW Austria
Vogelkop *see* Doberai, Jazirah
Vohimena, Tanjona *57 F4 Fr.* Cap Sainte Marie. *headland* S Madagascar
Voiron *69 D5* Isère, E France
Vojvodina *78 D3 Ger.* Wojwodina. Vojvodina, N Serbia
Volga *89 B7 river* NW Russian Federation
Volga Uplands *see* Privolzhskaya Vozvyshennost'
Volgodonsk *89 B7* Rostovskaya Oblast', SW Russian Federation
Volgograd *89 B7 prev.* Stalingrad, Tsaritsyn. Volgogradskaya Oblast', SW Russian Federation
Volkhov *88 B4* Leningradskaya Oblast', NW Russian Federation
Volkovysk *see* Vawkavysk
Volmari *see* Valmiera
Volnovakha *87 G3* Donets'ka Oblast', SE Ukraine
Volodymyr-Volyns'kyy *86 C1 Pol.* Włodzimierz, *Rus.* Vladimir-Volynskiy. Volyns'ka Oblast', NW Ukraine
Vologda *88 B4* Vologodskaya Oblast', W Russian Federation
Vólos *83 B5* Thessalía, C Greece
Volozhin *see* Valozhyn
Vol'sk *89 C6* Saratovskaya Oblast', W Russian Federation
Volta *53 E5 river* SE Ghana
Volta Blanche *see* White Volta
Volta, Lake *53 E5 reservoir* SE Ghana
Volta Noire *see* Black Volta
Volturno *75 D5 river* S Italy
Volunteer Island *see* Starbuck Island
Volzhskiy *89 B6* Volgogradskaya Oblast', SW Russian Federation
Võnnu *84 E3 Ger.* Wendau. Tartumaa, SE Estonia
Voorst *64 D3* Gelderland, E Netherlands
Voranava *85 C5 Pol.* Werenów, *Rus.* Voronovo. Hrodzyenskaya Voblasts', W Belarus
Vorderrhein *73 B7 river* SE Switzerland
Vóreies Sporádes *83 C5 var.* Vóreioi Sporádes, Vórioi Sporádhes, *Eng.* Northern Sporades. *island group* E Greece
Vóreioi Sporádes *see* Vóreies Sporádes
Vórioi Sporádhes *see* Vóreies Sporádes
Vorkuta *92 C2* Respublika Komi, NW Russian Federation
Vormsi *84 C2 var.* Vormsi Saar, *Ger.* Worms, *Swed.* Ormsö. *island* W Estonia
Vormsi Saar *see* Vormsi
Voronezh *89 B6* Voronezhskaya Oblast', W Russian Federation
Voronovo *see* Voranava
Voroshilov *see* Ussuriysk
Voroshilovgrad *see* Luhans'k, Ukraine
Voroshilovsk *see* Stavropol', Russian Federation
Võru *84 D3 Ger.* Werro. Võrumaa, SE Estonia
Vosges *68 E4 mountain range* NE France
Vostochno-Sibirskoye More *93 F1 Eng.* East Siberian Sea. *sea* Arctic Ocean
Vostochnyy Sayan *see* Eastern Sayans
Vostock Island *see* Vostok Island
Vostok *132 C3 Russian research station* Antarctica
Vostok Island *123 G3 var.* Vostock Island; *prev.* Stavers Island. *island* Line Islands, SE Kiribati
Voznesens'k *87 E3 Rus.* Voznesensk. Mykolayivs'ka Oblast', S Ukraine
Vranje *79 E5* Serbia, SE Serbia
Vranov *see* Vranov nad Topl'ou
Vranov nad Topl'ou *77 D5 var.* Vranov, *Hung.* Varannó. Prešovský Kraj, E Slovakia
Vratsa *82 C2* Vratsa, NW Bulgaria
Vrbas *78 C3* Vojvodina, NW Serbia
Vrbas *78 C3 river* N Bosnia and Herzegovina
Vršac *78 E3 Ger.* Werschetz, *Hung.* Versecz. Vojvodina, NE Serbia
Vsetín *77 C5 Ger.* Wsetin. Zlínský Kraj, E Czech Republic
Vučitrn *see* Vushtrri
Vukovar *78 C3 Hung.* Vukovár. Vukovar-Srijem, E Croatia
Vulcano, Isola *75 C7 island* Isole Eolie, S Italy
Vung Tau *115 E6 prev. Fr.* Cape Saint Jacques, Cap Saint-Jacques. Ba Ria-Vung Tau, S Vietnam
Vushtrri *79 D5 Serb.* Vučitrn. N Kosovo
Vyatka *89 C5 river* NW Russian Federation
Vyatka *see* Kirov
Vyborg *88 B3 Fin.* Viipuri. Leningradskaya Oblast', NW Russian Federation
Vyerkhnyadzvinsk *85 D5 Rus.* Verkhnedvinsk. Vitsyebskaya Voblasts', N Belarus
Vyetryna *85 D5 Rus.* Vetrino. Vitsyebskaya Voblasts', N Belarus
Vynohradiv *86 B3 Cz.* Sevluš, *Hung.* Nagyszöllös, *Rus.* Vinogradov; *prev.* Sevlyush. Zakarpats'ka Oblast', W Ukraine

W

Wa *53 E4* NW Ghana
Waag *see* Váh
Waagbistritz *see* Považská Bystrica
Waal *64 C4 river* S Netherlands
Wabash *18 C4* Indiana, N USA
Wabash River *18 B5 river* N USA
Waco *27 G3* Texas, SW USA
Wad Al-Hajarah *see* Guadalajara
Waddān *49 F3* NW Libya
Waddeneilanden *64 C1 Eng.* West Frisian Islands. *island group* N Netherlands
Waddenzee *64 C1 var.* Wadden Zee. *sea* SE North Sea
Wadden Zee *see* Waddenzee
Waddington, Mount *14 D5 mountain* British Columbia, SW Canada
Wādī as Sīr *97 B6 var.* Wadi es Sir. 'Ammān, NW Jordan
Wadi es Sir *see* Wādī as Sīr
Wadi Halfa *50 B3 var.* Wādī Ḥalfā'. Northern, N Sudan
Wādī Mūsā *97 B7 var.* Petra. Ma'ān, S Jordan
Wad Madanī *see* Wad Medani
Wad Medani *50 C4 var.* Wad Madanī. Gezira, C Sudan
Waflia *117 F4* Pulau Buru, E Indonesia
Wagadugu *see* Ouagadougou
Wagga Wagga *127 C7* New South Wales, SE Australia
Wagin *125 B7* Western Australia
Wāh *112 C1* Punjab, NE Pakistan
Wahai *117 F4* Pulau Seram, E Indonesia
Wahaybah, Ramlat Al *see* Wahībah, Ramlat Āl
Wahiawā *25 A8 var.* Wahiawa. O'ahu, Hawaii, USA, C Pacific Ocean
Wahībah, Ramlat Ahl *see* Wahībah, Ramlat Āl
Wahibah Sands *99 E5 var.* Ramlat Ahl Wahībah, Ramlat Al Wahaybah, *Eng.* Wahībah Sands. *desert* N Oman
Wahībah Sands *see* Wahībah, Ramlat Āl
Wahpeton *23 F2* North Dakota, N USA
Wahran *see* Oran
Waiau *129 A7 river* South Island, New Zealand
Waigeo, Pulau *117 G4 island* Maluku, E Indonesia
Waikaremoana, Lake *128 E4 lake* North Island, New Zealand
Wailuku *25 B8* Maui, Hawaii, USA, C Pacific Ocean
Waimate *129 B6* Canterbury, South Island, New Zealand
Waiouru *128 D4* Manawatu-Wanganui, North Island, New Zealand
Waipara *129 C6* Canterbury, South Island, New Zealand
Waipawa *128 E4* Hawke's Bay, North Island, New Zealand
Waipukurau *128 D4* Hawke's Bay, North Island, New Zealand
Wairau *129 C5 river* South Island, New Zealand
Wairoa *128 E4* Hawke's Bay, North Island, New Zealand
Wairoa *128 D2 river* North Island, New Zealand
Waitaki *129 B6 river* South Island, New Zealand
Waitara *128 D4* Taranaki, North Island, New Zealand
Waitzen *see* Vác
Waiuku *128 D3* Auckland, North Island, New Zealand
Wakasa-wan *109 C6 bay* C Japan
Wakatipu, Lake *129 A7 lake* South Island, New Zealand
Wakayama *109 C6* Wakayama, Honshū, SW Japan
Wake Island *130 C2 US unincorporated territory* NW Pacific Ocean
Wake Island *120 D1 atoll* NW Pacific Ocean
Wakkanai *108 C1* Hokkaidō, NE Japan
Walachei/Walachia *see* Wallachia
Wałbrzych *76 B4 Ger.* Waldenburg, Waldenburg in Schlesien. Dolnośląskie, SW Poland
Walcourt *65 C7* Namur, S Belgium
Wałcz *76 B3 Ger.* Deutsch Krone. Zachodnio-pomorskie, NW Poland
Waldenburg/Waldenburg in Schlesien *see* Wałbrzych
Waldia *see* Weldiya
Wales *14 C2* Alaska, USA
Wales *67 C6 Wel.* Cymru. *cultural region* Wales, United Kingdom
Walgett *127 D5* New South Wales, SE Australia
Walk *see* Valga, Estonia
Walk *see* Valka, Latvia
Walker Lake *25 C5 lake* Nevada, W USA
Wallachia *86 B5 var.* Walachia, *Ger.* Walachei, *Rom.* Valachia. *cultural region* S Romania
Walla Walla *24 C2* Washington, NW USA
Wallenthal *see* Haţeg
Wallis and Futuna *123 E4 Fr.* Territoire de Wallis et Futuna. *French overseas territory* C Pacific Ocean
Wallis et Futuna, Territoire de *see* Wallis and Futuna
Walnut Ridge *20 B1* Arkansas, C USA
Waltenberg *see* Zalău
Walthamstow *67 B7* Waltham Forest, SE England, United Kingdom
Walvisbaai *see* Walvis Bay
Walvis Bay *56 A4 Afr.* Walvisbaai. Erongo, NW Namibia
Walvish Ridge *see* Walvis Ridge
Walvis Ridge *47 B7 var.* Walvish Ridge. *undersea ridge* E Atlantic Ocean
Wan *see* Anhui

X

Y